Bilingual

English-Levantine Arabic
Levantine Arabic-English
Dictionary

Compiled by
Ayman Khalaf

STAR Foreign Language BOOKS

This Edition : 2021

Published by

STAR Foreign Language BOOKS

a unit of
ibs BOOKS (UK)

56, Langland Crescent
Stanmore HA7 1NG, U.K.
info@starbooksuk.com
www.starbooksuk.com

Printed in India at
Star Print-O-Bind, New Delhi-110 020

About this Dictionary

Developments in science and technology today have narrowed down distances between countries, and have made the world a small place. A person living thousands of miles away can learn and understand the culture and lifestyle of another country with ease and without travelling to that country. Languages play an important role as facilitators of communication in this respect.

To promote such an understanding, **STAR Foreign Language BOOKS** has planned to bring out a series of bilingual dictionaries in which important English words have been translated into other languages, with Roman transliteration in case of languages that have different scripts. This is a humble attempt to bring people of the word closer through the medium of language, thus making communication easy and convenient.

Under this series of *one-to-one dictionaries*, we have published almost 55 languages, the list of which has been given in the opening pages. These have all been compiled and edited by teachers and scholars of the relative languages.

Publishers

Bilingual Dictionaries in this Series

English-Afrikaans / Afrikaans-English	Abraham Venter
English-Albanian / Albanian-English	Theodhora Blushi
English-Amharic / Amharic-English	Girun Asanke
English-Arabic / Arabic-English	Rania-al-Qass
English-Bengali / Bengali-English	Amit Majumdar
English-Bosnian / Bosnian-English	Boris Kazanegra
English-Bulgarian / Bulgarian-English	Vladka Kocheshkova
English-Cantonese / Cantonese-English	Nisa Yang
English-Chinese (Mandarin) / Chinese (Mandarin)-Eng	Y. Shang & R. Yao
English-Croatian / Croatain-English	Vesna Kazanegra
English-Czech / Czech-English	Jindriska Poulova
English-Danish / Danish-English	Rikke Wend Hartung
English-Dari / Dari-English	Amir Khan
English-Dutch / Dutch-English	Lisanne Vogel
English-Estonian / Estonian-English	Lana Haleta
English-Farsi / Farsi-English	Maryam Zaman Khani
English-French / French-English	Aurélie Colin
English-Georgian / Georgina-English	Eka Goderdzishvili
English-Gujarati / Gujarati-English	Sujata Basaria
English-German / German-English	Bicskei Hedwig
English-Greek / Greek-English	Lina Stergiou
English-Hindi / Hindi-English	Sudhakar Chaturvedi
English-Hungarian / Hungarian-English	Lucy Mallows
English-Italian / Italian-English	Eni Lamllari
English-Japanese / Japanese-English	Miruka Arai
English-Korean / Korean-English	Mihee Song
English-Latvian / Latvian-English	Julija Baranovska
English-Levantine Arabic / Levantine Arabic-English	Ayman Khalaf
English-Lithuanian / Lithuanian-English	Regina Kazakeviciute
English-Malay / Malay-English	Azimah Husna
English-Nepali / Nepali-English	Anil Mandal
English-Norwegian / Norwegian-English	Samuele Narcisi
English-Pashto / Pashto-English	Amir Khan
English-Polish / Polish-English	Magdalena Herok
English-Portuguese / Portuguese-English	Dina Teresa
English-Punjabi / Punjabi-English	Teja Singh Chatwal
English-Romanian / Romanian-English	Georgeta Laura Dutulescu
English-Russian / Russian-English	Katerina Volobuyeva
English-Serbian / Serbian-English	Vesna Kazanegra
English-Sinhalese / Sinhalese-English	Naseer Salahudeen
English-Slovak / Slovak-English	Zuzana Horvathova
English-Slovenian / Slovenian-English	Tanja Turk
English-Somali / Somali-English	Ali Mohamud Omer
English-Spanish / Spanish-English	Cristina Rodriguez
English-Swahili / Swahili-English	Abdul Rauf Hassan Kinga
English-Swedish / Swedish-English	Madelene Axelsson
English-Tagalog / Tagalog-English	Jefferson Bantayan
English-Tamil / Tamil-English	Sandhya Mahadevan
English-Thai / Thai-English	Suwan Kaewkongpan
English-Tigrigna / Tigrigna-English	Tsegazeab Hailegebriel
English-Turkish / Turkish-English	Nagme Yazgin
English-Ukrainian / Ukrainian-English	Katerina Volobuyeva
English-Urdu / Urdu-English	S. A. Rahman
English-Vietnamese / Vietnamese-English	Hoa Hoang
English-Yoruba / Yoruba-English	O. A. Temitope

STAR Foreign Language BOOKS

English-Levantine Arabic

A

aback *adv.* للورا lelwaraa
abaction *n.* سرقة serqah
abactor *n.* حرامي harami
abandon *v.* تخلّى takhallah
abandonable *adj.* مهجور mahjur
abandonedly *adv.* بلا حدود bla hudud
anbandonee *n.* مهجور mahjur
abandoner *n.* هاجِر hajir
abase *v.* حقّر haqqar
abase *adv.* دوني duni
abasement *n.* تحقير tahkir
abash *v.* خجّل khajjal
abashed *adj.* مستحي mestehi
abashing *n.* إحراج ehraj
abate *v.* يهدِي yehaddi
abatement *n.* هدوء hudu'
abbey *n.* دير الراهبات dir elrahbat
abbot *n.* رئيس دير ra'es dir
abbreviate *v.* يختصر yekhteser
abbreviation *n.* إختصار ikhtisar
abdicate *v.t,* يستقيل yestaqil
abdication *n.* إستقالة istiqaleh
abdomen *n.* بطن batn
abdominal *adj.* بطني batni
abduct *v.* يخطف yekhtuf
abductee *n.* مخطوف makhtuf
abduction *n.* إختطاف ikhtitaf
abductor *n.* خاطف khatif
abed *adv.* بالتخت beltakhet

aberrance *n.* إنحراف inhiraf
aberration *n.* زيغان zayaghan
abet *v.* متمدد metmadded
abetment *n.* تحريض tahrid
abeyance *n.* عطالة ataleh
abeyant *adj.* معلَّق me'allaq
abhor *v.* كره kurh
abhorrence *n.* إشمئزاز eshme'zaz
abid *n.* إلتزام eltizam
abide *v.* يلتزم yeltezem
abideable *adj.* قابل للالتزام qabel lel'eltizam
abiding *adj.* مستمر mestamerr
ability *n.* قدرة qudrah
abject *adj.* حقير haqir
abject *v.* يذلّ yezell
abjection *n.* حقارة haqarah
abjure *v.* يرتدّ عن yertadd an
abjurer *n.* مرتدّ murtadd
ablaze *adv.* شاعل sha'el
ablaze *adv.* ملتهب melteheb
ablactate *v.* يفطم yeftum
ablactation *n.* فطام fitam
ablation *n.* تآكل ta'akul
ablative *adj.* تآكلي ta'akuli
ablate *v.* يتآكل yet'akal
able *adj.* قادر qader
ablegation *n.* تسفير tasfir
ablepsy *n.* عمى amah
ablush *adv.* محمر mehmarr
ablution *n.* وضوء wudu'
ablutionary *adj.* وضوئي wudu'i
abnegate *v.* يتنازل yetnazal
abnegation *n.* تنازل tanazul
abnormal *adj.* شاذ shazz
abnormalcy *n.* شذوذ shuzuz

abnormality *n.* شذوذ shuzuz

abnormally *adv.* بشذوذ beshuzuz

aboard *adv.* على المركب almarkab

abode *n.* مَسْكَن maskan

abolish *v.* يبطل yebtil

abolition *v.* إِبْطالَ ibtal

abolisher *n.* مُبطل mubtil

abolishment *n.* إبطال ibtal

abolitionism *n.* إِبْطاليّة ibtaleyyeh

abominable *adj.* كريه karih

abominably *adv.* بحقد beheqed

abominate *v.* يستنكر yestanker

abomination *n.* إِستِنكار estinkar

aboriginal *adj.* ساكن أصلي saken asli

abort *v.* تجهض tujhed

abortion *n.* إجهاض ijhad

abortive *adj.* إجهاضي ijhadi

abound *v.* يكثر yektar

aboundance *n.* كثرة ketreh

about *adv.* حوالي Iahawali

about *prep.* حوالي hawali

above *adv.* لفوق lafuq

above *prep.* فوق fuq

abrasion *n.* حَك hakk

abrasive *adj.* خشن kheshen

abrasively *adv.* بخشونة bekhushuneh

abrasiveness *n.* حَك hakk

abreast *adv.* جمب بعض jamb ba'ed

abridge *v.* يوجز yujez

abridged *adj.* موجز mujaz

abridgement *n.* مُوجَز mujaz

abroad *adv.* لبرا labarrah

abrogate *v.* يلغي yelghi

abrogation *n.* إلغاء elgha'a

abrupt *adj.* مفاجئ mufaje'

abruption *n.* تفاجئ tfaja'

abscess *n.* دملة dummaleh

absonant *adj.* نشاز nashaz

abscond *v.* يختفي yekhtfi

abscondence *n.* اختفاء ekhtifa'

absence *n.* غياب ghiyab

absent *adj.* غايب ghayeb

absent *v.* يغيب yeghib

absentee *n.* الغايب el ghayib

absist *v.* يترك ytruk

absolute *adj.* أكيد akeed

absolutely *adv.* عالأكيد al akeed

absolution *n.* تبرية tabriyeh

absolutism *n.* جبروت jbarout

absolve *v.* يبري yebri

absorb *v.* يتشرب yetsharab

absorption *n.* تشرب tashroub

absorptivity *n.* الامتصاص alemtisas

abstain *v.* يمتنع yemtene'

abstinence *n.* امتناع emtina'

abstract *adj.* معنوي ma'nawi

abstract *n.* ملخص mulakhkhas

abstract *v.* يلخّص yulakhkhes

abstraction *n.* تلخيص tlkhees

abstraction *n.* شرود shrood

absurd *adj.* تافه taafeh

absurdity *n.* تفاهة tfaha

abundance *n.* كترة ktreh

abundant *adj.* كتير kteer

abuse *v.* يسبسب ysbseb

abuse *n.* مسبة msabeh

abuser *n.* لعان la'aan

abusive *adj.* وقح weqeh

abusively *adv.* بوقاحة bwqaha

abut *v.* يتسند على yetsanad ala

abutment *n.* سنادة sannadeh

abyss *n.* هاوية hawyeh

acacia *n.* صمغ samgh

academic *adj.* جامعي jamei

academy *n.* كلية kliyeh

acarpous *adj.* ممحل mmhil

accede *v.* يلبي yelbie

acceder *n.* كفو kafoo

accelerate *v.* يسرع ysarre'

acceleration *n.* تسريع tasree'

accelerator *n.* مسرع msarre'

accend *v.* يشعل النار ysheul enaar

accent *n.* لهجة lahjeh

accent *v.* يركز على ykarek ala

accept *v.* يوافق ywafeq

acceptable *adj.* مقبول makbool

acceptance *n.* موافقة mwaka'a

access *n.* يدخل yedkhul

accessibility *n.* دخولية dkholiyeh

accession *n.* انتساب entisab

accessorise *v.* يزين yzyyen

accessory *n.* اكسسوار ikseswar

accident *n.* حادث hadith

accidental *adj.* فجائي fuja'i

accipitral *adj.* صقري saqri

acclaim *v.* يمدح ymdah

acclaim *n.* مديح mdih

acclamation *n.* تصفيق tsfiq

acclamation *n.* زغاريد zaghareed

acclimatise *v.* يتعود ytawaad

accommodate *v.* يستضيف ystadif

accommodate *v.* يسع ysae

accommodation *n.* بيت beit

accompaniment *n.* مرافقة murafaqa

accompany *v.* يترافق مع ytrafaq ma

accomplice *n.* قرين السوء areen esou'

accomplish *v.* ينتهي من ynthi mn

accomplished *adj.* خالص khales

accomplishment *n.* انتهاء entihaa'

accord *v.* يتفق مع ytfeq ma'

accord *n.* وفق wfq

accordance *n.* وفق wfq

accordancy *n.* توافق twafq

accordingly *adv.* لذا lza

accost *v.* يفاتح yefateh

account *n.* حساب hsab

account *v.* يحاسب yuhaseb

accountability *n.* مسؤولية mas'oliyeh

accountable *adj.* مسؤول mas'ool

accountancy *n.* محاسبة muhasabeh

accountant *n.* محاسب mhaseb

accredit *v.* يعتمد ye'tmd

accreditation *n.* اعتماد e'temad

accrementition *n.* نموة nmweh

accrete *v.* ينمو بلزق yenmou blzq

accrue *v.* يتكدس yetkaddas

accumulate *v.* يتراكم yetrakam

accumulation *n.* تراكم trakum

accuracy *n.* دقة deqqa

accurate *adj.* دقيق daqiq

accursed *adj.* ملعون mal'oon

accusation *n.* تهمة tehmeh

accusator *n.* متهم mutahim

accuse *v.* يتهم yetehm

accused *n.* متهم mutaham

accustom *v.* يعتاد على y'atad ala

accustomed *adj.* متعود على mt'awed ala

ace *n.* درة darra

acellular *adj.* غير خلوي ghir khalawi

acentric *adj.* غير مركزي ghir markazi

acephalous *adj.* بلا راس bla ras

acephaly *n.* عدم وجود راس adm wjood ras

acetate *n.* خل khall

acetifier *n.* تخليل takhlil

acetify *v.* يخلل yekhalil

acetone *n.* أسيتون aciton

ache *n.* وجع waja'

ache *v.* يوجع yuje'

achelike *adj.* بشبه الوجع beshbah el waja'

achieve *v.* ينجز yenjez

achievement *n.* إنجاز enjaz

achiever *n.* صاحب الانجاز sahin enjaz

achromatic *adj.* بلا لون bla loon

acid *adj.* حمضي hamdhi

acid *n.* حمض hamdh

acidic *adj.* حامض hamod

acidify *v.* يحمض yehmidh

acidity *n.* حموضة hmoodhaa

acknowledge *v.* يعترف yeateref

acknowledgement *n.* اعتراف eteraaf

acne *n.* حب الشباب hab eshabab

acolyte *n.* مساعد musa'ed

acorn *n.* بلوط baloot

acoustic *adj.* صوتي sawtti

acoustics *n.* صوتيات sawteyat

acquaint *v.* مطلع mttele'

acquaintance *n.* إطلاع etela'

acquest *n.* يكسب yeksab

acquiesce *v.* يخضع yakhdha'

acquiescence *n.* خضوع khodhoe'

acquire *v.* يحصل yahsal

acquirement *n.* حصول husool

acquisition *n.* تملك tmalook

acquit *v.* يعفو عن ye'fo an

acquittal *n.* إعفاء e'faa'

acre *n.* فدان faddan

acreage *n.* المساحة بالفدان el masaha bl faddan

acrid *adj.* حاد hadd

acrimony *n.* حدودية hdodiye

acritical *adj.* مو خطير mo khateer

acrobat *n.* مهرج muharej

acrobatic *adj.* تهريجي tehreji

acrobatics *n.* تهريج tehreej

acropolis *n.* قلعة أثينا kal'et athina

across *adv.* عبر abr

across *prep.* من طرف للتاني mn traf ll tani

acrylic *adj.* اكريليك acrilik

act *n.* تصرف tsaroof

act *v.* يتصرف yetsarraf

acting *n.* تمثيل tamtheel

action *n.* عمل 3mal

activate *v.* ينشط ynashet

active *adj.* نشط nshet

activist *n.* ناشط nasheth

activity *n.* نشاط nshat

actor *n.* ممثل mumathel

actress *n.* ممثلة mumatheleh

actual *adj.* فعلي fe'li

actually *adv.* فعلا fe'ln

acumen *n.* فطنة fetneh

acupuncture *n.* إبر صينية ebr siniyeh

acupuncturist *n.* مختص الابر الصينية mkhts ebr siniyeh

acute *adj.* قوي awi

acyclical *adj.* مو دوما mo dawmn

adage *n.* متل matal

adamant *adj.* معند meanned

adamant *n.* عند e'nd

adapt *v.* يتأقلم yet'aqlam

adaptation *n.* تأقلم ta'qlum

adays *adv.* خلال الأيام khilal el ayyam

add *v.* يزيد yzeed

adder *n.* شخص بيزيد sakhs byzeed

addict *v.* يدمن yedmn

addict *n.* مدمن mudmn

addiction *n.* إدمان edmaan

addition *n.* الزيادة el zeyadeh

additional *adj.* زيادة zeyadeh

addle *adj.* معفن meaffn

address *v.* يحكي مع yehki ma'

address *n.* عنوان enwan

addressee *n.* مخاطب mukhatab

addresser *n.* خطيب khatib

adduce *v.* يبرهن yebrhin

abduct *v.* يخطف yekhtuf

adept *n.* خبير khabeer

adept *adj.* شاطر shater

adequacy *n.* كفاية kfayeh

adequate *adj.* كافي kaffi

adhere *v.* يسمع كلمة yesma' klmeh

adherence *n.* طاعة ta'a

adhesion *n.* اندماج endimag

adhesive *n.* لاصق laseq

adhesive *adj.* لاصق laseq

adhibit *v.* يثبت yethbit

ad hoc *adj.* مشان هيك mshaan heik

adieu *n.* توديع twdie'

adieu *interj.* الله يحميك alla yehik

adiposity *n.* سمنة smneh

adjacent *adj.* بلزق blzq

adjective *n.* صفة sifa

adjoin *v.* يلزق ب ylzq be

adjourn *v.* يأجل yeajil

adjournment *n.* تأجيل ta'jil

adjudge *v.* يبت beit

adjunct *n.* ملحق mulhaq

adjure *v.* يترجى yetrajja

adjuration *n.* ترجي tarraji

adjust *v.* يضبط yadbt

adjustment *n.* ضبط dabt

adjuvant *n.* مادة مساعدة madeh musa'edeh

adjuvant *adj.* فرعي farei

administer *v.* يتولى yetwalla

administrate *v.* يدير yudir

administration *n.* إدارة iedara

administrative *adj.* إداري iedari

administrator *n.* مدير muddir

admirable *adj.* ملفت للنظر mulft llnazar

admiral *n.* قائد بحري ka'ed bhri

admiralty *n.* قوات بحرية kuwatt bhryeh

admiration *n.* إعجاب i'ejab

admire *v.* يعجب ب yuejab be

admirer *n.* معجب mu'jab

admissible *adj.* مقبول mkbuol

admission *n.* قبول kubul

admission *n.* اعتراف ietiraff

admit *v.* يعترف yetirf

admittance *n.* السماح بالدخول elssamah blddukhul

admittedly *adv.* باعتراف الكل be'tiraf elkll

admonish *v.* يعاتب yua'tb

admonisher *n.* عتبان atban

admonition *n.* عتاب itab

ado *n.* جعجعة jaja'a

adobe *n.* طوبة tubeh

adolescence *n.* مراهقة murahaqa

adolescent *adj.* مراهق murahiq

adopt *v.* يتبنى ytbnaa

adoption *n.* بني tbnni

adoptive *adj.* بالتبني bltbny

adorable *adj.* فتان fattan

adoration *n.* افتتان ifttan

adore *v.* يعشق yesha'

adorn *v.* رزين yzyn

adorner *n.* فزين mzyyen

adrenaline *n.* ادرينالين adrynalyn

adrenalise *v.* يحفز yhffz

adscititious *adj.* زايد zayid

adulate *v.* يمسح جوخ ymssh jwkh

adulation *n.* تمسيح الجوخ tmsih eljwkh

adult *adj.* راشد rashid

adult *n.* بالغ baligh

adulterate *v.* يغش yghsh

adulteration *n.* غش ghshsh

adultery *n.* زنا zinna

advance *v.* يمشي لقدام ymshi lqddam

advance *n.* سلفة slfeh

advancement *n.* تحسن thssun

advantage *n.* فايدة fayideh

advantage *v.* ينفع ynfae

advantageous *adj.* مفيد mufid

advent *n.* جية jyeh

adventure *n.* مغامرة mughamara

adventurous *adj.* متهور mthwur

adverb *n.* ظرف zrf

adverbial *adj.* ظرفي zrffi

adversary *n.* غريم ghrim

adverse *adj.* مزعج muze'j

adversity *n.* مصيبة msibeh

advert *v.* يأشر براسه ya'asher birash

advertise *v.* يُعلن yu'eln

advertisement *n.* إعلان i'elan

advice *n.* نصيحة nsiha

advisable *adj.* صايب sayib

advisability *n.* صواب swab

advise *v.* ينصح ynsah

advocacy *n.* دعم daem

advocacy *n.* دعوة daeweh

advocate *n.* محامي muhami

advocate *v.* يدافع yudafie

aerial *adj.* بالهوا blhwa

aerial *n.* انتيل antil

aeriform *adj.* وهمي whmy

aerify *v.* يهوي yhwwy

aerobic *adj.* هوائي hwaei

aerobics *n.* ايروبيك irobik

aerobiology *n.* علم الهوائيات e'lm elhawaeyiat

aerobot *n.* طيّارة بدون طيّار tyyara bdun tayyar

aerocraft *n.* طيّارة tyyara

aerodigestive *adj.* تنفسي علوي tnfusi elwy

aerodrome *n.* مطار matar

aerodynamic *adj.* متحرك بالهوا mtaharrik blhwa

aeronautics *n.pl.* علم الطيران e'lm elttayaran

aeroplane *n.* طيّارة tyyara

aeroponic *adj.* زراعة بالهوا zira'a blhwa

aerosol *adj.* مضبضب mdbdeb

aerostatic *adj.* متوازن الهوا والغاز mtawazn elhwa wlghaz

aerostatics *n.* توازن الهوا والغاز tawazn elhwa wlghaz

aesthetic *adj.* تجميلي tajmili

aesthetics *n.pl.* علم التجميل e'lim elttjmil

aestival *adj.* صيفي syfi

afar *adv.* من بعيد mn beid

affable *adj.* لطيف ltif

affair *n.* علاقة غرامية alaqa gharamiyh

affect *v.* يأثر على by'athr ala

affectation *n.* تصنع tsnue'

affection *n.* تعاطف ta'atuf

affectionate *adj.* حنون hnun

affidavit *n.* شهادة shahadeh

affiliate *v.* ينتسب إلى yntsib 'ila

affiliation *n.* انتساب intisab

affinity *n.* مصاهرة musahara

affirm *v.* يأكّد ya'kkd

affirmation *n.* تأكيد ta'kid

affirmative *adj.* مؤكّد mw'akkd

affirmative *adj.* إيجابي ijabi

affirmatively *adv.* عالأكيد al'akid

affix *v.* يبصم ybsum

affixation *n.* كعب الصفحة kaeb elssafha

afflict *v.* يعمّله مصيبة y'emllh msibeh

affliction *n.* مصيبة msibeh

afflictive *adj.* مفجع mufje'

affluence *n.* بطر btr

affluent *adj.* بطران btran

affluential *adj.* غني صاحب نفوذ ghani sahib nufuz

affluential *n.* الغني صاحب النفوذ elghani sahib elnnufuz

affluenza *n.* حب المال hubb elmal

afford *v.* يقدر يدفع yqdder ydfae

affordability *n.* القدرة ع الدفع elqudra alddfe'

afforest *v.* يزرع شجر yzra shajar

affray *n.* قتيلة qtileh

affront *v.* يهين yhin

affront *n.* إهانة ihaneh

afield *adv.* لبعيد lbeyd

aflame *adv.* شاعل نار shael nnar

afloat *adv.* على ملا وشه ala mala wshshh

afoot *adv.* ماشية الأمور تمام mashiyh el'umur tamam

afore *prep.* من قبل mn qbl

aforementioned *adj.* متل ما نحكا قبل mtl ma nhka abl

aforesaid *adj.* متل ما نحكا قبل mtl ma nhka abl

afraid *adj.* خوفان khwfaan

afresh *adv.* مرة تانية marra tanyeh

aft *n.* ورا wra

aft *adv.* لورا lwra

after *prep.* بعد ba'd

after *prep.* عن a'n

after *adv.* بعد ما baed ma

after *conj.* بخصوص bkhsws

after *adj.* متله mtluh

aftereffect *n.* الحاصل elhasil

aftergame *n.* اللعبة اللي بعد ellluebeh elly baed

aftergrowth *n.* المرحلة الجاي elmarhaleh eljay

afternoon *n.* المسا elmassa

afterthought *n.* بعد فوات الأوان baed fawwat al'awan

afterwards *adv.* وبعدا wba'da

again *adv.* مرة تانية marra tanyeh

against *prep.* مقابيل mqabyl

against *adj.* عكس aks

agamist *n.* مقابل muqabl

agape *adv.,* بدهشة bdahsheh

agape *n.* حب عذري hubb uzri

agaze *adv.* بحلقة bibahalaqa

age *n.* عمر eumr

aged *adj.* كبير بالعمر kbir bleumr

agency *n.* وكالة wkaleh

agenda *n.* جدول عمل jdwal a'mal

agent *n.* وكيل wakil

agglomerate *adj.* مكتّل mkttil

agglomerate *n.* كتّل ktll

agglomerate *v.* يتكتّل ytkttal

aggravate *v.* استفحل istafhal

aggravation *n.* استفحال istifhal

aggregate *v.* يجمّع yjmme'

aggression *n.* عدوانية edwanieh

aggressive *adj.* عدواني edwani

aggressor *n.* معتدي muetadi

aggrieve *v.* يجور على yjur ala

aggroupment *n.* تقسيم لمجموعات taqsim lmajmua'at

aghast *adj.* فزعان fza'an

agile *adj.* حرك hrik

agility *n.* خفّة khffeh

agitate *v.* يعمل بلبلة ye'ml balbaleh

agitation *n.* بلبلة balbaleh

agist *v.* يستأجر مزرعة yestajr mazra'a

aglare *adj.* زاهي zahi

aglow *adv.* لميع lmmye'

agnosticism *n.* شرك sherk

ago *adv.* مضيو mdyo

ago *adv.* قبل qbl

agog *adj.* بلهفة blahfeh

agonist *n.* منافس munafes

agonize *v.* يكركب ykrkib

agony *n.* هم hamm

agronomy *n.* هندسة زراعية handaseh ziraeih

agoraphobia *n.* الخوف من الفضا elkhwf mn elfadda

agrarian *adj.* حقلي haqly

agree *v.* يوآفق على ywafq ala

agreeable *adj.* متفق عليه muttafaq a'lyh

agreement *n.* اتفاقية ettifaqyeh

agricultural *adj.* زراعي zira'ei

agriculture *n.* زِراعة zira'a

agriculturist *n.* فلاح flaah

agrology *n.* دراسة التربة diraset eltturbeh

ague *n.* قشعريرة qasharira

ahead *adv.* لقدام lqddam

aheap *adv.* بكومةٍ bekumeh

aid *n.* مساعدة musaed

aid *v.* يساعد yusaed

aide *n.* مساعد musaed

aigrette *n.* طاقية taqyeh

ail *v.* يقلق yuqlq

ailment *n.* علّة elleh

aim *n.* نيّة nyeh

aim *v.* ينوي yenwi

air *n.* هوا hawa

airbag *n.* كيس هوا kys hwa

airborne *n.* محمول في الجو mahmul fi eljaww

airborne *adj.* محوقل mjwqal

airbrake *n.* مكبح عالهوا mukbbah a'lhwa

airbus *n.* طيارة ايرباص tayara ayrbas

aircraft *n.* طيارة tayara

aircrew *n.* طقم الطيارة taqm elttayara

airlift *n.* رحلة بالطيارة rihleh blttayara

airlift *v.* يركب بالطيارة yrkab blttayara

airy *adj.* جوّي jawwi

aisle *n.* ممر mamarr

ajar *adv.* مفتوح maftuh

akin *adj.* شبيه shbih

akinesia *n.* كساح kusah

alabaster *n.* مرمر mrmr

alabaster *adj.* رخامي rukhami

alacrious *adj.* نشيط nashit

alacrity *n.* نشاط nashat

alamort *adj.* تعبان كتير ta'ban ktir

alarm *n.* منبّه mnbbh

alarm *v.* ينبّه ynbbh

alarming *adj.* مزعج muzej

alas *interj.* للأسف lilasf

albeit *conj.* حتى لو hatta law

albino *n.* عنده وحمة eindh wahmmeh

album *n.* ألبوم album

albumen *n.* زُلال البيض zulal albid

alchemist *n.* كيميائي kimiaei

alchemy *n.* كيميا kimia

alcohol *n.* مشروب mashrub

alcoholic *n.* سكرجي sekarji

alcoholism *n.* شرب الخمر shrb alkhamr

alcove *n.* قبّة qbbeh

ale *n.* بيرة bayra

aleatory *adj.* حسب الحظ hsb alhazz

alegar *n.* خل الشعير khal alshaeir

alert *adj.* أخذ بالحسبان akhad bilhusban

alertness *n.* تحسّب thssb

alfa *n.* ألفا alfaa

alga *n.* طحالب tahalib

algal *adj.* فيو طحالب fiu tahalib

algebra *n.* الجبر aljabr

alias *n.* اسم مستعار ism musta'ar

alias *adv.* معروف كأن ب maroof kaman b

alibi *n.* تبرير غياب في الجرايم tabrir ghiab fi aljarayim

alien *adj.* غريب ghryb

alienate *v.* ينفّر yunffer

aliferous *adj.* مجنّح mjnnh

alight *v.* يتنزل من yenzil min

align *v.* يوقف بالدور ywqf bilddor

alignment *n.* وقفة بالدور waqfeh bilddor

alike *adj.* متساوي mutasawi

alike *adv.* بالتساوي blttasawi

aliment *n.* أكل akl

alimony *n.* نفقة nafaqa

aliquot *n.* قابل للقسمة دون كسور qabil lilqsma dun kusur

alive *adj.* عايش aysh

alkali *n.* مادة قلوية maddeh qulawia

alkaline *adj.* قلوي qulawi

all *adj.* كل kel

all *n.* الجميع aljamie

all *adv.* بكامل bikamel

all *pron* كلنا klna

allay *v.* يخفّف yukhaffef

allegation *n.* حجة hejjeh

allege *v.* يدّعي yaddaei

alleged *adj.* مزعوم mazoum

allegiance *n.* ولاء wala'

allegorical *adj.* مجازي majazi

allegory *n.* مجاز majaz

allergy *n.* حساسية hasasya

alleviate *v.* يخفف الوجع yukhaffef alwaja'

alleviation *n.* تسكين الوجع taskin alwaja'

alley *n.* طريق خلفي tariq khalfi

alliance *n.* حلف helf

alligator *n.* تمساح أمريكي temsah 'amriki

alliteration *n.* استخدام الجناس istikhdam aljinas

allocate *v.* يخصص yukhasses

allocation *n.* تخصيص takhsis

allness *n.* الاستماع بكل الحواس alaistimae bikull alhawas

allot *v.* قسم qassam

allotment *n.* تقسيم taqsim

allow *v.* يسمح yasmah

allowance *n.* سماح samah

alloy *n.* مزيج معادن mazij maadin

allude *v.* يلمّح yulammih

allure *v.* يغري yughri

allurement *n.* إغراء ighraa'

allusion *n.* تلميح talmih

allusive *adj.* بالتلميح bilttalmih

ally *v.* يتحالف yatahalaf

ally *n.* حلف helf

almanac *n.* رزنامة roznama

almighty *adj.* قادر qadir

almond *n.* لوز luz

almost *adv.* تقريبا taqriban

alms *n.* حسنة hasaneh

aloft *adv.* طاير بالعالي tayir bil aali

alone *adj.* لوحده lawahduh

along *adv.* عطول a'tul

along *prep.* جنب janb

aloof *adv.* بمعزل عن bimaezil aan

aloud *adv.* بصوت عالي bisawt ali

alp *n.* جبال الألب jibal el'alb

alpha *n.* أوّل awwal

alphabet *n.* أبجدية abjadiyeh

alphabetical *adj.* بالترتيب الأبجدي bilttartib el'abjadi

alpine *adj.* عالي كتير ali ketir

alpinist *n.* متسلق جبال الألب mutasalliq jibal el'alb

already *adv.* يا دوب ya dub

also *adv.* كمان kaman

altar *n.* هيكل haykal

alter *v.* يغيّر yughayir

alteration *n.* تغيير taghyir

altercation *n.* عدّ وصف a'd wesaff

alternate *adj.* بديل badil

alternate *v.* يبدّل yubaddil

alternative *n.* خيار khiar

alternative *adj.* اختياري ikhtiari

although *conj.* وغم berrghm

altimeter *n.* مقياس الأرتفاع miqyas elertifae

altitude *n.* ارتفاع ertifae

alto *n.* عالي aali

altogether *adv.* مع بعض mae ba'ad

altruism *n.* حُب الخير للناس hubb elkheyr lilnnas

altruist *n.* محّب للخير للناس muhebb lilkheyr lilnnas

altruistic *adj.* إيثاري ithari

aluminium *n.* الومنيوم alumenyum

alumna *n.* خريج جامعة khirrij jama'a

always *adv.* دوما dawman

alveary *n.* حفرة الأذن الخارجية hufret el'udhn elkharijiyeh

am *abbr* الصبح elssubh

amalgam *n.* خليط معدن khalit maedan

amalgamate *v.* يخلط مع معدن yakhlit mae maedan

amalgamation *n.* خلط المعادن khalt elma'adin

amass *v.* يكنّز yaknnuz

amateur *n.* هاوي hawi

amatory *adj.* محّب muhheb

amaurosis *n.* عمى a'ma

amaze *v.* يدهش yudhish

amazement *n.* دهشة dahsheh

ambassador *n.* سفير safir

amberite *n.* أمبريت ambrit

ambidexter *n.* شخص بشتغل بالإيدتين سوا shakhs beshteghel bil'idteyn suwa

ambient *adj.* حولنا hewlna

ambiguity *n.* غموض ghumood

ambiguous *adj.* غامض ghamid

ambissexual *adj.* يميل للجنسين yamil liljinsin

ambissexual *n.* ميال للجنسين mayal liljinsin

ambissexuality *n.* الميول للجنسين almuyul liljinsin

ambition *n.* طُموح tumuh
ambitious *adj.* طُموح tamuh
ambivalence *n.* تناقض tanaqud
ambivalent *adj.* متناقض mutanaqid
ambulance *n.* إسعاف isa'af
ambulant *adj.* مسعِف muse'f
ambulate *v.* يُسعف yuse'f
ambuscade *n.* كمين kamin
ambuscade *v.* ينصب كمين yunsub kamin
ambush *n.* فخ fakhkh
ameliorate *v.* يصلّح yusllih
amelioration *n.* تصليح taslih
amen *interj.* آمين amin
amenable *adj.* مطيع mutie'
amend *v.* يعدّل yueaddil
amendment *n.* تعديل ta'dil
amends *n.pl.* ترضية tardiyeh
amenorrhoea *n.* انقطاع الدورة enqitae elddawra
amiability *n.* لُطف lutf
amiable *adj.* لطيف latif
amicable *adj.* سلمي silmi
amid *prep.* بين bayn
amiss *adv.* بطريقة غلط bitariqa ghalat
amity *n.* صداقة sadaqa
ammonia *n.* نُشادر nashadir
ammunition *n.* ذخيرة dhakhira
amnesia *n.* فقدان ذاكرة fiqdan zhakira
amnesty *n.* عفو afw
among *prep.* بين bein
amongst *prep.* بين bein

amoral *adj.* بدون أخلاق bidun 'akhlaq
amorous *adj.* غرامي gharami
amortise *v.* يخصص مصاري لتسديد دين yukhasses masari litasdid din
amortization *n.* تخصيص مصاري لتسديد دين takhasses masari litasdid din
amount *n.* مبلغ mablagh
amount *v.* يساوي yusawi
amour *n.* علاقة غرامية alaqa gharamiyeh
ampere *n.* أمبير ampir
amphibious *adj.* برمائي barmaei
amphitheatre *n.* مدرج mudarraj
ample *adj.* واسع wase'e
amplification *n.* تكبير takbir
amplifier *n.* مكبِّر mukabber
amplify *v.* يكبِّر yukabber
amplitude *n.* وساعية wesa'yah
amputate *v.* يبتر yabter
amputation *n.* بتر bater
amputee *n.* أبتر abtar
amuck *adv.* جنون junun
amulet *n.* حجاب hejab
amuse *v.* يسلّي yusalli
amusement *n.* تسلية tasliyeh
amygdala *n.* لُوز luz
an *art.* أداة تعريف adat ta'rif
anabolic *adj.* بدائي bedaey
anachronism *n.* مفارقة تاريخية mufaraka tarikhiyeh
anaclasis *n.* انعكاس الضوء enekas eldaww

anaemia *n.* فقر الدم fiker eldamm

anaesthesia *n.* تخدير takhdir

anaesthetic *n.* المخدّر elmukhadder

anal *adj.* شرجي sharji

analogous *adj.* متطابق mutatabeq

analogy *n.* تطابق tatabuq

analyse *v.* يحلل yuhallel

analysis *n.* تحليل tahlil

analyst *n.* محلّل muhallil

analytical *adj.* تحليلي tahlili

anamnesis *n.* تذكّر tazakkur

anamnesis *n.* استرجاع esterjaa'

anamorphosis *adj.* انحراف enhiraf

anarchism *n.* فوضوية fawdawiyeh

anarchist *n.* فوضوي fawdawi

anarchy *n.* فوضى fawda

anatomy *n.* تشريح tashrih

ancestor *n.* جدّ jadd

ancestral *adj.* متوارث mutawarath

ancestry *n.* حَسَب hasab

anchor *n.* مرساة mersaat

anchorage *n.* مرفأ marfaa'

ancient *adj.* قديم kadim

ancon *n.* كوع kuwe'

and *conj.* و wa

androphagi *n.* أكل لحوم البشر aakel luhum el bashar

anecdote *n.* نكتة nekteh

anemometer *n.* مقياس سرعة الهوا mekyas sere't elhawwa

anew *adv.* مرة تانية mara tanyeh

anfractuous *adj.* مُتعرّج muta'rrej

angel *n.* ملاك malak

anger *n.* غِضب ghadab

angina *n.* ضيق النفس dhiq tanaffus

angiogram *n.* صورة للأوعية surah lilaweyeh

angle *n.* زاوية zawyeh

angle *n.* وجهة نظر wejhet nazar

angry *adj.* معصّب meassib

anguish *n.* حسرة hasra

angular *adj.* كتير نحيف ktir naheif

animal *n.* حيوان haywan

animate *v.* يحرّك yuharrek

animate *adj.* حيوي hayawi

animation *n.* تحريك tahrik

animosity *n.* حقد heqed

animus *n.* كراهية karaheyeh

aniseed *n.* ينسون yaansun

ankle *n.* كاحل kahel

anklet *n.* خلخال khelkhal

annalist *n.* مؤرّخ muarrekh

annals *n.pl.* تاريخ tarikh

annectent *adj.* رابِط rabit

annex *v.* يضُمّ yaddum

annexation *n.* ضمّ damm

annihilate *v.* يدمّر yudammer

annihilation *n.* تدمير tadmir

anniversary *n.* عيد سنوي eid sanawi

annotate *v.* يُعلّق أسفل كتاب yualleq asfal elkitab

announce *v.* يعلن yuelin

announcement *n.* إعلان eilan

annoy *v.* يزعِج yuzeij

annoyance *n.* إزعاج ezaaj

annoying *adj.* مزعج muzeij

annual *adj.* سنوي sanawi

annuitant *n.* متقاعد mutakaed

annuity *n.* راتب سنوي ratin sanawi

annul *v.* يفسخ yafsakh

annulet *n.* حلقة صغيرة halakah seghireh

annulment *n.* فسخ fasekh

anoint *v.* دهن dahen

anomalous *adj.* شاذ shaaz

anomaly *n.* شذوذ shuzuz

anon *adv.* فورا fawran

anonymity *n.* إخفاء الاسم ekhfaae' elesim

anonymosity *n.* عدم ذكر الاسم adam zekir elesim

anonymous *adj.* مجهول majhul

anorak *n.* أنوراك anorak

anorexic *adj.* فاقد الشهية faked elshaheyeh

another *adj.* تاني tani

answer *n.* جواب jawab

answer *v.* يجاوب yujawib

answerable *adj.* مسؤول mas'ul

ant *n.* نملة namleh

antacid *adj.* مضاد حموضة mudad humudah

antagonism *n.* عداوة a'daweh

antagonist *n.* عدو adu

antagonize *v.* يعادي yua'di

antarctic *adj.* قطبي جنوبي ketbi janubi

antecede *v.* يسبق yasbuq

antecedent *n.* سابق sabeq

antecedent *adj.* سبق sabaq

antedate *n.* يخط بتاريخ أقدم yenhatt bitarikh aqdam

antelope *n.* ظبي zabi

antenatal *adj.* قبل الولادة kabel elweladeh

antennae *n.* أنتيل هوائي antil hawaei

antenuptial *adj.* قبل الزواج kabel elzawaj

anthem *n.* نشيدة nashideh

anthology *n.* مقتطفات muktatafat

anthrax *n.* مرض الجمرة الخبيثة maradh eljamra elkhabitheh

anthropoid *adj.* يشبه البشر beyshbah elbashar

anti *pref.* مضاد muddad

anti-aircraft *adj.* مضاد طيران muddad tayaran

antibiotic *n.* مضاد حيوي muddad hayawi

antic *n.* غريب gharib

anticipate *v.* يتوقع yatawaqa'

anticipation *n.* توقع tawaque

antidote *n.* دوا للسم dawa lelsamm

antinomy *n.* تناقض tanaqudh

antipathy *n.* جفا jafa

antiphony *n.* استجابة صوتية estijabeh sawteyeh

antipodes *n.* ضدين dhuddin

antiquarian *adj.* أثري athari

antiquarian *n.* تاجر كتب عتيقة tajer kutub atiqa

antiquary *n.* خبير آثار khabir athar

antiquated *adj.* عتيق atiq

21

antique adj. انتيكا antika
antiquity n. قدم qidam
antiseptic n. مادة مطهّرة madeh mutahhera
antiseptic adj. مُطهّر mutahher
antithesis n. تناقض tanaqudh
antitheism n. تعصّب taessub
antitheist n. متعصّب mutaessib
antler n. قَرن karen
antonym n. عكس akes
anus n. شرج sharj
anvil n. سِندان sanadan
anxiety n. توتّر tawatur
anxious adj. متوتّر mutawater
anxiously adv. بتوتّر bitawatur
any adj. أي ayy
anyhow adv. كيف ما كان keif m kaan
anyone pron أي شخص ayy shakhes
anyplace pron أي مكان ayy makan
anything pron أي شي ayy shi
anytime adv. أي وقت ayy waet
anyway adv. بأي طريقة beayy tariqa
anywhen adv. أي وقت ayy wa'et
anywhere adv. أي مكان ayy makan
anywho adv. أي شخص ayy shakhes
aorta n. شالشريان الأبهر elshryan elabhar
apace adv. بسرعة beser'aa
apart adv. على جنب ala janab
apartment n. بيت beit

apathy n. نفُور nufur
ape n. قِرد kerd
ape v. يقلِّد yukalled
aperture n. ثقب thuqub
apex n. راس ras
aphasia n. فقدان النطق feqdan elnutuq
aphorism n. حكمة hekmeh
apiary n. منحلة manhaleh
apiculture n. تربية النحل tarbeit elnahel
apish adj. متل القرد metl elqerd
apnoea n. انقطاع النفس enqetaa' elnafas
apologize v. يعتذر yaetazer
apologue n. قصّة رمزية kessa razeyeh
apology n. اعتذار e'tizaar
apostle n. أسقف asquf
apostrophe n. فاصلة faseleh
apotheosis n. تمجيد tamjid
apotheosis n. مثل أعلى matal aala
apparatus n. عدّة uddeh
apparel n. لبس خاص lebes khas
apparel v. يلبِس لبس خاص yelbes lebes khas
apparent adj. واضح wadeh
appeal n. ترجّي tarajji
appeal v. يترجّى yetrajja
appear v. يظهر yazhar
appearance n. مظهر mazhar
appease v. يطمّن yetammen
appellant n. مقدم الطعن muqaddem eltaen

append v. يُضيف لكتاب yudef lekitab

appendage n. مُلحق mulhaq

appendicitis n. التهاب الزائدة الدودية eltihab elzaedeh eldudeyeh

appendix n. مُلحق mulhaq

appendix n. زِلدَة zaydeh

appetence n. شهوة shahweh

appetent adj. شهواني shahwani

appetite n. شهية shayyeh

appetizer n. مقبلات muqabelat

applaud v. يصفّق yusaffeq

applause n. تصفيق tasfiq

apple n. تفاحة teffaha

appliance n. جهاز jihaz

applicable adj. مطبّق mutabbaq

applicant n. مقدم الطلب mukaddem eltalab

application n. تطبيق tatbiq

application n. طلب talab

apply v. يطبّق yutabbeq

apply v. يقدم طلب yukaddem eltalab

appoint v. يعيّن yuaeyyen

appointment n. تعيين ta'eyyin

apportion v. يقسّم yukassem

apposite adj. عكس akes

appositely adv. بطريقة معاكسة betareqa mu'akeseh

appraise v. يمدح yamdah

appreciable adj. يستحق التقدير yastaheq eltaqdir

appreciate v. يقدّر yuqadder

appreciation n. تقدير taqdir

apprehend v. يستوعب yastaweb

apprehension n. استيعاب istiaab

apprehensive adj. خايف khayef

apprehensive adj. مستوعب mistaweb

apprentice n. صاحب مهنة saheb mehneh

apprise v. يبلّغ yuballegh

approach v. يصل إلى yasel ela

approach n. طريق tariq

approbate v. يوافق رسمياً على ywafiq rasmeyen ala

approbation n. موافقة رسميّة muwafaqa rasmeyeh

approbation n. اختبار ikhtibar

appropriate v. يرصد مصاري لشي yarsud masari leshi

appropriate adj. مناسب munasib

appropriation n. رصد مصاري لشي rased masari leshi

appropriation n. استيلاء istillae'

approval n. موافقة muwafaqa

approve v. يوافق yuwafiq

approximate adj. تقريبي taqribi

appurtenance n. مُلحق mulhaq

apricot n. مشمش meshmush

April n. نيسان nisan

apron n. مريولة maryuleh

apt adj. مناسب munasib

apt adj. موفّق muwaffaq

apt adj. بمحله bemahaluh

aptitude n. لياقة layaqa

aquarium n. حوض سمك huwdh samak

aquarius n. برج الدلو berj eldalu
aqueduct n. مجرى majra
Arab n. الشخص العربي elshakhes
elarabi
Arabic n. اللغة العربية ellugha
elarabeyeh
Arabic adj. عربي arabi
arable adj. صالح للزراعة saleh
lelzera'a
arbiter n. حَكَم hakam
arbitrary adj. تحكيمي tahkimi
arbitrate v. يحكّم yuhakkem
arbitration n. تحكيم tahkimi
arbitrator n. محكّم mukakkem
arc n. يلوي yalwi
arcade n. قنطرة qantara
arch n. قوس qaws
arch v. يقوّس yuqawwes
arch adj. مقوّس muqawwas
archaeology n. دراسة الآثار
القديمة deraset el'athar
elqademeh
archaic adj. مهجور mahjur
archangel n. جبريل عليه السلام
jibril aleh esalam
archbishop n. مطران mutraan
archer n. رامي السهام rami
elsiham
archery n. رماية السهام rimayet
elsiham
architect n. مهندس معماري
muhandes memari
architecture n. هندسة معمارية
handaseh memareyeh
archives n.pl. سجلات sijillat
Arctic n. القطب الشمالي elqutub
elshamali

ardent adj. متحمّس
mutahammes
ardour n. حماس hamas
arduous adj. حماسي hamasi
area n. منطقة metaqa
arefaction n. جفاف jafaf
arena n. حَلَبة halabeh
argil n. طين teyn
argonaut n. مغامر mughamir
argue v. يجادل yujadel
argument n. جدل jadal
argument n. حجّة hijjeh
argute adj. عالي الصوت aali esut
arid adj. يبسان yabsan
aries n. برج الحمل berj elhamal
aright adv. بالضبط beldabt
arise v. ينمو yanmu
aristocracy n. ارستقراطية
arustuqrateyeh
aristocrat n. شخص ارستقراطي
shakhes arustuqrati
arithmetic n. الحساب elhisab
arithmetical adj. حسابي hesabi
ark n. سفينة safineh
ark n. تابوت tabout
arm n. يد yad
arm v. يسلّح yusalleh
armada n. أسطول istul
armament n. سلاح silah
armature n. درع dere'
armature n. حافظة hafiza
armature n. عمود دوّار amud
dawwar
armistice n. هُدنة hudneh
armlet adj. اسوارة eswara
armlet adj. لسان lisan
armour n. درع dere'

armoury *n.* مستودع أسلحة
   mestawda' asleha
armpit *n.* باط bat
army *n.* جيش jish
aroma *n.* ريحة riha
aromatherapy *n.* العلاج بالروايح
   elelaj belrawayeh
around *prep.* حولين hawalin
around *adv.* حوالي hawali
arouse *v.* يفيق yafiq
arraign *v.* يستدعي yastade'i
arrange *v.* يرتّب yuratteb
arrangement *n.* ترتيبات
   tartibat
arrant *n.* بكل ماتعنيه الكلمة
   bekul ma ta'nehi elkalemeh
array *v.* يصِفّ yasuff
array *n.* صفّ saff
arrears *n.pl.* متأخّر
   muta'akhkher
arrest *v.* يعتقل ya'taqil
arrest *n.* اعتقال i'tiqal
arrival *n.* وصول wusul
arrive *v.* يصل yasil
arrogance *n.* غرور ghurur
arrogant *adj.* مغرور maghrur
arrow *n.* سهم sahem
arrowroot *n.* عرعروط ararut
arsenal *n.* ترسانة tirsaneh
arsenic *n.* زرنيخ zarnikh
arson *n.* حريق متعمد hariq
   muta'mmad
art *n.* فنّ fann
artery *n.* شريان sheryan
artful *adj.* داهية daheyeh
arthritis *n.* روماتيزم rumatizem

artichoke *n.* أرضي شوكي ardi
   shawki
article *n.* مقالة maqaleh
articulate *adj.* واضح wadeh
articulate *v.* يتكلّم بوضوح
   yatakallam bewuduh
artifice *n.* كيد kyd
artificial *adj.* إصطناعي istinaei
artillery *n.* مدفعية medfae'yeh
artisan *n.* حرفي hirafi
artist *n.* فنّان fannan
artistic *adj.* فنّي fanni
artless *adj.* ساذج sazaj
as *adv.* متل metal
as *conj.* بينما baynama
as *conj.* حسب hasab
as *prep.* كَ ka
as *pron.* أثناء athnaa'
asbestos *n.* حرير صخري harir
   sakhri
ascend *v.* يصعد yaşa'ad
ascendancy *n.* نفوذ nufuz
ascent *n.* صعود suood
ascertain *v.* يؤكّد yu'akkid
ascetic *n.* زاهد zahid
ascetic *adj.* متقشّف
   mutaqashshif
ascribe *v.* يعود لسبب yaood
   lesabab
asexuality *n.* إخصاء ikhsaa'
ash *n.* رماد ramad
ashamed *adj.* يخجل bikhajjil
ashen *adj.* شاحب shahib
ashore *adv.* عالشاطئ alshatie'
aside *adv.* جنب ajanab
aside *n.* كلام على انفراد kalam
   ala infirad

asinine *adj.* أهْبَل ahbal

ask *v.* يسأل yes'aal

asleep *adv.* أثناء النوم athnaa' ehnum

asparagus *n.* هليون hilyun

aspect *n.* ناحية nahyeh

asperse *v.* يغتَاب yeghtab

asphyxia *n.* اخْتِناق ikhtinaq

asphyxiate *v.* يَخْتنِق yakhnuq

aspirant *n.* شخص طموح shakhes tamuh

aspiration *n.* طُموح tumuh

aspire *v.* يطمح إلى yatmah ila

ass *n.* طيز teyz

assail *v.* يهاجِم yuhajim

assassin *n.* قاتل مأجور katil ma'jur

assassinate *v.* يغتال yaghtal

assassination *n.* اغتِيال ighteyal

assault *n.* إعتداء ietidaa'

assault *v.* يعتَدي على yatadi ala

assemble *v.* يجمع yatajammaa'

assembly *n.* جمعية jam'eyeh

assent *v.* يوافق على yuwafiq ala

assent *n.* إتفاق itifaq

assert *v.* يؤَكِّد على yuakkid ala

assertive *adj.* مؤكَّد muakkad

assess *v.* يقَيِّم yuqayyem

assessment *n.* تقييم taqyyem

asset *n.* ممتلكات mumtalakat

assign *v.* يَتنازَل عن ملكية yatanazal an mulkeyet

assignee *n.* متنازل له mutanazal lahu

assimilate *v.* يشُبّه yushabbeh

assimilation *n.* تَشبيه tashbeeh

assist *v.* يساعد yusaed

assistance *n.* مساعَدة musaadeh

assistant *n.* مساعِد musaed

associate *v.* يربط yarbut

associate *adj.* مرتبِط murtabit

associate *n.* شريك sharik

association *n.* رابِطة rabita

assoil *v.* يعَذِر ya'zur

assort *v.* يصنف yusannif

assuage *v.* يهدي yuhaddi

assume *v.* يفترض yaftared

assumption *n.* افتِراض iftiraad

assurance *n.* ضَمان daman

assure *v.* يضمَن yadman

astatic *adj.* مو مستقِر mu mistaqer

asterisk *n.* نجمة najmeh

asterism *n.* برج berj

asteroid *adj.* نجمي najmi

asthma *n.* ربو rabu

astir *adv.* بإنفعال beinfea'al

astonish *v.* يبهت yabhat

astonishment *n.* بهتة bahteh

astound *v.* يذهل yuzhil

astral *adj.* كوكبي kawkabi

astray *adv.,* بضياع bidayaa'

astrolabe *n.* أسطرلاب asterlaab

astrologer *n.* منجم munajjim

astrology *n.* تنجيم tanjiim

astronaut *n.* رائد فضاء raed fadaa'

astronomer *n.* عالم فلَك aalem falak

astronomy *n.* علم الفلَك ilim elfalak

asunder *adv.* شقفة shiqfeh shiqfeh

asylum *n.* لجوء lujouo'

asymmetrical *adj.* مو متناسق
mu metnaseq

at *prep.* في fi

atheism *n.* كُفر kufur

atheist *n.* كافِر kafir

athirst *adj.* عطشان atshaan

athlete *n.* شخص رياضي shakhes
reyaddi

athletic *adj.* رياضي reyyaddi

athletics *n.* رياضة ألعاب القوى
reyyadet alaab elqewa

athwart *prep.* من طرف للتاني
men taraf latani

atlas *n.* أطلس atlas

atmosphere *n.* جَو jaww

atmospheric *adj.* جوّي jawwi

atoll *n.* جزيرة مرجانيّة jazereh
merjaneyyeh

atom *n.* ذرّة zarra

atomic *adj.* ذرّي zarri

atone *v.* يكفّر عن yukaffir an

atonement *n.* تكفير عن takfiir
an

atrocious *adj.* فاحش fahish

atrocity *n.* كِبائِر kabair

atrophy *n.* ضُمور dumur

atrophy *v.* يضمر yadmur

atropine *n.* أتروبين artobin

attach *v.* يوصِل yuwassil

attach *v.* يوظّف في سفارة
yuwazzif fi safara

attache *n.* موظّف في سفارة
muwazzaf fi safara

attachment *n.* مرفق morfak

attack *n.* هجوم hojum

attack *v.* يهاجِم yuhajim

attain *v.* يحصل على yahsal ala

attainment *n.* الحصول على
elhusul ala

attaint *v.* يسبب العَار yusabib
el'aar

attempt *v.* يحاول yuhawil

attempt *n.* محاولة muhawaleh

attend *v.* يحضر yahdder

attendance *n.* حضور hudur

attendant *n.* حاضر hadir

attention *n.* إنتباه intibaah

attentive *adj.* مهتم muhtam

attest *v.* يوثّق yuwaththiq

attire *n.* لِبس lebes

attire *v.* يلبِّس yulabbis

attitude *n.* موقف mawqif

attorney *n.* محامي muhami

attract *v.* يلفت انتباه yalfit
intibah

attraction *n.* لفت انتباه lafet
intibah

attractive *adj.* مُلفت للانتباه
mulfit lelintibah

attribute *v.* يعود لسبب yaood
lesabab

attribute *n.* صفة مميزة sifa
mumayazeh

atypic *adj.* شاذّ shazz

aubergine *n.* باذنجان bazenjaan

auburn *adj.* كستنائي kastana'ei

auction *n.* مزاد علني mazad
alani

auction *v.* يبيع بالمزاد العلني yabei
belmazaad elalani

audacity *n.* وقاحة waqaha

audible *adj.* مسموع masmue'

audience *n.* جمهور jumhur

audiovisual *adj.* مسموع ومرئي masmue' w marei

audit *n.* تدقيق حسابات tadqiq hesabat

audit *v.* يدقق حسابات yudaqeq hesabat

auditive *adj.* سمعي samei

auditor *n.* مدقق حسابات mudaqeq hesabat

auditorium *n.* صالة saleh

auger *n.* ثقّابة thaqqabeh

aught *n.* ولا شي wla shi

augment *v.* مضاعفة mudaafeh

augmentation *n.* زيادة zeyadeh

August *n.* آب aab

august *adj.* فخم fakhem

aunt *n.* عمّة ammeh

aura *n.* نسمة nismeh

auriform *adj.* بشكل أذن beshakel uzun

aurilave *n.* نكّاشة أذن nakkashet uzun

aurora *n.* فجر fajer

auspicate *v.* يدعو yaduu

auspice *n.* فال faal

auspicious *adj.* مُبارك mubarak

austere *adj.* متزمّت mutazammit

authentic *adj.* موثوق mawthuq

author *n.* مؤلّف muallef

authoritative *adj.* متسلّط mutasallet

authority *n.* سلطة sulta

authorize *v.* يؤلّف yuallef

autobiography *n.* مذكّرات muzakkarat

autocracy *n.* استبداد istibeddad

autocrat *n.* شخص مستبّد shakhes mustabbed

autocratic *adj.* مستبّد mustabbed

autograph *n.* يوقّع بخط إيده yuwaqqee' bikhat yadeh

automatic *adj.* آلي aali

automobile *n.* سيّارة sayyarah

autonomous *adj.* مستقل mustaqqil

autumn *n.* خريف khariif

auxiliary *adj.* مساعد musaed

auxiliary *n.* فعل مساعد feil musaed

avail *v.* يوفّر yuwaffer

available *adj.* متوفّر mutawaffir

avale *v.* يبلع الإهانة yabla' elehaneh

avarice *n.* جَشع jashaa'

avenge *v.* ينتقم من yantaqim men

avenue *n.* جادّة jaddeh

average *n.* معدّل mu'addal

average *adj.* وسطي wasati

average *v.* يحسب معدّل yahsub mu'addal

average *v.* يقسّم بالتساوي yuqassem beltasawi

averse *adj.* طفران tafraan

aversion *n.* إشمئزاز ishme'zaz

avert *v.* يتحاشى yatahasha

aviary *n.* قفص عصافير qafas assafir

aviation *n.* طيران tayaran

aviator *n.* طيّار tayyar

avid *adj.* طمّاع tammaa'

avidity *adv.* طمَع tamaa'

avidly *adv.* بطمع betamaa'

avoid *v.* يَتَجَنّب yatajannab

avoidance *n.* تَجنُب tajannub

avow *v.* يصرّح عن yusarreh an

avulsion *n.* قَلَع qale'

await *v.* يَنتظر yantazir

awake *v.* يصحّي من النوم yusahhi men ennum

awake *adj.* صاحي من النوم sahi men enum

awakening *n.* صَحَيان من النوم sahayan men enum

award *v.* يكافِئ yukafe'

award *n.* مكافأة mukafa'a

aware *adj.* واعي waeii

awareness *n.* وعي waei

away *adv.* لبعيد labe'yed

awe *n.* هيبة haebeh

awesome *adj.* رهيب rahib

awful *adj.* بشع beshe'

awhile *adv.* لحظة lahza

awkward *adj.* محرِج muhrij

axe *n.* فأس fa's

axial *adj.* محوري mehwari

axis *n.* مدار madar

axle *n.* محور mehwar

ayield *v.* ينتهي من yantahi men

azote *n.* أزوت a'zut

azure *n.* سماوي samawi

B

babble *v.* يبربِر yebarber

babe *n.* غرّ gherr

babe *n.* مولود mawlud

babel *n.* ضجّة dajjeh

baboon *n.* قرد الميمون kerd elmaymun

baby *n.* مولود mawlud

babyface *n.* وجه طفولي wajeh tufuli

babyproof *adj.* آمن عالأطفال aamen alatfal

babysit *v.* يجلس مع الأطفال yajles ma' elatfal

babysitting *n.* الجلوس مع الأطفال eljulus ma' elatfal

baccalaureate *n.* بكالوريا bakaluria

bacchanal *n.* سَكّير sekkir

bacchanal *adj.* سَكّير sekkir

bachelor *n.* حامل إجازة جامعية hamil ijazeh jameyeh

bachelorette *n.* عازبة a'azebeh

back *n.* ظَهر zaher

back *adv.* لوَرا lawara

back *adj.* خلفي khalfi

back *v.* يدّعم yudae'm

backbite *v.* غيبة ghibeh

backbone *n.* صلَب solb

background *n.* معلومات عامة ma'lumat aameh

backhand *n.* ضربة بقفا الإيد darbeh biqafa eleyed

backfire *v.* يشعل النار قبل وقتا yeshul ennar abel waqta

backlash *n.* تَوجيع قطع الماكينة لورا tarje' kita' elmakina lawara

backlash *v.* يُرجع لورا yurajje' lawara

backlight *n.* إضاءة خلفيّة ida'a khalfeyeh

backlight *v.* يُشعل أضواء خلفيّة yush'el adwaa' khalfeyeh

backlit *adj.* مضاء من الخلف mudaa' men elkhalef

backpack *n.* حقيبة عالظهر haqibeh alzaher

backpack *v.* يحمل على الظهر yahmil alzaher

backpacker *n.* رحّال rahhal

backslide *v.* يتدهور yetdahwar

backstairs *n.* أدراج خلفيّة adraj khalfeyeh

backstairs *adj.* من ورا الظهر men wara elzaher

backtrack *n.* تراجُع عن الموقف tarajue' an elmawkif

backtrack *v.* يتراجع عن موقفه yetraja' an elmawkif

backup *n.* احتياطي ihtiyati

backup *adj.* داعم da'em

backward *adj.* متخلّف mutakhallef

backward *adv.* بالمقلوب belmaklub

bacon *n.* لحم خنزير lahem khanzir

bacteria *n.* بكتريا bakteria

bad *adj.* سيء saye'

badge *n.* وسام wisam

badger *n.* حيوان الجربوع haywan eljarbue'

badly *adv.* بطريقة سيئة betaraqa sayea'

badly *adv.* لأبعد حَدّ laabad hadd

badminton *n.* تِنِس الرّيشة tinis elrisheh

baffle *v.* يوقع في حيرة yuke' fi hireh

baffling *adj.* محيّر muhayyer

bag *n.* كيس kees

bag *v.* يحطّ في كيس yehut fi kis

bag *v.* ينتفخ yentafikh

baggage *n.* حقائب haqaeb

bagpipe *n.* مِزمار mezmaar

bagpiper *n.* عازف المِزمار aazif mezmaar

baguette *n.* صُمون طويل sammoun tawil

bail *n.* كَفالة kafaleh

bail *v.* يكفُل yakfal

bailable *adj.* ممكن إطلاق سراحه بكفالة mumken itlaq sarahu bekafaleh

bailiff *n.* مُحضِر المحكمة muhdir elmahkameh

bait *n.* طُعم للمصيدة tuem lelmasyadeh

bait *v.* يحط طُعم المصيدة yehet tuem lelmasyadeh

bake *v.* يخبز yakhbuz

baker *n.* فرّان farran

bakery *n.* مخبز makhbaz

balaclava *n.* طاقية صوف للرّاس والرقبة ta'eh suf lelras welraqabeh

balance *n.* توازن tawazun

balance *v.* يوازن yowazin

balcony *n.* بلكونة balkuneh

bald *adj.* أصلع aslaa'
bale *n.* حَزمة hezmeh
bale *v.* يَحزم yahzum
baleful *adj.* مؤذي muezi
baleen *n.* عظمة حنك الحوت azmet hanak elhut
ball *n.* طابة tabeh
ballad *n.* غنيّة تراثيّة gheneyeh turatheyeh
ballet *sn.* باليه baleh
ballistics *n.* دراسة القَذائف deraset elqazaef
balloon *n.* بالونة baluneh
ballot *n.* تصويت taswiit
ballot *v.* يصوّت yesawwet
ballpoint *n.* قلم حبر kalam heber
balm *n.* بَلسَم balsam
balmlike *adj.* متل البَلسَم metel elbalsam
balsam *n.* مرهم marham
balsamic *adj.* مرهمي marhami
bam *n.* غشّ gheshsh
bamboo *n.* خيزران khizaran
ban *n.* حظر hazer
ban *v.* يحظر yahzur
banal *adj.* تافه tafeh
banana *n.* موزة muzeh
band *n.* بد للشعر band lelshaer
bandage *n.* لزقة جرح lazqet jerh
bandage *v.* يحط لزقة جرح yehit lazqet jerh
bandit *n.* قاطع طريق kate' tariie
bane *n.* سم مميت samm mumiit
bane *v.* يسمم yesammem
bang *v.* ينطرق بشَي yentereq beshi

bang *n.* دقّة da'a
bangle *n.* اسوارة eswara
banish *v.* ينفي yanfi
banishment *n.* نفي nafi
banjo *n.* بانجو banjo
bank *n.* بنك bank
bank *n.* ضفّة diffeh
bank *v.* يكوّم yekawwem
bank *v.* يودع بالبنك yude' belbank
banker *n.* صاحب بنك sahib bank
banknote *n.* وراق نقديّة wraq nakdeyeh
bankrupt *n.* يفلّس yefallis
bankruptcy *n.* إفلاس iflaas
banner *n.* راية rayeh
bannister *n.* درابزون darabzun
banquet *n.* وليمة walimeh
banquet *v.* يعمل وليمة ye'mil walimeh
bantam *n.* قزم kazam
banter *v.* ينكّت yenakket
banter *n.* نكتة nikteh
bantling *n.* طفل زغير tefel zeghir
bantling *n.* ابن حرام ibn haram
banyan *n.* شجر التين الهندي shajar ettiin elhindi
baptism *n.* تعميد ta'amiid
baptize *+v.t.* يعمّد yu'ammid
bar *n.* بار bar
bar *n.* لوح luh
bar *v.* يقفل yukfil
barb *n.* دقن da'en
barbarian *adj.* همجي hamaji
barbarian *n.* الهمجي elhamaji

barbarism *n.* هَمَجِيّة hamajeyeh

barbarity *n.* رَبَرِيّة barbareyeh

barbarous *adj.* رَبَري barbari

barbed *adj.* شائِك sha'ek

barber *n.* حَلّاق hallaq

bard *n.* شاعِر ملاحِم shaiir malahim

bare *adj.* بِلا لِبس bla lebes

bare *v.* يِشَلِّح yeshalleh

barefoot *adj.* حَفيان hafyan

barely *adv.* يا دوب ya dub

bargain *n.* تَجرة tajraa

bargain *v.* يِساوِم بالسِعر yesawem belser

barge *n.* زورَق zawra'a

baritone *n.* صوت جهوري saut jahuri

barium *n.* باريوم barium

bark *n.* تِعواية te'wayeh

bark *v.* يِعوي yeawwi

bark *v.* يِقشِر لِحاء الشَجَر yekasher lihaa' eshajar

barley *n.* شعير sha'ir

barman *n.* سَقّا البار saqqa elbar

barn *n.* إسطَبل istabel

barnacle *n.* شَخص دِبِق shakhes debe'

barometer *n.* مِقياس ضَغط الهوا mekyas daghet elhawa

baron *n.* بارون baron

baroque *adj.* مدوكَر زيادة mdukar zeyadeh

barouche *n.* عَربة بِجَرّا حصان arabeh yejerra hesaan

barrack *n.* ثَكَنة thakaneh

barrage *n.* سَدّ sadd

barrel *n.* بَرميل barmil

barren *n.* عقيم akiim

barricade *n.* حاجِز hajiz

barrier *n.* ساتِر satir

barrister *n.* مُحامي muhami

bartender *n.* نادِل في بار nadil fi bar

barter *v.* يِقايِض yukayed

barter *n.* مُقايَضة mukadadah

basal *adj.* قاعِدي kaeydi

base *n.* قاعِدة ka'edeh

base *adj.* دَنيء danie'

base *v.* يِبني قاعِدة عَسكَرية yebni kaedeh askaryeh

baseborn *adj.* مولود مِن بيئة مِنحَطّة mawlud men bea'a monhattah

baseless *adj.* مالُه مُبَرِّر malu mubarir

basement *n.* قَبو abu

bash *n.* خَبْطة khabtah

bash *v.* يِخبُط yakhbut

bashful *adj.* خَجول khajul

basic *adj.* أساسي asasi

basically *adv.* بِشَكل أساسي beshakel asasi

basil *n.* حَبَق habae'

basin *n.* طَشت tesht

basis *n.* أساس asas

bask *v.* يِتشَمَّس yetshammas

basket *n.* سَلّة salleh

basketball *n.* كرة السَلّة kuret salleh

bass *n.* فَرخ farkh

bastard *n.* ابن حَرام ibn haram

bastard *adj.* حَقير hakiir

bastion *n.* حِصن hesen

bat *n.* خُفّاش khaffash

bat *n.* مضرَب miḍrab

bat *v.* يضرب بالمضرب yadrub belmidrab

batch *n.* عجنة ajneh

bath *n.* حمّام hammam

bathe *v.* يتحمّم yetehammam

baton *n.* عصاية asayeh

batsman *n.* ضارب المضرب darib elmadrab

battalion *n.* كتيبة katibeh

battlement *n.* سور إله فتحات sur elu fatehat

batter *n.* مهتري mehteri

batter *v.* يقصف yaqsuf

battery *n.* بطّارية batareyeh

battle *n.* معركة maarakeh

battle *v.* يقاتل بالمعركة yeaatil bilmaarakeh

battlefield *n.* ميدان المعركة midan elmaarakeh

battleground *n.* أرض المعركة ared elmaarakeh

battlezone *n.* منطقة المعارك metaet maarek

baulk *n.* غَلَط ghalat

bawd *n.* صاحب sahib

bawl *v.* صِياح siyah

bawn *n.* بيدق baydae'

bay *n.* نباح الكلب nubah elkaleb

bayonet *n.* حَربة herbeh

bayou *n.* جدوَل مي jadwal mai

bayside *adj.* عشاطئ خليج ashate' khalij

bazaar *n.* بازار bazar

bazooka *n.* سلاح عالكتف silah al ketef

be *v.* يكون yekun

beach *n.* شاطئ shate'

beachfront *adj.* على شاطئ البحر ala shate' elbaher

beachside *adj.* شط البحر shatt elbaher

beacon *n.* مَنَارة manara

bead *n.* حبّة habbeh

beads *n.* مسبحة masbaha

beadle *n.* شمّاس الكنيسة shammas elkaniseh

beadwork *n.* تطريز tatriiz

beady *adj.* مطرّز mutarraz

beak *n.* منقار mena'ar

beaker *n.* قدَح كبير qadah kbir

beam *n.* شعاع shuaa'

beam *v.* يتلالا yetla'l'

beamless *adj.* كيبي kebi

bean *n.* فول ful

bear *n.* دب debb

bear *v.* يتحمّل yetehammal

bear *v.* يطيق yetiie'

beard *n.* دقن da'en

bearded *adj.* مطوّل دقنه metawwel da'enuh

beardless *adj.* ماله دقن malu da'en

bearing *n.* حمَل hamel

beast *n.* بهيم bahiim

beastly *adj.* بيهامة bebahameh

beat *v.* يهزم yahzim

beat *v.* يسحق yaseha'

beat *n.* طرقة tarqa

beautiful *adj.* حلو helu

beautify *v.* يحلّي yehalli

beauty *n.* جمّال jamal

beaver *n.* قندس qundus

becalm *v.* يهدّي yuhaddi
because *conj.* لأنّه le'annu
beck *n.* إشارة isharah
beckon *v.* يؤشّر على yu'ashsher ala
beckon *v.* يغري yughri
become *v.* يصير yesir
becoming *adj.* لايق layeq
bed *n.* تخت takhit
bed *v.* يستريح yestrih
bedevil *v.* يغوي yaghwi
bedding *n.* شراشف sharshif
bedight *v.* زيّن yuzayyen
bedlamp *n.* ضوّ التخت daww ettakhit
bedrobe *n.* لبس النوم lebes ennum
bedroom *n.* غرفة النوم ghirfit ennum
bedsheet *n.* غطا التخت ghata ettakhit
bedsore *n.* قرحة الفراش qarhet elfirash
bed-time *n.* وقت النوم waqet ennum
bee *n.* نحلة nahleh
beech *n.* شجر زان shajar zaan
beef *n.* لحم بقر lahem baqar
beefy *adj.* سمين samiin
beehive *n.* خليّة النحل khaleyyet elnahil
beekeeper *n.* مُربّي النحل murabbi elnahil
beer *n.* بيرة bira
beet *n.* شوندر shawandar
beetle *n.* خنفسة khenifseh

beetroot *n.* جذر الشوندر jazer elshawandar
befall *v.* يصيب yusiib
before *prep.* تجاه tijah
before *prep.* قدّام kiddam
before *adv.* قبل kabel
before *conj.* سبق sabaq
beforehand *adv.* صدارة sadarah
befriend *v.* يعاشر ye'aashir
beg *v.* يشحد yeshehad
beget *v.* تولّد tulad
beggar *n.* شحّاد shahhad
begin *v.* يبدى yebda
beginner *n.* مبتدئ mubtade'
beginning *n.* بداية bedayeh
begird *v.* زنّر yezanner
begrudge *v.* يحسد yehsud
begrudging *adj.* حسّاد hessad
beguile *v.* يفتن yaftun
beguile *v.* يخدع yakhdaa
beguiling *adj.* خدعة khedaa
behalf *n.* مصلحة maslaha
behave *v.* يتصرّف yetsarraf
behaviour *n.* تصرف tasarruf
behead *v.* يقطع راس yektaa ras
behind *n.* مؤخّرة muakhkhera
behind *adv.* لورا lawara
behind *adj.* خلفي khalfi
behind *prep.* ورا wara
behold *v.* يلمح yulammeh
being *n.* مخلوق makhluuq
bejewel *v.* يتزيّن بالجوهرات yetzayyan belmujawharat
belabour *v.* يقتل حشك ولبك yektel hashek w labek
belated *adj.* متأخّر met'akhkher

belch *v.* يَتَجَشّأ yetejashae'	**beluga** *n.* الحوت الأبيض elhut elabyad
belch *n.* تَجَشُؤ tajashu'	**belvedere** *n.* مبنى مع إطلالة رائعة mabna ma itlaleh rae'a
belief *n.* إيمان iman	
belief *n.* اعتقاد ie'tikaad	**bemask** *v.* يغطّي بقناع yeghatti beqenaa'
believe *v.* يؤمن yu'emin	
believe *v.* يعتقد ya'teked	**bemire** *v.* يلوّث yelawweth
belittle *v.* يستضغر yestasgher	**bemuse** *v.* يلبك yelabbek
bell *n.* جرس jaras	**bench** *n.* مصطبة mastabeh
bellboy *n.* عامل الفندق aamel elfunduq	**bencher** *n.* عضو بنقابة المحامين edu be naqabet elmuhamin
belle *n.* مرًا حلوة كثير mara helweh ktir	**benchtop** *n.* سطح المصطبة sateh elmastabeh
bellhop *n.* عامل الفندق aamel elfuduq	**bend** *n.* يحني yehni
bellicose *adj.* عدواني edwani	**bend** *v.* حنيّة hanyeh
belligerency *n.* وضع حربي wade' harbi	**beneath** *adv.* لتحت la tahit
	beneath *adv.* لأوطى la awta
belligerent *adj.* حربي harbi	**beneath** *prep.* تحت tahet
belligerent *n.* محارب muhareb	**beneath** *prep.* أوطى awtaa
bellow *v.* يخوّر yekhwwer	**benediction** *n.* وركة barakeh
bellows *n.* منفاخ menfaakh	**benefaction** *n.* حسنة hasaneh
belly *n.* بطن baten	**benefactor** *n.* محسن muhsen
belong *v.* يخص yekhuss	**benefic** *adj.* خيري khayri
belongings *n.* ممتلكات mumtalakat	**benefice** *n.* إقطاعة للكنيسة iqtaa' lelkaniseh
beloved *adj.* محبوب mahbub	**beneficial** *adj.* نافع nafe'
beloved *n.* حبيب habib	**benefit** *n.* فائدة fa'edeh
below *adv.* لتحت latahit	**benefit** *v.* يفيد yefid
below *adv.* لجهنم lajhannam	**benevolence** *n.* صدقة sadaqa
below *prep.* تحت tahit	**benevolent** *adj.* متصدّق mutasadeq
below *prep.* أوطى awtaa	
bellowing *n.* خوار khiwar	**benight** *v.* يضلل yudallel
belly *n.* معدة me'deh	**benign** *adj.* حميد hamid
belong *v.* ينتمي yentimi	**benignly** *adv.* وقّة bereqqa
belonging *n.* انتماء intimaa'	**benison** *n.* وركة barakeh
belt *n.* كمر kamar	**bent** *n.* رغبة raghbeh
	bent *n.* إتجاه itijah

bent *adj.* محدَّب mohaddab
bent *adj.* مايل mayel
benzene *n.* بنزين benzyn
benzidine *n.* بنزيدين benzydin
bequeath *v.* يورث yowarreth
bereave *v.* يفقد تخص yafkud shakhes
bereaved *adj.* مفجوع mafjue'
bereavement *n.* فقدان شخص feqdan shakhes
bereavement *n.* فاجعة fajiaa
beret *n.* قلنسوة kelensuweh
berm *n.* علاوة بالأرض alaweh beared
berry *n.* توت tut
berserk *n.* جنون junun
beserk *adj.* جائن جنونه janen jununu
beserker *n.* شخص جائن جنونه shakhes janen jununu
berth *n.* مرسى marsah
beryllium *n.* بيريليوم berylyum
beseech *n.* توسل tawassul
beseech *v.* يتوسل yetwassal
beseeching *n.* توسل tawassal
beshame *v.* يستعر من yesta'err men
beside *prep.* لجنب lejanab
besides *prep.* لطرف letaraf
besides *adv.* كمان kaman
besiege *v.* يحاصر yehaser
besmirch *v.* ينجس yenajjes
bespeak *v.* يعطي إشارة yeti esharah
bespectacled *adj.* لابس نظارات labes nazarat

bespoken *adj.* حسب الطلب hasab eltalab
bestial *adj.* همجي hamaji
bestow *v.* يمنح yemnah
bestrew *v.* يرش yerush
bet *v.* يراهن yerahin
bet *n.* رهان rihan
beta *adj.* ثاني thani
beta *n.* بتا betta
betel *n.* نبات متسلق nabat mutasalleq
betray *v.* يخون yekhun
betrayal *n.* خيانة kheyaneh
betroth *v.* يخطب yakhtub
betrothal *n.* خطبة khutbeh
betrothed *adj.* خطيب khatib
better *adj.* أحسن ahsan
better *adv.* للأحسن lelahsan
better *v.* يحسن yehassin
betterment *n.* تحسين tahsiin
betting *adj.* مراهنة murahaneh
bettor *n.* مراهن murahin
between *prep.* بين bein
betwixt *prep.* بين bein
beverage *n.* مشروب mashrub
bewail *v.* ينوح على yenuuh ala
beware *v.* يحتاط yehtaat
bewilder *v.* يحير yehayyer
bewilderment *n.* حيرة hireh
bewind *v.* يتمايل yetmayal
bewitch *v.* يسحر yasehar
bewitched *adj.* مسحور masehur
bewitching *adj.* ساحر saher
bewitching *n.* كاتب سحور kateb sehur
beyond *prep.* ورا wara
beyond *adv.* لبعد labaed

biangular *adj.* إلى زاويتين elu zawitin

biannual *adj.* مرتين بالسنة martin belsineh

biannually *adv.* يصير مرتين بالسنة yesir martin belseneh

biantennary *adj.* إلى انتيلين elu antilin

bias *n.* تحيّز tahayyuz

bias *v.* يتحيّز yetehayyaz

biased *adj.* متحيّز metehayyez

biaxial *adj.* إلى محورين elu mehwarin

bib *n.* دقّونة daquneh

bib *v.* يشرب yashrab

bibber *n.* شرّيب sharriib

bible *n.* إنجيل injil

bibliography +n صفحة مؤلفات الكاتب safhet mualafat elkatib

bibliographer *n.* عالم كتب aalem ketub

bicellular *adj.* إلى خليتين elu khalitin

bicentenary *adj.* ذكرى مئوية تانية zikra meaweyeh taneyeh

biceps *n.* عضلة براسين adaleh brasin

bicker *v.* نقاش nikash

bicycle *n.* مسكليت misklit

bid *v.* يقدّم عرض سعر yuqaddem ared se'r

bid *v.* يقدّم عمناقصة yuqaddem ala munaqasa

bid *n.* مناقصة munaqasa

bidder *n.* مناقص munaqis

bide *v.* ينتظر yentuzer

bidet *n.* شطّافة shattafeh

bidimensional *adj.* ثنائي الأبعاد thunaei elabaad

biennial *adj* مرة كل سنتين marah kel sintin

bier *n.* نعش na'esh

bifacial *adj.* إلى وجهين elu wajhin

biff *n.* كفّ kaff

biff *v.* يضرب كفّ yedrub kaff

biformity *n.* تطابق tatabuq

bifurcate *v.* يتفرّع yetfarra'

bifurcation *n.* تفرّع tafarru'

big *adj.* كبير kbir

bigamist *n.* شخص متزوج تنتين shakhes metzawwej tentiin

bigamous *adj.* متزوج تنتين metzawwej tentiin

bigamy *n.* تعدد الزوجات taadud elzawjat

bighead *n.* ضخامة الراس dakhamet elras

bighearted *adj.* طيّب tayyeb

bight *n.* عقدة uqdeh

bigot *n.* تعصب taassub

bigotry *n.* رجعية rajeyeh

bike *n.* مسكليت misklit

biker *n.* سوّاق المسكليت sawaq elmesklit

bikini *n.* بكيني bekini

bilateral *adj.* ثنائي thunaei

bile *n.* المادة الصفراوية elmadeh elsafraweyeh

bile *n.* تعكّر المزاج taakkur elmizaj

bilingual *adj.* ثنائي اللغة thunaei ellugha

bill *v.* يفوتر yefuter
bill *n.* فاتورة fatura
billable *adj.* بتفوتر betfutar
billboard *n.* لوحة إعلانات lawhit e'elanat
billiard *n.* بيلياردو bilyardu
billion *n.* بليون bilyon
billionaire *n.* بليونير bilyunir
billow *n.* موجة عارمة mawjeh aarmeh
billow *v.* يهوج yehuuj
billow *v.* يتموج yetmawwaj
bimonthly *adj.* كل نص شهر kel nes shaher
binary *adj.* زوجي zawji
bind *v.* يلزم yulzim
binding *adj.* ملزم mulzim
binge *v.* حفلة سكر haflet sukr
binocular *adj.* إلو عينتين elu eyntin
binoculars *n.* ناظور nazur
bioabsorption *n.* امتصاص حيوي imtisas hayawi
bioactivity *n.* تأثير حيوي taa'thir hayawi
bioagent *n.* عامل حيوي aamel hayawi
biochemical *adj.* كيميا حيوية kimia hayaweyeh
bioclimate *n.* مناخ حيوي manakh hayawi
biodegradation *n.* تحلّل حيوي tahalul hayawi
bioengineering *n.* هندسة حيوية hanadeh hayaweyeh
biofuel *n.* وقود حيوي wuqud hayawi

biographer *n.* كاتب سيرة ذاتيّة katib elsireh elzateyeh
biography *n.* كتابة السيرة الذاتيّة kitabet elsireh elzateyeh
biohazardous *adj.* سامّ عضوياً samm udweyan
biologist *n.* مختصّ بعلم الأحياء mukhtas be'elem elahyaa'
biology *n.* علم الأحياء elem elahyaa'
biomass *n.* كتلة حيويّة keteleh hayaweyeh
biometric *adj.* إحصاء حيوي ihsaa' hayawi
bionic *adj.* إلو أطراف صناعيّة elu atraaf sinaeyeh
biopsy *n.* خُزعَة khuza'a
biopsy *v.* ياخد خزعة yakhud khuza'a
bioscope *n.* جهاز عرض سينمائي jihaz ared sinamaei
bioscopy *n.* فحص حيوي fahes hayawi
biped *n.* حيوان يمشي عرجلتين heywan bemshi arejltin
bipolar *adj.* إلو قطبين elu ketbin
biracial *adj.* جاي من عرقين jay men erein
birch *v.* يجلد yajlud
birch *n.* عصاية التأديب asayet taa'dib
bird *n.* عصفور asfur
birdcage *n.* قفص العصفور kafas elasfur
birdlime *n.* دَبَق dabaq
birth *n.* ولادة weladeh

birthdate *n.* تاريخ الولادة tarikh elweladeh

birthmark *n.* علامة الولادة alamet elweladeh

biscuit *n.* بسكويت biskwit

bisect *v.* يقسم قسمين yeksem kesmin

bisexual *adj.* مخنّث mukhannath

bisexual *adj.* للجنسين leljensin

bishop *n.* قسيس kasis

bison *n.* ثور أمريكي thawr amriki

bisque *n.* شوربة دسمة shurabah desmeh

bistro *n.* نادي ليلي nadi layli

bit *n.* عضّة adda

bitch *n.* شرموطة sharmuta

bite *v.* يعضّ ye'add

bite *n.* لقمة leqmeh

bitter *adj.* مرّ murr

bi-weekly *adj.* مرتين بالأسبوع martin belesbue'

bizarre *adj.* شاذّ shazz

blab *v.* يحكي حكي فاضي yehki haki fadi

blab *n.* حكي فاضي haki fadi

blabber *n.* علّاك allak

black *adj.* أسود aswad

blacken *v.* يسوّد yesawwed

blacklist *n.* القائمة السودا elqaemeh elsuda

blacklist *v.* يدخّله عالقائمة السودا yedakhkhluh alqaemeh elsuda

blackmail *n.* ابتزاز ibtizaz

blackmail *v.* يبتزّ yebtazz

blackmailer *n.* مبتزّ mubtazz

blacksmith *n.* حدّاد haddad

bladder *n.* مثانة mathaneh

blade *n.* شفرة shafra

blain *n.* ناسور nasur

blame *v.* يلوم yeluwm

blame *n.* لوم luwm

blanch *v.* يبيّض yebayyed

bland *adj.* أنيس anis

bland *adj.* خفيف khafif

blank *adj.* فاضي fadi

blank *adj.* أبيض abyad

blank *n.* فضا fada

blank *n.* بياض bayad

blanket *n.* حرام heram

blare *v.* يعلن yuelin

blare *v.* يدوي yedwi

blasé *adj.* لا مبالي la mubali

blast *n.* تفجير tafjir

blast *v.* يفجّر yefajjer

blastoff *n.* انطلاق intilaq

blatant *adj.* وقح weqeh

blaze *n.* حريق hariq

blaze *v.* يحترق yehterq

blazing *adj.* مشتعل mushta'el

blazon *n.* درع مزركش dere' muzarkash

blazon *v.* يزركش yezarkesh

blazoned *adj.* مزركش muzarkash

bleach *v.* يبيّض yebayyed

bleach *n.* مبيّض mubayyed

bleak *n.* سمك أبيض samak abyad

bleak *adj.* كئيب ka'eyb

blear *v.* يدمع العينين yedamme' eleynin

bleat n. صوت الخروف sut elkharuf

bleat v. يحكي متل السكارى yehki metel elsakara

bleb n. حبّاية habbayeh

bleed v. ينزف yenzuf

blemish n. عيبة eybeh

blemish v. يعيب yeayyeb

blend v. يخلط yekhlut

blend n. خليط khalit

bless v. يبارك yebarek

blether v. يحكي بغباء yehki beghabaa'

blether n. حكي فاضي haki fadi

blight n. آفة a'afeh

blind adj. أعمى a'ama

blindage n. درع derę'

blindfold v. يعصب عيون yaesub uyun

blindfold n. عصب العيون aseb eluyun

blindness n. عمى ama

bling n. اكسسوارات معدن ikseswarat maadan

blink v. يرمش yermush

blip n. صوت الكتروني عالي sut elkitroni aali

blip v. يطلّع صوات ورا بعض yetalle' sut wara baad

bliss n. نعيم maeyem

blister n. حبّاية habbayeh

blizzard n. عاصفة ثلجية asefeh thaljeyyeh

blob n. فقّاعة fuqa'a

bloc n. جهة jabha

block n. حظر hazur

block v. يحظر yahzur

blockade n. حصار hisar

blockhead n. متخلّف mutakhallef

blood n. دمّ damm

bloodshed n. سفك دمّ safek damm

bloody adj. دموي damawi

bloom n. تفتّح الوردة tafattuh elwardeh

bloom v. تتفتّح الوردة tetfattah elwardeh

blossom n. زهرة zahra

blossom v. تزهر tuzhir

blot n. لطخة latekha

blot v. يلطّخ yelattekh

blotted adj. متلطّخ metlattekh

blouse n. بلوزة bluzeh

blow v. يهجم yehjum

blow n. مصيبة musibeh

blowout n. انفجار infijar

blue n. لون أزرق lun azraq

blue adj. أزرق azraq

bluff v. يغش yeghush

bluff n. غش ghesh

blunder n. خطأ كبير khata' kebir

blunder v. يخطئ خطأ كبير yekhte' khata' kebir

blundering v. يتخبّط yetkhabbat

blundering n. تخبّط takhabbut

blunt adj. خشن kheshen

blunt adj. مسنّن mesannan

bluntly adv. بخشونة bekhushuneh

blur n. غباش ghabash

blur n. لطخة latkha

blur v. يغبّش yeghabbesh

blurt v. يَلْطِّخ yelattekh

blush n. تَوَرُّد tawarrud

blush v. يَحْمَرّ yehmarr

blushing adj. مُحْمَرّ muhmarr

blushing n. إحْمِرار من الخجل ihmirar men elkhajal

boa n. أفعى كبيرة afaa kibireh

boar n. خنزير بري khinzir barri

board n. لوح luh

board n. مجلِس majlis

board n. كَرتون مُقَوّى kartun muqawwa

board v. يركب سفينة yerkab a'safineh

board v. يكسي بالخشب yeksi belkhashab

boast v. يَتِبَرْوَظ yetbarwaz

boast n. بَرْوَظة barwazah

boat n. زورق zawraq

boat v. يركب بالزورق yerkab belzawareq

boathouse n. مكان صَفّ الزوارق makan saff elzawareq

boatman n. بحّار bahhar

bob n. قصّة عالقصير qassa al qasir

bob v. يقصّر شعره yeqassir sharu

bobbin n. وشيعة washi'a

bodice n. سِتْيانة sityaneh

bodily adv. كلّه kulluh

body n. جسم jesem

body n. جُثّة jeththeh

bodyboard v. يسبح ع لوح سباحة yesbah a luh sibaha

bodyboard n. لوح سباحة قصير lawh sibaha kasir

bodyguard n. مُرافِق murafiq

bog n. مُسْتَنْقَع mustanaqaa

bog n. سبخة sabkha

bog v. يغوص بالوحل yeghus belwahel

bogland n. أرض مستنقعات ared mustanqaat

boglet n. مُسْتَنْقَع صغير mustanqa' sighir

bogus adj. مُزَيَّف muzayyaf

bohemian n. سكان بوهيميا sukkan buhimia

bohemian adj. بوهيمي buhimi

boil n. غليان ghalayan

boil v. يغلي غلي yeghli ghali

boiler n. غلّاية ghallayeh

boisterous adj. عاصف aasif

bold adj. جريء jari'e

boldly adv. بجرأة bejura'a

boldness n. جرأة jura'a

bolero n. بوليرو buliru

bollocks n. حكي فاضي haki fadi

bollocks v. يحكي حكي فاضي yehki haki fadi

bolt n. دربّاس الباب derbas elbab

bolt v. يدربِس الباب yedarbes elbab

bomb n. قنبلة kunbula

bomb v. يفجّر yefajjer

bombard v. يقصف بالقنابل yeksuf belkanabel

bombardment n. قَصف بالقنابل kasuf belkanabel

bomber n. قاذفة kazifah

bonafide adv. بصحّتك bisahtik

bonafide adj. أصلي asli

bond n. صِلة silah

bondage *n.* استعباد iste'bad

bonds *n.* سندات sanadat

bone *n.* عضمة admeh

bonefish *n.* سمك عظمي samak azmi

bonehead *n.* شخص غبي shakhes ghabi

boneheaded *adj.* غبي ghabi

boneless *adj.* بلا عضم bla adem

bonfire *n.* دفاية daffayeh

bonnet *n.* غطا ghata

bonus *n.* مكافأة mukafa'a

book *n.* كتاب kitab

book *v.* يحجز yehjuz

book-keeper *n.* محاسب muhasib

book-keeping *n.* مسك الدفاتر masek dafater

book-mark *n.* فاصل كتاب fasel kitab

book-seller *n.* بياع كتب bayaa' ketub

book-worm *n.* مثقف muthaqqaf

bookish *n.* شخص مهووس كتب shakhes mahwwus ketub

booklet *n.* دفتر daftar

boom *n.* ازدهار izdihar

boom *v.* يزدهر yezdiher

boon *n.* نعمة ne'meh

boor *n.* فلاح ريفي fallah rifi

boost *n.* دعم da'em

boost *v.* يدعم yedaam

boost *v.* يعزز yeazziz

boot *n.* بوط buwt

booth *n.* كبينة التلفون kabenet eltalifon

booty *n.* غنيمة ghanimeh

booze *v.* يشرب ليسكر yeshrab layeskar

border *n.* حدّ hadd

border *v.* يحدد الحدود yehadded elhudud

bore *v.* يثقب thuqub

bore *n.* يثقب yethqub

born *v.* يولد yulad

born rich *adj.* ولدان بتّه ملعقة دهب waldan betumuh malaqet dahab

borne *adj.* محمول mahmul

borough *n.* بلدة baldeh

borrow *v.* يستعير yesta'ir

bosom *n.* ثدي thadi

boss *n.* مدير mudir

bossy *adj.* مستبد mustabbed

botany *n.* دراسة النبات deraset elnabat

botch *v.* يرقع yeraqqe'

both *adj.* سوا sawa

both *pron* التنين eltenin

both *adv.* مع بعض ma baad

both *conj.* هاد وهاد had w had

bother *v.* يدايق yedayeq

botheration *n.* مدايقة mudayaqah

bottle *n.* قنينة qannineh

bottle *v.* يعبي بقناني yeabbi beqanani

bottler *n.* شخص متفهم shakhes metfahhim

bottler *n.* مصنع قناني musanne' kenani

bottler *n.* سقّا saqqa

bottom *n.* سفل sefel

bottom *n.* عُمق umuq
bough *n.* غصن ghesun
boulder *n.* صخر كبير sakher kbir
bouncer *n.* حارس بار haris bar
bound *adj.* مقيّد muqayyad
bound *v.* يقيّد yeqayyid
bound *n.* قيد qid
boundary *n.* حدّ hadd
bountiful *adj.* سخي sakhi
bounty *n.* سخا sakha
bouquet *n.* بوكيه buqeyh
bourgeois *adj.* وجوازية burjwazeyeh
bourgeoise *n.* برجوازي burjwazi
bout *n.* وعكة waekeh
bow *v.* يحني yehni
bow *n.* تحيّة احترام taheyyet ihtiram
bow *n.* عُقدة uqdeh
bowel *n.* أمعاء amaa'
bower *n.* عريشة arisheh
bowl *n.* زبديّة zebdeyeh
bowl *v.* يلعب بولينغ yelaab buling
box *n.* صندوق sinduq
boxing *n.* ملاكمة mulakameh
boy *n.* صبي sabi
boycott *v.* يقاطع yuqate'
boycott *n.* مقاطعة muqata'a
boyhood *n.* صبا siba
boyish *adj.* صبياني sibyani
brace *n.* منصب mansab
bracelet *n.* سوارة swara
braces *n.* حمّالة hammaleh
bracket *n.* قوسين qusin

bracket *v.* يكتب بين قوسين yektub bin qusin
brag *v.* يتباهى yetbaha
brag *n.* تباهي tabahi
braid *n.* ضفرة dafra
braid *v.* يضفر yedaffer
braille *n.* طريقة بريل للقراءة tariqet bril lelqera'a
brain *n.* دماغ dimakh
brainless *adj.* مجنون majnun
brainstorm *n.* عصف ذهني asef zihni
brainstorm *v.* يعصف ذهنيّاً yaasuf zehneyan
brake *n.* مكابح makabeh
brake *v.* يستخدم المكابح yestakhdim elmakabeh
branch *v.* يفرع yefarre'
branch *n.* فرع fare'
brand *n.* علامة تجارية alameh tijareyeh
brand *n.* وصمة wasmeh
branding *n.* تمييز العلامة التجارية tamyyez elalameh eltijareyeh
brandy *n.* كونياك konyak
brangle *v.* يجادل yejadel
brass *n.* نحاس أصفر nehas asfar
brat *n.* صبي sabi
brave *adj.* شجاع shujaa'
bravery *n.* شجاعة shaja'a
brawl *v.* يتقاتل yetqatal
brawl *n.* قتيلة qetileh
bray *n.* نهيق الحمار nahiq elhimar
bray *v.* ينهق yanhaq

braze v. نحاس يلبّس yelabbes nehas	**breviary** n. مُختَصَر mukhtasar
brazen adj. بذيء bazei'	**brevity** n. اختصار ikhtisar
brazen v. ببذاءة يحكي yehki bebaza'a	**brew** v. يَخمّر yekhammer
breach n. تعدّي ta'addi	**brew** v. يشكّل yeshakkel
breach v. يتعدّى yet'adda	**brew** n. بيرة مشروب mashrub bira
bread n. خبز khebez	**brewery** n. بيرة مصنع masna bira
breaden v. يخبز yekhbiz	**bribe** n. رشوة rashweh
breadth n. عرض ared	**bribe** v. يرشي yershi
break v. يكسر yeksur	**brick** n. طوبة tubeh
break v. يستريح yestrih	**bride** n. عروس arus
break n. استراحة istiraha	**bridegroom** n. عرّيس arris
breakage n. كسر kaser	**bridge** n. جسر jiser
breakdown n. تعطّل ta'attul	**bridge** v. جسر يبني yebni jiser
breakfast n. فطور fetur	**bridle** n. يكبت yakbut
breakfront n. أمامي كسر keser amami	**brief** adj. موجز mujaz
breaking n. تكسير taksir	**brigade** n. سريّة sareyyeh
breakneck n. الفجر طلوع tulue' elfajer	**brigadier** n. لواء liwae'
breakoff n. انقطاع inqitaa'	**brigand** n. طريق قاطع qate' tariq
breakout n. إندلاع indilaa'	**bright** adj. كاشف kashif
breakpoint n. توقف نقطة niqtet tawaqquf	**brighten** v. يفتّح yefatteh
breaktime n. استراحة istiraha	**brilliance** n. نورانية nuraneyeh
breakup n. إنقسام inqisam	**brilliant** adj. ذكّي zaki
breast v. يواجه yewajih	**brim** n. فنجان حرف herif finjan
breast n. ثدي thadi	**brine** n. مالحة مي mai malha
breath n. نفّس nafas	**bring** v. يجيب yijib
breathe v. يتنفّس yetnaffas	**brinjal** n. باذنجان banjan
breeches n. للركبة بنطلون bantalun lelrekbeh	**brink** n. حافّة haffeh
breed v. يربّي yerabbi	**briquet** n. قالب qalib
breed n. سلالة sulaleh	**brisk** adj. رشيق rashiq
breed n. نسَل nasel	**bristle** n. خشن قصير شعر shaer kasir khishin
breeze n. نسمات nasmat	**british** adj. بريطاني britani
	brittle adj. هشّ hashsh
	broad adj. عريض ariid

broadcast *n.* إذاعي izaei

broadcast *v.* يذيع عالتلفزيون yeze' al telfezyun

brocade *n.* تطريز tateriz

brocade *v.* يطرز yutarriz

broccoli *n.* بروكولي brukuli

brochure *n.* برشور brushur

brochure *n.* نشرة nashra

broker *n.* دلال dallal

bromite *n.* بروميت bromit

bronchial *adj.* قصبي qasabi

bronze *n.* برونز bronz

bronze *adj.* برونزي bronzi

brood *n.* تفكير كتير tafkir ktir

brood *n.* تفقيس البيض tafqis elbid

brood *v.* يفكّر كتير yefakker ktir

brood *v.* يفقّس البيض yefaqqes elbid

brood *adj.* تفقيسي tafqisi

broom *n.* مكنسة mekneseh

broth *n.* مرقة maraqa

brothel *n.* بيت دعارة bit da'ara

brother *n.* أخ akhkh

brotherhood *n.* أخوة ukhkhuweh

brow *n.* جبين jebin

brown *adj.* بني benni

brown *n.* لون بني luwn benni

brownnoser n مسيح جوخ massih jukh

browse *n.* تصفّح tasaffuh

browse *v.* يتصفّح yesaffah

browser *n.* متصفّح mutasaffeh

bruise *n.* كدمة kadmeh

bruit *v.* ينشر إشاعة yeshur isha'a

bruit *n.* إشاعة isha'a

brunt *n.* قوّة الصدمة qwet elsadmeh

brush *n.* فرشاية firshayeh

brush *v.* يفرشي yefarshi

brustle *v.* يطقطق yetaqteq

brutal *adj.* ظالم zalim

brute *n.* حيوان hayawan

brutify *v.* يظلم yazlum

brutish *adj.* حيواني hayawani

bubble *n.* فقاعة fuqa'a

buck *n.* دولار dular

buck *v.* يقاوم بقوّة yeqawem beqweh

bucket *n.* سطل satel

buckle *n.* بكلة شعر biklet shaer

buckle *v.* يبكّلَ الشعر bebakkel shaer

bud *n.* برعمة burumeh

buddy *n.* زميل zamil

budge *v.* يتزحزح yezahzah

budge *n.* زحزح tazahzuh

budget *n.* ميزانية mizaneyeh

buff *n.* أصفر برتقالي asfar burtuqli

buff *n.* بدلة عسكرية badleh askareyeh

buffalo *n.* جاموس jamus

buffoon *n.* بهلول bahlul

bug *n.* بق baqq

bugle *n.* بوق buq

build *v.* يبني yebni

build *n.* بناء binaa'

building *n.* بناية binayeh

bulb *n.* لمبة lamba

bulb *n.* بصلة basaleh

bulimia *n.* شره sharah

bulk *n.* ضخامة dakhameh

bulky *adj.* ضخم dakhem

bull *n.* ثور thur

bulldog *n.* طبنجة tabanjeh

bull's eye *n.* رمية موفقة ramyeh mwaffaqa

bullet *n.* رصاصة resasa

bulletin *n.* نشرة nashra

bullock *n.* عجل ejel

bully *n.* متنمر mutanammer

bully *v.* يتنمر yetnammar

bulwark *n.* حصن hesun

bumper *n.* واقي صدمات waqi sadmat

bumpy *adj.* مليان مطبات malyan metabbat

bunch *n.* رزمة ruzmeh

bundle *n.* صرة serrah

bungalow *n.* بيت قش beit qashsh

bungee *n.* حبل مطاطي habel mattati

bungle *v.* يشتغل من قفا الكيف yeshteghel men qafa elkif

bungle *n.* شغل من قفا الكيف sheghul men qafa elkif

bunk *n.* حكي فاضي haki fadi

bunk *n.* معلف ma'laf

bunker *n.* مخزن محروقات makhzan waqud

buoy *n.* عوامة awwameh

buoyancy *n.* عوم uum

burden *n.* حمل hemel

burden *v.* يحمل حمل yehmel hemel

burdensome *adj.* صعب تحمله saeb tahamulu

bureau *n.* مكتب maktab

Bureacuracy *n.* بروقراطية beruqrateyeh

bureaucrat *n.* بروقراطي beruqrati

burglar *n.* حرامي harami

burglary *n.* سرقة serqa

burial *n.* دفن dafen

burke *v.* يكتم ع نفس yektum a nafas

burlesque *adj.* مسخرة maskharah

burlesque *n.* مسخرة maskharah

burlesque *v.* يسخر من yeskhar men

burn *v.* يحرق yahruq

burn *n.* حرق herq

burp *n.* تجشؤ tajashue'

burp *v.* يتجشأ yejasha'

burrow *n.* يحفر جحر yehfur jeher

burst *v.* يفجر yefajjer

burst *n.* تفجير tafjir

bury *v.* يدفن yedfun

bus *n.* باص bas

bush *n.* غصن ghusen

business *n.* أعمال تجارية a'maal tijareyeh

businessman *n.* رجل أعمال rajul a'maal

bustle *v.* يستعجل yesta'jil

busy *adj.* مشغول mashghul

but *prep.* إلا ella

but *conj.* بس bas

butcher *n.* قصاب qassab

butcher *v.* يذبح yezbah

butt *n.* نطحة hateha

butt *v.* يحشر انفه yehshur infu

butter *n.* زبدة zebdeh

butter *v.* يَمَسِح جوخ yemasseh jukh

butterfingers *n.* شخص رخُو shakhes rakhu

butterfly *n.* فراشة farasheh

buttermilk *n.* لبن مروب laban mrawwab

buttock *n.* ردف redef

button *n.* زرّ zerr

button *v.* يُخيّط زرار yekhayyet zerar

buy *v.* يشتري yeshteri

buy *n.* صفقة شراء safqet shiraa'

buyer *n.* شرا sharra

buzz *v.* يطنطن yetanten

buzz *n.* طنطنة tantaneh

by *prep.* جنب janb

by *prep.* ورا wara

by *prep.* بـ bi

by *adv.* باسم bi'esm

bye-bye *interj.* خاطركم khaterkum

by-election *n.* انتخابات فرعيّة intikhabat fareyyeh

bylaw *n.* قانون داخلي qanun dakhli

bypass *n.* شارع فرعي share' farei

by-product *n.* منتج ثانوي muntaj thanawi

byre *n.* زريبة zribeh

byte *n.* بايت bayt

bywalk n تمشاية خاصة temshayeh khassah

byway *n.* شارع فرعي share' farei

byword *n.* مثل mathal

C

cab *n.* تكسي taksi

cabana *n.* شاليه shaleh

cabaret *n.* كباريه kabareh

cabbage *n.* ملفوف malfuf

cabby *n.* سائق تكسي saeq taksi

cabin *n.* غرفة صغيرة gherfeh zeghereh

cabinet *n.* مرحاض merhad

cabinet *n.* مجلس الوزراء majles elwuzara

cable *n.* كبل kabel

cable *v.* يكبّل yekabbel

cache *n.* مونة muneh

cachet *n.* دمغة damgha

cackle *v.* يبربر yebarber

cactus *n.* صبّار sabbar

cad *n.* لدل nadel

cadaver *n.* جثّة jeththeh

cadaverous *adj.* متل الأموات metel elamwat

cadence *n.* إيقاع iqaa'

cadence *v.* يضبط الإيقاع yedbut eliqaa'

cadet *n.* غرّ ghirr

cadge *n.* تسوّل tasawwul

cadge *v.* يتسول yetsawwal

cadmium *n.* كادميوم kademyum

cafe *n.* كافيه kafeh

cage *n.* قفص qafas

cage *v.* يحبس بقفص yehbus belqafas

caged *adj.* محبوس بالقفص
mahbus belqafas

cajole *v.* يلعب بعقله yelab
beaqluh

cake *n.* كاتو kato

calamity *n.* مصيبة mesibeh

calcite *n.* كالسيت kalsit

calcium *n.* كالسيوم kalsiyum

calculate *v.* يحسب yehsub

calculator *n.* آلة حاسبة aleh
hasebeh

calculation *n.* حساب hisab

calendar *n.* روزنامة ruznameh

calf *n.* عجل ejel

calibrate *v.* يعاير yeayir

calibration *n.* تعيير ta'yyir

call *v.* يتصل yettesel

call *v.* يستدعي yestadei

call *n.* اتصال ittisal

call *n.* استدعاء istida'a

caller *n.* متصل muttasil

calligraphy *n.* خط الإيد khatt
eleyed

calling *n.* اتصال ittisal

callow *adj.* ما عنده خبرة ma
andu khebra

callous *adj.* مقسّى muqassa

calm *n.* هادي hadi

calm *v.* يهدّي yehaddi

calmative *adj.* مُسكّن
musakken

calorie *n.* وحدة حرارية wehdeh
harariyeh

calorific *adj.* حراري harari

calumniate *v.* يشوّه سمعة
yeshawweh sima'a

calumny *n.* تشويه سمعة tashwih
simaa'

camel *n.* جمل jamal

cameo *n.* حجر كريم hajar karim

camera *n.* كاميرا kamira

camlet *n.* لبس من وبر الجمل lebes
men wabar eljamal

camouflage *n.* تمويه tammwih

camouflage *v.* يموّه yemawweh

camouflaged *adj.* مموّه
mumawwah

camp *n.* مخيّم mukhayyam

camp *v.* يخيّم yekhayyem

campaign *n.* حملة hamleh

campaign *v.* يشنّ حملة yeshenn
hamleh

camper *n.* عايش بالمخيّم ayesh
belmukhayyam

campfire *n.* نار المخيّم nar
elmukhayyam

camphor *n.* كافور kafur

campsite *n.* مكان المخيّم makan
elmukhayyam

campus *n.* حرم جامعي haram
jamei'

can *n.* علبة elbeh

can *v.* يقدر yeqder

can *v.* يعلّب yealleb

canal *n.* قناة kanah

canard *n.* إشاعة كذب isha'a
kizib

canary *n.* كناري kanari

canary *adj.* فسّاد fassad

canary *v.* يفسّد yefassid

cancel *v.* يلغي yehlghi

cancellation *n.* إلغاء elghaa'

cancer *n.* سرطان saratan

cancerogenic *adj.* مسرطن
musartin

candid *adj.* صريح sarih

candidacy *n.* ترشيح tarshih

candidate *n.* مرشّح murashshah

candle *n.* شمعة shama'

candle *v.* يفحص صلاحيّة البيض
yefhas salaheyet elbeid

candour *n.* صراحة saraha

candy *n.* حلويّات helweyat

candy *v.* يحلّي yehalli

cane *n.* خيزرانة khizaraneh

cane *v.* يضرب بالخيزرانة yedrub
belkhizaran

canine *adj.* يخصّ الكلاب
bekhuss elkilab

caning *n.* الضرب بالخيزران
eldareb belkhizaran

canister *n.* كِلة keleh

cannibal *n.* آكل لحوم البشر aakel
luhum elbashar

cannibalise *v.* ياكل لحوم البشر
yakul luhum elbashar

cannibalism *n.* أكل لحوم البشر
akel luhum elbashar

cannon *n.* مدفع medfae'

cannonade *v.* يقصف بالمدافع
yeqsuf belmadafe'

canny *adj.* ماكر maker

canon *n.* قانون qanun

canonize *v.* يقدّس yeqaddes

canopy *n.* قبّة qubbeh

canteen *n.* مطرة matarah

canter *n.* شحّاد shahhad

canton *n.* ولاية welayeh

cantonment *n.* ثكنة عسكريّة
thaqaneh askareyeh

canvas *n.* لوحة زيتيّة lawha
zeyteyeh

canvass *v.* جمع الأصوات jame'
elaswat

canyon *n.* وادي ضيّق wadi
dayyeq

cap *n.* قبوعة qabua'a

cap *v.* يغطّي yeghatti

capability *n.* قدرة qudrah

capable *adj.* قادر qader

capacious *adj.* فسيح fasih

capacity *n.* سعة sia'a

cape *n.* رأس ras

cape *n.* كاب kab

capillary *n.* أنبوب شعري inbub
sha'ri

capillary *adj.* شعري sha'ri

capital *n.* عاصمة asemeh

capital *n.* رأس مَال ras mal

capital *n.* حرف كبير haref kbir

capital *adj.* رئيسي raeysi

capital *adj.* رسمالي rasmali

capitalist *n.* شخص رأسمالي
shakhes rasmali

capitulate *v.* يستسلم بشروط
yestaslim beshrut

caprice *n.* نزوة nazweh

capricious *adj.* متقلّب
mutaqalleb

Capricorn *n.* برج الجدي berj
eljadi

capsicum *n.* فليفلة حمرا flifleh
hamrah

capsize *v.* ينقلب قلب yeqelib
qaleb

capsular *adj.* مكبسَن mekabsan

capsule *n.* كبسولة kapsuleh

captain *n.* كابتن kaptin
captaincy *n.* رئاسة riyaseh
caption *n.* شرح shareh
captivate *v.* أيسر ya'sir
captive *n.* أسير asir
captive *adj.* مأسور ma'sur
captivity *n.* أسر aser
capture *v.* يستولي على yestawli ala
capture *n.* استيلاء istilaa'
car *n.* سيّارة sayyarah
carbine *n.* بارودة barudeh
carat *n.* قيراط kirat
caravan *n.* مَوكب mawkib
carbide *n.* كَربيد kerbid
carbon *n.* كربون karbun
carbonization *n.* كَربنة karbaneh
carbonize *v.* يكربن yekarben
cabuncle *n.* عقيق أحمر aqiq ahmar
card *n.* كرت kart
cardamom *n.* هيل heal
cardboard *n.* كَرتون kartun
cardiac *adj.* قلبي kalbi
cardinal *adj.* جوهري jawhari
cardinal *n.* كاردينال kardinal
cardio *adj.* يخص القلب bekhuss elqaleb
cardio *n.* القلب elqaleb
cardiology *n.* أمراض القلب amraad elqaleb
care *n.* رعاية reayeh
care *v.* يرعى year'a
career *n.* مهنة mehneh
careful *adj.* متأنّي metanni
careless *adj.* لا مبالي la mubali

caress *v.* يبوّس yebawwes
caretaker *n.* مشرف mushref
caretaker *adj.* مشرف mushref
cargo *n.* حمولة hmuleh
caricature *n.* كاريكاتير karikatir
carious *adj.* نخر nakher
carl *n.* وضيع wadei'
carnage *n.* مجزرة majzarah
carnal *adj.* جسدي jasadi
carnival *n.* مهرجان mahrajan
carnivore *n.* آكل لحوم aakel luhum
carol *n.* ترنيمة tarnemeh
carp *n.* سمك شبوط samak shabbut
carpal *adj.* رسغي resghi
carpenter *n.* نجّار najjar
carpentry *n.* نجارة nejarah
carpet *n.* سجّادة sijjadeh
carrack *n.* سفينة كبيرة safineh kbereh
carriage *n.* حمولة humuleh
carriage *n.* توصيل tawsil
carrier *n.* حمّال hammal
carrier *n.* شركة نقل sherkit naqel
carrot *n.* جزرة jazarah
carry *v.* يحمل yehmil
carsick *adj.* مصاب بغثيان من الحركة السيارة musab beghathayan men haraket al sayyarah
carsickness *n.* غثيان من حركة السيارة ghathayan men haraket al sayyarah
cart *n.* طنبر tunbur
cart *n.* عرباية arabayeh

cartage n. أجرة نقل ejret naqel

cartilage n. غضروف ghudruf

cartographer n. رسام خرايط rassam kharyet

carton n. كرتون kartun

cartoon n. أفلام كرتون aflam kartun

cartoonist n. رسام كرتون rassam kartun

cartridge n. محبرة mahbarah

carve v. ينحت yenhat

carve v. يحفر yehfur

cascade n. شلال shallal

case n. شنتا shanta

case n. قضية kadeyeh

case n. مطلب matelab

case n. صندوق sanduq

case v. يحط في الصندوق yehut fi elsanduq

casern n. ثكنة عسكرية thakaneh askareyyeh

cash n. مصاري نقدي masari naqdi

cash v. يدفع نقدي yeda' naqdi

cashier n. أمين صندوق amin sanduq

cashmere n. كشمير kashmir

casing n. تلبيس talbis

casino n. كازينو kazino

cask n. برميل خشب barmil khasab

casket n. علبة صيغة elbet sigha

casserole n. كسرولة kasruleh

cassette n. كاسيت kasit

cast v. يقشر الجلد yeqshur eljeld

cast v. زِت yezett

cast v. يقولب yequlib

cast n. قولبة qulabeh

cast n. زتّ zatt

cast n. جبيرة jbireh

caste n. طبقة اجتماعية tabaqah ejtimaeyeh

castellan n. مالك القلعة malek elqalaa

caster n. رشّاشة التوابل rashashet tawabel

castigate v. يعاقب yeaaqeb

casting n. عملة معدنية emleh ma'daneyeh

cast-iron adj. حديد صبّ hadid sabb

castle n. قلعة kalaa

castor n. مملحة mamlaha

castor oil n. زيت خروع zit khuwe'

casual adj. عارض ared

casualty n. خسائر khasaer

cat n. قطة qettah

cataclysm n. طوفان tufan

catacomb n. مقبرة maqbarah

catalogue n. كاتالوج katalug

catalogue v. يحط بالكاتالوج yehut bekatalug

catalyst n. دافع dafe'

catalyzer n. عامل تحفيز amel tahfiz

catapult n. نقّيفة neqqefeh

catapult v. ينقف yequf

cataract n. إعتام عدسة العين ietam adaset eÍein

catastrophe n. كارثة karetheh

catastrophic adj. كارثي karethi

catch v. يمسك yemsík

catch n. سقّاطة saqqatah

categorical *adj.* فاصل fasel

category *n.* صنف senef

cater *v.* يقدّم أكل yeqaddem akel

caterer *n.* متعهّد حفلات meahhed haflat

caterpillar *n.* دودة dudeh

catfight *n.* قتيل القطاط ketil elqatat

catfish *n.* سمك السلّور samak elsallur

catharsis *n.* إسهال شديد ishal shadid

cathartical *adj.* مُسهّل musahhil

cathedral *n.* كاتدرائية katedraeyeh

catholic *adj.* كاثوليكي kathuliki

catholicism *n.* كاثوليكية kathulikeyeh

cattle *n.* مواشي mawashi

catwalk *n.* منصّة عرض الأزياء menasset ared elazya'

caudal *adj.* يخصّ الذنب bekhus eldanab

cauldron *n.* غلّاية ghallayeh

cauliflower *n.* قرنبيط karnabit

causal *adj.* سببي sababi

causality *n.* سببية sababeyyeh

causative *adj.* مسبّب musabbeb

cause *n.* قضية kadeyeh

cause *n.* سبب sabab

cause *v.* يسبّب yesabbeb

causeway *n.* طريق معبد tariq mumahhad

caustic *adj.* كاوي kawi

caution *n.* تحذير tahzir

caution *n.* تحفّظ tahaffuz

caution *v.* يحذّر yehzar

cautious *adj.* حذِر hazar

cavalry *n.* فرسان fursan

cave *n.* كهف kahef

cavern *n.* مغارة magharah

caviar *n.* كافيار kafiyar

cavil *v.* يعترض بسخافة yetured bisakhafeh

cavity *n.* فجوة fajweh

cavort *v.* ينطوط yenatwet

cavorting *n.* نطّ natt

caw *n.* نعيق naeyq

caw *v.* ينعق yea'q

cease *v.* يوقف yuqef

ceasefire *n.* وقف إطلاق النار waqef itlaq ennar

ceaseless *adj.* مستمرّ mustamerr

cedar *n.* شجرة الأرز shajaret elarz

cede *v.* يترك yetruk

ceiling *n.* سقف saqf

celebrate *v.* يحتفل yehtifil

celebration *n.* احتفال ihtifal

celebrity *n.* شخص مشهور shakhes mashehur

celebrity *n.* صيت sit

celerity *n.* عجلة ajaleh

celery *n.* كرفس krafs

celestial *adj.* سماوي samawi

celibacy *n.* عزوبية uzubeyeh

celibacy *n.* امتناع عن الزواج imtina' am ezzawaj

celibate *adj.* أعزب a'zab

cell *n.* خلية khaleyyeh

cell *n.* زنزانة zinzaneh

cell *n.* غرفة صغيرة gherfeh seghereh

cellar n. دِهليز dahliz
cello n. كَنجة kamanja
cellular adj. خَلِيوي khalyawi
Celsius adj. مِئوي meawwi
cement n. إسمَنت ismant
cement v. يبني بالاسمنت yebni
belismant
cemetery n. جَبّانة jabbaneh
cense v. يَبخَر بالبخور yebakhkher
belbakhur
censer n. مبخَرة mabkharah
censor n. مُراقِب muraqib
censor v. يُراقِب yeraqib
censorious adj. انتقادي
intiqadi
censorship n. مُراقِبة
muraqabeh
censure n. لَوم lum
censure v. يَلوم yelum
census n. تعدادّ سكّاني te'dad
sukkani
cent n. سِنت sint
centenarian n. سنة 100 عمره
umru 100 sineh
centenary n. ذِكرى مِئوِية zikra
meaweyyeh
centennial n. ذِكرى مِئوِية zikra
meaweyyeh
center n. مَركَز markaz
centigrade adj. دَرَجة مِئوِية
darajeh meaweyyeh
centipede n. أم أربع وأربعين em
arba' wu arbeyin
central adj. مَركَزي markazi
centre n. مَركَز markaz
centrical adj. مَركَزي markazi

centrifugal adj. طرد مَركَزي
tard markazi
centuple n. & adj. مية ضعف
meyyet de'f
century n. قَرن karn
cephaloid adj. رأسِية ra'seyeh
ceramics n. سيراميك seramik
cerated adj. مشمَع meshamma'
cereal n. حَنطة hentah
cereal adj. يَخصّ الحبوب bekhuss
elhubub
cerebral adj. دماغي demaghi
ceremonial adj. مَراسمي
marasmi
ceremonious adj. رسمي rasmi
ceremony n. مَراسم marasim
certain adj. أكّيد akid
certain adj. حازِم hazim
certainly adv. بالتأكيد betta'kid
certainty n. يقين yaqin
certificate n. شهادة shahadeh
certify v. يَشهَد yeshehad
cerumen n. صملاخ الإذن
simlakh eleden
cervical adj. رقَبي raqabi
cesarean n عمليّة قيصَريّة
amaleyeh kaysareyyeh
cesarean adj. قيصَري kaysari
cessation n. إلغاء elghaa'
cesspool n. بالوعة balua'a
cetin n. سيتين sitin
cetylic adj. سيتيلي sitili
chain n. جَنزير janzir
chain v. يَجنزِر yejanzir
chair n. منصِب mansib
chairman n. رئيس raeyis
chaise n. ديوانة diwaneh

chalice *n.* كاس القدّاس kas
elquddas

chalice *n.* كاس kas

chalk *n.* طبشورة tabshurah

chalk *v.* يكتب بالطباشير yektub
beltabashir

chalkdust *n.* غبرة الطباشير
ghabret eltabashir

challenge *n.* تحدّي tahaddi

challenge *v.* يتحدّى yetehadda

chamber *n.* غرفة ghurfeh

chamberlain *n.* حاجِب الملك
hajib elmalek

champion *n.* بطولة butuleh

champion *v.* يدافع عن yedafe'
am

chance *n.* فرصَة fursah

chancellor *n.* مستشار
mustashar

chancery *n.* أرشيف arshif

change *v.* يغيّر yeghayyer

change *n.* تغيير taghyyir

channel *n.* قناة kanat

chant *n.* نشيدة nashideh

chant *v.* يغنّي نشيدة yeghanni
nashideh

chaos *n.* فوضى fawda

chaotic *adv.* بفوضوية
befawdaweyeh

chapel *n.* كنيسة صغيرة keniseh
seghireh

chapter *n.* فصل fasel

character *n.* شخصية
shakhseyyeh

charade *n.* تمثيليّة تحزورات
tamtheleyeh tahzurat

charge *v.* يتّهم yettehim

charge *n.* إتّهام ittiham

charger *n.* شاحِن shahen

chariot *n.* عربة خَيل arabet khil

charisma *n.* حضور الشخصية
hudur elshakhseyeh

charismatic *adj.* ملهِم mulhem

charitable *adj.* خيري khiri

charity *n.* عمل خير amal khir

charm *n.* سِحر seher

charm *v.* يسحر yesehar

chart *n.* جدوَل jadwal

chart *n.* مخطط mukhattat

charter *n.* ميثاق mithaq

chase *v.* يطارد yetared

chase *n.* مطاردة mutaradeh

chaste *adj.* عفيف afif

chasten *v.* يعفّ ye'eff

chastise *v.* يأدب yeaddeb

chastity *n.* عفّة effeh

chat *n.* دردشة dardasheh

chat *v.* يدردش yedardesh

chatter *v.* يحكي كتير yehki ktir

chauffeur *n.* شوفير shufir

chauvinism *n.* تعصب قومي
ta'assub qawmi

chauvinist *adj.* متعّصب قوميا
muta'assib qawmeyyan

chauvinist *n.* شخص متعصب قوميا
shakhes muta'assib
qawmeyyan

cheap *adj.* رخيص rekhis

cheapen *v.* يرخّص yerakhkhes

cheat *v.* يغشّ yeghushsh

cheat *n.* غشّ ghishsh

cheat *n.* إحتيال ihteyal

cheater *n.* شي مزيف shi
mezayyaf

check v. يفحَص yefhas
check n. فحص fahes
checkers n. لعبة الداما lebet eldama
checklist n. قائمة تدقيق qaemet tahqiq
checkmate n. كش مَلِك kish malik
checkout n. خروج khuruj
checkpoint n. حاجز تفتيش hajiz taftish
checkpoint v. يفتّش عالحاجِز yefattish alhajiz
checkup n. فحص طبّي fahes tebbi
checkup v. يفحَص yefhas
cheddar n. جبنة شيدر jebneh shidar
cheek n. خدود khudud
cheek n. وقاحة waqahah
cheep v. يزقزِق yezaqzeq
cheer n. زَقْزَقة zaqzaqah
cheer v. يفرِح yefarreh
cheerful adj. مفرِح mufrih
cheerless adj. موحِش muwhish
cheese n. جبنة jebneh
cheesy adj. يِشبه الجبنة beyshbah ejjebneh
chef n. شيف shifra
chemical adj. كيميائي kimyae'
chemical n. مادة كيماوِية madeh kimaweyyeh
chemise n. قميص qamis
chemist n. كيميائي kimyaei'
chemistry n. كيميا kimia
cheque n. شيك shik
cherish v. يدلِل yedallel

cheroot n. نوع من السيجار nue' men essigar
cherry n. كرز karaz
cherry adj. كرزي karazi
cherub n. طفل بريء tefil bare'
chess n. شطرنج shatranj
chest n. صدر sader
chestnut n. كستنا kastanah
chew v. يعلِك yeallek
chevalier n. فارس faris
chia n. نبات الشيا nabat elshya
chic adj. أنيق aniq
chick n. صوص sus
chicken n. دِجاجة dajajeh
chicken adj. جبان jaban
chide v. يَنهَر yenhar
chief adj. أساسي asasi
chieftain n. شيخ قبيلة sheikh qabeleh
child n. طفل tefil
childhood n. طفولة tufuleh
childish adj. طفولي tufuli
chiliad n. ألف سنة alif seneh
chill n. قشعَريرة qasharereh
chilli n. فليفلة filfleh
chilly adj. كتير بارد ktir bared
chime n. انسِجام insijam
chime v. يَنسجِم yensijim
chimera n. وِهم wahm
chimney n. مدخنة madkhaneh
chimpanzee n. شمبانزي shambanzi
chin n. دقن daqen
China n. الصين elsin
china n. بورسلان bursalan
chip n. رقاقة ruqaqah

chip v. يقطّع شرايح yeqatte'
sharayeh

chirp v. يغرّد yegharred

chirp n. تغريد taghrid

chisel n. إزميل izmil

chisel v. ينحت yenhat

chit n. بنت وحْقَة bent weqha

chit n. فاتورة مطعم fatwret
matam

chivalrous adj. بطولي butuli

chivalry n. بطولة butuleh

chlorine n. كلور klur

chloroform n. كلوروفورم
klurufurm

choice n. خِيار khayar

choir n. كورال kural

choke v. يخنق yekhnuq

cholera n. كوليرا kulira

chocolate n. شوكولا shukula

choose v. يختار yekhtar

chop v. يفرم yefrum

chord n. سلك silk

choroid n. مَشيمة العين
mashymet elein

chorus n. جوقَة juqa

Christ n. المسيح welmasyh

Christendom n. النَصرانيّة
elnasraneyyeh

Christian n. المسيحي elmasyhi

Christian adj. مسيحي masyhi

Christianity n. المسيحية
elmasyheyyeh

Christmas n. عيد ميلاد المسيح
eid milad elmasyh

chrome n. كروم krum

chromosome n. كروموزوم
krumuzum

chronic adj. مُزمِن muzmin

chronicle n. تسجيل الأحداث
tasjil elahdath

chronological n. مُتَسلسل زمنيًا
mutasalsil zamaneyyan

chronology n. تَسلسل زمني
tasalsul zamani

chronograph n. آلة قياس الوقت
alet qyas elwaqt

chrysalis n. شرنَقَة sharnaqah

chubby adj. مربرب merabrab

chuckle v. يضحك بالمخفي yedhak
belmekhfi

chum n. صديق حميم sadiq
hamim

chum v. يعيش مع شخص تاني
yeish ma' shakhes tani

church n. كنيسة keniseh

churchyard n. باحة الكنيسة
bahit elkeniseh

churl n. غليظ ghaliz

churn v. يخفق اللبن yekhfuq
ellaban

churn n. خفق اللبن khafeq
ellaban

cicada n. صرصور الليل sarsur
ellil

cider n. عصير تفّاح asir tiffah

cigar n. سيجار sijar

cigarette n. سيكارة sikarah

cinema n. سينما sinamah

cinnabar n. أحمر لمّيع ahmar
lammei'

cinnamon n. قرفة qerfeh

cipher n. شيفرة shifra

cipher v. يشفّر yeshaffer

circle n. دائرة daera

circle v. يدوّر yedawwer

circuit n. دارة كهربا daret kahrabah

circuit n. دورة dawra

circumfluence n. إحاطة بالسوائل ihatah belsawael

circumspect adj. منتبه mentebeh

circular adj. مدوّر mudawwar

circular n. تعميم ta'mim

circulate v. يعمم ye'amem

circulation n. تعميم ta'mim

circumference n. محيط الدائرة muhit eddaera

circumstance n. ظرف zaref

circumstantial adj. ظرفي zarfi

circumvent v. يراوغ yerawegh

circumvention n. مراوغة murawagha

circus n. سيرك sirk

cirrhosis n. تشمّع الكبد tashammu' elkabed

cirrhotic adj. متشمّع metshamme'

cist n. جوهر jawhar

cistern n. صهريج sahrij

citadel n. قلعة qala'a

cite v. ينقل عن yenqul an

citizen n. مواطن muwatin

citizenship n. مواطنة muwateneh

citric adj. حمضي hamdi

citrine n. سترين sitrin

citrine adj. مزيف muzayyaf

citrus n. حمضي hamdi

city n. مدينة madineh

civic adj. مدني madani

civics n. التربية الوطنية eltarbeyeh elwataneyeh

civil adj. مدني madani

civilian n. مواطن muwaten

civilization n. حضارة hadarah

civilize v. يتحضّر yetehaddar

clack v. يطقطق yetaqteq

clack n. طقطقة taqtaqah

claim n. إدعاء iddea'a

claim v. يدّعي yeddei'

claimant n. مدّعي muddaei

clam n. صمت samt

clam v. يصمت yesmut

clamber v. يتسلّق بصعوبة yesallaq besu'ubeh

clamour n. ضجّة dajjeh

clamour v. يطلب بصوت عالي yetlub besut aali

clamp n. لقّاطة laqqatah

clandestine adj. مخفي mekhfi

clap v. يصفّق yesaffiq

clap n. تصفيق tasfiq

claque n. مصفقين بالمصاري mesafqin belmasari

clarification n. توضيح tawdih

clarify v. يوضّح yewaddeh

clarion n. بوق buq

clarity n. وضوح wuduh

clarinet n. مزمار mezmar

clash n. قتيل qtil

clash v. يتقاتل مع yetqatal ma'

clasp n. حبسة habseh

clasp v. يثبّت yethabbit

class n. درجة darajeh

class n. صف saff

classic adj. كلاسيكي klasiki

classic n. شخص كلاسيكي shakhes klasiki

classical adj. كلاسيكي klasiki

classification n. تصنيف tasnif

classify v. يصنف yesannif

clatter n. خشخشة khashekhasheh

clatter v. يخشخش yekhashekhis

clause n. عبارة ebarah

clausula n. بند band

clave n. عصاية asayeh

claw n. مخلب makhlab

claw v. يخرمش yekharmish

clay n. صلصال silsal

clean adv. بنظافة benazafeh

clean adj. نظيف nazif

clean v. ينظف yenazzef

cleanliness n. النظافة elnazafeh

cleanse v. يطهّر yetahher

clear adj. صافي safi

clear v. يصفّي yesaffi

clear v. يمحي yemhi

clearance n. وضوح wuduh

clearly adv. بوضوح bewuduh

cleft n. شقّ seqq

clergy n. راهب rahib

clerical adj. كاهني kahini

clerk n. موظف muwazzaf

clever adj. ذكي zaki

clew n. كبكوبة kabkubeh

cliché n. كليشيه klisheh

click n. نقرة naqrah

click v. ينقر yequr

client n. عميل amil

cliff n. منحدر munhadar

climate n. مناخ manakh

climax n. ذروة zarweh

climb n. تسلّق tasalluq

climb v. يتسلّق yetsallaq

climber n. متسلّق mutasalleq

cling v. يلتزم ب yeltezem bi

clingy adj. دبق debeq

clinic n. عيادة eyadeh

clinical adj. سريري sariri

clink n. طنين tanin

clip n. حبسة habseh

clip v. يجزّ yejezz

cloak n. عباية abayeh

clock n. ساعة sa'ah

clod n. تراب turab

cloister n. دير dir

close n. إغلاق ighlaq

close adj. مغلق mughlaq

close v. يغلق yughleq

closet n. خوانة khizaneh

closet v. يختلي بحاله yekhteli behalu

closure n. قفل qefel

clot n. جلطة jaltah

clot v. يتختّر yetkhaththar

cloth n. قماش qmash

clothe v. يكسي yeksi

clothes n. لبس lebes

clothing n. كسوة kisweh

cloud n. غيمة ghemeh

cloudy adj. مغيّم meghayyim

clove n. فصّ fass

clown n. مهرّج muharrej

club n. نادي nadi

clue n. دليل dalil

clumsy adj. طايش tayesh

cluster n. عنقود anqud

cluster v. يتجمّع yetjamma'

clutch n. دبرياج deberyaj

clutch v. يِمسُك yemsuk

clutter v. يتشوّش yetshawwash

coach n. مُدرِّب mydarreb

coach v. يدرِّب yedarreb

coachman n. سوّاق عربة
sawwaq arabeh

coal n. فَحم fahim

coalition n. إئتلاف ietilaf

coarse adj. خشِن kheshin

coast n. ساحِل sahil

coastal adj. ساحلي sahli

coat n. مانطو mantu

coat v. يطلي yetli

coating n. تغليفة taghlifeh

coax v. ياخد بالمحايلة yakhud belmehayaleh

cobalt n. كوبالت kubalt

cobble n. حصوة hasweh

cobble v. يرقّع yeraqqe'

cobbler n. إسكافي iskafi

cobblestone n. جمرة jamrah

cobra n. كوبرا kubra

cobweb n. بيت العنكبوت beit elankabut

cocaine n. كوكائين kukaen

cock n. ديك dik

cocker v. يدلِّع yedalle'

cockle v. يتجعّد yetja'ad

cock-pit n. مقصورة الطيار maqsuret ettayyar

cockroach n. صرصور sarsur

coconut n. جوز هند juz hind

cod n. سمك القدّ samak elqedd

code n. رمز ramz

code v. يرمِز yerammiz

coding n. ترميز tarmiz

coeducation n. تعليم مُختلط ta'lim mukhtalat

coefficient n. معامِل muaamel

coerce v. يجبر yejbur

coexist v. يتعايش yetayash

coexistence n. تعايش ta'ayush

coffee n. قهوة kahweh

coffer n. تابوت tabut

coffin n. كفن kafan

cog n. سنّ الدولاب sann eddulab

cogent adj. حاسِم hasim

cognate adj. قريب من الأرحام qarib men elarham

cognitive adj. مقرّب muqarrab

cognizance n. بصيرة basirah

cohabit v. يعاشِر ye'asher

coherent adj. مترابِط mutarabet

coherent adj. متين matin

cohesive adj. ملحوم malhum

cohesive adj. ملصوق malsuq

cohort n. فوج fuj

coif n. تسريحة شعر tasrihit shaer

coif n. غطا ghata

coin n. عملة معدن emleh ma'daneyyeh

coinage n. سكّ العملة المعدنيّة sakk elemleh elma'daneyyeh

coincide v. يتزامَن yetzaman

coir n. ليف جوز الهند lif juz hind

coke v. يحوّل لفحم yehawwel lafahim

coky adj. مغرور maghrur

cold adj. بارد bared

cold n. برد bard

cold n. انفلونزا influwanza

collaborate v. يتعاون مع yeta'awan ma

collaboration n. تعاون ta'awun

collapse v. ينهار yenhar

collar n. قبة قميص qabbet qamis

colleague n. زميل zamil

college n. كلية keliyyeh

collect v. يحصّل yehassil

collection n. تحصيل tahsil

collective adj. جماعي jamaei

collector n. جابي jabi

collide v. ينطرق ب yetureq bi

collision n. طرقة tarqa

colloquial adj. عامّي aammi

colloquialism n. عاميّة aameyyeh

collusion n. تآمر ta'amur

colon n. قولون kulun

colonel n. كولونيل kulunil

colonial adj. إستعماري iste'mari

colony n. استعمار iste'mar

colour n. لون lun

colour v. يلوّن yelawwen

colour-blind adj. مصاب بعمى ألوان musab be ama alwan

colourful adj. ملوّن mulawwan

coclourless adj. باهت bahet

colter n. سكة المحراث sikket elmihrath

column n. عمود amud

columnist n. كاتب عمود في جريدة katib amud fi jarideh

coma n. غيبوبة ghaybubeh

comatose adj. بغيبوبة beghaybubeh

comb v. يمشّط yemashshet

comb n. مشط musht

combat n. إشتباك ishtibak

combat v. يشتبك مع yeshtebek ma'

combatant n. مقاتل muqatil

combative adj. قتالي qitali

combination n. مجموع majmu'

combine v. يجمع سوا yejma' sawa

combust v. يحترق yehteriq

combustile adj. قابل للاشتعال qabel lelishti'al

combustion n. إحتراق ihtiraq

combustor n. محرقة mehraqa

come v. يجي yeji

comedian n. كوميدي kumidi

comedy n. كوميديا kumidya

comely adj. مليح melih

comet n. مذنّب muzannab

comfit n. فواكه مجففة fawakeh mejaffafeh

comfort n. راحة raha

comfort v. يريّح yerayyeh

comfort v. يعزّي ye'azzi

comfortable adj. مريح murih

comforter n. بطانية bataneyyeh

comfy adj. مريح murih

comic adj. فكاهي fukahi

comic n. فكاهة fukaha

comical adj. كوميدي kumidi

comma n. فاصلة fasleh

command n. أمر amr

command n. سلطة sulta

command v. يأمر ye'mur

commandant n. حاكم hakim

commander n. قائد qaed

commandment *n.* وصيّة
waseyyeh

commemorate *v.* يحيي ذكرى
yehyi zikra

commemoration *n.* إحياء
ذكرى ihya' zikra

commence *v.* يبدى yebda

commencement *n.* بداية
bidayeh

commend *v.* يمدَح yemḍah

commendable *adj.* ممدوح
mamduh

commendation *n.* مديح madih

comment *v.* يُعلّق yualliq

comment *n.* تعليق ta'liq

commentary *n.* شرح shareh

commentator *n.* معلّق mualleq

commerce *n.* تجارة tijarah

commercial *adj.* تجاري tijari

commiserate *v.* يحن على
yehenn ala

commission *n.* عمولة umuleh

commission *n.* مهمّة
mahammeh

commissioner *n.* سمسار simsar

commissure *n.* وصلة عصبية
wasleh asabeyeh

commit *v.* يرتكب yertikib

commit *v.* يلزم yulzim

commitment *n.* التزام iltizam

committee *n.* لجنة lajneh

commodity *n.* سلعة sila'a

common *adj.* عام a'm

commoner *n.* شخص عامّي
shakhes a'mmi

commonplace *adj.* مكان عامّ
makan a'm

commonwealth *n.* ثروة عامّة
tharweh a'mmeh

commotion *n.* فوضى fawda

commove *v.* يحرّك العواطف
yeharrek elawatef

communal *adj.* مشاع masha'

commune *n.* بلديّة baladeyyeh

commune *v.* يناجي yenaji

commune *v.* يحكي عالهمس
yehki alhames

communicate *v.* يتواصل
yetwasal

communication *n.* تواصل
tawasul

communiqué *n.* بلاغ رسمي
balagh rasmi

communism *n.* شيوعيّة
shiueyeh

communist *n.* شيوعي shiuei

community *n.* مجتمع mujtama'

commute *v.* يخفف الحكم
yekhaffef elhukum

commute *v.* يعدّل yeaddel

compact *adj.* مضغوط madghut

compact *n.* ميثاق mithaq

compact *n.* عقد aqed

companion *n.* صحبة suhbeh

company *n.* شركة sharikeh

comparative *adj.* مقارن
muqaran

compare *v.* يقارن yeqaren

comparison *n.* مقارنة
muqaraneh

compartment *n.* غرفة ghurfeh

compass *n.* بوصلة busleh

compassion *n.* عاطفة a'tifeh

compel *v.* يجبر yejbir

compensate v. يعوّض
yeawwed

compensation n. تعويض
ta'wid

compete v. ينافس yunafes

competence n. جَدارة jadarah

competent adj. مؤهّل mu'ahhal

competition n. منافسة
munafaseh

competitive adj. مُنافِس
munafes

compilation n. تجميع tajmei'

compile v. يجمع yejammei'

complacent adj. راضي radi

complain v. يشتكي yeshtiki

complaint n. شكوة shakweh

complaisance n. مجامَلة
mujamaleh

complaisant adj. مُجَامِل
mujamil

complement n. يكمّل
yekammil

complementary adj. مكمّل
mukammel

complete adj. منتهي mentihi

complete v. ينهي yenhi

completion n. إنهاء inha'

complex adj. معقّد muaqqad

complex n. عقدة uqdeh

complexion n. سحنة sihneh

compliance n. طاعة ta'a

compliant adj. مطيع mutei'

complicate v. يعقّد yeaqqid

complication n. تعقيد ta'qid

compliment n. غزَل ghazal

compliment v. يتغزل
yetghazzal

comply v. يطيع yetei'

component adj. مكوِّن
mukawwan

compose v. ألّف yeallef

compose v. يركّب yurakkeb

composition n. مركّب
murakkab

compositor n. جامِع jame'

compost n. سماد samad

composure n. رزانة razaneh

compound n. مركّب
murakkab

compound adj. مركّب
murakkab

compound n. مجمّع mujamma'

compound v. يركّب yerakkeb

compounder n. مركّب
murakkab

comprehend v. يستوعِب
yestaweb

comprehension n. استيعاب
isti'ab

comprehensive adj. شامِل
shamil

compress v. يعصر yu'sur

comprise v. يحوي yehwi

compromise n. تسوية
tasweyeh

compromise v. يسوّي yesawwi

compulsion n. إجبار ijbar

compulsory adj. إجباري ijbari

compunction n. تأنيب الضمير
ta'nib damir

computation n. إحصاء ihsa'

compute v. يحسب yehsub

computer n. حاسوب hasub

computeracy n. حاسوب hasub

comrade n. رِفقَة rifqa

concave adj. مقعَر muqa'ar

conceal v. يخفي yekhfi

concede v. يمنح yemnah

conceit n. غرور ghurur

conceive v. يعتبر ye'teber

conceive v. يتصور yetsawwar

concentrate v. يركّز yerakkiz

concentration n. تركيز tarkiz

concept n. مفهوم mafhum

conception n. تصور tasawwur

concern v. يقلق yuqliq

concern n. اهتمام ihtimam

concert n. حفلة موسيقية hafleh musiqeyyeh

concert v. ينسّق yenasseq

concession n. إمتياز imteyaz

conch n. صدفة sadafeh

conciliate v. يعمل صلحة ye'mul silha

concise adj. موجز mujaz

conclude v. يستنتج yestantej

conclusion n. نتيجة natijeh

conclusive adj. نهائي nihaei

concoct v. يفتعل yefe'l

concoction n. إفتعال ifti'al

concord n. انسجام insijam

concrescence n. التحام ملاطي iltiham malati

concrete n. باطون batun

concrete adj. صلب selb

concrete v. يقسّي yeqassi

concubinage n. ملك يمين melk yamin

concubine n. حبيبة سريّة habibeh seryyeh

condemn v. يدين yedin

condemnation n. إدانة idaneh

condensate n. تكثيف takthiif

condense v. يكثّف yekaththif

condescend v. يتفضّل على yetfaddal ala

condescending dj. متنازل mutanazil

condign adj. مُناسب munasib

condition n. حَالة haleh

condition n. شرط shart

conditional adj. شرطي sharti

condole v. يعزّي yeazzi

condolence n. تعزية te'zayeh

condonation n. عفو afu

condor n. نسر أمريكي neser amriki

conduce v. يسبّب yesabbeb

conduct n. تعامل ta'amul

conduct v. يتعامل yeaamal

conduct v. يقود yequd

conductor n. مايسترو maystru

conductor n. دليل dalil

conductor n. قاطع تذاكر qate' tazaker

cone n. مخروط makhrut

confectioner n. حلواني helwani

confectionery n. حلويّات helweyyat

confer v. يقدّم yeqaddem

confer v. يتشاور yetshawar

conference n. مؤتمر mu'tamar

confess v. يعترف yeteref

confession n. اعتراف ietiraf

confidant n. مؤتمن mu'taman

confide v. يوثق ب yuthaq bi

confidence n. ثقة thiqa

confident *adj.* واثق wathiq
confidential *adj.* سري serri
config *n.* إعداد e'dad
configuration *n.* تهيئة tahye'a
configure *v.* يهيئ yehayye'
confine *v.* يحبس yehbus
confinement *n.* حبس habes
confirm *v.* يؤكّد yu'akkid
confirmation *n.* تأكيد ta'kid
confiscate *v.* يصادر yuṣader
confiscation *n.* مصادرة musadarh
conflict *n.* تعارض taarud
conflict *v.* يتعارض مع yetarad ma'
confluence *n.* التقاء نهرين eltiqa' ennahrin
confluent *adj.* رافد rafid
conformity *n.* مطابقة mutabaqa
confraternity *n.* أخوية akhaweyyeh
confrontation *n.* مواجهة muwajaha
confuse *v.* يشوّش yeshawwesh
confuse *v.* يخلط yekhlut
confusion *n.* تشويش tashwish
confute *v.* يكذّب yekazzib
conge *n.* عطلة eteleh
congeal *v.* يتجمّد yetjammad
congenial *adj.* متوافق بالعقل والروح metwfeq beaqel welruh
conglomerate *n.* تكوّر takawwur
conglomerate *adj.* يتكوّر yetkawwar
conglutinate *v.* يلزق yelzuq

congratulate *v.* يهنّي yehanni
congratulation *n.* تهنئة tahne'a
congregate *v.* يحشد yehshud
congregation *n.* حشد hashed
congress *n.* كونغرس kungres
congruency *n.* تطابق tatabuq
congruent *adj.* متطابق mutatabiq
conical *adj.* مخروطي makhruti
conjecture *n.* حدس hades
conjecture *v.* يحزر yehzur
conjugal *adj.* زوجي zawji
conjugate *v.* يشتق yeshtaqq
conjunct *adj.* مقترن muqtaren
conjunction *n.* إقتران iqtiran
conjunctiva *n.* الملتحمة elmultahimeh
conjuncture *n.* وضع wade'
conjure *v.* يستحضر أرواح yestahder arwah
connaisseur *n.* ذوّاق zawwaq
connect *v.* يوصّل yewassel
connection *n.* توصيل tawsil
connivance *n.* تغاضي taghadi
connive *v.* يتغاضى yetghada
conniving *adj.* متغاضي mutaghadi
conquer *v.* يغزو yaghzu
conquer *v.* ينتصر على yentuser ala
conquerer *n.* غازي ghazi
conquest *n.* غزوة ghazweh
conscience *n.* ضمير damir
conscious *adj.* متعمد mutaammad
consecrate *v.* يكرّس حياته yekarres hayatuh

consecutive adj. مُتَسَلْسِل
mutasalsel

consecutively adv. بِالتَّسَلْسُل
beltasalsul

consensual adj. بتوافق الآراء
betwafuq elara'

consensus n. إجْماع ijmaa'

consent n. رِضى rida

consent v. يَرْضى yerda

consequence n. نَتِيجة سلبيّة
natijeh salbeyeh

consequent adj. ناتِج natij

conservation n. حِفْظ hefez

conservative adj. مُحافِظ
muhafez

conservative n. شَخْص محافظ
shakhes muhafez

conserve v. يَحفظ بالسكّر yehfaz
belsekkar

consider v. يَعتَبِر ye'teber

considerable adj. مهمّ
muhemm

considerate adj. متفهّم
mutafahhem

consideration n. إعْتِبار i'tibar

considering prep. بِما إنّو bima
ennu

consign v. يرسل yersel

consignment n. إرساليّة
irsaleyyeh

consist v. يتكوّن من yekawwan
mn

consistence n. كَثافة kathafeh

consistency n. إنْسِجام insijam

consistency n. تَماسُك tamasuk

consistent adj. منسجم
mensejim

consolation n. تعزِاية te'zayeh

console v. يعزّي yeazzi

consolidate v. يمتّن yemattin

consolidation n. تَمتين tamtin

consonance n. تناغم tanaghum

consonant n. حرف ساكِن
haref saken

consort n. قرين qarin

conspectus n. لَمحة عامة lamha
ammeh

conspicuous adj. بارِز barez

conspiracy n. مؤامرة
mu'amarah

conspirator n. مُتآمِر
mutaamer

conspire v. يِتآمَر yetamar

constable n. مسؤول أمن masul
amen

constant adj. ثابِت thabit

constellation n. صورة فلكيّة
sura falakeyeh

constipation n. إمْساك imsaak

constituency n. دائرة انْتخابيّة
daera intikhabeyeh

constituent n. مصوّت
musawwet

constituent adj. تأسيسي ta'sisi

constitute v. يؤسّس yuassis

constitution n. دستور dastur

constrict v. يتشنّج yetshannaj

construct v. يبني yebni

construction n. بناء bina'

consult v. يستشير yestashir

consultation n. استشارة
istisharah

consume v. يستهلك yestahlek

consumption n. استهلاك istihlak

contact n. تواصل tawasul

contact v. يتصل yettsel

contagious adj. معْدي mu'di

contain v. يحتوي yehtwi

containment n. إحتواء ihtiwa'

contaminate v. يلوّث yelawweth

contemplate v. يتأمّل yetammal

contemplation n. تأمّل ta'ammul

contemporary adj. مؤقّت muaqqat

contempt n. تحقير tahqir

contemptuous adj. محتقر muhtaqer

contend v. يكافح yekafeh

content adj. راضي radi

content v. يراضي yeradi

content n. رضى rida

content n. محتوى muhtawah

contention n. خلاف khilaf

contentment n. قناعة qana'a

contest v. يتبارى yetbarah

contest n. مباراة mubarah

context n. سياق seyaq

contiguous adj. قريب qarib

continent n. قارّة qarrah

continental adj. قارّي qarri

contingency n. إحتمال ihtimal

continual adj. متتابع mutatabe'

continuation n. إستمرار istimrar

continue v. يستمرّ yestemerr

continuity n. إستمرارية istimrareyeh

continuous adj. مُستَمِرّ mustamerr

continuum n. سلسلة متّصلة silseleh muttesleh

contour n. تحديد tahdid

contra pref. عكس akes

contraception n. منع حمل mae' haml

contraceptive adj. مانع حمل mane' haml

contract n. عقد aqed

contract v. يتعاقد yetaaqad

contraction n. تشنّج tashannuj

contractor n. مقاول muqawel

contradict v. يعارض yuaared

contradiction n. تعارض taarud

contrarian n. مضارب mudareb

contrary adj. معاكس muakes

contrast v. يعاكس yuakes

contrast n. تعاكس taakus

contribute v. يساهم yesahem

contribution n. إسهام iseham

control n. تحكّم tahakkum

control v. يتحكّم yetehakkam

controller n. مراقب muraqeb

controversy n. خصومة khusumeh

contuse v. يعمل رض yamul ridd

contusion n. رضّ radd

conundrum n. لغز lughez

convalesce v. يتعافى yetaafa

convalescence n. نقاهة naqaha

convalescent adj. معافى muaafa

convene v. يدعي لاجتماع yedei lelijtima'

convener n. داعي لاجتماع daei lelijtima'

convenience n. راحة raha

convenient adj. مريح murih

convent n. دير dir

convention n. مُعَاهَدة mu'ahadeh

conventional adj. تَقْليدي taqlidi

convergence n. لقاء liqa'

convergent adj. قريب qarib

conversant adj. عرفان arfan

conversation n. حديث hadith

converse v. يتحادث yetehadath

conversion n. تَحْويل tahwil

convert v. يحوّل yehawwel

convert n. تَحْويل tahwil

convertible n. سيّارة كشف sayyara kashef

convertible adj. ممكن تحويله mumken tahwelu

convey v. ينقل حكي yenqul haki

conveyance n. نقل الحكي naql elhaki

convict v. يدين yedin

convict n. مجرم محكوم عليه mujrem mahkum aleh

conviction n. إدَانة idaneh

convince v. يَقنع yuqne'

convivial adj. معشراني ma'sharani

convocation n. دعوة لاجتماع da'eweh leijtima'a

convoke v. يدعي لاجتماع yedei leijtima'a

convolve v. يلفّ yeleff

convoy n. مُرَافقَة murafaqah

convoy v. يرافق yerafeq

convulse v. يختلج yekhtilij

convulsion n. اختلاج ikhtilaj

coo n. هَديل الحَمام hadil elhamam

coo v. يهدُل الحَمام yehdul elhamam

cook v. يطبخ yetbukh

cook n. طبّاخ tabbakh

cooker n. غاز الطبخ ghaz ettabekh

cool adj. بارد bared

cool v. يبرّد yebarred

cooler n. مبرّد mubarred

cooperate v. يتعاون yetawan

cooperation n. تعاون ta'awun

cooperative adj. تعاوني ta'awuni

coordinate adj. منسّق munassiq

coordinate v. ينسّق yenassiq

coordination n. تنسيق tansiq

coot n. مختلّ mughtall

copartner n. شريك متضامن shrik mutadamin

cope v. يجاري yejari

copier n. آلة تصوير ورق alet taswir waraq

copper n. نحاس nhas

coppery adj. نحاسي nehasi

coppice n. أرض دغلة ared deghleh

coprology n. دراسة البُراز diraset elburaz

copulate *v.* ينام مع yenam ma'

copy *n.* نسخ naskh

copy *v.* ينسخ yensakh

coral *n.* مرجان marjan

corbel *n.* ركيزة معدن rakizeh ma'dan

cord *n.* حَبْل habel

cordate *adj.* ع ع شكل قلب shakil qalib

corded *adj.* مشدود بالحبال mashdud belhibal

cordial *adj.* ينعش القلب yenesh elqalib

cordless *adj.* لا سلكي la silki

cordon *v.* يطوق yetawweq

cordon *n.* طوق من الشرطة tuq men eshshurtah

corduroy *n.* لبس قطني lebes qutni

core *n.* صميم samim

coriander *n.* كزبرة kezbarah

cork *n.* سدّادة saddadeh

cork *n.* فلّينة fallyneh

cormorant *n.* طائر الغاق taer elghaq

corn *n.* ذرة zurah

cornea *n.* القرنية elqarneyeh

corner *n.* زاوية zawyeh

cornet *n.* بوق buq

conical *n.* منخل صيني mankhal syni

coronation *n.* تتويج tatwij

coronet *n.* إكليل iklil

corporal *adj.* بدني badani

corporate *adj.* مؤسساتي muassasati

corporation *n.* مؤسسة muassaseh

corps *n.* كتيبة katibeh

corpse *n.* جثّة jiththeh

correct *adj.* صح sahh

correct *v.* يصحح yesahehhih

correction *n.* تصحيح tashih

correlate *v.* يترابط yetrabat

correlation *n.* ترابط tarabut

correspond *v.* يراسل yeraşil

correspondence *n.* مراسلة murasaleh

correspondent *n.* مُراسل murasil

corridor *n.* ممرّ mamarr

corroborate *v.* يأسّس yeassis

corroborative *adj.* تأسيسي ta'sisi

corrosive *adj.* متآكل metaakil

corrupt *v.* يفسد yefsid

corrupt *adj.* فاسد fasid

corruption *n.* فسَاد fasad

cosmetic *adj.* تجميلي tajmili

cosmetic *n.* مستحضرات تجميل mustahdarat tajmil

cosmic *adj.* كوني kuni

cosmopolitan *adj.* أممي umami

cosmos *n.* الكون elkun

cost *v.* يكلف yekallef

cost *n.* تكلفة taklifeh

costal *adj.* ضلعي dilei

cote *n.* حظيرة hazirah

costly *adj.* غالي ghali

costume *n.* بدلة badleh

cosy *adj.* مريح murih

cot *n.* تخت الطفل takhet eltifil

cotemporal *adj.* صدغي sidghi

cottage *n.* كوخ kukh

cotton *n.* قطن qutun

couch *n.* ديوانة diwaneh

cough *n.* سعلة saelih

cough *v.* يسعل yesul

could *v.* يقدر yeqdir

council *n.* مجلس majlis

councillor *n.* عضو في المجلس
udu fi elmajlis

counsel *n.* استشارة istisharah

counsel *v.* يستشير yeştishir

counsellor *n.* مستشار
mustashar

count *n.* عدّ a'dd

count *v.* يعدّ yeudd

countable *adj.* معدود maedud

countdown *n.* عدّ تنازلي a'dd
tanazuli

countenance *n.* ملامح malamih

counter *n.* عدّادة addadeh

counter *v.* يواجه yewajih

counteract *v.* يناقض yenaqid

countercharge *n.* اتهام معاكس
itiham muakis

counterfeit *adj.* مقلّد meqallad

counterfeiter *n.* مقلّد meqallad

countermand *v.* فسخ fasekh

counterpart *n.* ندّ nidd

countersign *v.* يصدّق ع التوقيع
yesaddeq altawqi'e

countess *n.* كونتيسا kuntissa

countless *adj.* ما بينعد ma
beynad

country *n.* بلد balad

county *n.* ناحية nahyeh

coup *n.* إنقلاب inqilab

couple *n.* زوج من zuj men

couple *v.* يرتبط ب yertubet bi

couplet *n.* زوج من zuj men

coupon *n.* كوبون kubun

courage *n.* شجاعة shaja'a

courageous *adj.* شجاع shuja'e

courier *n.* بريد سريع barid
sari'e

course *v.* يركض yerkud

course *n.* دورة dawrah

court *n.* محكمة mahkameh

court *v.* يحتكم ل yehtikim la

courteous *adj.* مأدّب meaddab

courtesan *n.* شرموطة
sharmutah

courtesy *n.* أدب addab

courtier *n.* متودّد metwadded

courtship *n.* تودّد tawaddud

courtyard *n.* حوش hush

cousin *n.* ابن عمّ ibn amm

coven *n.* اجتماع سحرة ijtima'
saharah

covenant *n.* عهد ahed

cover *v.* يغطّي yeghatti

cover *n.* غطا ghata

coverlet *n.* غطا التخت ghata
ettakhit

covet *v.* يرغب ب yerghab bi

cow *n.* بقرة baqarah

cow *v.* يخوّف yekhawwif

coward *n.* جبان jaban

cowardice *n.* جبن jubin

cower *v.* يصير جبان yesir jaban

coy *adj.* محتشم mehtishim

coy *n.* نجل khajal

cozy *adj.* ناعم naem

crab *n.* سلطعون saltaun

crack *n.* صدع sade'

crack v. يتصدّع yetsadda'	create v. يجعلك yeja'lik
cracker n. بسكويت رقيق biskwit rqiq	creation n. إبداع ibda'
cracker n. كسّارة kassarah	creative adj. يبدع yebde'
cracker n. فتّاش ناري fattash nari	creator n. خلّاق khallaq
crackle v. يفرقع yefarqi'e	creature n. مخلوق makhluq
cradle n. يهدهد yehadhid	credential n. اعتماد ietimad
craft n. مهارة maharah	credential adj. اعتمادي ietimadi
craftsman n. حرفي hirafi	credible adj. موثوق mawthuq
crafty adj. داهية dahyeh	credit n. مديونيّة madyuneyyeh
cram v. يحشي yehshi	creditable adj. يتصدّق beytsaddaq
crambo n. لعبة القافية le'bet elqafyeh	creditor n. دائن da'n
crane n. رافعة rafe'ah	credulity n. سذاجة sazajeh
crane n. عصفور الكركي asfur elkirki	credulous adj. ساذج sazaj
crankle v. يحني yehni	creed n. عقيدة aqideh
crash v. يحطّم yethattam	creek n. جدول مي jadwal mai
crash n. تحطّم tahattum	creep v. يتسلّل yetsallal
crasher n. طفيلي tufayli	creeper n. نبات معرّش nabat mu'arresh
crass adj. كتير ktir	creepy adj. زاحف zahif
crate n. صندوق sinduq	cremate v. يحرقه لرماد yehruquh laramad
crater n. حفرة الانفجار hufrit elinfijar	cremation n. حرق الجثث hareq eljuthath
crave v. يشتاق ل yeshtaq li	crematorium n. محرقة mihraqah
craving n. شوق shuq	creole n. أمريكي من أصل أوربي amriki men asel urubi
craw n. كرش kerish	crepe n. زلابية zelabeyeh
crawl v. يزحف yezhaf	crepitate v. يطق yetuqq
crawl n. زحف zahef	crepitation n. طق taqq
crayfish n. روبيان rubyan	crest n. عرف الديك urf eddik
craze n. صرعة sar'ah	cretin n. مختل عقليّا mukhtall aqleyan
crazy adj. مجنون majnun	
creak v. يصرصر yesarsir	crevette n. جمبري jambari
creak n. صرير sarir	crew n. طاقم taqim
cream n. كريم krym	
crease n. جعلكة ja'lakeh	

crib *n.* تخت الطفل takhit eltefel

cricket *n.* صرصور الليل sarsur ellil

cricket *n.* رياضة الكريكت riyadet elkrikit

crime *n.* جريمة jarimeh

criminal *adj.* إجرامي ijrami

crimp *n.* تجعيدة tajeydeh

crimple *v.* يجعد yeja'ed

crimson *n.* اللون القرمزي ellun elqurmuzi

crimson *v.* يحمّر وجهه yehmarr wejhuh

cringe *v.* يقرفص yeqarfes

cripple *n.* عاجز ajiz

crisis *n.* أزمة azmeh

crisp *adj.* مقرمش meqarmesh

crisp *adj.* مموج mumawwaj

crispen *v.* يخليه مقرمش yekhalleyh meqarmesh

criterion *n.* معيار meyar

critic *n.* ناقد naqid

critical *adj.* خطير khatir

criticism *n.* نقد naqed

criticize *v.* ينقد yenqud

croak *n.* نعيق naeyq

crockery *n.* فخّارة fakhkharah

crocodile *n.* تمساح timsah

croesus *n.* قارون qarun

croft *n.* حقل صغير haqel seghir

crone *n.* شمقرين shimmeqrin

crook *adj.* عصاية الراعي asayet erraei

crooked *adj.* معقوف ma'quf

crookery *n.* شغل غير قانوني shughul ghir qanuni

crooning *n.* ندندة dandaneh

crop *n.* محصول mahsul

cross *v.* يصالب yusalib

cross *n.* مصالبة musalabeh

cross *adj.* متصالب mutasalib

cross *adj.* معاكس mu'akes

crossbar *n.* عارضة a'redah

crossbeam *n.* عارضة ضخمة a'redah dakhmeh

crossbench *adj.* عضو محايد في برلمان udu muhayd filbarlaman

crosscut *v.* يقطع بالعرض yeqta' belared

crossfire *n.* تبادل إطلاق نار tabadul itlaq nar

crossing *n.* تصالب tasalub

crotch *n.* مشطور بالنصّ mashtur elnuss

crochet *v.* يشتغل كروشيه yeshtughil krusheh

crochet *n.* كروشيه krusheh

crouch *v.* يقرفص yeqarfes

crow *n.* غراب ghurab

crow *v.* يصيح الديك yesih eddik

crowbar *n.* رافعة rafe'ah

crowd *n.* زحام zham

crowded *adj.* زحمة zahmeh

crowdy *adj.* عصيدة asideh

crown *n.* تاج taj

crown *v.* يتوج yetawwej

crowned *adj.* متوج mutawwaj

crucial *adj.* مصيري masiri

crucified *adj.* مصلوب maslub

crucifix *n.* صليب salib

crucify *v.* يصلب yeslub

crude *adj.* خام kham

cruel *adj.* وحشي wahshi

cruelty *n.* وحشيّة wahsheyyeh

cruise *v.* سفرة بحرية safrah bahreyyeh

cruiser *n.* سفينة حربيّة safineh harbeyyeh

crumb *n.* لبّ الصمن lebb elsumen

crumble *v.* يتفتفت yetfatfat

crump *v.* يطلع صوت طحن yetalle' sut tahen

crunch *n.* طحن tahen

crunch *v.* يطحن بسنانه yetehan bisnanuh

crusade *n.* حملة صليبيّة hamleh salibeyyeh

crusader *n.* مشترك بحملة صليبيّة mushtark behamleh salibeyyeh

crush *v.* يهرس yehrus

crust *n.* قشرة qishreh

crutch *n.* شاكوش shakush

cry *n.* بكي beke

cry *v.* يبكي yebki

cry *v.* يندب yendub

cryogenics *n.* فيزيا الحرارة المتدنية fizya elhararah elmutadaneyeh

cryptography *n.* كتابة مشفّرة kitabeh meshaffarah

crystal *n.* كريستال kristal

crystalize *v.* يتبلور yetbalwar

cub *n.* جرو jaru

cubby *n.* صندوق صغير sinduq seghir

cube *n.* مكعّب muka'ab

cubical *adj.* تكعيبي takeybi

cubiform *adj.* شكله متل المكعّب shakluh metel elmuka'ab

cubit *n.* ذراع zira'a

cuckold *n.* مركّب قرون mrakkib qrun

cuckoo *n.* وقواق waqwaq

cucumber *n.* خيار khyar

cuddle *n.* حضن hudun

cuddle *v.* يحضن yehdun

cudgel *n.* باكورة bakurah

cue *n.* ضفرة dafrah

cuff *n.* كلبشة kalabshah

cuff *v.* يكلبش yekalbesh

cuisine *n.* مطبخ matbakh

cullet *n.* كسارة بلّور kasaret elballur

culminate *v.* يسقّف yesaqqef

culpable *adj.* مذنب muzneb

culprit *n.* الجاني eljani

cult *n.* عبادة ibadeh

cultivate *v.* يحصد yehsud

cultivation *n.* حصاد hasad

cultural *adj.* ثقافي thaqafi

culture *n.* ثقافة thaqafeh

culvert *n.* مصرف masraf

cunning *adj.* داهية dahyeh

cunning *n.* كيد kayd

cup *n.* فنجان finjan

cupboard *n.* خزانة إلها رفوف khizaneh elha rfuf

Cupid *n.* إله الحب elah elhub

cupidity *n.* طمع tama'e

curable *adj.* يتعالج beyta'alaj

curative *adj.* علاجي eilaji

curb *n.* لجام الحصان lijam elhusan

curb v. يلجُم الحصان yeljum elhusan

curcumin n. كُركُم kurkum

curd n. تخثُّر takhaththur

curd v. يتخثَّر yetekhaththar

cure n. علاجي eilaji

cure v. يعالِج yealij

curfew n. حظر تجوّل hazer tijwal

curiosity n. فضول fudul

curious adj. فضولي fuduli

curl n. تجعيدة tajeydeh

curly adj. مجعد muja'ad

currant n. زبيب zbib

currency n. عملة emleh

current n. تيّار tayyar

current adj. جاري jari

curriculum n. مقرّر muqarrar

curse n. لعنة la'neh

curse v. يلعَن yelan

cursory adj. سريع sari'e

curt adj. دفش difish

curtail v. يوجِز yujiz

curtain n. وداية berdayeh

curvature n. حدبة hadbeh

curve n. عكفة akfeh

curve v. يعكِف yekuf

cushion n. مخدّة mekhaddeh

cushion v. يفرُش yefrush

custard n. كاسترد kastard

custodian n. وصي wasi

custody n. عهدة uhdeh

custody n. وصاية wisayeh

custom n. عرْف urf

customary adj. عرفي urfi

customer n. زبون zbun

cut v. يقص yequss

cut n. قصّة qassah

cutis n. أدمة الجلد adamet el-jeld

cutter n. قطّاعة katta'a

cuvette n. زبدية zebdeyyeh

cyan n. لون سماوي lun samawi

cyan adj. سماوي samawi

cyanide n. سيانيد syanid

cyber adj. الكتروني elktruni

cybercafé n. قهوة انترنت kahwet enternit

cyberchat n. محادثة الكترونيّة muhadatheh elktruneyyeh

cybercrime n. جريمة الكترونيّة jarimeh elktruneyyeh

cycle n. دورة dawrah

cycle v. يركب مسكليت yerkab misklit

cyclic adj. مدوّر medawwar

cyclist n. راكب المسكليت rakeb elmisklit

cyclone n. إعصار iesar

cyclops n. عملاق بعين وحدة emlaq bein wehdeh

cylinder n. اسطوانة istwaneh

cylindrical adj. اسطواني istwani

cynic n. مسخرة maskharah

cynical adj. مسخرجي maskharji

cypher n. شيفرة shifra

cypress n. شجرة السرو shajaret essaru

D

dabble v. ينّدي yenaddi
dacoit n. أزَعر az'ar
dacoity n. زعرَنة zaeraneh
dad n. بابا baba
daddy n. بابا baba
daffodil n. نرجِس برّي narjis barri
daft adj. أهْبَل ahbal
dagger n. خَنجَر khanjar
daily adj. يوِمي yumi
daily adv. يومياً yumeyyan
daily n. صحيفة يوميّة sahifeh yumeyyeh
dainty adj. بيشهّي byshahhi
dainty n. أكل طيّب akel tayyeb
dairy n. مصنع أَلبان masna' alban
dais n. مِنبَر menbar
daisy n. أُقحُوان uqhuwan
dale n. خَور khur
dam n. سد sadd
damage n. ضَرَر darar
damage v. يتضرّر yetdarrar
damask n. لون أحمر رمادي lun ahmar ramadi
damask adj. أحمر رمادي ahmar ramadi
dame n. رِبّة rabbeh
damn v. يلعن yel'an
damn n. لعنة la'neh
damn adj. ملعون mal'un

damn int. الله يلعنَك allah yelanak
damnable adj. رَجيم rajim
damnation n. عذاب جهَنم azab jahanam
damned adj. ملعون mal'un
damp adj. ندِيان nadyan
damp n. تندِية tandeyeh
damp v. ينّدي yenaddi
dampen v. ينّدي شوي yenaddi shway
damsel n. آنسة aniseh
dance n. رقصة raqsah
dance v. يرقص yerqus
dancer n. رقّاصة raqqasah
dancing adj. راقص raqes
dandelion n. هِندبة hendbeh
dandle v. يلعّب الولد yela'eeb elwalad
dandruff n. قشرة qishreh
dandy n. شَخص متأتّق shakhes metanniq
danger n. خطَر khatar
dangerous adj. خطير khatir
dangle v. يتدندل yetdandal
dangling adj. مدلدل mdaldal
dank adj. كتير رطب ktir reteb
dank n. رطوبة كبيرة rutubeh kbireh
dap v. يصطاد برواق yestad berawaq
dapper adj. متأتّق metanniq
dare v. يتجرّأ yetjarra'
dare n. جرأة jur'a
daredevil adj. طايش tayesh
daredevil n. طيّاشة tayasheh
daresay v. يظنّ yezunn

daring *n.* جرأة jur'a
daring *adj.* جريء jare'
dark *adj.* معتم muattem
dark *n.* عتمة utmeh
darken *v.* يعتّم ye'attem
darkle *v.* يميل للسواد yemil lelsawad
darkly *adv.* بتعتيم beta'tim
darkness *n.* العتمة elutmeh
darling *n.* حبيب habib
darling *adj.* حبيبي habibi
dart *n.* سهم sahem
dart *v.* يرمي السهم yermi essahem
darting n إطلاق itlaq
dash *v.* يمشي بعجلة yemshi beajaleh
dash *n.* مشي بعجلة mashi beajaleh
dashing *adj.* على عجلة ala ajaleh
data *n.* بيانات bayanat
databank *n.* بنك المعلومات bank elma'lumat
database *n.* قاعدة بيانات qaedit bayanat
date *n.* تاريخ tarikh
date *n.* نخلة nakhleh
date *n.* موعَد maw'ed
date *v.* يتّرخ yetarrekh
dated *adj.* متّرخ mtarrakh
daub *n.* جبصين jabsin
daub *v.* يجبصن yejabsen
daughter *n.* بنت bent
daunt *v.* يرعّب year'eeb
daunting *adj.* مرعب mur'eb
dauntless *adj.* قلبه قوي qalbu qawi

dawdle *v.* يتلكّع yetlakka'
dawdler *n.* متسكّع metsakke'
dawn *n.* الفجر elfajr
dawn *v.* يطلع الفجر yetla' elfajr
dawnlight *n.* طلوع الفجر tulue elfajr
day *n.* يوم yum
daydream *n.* حلم يقظة helim yaqazah
daydream *v.* يحلم وهو صاحي yehlam w hueh sahi
daylight *n.* ضوّ النهار daww ennehar
daze *n.* دوخة dukha
daze *v.* يدوخ yedukh
dazed *adj.* دايخ dayekh
daziness *n.* الدوخة eddukha
dazzle *n.* انبهار inbihar
dazzle *v.* ينبهر yenbher
dazzling *adj.* مبهر mubher
dazzlingly *adv.* بشكل مبهر beshakel mubher
deacon *n.* شمّاس الكنيسة shammas elknisèh
deaconship *n.* منصِب شمّاس الكنيسة mansib shammas elkniseh
deactivate *v.* يعطّل yeattil
deactivator *n.* معطّل muattal
deactivation *n.* تعطيل ta'til
dead *adj.* ميّت mayyet
dead *n.* الشخص الميّت elshakhes elmayyet
deadbeat *n.* المتسكّع elmetsakke
deadbeat *adj.* متسكّع metsakke'

deadbolt n. قفل مركّب qufel mrakkab

deadbolt v. يقفل بقفل مركّب yeqful bequfel mrakkab

dead-end adj. مسدود masdud

dead-end n. طريق مسدود tariq masdud

dead-end v. يسدّ yesedd

deadline n. الموعد النهائي elmawed eniha'i

deadlock n. مأزق ma'ziq

deadlock v. يتورط بمأزق yetwarrat bema'ziq

deadly adj. بيموت bymawwet

deaf adj. أطرش atrash

deafen v. يطرش yetrush

deafening adj. بيطرش beyutrush

deal n. صفقة safaqah

deal v. يتعامل yet'amal

dealer n. متعامل muta'amil

dealership n. بيع بالمفرّق bei' belmfarraq

dealings n. تعاملات ta'amulat

dealmaker n. منظّم الصفقات munazzim elsafaqat

dean n. عميد amid

dear adj. روحي ruhi

dearth n. قلّة qelleh

death n. موتة muteh

deathbed n. فراش الموت firash elmut

deathblow n. ضربة قاضية darbeh qadeyeh

deathly adj. بيموت bymawwet

debar v. يمنع yemna'

debase v. يحتقر yehteqir

debate n. جدل jadal

debate v. يجادل yejadel

debated adj. محكي فيه mehki fih

debauch v. يفسق yefsuq

debauch n. فسق fesq

debauchee n. فاسق fasiq

debauchery n. دعارة da'arah

debile adj. ضعيف da'if

debilitant n. مضعف mud'ef

debilitation n. إضعاف id'af

debilitating adj. بيضعف byd'af

debility n. ضعف daef

debit n. مبلغ مدين mablagh madin

debit v. يخصم من yekhsum men

debris n. أنقاض anqad

debt n. دين din

debtor n. مدين madin

debug v. ينقّح yenaqqeh

debutant n. ظهور لأوّل مرّة zuhur la awwal marrah

decade n. عشر سنين asher snin

decadent adj. معفّن meaffin

decalcification n. إزالة الكلس ezalet elkles

decalcifiy v. يروّح الكلس yerawweh elkles

decamp v. يرحل فجأة yerhal faj'a

decay n. تلف talaf

decay n. إنحلال inhilal

decay v. ينحلّ yenhall

decease n. موتة muteh

decease v. يموت yemut

deceased adj. ميّت mayyet

deceit n. غش ghishsh

deceitful *adj.* غشّاش
ghashshash

deceive *v.* يخدع yekhda'

decelerate *v.* يخفّف السرعة
yekhaffif essur'a

deceleration *n.* تخفيف السرعة
takhfif essur'a

december *n.* كانون الأول kanun
elawwal

decency *n.* لَبَاقَة labaqah

decennary *n.* عشر سنين asher
snin

decent *adj.* لايق layq

decentralized *adj.* لا مركزي la
markazi

decentre *v.* يبعّد عن المركز
yeba'eed am elmarkaz

deception *n.* إحتيال ihtyal

deceptive *adj.* كاذب kazib

decibel *n.* ديسيبل disibil

decide *v.* يقرّر yeqarrer

decided *adj.* مقرر muqarrar

decidedly *adv.* قطعا qat'an

decidedness *n.* حتميّة
hatmeyyeh

decillion *n.* ديسيليون disilyyun

decimal *adj.* عشري ushri

decimate *v.* يهلك أكبر قسم
yuhlik akbar qesem

decimetre *n.* العشر المتري
elushur elmitri

decipher *v.* يقرأ الشفرة yeqra'
eshshifra

decision *n.* قرار qarar

decisive *adj.* حاسم hasim

deck *n.* سطح sateh

deck *v.* يزيّن yezayyin

declaration *n.* تصريح tasrih

declare *v.* يصرّح yesarreh

decline *n.* انحدار inhidar

decline *v.* ينحدر yenheder

declinous *adj.* منحدر menheder

declutter *v.* يرتّب yerattib

decode *v.* يقرأ الشفرة yeqra'
eshshifra

decoder *n.* جهاز فكّ الرموز jihaz
fakk elrumuz

decolonization *n.* إنهاء الاستعمار
inha' eliste'mar

decolonize *v.* ينهي الاستعمار
yenhi eliste'mar

decommission *v.* ينهي خدمة
yenhi khedmet

decompose *v.* يفكّك yefakkik

decomposition *n.* تفكيك
tafkik

decompress *v.* يفكّ الضغط
yefkk daghet

decompression *n.* فكّ الضغط
fakk eddaghet

deconstruct *v.* يهدم yehdum

deconstruction *n.* هدم hadm

deconstructively *adv.* بطريقة
هدمية betariqah hammyyeh

decontrol *v.* يلغي الرقابة yeghi
erraqabeh

decor *n.* ديكور dikur

decorate *v.* يدوكر yedukir

decoration *n.* ديكور dikur

decorative *adj.* ديكوري dikuri

decorum *n.* ذوق zuq

decoy *n.* استدراج istidraj

decoy *v.* يستدرج yestadrij

decrease *v.* يخفّض yekhaffid

decrease *n.* تخفيض takhfid

decreasingly *adv.* بتخفيض betakhfid

decree *n.* مرسوم marsum

decree *v.* يصدر مرسوم yeder marsum

decrement *n.* نقصان neqsan

decrepitate *v.* يغلي غلي yeghli ghali

decrepitation *n.* كتر الغليان kter elghalayan

decriminalization *n.* شيل من قائمة المجرمين shil men qaement elmejrmin

decriminalize *v.* يشيل من قائمة المجرمين yeshil men qaemet elmejrmin

decrypt *v.* يفكّ تشفير yfekk tashfir

decrypt *n.* فكّ تشفير fakk tashfir

decryption *n.* فكّ التشفير fakk ettashfir

dedicate *v.* يكرّس yekarris

dedication *n.* تكريس takris

dedicatory *n.* إهداء ihda'

dedicatory *adj.* مكرس mukarras

deduce *v.* يستخلص yestakhlis

deduct *v.* يحسم yehsum

deduction *n.* حسم hasim

deed *n.* صكّ sakk

deem *v.* يعتبر ye'teber

deep *adj.* عميق amiq

deepen *v.* يعمق yeammeq

deeply *adv.* بعمق beumeq

deer *n.* ظبي zabi

defamation *n.* تشهير tashehir

defamatory *adj.* تشهيري tashehiri

defame *v.* يشهّر yeshahhir

default *n.* تقصير taqsir

defeat *n.* هزيمة hazimeh

defeat *v.* يهزم yehzum

defect *n.* عيب ayeb

defecate *v.* يقضي حاجته yeqdi hajtuh

defence *n.* دفاع fifa'

defenceless *adj.* أعزَل a'zal

defend *v.* يدافع yedafe'

defendant *n.* مدعى عليه mudda'a alyh

defensive *adv.* بدفاع bidifa'

defer *v.* يأجّل ye'ajjil

deference *n.* فرق farq

defiance *n.* تصدّي tasaddi

defiant *adj.* جريّء jari'e

deficiency *n.* نقص naqes

deficit *n.* عيب ayeb

deficient *adj.* معيوب ma'yub

deficit *n.* قصور qusur

defile *n.* نجس nejis

define *v.* يعرّف ye'arrif

definite *adj.* مؤكّد mu'akkad

definition *n.* تعريف ta'rif

deflate *v.* يفضي من الهوا yefaddi men elhawa

deflation *n.* تفضاية من الهوا tifdayeh men elhawa

deflect *v.* يشتّت yeshattit

deflection *n.* تشتيت tashtit

deflesh *v.* يسلخ yeslakh

deflower *v.* يفض البكارة yefudd elbakarah

defoliant n. مزيل أوراق الشجر
muzil awraq eshshajar

defoliate v. ينزع ورق الشجر
yenza' waraq eshshajar

deforest v. يصحّر yasahher

deform v. يشوّه yeshawweh

deformity n. تشويه tashwih

defragment v. يلغي تجزأة yeghi
tajzy'et

defragmentation n. إلغاء التجزئة
elgha'e ettajzy'a

deft adj. متفوّق mutafawwiq

degenerate v. ينحطّ yenhatt

degenerate n. إنحطاط inhitat

deglutination n. استخلاص
istikhlas elglutin الغلوتين

degrade v. يحدر yenheder

degrading adj. مخجل mukhjil

degree n. درجة darajeh

degustation n. التذوّق
ettazawwuq

dehort v. يرجّعه عن رأيه yerajje'u
am ra'yu

dehumidify v. يزيل الرطوبة yezil
elrutubeh

dehydrate v. ينشّف yenashshef

dehydration n. تنشيف tanshif

deify v. يعبد ye'bud

deign v. يفضّل على yefaddel ala

deism n. ربوبية rbubeyyeh

deist n. ربّاني rabbani

deity n. ربّ rabb

deject v. يكئب yek'ub

dejection n. كآبة ka'abeh

delay v. يأخّر ye'akhkhir

delay n. تأخير ta'ekhir

delayment n. مانع mane'

delectability n. لذّة lizzeh

delegacy n. تفويض tafwid

delegator n. مفوّض mufawwad

delegate n. تفويض tafwid

delegate v. يفوّض yefawwid

delegation n. تفويض tafwid

deletable adj. ينحذف bynhezef

delete v. يحذف yéhzuf

deliberate adj. عن قصد an qasd

deliberate v. يتناقش yetnaqash

deliberation n. مناقشة
munaqasheh

delicacy n. هشاشة hashasheh

delicate adj. هشّ hash

delicious adj. بيشهّي byshahhi

delight n. بهجة bajeh

delight v. يفرح yefarreh

delightedly adv. ببهجة bibahjeh

delightful adj. مبهج mubhij

delimit v. يحدّد yehaddid

delimitate v. يعيّن yeayyin

delimitation n. تحديد الحدود
tahdid elhudud

delinquency n. جنحة jinha

delinquent adj. مذنب muznib

delinquent n. جاني jani

delipidate adj. مزيل للشحوم
muzil eshshuhum

delipidate v. يزيل الشحوم yezil
eshshuhum

delipidation n. إزالة الشحوم
ezalet elshshuhum

deliriant n. هذيان hazayan

deliver v. يسلّم yesallem

deliverance n. نجاة najat

delivery n. تسليم taslim

delta n. دلتا delta

deltoid *n.* عضلة دالِيّة adaleh daleyyeh

delude *v.* يوهِم yuhim

deluded *adj.* موهوم mawhum

delusion *n.* وهم wahm

delusional *adj.* وهمي wahmi

demagnatize *v.* يروّح المغنطة yerawweh elmaghnatah

demagogue *n.* غوغائي ghawgha'ei

demagogy *n.* غوغائِيّة ghawgha'eyyeh

demand *n.* طلب talab

demand *v.* يطلب yetlub

demarcate *v.* يحدّد الحدود yehaddid elhudud

demarcation *n.* تحديد الحدود tahdid elhudud

demasculinization *n.* زوال الذكورة zawal zukuret

dematerialisation *n.* زوال المادِيّة zawal madeyyet

dematerialize *v.* يروّح مادِيّة yerawweh madeyyet

dement *v.* يجنّ yejenn

demented *adj.* مجنون majnun

demerit *n.* عيبة eybeh

demicircle *n.* نصف دائرة nesef da'era

demilitarized *adj.* منزوع السلاح manzu'e essilah

demise *n.* موت mut

demobilization *n.* تسريح العساكر tasrih elasaker

demobilize *v.* يسرّح yesarreh

democracy *n.* ديموقراطِيّة dimukrateyyeh

democratic *adj.* ديموقراطي dimukrati

demolish *v.* يهدُم yehdum

demolition *n.* هدم hadem

demon *n.* عفريت afrit

demonetize *v.* يسحب من التداول yesehab men ettadawul

demonstrate *v.* يثبِت yethbit

demonstration *n.* إثبات ithbat

demoralize *v.* يفسِد أخلاق yefsid akhlaq

demur *n.* اعتراض ietirad

demur *v.* يعتَرض ye'terid

demurrage *n.* غرامة تأخير gharamet ta'khir

den *n.* وكر waqer

dengue *n.* حمّى الضنك humma eddank

denial *n.* إنكار inkar

denominate *v.* يسمّي yesammi

denomination *n.* تسمِية tasmeyeh

denote *v.* يدّل yeddel

denounce *v.* يستنكِر yestankir

dense *adj.* أبله ablah

density *n.* سماكة samakeh

dentist *n.* دكتور أسنان dektur asnan

denude *v.* يشلّح yeshalleh

denunciation *n.* ابلاغ iblagh

deny *v.* ينكر yenkr

deodorant *n.* ديودوران diuduran

deodorant *adj.* مزيل عرق muzil araq

deontological *adj.* يخصّ
الأخلاق الواجبة bekhuss
elakhalq elwajbeh

deontology *n.* الأخلاق الواجبة
elakhlaq elwajbeh

deoxidation *n.* شيل الأكسجين
shil eluksijin

deoxy *adj.* بلا أكسجين bla
uksijin

depart *v.* يرحَل yerhal

department *n.* رحيل rahil

departmentalization *n.* تقسيم
لدوائر taksim ledawa'r

departure *n.* مغادرة
mughadarah

depend *v.* يعتمد على ye'temed
ala

dependant *n.* شخص تابع shakhes
tabe'

dependence *n.* إتكال ittikal

dependent *adj.* إتكالي ittikali

depict *v.* يشرح بالصور yeshrah
belsuwar

depiction *n.* شرح بالصور sharh
belsuwar

depilatory *adj.* مزيل للشَعر
muzil lelsha'er

deplete *v.* يستنفد yestanfiz

depleted *adj.* مستنفذ mustanfiz

depletion *n.* إِسْتِنْفَاد istinfaz

deplorable *adj.* يبزعِل beyza'el

deploy *v.* ينشُر العساكر yeshur
elasaker

depolarize *v.* يشيل استقطاب
yeshil istektab

deponent *n.* شاهد مُحلّف shahid
muhallaf

deport *v.* يرحّل yerahhel

depose *v.* يعزل ye'zul

deposit *n.* إيداع بالبنك iyda'
belbank

deposit *v.* يودع بالبنك yude'
belbank

depot *n.* مستودع mestawda'

depravation *n.* فَساد fasad

deprave *v.* يفسد yefsed

depraved *adj.* فاسد fased

depreciate *v.* ينزِّل قَيمة yenazzil
qimet

depreciating *adj.* بينزّل قيمة
beynazzil qimet

depreciatory *adj.* يقلِّل من قدر
شخص beqallel mn qadr
shakhes

depredate *v.* يسلُب yeslub

depress *v.* يحبِط yehbit

depress *v.* يضغط عَل yedeghat
ala

depression *n.* إحبَاط ihbat

depression *n.* ضغط daghet

depression *n.* كساد kasad

depression *n.* إنحسار inhisar

deprive *v.* يحرم yehrum

depth *n.* عمق umq

deputation *n.* إنابة inabeh

depute *v.* ينيب yenib

deputy *n.* إنابة inabeh

derail *v.* يطلع عن السكّة yetalle'
an essekkeh

derailment *n.* طلوع عن السكّة
tlu'e an essekkeh

derive *v.* يستخرج yestakhrej

dermabrasion *n.* حكّ الجلد
hakk eljeld

dermatologist *n.* دكتور جلديّة duktor jeldeyyeh

dermic *adj.* جلدي jildi

derogatory *adj.* احتقاري ihtiqari

derrick *n.* رافعة raf'a

desalt *v.* يروّح ملوحة yerawweh mluhet

descend *v.* يجي من نَسَب yeji mn nasab

descendant *n.* جاي من نَسَب jay mn nasab

descent *n.* أصل asel

describe *v.* يوصف yusef

description *n.* وصف wasef

descriptive *adj.* توصيفي tawsifi

desert *v.* يصحّر yesahher

desert *n.* صحرا sahrah

desert *n.* هجر hajer

deserve *v.* يستاهل yetsahal

design *v.* يصمّم yesammem

design *n.* تصميم tasmim

designate *v.* يعيّن yeayyen

designated *adj.* معيّن muayyan

designer *n.* مصمّم musammem

desirable *adj.* مرغوب marghub

desire *n.* رغبة raghbeh

desire *v.* يرغب yerghab

desirous *adj.* طمّاع tamma'e

desk *n.* مكتب maktab

desktop *n.* سطح المكتب sateh elmaktab

desocialization *n.* عزلة اجتماعيّة ezleh jamaeyyeh

desolate *adj.* مهجور mahjur

despair *n.* يأس ya's

despair *v.* يأس yey'as

desperate *adj.* يائس ya'es

despicable *adj.* خسيس khasis

despise *v.* يستهين ب yestehin bi

despiteful *adj.* حقود haqud

despot *n.* طاغية tagheyeh

dessert *n.* حلويّات helweyyat

destabilization *n.* زعزعة الاستقرار zaezaet elistiqrar

destabilize *v.* يزعزع استقرار yezaze' istiqrar

destination *n.* الوجهة elwejha

destiny *n.* قدر qadar

destitute *adj.* محروم mahrum

destress *v.* يخفّف توتّر yekhaffef tawattur

destroy *v.* يدمّر yedammer

destroyer *n.* مخرّب mukharreb

destruction *n.* دمار damar

detach *v.* يفكّ yefekk

detachment *n.* فكّ fakk

detail *n.* تفصيل tafsil

detail *v.* يفصّل yefassil

detain *v.* يوقف بالسجن yuqef belsejn

detect *v.* يكتشف yekteshef

detective *adj.* بوليسي bulisi

detective *n.* محقّق muhaqqeq

determination *n.* حزم hazm

determination *n.* إصرار israr

determine *v.* يصرّ yeserr

detest *v.* يشمئزّ yeshmaezz

dethrone *v.* يخلع عن العرش yekhla' an elarsh

detonate *v.* يفجّر yefajjer

detoxication *n.* إزالة التسمّم izalet summum

detractor *n.* ناقد naqid

devaluate *v.* ينزّل قيمَة yenazzil qimet

devastate *v.* يدمّر yedammer

develop *v.* يطوّر yetawwir

development *n.* تطوير tatwir

deviate *v.* ينحرف yenhrif

deviation *n.* انحراف inhiraf

device *n.* جهاز jihaz

devil *n.* شيطان shitan

devise *v.* يدبّر yedabber

devoid *adj.* فاضي fadi

devote *v.* يخصّص yekhassis

devotee *n.* معجب mujab

devotion *n.* تخصيص takhsis

devour *v.* يبلع بلع yebla' bala'e

dew *n.* ردّ barad

diabetes *n.* مرض السكّري marad essikkari

diagnose *v.* يشخّص yeshakhkhes

diagnosis *n.* تشخيص tashekhiss

diagram *n.* مخطّط mukhattat

dial *n.* يتّصل ب yettesel bi

dialect *n.* لهجة lahjeh

dialogue *n.* حوار hiwar

diameter *n.* قطر الدائرة qeter eddaerah

diamond *n.* ألماس almas

diaper *n.* حفوضة haffudah

diarrhea *n.* إسهال ishal

diary *n.* يومية yawmeyyeh

dib *n.* صيد بالصنّارة sid belsinnarah

dib *v.* يصطاد بالصنّارة yestad belsinnarah

dice *n.* زهر الطاولة zaher eltawleh

dice *v.* يلعَب طاولة yela'b tawleh

dictate *v.* ينقّل yenaqqel

dictation *n.* تنقيل tanqil

dictator *n.* دكتاتور diktatur

diction *n.* أسلوب uslub

dictionary *n.* قاموس qamus

dictum *n.* قول مأثور qul ma'thur

didactic *adj.* تعليمي ta'limi

die *v.* يموت yemut

die *n.* قالِب qalib

die *n.* توقّف tawaqquf

diesel *n.* ديزل dizel

diet *n.* ريجيم rijim

diet *v.* يعمل ريجيم yemul rijim

differ *v.* يختلف yekhtelef

difference *n.* اختلاف ikhtelaf

different *adj.* مختلف mekhtelef

difficult *adj.* صعب saeb

difficulty *n.* صعوبة su'ubeh

diffuse *v.* ينشر yenshur

diffuse *adj.* منتشر mentesher

dig *n.* حفرِ hafr

dig *v.* يحفِر yehfur

digest *v.* يهضم yehdum

digest *n.* خلاصة khulasah

digestion *n.* هضم hadem

digit *n.* رقم raqam

digital *adj.* رقمي raqami

dignify *v.* يكرّم yekarrem

dignity *n.* هيبة hebeh

digress *v.* يحرف عن الموضوع yeharref an elmawdu'e

digression *n.* انحراف عن الموضوع
inhiraf an elmawdu'e

dilaceration *n.* تفتيت taftit

dilemma *n.* مأزق ma'ziq

diligence *n.* إجتهاد ijtihad

diligent *adj.* مجدّ mujidd

dilute *v.* يمرّق yemarreq

dilute *adj.* مريق mriq

dim *adj.* معتم m'attem

dim *v.* يعتم yeattem

dimension *n.* أبعاد aba'ad

diminish *v.* ينقّص yenaqqis

diminutive *adj.* مصغّر
musaghghar

dimly *adv.* بغباء bighaba'

dimness *n.* تعتيم ta'tim

din *n.* ضِرعة sar'a

dine *v.* يتعشّى yetashshah

diner *n.* مطعم mat'am

dingy *adj.* معكّر meakkar

dinner *n.* عشا asha

diocese *n.* أبرشيّة abrasheyyeh

dioxide *n.* ثاني أكسيد thani
uksid

dip *n.* غطس ghates

dip *v.* يغطس yeghtus

diploma *n.* ديبلوما diploma

diplomacy *n.* ديبلوماسيّة
diplomaseyyeh

diplomat *n.* ديبلوماسي
diplumasi

diplomatic *adj.* ديبلوماسي
diplumasi

dire *adj.* مخيف mukhif

direct *adj.* مباشر mubashar

direct *v.* يوجّه yewajjeh

direction *n.* اتّجاه ittijah

director *n.* مخرج mukhrij

directory *n.* دليل dalil

dirt *n.* وسخ wasakh

dirty *adj.* وسخ wesekh

disability *n.* إعاقة iaqah

disable *v.* يبطل yebtil

disabled *adj.* معاق muaaq

disadvantage *n.* ضرر darar

disagree *v.* يعترض yetered

disagreeable *adj.* مكروه
makruh

disagreement *n.* إختلاف
ikhtilaf

disappear *v.* يختفي yekhtifi

disappearance *n.* اختفاء
ikhtifa'

disappoint *v.* يخيّب yekhayyeb

disapproval *n.* رفض rafd

disapprove *v.* يرفض yerfud

disarm *v.* ينزع سلاح yenza'
slah

disarmament *n.* نزع السلاح
naze' slah

disaster *n.* كارثة karitheh

disastrous *adj.* كارثي karithi

disband *v.* يفرّق yefarreq

disbelief *n.* إلحاد ilhad

disbelieve *v.* يلحد yehid

disc *n.* قرص qrs

discard *v.* يرذت yezett

discharge *v.* يخلّي yekhli

discharge *v.* يسرّح yesarreh

discharge *n.* إخلاء ikhla'

discharge *n.* تسريح tasrih

disciple *n.* حواري hiwari

discipline *n.* إنضباط indibat

disclose *v.* يكشف yekshuf

discomfort *n.* إزْعاج izaaj

disconnect *v.* يفصِل yefsil

discontent *n.* تأفّف ta'affuf

discontinue *v.* يوقّف yewaqqef

discord *n.* خلاف khilaf

discount *n.* حسم hasm

discourage *v.* يبرِّد همّة yebarred hemmet

discourse *n.* حديث مهمّ hadith muhimm

discourteous *adj.* دجّ dajj

discover *v.* يكتشف yekteshif

discovery *n.* اكتشاف iktishaf

discredit *v.* عار aar

discretion *n.* تقدير taqdir

discriminate *v.* يميِّز yemayyez

discrimination *n.* تمييز tamyyiz

discuss *v.* يناقش yenaqesh

disdain *n.* استحقار istehqar

disdain *v.* يستحقر yestahqer

disease *n.* مرَض maradh

disembody *v.* يطلّع الروح من الجسم yetalle' elruh mn eljesm

disfigure *v.* يشوّه yeshawweh

disguise *n.* تنكُّر tanakkur

disguise *v.* يتنكّر yetnakkar

disgusting *adj.* مقرف muqref

dish *n.* صحن sahn

dishearten *v.* يحبِط yehbet

dishonest *adj.* غشّاش ghashshash

dishonesty *n.* خيانة kheyaneh

dishonour *v.* يهين yehin

dishonour *n.* إهانة ihaneh

dislike *v.* يكرَه yekrah

dislike *n.* كُره kereh

disloyal *adj.* عاقّ aaqq

dismay *n.* حيرة hireh

dismiss *v.* يطرد yetrud

dismiss *v.* يخلَع yekhla'

dismissal *n.* طرد tard

disobey *v.* يعصي ye'si

disorder *n.* إضطِراب ittirab

disparity *n.* تفاوُت tafawut

dispensary *n.* مستوصف mestawsaf

disperse *v.* يشتِّت yeshattet

displace *v.* يشرِّد yesharred

display *v.* يعرِض ye'rud

display *n.* عرْض ared

displease *v.* يزعِج yez'uj

displeasure *n.* ضجر dajar

disposal *n.* تصريفة tasrifeh

dispose *v.* يتصرّف yetsarraf

disprove *v.* يكذِّب yekazzib

dispute *n.* ملاسنة mlasaneh

dispute *v.* يتلاسَن yetlasan

disqualification *n.* عدم أهليّة adam ahleyyeh

disqualify *v.* يستبعِد yestabed

disquiet *n.* إرباك irbak

disregard *n.* إهمال ihmal

disregard *v.* يهمِل yehmil

disrepute *n.* سمعة سيّئة sem'a say'a

disrespect *n.* قلّة احترام qellet ihtiram

disrupt *v.* يشوِّش yeshawwesh

dissatisfaction *n.* عدم رضى adam ridah

dissatisfy *v.* يخلِّيه مو رضيان yekhalleh mu radyan

dissect v. يشرّح yesharreh

dissection n. تشريح tashrih

dissimilar adj. ما يشبه ma byshbah

dissolve v. يدوّب yedawweb

dissolve v. يحلّ yehhel

dissuade v. يصدّه عن yesudduh an

distance n. مسافة masafeh

distant adj. بعيد beid

distil v. يقطّر yeqatter

distillery n. تقطير taqtir

distinct adj. ظاهر zaher

distinction n. تمييز tamyyiz

distinguish v. يفرّق yefarriq

distort v. يشوّه yeshawweh

distress n. ضيقة diqah

distress v. يدايق yedayeq

distribute v. يوزّع yewazze'

distribution n. توزيع tawzi'e

district n. حيّ hayy

distrust n. ظنّ zann

distrust v. يظنّ yezunn

disturb v. يدايق yedayeq

ditch n. خندق khandaq

ditto n. نفس الشي nafs eshshi

dive v. يغوص yeghus

dive n. غوص ghus

diverse adj. متنوّع metnawwe'

divert v. يآنس ye'anis

divide v. يقسّم yeqassim

divine adj. إلهي elahi

divinity n. ألوهيّة uluheyyeh

division n. قسم qesm

divorce n. طلاق talaq

divorce v. يطلّق yetalleq

divulge v. يفشي سر yefshi srr

do v. يعمل yemil

doable adj. بينعمل ben'emil

docent n. محاضر muhader

docile adj. سلس seles

dock n. قفص الاتّهام qafas elittiham

dock n. مرسى marsah

dock v. يرسى yersah

dockmaster n. مدير المرسى mudir elmarsah

dockworker n. عامل المرسى aamel elmarsah

dockyard n. أرض المرسى ard elmarsah

doctor n. دكتور diktur

doctor v. يعالج yealij

doctored adj. آخد علاج aakhid elaj

doctorate n. دكتوراه dikturah

doctrine n. فقه feqeh

document n. مستند mustanad

documentary adj. وثائقي wathaeiqi

documentary n. برنامج وثائقي brnamej watheiqi

dodge n. هريبة hribeh

dodge v. يهرب yehrub

dodo n. طير الدودو tir eldudu

doe n. ظبية zabyeh

doer n. فاعل fael

doeskin n. جلد ناعم jld naem

dog n. كلب kalb

dog v. يدايق yedayeq

dogcatcher n. صيّاد كلاب sayyad klab

dogeared adj. مطويّة زواياه mtawwayeh zawayah

dogfight *n.* قتال جوّي qital jawwi

dogfight *v.* يتقاتل بالجوّ yetqatal beljaww

doghole *n.* سكَن وسخ sakan wesekh

doghouse *n.* بيت الكلب beit elkalb

dogma *n.* عَقيدة aqideh

dogmatic *adj.* عَقائدي aqaeidi

dole *n.* صدَقة sadaqah

dole *v.* يتصدق yetsaddaq

doll *n.* لعبة lebeh

dollar *n.* دولار dular

dolman *n.* كاب kab

dolmen *n.* قبر قديم qaber qadim

dolorous *adj.* حزنان haznan

dolphin *n.* دلفين delfin

domain *n.* نطاق netaq

dome *n.* قبّة qebbeh

domestic *adj.* محلّي mahalli

domestic *n.* سوق محلّي suq mahalli

domestical *adj.* محلّي mahalli

domesticate *v.* يروّض yerawwedh

domesticator *n.* المروّض elmrawwedh

domicile *n.* مَسكَن maskan

domiciled *adj.* ساكن saken

domiciliary *adj.* منزلي manzli

dominant *adj.* مهيمن mehaymen

dominate *v.* يهيمن yehaymin

domination *n.* هيمنة haymaneh

dominion *n.* سيادة siyadeh

domino *n.* دومينو dumino

donate *v.* يتبرّع yetbarra'

donation *n.* تبرع tabarru'

donkey *n.* حمار hmar

donor *n.* متبرع metbarre'

doom *n.* حكم ربنا hkem rabna

doom *v.* يحدّد مصير yehadded masir

doomed *adj.* محكوم عليه mahkum aleh

doomsday *n.* يوم القيامة yum elqyameh

door *n.* باب bab

doorbell *n.* جرس الباب jaras elbab

doorknob *n.* سقَّاطة الباب saqqatet elbab

doormat *n.* مسَّاحة الرجلين massahit elrejlin

dope *n.* مخدّر mukhadder

dope *v.* يخدّر yekhadder

doped *adj.* مخدر mukhadder

dopey *adj.* بليد balid

dorky *adj.* غبي ghabi

dormant *adj.* هيمد hemid

dormitory *n.* مهجع mahja'

dorsal *adj.* ظهري zahri

dosage *n.* جرعة jar'a

dose *n.* جرعة jar'a

dot *n.* نقطة nuqtah

dot *v.* ينقّط yenaqqet

double *adj.* زيادة zyadeh

double *v.* يضاعف yedaef

double *n.* شبيه shabih

double *n.* ضعف de'f

doubt *v.* يشكّ yeshekk

doubt *n.* شكّ shakk

doubtful *adj.* مشكوك فيه
mashkuk fi

doubtless *adj.* ما فيو شكّ
mafeyyu shakk

dough *n.* عجين ajin

doughnut *n.* دونات dunat

dour *adj.* عنيد anid

douse *v.* يغطس yeghtus

dove *n.* حمامة hamameh

dowery *n.* مهر mher

down *adv.* لتحت latahet

down *prep.* تحت tahet

down *v.* يخفّف yekhaffef

downfall *n.* انهيار inhyar

downpour *n.* مطر غزير matar
ghazir

downright *adv.* بالتّمام
beltamam

downright *adj.* أكيد akid

downstairs *adj.* تحتاني tehtani

downward *adj.* نازل nazil

downward *adv.* بنزول benzul

downwards *adv.* لنزول lanzul

doze *n.* غفوة ghafweh

doze *v.* يغفى yeghfah

dozen *n.* دزينة dazzineh

drab *n.* قحبة qahbeh

drab *adj.* شاحب shahib

drab *v.* يعاشر قحبة yeasher
qahbeh

draconic *adj.* وحشي wahshi

draft *v.* يسحب yesehab

draft *v.* يطوّع yetawwe'

draft *n.* مسودة meswaddeh

draft *n.* سحب saheb

draft *n.* تطويع tatwe'

drafty *adj.* معرَّض لريح قويّة
muarrad larih qawweyyeh

draftsman *adj.* رسّام rassam

drag *n.* جرّ jarr

drag *v.* يجر yejurr

dragon *n.* تنّين tennin

dragonfly *n.* يعسوب ya'sub

drain *n.* مجرور majrur

drain *v.* يفضي yefaddi

drainage *n.* صرف صحّي sarf
sehhi

drainpipe *n.* ماسورة الصرف
masuret elsarf

dram *n.* درهم drham

drama *n.* دراما drama

dramatic *adj.* مسرحي masrahi

dramatist *n.* كاتب مسرحي
kateb masrahi

drape *n.* برداية bardayeh

drape *v.* يعلّق برداية yealleq
bardayeh

draper *n.* تاجر جوخ tajer jukh

drapery *adj.* تجارة الجوخ tejaret
eljukh

drastic *n.* قاسي qasi

draught *n.* مسودة meswaddeh

draught *n.* تيّار هوا tayyar hawa

draw *v.* يرسم yrsum

draw *v.* يستدرج yestadrej

draw *v.* يسحب yeshab

draw *v.* يجر yejurr

draw *n.* استدراج istedraj

draw *n.* سحب saheb

draw *n.* جر jarr

drawback *n.* علّة elleh

drawbridge *n.* جسر متحرّك jser
meteharrek

drawer *n.* جارُور jarur

drawing *n.* رسم rasm

drawing-room *n.* غرفة الرسم ghurfet elrasm

dread *n.* يرهب yerheb

dread *v.* رهبة rahbeh

dread *adj.* إلو رهبة elu rahbeh

dreadful *adj.* مرعب mureb

dreadful *n.* مجلّة رخيصة majalleh rekhisah

dreadfully *adv.* بقوّة beqwweh

dreadlock *n.* شعر مجدّل shaer mejaddal

dreadlock *v.* يجدّل الشعر yejaddel elsaer

dream *n.* حلم hlem

dream *v.* يحلَم yehlam

dreamer *n.* صاحب حلم sahin hlem

dreamily *adv.* بخياليّة bekhayalleyyeh

dreamworld *n.* عالم الأحلام alam elahlam

dreamy *adj.* خيالي khayali

drench *v.* ينقَع yenqa'a

dress *n.* روب rub

dress *v.* يلبّس yelabbes

dressing *n.* لبس lebes

dressmaker *n.* مصمم أزياء musammem azya'

drib *n.* كمّ قليل kamm qalil

dribble *n.* رذاذ razaz

dribble *v.* ينقّط قطرة قطرة yenaqqet qatra qatra

dried *adj.* ميبّس meyabbas

drift *n.* مغزى maghza

drift *v.* يشطّ عن yesh

drill *n.* حفّارَة haffarah

drill *v.* يحفُر yehfur

drink *n.* شراب shrab

drink *v.* يشرب yeshrab

drip *n.* نقطة nuqtah nuqtah

drip *v.* ينقّط yenaqqet

drive *v.* يسوق yesuq

drive *n.* سواقة sawwaqah

drive *n.* حافز hafiz

drive *n.* دافِع dafe'

driver *n.* سوّاق sawwaqah

drizzle *n.* دوخة dukhah

drizzle *v.* يدوخ yedukh

droid *n.* روبوت rubut

drone *n.* طنطنة tantaneh

drool n رويل rewel

drool *v.* يسيل رويله yesil rewelu

droop *v.* يتدلّى yetdallah

droop *n.* تدلاية tedlayeh

droopy *adj.* مدلّى mdallah

drop *n.* نقطة nuqtah

drop *v.* ينقّط yenaqqet

dropout *n.* ترك الدراسة tark edderaseh

dropzone *n.* درابزون drabzun

drought *n.* جفاف jafaf

drown *v.* يغرق yeghraq

drug *n.* دوا dawah

druggist *n.* صيدلي saydali

druid *n.* كاهن kahin

drum *n.* دربكّة derbakkeh

drum *v.* يدقّ عالدربكّة yeduqq alderbakkeh

drumbeat *n.* صوت الطبل sut eltabl

drumfish *n.* طبلة tableh

drunk *adj.* سكران sakran
drunkard *n.* سكّير sakkir
dry *adj.* ناشف nashif
dry *v.* يَنشّف yenashshif
dual *adj.* ثنائي thunaei
duality *n.* ثائيّة thunaeyyeh
dub *n.* دبلجة dablajeh
dub *v.* يدبلج yedablej
dubious *adj.* مشبوه mashbuh
ducat *n.* الدوقيّة elduqeyyeh
duchess *n.* دوقة duqah
duck *n.* بطّة battah
duck *v.* يطاطي رأسه tetati rasuh
duct *n.* ماسورة masurah
duct *v.* ينقل بالماسورة yenqul
belmasurah
dude *n.* مِتأنّق metanneq
due *adj.* مستحِق mestahaqq
due *n.* المستحقّات
elmustahaqqat
due *adv.* وقت الاستحقاق waqt
elistehqaq
duel *n.* مبارزة mubarazeh
duel *v.* يبارز yebariz
duet *n.* دويتو duwitto
duet *v.* يغنّي دويتو yeghanni
duwitto
duke *n.* دوق duq
dull *adj.* ممل mumell
dull *v.* يكسد yeksad
duly *adv.* حسب الأصول hasab
elusul
dumb *adj.* أبله ablah
dumbbell *n.* أثقال رياضيّة athqal
reyadeyyeh
dumbfound *v.* يسطل yesattel

dumbfounded *adj.* مسطول
mastul
dumbo *n.* الغبي elghabi
dummy *n.* شخص وهمي shakhes
wahmi
dummy *v.* يجهّز واجهة كتاب
yejahhiz wajehet ktab
dump *n.* مزبلة mazbaleh
dump *v.* يكبّ الوسخ yekebb
elwasakh
dumpster *n.* سلّة المهملات sallet
elmuhmalat
dunce *n.* الغبي elghabi
dune *n.* تلّ رمل tall raml
dung *n.* بعر baer
dungeon *n.* زنزانة zinzaneh
dunk *n.* غمر ghamr
dunk *v.* يغمر بالمرقة yeghmur
belmarqah
duo *n.* تنين tenin
dup *v.* يضاعِف yedaef
dupe *v.* يخدَع yekhda'
dupe *n.* جدبة jadbeh
duplex *n.* بيت بطابقين beit
btabqin
duplicate *adj.* مضاعف muda'af
duplicate *n.* نُسخة طبق الأصل
nesekha tbeq elasel
duplicate *v.* يضاعف yedaef
duplicity *n.* نفاق nefaq
durable *adj.* مِتين matin
duration *n.* مداومة
mudawameh
during *prep.* خلال khilal
dusk *n.* غروب ghurub
dust *n.* غبرا ghabrah
dust *v.* يغبِّر yeghabber

duster *n.* نفاضة الغبرا nafadet elghabra

dutiful *adj.* مطيع mute'

duty *n.* واجب wajib

duvet *n.* لحاف lhaf

dwarf *n.* قزم qazam

dwarf *v.* يقزم yeqazzim

dwarf *adj.* قزم qazam

dwell *v.* يسكن yeskun

dwelling *n.* سكن sakan

dwindle *v.* يقل yequll

dye *v.* يصبغ yesbugh

dye *n.* صباغ sbagh

dynamic *adj.* حرك hirik

dynamics *n.* دراسة الحركة diraset elharakeh

dynamite *n.* ديناميت dinamit

dynamo *n.* مولدة كهربا muwalledet kahrabah

dynasty *n.* أسرة حاكمة usrah hakmeh

dysentery *n.* زحار zuhar

dystopia *n.* الواقع المر elwaqe' elmurr

E

each *adj.* كل kell

each *adv.* لكل lakell

eager *adj.* متحمس metehammes

eagle *n.* نسر nser

ear *n.* إدن eden

early *adv.* عبكّير abakkir

early *adj.* بكّير bakkir

earn *v.* يكسب yeksab

earnest *adj.* جدّي jaddi

earth *n.* الأرض elared

earthen *adj.* دنيوي denyawi

earthly *adj.* أرضي ardi

earthquake *n.* هزّة أرضيّة hazzeh ardeyyeh

ease *n.* بحبوحة bahbuha

ease *v.* يسكن yeskun

east *n.* شرق sharq

east *adv.* للشرق lelsharq

east *adj.* شرق sharq

easter *n.* فصح fseh

eastern *adj.* شرقي sharqi

easy *adj.* سهل sahl

eat *v.* ياكل yakul

eatable *n.* أكل akl

eatable *adj.* يتاكل beyttakal

eave *n.* رواق rawaq

eavesdrop *v.* يتنصّت yetnassat

eavesdrop *n.* تنصت tanassut

ebb *n.* جزر jazr

ebb *v.* ينحسر المد yenhsir elmadd

ebony *n.* خشب الابنوس khashab elabanus

e-book *n.* كتاب الكتروني ktab elketruni

ebulliate *v.* يفور yefur

ebullience *n.* فورة furah

ebullient *adj.* فاير fayer

eccentric *adj.* غريب الاطوار gharib elatwar

ecclesiastical *adj.* كنَسي kanasi

echinid *adj.* توتيائي tutya'ei

echo *n.* صدى sadah

echo *v.* يطلّع صدى yetalle' sadah

echocardiogram *n.* مُخَطَّطُ صَدَى القَلْب mukhattat sadah elqalb

eclampsia *n.* تَشَنُّج أثناء الحمل tashannuj athna' elhamel

eclectic *adj.* انتقائي intiqa'i

eclipse *n.* خسوف khusuf

eclipse *v.* يخسف القمر yekhsuf elqamar

eclipsis *n.* الكسوف elkusuf

ecological *adj.* بيئي be'i

ecologist *n.* عالم بيئة aalim bi'a

ecology *n.* علم البيئة elim elbi'a

economic *adj.* اقتصادي iqtisadi

e-commerce *n.* تجارة الكترونية tejarah elketruneyyeh

economical *adj.* اقتصادي iqtisadi

economics *n.* علوم اقتصادية ulum iqtisadeyyeh

economy *n.* اقتصاد iqtisadi

ecosystem *n.* نظام بيئي nizam bi'e

ecoterrorism *n.* إرهاب بيئي irhab bi'e

ectasy *n.* نشوة nashweh

ecstatic *adj.* منتشي menteshi

ectoplasm *n.* اكتوبلازم aktublazm

ecumenic *adj.* عالمي aalami

ecumenical *adj.* عالمي aalami

eczema *n.* أكزيما akzimah

edema *n.* استسقا istisqah

edge *n.* حرف harf

edible *adj.* صالح للأكل saleh lelakel

edifice *n.* بناية كبيرة benayrh kbireh

edict *n.* مرسوم marsum

edificant *adj.* مهذّب muhazzab

edification *n.* تهذيب tahzib

edify *v.* يهذّب yehazzib

edit *v.* يحرّر yeharrir

edition *n.* تحرير tahrir

editor *n.* محرر muharrer

editorial *adj.* تحريري tahriri

editorial *n.* إفتتاحية iftitaheyyeh

educate *v.* يعلّم yeallim

education *n.* تعليم ta'lim

eel *n.* سمك الانكليس samak elanklis

eerie *adj.* غريب gharib

effable *adj.* بنشرح بكم كلمة bnshereh bekam klmeh

efface *v.* يطمس yetmus

effect *n.* تأثير ta'thir

effect *v.* يسبّب yesabbeb

effective *adj.* فعّال fa'al

effeminate *adj.* مخنّث mekhannath

efficacy *n.* كفاءة kafa'ah

efficiency *n.* فعّالية fa'aleyyeh

efficient *adj.* كفؤ kufu'e

effigy *n.* تمثال temthal

effort *n.* جهد hjhed

effortless *adj.* هيّن hayyen

effusive *adj.* متدفّق metdaffeq

egg *n.* بيضة bedah

ego *n.* الأنا el'anna

egocentric *adj.* أَنَانِي anani
egotism *n.* أَنَانِيّة ananeyyeh
eight *n.* الرقم 8 elraqam 8
eighteen *adj.* الرقم 18 elraqam 18
eighty *n.* الرقم 80 elraqam 80
either *pron.* حدا مِن hada mn
either *adv.* إمّا emma
ejaculate *v.* يقذف المني yeqzuf elmani
ejaculate *n.* قذف المني qazf elmani
ejaculation *n.* القذف elqazf
ejaculatory *adj.* قذفي qazfi
eject *v.* يطلع yetalle'
elaborate *v.* يفصل yefassel
elaborate *adj.* تفصيلي tafsili
elapse *v.* يمرّ الوقت yemurr elwaqt
elastic *adj.* رخْو rakhu
elasticity *n.* رخاوة rakhaweh
elate *v.* يبسط yebsit
elate *adj.* بشوشَ bashush
elated *adj.* فرحان farhan
elation *n.* فرح farah
elbow *n.* كوع ku'e
elder *adj.* أكبَر akbar
elder *n.* الكبير بالعمر elkbir belumer
elderly *adj.* كبير بالعمر kbir belumur
elect *v.* ينتخب yentuhkib
election *n.* انتخاب intikhab
electorate *n.* ناخِب nakhib
electric *adj.* كهرَبائي kahrubae'i
electricity *n.* كهرباً kahrabah
electrify *v.* يكهرب yekahreb

electrocute *v.* يعدِم بالكهربا ye'dim belkahraba
electrocution *n.* إعدام بالكهربا e'dam belkahraba
electrolyte *n.* محلول كهربائي mahlul kahruba'i
electron *n.* الكترون elektron
electronic *adj.* الكتروني elketroni
elegance *n.* ظَرَافة zarafeh
elegant *adj.* ظريفَ zarif
elegy *n.* لدبة nadbeh
element *n.* عنصر ensur
elemental *adj.* عنصُري unsuri
elementary *adj.* إبتدائي ibteda'i
elephant *n.* فيل fil
elephantine *adj.* سمين smin
elevate *v.* يرفَع yerfa'e
elevation *n.* رفع rafe'
elevator *n.* مصعد mas'ad
eleven *n.* الرقم 11 elraqm 11
elf *n.* عفريت afrit
elicitate *v.* يثير yuthir
eligibility *n.* جَدَارة jadarah
eligible *adj.* جدير jadir
eliminate *v.* يلغي yelghi
elimination *n.* إلغَاء elgha'
eliminator *n.* مزيل muzil
eliminatory *adj.* إلغائي elgha'ei
elision *n.* إدغام edgham
elite *adj.* يخص النخبة bekhuss elnughbeh
elite *n.* النخبة elnughbeh
elitism *n.* النخبويّة elnakhbaweyyeh
elitist *n.* نخبوي nakhbawi
elixir *n.* إكسير iksir

elk *n.* ظبي zabi

ellipse *n.* شكل بيضاوي shakel baydawi

elliptic *adj.* بيضاوي baydawi

elocution *n.* خطابة khatabeh

elope *v.* يهرب مع العشيقة yehrub ma elashiqah

eloquence *n.* فَصَاحة fasaha

eloquent *adj.* فصيح fasih

else *adj.* ثاني tani

else *adv.* كمان kaman

elucidate *v.* يبسّط yebsit

elude *v.* يتهرّب من yeteharrab mn

elusion *n.* تهرّب taharrub

elusive *adj.* متهرّب meteharrab

emaciate *v.* يخف كتير yenhaf ktir

emaciated *adj.* نحيف nahif

emaculate *v.* يروّح النمش yerawweh elnamsh

emaculation *n.* إزالة النمش ezalet elnamash

email n بريد الكتروني barid elketroni

emanate *v.* يتطاير yettayar

emanation *n.* تطاير tatayur

emancipate *v.* يعتق ye'tuq

emancipation *n.* عتق eteq

embalm *v.* يحنّط yehannit

embalming *n.* تحنيط tahnit

embank *v.* يسد yesedd

embankment *n.* سد sadd

embargo *n.* حظر hazer

embark *v.* يركب سفينة yerkab safeneh

embarrass *v.* يحرج yehrej

embarrassing *adj.* محرج muhrej

embarrassment *n.* إحراج ihraj

embassy *n.* سفارة safarah

embitter *v.* ينغّص yetnaghghas

emblem *n.* شارة sharah

embodiment *n.* تجسيم tajsim

embody *v.* يجسّم yejassim

embolden *v.* يقوّي yeqawwi

embrace *v.* يحضن yehdun

embrace *n.* حضن heden

embroidery *n.* تطريز tatriz

embryo *n.* جنين janin

embryonic *adj.* جنيني janini

embush *v.* يخفي بالغابة yekhfi belghabeh

emend *v.* ينقّح yenaqqeh

emendate *v.* يصحّح yesahhih

emerald *n.* زمرّد zumurrud

emerge *v.* يطلع yetalle'

emergency *n.* طوارئ taware'

emigrate *v.* يهاجر yehajer

emigration *n.* هجرة hejrah

eminence *n.* سمو sumuu

eminent *adj.* مرموق marmuq

emissary *n.* مبعوث mabuth

emission *n.* انبعاث inbe'ath

emit *v.* يطلق yetleq

emittance *n.* إطلاق itlaq

emmet *n.* نملة namleh

emoji *n.* رموز تعبيرية rumuz ta'bereyyeh

emolument *n.* معاش ma'ash

emote *v.* يتظاهر بمشاعر yetzahar bemasher

emoticon *n.* وجه تعبيري wajeh ta'beri

emotion *n.* عاطفة a'tefeh

emotional *adj.* عاطفي a'tefi

emotive *adj.* يحرّك المشَاعر
beyharrek elmasha'er

empath *n.* متقمّص عاطفي
metqammes aatefi

empathic *adj.* تقمّصي taqmmusi

empathy *n.* التقمّص
eltaqammus

emperor *n.* امبراطور embratur

emphasis *n.* تأكيد ta'kid

emphasize *v.* يؤكّد yeakkid

emphatic *adj.* مؤكّد mu'akkad

empire *n.* إمبراطوريّة
embratureyyeh

empirical *adj.* تجريبي tajribi

empiricism *n.* تجريبيّة
tajrebeyyeh

empiricist *n.* التجريبي eltajribi

employ *v.* يوظّف yewazzif

employee *n.* موظّف muwazzaf

employer *n.* صاحب الشغل
saheb elshughul

employment *n.* توظيف tawzif

empower *v.* يفوّض yefawwed

empress *n.* إمبراطورة
embraturah

empty *adj.* فاضي fadi

empty *v.* يفضّي yefaddi

emulate *v.* يقلّد yeqalled

emulation *n.* تقليد taqlid

emulsifier *n.* مستحلب
mustahlab

emulsify *v.* يستحلب yestahlib

enable *v.* يَسمَح yesmah

enact *v.* يشرّع yesharre'

enamel *n.* مينا السنين mina
elsnin

enamour *v.* يعجب ye'jjb

enamoured *adj.* معجب mu'jab

enamourment *n.* إعجاب e'jab

encage *v.* يحبس بقفص yehbus
beqafas

encapsulate *v.* يحطّ بكبسولة
yehutt bekabsuleh

encase *v.* يعبّي بصندوق ye'abbi
besanduq

enchant *v.* يسحر yeshar

encircle *v.* يطوّق yetawweq

enclose *v.* يسيّج yesayyej

enclosure *n.* سياج syaj

encompass *v.* يشمل yeshmal

encounter *n.* مواجهة
muwajaha

encounter *v.* يواجه yewajeh

encourage *v.* يشجّع yeshajje'

encroach *v.* يعتدي على ye'tedi
ala

encrust *v.* يلبّس yelabbes

encrusted *adj.* ملبّس mlabbas

encrypt *v.* يشفّر yeshaffer

encrypted *adj.* مشفّر meshaffer

encryption *n.* تشفير tashfir

encumber *v.* يكبّل بالديون
yekabbel beldyun

encyclopaedia *n.* موسوعة
mawsu'ah

end *v.* ينهي yenhi

end *n.* نهاية nihayeh

endanger *v.* يعرّض للخطر
ye'arred lelkhatar

endangered *adj.* معرَّض للخطر
mu'arrad lelkhatar

endear *v.* يحبّب yehabbeb

endearment *n.* تحبيب tahbib

endeavour *n.* محاولة
muhawaleh

endeavour *v.* يحاول yehawel

endemic *adj.* مستوطن
mestawten

endemic *n.* مرض مستوطن
marad mestawten

endemiology *n.* دراسة الأمراض
المستوطنة deraset elamrad
elmestawteneh

endless *adj.* مؤبد mu'abbad

endorse *v.* يجير شيك yejayyer
shik

endorsement *n.* تجيير الشيك
tajyyr elshik

endorser *n.* مظهّر الشيك
muzahher elshik

endoscopic *adj.* تنظيري tanziri

endoscopy *n.* تنظيري tanziri

endow *v.* يعطي مهر ye'ti mahr

endowed *adj.* مقدم muqaddam

endurable *adj.* ينحمل
beynhemel

endurance *n.* تحمّل tahammul

endure *v.* يتحمّل yethammal

enemy *n.* عدو adu

energetic *adj.* نشيط nashit

energize *v.* ينشّط yenashshet

energy *n.* نشاط nashat

enervate *v.* ينهك yenhik

enervated *adj.* منهك munhak

enfeeble *v.* يتعب yet'eb

enforce *v.* يجبر yejbur

enfranchise *v.* يعطي حق
ye'ti haq elíqtera' الاقتراع

engage *v.* يخطب yenkhutib

engagement *n.* خطبة khutbeh

engaging *adj.* جذّاب jazzab

engine *n.* محرّك muharrek

engineer *n.* مهندس muhandes

engineering *n.* هندسة
handaseh

English *n.* اللغة الانكليزيّة
ellugha elinklizeyyeh

englobe *v.* يشمل yeshmal

engorge *v.* يحتقن yehtuqen

engrave *v.* ينقش yenqush

engross *v.* يحتكر yehteker

engulf *v.* يطم yetumm

enhance *v.* يحسّن yehassin

enhancement *n.* تحسين tahsin

enigma *n.* معضلة mu'deleh

enigmatic *adj.* غامض ghamed

enigmatical *adj.* غامض
ghamed

enigmatically *adv.* بغموض
beghumud

enjoy *v.* ينبسط yenbeset

enjoyability *n.* القدرة عالبسط
elqudrah albast

enjoyable *adj.* بيبسط beybset

enjoyment *n.* بسط bast

enlarge *v.* يكبّر yekabber

enlighten *v.* يضوّي yedawwi

enlist *v.* يحطّ بقوائم yehut
beqawaem

enliven *v.* ينعش yen'esh

enmity *n.* عداوة adaweh

ennoble *v.* يبجّل yebajjel

enormous *adj.* ضخم dakhem

enough *adj.* كافي kafi

enough *adv.* بطريقة كافية
betareqa kafeyeh

enrage *v.* يعصّب ye'assib

enrapture v. يفرّح yefarreh
enrich v. يغني yeghanni
enrol v. يسجّل بـ yesajjel bi
enshrine v. يقدّس yeqaddes
enslave v. يستعبد yesteid
ensue v. يجي من yeji mn
ensure v. يضمن yedman
entangle v. يوقع بالفخ yewaqqe' belfakh
enter v. يدخل yedkhul
enterprise n. مشروع mashru'e
entertain v. يسلّي yesalli
entertainment n. تسلية tasleyeh
enthral v. يشدّ yeshedd
enthrone v. يتوّج yetawwej
enthusiasm n. حماس hamas
enthusiastic adj. يحمّس byhammes
entice v. يغرّر yegharrer
enticement n. تغرير taghrir
enticer n. مغري mughri
enticing adj. فتّان fattan
entire adj. كامل kamil
entirely adv. بالكامل belkamel
entitle v. يعنون ye'anwen
entity n. كائن ka'en
entomb v. يدفن yedfun
entomology n. علم الحشرات elm elhasharat
entrails n. مصران musran
entrance n. دخول dukhul
entrap v. يوقع بالفخ yeqwaqqe' belfakh
entrapment n. توقيع بالفخ tawqi'e belfakh
entreat v. يترجّى yetrajja
entreaty n. ترجّي tarajji

entrench v. يتحصّن yetehassan
entrenchment n. تحصين tahsin
entropic adj. مقصور حراريّا maqsur hararyyan
entropy n. قصور حراري qusur harari
entrust v. يفوّض yefawwed
entry n. إنتساب intisab
enumerate v. يعدّ ye'edd
enumerative adj. حسابي hesabi
enunciate v. ينطق yentuq
enunciation n. نطق nutuq
enunciatory adj. نطقي netqi
envelop v. يحطّ بظرف yehett bezarf
envelope n. ظرف zarf
envelopment n. تغليف taghlif
enviable adj. محسود mahsud
envious adj. حسود hasud
environment n. بيئة be'aa
environmental adj. بيئي be'ei
environmentalism n. علم البيئة elm elbe'aa
environmentalist n. مختصّ بيئة mekhtass be'aa
envisage v. يتخيّل yetkhayyal
envision v. تخيّل takhayyul
envoy n. يوفد yufid
envy v. يحسد yehsud
envy n. حسد hasad
enzyme n. انزيم enzym
enzymic adj. انزيمي enzymi
eon n. دهر dahr
ephemera n. دبّانة مايو debbanet mayo
ephemeral adj. عابر a'ber
ephemeric adj. عابر a'ber

epic *n.* ملحَمة malhameh

epical *adj.* ملحَمي malhami

epicentre *n.* مركز الزلزال السطحي
markaz elzalazel elsatehi

epicure *n.* ذَوّاق zawwaq

epicurean *adj.* لذّاتي lazzati

epicurean *n.* لذّاتي lazzati

epidemic *n.* وباء waba'

epidural *n.* فوق الجافية fuq
eljafeyeh

epiglittis *n.* لحمة الحلق lahmet
elhaleq

epigram *n.* مثَل مسخرجي matal
maskharji

epilepsy *n.* صرْع، sara'

epileptic *adj.* مصروع masru'e

epileptic *n.* مصروع masru'e

epilogue *n.* ختام khetam

epiphany *n.* عيد الغطاس eid
alghattas

episode *n.* حلقَة halaqah

epitaph *n.* نقش ع قبر naqesh a
qabr

epoch *n.* زَمَن zaman

equal *adj.* متساوي metsawi

equal *v.* يساوي yesawi

equal *n.* تساوي tasawi

equality *n.* مساواة musawat

equalize *v.* يوازِن yewazin

equate *v.* يعادِل ye'adil

equation *n.* عملية حسابية
amaleyyeh hesabeyyeh

equator *n.* خط الأستواء khatt
elistewa'e

equilateral *adj.* تساوى الاضلاع
tasawi eladla'

equinox *n.* الاعتدال الربيعي
ele'tedal elrabe'i

equip *v.* يجهِز yejahhez

equipment *n.* معدِات mu'eddat

equitable *adj.* حقّاني haqqani

equivalent *adj.* متساوي
metsawi

equivocal *adj.* غامض ghamed

era *n.* عهد ahed

eradicate *v.* يستأصل yesta'sel

eradication *n.* استئصال este'sal

eradicator *n.* أداة استئصال adat
este'sal

erase *v.* يمحي yemhi

eraser *n.* محاية mahayyeh

erect *v.* يعمِر ye'ammer

erect *adj.* مبني mabni

erectile *adj.* انتصابي intisabi

erection *n.* انتصاب intisab

erode *v.* يتآكل yettakal

erosion *n.* تآكل ta'akul

erosive *adj.* تآكلي ta'akuli

erotic *adj.* جنسي jensi

erotica *n.* أفلام جنسية aflam
jenseyyeh

eroticism *n.* إثارة جنسية etharah
jenseyyeh

eroticize *v.* يثير الغريزة الجنسية
yethir elgharezeh
eljinseyyeh

err *v.* غلط ghalat

errand *n.* مرسال mersal

erroneous *adj.* غلطان ghaltan

error *n.* خطأ ghata'

erupt *v.* ينفجر البركان yenfejr
elburkan

eruption n. انفجار البركان infijar elburkan

escalator n. درج متحرّك daraj meteharrek

escapable adj. بيقدر يتجنّبه beyqder yetjannabuh

escape n. هروب hurub

escape v. يهرب yeharreb

escapee n. فراري frari

escapism n. التهرّب من الواقع eltaharrub mn elwaqe'

escapist n. إنهزامي inhizami

escapology n. فنّ الهروب fann elhurub

escargot n. حلزون halazun

eschew v. يتجنّب yetjannab

eschewment n. تجنّب tajannub

escort n. حراسة hiraseh

escort v. يحرس yehrus

escorted adj. محروس mahrus

escrow n. حساب ضمان hesab daman

escrow v. يودع بحساب الضمان yude' behsab eldaman

esophageal adj. بلعومي bal'umi

esoteric adj. سري serri

esoterism n. سرية serreyyeh

espace n. مسافة masafeh

especial adj. خصوصي khususi

especially adv. وخصوصا wekhsusan

espouse v. يتزوج yetzawwaj

essay n. مقالة maqaleh

essay v. يجرّب yejarreb

essayist n. كاتب مقالات katb maqalat

essence n. جوهر jawhr

essential adj. جوهري jawhari

establish v. يأسس ye'assis

establishment n. تأسيس ta'sis

estate n. أملاك amlak

esteem n. تقدير taqdir

esteem v. يقدر yeqadder

estimate n. تقييم taqyyem

estimate v. يقيم yeqayyem

estimation n. تقييم taqyyem

estimative adj. تقييمي taqyyimi

estragon n. طرخون tarkhun

estrange v. يبعد yeb'ed

estranged adj. متباعد metba'ed

estrogen n. إستروجين estrojin

estuary n. مصب النهر masabb ennaher

etcetera adv. وهيك wuhik

etch v. يحفر كليشيه yehfur klisheh

etched adj. محفور mahfur

etching n. حفر كليشيه hafr klisheh

eternal adj. خالد khaled

eternalize v. يخلّد yekhalled

eternally adv. للأبد lelabad

eternity n. أبدية abadeyyeh

ether n. أثير athir

ethical adj. أخلاقي akhlaqi

ethics n. آداب aadab

ethnic adj. عنصري unsuri

ethnicity n. عرقية erqeyyeh

ethos n. أخلاقيات akhlaqyyat

etiquette n. اتيكيت etikit

etymology n. اشتقاق eshtiqaq

eunuch n. مخصي makhsi

eucalypt n. الاوكالبتوس elukalebtus

euphemistic *adj.* كلامه منيح klamuh mneh

euphoria *n.* نشوة nashweh

eureka *int.* وجدتها wajadtuha

euthanize *v.* يموت ببطء yemut bebute'

eutopia *n.* المثاليّة elmethalyyeh

evacuate *v.* يخلي yekhli

evacuation *n.* إخلاء ekhla'

evade *v.* يتملّص yetmallas

evaluate *v.* يثمّن yetammen

evangel *n.* إنجيل enjil

evangelic *adj.* إنجيلي enjili

evaporate *v.* يتبخّر yetbakhkhar

evasion *n.* تملّص tamallus

evasive *adj.* مراوغ mrawegh

even *adj.* متساوي metsawi

even *adj.* تامّ tamm

even *adj.* منتظم mentezem

even *v.* يسوّي yesawwi

even *adv.* تماما tamaman

evening *n.* مسا msa

evenly *adv.* بالتساوي beltasawi

event *n.* حدث hadath

eventually *adv.* وأخيرا wa'akhiran

ever *adv.* أبدا abdan

evergreen *adj.* دائمة الخضرة da'emet elkhudrah

evergreen *n.* شجر دائم الخضرة shajr da'em elkhudrah

everlasting *adj.* دائم da'em

evert *v.* يقلب لبرا yeqleb labarrah

every *adj.* كلامه منيح klamuh mnih

everybody *pron.* كل حدا kel hada

everyday *adj.* كل يوم kel yum

everyone *pron.* كل حدا kel hada

everything *pron.* كلشي klshi

everywhere *pron.* كل مكان kel makan

evict *v.* يستردّ ملكيّة yestredd melkeyyet

eviction *n.* استرداد ملكيّة esterdad melkeyyet

evictor *n.* مستردّ الملكيّة mestaredd elmelkeyyeh

evidence *n.* دليل dalil

evident *adj.* واضح wadeh

evil *n.* شرّ sharr

evil *adj.* شرير sherrir

evince *v.* يثبت yethabbit

eviscerate *v.* يطالع أحشاء yetale' ahsha'a

evisceration *n.* تطليع الأحشاء tatli'e ahsha'a

evitability *n.* حتميّة hatmeyyeh

evocate *v.* يرجّع الذكريات yerajje' ezzekrayat

evocation *n.* ترجيع الذكريات tarje' ezzekrayat

evocative *adj.* بيرجّع الذكريات berajje' ezzekrayat

evoke *v.* يستحضر yestahder

evolution *n.* تطوّر tatawwur

evolutionary *adv.* تطوّري tatawwuri

evolve *v.* يطلق yetleq

ewe *n.* نعجة na'jeh

exact *adj.* دقيق daqiq

exactly *adv.* بدقَّة bedeqqah

exaggerate *v.* يبالغ yebalegh

exaggeration *n.* مبالغة mubalaghah

exalt *v.* يرفع yeraffe'

examination *n.* امتحان emtihan

examine *v.* يمتحن yemtehen

examinee *n.* مقدّم امتحان muqaddem emtihan

examiner *n.* صاحب الامتحان saheb elemtihan

example *n.* مثال methal

excavate *v.* يحفر yehfur

excavation *n.* حفر hafr

exceed *v.* يتجاوز yetjawaz

excel *v.* يتفوّق yetfawwaq

excellence *n.* تفوّق tafawwuq

excellency *n.* صاحب السعادة saheb elsa'adeh

excellent *adj.* ممتاز mumtaz

except *v.* يستثني yestathni

except *prep.* ما عدا ma ada

exception *n.* استثناء estethna'

exceptional *adj.* استثنائي estethna'e

excerpt *n.* اقتباس iqtebas

excess *n.* فايض fayed

excess *adj.* فايض fayed

excessive *adj.* مفرط mufret

exchange *n.* تصريف عملة tasrif emleh

exchange *v.* يصرّف عملة yesarref emleh

excise *n.* ضريبة darebeh

excite *v.* يثير yethir

exclaim *v.* يهتف yehtuf

exclamation *n.* تعجُّب ta'ajjub

exclude *v.* يستبعد yestab'ed

exclusive *adj.* حصري hasri

excommunicate *v.* يحرم كنسيّاً yehrum kanaseyyan

excursion *n.* رحلة rehleh

excuse *v.* يعذر ye'zur

excuse *n.* عذر uzer

execute *v.* يعدم ye'dim

execution *n.* إعدام e'dam

executioner *n.* جلّاد jallad

exempt *v.* يعفي ye'fi

exempt *adj.* معفي me'fi

exercise *n.* تمرين tamrin

exercise *v.* يتمرّن yetmarran

exhaust *v.* يستنفذ yestanfiz

exhibit *n.* شي معروض shi ma'rud

exhibit *v.* يعرض ye'rud

exhibition *n.* معرض ma'rad

exile *n.* منفي manfi

exile *v.* ينفي yenfi

exist *v.* يكوّن yekun

existence *n.* كينونة kenuneh

existential *adj.* وجودي wujudi

existentialism *n.* وجودية wujudeyyeh

exit *n.* مخرج mukhrej

exit *v.* يطلع برا yetalle' labarrah

expand *v.* يوسّع yewasse'

expansion *n.* توسيع tawse'

ex-parte *adj.* متحيّز methayyez

ex-parte *adv.* بتحيّز betahayyuz

expect *v.* يتوقّع yetwaqqa'

expectation *n.* توقّع tawaqqu'e

expedient *adj.* مناسب munaseb

expedite v. يبعَت لبرا yebat labarra

expedition n. بعثة be'theh

expel v. يرحّل من البلد yerahhil mn elbalad

expend v. يصرف yesruf

expenditure n. مصروفات masrufat

expense n. نفقة nafaqah

expensive adj. غالي ghali

experience n. تجربة tajrubeh

experience v. يجرب yejarreb

experiment n. اختبار ikhteyar

expert adj. خبير khabir

expert n. الخبير elkhabir

expire v. ينتهي صلاحيته yentehi salahetuh

expiry n. تاريخ الصلاحية tarikh elsalaheyyeh

explain v. يشرح yeshrah

explanation n. شرح shareh

explicit adj. صريح sarih

explode v. يفجر yefajjer

exploit n. استغلال estighlal

exploit v. يستغل yestaghghel

exploration n. تصفح tasaffuh

explore v. يتصفح yestaffah

explosion n. انفجار enfijar

explosive n. مواد متفجرة mawad metfajrah

explosive adj. تفجيري tafjiri

exponent n. أس uss

export n. تصدير tasdir

export v. يصدّر yesadder

expose v. يكشف yekshuf

expose v. يفضح yefdah

express v. يعبّر ye'abber

express adj. سريع sare'

express n. البريد السريع elbarid essare'

expression n. تعبير ta'bir

expressive adj. تعبيري ta'biri

expulsion n. ترحيل tarhil

exquisite adj. حسّاس كتير hassas ktir

exquisitive adj. فضولي fduli

extend v. يمدّد yemadded

extent n. درجة darajeh

external adj. خارجي kharji

extinct adj. منقرض menqured

extinguish v. يطفّي النار yetaffi ennar

extol v. يمدَح yemdah

extra adj. زيادة zydeh

extra adv. بزيادة bezyadeh

extract n. خلاصة khulasah

extract v. يستخلص yestakhles

extrajuducial adj. برات القانون barrat elqanun

extramarital adj. برّا إطار الزواج brra eitar ezzawaj

extranet n. شبكة خارجية shabakeh kharejeyyeh

extraordinary adj. إستثنائي estithna'e

extrapolate v. يقدّر بالاستدلال yeqadder bel'estedlal

extrapolation n. تقدير بالاستدلال taqdir bel'estedlal

extraspecial adj. كتير خاص ktir khas

extraterrestrial adj. برّا الكرة الأرضية brra elkurah elardeyyeh

extraterrestrial *n.* مخلوق فضائي
makhluq fadae'i

extravagance *n.* تبذير tabzir

extravagant *adj.* مبذّر
mubazzer

extreme *adj.* تطرّفي tatarrufi

extreme *n.* درجة قصوى
darajeh quswa

extremist *n.* متطرّف mettarref

extremity *n.* تطرّف tatarruf

extricate *v.* يخلّص yekhalles

extrinsic *adj.* عرَضي aradi

extrinsically *adv.* بعرضية
be'aradeyyeh

extrovert *n.* منبسط menbeset

exude *v.* يشكّل المعدن yeshakkel
elma'dan

exultant *adj.* مبتهج mebtehej

exult *v.* ابتهاج ibtihaj

eye *n.* عين eyn

eyeball *n.* مقلة العين meqlet
eleyn

eyebrow *n.* حاجب العين hajeb
eleyn

eyecatcher *n.* شي بلفت النظر shi
belfet ennazar

eyelash *n.* رموش العين rumush
eleyn

eyelet *n.* عروايه erwayeh

eyelid *n.* جفن العين jfn eleyn

eyespot *n.* بقعة العين buq'et
eleyn

eyewash *n.* قَطْرة qatrah

F

fable *n.* خُزَعْبَلات khuza'balat

fabric *n.* نسيج nasij

fabricate *v.* يلفّق yelaffeq

fabrication *n.* تلفيق talfiq

fabulous *adj.* خرافي khurafi

facade *n.* دّياجة dibajeh

face *n.* وجه wajeh

face *v.* يواجه yewajeh

facelift *n.* تجميل وجه tajmil
wajeh

facelift *v.* يعمل تجميل للوجه
ye'mil tajmil lelwajeh

facet *n.* جانب janib

facet *n.* سطح صغير sateh sghur

facial *adj.* وجهي wajhi

facile *adj.* هيّن hayyem

facilitate *v.* يسهّل yesahhel

facility *n.* منشأة munsha'a

fac-simile *n.* صورة طبق الأصل
surah tebq elasel

fact *n.* حقيقة haqeqah

faction *n.* خيال khayal

factious *adj.* خيالي khayali

factor *n.* عامل aamel

factory *n.* معمل ma'mal

faculty *n.* كلية kleyyeh

fad *n.* بدعة bed'a

fade *v.* يكبي yekbi

faggot *n.* حزمة الحطب hezmet
elhatab

fail *n.* فشل fashal

fail *v.* يفشل yefshal

failure *n.* إخفاق ekhfaq	**famous** *adj.* مشهور mashhur
faint *adj.* مغمى عليه mughma alyh	**fan** *n.* معجب mu'jab
	fan *n.* مروحة marwaha
faint *v.* يغمى عليه yughma alyh	**fanatic** *adj.* أرعن ar'an
fair *adj.* عادِل adel	**fanatic** *n.* الأرعن elar'an
fair *n.* معرَض ma'rad	**fanciful** *adj.* خيالي khayali
fairly *adv.* لحدّ ما lahadd ma	**fancy** *n.* خيال khayal
fairy *n.* جان jan	**fancy** *v.* يتخيّل yetkhayyal
faith *n.* إيمان eyman	**fancy** *adj.* خيالي khayali
faithful *adj.* مؤمن mu'men	**fantastic** *adj.* رائع ra'e
fake *adj.* مزوَّر mzawwar	**fantasy** *n.* مخيّلة mukhayyeleh
fake *n.* تزوير tazwir	**far** *adv.* لبعيد labeyed
fake *v.* يزوِّر yezawwer	**far** *adj.* بعيد beyed
falcon *n.* صقر saqr	**farce** *n.* مهزلة mahzaleh
fall *v.* يوقع yuqa'	**fare** *n.* أجرة المواصلات ejret elmuwasalt
fall *n.* وقوع wuqu'e	
fallacy *n.* فكرة خطأ fekrah ghalat	**farewell** *n.* وَداع wada'
	farewell *interj.* وداعا wada'an
fallen *adj.* ساقط saqet	**farm** *n.* مزرعة mazra'a
fallen *n.* السَاقط elşaqet	**farmer** *n.* مزارِع muzare'
fallout *n.* غبار نووَي ghubar nawawi	**fascinate** *v.* ينفتن yenften
	fascination *n.* فتنة fetneh
fallow *v.* يريّح الأرض yerayyeh elard	**fashion** *n.* موضة mudah
	fashionable *adj.* عالموضة almudah
fallow *n.* تريح الأرض taryyeh elard	
	fast *adj.* سريع sari'e
falls *n.* شَلَّال shallal	**fast** *adj.* عجول ajul
false *adj.* مزيَّف mzayyaf	**fast** *adv.* بسرعة bser'a
falsehood *n.* زور zur	**fast** *n.* صيام syam
falsetto *n.* صوت عالي sut ali	**fast** *v.* يصوم yesum
falsification *n.* تزييف tazyyif	**fasten** *v.* يُثبِت yethabbit
falsify *v.* يزيِّف yezayyef	**fat** *adj.* سمين smin
falter *v.* يتَرنَّح yetrannah	**fat** *n.* دهون dehun
fame *n.* سمعة sim'ah	**fatal** *adj.* مميت mumit
familiar *adj.* مألوف ma'luf	**fatalism** *n.* الايمان بالقضاء والقدر eleyman belqada' welqadar
family *n.* عائلة ayleh	
famine *n.* مجاعة maja'a	**fatality** *n.* نحس nahs

fate v. يقدّر yeqadder

fate n. قدَر qadar

father n. أبّ abb

father v. يجيب ولد yejib walad

fathom v. يقيس عمق المي yeqis umq elmay

fathom n. مقياس لعمق المي meqyas la umq elmay

fatigue n. تعب ta'ab

fatigue v. يتعب yet'ab

fault n. غلطة ghaltah

faulty adj. غلطان ghaltan

fauna n. حيوانات المنطقة haywanat elmantiqah

favour n. معروف ma'ruf

favour n. نكهة nakha

favour v. يعمل معروف ye'mel ma'ruf

favourable adj. مؤيِّد mu'ayyed

favourite adj. مفضّل mudfaddal

favourite n. المحبوب elmahbub

fax n. فاكس faks

fax v. يبعت بالفاكس yeb'at belfaks

fealty n. برّ berr

fear n. خوف khuf

fear v. يخاف yekhaf

fearful adj. جبان jaban

feasible adj. عملي amali

feast n. وليمة walemeh

feast v. يقصف yuqsuf

feat n. عمل بطولي amal butuli

feather n. ريشة risheh

feature n. ميزة mezeh

feature v. يميّز yemayyez

febrile adj. حمّي hemmi

February n. شباط shebat

fecal adj. برازي burazi

feces n. براز buraz

fecund adj. ولود walud

fecundation n. إخصاب ikhsab

federal adj. فيدرالي fedrali

federation n. فيدرالية fedraleyyeh

fee n. رسم rasm

feeble adj. ضعيف da'ef

feed v. يعلف ye'luf

feed n. علَف alaf

feel v. يشعر yash'ur

feeling n. شعور shu'ur

feign v. يلفّق yelaffeq

felicitate v. يهنّي yehanni

felicitations int. تهاني tahani

felicity n. سعْد sa'd

feline adj. ماكر maker

felinity n. مكر makr

fell v. يوقع yewaqqe'

fellatio n. لحس القضيب lahs elqadib

fellow n. زميل zamil

felony n. جناية jenayeh

female adj. مؤنّث mu'annath

female n. أنثى untha

feminine adj. نسائي nisa'e

feminist adj. نسائي nisa'e

feminist n. النسائي elnisa'e

femur n. عظمة الفخد azmet elfalhd

fence n. سور sur

fence v. يسوّر yesawwer

fencer n. مقاتل بالسيف muqatel belsif

fend v. يحتاط yehtat

ferment *n.* لبس الخمار lebs elkhimar

ferment *v.* يلبس خمار yelbes khimar

fermentation *n.* اختمار ikhtimar

fern *n.* سرخس sarkhas

ferocious *adj.* شرس shares

ferret *n.* تحري taharri

ferret *v.* يتحرى yetharrah

ferry *n.* قارب qareb

ferry *v.* يطلع بقارب العبّارة yetla' beqareb elabbarah

ferryboat *n.* قارب عبّارة qareb elabbarah

fertile *adj.* خصب kheseb

fertility *n.* خصوبة khusubeh

fertilize *v.* يخصّب yekhassib

fertilizer *n.* سماد samad

fervent *adj.* متحمّس metehammes

fervour *n.* حماسة hamaseh

fester *v.* يقيّح yeqayyeh

festival *n.* مهرجان mahrajan

festive *adj.* إحتفالي ehtifali

festivity *n.* احتفاليّة ehtifalyyeh

festoon *n.* حبل زينة habel zyneh

fetal *adj.* جنيني janini

fetch *v.* يجيب yejib

fetish *n.* حجاب hijab

fetishism *n.* شهوة جنسيّة shahweh jinseyyeh

fetter *n.* كلبشة klabshah

fetter *v.* يلكبش yekalbesh

feud *n.* عداوة adaweh

feud *v.* يعادي ye'adi

feudal *adj.* إقطاعي eqta'e

feudalism *n.* نظام إقطاعي nizam eqta'e

fever *n.* حمّى hummah

feverish *adj.* محموم mahmum

few *adj.* شوي shway

fiancé *n.* خطيب khatib

fiasco *n.* خيبة khybeh

fibre *n.* ليف lif

fiberglass *n.* ألياف زجاجيّة alyaf zujajeyyeh

fibrillate *v.* يرجف yerjuf

fibroid *adj.* ليفي lifi

fibromuscular *adj.* ورمٌ ليفي waram lifi

fibrosis *n.* تليّف talayyuf

fibrosity *n.* تليّف talayyuf

fibrous *adj.* ليفي lifi

fickle *adj.* مقلقل mqa;qal

fiction *n.* حكاية hkayeh

fictional *adj.* خيالي khalali

fictitious *adj.* خرافي khurafi

fiddle *n.* كمنجة kamanjah

fiddle *v.* يضيّع الوقت yedayye' elwaqt

fidelity *n.* أمانة amaneh

fidget *n.* تململ tmulmul

fidget *v.* يتململ yetmalmal

fie *interj* تفه عليك tfeh alik

field *n.* حقل hakl

fiend *n.* إبليس eblis

fierce *adj.* عنيف anif

fiery *adj.* ناري nari

fifteen *n.* الرقم 15 elraqm 15

fifty *n.* الرقم 50 elraqm 50

fig *n.* تين tin

fight *n.* قتيل qtel

fight v. يتقاتل yetqatal

figment n. تلفيق talfiq

figurative adj. مجازي majazi

figure n. رقم raqm

figure n. رسم rasm

figure v. يرسم yersum

filament n. خيط khit

filamentation n خيوط khyut

filamented adj. خيطي khyti

file n. ملف malaf

file n. إضبارة edbarah

file n. طابور tabur

file v. يقدّم طلب yeqaddem talab

file v. يحفظ بالإضبارة yehfaz bel edbarah

file v. يمشي بالدور yemshi beldur

fill v. يعبّي ya'abbi

fillet n. فيليه fileh

fillet v. يقطّع شرايح yeqatte' sharayeh

film n. فلم felm

film v. يصوّر فلم yesawwer felm

filmmaker n. مخرج mukhrej

filter n. فلتر feltr

filter v. يفلتر yefalter

filth n. بذاءة baza'a

filthy adj. بذيء baze'

fin n. زعنفة ze'enfeh

final adj. نهائي niha'e

finance n. تمويل tamwil

finance v. يموّل yemawwel

financial adj. مالي mali

financier n. خبير مالي khabir mali

find v. يلاقي yelaqi

fine n. غرامة gharameh

fine v. يفرض غرامة yefrud gharameh

fine adj. منيح mneh

finger n. أصبع esba'

finger v. يلمس yelmes

fingernail n. أظفر uzfur

fingerpaint n. مناكير manakir

finish v. ينهي yenhi

finish n. تلميع talme'

finite adj. محدود mahdud

fir n. مفصول mafsul

fire n. حريق hareq

fire v. يحرق yehruq

fireball n. قذيفة qazefeh

firefight n. إطفاء الحريق itfa' hariq

firefighter n. إطفائي itfa'e

firehose v. يطفي حريق بالخرطوم yetfi hariq belkhartum

firehouse n. إطفائية itfa'eyyeh

firepit n. حفرة الحريق hifret elhariq

fireproof adj. ضدّ الحريق dedd elhariq

fireproof v. يقاوم الحريق yeqawm elhariq

firesuit n. لبس الإطفائي lebs elitfa'e

firetruck n. سيّارة إطفاء sayyaret itfa'

fireworks n. ألعاب ناريّة alaab nareyyeh

firm adj. ثابت thabit

firm n. شركة sherkeh

firmament n. سما sama

firmness n. ثبات thabat

first *adj.* أوّل awwal
first *n.* الأوّل elawwal
first *adv.* بالأوّل belawwal
fiscal *adj.* مالي mali
fish *n.* سمكة samakeh
fish *v.* يصطاد سمك yestad samk
fisherman *n.* صيّاد sayyad
fissure *n.* شقّ sheqq
fist *n.* قبضة الإيد qabdet eleyd
fist *v.* يضرب بوكس yedrub boks
fistula *n.* ناسور nasur
fit *v.* يناسب yenasib
fit *adj.* مناسب mnaseb
fit *n.* لياقة layakah
fit *n.* نوبة nubeh
fitful *adj.* متقطّع metqatte'
fitter *n.* مصلّح محرّكات msalleh muharekat
five *n.* الرقم 5 elraqm 5
fix *v.* يصلّح yesalleh
fix *n.* ورطة wartah
fixer-upper *n.* مُثبت علوي muthabbit ulwi
fizz *n.* فوران fawaran
fizz *v.* يفور yefur
fizzy *adj.* فوّار fawwar
flabbergast *n.* بهتة bahteh
flabbergast *v.* ينبهت yenbehet
flabbergasted *adj.* مبهوت mabhut
flabby *adj.* مترهّل metrahhel
flag *n.* علم elm
flagrant *adj.* فاضح fadeh
flake *n.* رقاقة ruqaqah
flake *v.* يفتّت yefattet
flaking *adj.* متفتّت metfattet

flambé *adj.* شاعل نار sha'el nar
flambé *n.* أكل شاعل نار akel sha'el nar
flambé *v.* يشعل نار عالأكل yesh'ul nar alakel
falmboyance *n.* أناقة زايدة anaqah zaydeh
falmboyant *adj.* كتير متأنّق ktir metanneq
falmboyant *n.* المتأنّق زيادة elmetanneq zyadeh
flame *n.* لهب lahab
flame *v.* يشعل نار yesh'ul nar
flank *adj.* جانبي janbi
flank *n.* خصر khasr
flank *v.* يهاجم الجناح yehajem eljanah
flannel *n.* فلانيلا vanilya
flap *n.* كفّ kaff
flap *v.* يدقّ كفّ yduqq kaff
flapping *adj.* بيرفرف berafref
flapping *n.* خفقان khafaqan
flapping *v.* يرفرف yerafref
flapper *n.* فرخ farkh
flare *v.* يشعل قنبلة إشارة yesh'ul qunblet isharah
flare *n.* قنبلة إشارة qunblet isharah
flash *n.* فلاش flash
flash *v.* يشعل فلاش yesh'ul flash
flashback *n.* مشهد عودة للماضي mashhad udeh lelmadi
flashbulb *n.* ضوّ الكاميرا daww elkamirah
flashcard *n.* بطاقة ذاكرة مدمجة betaqet zakrah mudmajeh

flasher *n.* غمّاز ghammaz

flashing *n.* حشوة معدنية بتمنع التسرب hashweh ma'daneyyeh btmna' ettasarrub

flask *n.* بطحة bateha

flat *adj.* مسطّح musattah

flat *n.* بيت beit

flatbed *n.* شاحنة مسطّحة shahneh musattaha

flatbed *adj.* مسطّح musattah

flatfoot *n.* رجل مسطّحة mjel mesttahah

flatland *n.* أرض مسطّحة ard mesttahah

flatter *v.* يجامل yejamel

flattery *n.* مجاملة mujamaleh

flatulence *n.* انتفاخ البطن بالغازات intifakh elbatn belghazat

flatulent *adj.* مطبلة mtableh

flaunt *v.* يغترّ yeghtarr

flavour *n.* نكهة nakha

flaw *n.* عيب eyb

flea *n.* برغوت barghut

flee *v.* يهرب yehrub

fleece *n.* صوف الخروف suf elkharuf

fleece *v.* يجزّ الصوف yejzz elsuf

fleet *n.* أسطول ustul

flesh *n.* لحم lahm

flexible *adj.* مرِن mren

flicker *n.* نقّار الخشب naqqar elkhashab

flicker *v.* يومض yumed

flight *n.* طيران tayaran

flimsy *adj.* ركيك rakik

fling *v.* رفس rafs

flip *n.* نقف naqf

flip *v.* ينقُف yenquf

flippancy *n.* وقاحة waqahah

flirt *n.* غزل ghazl

flirt *v.* يتغزّل yetghazzal

float *v.* يطوف yetuf

flock *n.* قطيع qate'

flock *v.* يتجمّع yetjamma'

flog *v.* يجلد yejlud

flood *n.* طوفان tufan

flood *v.* يطوف yetuf

floor *n.* أرض ard

floor *n.* بلاط blat

floor *v.* يبلّط yeballet

flora *n.* الحياة النباتية elhayat elnabateyyeh

florist *n.* محل زهور mahl zhur

flour *n.* طحين tehin

flourish *v.* يزخرف yezakhref

flow *n.* سيلان syalan

flow *v.* يسيل yesil

flower *n.* وردة wardeh

flowery *adj.* مورّد mwarred

fluent *adj.* طليق taliq

fluid *adj.* مايع may'e

fluid *n.* سائل sa'el

flush *v.* يحمّر yehammer

flush *v.* يشطف yeshtuf

flush *n.* إحمرار ihmirar

flush *n.* تورّد tawarrud

flute *n.* مزمار mezmar

flute *v.* يعزف عالمزمار ye'zuf almezmar

flutter *n.* رعشة ra'sheh

flutter *v.* يرتعش yerte'esh

fly *n.* دبّانة debbaneh

fly *v.* يطير yetir
foal *n.* مهر muhr
foal *v.* تولد مهر twlad elmuhr
foam *n.* رغوة raghweh
foam *v.* يرغي yerghi
foamy *adj.* بيرغي byerghi
focal *adj.* بؤري bu'eri
focalization *n.* توكيز tarkiz
focalize *v.* يركز yerakkiz
focus *n.* نقطة تركيز nuqtet tarkiz
focus *v.* يركز yerakkiz
focused *adj.* مركز mrakkaz
focusing *adj.* تركيزي tarkizi
fodder *n.* علف alaf
foe *n.* غريم gharim
fog *n.* ضباب dabab
foggy *adj.* ضبابي dababi
foil *v.* يلف بورق معدن yelf bwaraq ma'dan
fold *n.* طوية taweyeh
fold *v.* يطوي yetwi
folding *adj.* مطوى metawwah
folding *n.* تطواية tetwayeh
foldup *adj.* طوية ṭawyeh
foliage *n.* وراق النبات wraq elnabat
foliate *adj.* مورق mwarreq
foliate *v.* يورق ywarreq
foliation *n.* توريق tawwriq
folic *n.* فوليك folik
folio *n.* ملف malaf
folk *adj.* شعبي sha'bi
folk *n.* شعب sha'b
folklore *n.* فلكلور flklur
folkloric *adj.* فلكلوري flkluri
follies *n.* غباء ghaba'

follow *v.* يلحق yelhaq
follower *n.* تابع tabe'
folly *n.* جهل jahl
foment *v.* يحط كمادات yehett kammadat
fond *adj.* غرمان gharman
fondant *n.* فوندان fundan
fondle *v.* يدلل yedallel
fondler *n.* حنون hanun
fondling *n.* دلال dalal
font *n.* خط khatt
food *n.* أكل akel
fool *v.* يكذب على yekazzeb ala
fool *v.* يحتال yehtal
fool *n.* الغبي elghabi
foolish *adj.* غبي ghabi
foot *n.* قدم qadam
foot *v.* يمشي yemshi
football *n.* طابة tabeh
foothold *n.* موطئ قدم mawte' qadam
footman *n.* خدام khaddam
footsore *adj.* متقرحة أجريه metqarrha rejleh
footwork *n.* حركة الرجلين haraket elrejlin
for *prep.* مشان mshan
for *conj.* مشان mshan
forage *n.* علف alaf
forage *v.* يعلف ye'luf
forager *n.* علاف allaf
foraging *n.* علف alaf
foray *n.* غارة gharah
foray *v.* يغير yeghayyer
forbear *v.* يكف عن yekeff an
forbearance *n.* تسامح tasamuh
forbid *v.* يمنع yemna'

forbidden *adj.* ممنوع mamnu'e

force *n.* قوّة qwweh

force *v.* يجبر yejbur

forceful *adj.* عنيف anif

forceps *n.* ملقط الجرّاح mlaqat eljarrah

forcible *adj.* إلزامي elzami

forearm *n.* زَند znd

forearm *v.* يستعدّ yesta'edd

forecast *n.* تنبّؤ tanabbu'e

forecast *v.* يتنبّأ yetnabba'

forefather *n.* جدّ jadd

forefinger *n.* سبّابة sabbabeh

forehead *n.* جبين jbin

foreign *adj.* أجنبي ajnabi

foreigner *n.* غريب gharib

foreknowledge *n.* بَداهة badaha

foreleg *n.* أجر أماميّة ejr amameyyeh

forelock *n.* خصلة شعر kheslet sha'er

foreman *n.* رئيس العمال ra'es elummal

foremost *adj.* أهمّ ahamm

forenoon *n.* ضحوة dahweh

forerunner *n.* بشاير bashayer

foresee *v.* يتوقّع yetwaqqa'

foresight *n.* توقّع tawaqqu'

forest *n.* غابة ghayeh

forestall *v.* يستبق yestebeq

forester *n.* حارس الغابة hares elghabeh

forestry *n.* زراعة الغابات zera'et elghabat

foretell *v.* يتكهّن yetkahhan

forethought *n.* روية raweyyeh

forever *adv.* للأبد lelabad

forewarn *v.* ينبّه yenabbeh

foreword *n.* مقدمة الكتاب muqademet ktab

forfeit *v.* يصادر yesader

forfeit *n.* غرامة gharameh

forfeiture *n.* مصادرة msadarah

forge *n.* تزوير tazwir

forge *v.* يزوّر yezawwer

forge *v.* يطرق الحديد yetruq elhadid

forge *v.* يصفّح yesaffeh

forgery *n.* تزوير tazwir

forget *v.* ينسى yensa

forgetful *adj.* نَسيان nsyan

forgive *v.* يسامح yesameh

forgo *v.* يتخلّى yetkhallah

forlorn *adj.* مهمل mehmel

form *n.* شكل shakel

form *n.* صيغة sheghah

form *v.* يشكّل yeshakkel

formal *adj.* رسمي rasmi

format *n.* فورمات furmat

formation *n.* تشكيل tashkil

former *adj.* سابق sabeq

former *pron* من قبل mn qabl

formerly *adv.* فيما مضى fima mada

formidable *adj.* مُوقَّر mwaqqar

formula *n.* صيغة sheghah

formulate *v,* يصيغ yesegh

forsake *v.* يهجر yehjur

forswear *v.* يحلف كذب yehlef kzeb

fort *n.* حصن hsen

forte *n.* نقطة قوّة neqtet qwweh

forth *adv.* من هون ورايح mn
hun wrayeh

forth *adv.* لبعدين laba'din

forthcoming *adj.* قَريب qarib

forthwith *adv.* حالاً halan

fortify *v.* يقوّي yeqawwi

fortitude *n.* جلد jalad

fort-night *n.* أسبوعين esbu'en

fortress *n.* قلعة qal'ah

fortunate *adj.* محظوظ mahzuz

fortune *n.* ثُروة tharweh

forty *n.* الرقم 40 elraqm 40

forum *n.* ندوة nadweh

forward *adj.* أمَامي amami

forward *adv.* لقدّام lqeddam

forward *v.* يعاوِن ye'awen

fossil *n.* مستحاثة
mustahaththeh

foster *v.* يربّي yerabbi

foster *v.* يعزّز ye'azziz

foul *n.* الخبيث elkhabith

foul *adj.* خبيث khabith

foul *v.* يعلّق مع ye'laq ma

found *v.* يأسّس ye'assis

foundation *n.* مؤسسة
mu'assaseh

founder *n.* مؤسّس mu'asses

foundry *n.* صبّ sabb

fountain *n.* نبعة nab'ah

four *n.* الرقم 4 elraqm 4

fourteen *n.* الرقم 14 elraqm
14

fowl *n.* دواجِن dwajen

fowler *n.* صياد عصافير sayyad
asafir

fox *n.* ثعلب tha'lab

fraction *n.* كسر kasr

fracture *n.* صَدْع sade'

fracture *v.* يتصدّع yetsadda'

fragile *adj.* قابل للكسر qabel
lelkasr

fragment *n.* جزء jeze'

fragrance *n.* عطر uter

fragrant *adj.* فوّاح fawwah

frail *adj.* زنبيل zanbil

frame *v.* يبروز yebarwez

frame *v.* يصيغ yesigh

frame *n.* برواز brwaz

franchise *n.* إمتياز imtyaz

frank *adj.* صريح sarih

frantic *adj.* فاير fayr

fraternal *adj.* أخوي akhawi

fraternity *n.* أخوية
akhaweyyeh

fratricide *n.* قتل الأخّ qatl
elakhkh

fraud *n.* تلاعُب talaub

fraudulent *adj.* نصّاب nassab

fraught *adj.* مشحون mashhun

fray *n.* شغب shaghab

freak *n.* نزوة nazweh

freak *adj.* شاذّ shazz

freak *v.* يخالف yekhalef

free *adj.* مجّاني majjani

free *v.* يحرّر yeharrer

freedom *n.* حرية hureyyeh

freeze *v.* يجمّد yejammed

freight *n.* شحن shahen

French *adj.* فرنسي fransi

French *n.* اللغة الفرنسية ellugha
elfaranseyyeh

frenzy *n.* جنون jnun

frequency *n.* تردد taraddud

frequent *adj.* متكرّر metkarrer

fresh *adj.* تازه tazah
fret *n.* تآكل ta'akul
fret *v.* يتآكل yet'akal
friction *n.* إحْتكاك ihtikak
Friday *n.* الجمعة eljum'a
fridge *n.* براد barrad
friend *n.* رفيق rfiq
fright *n.* هول hul
frighten *v.* يخوّف yekhawwef
frigid *adj.* بارد bared
frill *n.* كشكش kashkash
fringe *n.* حافة haffeh
fringe *n.* جناح janah
fringe *v.* يحشي اللبس yehshi
ellebs
frivolous *adj.* أرْعَن ar'an
frock *n.* عباية abayeh
frog *n.* ضِفْدَع defda'
frolic *n.* مقلب maqlab
frolic *v.* يعمل مقلب ye'mel
maqlab
from *prep.* من mn
front *n.* مقدمة muqademeh
front *adj.* أمامي amami
front *v.* يواجه yewajeh
frontier *n.* حد hadd
frost *n.* جليد jalid
frown *n.* عبسة abseh
frown *v.* يعبس ye'bus
frugal *adj.* بخيل bakhil
fruit *n.* فاكهة fakha
fruitful *adj.* مثمر muthmir
frustrate *v.* يحبط yehit
frustration *n.* إحباط ihbat
fry *v.* يقلي yeqli
fry *n.* مقالي maqali
fuel *n.* فيول fyul

fugitive *adj.* مُلاحَق mulaheq
fugitive *n.* فار farr
fulfil *v.* يحقق yehaqqeq
fulfilment *n.* إنجاز injaz
full *adj.* مليان malyan
full *adv.* بالكامل belkamel
fullness *n.* إمتلاء imtila'e
fully *adv.* بالكامل belkamel
fumble *v.* يختل yekhtall
fun *n.* مرح marah
function *n.* شغل shughl
function *v.* يشتغل yeshteghel
functionary *n.* شغيل
shaghghil
fund *n.* مصاري masari
fundamental *adj.* أساسي asasi
funeral *n.* جنازة jnazeh
fungus *n.* فطر fter
funny *n.* مزحة mazha
fur *n.* فرو faru
furious *adj.* معصّب me'assib
furl *v.* يلفّ yelff
furlong *n.* فرسخ farsakh
furnace *n.* تنور tannur
furnish *v.* يفرش yefrush
furniture *n.* فرش farsh
furrow *n.* غصن ghesn
further *adv.* لحد ما lahdd ma
further *adj.* زيادة zyadeh
further *v.* يأيّد ya'ayyed
fury *n.* غيظ ghiz
fuse *v.* يصهر yeshehar
fuse *n.* قاطع تيّار qate' tayyar
fusion *n.* صهر sahr
fuss *n.* ضجّة dajjeh
fuss *v.* ينفعل yenfe'el
futile *adj.* عقيم aqim

futility n. عقم uqm
future adj. مستقبلا mustaqbalan
future n. مستقبل mustaqbal
futuristic adj. مستقبلي mustaqbali
futurology n. علم المستقبل elm elmustaqbal
fuzz n. وبر wabar
fuzz v. يغشي yeghashshi
fuzzy adj. مغشى meghashsha

G

gabble v. يبربر yebarber
gadfly n. دبانة الحصان debbanet elhsan
gadget n. أداة adat
gaffe n. زلية zelleyeh
gag v. ينكت yenakket
gag v. يكمم yekammem
gag n. نكتة nekteh
gag n. كمامة kammameh
gaiety n. بهجة bahjeh
gain v. يربح yerbah
gain n. ربح rebh
gainful adj مربح murbeh
gainly adj مناسب munasib
gainsay v. يكذب yekazzib
gait n. مشية mashyeh
gala n. احتفال ihtifal
galactic adj مجري majarri
galaxy n. مجرة majarrah

gale n. جرب jarab
gallant adj. ظريف zarif
gallant n. الظريف elzarif
gallantry n. نخوة nakhweh
gallery n. جالري galiri
gallon n. غالون galun
gallop n. ركض raked
gallop v. يركض yerkud
gallows n. . مشنقة mashnaqah
galore adv. بكترة bketreh
galvanize v. يجلفن yejalfen
galvanometer n. جلفانوميتر jelfanometer
gambit n. مناورة mnawarah
gamble v. يلعب قمار yel'ab qmar
gamble n. قمار qmar
gambler n. لعيب قمار la'eyb qmar
game n. لعبة le'beh
game n. مباراة mubarah
game v. يلعب yel'ab
gamemaster v. سيد اللعبة sayyed elle'beh
gameplayer n. لاعب la'eb
gamma n. أشعة غاما ashe'et gamma
gander n. وز wazz
gang n. عصابة asayeh
gangrene n. غنغرينا gangarina
gangster n. قاطع طريق qate' tariq
gap n. حفرة hufrah
gap v. يحفر yehfur
gape v. يتاوب yettawab
garage n. كراج karaj
garb n. مأنطو mantu

garb v. يلبس مانطو yelbs mantu
garbage n. زبالة zbaleh
garden n. حَديقة hadiqah
gardener n. بستاني bestani
gargle v. غَرْغَرَة gargarah
garland n. إكليل iklil
garland v. يكلّل بالغار yekallel belghar
garlic n. توم tum
garlicky adj. متوَّم mtawwam
garment n. جاكيت طويل jakit twil
garnish v. زَيّن yezayyen
garnish n. زينة zineh
garnishment n. تَزيين tazyyin
garrisson n. حامية hamyeh
garrisson v. يألِف حامية ye'allef hamyeh
garrotte n. إعدام خنقا e'dam khanqan
garrotte v. يعدم خنقا ye'dim khanqan
garter n. رباطة rabbatah
gas n. غاز ghaz
gasesous adj. غازي ghazi
gash n. جرح jreh
gash v. يجرح yejrah
gashing adj. جرح jreh
gasification n. تحويل لغاز tahwil laghaz
gasified adj. محوَّل لغاز mehawwal laghaz
gasify v. يحوّل لغاز yehawwel laghaz
gasket n. جوان jwan
gasmask n. قناع غاز qina' ghaz
gasoline n. بنزين bnzin

gasp n. لهتة lahteh
gasp v. يلهت yelhat
gassy adj. غازي ghazi
gastric adj. معدي me'di
gastronomy n. فنّ الطهي fann ettahi
gate n. بوابة bawwabeh
gatehouse n. بيت الحارس beit elhares
gatekeeper n. ناطُور natur
gateway n. مدخل madkhal
gather v. يتجمع yetjamma'
gaudy adj. مزِوق mezweq
gauge n. مقياس meqyas
gaunt adj. نحيف nahif
gauntlet n. كفوف kfuf
gawk n. الجدبة eljadbeh
gawk v. يطلّع بهبل yettala' bihabal
gawky adj. جدبة jadbeh
gay adj. لوطي luti
gay n. اللوطي elluti
gaze v. يحدق yehaddeq
gaze n. تحديق tahdiq
gazelle n. غزال ghazal
gazette n. جريدة jarideh
gear n. ترس tres
gearbox n. علبة تروس elbet trus
gearset n. مجموعة تروس majmu'et trus
gearwheel n. دولاب مسنَّن dulab msannan
geek n. مهووس mahwwus
geek v. ينهوس yenhuwes
geeky adj. فيو خضّة fyyu khaddah
gel n. جلّ jill

gel v. يحوّل لجلّ yehawwel lajell

gelatin n. جيلاتين jilatin

gelatinous adj. دبق dayyeq

gelatinize v. يحوّل لجيلاتين yehawwel lajilatin

geld v. يخصي yekhsi

gelded adj. مخصي makhsi

gelding n. المخصي elmakhsi

gem n. جوهرة juharah

geminate adj. مضاعَف muda'af

geminate v. يضاعف yeda'ef

Gemini n. برج الجوزاء burj eljawza'

gender n. جنس jens

gene n. جينة jeneh

genealogical adj. يخصّ النسب bekhuss elnasab

genealogy n. نَسَب nasab

generable adj. بيولّد bywalled

general adj. عامّ aamm

generally adv. عموماً umuman

generate v. يولّد yewalled

generation n. جيل jil

generator n. مولّدة muwalledeh

generosity n. كرَم karam

generous adj. كريم karim

genetic adj. جيني jini

geneticist n. أخصائي جينات akhessa'e jinat

genial adj. عبقري abkari

geniality n. عبقرية abkareyyeh

genie n. جنّي jenni

genital adj. تناسلي tanasuli

genitalia n. الأعضاء التناسلية ela'da' ettanasuleyyeh

genius n. العبقري elabkari

genocide n. مذبحة mazbaha

genome n. جينوم jinum

genre n. نوع nu'

genteel adj. أنيق anik

gentility n. رقة reqqah

gentle adj. جنتل jentil

gentleman n. جنتل jentil

gentry n. ارستقراطية arusteqrateyyeh

genuine adj. أصيل asil

geographer n. مصوّر mesawwar

geographical adj. جغرافي jughrafi

geography n. جغرافيا jughrafya

geological adj. جيولوجي jiuluji

geologist n. عالم طبقات الأرض alem tabaqat elard

geology n. دراسة طبقات الأرض deraset tabaqat elard

geometrical adj. هندسي handasi

geometry n. هندسة رياضيّة handaseh riyadeyyeh

geopolitical adj. جغرافي سياسي jughrafi syasi

geranium n. ابرة الراعي ebret elra'e

germ n. جرثومة jrthumeh

germicide n. مبيد للجراثيم mubid leljarathim

germinate v. يفرّخ yefarrekh

germination n. تفريخ tafrikh

gerund n. مصدر masdar

gesture n. إشارة isharah

get v. يجيب yejib

geyser n. سخّان sakhkhan

ghastly *adj.* بيرعِب bera'eb
ghetto *n.* حيّ اليهود hayy elyahud
ghost *n.* شبح shabah
ghostwriter *n.* كاتب باسم مستعار katb be'işm musta'ar
ghoul *n.* غُول ghul
ghoulish *adj.* غولي ghuli
giant *n.* عملاق emlaq
giantess *n.* ضخامة dakhameh
gibber *n.* بَرِرة barbarah
gibber *v.* يبرر yebarbr
gibbon *n.* نوع من القرود nu' mn elqrud
gibe *v.* يعيّر ye'ayyer
gibe *n.* تعيير ta'yyir
giddy *adj.* دايخ daykh
gift *n.* هدية hadeyyeh
gift *v.* يهدي yehdi
gifted *adj.* موهوب mawhub
gift-wrap *v.* لفّ الهدايا laff elhadayah
gig *n.* صنارة صيد sinnaret sid
gigabit *n.* جيغابت jigabet
gigabyte *n.* جيغابايت jigabayt
gigantic *adj.* عملاق emlaq
giggle *v.* يضحك yedhak
gild *v.* يلبس دهب yelabbes dahab
gilt *adj.* مدهّب mdahhab
gimmick *n.* نصِب nasb
gimmick *v.* ينصب yensub
gimmickry *n.* حِيل hyal
gimp *v.* يعرج yu'ruj
gimp *adj.* أعرج a'raj
gin *n.* محلج قطن mahlaj kutn
ginger *adj.* نشيط nashit

ginger *n.* زَنْجَبيل zanjabil
giraffe *n.* زرافة zarafeh
gird *v.* يلبس زنار yelabbes zennar
girder *n.* عارضة ardah
girdle *n.* حِزام hizam
girdle *v.* يلبّس حِزام yelabbes hizam
girl *n.* بنت bent
girlish *adj.* بنّاتي bennati
gist *n.* لُبّ lebb
give *v.* يعطي ye'ti
gizmo *n.* أداة adat
glacier *n.* نهر جليدى nahr jalidi
glad *adj.* مبسوط mabsut
gladden *v.* يبسوط yebsut
glade *n.* فسحة بالغابة feseha belghabeh
gladiator *n.* مُصارِع musare'
gladly *adv.* ببسط bebst
glam *adj.* جذّاب jazzab
glamour *n.* جاذبية jazbeyyeh
glance *n.* لمحة lamha
glance *v.* يلمح yelmah
gland *n.* غُدّة ghuddeh
glare *n.* تألّق ta'alluq
glare *v.* يتألّق yetallaq
glass *n.* بلّور ballur
glasses *n.* نظارات ņazarat
glasshouse *n.* بيت بلّوري beit balluri
glassmaker *n.* صانع بلّور sane' ballur
glaucoma *n.* المى الزرقا بالعين elmay ezzarqah beleyn
glaze *v.* يلمّع yelamme'
glaze *n.* لمعان التلج laman eltalj

glazier *n.* بلّورجي ballurji

gleam *n.* ضو ضعيف daww da'ef

gleam *v.* يضوي yedawwi

gleaming *adj.* مضوي mdawwi

glee *n.* طرب tarab

gleeful *adj.* مطروب matrub

gleefully *adv.* بفرح befarah

glide *n.* انزلاق inzilaq

glide *v.* زلق yezalleq

glider *n.* مزلّق muzalleq

glimmer *n.* بصيص basis

glimmer *v.* يطلع بصيص yetla' basis

glimpse *n.* نظرة خاطفة nazrah khatfeh

glitter *v.* يبرق yebruq

glitter *n.* وق barq

gloat *v.* يشمت yeshmat

gloat *n.* شماتة shamateh

gloatingly *adv.* بشماتة beshamteh

global *adj.* عالمي aalami

globe *n.* العالم elaalm

gloom *n.* كآبة ka'abeh

gloomy *adj.* كئيب ka'ib

glorification *n.* تمجيد tamjid

glorify *v.* يمجّد yemajjed

glorious *adj.* مجيد majid

glory *n.* مجد majd

gloss *n.* لمعان lama'an

glossary *n.* فهرس fehres

glossy *adj.* ملمع mulamma'

glove *n.* كفوف kfuf

glow *v.* يحمر من الخجل yehmarr mn elkhajal

glow *n.* إحمرار ihmirar

glucose *n.* سكّر العنب sekkar elenib

glue *n.* غري ghreh

glue *v.* يغري yegharri

glut *v.* يتخم yetkhum

glut *n.* تخمة tekhmeh

glutton *n.* بجعان fajaan

gluttony *n.* بجع faja'

glycerine *n.* غليسيرين gliserin

gnarl *n.* شي معقود shi ma'kud

gnarl *v.* يعقد ye'qud

gnaw *v.* يقرض yeqrud

gnome *n.* قزم qazam

go *v.* يروح yruh

goal *n.* هدف hadaf

goalkeeper *n.* حارس المرمى hares marmah

goalpost *n.* عارضة ardah

goalscoring *n.* إدخال هدف idkhal hadf

goat *n.* تيس tys

gobble *n.* صوت الديك sut eddik

goblet *n.* قدح kadah

god *n.* إله elah

goddess *n.* إلهة aleha

godhead *n.* ربوبية rebubeyyeh

godly *adj.* تقي taqi

godown *n.* مخزن بضايع makhzan badaye'

godsend *n.* صدفة حلوة sedfeh helweh

goggles *n.* نظارات سباحة nazarat sbaha

gold *n.* دهب dahab

golden *adj.* دهبي dahabi

goldsmith *n.* صايغ sayegh

golf *n.* غولف gulf

gonads *n.* غدد تناسلية ghedad tanasuleyyeh

gondola *n.* جندول jandul

gong *n.* جرس jaras

goo *n.* مادة دبقة maddeh debqa

goo *v.* يدبق yedabbeq

good *adj.* منيح mnih

good *adj.* حلو helu

good *n.* فايدة faydeh

good *n.* عمل خير amal khir

good-bye *interj.* مع السلامة ma' essalameh

goodness *n.* صلاح salah

goodwill *n.* ود wedd

goof *n.* يغلط yeghlat

goof *v.* غلطة ghaltah

goofy *adj.* غلطان ghaltan

google *v.* يدور بالغوغل yedawwer belgugel

goose *n.* وزة wazzeh

gooseberry *n.* كشمش kishmesh

gorgeous *adj.* رائع ra'e

gore *n.* نطحة nateha

gore *v.* ينطح yentah

gorge *n.* حلق halq

gorge *v.* يبلع yebla'

gorge *adj.* متخوم matkhum

gorilla *n.* غوريلا gurilla

gospel *n.* بشارة bsharah

gossip *n.* غيبة ghybeh

gossip *v.* يغتاب yeghtab

gothic *n.* قوطي quti

gothic *adj.* قوطي quti

gourd *n.* يقطين yaqtin

gout *n.* نقرس nuqrus

govern *v.* يحكم yehakkim

governance *n.* حكم hukm

governess *n.* مرت المحافظ mart elmuhafez

government *n.* حكومة hukumeh

governor *n.* محافظ muhafez

gown *n.* عباية abayeh

grab *v.* يغتصب yeghteseb

grace *n.* شرف sharaf

grace *v.* يشرف بوجوده yesharref bewjuduh

gracious *adj.* لطيف latif

gradation *n.* تدرج tadarruj

grade *n.* درجة darajeh

grade *n.* صف saff

grade *v.* يدرج yedarrej

gradual *adj.* تدريجي tadriji

graduate *v.* يتخرج yetkharraj

graduate *n.* خريج kherrij

graft *n.* طعم tu'em

graft *n.* ابتزاز ibtizaz

graft *v.* يبتز yebtazz

grain *n.* حبة hayyeh

grammar *n.* نحو nahu

grammarian *n.* نحوي nahawi

gramme *n.* غرام gram

gramophone *n.* فونوغراف funugraf

granary *n.* مخزن قمح makhzan kamh

grand *adj.* كبير kbir

grandeur *n.* جبروت jabarut

grant *v.* يعطي ye'ti

grant *n.* منحة menhah

grape *n.* عنب enb

graph *n.* رسم بياني rasm byani

graphic *adj.* مرسوم marsum
grapple *n.* مرساية mersayeh
grapple *v.* يمسك yemsik
grasp *v.* يمسك yemsik
grasp *n.* مسكة maskeh
grass *n.* عشب esheb
grate *n.* بشر bashr
grate *v.* يبشر yebshur
grateful *adj.* ممنون mamnun
grater *n.* مبشرة mabsharah
gratification *n.* إشباع eshba'
gratis *adv.* مجاناً majanan
gratitude *n.* إمتنان imtinan
gratuity *n.* بخشيش bakhshish
grave *n.* قبر qabr
grave *adj.* رزين razin
gravitate *v.* ينجذب yenjzeb
gravitation *n.* تجاذب tajazub
gravity *n.* جاذبية jazbeyyeh
graze *v.* يرعى مواشي yer'a mwashi
graze *v.* يقشط yeqshut
graze *n.* رعاية المواشي re'ayet elmawashi
grease *n.* شحم shahm
grease *v.* يشحّم yeshahhim
greasy *adj.* مشحّم mshahham
great *adj.* رائع ra'e
greed *n.* طمع tama'
greedy *adj.* طمّاع tamma'
Greek *n.* اليونان elyunan
Greek *adj.* يوناني yunani
green *adj.* أخضر aghdar
green *n.* اللون الأخضر ellun elakhdar
greenery *n.* نباتات خضرا nabatat khadrah

greet *v.* يسلّم على yesallem ala
grenade *n.* قذيفة kazifeh
grey *adj.* رمادي rmadi
greyhound *n.* كلب صيد kleb syd
grief *n.* زعل za'al
grievance *n.* مظلمة mazlameh
grieve *v.* زعل yez'al
grievous *adj.* بيزعل byza'el
grind *v.* يطحن yetehan
grinder *n.* طاحونة tahuneh
grip *v.* يمسك yemsek
grip *n.* قبضة qabdah
groan *v.* يقول آه byqul ah
groan *n.* آهات aahat
grocer *n.* سمّان samman
grocery *n.* سمانة smaneh
groom *n.* عريس aris
groom *v.* يسوس الحصان yesus elhsan
groove *n.* أخدود akhdud
groove *v.* يحفر أخدود yehfur akhdud
grope *v.* يدوّر عطريقه yedawwer atareqah
gross *n.* الإجمالي elejmali
gross *adj.* إجمالي ejmali
gross *adj.* رخيص rkhis
grotesque *adj.* غريب ghrib
ground *n.* أرض ard
ground *n.* أساس asas
ground *v.* يحط عالأرض yehett alard
group *n.* مجموعة majmu'a
group *v.* يجمع بمجموعات yejamme' bemajmu'at
grow *v.* يكبّر yekabber

grower *n.* مُزَارِع nmuzare'

growl *v.* يدمدم yedamdm

growl *n.* دمدمة damdmeh

growth *n.* نُمو munwu

grudge *v.* يحقد yehqud

grudge *n.* حقد heqd

grumble *v.* يتأفَّف yetaffaf

grunt *n.* صوت الخنزير sut elkhenzir

guarantee *n.* ضَمان daman

guarantee *v.* يضمن yedman

guard *v.* يحرس yehrus

guard *n.* حارس hares

guardian *n.* وصي wasi

guava *n.* جَوَّافة jawwafeh

guerilla *n.* فدائي fida'e

guess *n.* تخمين takhmin

guess *v.* يخمِّن yekhammen

guest *n.* ضَيف dif

guidance *n.* دليل dalil

guide *v.* يدلّ yedell

guide *n.* دليل dalil

guild *n.* نقابة التجار naqabet eltejjar

guile *n.* نفاق nifaq

guilt *n.* ذنب zanb

guilty *adj.* مذنب muzneb

guise *n.* مظهر mazhar

guitar *n.* غيتار gitar

gulf *n.* خليج khalij

gull *n.* نورس nawras

gull *n.* خداع khida'

gull *v.* يخدع yekhda'

gulp *v.* يغص yeghuss

gulp *n.* غصة ghassah

gum *n.* علكة elkeh

gun *n.* مسدس musaddas

gust *n.* هبّة habbeh

gutter *n.* مزراب mzrab

guttural *adj.* بلعومي bal'umi

gymnasium *n.* قاعة جمباز qa'et jmbaz

gymnast *n.* جمبازي jmbazi

gymnastic *adj.* جمبازي jmbazi

gymnastics *n.* الجمباز eljmbaz

habeas corpus *n.* أمر قضائي amr qada'i

habit *n.* عادة adeh

habitable *adj.* مسكون maskun

habitat *n.* ساكن saken

habitation *n.* سكّان sukkan

habituate *v.* يعوّد yeawwed

hack *v.* فاس fas

hacker *n.* هكر hakar

hag *n.* عرّافة arrafeh

haggard *adj.* شرِس sheres

haggle *v.* يساوم yesawm

hail *n.* ترحيب tarhib

hail *v.* يرحب yerahhib

hair *n.* شَعر sha'er

hale *adj.* معافى me'afah

half *n.* نص ness

half *adj.* نص ness

hall *n.* صالة saleh

hallmark *n.* دمغة الدهب damghet eddahab

hallow v. يقدّس yeqaddes

halt v. يوقّف yewaqqef

halt n. موقَف mawqef

halve v. يقسم نصين yeqsm nessin

hamlet n. ضيعة de'a

hammer n. شاكوش shakush

hammer v. يدقّ بالشاكوش yeduq belshakus

hand n. إيد eyd

hand v. يسلّم بالإيد yesallem be'eyd

handbill n. إعلان يدوي e'lan yadawi

handbook n. دليل السيّاح dalil essyyah

handcuff n. كلبشة kalabshah

handcuff v. يكلبش yekalbesh

handful n. مقدار كف الإيد meqdar kaff eleyd

handicap v. يعمل إعاقة ye'mel ey'aqa

handicap n. إعاقة ey'aqah

handicraft n. شغل إيد shughl eyd

handiwork n. شغل إيد shughl eyd

handkerchief n. محرمة mahrameh

handle n. تعامل ta'amul

handle v. يتعامل yet'amal

handsome adj. أنيق aniq

handy adj. بنمسك بالإيد benmesek beleyd

hang v. يعلّق yealleq

hanker v. يشتاق yeshtaq

haphazard adj. كيف ما كان kif ma kan

happen v. يصير yesir

happening n. حدوث huduth

happiness n. سعادة sa'adeh

happy adj. سعيد sa'ed

harass v. يتحرّش yeteharrash

harassment n. تحرّش taharrush

harbour n. مرفا mara'

harbour v. يخفي yekhfi

hard adj. صعب sa'eb

hard adj. قاسي qasi

hard adv. بصعوبة besu'ubeh

harden v. يقسّي yeqassi

hardihood n. شجاعة shaja'a

hardly adv. يادوب yadub

hardship n. حرمان herman

hardy adj. قلبه قوي kabu qawi

hare n. أرنب برّي arnab barri

harm n. أذى aza

harm v. يأذي ye'zi

harmonious adj. متوافق metwafeq

harmony n. توافق tawafuq

harness n. روتين الشغل rutin elshughel

harness v. يستخدم yestakhdem

harp n. قيثارة qitharah

harsh adj. دفش dfesh

harvest n. حصاد hasad

harvest v. يحصد yehsud

harvester n. حصاد hasad

haste n. عجلة ajaleh

hasten v. يستعجل yesta'jel

hasty adj. مستعجل mesta'jil

hat n. قبوعة qabbu'a

hatchet *n.* فاس صغير fas sghir
hate *n.* كره kurh
hate *v.* يكره yekrah
haughty *adj.* متعجرف met'ajref
haunt *v.* يرتاد yertad
haunt *n.* مأوى ma'wa
have *v.* يملك yemluk
haven *n.* ملاذ malaz
havoc *n.* خراب kharab
hawk *n.* صقر saqr
hawker *n.* بيّاع جوّال bayya' jawwal
hawthorn *n.* زعرور za'rur
hay *n.* قشّ qashsh
hazard *n.* مخاطرة mukhatarah
hazard *v.* يخاطر yekhater
haze *n.* غشاوة ghashaewh
hazy *adj.* مضبضب medabdeb
he *pron.* هوه hewweh
head *n.* راس ras
head *v.* يترأس yetra'as
headache *n.* وجع راس waja' ras
heading *n.* ترأس tara'us
headlong *adv.* بطيش betish
headstrong *adj.* عنيد anid
heal *v.* يطيب yetayyeb
health *n.* صحة sahhah
healthy *adj.* صحّي sihhi
heap *n.* كومة kumeh
heap *v.* يكوّم yekawwem
hear *v.* يسمع yesma'
hearsay *n.* أقوال الناس aqwal ennas
heart *n.* قلب qalb
hearth *n.* دفّاية daffayeh
heartily *adv.* من قلبه mn qlbuh

heat *n.* سخونة skhuneh
heat *v.* يسخّن yesakhkhen
heave *v.* يتنهّد yetnahhad
heaven *n.* جنّة janneh
heavenly *adj.* مقدّس muqaddas
hedge *n.* سياج شجر syaj shajr
hedge *v.* يغطّي بالمصاري yeghatti belmasari
hedge *v.* يسيّج بالشجر yesayyej belshajr
heed *v.* ينتبه yentebeh
heed *n.* انتباه intibah
heel *n.* كعب ka'eb
hefty *adj.* كتير تقيل ktir tqil
height *n.* طول tul
heighten *v.* يطوّل yetawwil
heinous *adj.* بشع beshe'
heir *n.* وريث warith
hell *n.* جهنم jehannam
helm *n.* دفّة القارب daffet elqareb
helmet *n.* خوذة khuzeh
help *v.* يساعد yesa'ed
help *n.* مساعدة musa'adeh
helpful *adj.* مساعد musa'ed
helpless *adj.* عاجز aajiz
helpmate *n.* رفيق مساعد rfiq musa'ed
hemisphere *n.* نصّ الكرة الأرضيّة nuss elkurah elardeyyeh
hemp *n.* خيش khish
hen *n.* جاجة jajeh
hence *adv.* من هون وراي mn hum wray

henceforth *adv.* من هلق وراي
mn hallaq wray

henceforward *adv.* من اليوم
وبعد mn elyum wba'ed

henchman *n.* تابع أمين tabe'
amin

henpeck *v.* يسيطر yesyter

her *pron.* إلها elha

her *adj.* لها laha

herald *n.* نذير nazir

herald *v.* ينذر yenzir

herb *n.* عشبة eshbeh

herd *n.* قطيع qate'

herdsman *n.* راعي ra'ey

here *adv.* هون hun

hereabouts *adv.* بأقرب مكان
be'aqrab makan

hereafter *n.* مستقبل mestakbal

hereafter *adv.* لبعدين laba'dyn

hereditary *adj.* موروث
mawruth

heredity *n.* وراثة wiratheh

heritable *adj.* بتورث
betwarrath

heritage *n.* تركة terkeh

hermit *n.* ناسك nasek

hermitage *n.* دير dir

hernia *n.* فتق fetq

hero *n.* بطل batl

heroic *adj.* بطولي butuli

heroine *n.* بطلة bataleh

heroism *n.* بطولية butulyyeh

herring *n.* سمك مملّح samak
memallah

hesitant *adj.* حيران hyran

hesitate *v.* يحتار yehtar

hesitation *n.* حيرة hireh

hew *v.* ينحت yenhat

heyday *n.* ذروة zarweh

hibernation *n.* سبات شتوي
sbat shatwi

hiccup *n.* حازوقة hazuqah

hide *n.* تخبية tekhbyeh

hide *v.* يخبّي yekhabbi

hideous *adj.* دميم damim

hierarchy *n.* هرمية harmeyyeh

high *adj.* عالي aali

highly *adv.* لفوق lafuq

Highness *n.* سمو sumwu

highway *n.* طريق سريع tariq
sare'

hilarious *adj.* فرحان farhan

hilarity *n.* فرح كبير farah kbir

hill *n.* هضبة hadabeh

hillock *n.* رابية rabyeh

him *pron.* إلو elu

hinder *v.* يمنع yemna'

hindrance *n.* مانع mane'

hint *n.* تلميح talmih

hint *v.* يلمّح yelammeh

hip *n.* ورك wrek

hire *n.* إجرة ejrah

hire *v.* يستأجر yesta'jer

hireling *n.* مرتزق murtazaq

his *pron.* إلو elu

hiss *n.* هسهسة hasehaseh

hiss *v.* يهسهس yehasehes

historian *n.* مؤرخ mu'arrekh

historic *a.* تاريخي ta'rikhi

historical *adj.* تاريخي tarikhi

history *n.* تاريخي traikhi

hit *v.* يضرب yedrub

hit *n.* ضربة darbeh

hitch *n.* حركة سريعة harakeh sare'a	**honeymoon** *n.* شهر العسل shahr elasal
hither *adv.* لهون lahun	**honorarium** *n.* مكافأة فخرية mukafa'a fakhreyyeh
hitherto *adv.* لليوم lelyum	**honorary** *adj.* فخري fakhri
hive *n.* خلية نحل khaleyyeh nahl	**honour** *n.* شرف sharaf
hoarse *adj.* مبحوح mabhuh	**honour** *v.* يشرّف yesharref
hoax *n.* حيلة hyleh	**honourable** *adj.* مشرِّف musharref
hoax *v.* يحتال yehetal	**hood** *n.* طاقية taqeyyeh
hobby *n.* هواية hewayeh	**hoodwink** *v.* يحتال على yehtal ala
hobbyhorse *n.* حصان خشب hsan khashab	**hoof** *n.* حافر hafez
hockey *n.* الهوكي elhuki	**hook** *n.* صنّارة sinnarah
hoist *v.* آلة رافعة aleh raf'a	**hooligan** *n.* سفّاح saffah
hold *n.* دعامة di'ameh	**hoot** *n.* صوت البوم sut elbum
hold *n.* احتجاز ihtejaz	**hoot** *v.* يستهزئ yestahze'
hold *v.* يحجز yehjuz	**hop** *v.* يطّ yenutt
hold *v.* يمسك yemsik	**hop** *n.* نطّة nattah
hold *v.* يحوي yehwi	**hope** *v.* يتأمّل yetammal
hole *n.* حفرة hefrah	**hope** *n.* أمل amal
hole *v.* يحفر حفرة yehfur hefrah	**hopeful** *adj.* يعطي أمل yeya'ti amal
holiday *n.* عطلة eteleh	**hopeless** *adj.* يائس ya'es
hollow *adj.* مجوّف mjawwaf	**horde** *n.* قبيلة qabeleh
hollow *n.* ثقب thuqb	**horizon** *n.* أفق ufuq
hollow *v.* يقعور yeqa'wir	**horn** *n.* قرن grn
holocaust *n.* محرقة mahraqah	**hornet** *n.* دبور dabbur
holy *adj.* مقدّس muqaddas	**horrible** *adj.* مخيف mukhif
homage *n.* مبايعة mubaya'ah	**horrify** *v.* يخوّف yekhawwef
home *n.* وطن watan	**horror** *n.* رعب ru'b
homicide *n.* قاتل qatel	**horse** *n.* حصان hisan
homogeneous *adj.* متجانس mutajanis	**horticulture** *n.* بستنة bastaneh
honest *adj.* شريف sharif	**hose** *n.* خرطوم khartum
honesty *n.* صدق sedq	**hosiery** *n.* جراب jrab
honey *n.* عسل asal	**hospitable** *adj.* مضياف medyaf
honeycomb *n.* شهد العسل shahd elasal	**hospital** *n.* مستشفى mestashfah

hospitality *n.* ضيافة dyafeh
host *n.* عائل ayel
hostage *n.* رهينة rahineh
hostel *n.* مضيفة mudefeh
hostile *adj.* عدواني edwani
hostility *n.* عدوانية edwaneyyeh
hot *adj.* حدّ hadd
hotchpotch *n.* خلْطة khaltah
hotel *n.* فندق fenduq
hound *n.* كلب صيد kleb syd
hour *n.* ساعة sa'ah
house *n.* بيت beit
house *v.* يستضيف yestadif
how *adv.* كيف keif
however *adv.* مع هيك ma' hik
however *conj.* بس bas
howl *v.* ينبح uyenbah
howl *n.* نباح nbah
hub *n.* محور mehwar
hubbub *n.* ضوجة dujeh
huge *adj.* ضخم dakhem
hum *v.* ينغّم yenaghghem
hum *n.* تنغيم tanghym
human *adj.* بشري bashari
humane *adj.* إنساني ensani
humanitarian *adj.* مدافع عن حقوق الإنسان mudafe' am huquq elensan
humanity *n.* إنسانية ensanyyeh
humanize *v.* يمدّن yemadden
humble *adj.* متواضع metwade'
humdrum *adj.* ببلل beymallel
humid *adj.* رطب retb
humidity *n.* رطوبة rutubeh
humiliate *v.* يذلّ yezll
humiliation *n.* إذلال izlal

humility *n.* مهانة mahaneh
humorist *n.* منكّت mnakket
humorous *adj.* بيضحّك bydahhek
humour *n.* خفّة الدم kheffet damm
hunch *n.* حدبة hadbeh
hundred *n.* الرقم 100 elraqm 100
hunger *n.* جوع ju'e
hungry *adj.* جوعان ju'aan
hunt *v.* يصطاد yestad
hunt *n.* صيد syd
hunter *n.* صيد syd
huntsman *n.* الصياد essayyad
hurdle *n.* حاجز hajez
hurdle *v.* يطّ من عالحاجز yenutt mn alhajz
hurl *v.* يدفش yedfush
hurricane *n.* بركان burkan
hurry *v.* يستعجل yesta'jil
hurry *n.* عجلة ajaleh
hurt *v.* يجرح yejrah
hurt *n.* جرح jreh
husband *n.* زوج zuj
husbandry *n.* تقتير بالنفقة taqtir belnafakah
hush *n.* سكوت skut
hush *v.* يسكّت yesakket
husk *n.* قشر qeshr
hut *n.* سقيفة sqifeh
hyaena, hyena *n.* ضبع dabe'
hybrid *adj.* هجين hajin
hybrid *n.* نغل naghl
hydrogen *n.* هيدروجين hydrojin

hygiene *n.* علم الصحّة elm essahhah

hygienic *adj.* صحّي sihhi

hymn *n.* تَرتيلة tartyleh

hyperbole *n.* مُبالَغة mubalaghah

hypnotism *n.* تنويم مغنطيسي tanwim maghnatisi

hypnotize *v.* ينوّم مغنطيسياً yenawwim maghnatisyyan

hypocrisy *n.* رِياء rya'

hypocrite *n.* مُنافِق munafeq

hypocritical *adj.* رِيائي rya'i

hypothesis *n.* فرَضيّة faradeyyeh

hypothetical *adj.* إفتِراضي ifteradi

hysteria *n.* هستيريا hesteryah

hysterical *adj.* هستيري hestiri

I

I *pron.* أنا ana

ice *n.* جليد jalid

ice *v.* يجمّد yejammed

iceberg *n.* جبل تلج jabl talj

iceblock *n.* كُتلة تلج ketlet talj

iced *adj.* مجمّد mejammad

icy *adj.* جليدي jalidi

icon *n.* أيقونة ayquneh

iconic *adj.* أيقوني ayquni

idea *n.* فكرة fekrah

ideal *adj.* مثالي methali

ideal *n.* مثَل أعلى matal a'la

idealism *n.* مثالية methalyyeh

idealist *n.* مثالي methali

idealistic *adj.* مثالي methali

idealize *v.* يخلّيه مثالي yekhalleh methali

identical *adj.* متطابقين metabqin

indentification *n.* تطابُق tatabuq

identify *v.* يعرّف ye'arref

identity *n.* هويّة haweyyeh

idiocy *n.* جدبنة jadbaneh

idiom *n.* مصطلَح mustalah

idiomatic *adj.* إصطلاحي istilahi

idiot *n.* أبلَه ablah

idiotic *adj.* معتوه ma'tuh

idle *adj.* خامل khamil

idleness *n.* خمول khumul

idler *n.* متسكّع metsakke'

idol *n.* محبوب mahbub

idolater *n.* وثني wathani

if *conj.* إن enn

igloo *n.* كوخ مقبّب kukh mqabbab

ignition *n.* تشعيل tash'il

ignoble *adj.* لئيم la'ym

ignorance *n.* إهمال ihmal

ignorant *adj.* مهمل muhmel

ignore *v.* يهمل yehmil

ill *adj.* مريض marid

ill *adv.* بطريقة سيّئة betareqah say'a

ill *n.* بلوة balweh

illegal *adj.* مو قانوني mu qanuni

illegibility n. عدم الوضوح adam elwuduh

illegible adj. مو واضح mu wadeh

illegitimate adj. مو شرعي mu shar'e

illicit adj. مو مشروع mu mashru'e

illiteracy n. أُمِّيَّة ummeyyeh

illiterate adj. أُمِّي ummy

illness n. مرض marad

illogical adj. مو منطقي mu mantiqi

illuminate v. ينوّر yenawwer

illumination n. تنوير tanwir

illusion n. وهم wahm

illustrate v. يشرح yeshrah

illustration n. شرح sharh

image n. صورة surah

imagery n. تخيّلات takhayyulat

imaginary adj. مُتخيّل mutakhayyal

imagination n. خيال khayal

imaginative adj. خيالي khayali

imagine v. يتخيّل yetkhayyal

imitate v. يقلّد yeqallid

imitation n. تقليد taqlid

imitator n. مقلّد mqalled

immaterial adj. روحي ruhi

immature adj. خام kham

immaturity n. عدم نضوج adam nuduj

immeasurable adj. ما بنقاس ma bnqas

immediate a مباشر mubashr

immemorial adj. قَديم qadim

immense adj. ضَخْم dakhm

immensity n. ضَخَامة dakhmeh

immerse v. يعمّد ye'ammed

immersion n. تعميد ta'mid

immigrant n. مهاجِر muhajer

immigrate v. يهاجِر yehajer

immigration n. هجرة hijrah

imminent adj. وشيك washik

immodest adj. وقح weqeh

immodesty n. وقاحة waqahah

immoral adj. خليع khale'

immorality n. خلاعة khala'ah

immortal adj. خالد khalid

immortality n. خلود khulud

immortalize v. يخلّد yekhalled

immovable adj. جامد jamid

immune adj. مناعي mana'e

immunity n. مناعة mana'ah

immunize v. يلقّح yelaqqeh

impact n. أثر athar

impart v. ينقل yenqul

impartial adj. حقّاني haqqani

impartiality n. نزاهة nazaha

impassable adj. تعجيزي ta'jizi

impasse n. طريق مسدود tariq masdud

impatience n. قلّة الصبر qellet sabr

impatient adj. قليل صبر qalil sabr

impeach v. يتّهم yettehm

impeachment n. إتّهام ettiham

impede v. يعيق ye'yq

impediment n. عائق a'eiq

impenetrable adj. كتيم katim

imperative adj. إلزامي elzami

imperfect adj. ناقص naqes

imperfection *n.* نَقْص naqs

imperial *adj.* مُلوكي mluki

imperialism *n.* إمْبِرْيالِية emberyaleyyeh

imperil *v.* يُهوّر yehawwer

imperishable *adj.* خالِد khalid

impersonal *adj.* مُجرّد mjarrad

impersonate *v.* يَنتحل شَخصِية yentehil shakhseyyet

impersonation *n.* انتِحال شَخصِية entihal shakhseyyet

impertinence *n.* سَفاهة safaha

impertinent *adj.* سَفيه safih

impetuosity *n.* طَيش tish

impetuous *adj.* طايِش tayesh

implement *n.* تَنفيذ tanfiz

implement *v.* يُنفّذ yenaffiz

implicate *v.* يُورّط yewarret

implication *n.* تَوريط tawrit

implicit *adj.* خَفي khafi

implore *v.* يَستحْلِف yestahlef

imply *v.* يَتضمّن yetjamman

impolite *adj.* وَقِح weqh

import *v.* يَستورد yestawred

import *n.* استيراد estirad

importance *n.* أهمِية ahameyyeh

important *adj.* مهم mehem

impose *v.* يَفرُض yefrud

imposing *adj.* مُلزِم mulzem

imposition *n.* فَرض fard

impossibility *n.* استِحالة estihaleh

impossible *adj.* مُستحيل mustahil

impostor *n.* نَصّاب nassab

imposture *n.* دجَل dajl

impotence *n.* ضَعْف جِنْسي de'f jinsi

impotent *adj.* عاجِز جِنسياً a'jez jinseyyan

impoverish *v.* يُخلّيه فَقير yekhallih faqir

impracticability *n.* استِحالة estihaleh

impracticable *adj.* مُستحيل mustahil

impress *v.* يِبصُم بالإبْهام yebsum belibham

impression *n.* بَصْمة basmeh

impressive *adj.* مُؤثّر mu'athther

imprint *v.* يِدمغ yedma'

imprint *n.* دمغة dam'ah

imprison *v.* يَسجُن yesjun

improper *adj.* بَذيء baze'

impropriety *n.* بَذاءَة baza'a

improve *v.* يُحسّن yehassin

improvement *n.* تَحسين tahsin

imprudence *n.* جَهل jahl

imprudent *adj.* جاهِل jahel

impulse *n.* خَفْقَة khafqah

impulsive *adj.* عَفوي afwi

impunity *n.* حَصانة hasaneh

impure *adj.* نَجِس nejs

impurity *n.* نَجاسة najaseh

impute *v.* يلزق التِهمة ب yelzuq ettihmeh bi

in *prep.* في fi

inability *n.* عَجز ajez

inaccurate *adj.* مو دقيق mu daqiq

inaction *n.* هُمود humud

inactive *adj.* هامِد hamed

inadmissible *adj.* مَرْفُوض marfud

inanimate *adj.* جَمَاد jamad

inapplicable *adj.* ما يتطبّق ma beyntaq

inattentive *adj.* سهيان sahyan

inaudible *adj.* ما بنسمع ma benseme'

inaugural *adj.* إفْتِتَاحِي iftitahyeh

inauguration *n.* تدشين tadshin

inauspicious *adj.* منحوس manhus

inborn *adj.* غريزي gharizi

incalculable *adj.* ما بينحصى ma beynhasa

incapable *adj.* عاجِز ajez

incapacity *n.* تقْصير taqsir

incarnate *adj.* مجسّم mejassam

incarnate *v.* يجسّم yejassem

incarnation *n.* تجسيم tajseem

incense *v.* يبخّر yebakhkher

incense *n.* بخور bakhur

incentive *n.* حافِز hafez

inception *n.* بدَايَة bedayeh

inch *n.* إنْش insh

incident *n.* حدَث hadath

incidental *adj.* عرَضِي aradi

incite *v.* يحفّز yehaffez

inclination *n.* ميول myul

incline *v.* يميل ل yemil la

include *v.* يحتوي yehtwi

inclusion *n.* احتواء ihtiwa'

inclusive *adj.* شامِل shamil

incoherent *adj.* متنافر metnafer

income *n.* دخل dakhl

incomparable *adj.* فَرِيد farid

incompetent *adj.* مالو كفؤ malu kafu

incomplete *a.* ناقص naqes

inconsiderate *adj.* متهوّر metehawwer

inconvenient *adj.* مُتْعِب mut'eb

incorporate *v.* يأسّس ye'asses

incorporate *adj.* مؤسّس mu'asses

incorporation *n.* مؤسّسة mu'assaseh

incorrect *adj.* غَلَط ghalat

incorrigible *adj.* أخلاقه سيئة akhlaquh say'ah

incorruptible *adj.* عفيف afif

increase *v.* يزيد yezid

increase *n.* زيادة zyadeh

incredible *adj.* مو معقول mu ma'qul

increment *n.* علاوة alweh

incriminate *v.* يدين yedin

incubate *v.* يحضن yehdun

inculcate *v.* ينطبع بالراس yentebe' belras

incumbent *n.* موظف مثبّت muwazzaf methabbat

incumbent *adj.* واجب wajb

incur *v.* يجيب ع حاله yejib a halu

incurable *adj.* عُضَال udal

indebted *adj.* مَدِيون madyun

indecency *n.* سفَالة safaleh

indecent *adj.* سافِل safil

indecision *n.* تَردّد taraddud

indeed *adv.* عن حقّ an haqq

indefensible *adj.* ما بتبرر ma beytbarrar

indefinite *adj.* مو محدّد mu mhaddad

indemnity *n.* تعويض ta'wid

independence *n.* استقلال istiqlal

independent *adj.* مستقلّ metaqell

indescribable *adj.* ما بتنوصف ma beynwesef

index *n.* فهرس fahras

Indian *adj.* هندي hendi

indicate *v.* يأشر ye'ashsher

indication *n.* تأشير ta'shir

indicative *adj.* تأشيري ta'shiri

indicator *n.* مؤشّر mu'ashsher

indict *v.* يشتبه ب yeshtebeh be

indictment *n.* إتّهام ittiham

indifference *n.* لا مبالاة la mubalat

indifferent *adj.* لا مبالي la mubali

indigenous *adj.* بلَدي baladi

indigestible *adj.* ما بنهضَم ma beynhedm

indigestion *n.* هضم hadem

indignant *adj.* ناقم naqem

indignation *n.* نقمة naqmeh

indigo *n.* اللون النيلي ellun elnili

indirect *adj.* مراوغ mrawegh

indiscipline *n.* عصيان esyan

indiscreet *adj.* أبرعن ar'an

indiscretion *n.* رعونة ru'uneh

indiscriminate *adj.* عشوائي ashwa'e

indispensable *adj.* لازم lazem

indisposed *adj.* مرضان mardan

indisputable *adj.* أكيد akid

indistinct *adj.* عويص awes

individual *adj.* فردي fardi

individualism *n.* فردية fardeyyeh

individuality *n.* فردية fardeyyeh

indivisible *adj.* مابتقسّم ma beynqsem

indolent *adj.* كسُول kasul

indomitable *adj.* محصّن muhassan

indoor *adj.* جوّاني jwwani

indoors *adv.* جوّا jwwah

induce *v.* يحرّض yeharred

inducement *n.* تحريض tahrid

induct *v.* يطوّع عساكر yetawwe' asaker

induction *n.* تطويع tatwe'

induction *n.* تنصيب tansib

indulge *v.* يدلّع yedalle'

indulgence *n.* دلع dala'

indulgent *adj.* حليم halim

industrial *adj.* صناعي sina'e

industrious *adj.* مجدّ mujedd

industry *n.* صناعة sina'ah

ineffective *adj.* مالو أثر malu athar

inert *adj.* مطفى metaffa

inertia *n.* إنطفاء intifa'

inevitable *adj.* محتوم mahtum

inexact *adj.* مو دقيق mu daqiq

inexorable *adj.* عنيد anid

inexpensive *adj.* رخيص rkhis

inexperience *n.* قلّة الخبرة
qellet khebrah

inexplicable *adj.* مابتفسّر ma
beytfassar

infallible *adj.* مَعْصوم ma'sum

infamous *adj.* سيئ السمعة saye'
essem'a

infamy *n.* سُوء السُّمْعَة su'e
essem'a

infancy *n.* طُفُولة tufuleh

infant *n.* طَفَل tefl

infanticide *n.* قَتْل الرَّضيع qatl
elrade'

infantile *adj.* طفولي tufuli

infantry *n.* المُشاة elmushat

infatuate *v.* يسلب عقل yeslub
aqel

infatuation *n.* هيام hyam

infect *v.* يعدي ye'di

infection *n.* عدوة adweh

infectious *adj.* معدي me'di

infer *v.* يتدخّل yetdakhkhal

inference *n.* تدخّل tadakhkhul

inferior *adj.* تافه tafeh

inferiority *n.* دونيّة duneyyeh

infernal *adj.* شيطاني shitani

infinite *adj.* لا نهاأى la niha'e

infinity *n.* لا نهاأيه la
niha'eyyeh

infirm *adj.* عاجز a'jez

infirmity *n.* عَجْز ajez

inflame *v.* ينغاظ yenghaz

inflammable *adj.* سريع
الاشتعال sare' eleshti'al

inflammation *n.* إشْتعال
eshti'al

inflammatory *adj.* التهابي
eltihabi

inflation *n.* إنْتفاخ intifakh

inflexible *adj.* قاسي qasi

inflict *v.* يصيب yesib

influence *n.* تأثير ta'thir

influence *v.* يأثر ye'athther

influential *adj.* مؤثّر
mu'athther

influenza *n.* انفلونزا influwanza

influx *n.* تدفّق tadaffuq

inform *v.* يخبر yekhayyer

informal *adj.* مو رسمي mu
rasmi

information *n.* معلومات
ma'limat

informative *adj.* إخباري
ikhbari

informer *n.* مُبلّغ muballegh

infringe *v.* يخالف yekhalef

infringement *n.* مخالفة
mukhalafeh

infuriate *v.* ينهّر yenhar

infuse *v.* ينقَع yenfa'

infusion *n.* نقَع nafe'

ingrained *adj.* متأصّل
nmet'assel

ingratitude *n.* نكران الفضل
neqran ejjamil

ingredient *n.* مكونات
mukawwenat

inhabit *v.* يسكن yeskun

inhabitable *adj.* صالح للسكن
saleh lelsakan

inhabitant *n.* ساكن saken

inhale *v.* يستنشق yestansheq

inherent *adj.* فطري fitri

inherit v. يورَت yewarret	innocent adj. بريء bare'
inheritance n. ورثة werteh	innovate v. يبتكر yebteker
inhibit v. يردَع yerda'	innovation n. ابتكار ibtikar
inhibition n. ردْع rade'	innovator n. مبتكر mebteker
inhospitable adj. وحْشي wahshi	innumerable adj. مابينعدّ ma beyn'add
inhuman adj. همَجي hamaji	inoculate v. يلقّح yelaqqeh
inimical adj. عدْواني udwani	inoculation n. تلقيح talqih
inimitable adj. خارِق khareq	inoperative adj. مالو مفعول malu maf'ul
initial adj. أوَّلي awwali	inopportune adj. مو بمحلّه mu bemahalluh
initial n. أحرِف أوَّلى ahruf ula	input n. إدخال idkhal
initial v. يوقِّع بأوّل حرف yewaqqe' beawwal harf	inquest n. إسْتجْواب estijwab
initiate v. يبادر yebader	inquire v. يتساءَل yetsa'al
initiative n. مبادرة mubadarah	inquiry n. تساؤل tasa'ul
inject v. يضرب إبرة yedrub ibreh	inquisition n. إسْتجْواب estijwab
injection n. ضرب الإبرة dareb ibreh	inquisitive adj. فضُولي fuduli
injudicious adj. طايش tayesh	insane adj. مجنون majnun
injunction n. إيعاز ey'az	insanity n. جنون jnun
injure v. يجرح yejrah	insatiable adj. جَعان faj'an
injurious adj. جارح jareh	inscribe v. ينقش yenqush
injury n. جرح jerh	inscription n. نقش naqsh
injustice n. تعسف ta'assuf	insect n. حشرة hasharah
ink n. حبر hebr	insecticide n. مبيد حشرات mubid hasharat
inkling n. تلميح tamlih	insecure adj. متَزعزِع metza'ze'
inland adj. داخِلي dakhli	insecurity n. تزعزُع taza'zu'
inland adv. من جوّا mn jwwah	insensibility n. فقدان الحس fiqdan
in-laws n. مصاهرة musaharah	insensible adj. ما عنده حسّ ma andu hess
inmate n. موقوف mawquf	inseparable adj. متَرابِط metrabet
inmost adj. عميق amiq	insert v. يدخِّل yedakhkhel
inn n. خان khan	insertion n. إدخال edkhal
innate adj. فطْري fitri	
inner adj. داخِلي dakhli	
innings n. جولات jawlat	
innocence n. براءة bra'ah	

inside *n.* باطن baten

inside *prep.* جوّات jwwat

inside *adj.* جوّا jawwah

inside *adv.* لجوّا lajuwwah

insight *n.* بصيرة basirah

insignificance *n.* حَقَارَة haqarah

insignificant *adj.* حَقِير haqir

insincere *adj.* مُنافِق munafiq

insincerity *n.* نفاق nifaq

insinuate *v.* يوسوس yewaswes

insinuation *n.* وسوسة waswaseh

insipid *adj.* مالو طعمة malu ta'meh

insipidity *n.* تفاهة tafaha

insist *v.* يصر yeserr

insistence *n.* إصرار esrar

insistent *adj.* مصر muserr

insolence *n.* جِّفة ajrafeh

insolent *adj.* متجرف met'ajref

insoluble *n.* مابينحَل ma beynhall

insolvency *n.* إفْلاس iflas

insolvent *adj.* مفلس mufles

inspect *v.* يتحرى yeteharrah

inspection *n.* تحرّي taharri

inspector *n.* متحري meteharri

inspiration *n.* إلهام elham

inspire *v.* يلهم yehem

instability *n.* عدم استقرار adam isteqrar

install *v.* يركّب yerakkeb

installation *n.* تركيب tarkib

instalment *n.* قسط qest

instance *n.* مثَال methal

instant *n.* لَحظَة lahzah

instant *adj.* سريع sari'

instantaneous *adj.* فوري fawri

instantly *adv.* فورا fawran

instigate *v.* يحرّض yeharred

instigation *n.* تحريض tahrid

instil *v.* يغرس yeghrus

instinct *n.* غريزة gharezeh

instinctive *adj.* غريزي gharizi

institute *n.* معهد ma'had

institution *n.* مُؤَسّسة mu'assaseh

instruct *v.* يدرّس yedarres

instruction *n.* تعليمات ta'limat

instructor *n.* مدرّس mdarres

instrument *n.* أَدَاة adat

instrumentalist *n.* عازِف azef

insubordinate *adj.* متمرِّد metmarred

insubordination *n.* تمَرُّد tamarrud

insufficient *adj.* قليل qalil

insular *adj.* منفصل menfesl

insularity *n.* تقوقع taququ'

insulate *v.* يعزل ye'zul

insulation *n.* عزل azl

insulator *n.* عازِل azel

insult *n.* مسبِّة mesabbeh

insult *v.* يسَبّ yesbb

insupportable *adj.* مابينطاق ma beyntaq

insurance *n.* تأمين ta'min

insure *v.* يأمّن ye'ammen

insurgent *adj.* منْشق menshaqq

insurgent *n.* منْشَق menshaqq

insurmountable *adj.* تعجِيزي ta'jizi

insurrection *n.* عصيان esyan
intact *adj.* سليم salim
intangible *adj.* مو ملموس mu malmus
integral *adj.* كامل kamel
integrity *n.* كمال kamal
intellect *n.* فكر feker
intellectual *adj.* مثقف muthaqqaf
intellectual *n.* مثقف muthaqqaf
intelligence *n.* ذكاء zaka'
intelligence *n.* استخبارات estikhbarat
intelligent *adj.* ذكي zaki
intelligentsia *n.* فئة مثقفة fe'ah muthaqqafeh
intelligible *adj.* مفهوم mafhum
intend *v.* ينوي yenwi
intense *adj.* سميك smik
intensify *v.* يسمك yesammek
intensity *n.* سماكة samakeh
intensity *n.* شدة sheddeh
intensive *adj.* سميك smik
intent *n.* نية neyyeh
intention *n.* قصد qasd
intentional *adj.* عن قصد an qasd
intercept *v.* يعترض ye'terd
interception *n.* اعتراض e'terad
interchange *n.* تبادل tabadul
interchange *v.* يتبادل yetbadl
intercourse *n.* جماع jema'
interdependence *n.* ارتباط ertibat

interdependent *adj.* ترتبط tertebet
interest *n.* مصلحة maslahah
interested *adj.* مهتم mehtamm
interesting *adj.* بيهم beyhemm
interfere *v.* يحشر إنفه yehshur infuh
interference *n.* حشرية heshreyyeh
interim *n.* فاصل fasel
interior *adj.* داخلي dakhli
interior *n.* الداخلية eddakhleyyeh
interjection *n.* صيغة تعجب sighet ta'ajjub
interlock *v.* يشتبك yeshtebek
interlude *n.* إستراحة estirahah
intermediary *n.* الوسيط elwasit
intermediate *adj.* وسيط wasit
interminable *adj.* مطول metawwel
intermingle *v.* يخلط yekhlut
intern *n.* دكتور مقيم diktur muqim
internal *adj.* داخلي dakhli
international *adj.* دولي duwali
interplay *n.* تفاعل tafa'ul
interpret *v.* يفسر yefasser
interpreter *n.* مترجم شفهي mtarjem shafahi
interrogate *v.* يستجوب yestajweb
interrogation *n.* استجواب istijwab
interrogative *adj.* استجوابي istijwabi

interrogative *n.* مُحَقِّق
muhaqqeq

interrupt *v.* يقاطع yeqate'

interruption *n.* مقاطعة
maqata'ah

intersect *v.* يتصالب yetsalab

intersection *n.* تصالب tasalub

interval *n.* فاصل fasel

intervene *v.* يتطَفَّل yettaffal

intervention *n.* تطفُّل tatafful

interview *n.* مقابلة muqabaleh

interview *v.* يعمل مقابلة ye'mel
muqabaleh

intestinal *adj.* معوي me'awi

intestine *n.* أمعاء am'ae

intimacy *n.* علاقة جنسية مو
alaqah jinseyyeh mu
شرعيّة shar'eyyeh

intimate *adj.* صاحب sahib

intimate *v.* يصاحب yesahib

intimation *n.* تنويه tanwih

intimidate *v.* يخوّف yekhawwef

intimidation *n.* تخويف
takhwif

intolerable *adj.* مابنطاق ma
beyntaq

intolerance *n.* عدم تحمّل adam
tahammul

intolerant *adj.* متعصّب
met'assib

intoxicant *n.* يسطلي beystul

intoxicate *v.* يسطل yestul

intoxication *n.* سكرة sakrah

intransitive *adj.* (*verb*) لازم
lazem

intrepid *adj.* جريء jare'

intrepidity *n.* جرأة jur'ah

intricate *adj.* مستعصي mesta'si

intrigue *v.* يتآمر yet'amar

intrigue *n.* مؤامرة mu'amarah

intrinsic *adj.* حقيقي haqiqi

introduce *v.* يقدّم yeqaddem

introduction *n.* مقدّمة
muqademeh

introductory *adj.* تقديمي
taqdimi

intrude *v.* يقتحم yeqtehim

intrusion *n.* اقتحام iqtiham

intuition *n.* بديهة badihah

intuitive *adj.* بديهي badihi

invade *v.* يغزو yeghzu

invalid *adj.* باطل batel

invalid *n.* عاجز ajez

invalidate *v.* يبطل yebtel

invaluable *adj.* نفيس nafis

invasion *n.* غارة gharah

invective *n.* تشهير tashehir

invent *v.* يخترع yekhter'

invention *n.* اختراع ikhtera'

inventive *adj.* اختراعي ikhtera'i

inventor *n.* مخترع mukhtare'

invert *v.* يقلب yeqaleb

invest *v.* يستثمر yestathmer

investigate *v.* يتحرّى yeteharrah

investigation *n.* تحري taharri

investment *n.* استثمار
istithmar

invigilate *v.* يراقب yeraqib

invigilation *n.* مراقبة الإمتحانات
muraqabet elemtihanat

invigilator *n.* مراقب إمتحانات
muraqb emtihanat

invincible *adj.* مابنغلب ma
beyngheleb

inviolable *adj.* حَرَام haram
invisible *adj.* مخفي mekhfi
invitation *n.* دعْوة da'weh
invite *v.* يدعِي yed'e
invocation *n.* دعاء du'a
invoice *n.* فاتورة faturah
invoke *v.* يبتهل yebtehel
involve *v.* يشمل yeshmal
inward *adj.* داخلي dakhli
inwards *adv.* لجوّاً lajuwwah
irate *adj.* معصّب me'assib
ire *n.* تعصيب ta'sib
Irish *adj.* ايرلندي erlandi
Irish *n.* إيرلندي erlandi
irksome *adj.* مِل mumell
iron *n.* حديد hadid
iron *v.* يكوي yekwi
ironical *adj.* مسخرجي maskharji
irony *n.* مسخرة maskharah
irradiate *v.* يعالج بالأشعّة ye'alej belashe'ah
irrational *adj.* مو منطقي mu manteqi
irreconcilable *adj.* متضارب metdareb
irrecoverable *adj.* ما بيسترّد me beystaradd
irrefutable *adj.* مُفحِم mufhim
irregular *adj.* مُخالِف mekhalef
irregularity *n.* شذوذ shuzuz
irrelevant *adj.* مالو علاقة malu alaqah
irrespective *adj.* بصرف النظر yesruf nazar
irresponsible *adj.* مستهتِر mestahter

irrigate *v.* يسقي yesqi
irrigation *n.* سقاية sqayeh
irritable *adj.* عصبي asabi
irritant *adj.* مهيّج mehayyej
irritant *n.* مادّة مهيّجة maddeh mehayyjeh
irritate *v.* يفوّر دم yefawwer damm
irritation *n.* إثارة etharrah
irritation *n.* تهييج tahayyuj
irruption *n.* اقتحام iqtiham
island *n.* جزيرة jazireh
isle *n.* جزيرة صغيرة jazireh sghireh
isolate *v.* يعزل ye'zul
isolation *n.* عزل azel
issue *v.* يصدِّر yesder
issue *n.* قضيّة qadeyyeh
issue *n.* إصدار isdar
Italian *adj.* إيطالي itali
Italian *n.* الإيطالي elitali
italic *adj.* مايِل mayl
italics *n.* الخطّ المايل elkhatt elmayl
itch *n.* حكّة hakkeh
itch *v.* يحكّ yehekk
item *n.* مادّة maddeh
ivory *n.* عاج aaj
ivy *n.* لبلاب leblab

J

jab *v.* يشكّ إبرة yeshekk ebreh

jack *n.* رافعة raf'ah

jack *v.* يرفع yerfa'

jackal *n.* واوي wawi

jacket *n.* جاكيت jakit

jail *n.* سجن sejn

jail *v.* يسجن yesjun

jailer *n.* سجّان sajjan

jam *n.* مربى mrabbah

jam *v.* يهرس yehrus

janitor *n.* ناطور natur

January *n.* كانون الثاني kanun ettani

jar *n.* مطربان matraban

jasmine, jessamine *n.* ياسمين yasmin

jaundice *n.* أبو صفار abu safar

jaundice *v.* ينصاب بأبو صفار yensab be abu safar

javelin *n.* رمح remh

jaw *n.* حنك hanak

jay *n.* قاق qaq

jealous *adj.* غيور ghayyur

jealousy *n.* غيرة ghereh

jeer *v.* يتمسخر yetmaskhar

jelly *n.* جيليه jelyh

jeopardize *v.* يعرّض للخطر ye'arred lelkhatar

jeopardy *n.* خطر khatar

jerk *n.* رجفة rajfeh

jerky *adj.* متقلّب metqalleb

jersey *n.* قميص صوف qamis suf

jest *n.* مزحة mazha

jest *v.* يمزح yemzah

jet *n.* طيّارة نفاثة tayyarah nafatheh

Jew *n.* يهودي yahudi

jewel *n.* جوهرة juharah

jewel *v.* يزيّن بالمجوهرات yezayyen belmjawharat

jeweller *n.* صايغ sayegh

jewellery *n.* مجوهرات mjawharat

jingle *n.* خشخشة khashkhasheh

jingle *v.* يخشخش yekhashkhesh

job *n.* شغل sheghl

jobber *n.* تاجر جملة tajer jumleh

jobbery *n.* فساد إداري fasad idari

jocular *adj.* مزوح mazuh

jog *v.* ركض raked

join *v.* ينتسب yentseb

joiner *n.* نجّار najjar

joint *n.* مفصل mefassal

joint *adj.* مربوط marbut

jointly *adv.* سوا sawa

joke *n.* نكتة nekteh

joke *v.* ينكّت yenakket

joker *n.* جوكر juker

jollity *n.* روح مرحة ruh mrhah

jolly *adj.* فرحان farhan

jolt *n.* خضّ khadd

jolt *v.* يخضّ yekhudd

jostle *n.* إصطدام istidam

jostle *v.* يصطدم yestedem

jot *n.* مثقال ذرّة methqal zarrah

jot *v.* يسجّل yesajjel

journal *n.* مجلة majalleh

journalism *n.* صحافة sahafeh

journalist *n.* صحفي sahafi

journey *n.* رحلة rehleh

journey *v.* يسوح yesuh

jovial *adj.* بشوش bashush
joviality *n.* بشاشة bashasheh
joy *n.* مَرَح marah
joyful *n.* مرِح merih
joyous *n.* مفرِح mefreh
jubilant *adj.* فرْحان farhan
jubilation *n.* فرَح farah
jubilee *n.* يوبيل yubil
judge *n.* قاضي qadi
judge *v.* يحكُم yehkum
judgement *n.* حكَم hekm
judicature *n.* قضاء qada'
judicial *adj.* قضائي qada'e
judiciary *n.* سلطة قضائية sultah qada'eyyeh
judicious *adj.* متّزن mettezen
jug *n.* إبريق ibreq
juggle *v.* يتلاعب yetla'ab
juggler *n.* مشعوذ musha'wez
juice *n.* عصير asir
juicy *adj.* غضّ ghadd
jumble *n.* بلبلة balbaleh
jumble *v.* يتبلبل yetbalbal
jump *n.* نطة nattah
jump *v.* يطّ yenutt
junction *n.* لحم lahm
juncture *n.* نقطة اتصال neqtet ettisal
jungle *n.* غابة ghabeh
junior *adj.* أصغر asghar
junior *n.* شبّ shabb
junk *n.* حثالة huthaleh
jupiter *n.* المشتري elmushtari
jurisdiction *n.* صلاحيّة salaheyyeh
jurisprudence *n.* فقْه feqh
jurist *n.* فقَيه faqih

juror *n.* مُحلّف muhallaf
jury *n.* لجنة التحليف lajnet tahlif
juryman *n.* عضو في لجنة محلّفين udu fi lejnet muhallafin
just *adj.* بس bas
justice *n.* عدالة adaleh
justifiable *adj.* مبرّر mubarrar
justification *n.* تبرير tabrir
justify *v.* يبرّر yebarrer
justly *adv.* بالحق belhaqq
jute *n.* خيش khish
juvenile *adj.* حدث hadath
juxtapose *v.* يحطّ شي جمب شي yehutt shi jmb shi
juxtaposed *adj.* محطوط جمب بعضه mahtut jmb ba'duh
juxtaposition *n.* مجاورة mejawarah

K

kaki *n.* كاكي kaki
kamikaze *n.* إنتحاري intihari
kangaroo *n.* كنغارو kangaru
karat *n.* كراتيه karatih
keen *adj.* حريص haris
keenness *n.* حرص hers
keep *v.* يحفظ yehfaz
keeper *n.* أمين صندوق amin sanduq
keepsake *n.* تذكار tizkar

kennel *n.* بيت الكلب beit elkalb

kerchief *n.* حجاب المرا hijab elmarah

kernel *n.* نَوَاة nawat

kerosene *n.* كيروسين kirusin

ketchup *n.* كتشب katshap

kettle *n.* إبريق ibriq

key *n.* مفتاح meftah

key *v.* يفتح بالمفتاح yeftah bel mftah

key *adj.* رئيسي ra'isi

keyhole *n.* ثقب المفتاح thuqb el meftah

keypad *n.* لوحة المفاتيح luhet elmafatih

keystone *n.* قُطْب qutub

keyword *n.* كلمة أساسية kelmeh asasyyeh

kick *n.* يرفس yerfus

kick *v.* رفسة rafseh

kid *n.* طَفل tefl

kidnap *v.* يخطف yekhtuf

kidney *n.* كلية klyeh

kill *v.* يقتل yeqtul

kill *n.* قتل qatl

kiln *n.* تنور tannur

kilo *n.* كيلو kilo

kilogram *n.* كيلوغرام kilogram

kilt *n.* تنورة بكسرات tannurah be kasrat

kin *n.* أهْل ahel

kind *n.* نوع nu'

kind *adj.* لطيف latif

kindergarten *n.* حضانة hadaneh

kindle *v.* يشعل yesh'ul

kindly *adv.* بلطف belutf

kindness *n.* لطافة latafeh

kinetic *adj.* حرَكي haraki

king *n.* ملك malek

kingdom *n.* مملكة mamlakeh

kinship *n.* قرابة qrabeh

kiss *n.* بوسة buseh

kiss *v.* يبوس yebus

kit *n.* عدة eddeh

kitchen *n.* مطبخ matbakh

kite *n.* طيّارة ورق tayyarah waraq

kith *n.* قرايب qrayeb

kitten *n.* قطة صغيرة qettah sghereh

knave *n.* محتال mehtal

knavery *n.* إحتيال ihtyal

knee *n.* ركبة rekbeh

kneel *v.* يسجد yesjud

knife *n.* سكّينة sekkyneh

knight *n.* فارس fares

knit *v.* يشتغل صوف yeshteghel suf

knock *v.* طَرْقَة tarqah

knot *n.* عقْدة uqdeh

knot *v.* يعقُد ye'qud

know *v.* يعرف ye'ref

knowledge *n.* معرفة ma'refeh

knowledgeable *adj.* لبيب labib

knuckle *n.* مفصل الإصبع mefsal elusba'

knuckle *v.* ينشغل yensheghel

koala *n.* كوالا kuala

krill *n.* قوقعة qawqa'ah

L

label n. عنوان unwan
label v. يعنون y'anwen
labial adj. شفهي shafahi
laboratory n. مختبر mukhtabar
laborious adj. كادح kadeh
labour n. شغل sheghl
labour v. يشتغل yeshteghl
laboured adj. مشغول mashghul
labourer n. شغيل shaghghil
labyrinth n. متاهة matahah
lace n. دنتيل dantil
lace n. رباط الحذاء rabbat elhiza'
lace v.t. يجلد yejlud
lacerate v. يشق yesheqq
lachrymose adj. مسيل للدموع musil leldumu'
lack n. نقص naqs
lack v. ينقص yenaqqes
lacklustre adj. باهت bahet
laconic adj. موجز mujaz
lactate v. يطلع حليب yetalle' halib
lactometer n. مقياس كثافة اللبن meqyas kathafet ellaban
lactose n. لاكتوز laktuz
lacuna n. فتحة fatehah
lacy adj. شريطي shariti
lad n. صبي sabi
ladder n. سلّم sullam
lade v. يشحن shahn

ladle n. مغرفة maghrafeh
ladle v. يغرف yeghruf
lady n. سيدة sayyedeh
lag v. يتباطأ yetbata'
laggard n. بطئ betu'
lagoon n. بحيرة buhayrah
lair n. عرين arin
lake n. بحيرة buhayrah
lamb n. حمل hamal
lambaste v. ينتقد yentqed
lame adj. كسيح kasih
lame v. يعرج ye'ruj
lament v. ينوح yenuh
lament n. نواح nwah
lamentable adj. ببكي bebakki
lamentation n. مناحة manahah
laminate v. يصفح yesaffeh
lamp n. لمبة lambah
lampoon n. هجاء hija'
lampoon v. يهجي yehji
lance n. حربة harbeh
lance v. يرمي الحربة yermi harbeh
lancer n. حامل الرمح hamel elremeh
lancet adj. رمحي remhi
land n. أرض ard
land v. يهبط yehbut
landing n. هبوط hubut
landscape n. مشهد mashhad
lane n. سكة sekkeh
language n. لغة lughah
languish v. يتراخى yetrakha
languor n. تراخي tarakhi
lantern n. فانوس fanus
lanugo n. زغب zaghab

lap n. حِضْن heden

lapse v. يتقادم yetqadm

lapse n. تقادم taqadm

laptop n. لابتوب labtup

lard n. دهن الخنزير dehn elkhanzir

large adj. واسع wase'

largesse n. هِبة hebah

lark n. كَروان krawan

lascivious adj. فاجر fajer

lash n. كُرْباج kerbaj

lass n. صَبِيّة sabeyyeh

last adj. آخِر akher

last adv. بالآخِر belakher

last v. يستمرّ yestmerr

last n. نهاية nihayeh

lastly adv. وبالنهاية wu belnihayeh

lasting adj. دائِم da'em

latch n. دَرْياس derbas

late adj. مُتَأخِر met'akhkher

lately adv. من فترة قريبة mn fatrah qarebeh

latent adj. مكتوم maktum

lath n. خَشبة khashabeh

lathe n. مَخْرَطة makhratah

lather n. رغوة الصابون raghwet elsabun

latitude n. خط عرض khatt arid

latrine n. مِرْحاض merhad

lattice n. شَعْرية sa'reyyeh

laud v. يَمدح yemdah

laud n. مديح madih

laudable adj. محمود mahmud

laugh n. ضَحكة dehkeh

laugh v. يضحك yedhak

laughable adj. بيضحّك beydahhek

laughter n. ضَحكة dehkeh

launch v. يفتتح yefteteh

launch n. إفتتاح iftitah

launder v. يغسل اللبس yeghsel ellebes

laundress n. غَسّالة ghassaleh

laundry n. مصبغة masbaghah

laurel n. يكلّل بالغار yekallel belghar

laureate adj. مكلَّل بالغار mkallal belghar

lava n. حمم بركانية hemam burkaneyyeh

lavatory n. حَمّام hammam

lavender n. لافندر lavendar

lavish adj. مبذِّر mubazzer

lavish v. يبذِّر yebazzer

law n. قانون qanun

lawful adj. قانوني qanuni

lawless adj. مو قانوني mu qanuni

lawn n. مَرْج marj

lawyer n. محامي muhami

lax adj. مسهِّل mesahhel

laxative n. دوا مسهِّل dwa mesahhel

laxative adj. مُلَيِّن mulayyen

laxity n. لِين lyn

lay v. تبيض tabyyid

lay adj. علماني elmani

lay n. مَطرح matrah

layer n. طبقة tabaqah

layman n. علماني elmani

laze v. يضيّع وقت yedayye' waqt

laziness *n.* كسل kasal
lazy *n.* كسلان kaslan
lea *n.* مرعى mar'e
leach *v.* يقطر yeqatter
lead *n.* رصاص rsas
lead *v.* يقود yequd
lead *n.* قيادة qyadeh
leaden *adj.* رصاصي rsasi
leader *n.* قائد qa'ed
leadership *n.* قيادة qyadeh
leaf *n.* ورقة شجر warqet shajar
leaflet *n.* نشرة nashrah
leafy *adj.* مورق mwarreq
league *n.* جامعة jam'ah
leak *n.* تسرب tasarrub
leak *v.* يتسرب yetsarrab
leakage *n.* تسريب tasrib
lean *n.* ميل myl
lean *v.* يميل yemil
leap *v.* يقفز yeqfez
leap *n.* قفزة qafzeh
learn *v.* يتعلم yet'allam
learned *adj.* مطلع على mettele' ala
learner *n.* متعلم met'allem
learning *n.* تعليم ta'lim
lease *n.* استئجار este'jar
lease *v.* يستأجر yesta'jer
least *adj.* أقل aqall
least *adv.* أرخص arkhas
leather *n.* جلد jeld
leave *n.* إجازة ejazeh
leave *v.* يترك yetruk
lecture *n.* محاضرة muhadarah
lecture *v.* يحاضر yehader
lecturer *n.* محاضر muhader

ledger *n.* دفتر الأستاذ daftar elistaz
lee *n.* عكر akar
leech *n.* متطفل metataffel
leek *n.* كرات kurrat
left *adj.* يسار yasar
left *n.* اليسار elyasar
leftist *n.* يساري yasari
leg *n.* ركبة rekbeh
legacy *n.* وصية waseyyeh
legal *adj.* شرعي shar'i
legality *n.* شرعية shar'eyyeh
legalize *v.* يصدق على yesaddeq ala
legend *n.* أسطورة usturah
legendary *adj.* أسطوري usturi
leghorn *n.* طاقية قش taqeyyeh qash
legible *adj.* مقروء maqrue'
legibly *adv.* بوضوح bewuduh
legion *n.* فيلق faylaq
legionary *n.* عسكري في فيلق askari fi fylaq
legislate *v.* يشرع yesharre'
legislation *n.* تشريع tashre'e
legislative *adj.* تشريعي tashre'i
legislator *n.* مشرع musharre'e
legislature *n.* السلطة التشريعية elsultah eltashre'eyyeh
legitimacy *n.* شرعية shar'eyyeh
legitimate *adj.* شرعي shar'ei
leisure *n.* راحة raha
leisurely *adj.* على مهل ala mahl
leisurely *adv.* بروية beraweyyeh
lemon *n.* ليمون limon
lemonade *n.* ليمونادا limonadah

lend v. يعير ye'ir
length n. طول tul
lengthen v. يطوّل yetawwel
lengthy adj. مطوّل metawwal
lenience n. لين lyn
leniency n. حلم helm
lenient adj. حليم halim
lens n. عدسة adaseh
lentil n. عدس ades
Leo n. برج الأسد berj elasad
leonine adj. أسدي asadi
leopard n. فهد fahd
leper n. أبرص abras
leprosy n. برص baras
leprous adj. أبرص abras
less adj. أخفّ akhaff
less adv. أقلّ aqall
less prep. ناقص naqes
lessee n. مستأجر mesta'jer
lessen v. يخفّ yekheff
lesser adj. مؤجّر mu'ajjer
lesson n. درس dars
lest conj. وإلا w ella
let v. يترك yetruk
lethal adj. فتّاك fattak
lethargic adj. متكاسل metkasel
lethargy n. خمول khumul
letter n. رسالة risaleh
level n. مستوى mestawah
level adj. مستوي mestwi
level v. يسوّي yesawwi
lever n. عتلة الرافعة atalet elrafe'
lever v. يرفع yerfa'
leverage n. سطوة satweh
levity n. زنق nezeq
levy v. يجبي yejbi

levy n. جباية jibayeh
lewd adj. إباحي ebahi
lexicography n. تأليف القواميس ta'lif qwamis
lexicon n. قاموس qamus
liability n. مطلوب matlub
liable adj. مسؤول mas'ul
liaison n. صلة silah
liar n. الكذّاب elkazzab
libel n. تجريح tajrih
libel v.t. يجرح yejarreh
liberal adj. ليبرالي liberali
liberalism n. ليبرالية liberaleyyeh
liberality n. سخاء sakha'
liberate v. يحرّر yeharrer
liberation n. تحرير tahrir
liberator n. محرّر muharrer
libertine n. فاجر fajer
liberty n. تحرّر taharrur
librarian n. أمين مكتبة amin elmaktabeh
library n. مكتبة maktabeh
licence n. رخصة rekhsah
license v. يرخّص yerakhkhes
licensee n. صاحب الرخصة sahib elrukhsah
licentious adj. متحرّر mutaharrer
lick v. يلحس yelhas
lick n. لحس lahs
lid n. جفن العين jefn eleyn
lie v. يكذب yekazzeb
lie v. يتسطّح yetsattah
lie n. كذبة kezbeh
lien n. رهن rahn
lieu n. بديل badyl

lieutenant *n.* مُلازِم mulazem

life *n.* حياة hayat

lifeless *adj.* مو مأهول mu ma'hul

lifelong *adj.* مُؤبّد mu'abbad

lifestyle *n.* أسلوب حياة eslub hayat

lift *n.* مصعد mes'ad

lift *v.* يرفع yerfa'

light *n.* ضو daww

light *adj.* خفيف khafif

light *v.* يضوي yedawwi

lighten *v.* يخفف yekhaffef

lighter *n.* قدّاحة qaddahah

lightly *adv.* شوي shwai

lightening *n.* إضاءة eda'ah

like *adj.* متل matal

like *n.* إعجاب e'jab

like *v.* يحب yehb

likelihood *n.* ترجيح tarjih

likely *adj.* أرجح arjah

liken *v.* يشبّه yeshabbeh

likeness *n.* تشبيه tashbih

likewise *adv.* بالمتل belmetl

liking *n.* إعجاب e'jab

lilac *n.* ليلك lilak

lily *n.* زنبق zanbaq

limb *n.* عضو udu

limber *adj.* رشيق rashiq

limber *n.* رشيق rashiq

lime *n.* حامض hamud

lime *v.* يحمّض yehammed

lime *n.* جير jir

limelight *n.* ضو المسرح daww elmasrah

limit *n.* حدّ hadd

limit *v.* يحدّ yehedd

limitation *n.* حدود hdud

limited *adj.* محدود mahdud

limitless *adj.* مايبحصر ma beynheser

line *n.* صفّ saff

line *v.* يصطفّ yestaff

lineage *n.* نسب nasab

linen *n.* كتّان kettan

linger *v.* يمشي ع مهل yemshi a mahl

lingo *n.* لغة أجنبيّة lughah ajnabeyyeh

lingual *adj.* لغوي lughawi

linguist *n.* لغوي lughawi

linguistic *adj.* لغوي lughawi

linguistics *n.* علم اللغة elm ellughah

lining *n.* تبطين tabtin

link *n.* رابط rabit

link *v.* يربط yerbut

linseed *n.* بزر الكتّان bezer elkettan

lintel *n.* عتبة الباب atabet elbab

lion *n.* أسد asad

lioness *n.* لبوة labweh

lip *n.* شفّة sheffeh

liquefy *v.* يميّع yemayye'

liquid *adj.* مايع maye'

liquid *n.* سائل sa'el

liquidate *v.* يصفّي yesaffi

liquidation *n.* تصفية tasfeyeh

liquor *n.* خمر khamr

list *n.* قائمة qa'emeh

list *v.* يعمل قائمة ye'mel qa'emeh

listen *v.* يسمع yesma'

listener *n.* مستمع mesteme'

listless *adj.* متقاعس metqa'es

literacy n. معرفة القراءة ma'reft elqira'ah

literal adj. حرفي harfi

literary adj. أدبي adabi

literate adj. متعلّم met'allem

literature n. أدب adab

litigant n. خصم khasm

litigate v. يقاضي yeqadi

litigation n. خصومة khusumeh

litre n. لتر letr

litter n. نقّالة جرحى naqallet jarha

litter v. تولد الحيوانات tulad elhaywanat

litterateur n. أديب adib

little adj. قليل qalil

little adv. شوية shwayyeh

littoral adj. ساحلي sahli

liturgical adj. شعَائُوي sha'yri

live v. يعيش ye'ish

live v. يسكن yeskun

live adj. عايش ayesh

live adv. مباشر mubashar

livelihood n. رِزْق rezq

lively adj. نشيط nashit

liver n. كبِد kabed

livery n. علف الحصان alaf elhusan

living adj. نشيط nashit

living n. عيشة eysheh

lizard n. جردون jardun

load n. حمل heml

load v. يحمّل yehammel

loadstar n. نجم القطب najm elqutub

loadstone n. حجر المغنطيس hajar elmaghnatis

loaf n. رغيف rghif

loaf v. يتسكّع yetsakka'

loafer n. متسكّع metsakke'

loan n. قرض qard

loan v. يقرض yuqred

loath adj. مشمئزّ mushma'ezz

loathe v. يشمئزّ yeshma'ezz

loathsome adj. مقزّز muqazzez

lobby n. دهليز dahliz

lobe n. شحمة الأذن shahmet elezen

lobster n. روبيان rubyan

local adj. محلّي mahalli

locale n. موقع mawqe'

locality n. محلية mahaleyyeh

localize v. يتمركز yetmarkaz

locate v. يقع yeqa'

location n. موقع mawqe'

lock n. قفل qefl

lock v. يقفل yeqfel

locker n. خزانة بقفل khezaneh beqefl

locomotive n. قاطرة qatrah

locus n. محلّ mahall

locust n. خرنوب kharnub

locution n. أسلوب كلام eslub klam

lodge n. مأوى ma'wa

lodge v. يأوي ye'wi

lodging n. مسكن maskan

loft n. سقيفة sqefeh

lofty adj. عالي a'li

log n. سجل يومي sejell yumi

log n. جزع شجرة jeze' shajarah

log v. يسجّل بالسجل yesajjel belsejl

logarithim n. لوغاريتم lugaritm

loggerhead *n.* أهبل ahbal	**lordship** *n.* سيادة syadeh
logic *n.* علم المنطق elm elmateq	**lore** *n.* معرفة خاصة ma'refeh khassah
logical *adj.* منطقي mateqi	
logician *n.* عالم منطقي alem mateq	**lorry** *n.* شاحنة shahneh
loin *n.* عورة urah	**lose** *v.* يَضيع yedayye'
loiter *v.* يتأخر yetakhkhar	**loss** *n.* ضياع daya'
loll *v.* يترهل yetrahhal	**lot** *n.* قرعة qur'ah
lollipop *n.* مصاصة masasah	**lot** *n.* قسم qesm
lone *adj.* وحيد wahid	**lotion** *n.* لوشن lushen
loneliness *n.* وحدة wehdeh	**lottery** *n.* ياناصيب yanasib
lonely *adj.* وحيد wahid	**lotus** *n.* لوتس lutus
lonesome *adj.* مهجور mahjur	**loud** *adj.* عالي a'li
long *adj.* مديد madid	**lounge** *v.* يتمشى yetmashsha
long *adv* لوقت طويل lwaqet tawil	**lounge** *n.* غرفة القعدة gherfet elqa'deh
long *v.* يشتاق yeshtaq	**louse** *n.* قملة qamleh
longevity *n.* تعمير ta'mir	**lovable** *adj.* محبوب mahbub
longing *n.* شوق shuq	**love** *n.* حبّ hubb
longitude *n.* خط الطول khatt ettul	**love** *v.* يحبّ yehebb
	lovely *adj.* محبوب mahbub
look *v.* يطلّع yetalle'	**lover** *n.* حبيب habib
look *n.* شكل shakl	**loving** *adj.* عطوف atuf
loom *n.* نول nul	**low** *adj.* سافل safel
loom *v.* يشتغل ع النول yeshteghel alnul	**low** *v.* يبخس yebkhas
	low *n.* منخفض menkhefed
loop *n.* عروة urweh	**lower** *v.* يخفّض yekhaffed
loop-hole *n.* فتحة للرمي fateha lelrami	**lowliness** *n.* حقارة haqarah
	lowly *adj.* وضيع wade'
loose *adj.* مفكوك mafkuk	**loyal** *adj.* وفي wafi
loosen *v.* يفكّ yefekk	**loyalist** *n.* موالي mwali
loot *n.* غنيمة ghanimeh	**loyalty** *n.* إخلاص ikhlas
loot *v.* يغنم yeghnam	**lubricant** *n.* مزلّق mezalleq
lop *v.* يتدلّى yetdallah	**lubricate** *v.* يشحم yeshahhem
lop *n.* تدلّي tadalli	**lubrication** *n.* تشحيم tashehim
lord *n.* لورد lurd	**lucent** *adj.* شفّاف shaffaf
lordly *adj.* جليل jalil	**lucerne** *n.* فصة fassah
	lucid *adj.* فصيح fasih

lucidity *n.* صفاء safa'

luck *n.* حظّ hazz

luckily *adv.* لحسن حظّه lahesn hazzuh

luckless *adj.* مَنْحُوس manhus

lucky *adj.* مَحْظُوظ mahzuz

lucrative *adj.* مُرْبِح murbih

lucre *n.* رِبْح rebeh

luggage *n.* شناتي السفر shanati elsafar

lukewarm *adj.* فاتِر fater

lull *v.* يهزّ الرضيع yehezz elrade'

lull *n.* هزّ الرضيع hazz elrade'

lullaby *n.* غنيّة النوم ghennyt elnum

luminary *n.* نَجْم najm

luminous *adj.* مُشِعّ mushe'

lump *n.* كُتْلة ketleh

lump *v.* يجمع yejma'

lunacy *n.* جنون jnun

lunar *adj.* هلالي helali

lunatic *n.* مَجْنُون majnun

lunatic *adj.* مَمْسُوس mamsus

lunch *n.* غدا ghada

lunch *v.* ياكل الغدا yakul elghada

lung *n.* رِئة re'ah

lunge *n.* طَعْنة ta'neh

lunge *v.* يطعَن yet'an

lurch *n.* ميلان myalan

lurch *v.* يميل yemil

lure *n.* إغراء eghra'

lure *v.* يغري yeghri

lurk *v.* يترقّب yetraqqab

luscious *adj.* طَيِّب tayyeb

lush *adj.* حافِل hafil

lust *n.* شهوة shahweh

lustful *adj.* شهواني shahwani

lustre *n.* رونق runaq

lustrous *adj.* لَمِيع lamme'

lusty *adj.* شهواني shahwani

lute *n.* طين tyn

luxuriance *n.* فَخامة fakhmeh

luxuriant *adj.* فَخْم fakhm

luxurious *adj.* مترَف mutraf

luxury *n.* رفاهيّة rafaheyyeh

lynch *v.* يعدم بدون مَحاكمة ye'dem bdun muhakameh

lyre *n.* قيثارة qitharah

lyric *n.* كلِمات أغْنيَة kalimat ughneyeh

lyrical *adj.* غِنائي ghena'e

lyricist *n.* شاعر غنائِي sha'er ghena'e

M

mace *n.* صولَجان sulajan

machinate *v.* يدبِّرله مكيدة yedaberluh makideh

machination *n.* مَكيدة makideh

machine *n.* ماكينَة makinah

machinery *n.* آلاتَ alat

machinist *n.* ميكانِسيان mikanisyan

mack *n.* مشمَّع meshamma'

macro *adj.* كبير kbir

macrobiotic *adj.* نباتي nabati

macrocephaly n. كبر الرأس
kebr elras

maculate v. يبقّع yebaqqe'

maculate adj. مبقّع mebaqqe'

mad adj. مسعور mas'ur

mad adv. بغباء beghaba'

madam n. مدام madam

madden v. يجنّن yejannin

maddening adj. بيهستر
beyhaster

madhouse n. بيمارستان
bymarstan

madness n. جنون jnun

mafia n. مافيا mafya

magazine n. مجلّة majalleh

maggot n. يرقة yaraqah

magic n. سحر sehr

magical adj. سحري sehri

magician n. ساحر saher

magisterial adj. وقور waqur

magistracy n. هيئة القضاة
haye't elqudat

magistrate n. قاضي qadi

magistrature n. منصب القاضي
manseb elqadi

magma n. حمم بركانية hemam
burkaneyyeh

magnanimity n. نخوة
nakhweh

magnanimous adj. شهم
shahem

magnate n. شخصيّة كبيرة
shakhseyyeh kbireh

magnet n. مغنطيس maghnatis

magnetic adj. مغنطيسي
maghnatisi

magnetism n. مغنطيسيّة
maghnateseyyeh

magnificent adj. عظيم azim

magnify v. يعظّم ye'azzem

magnitude n. ضخامة
dakhameh

mahout n. سوّاق الفيل swwaq
elfil

maid n. وصيفة wasifeh

maiden n. بكر bekr

maiden adj. عذراء azra'e

maiden adj. عذري uzri

mail n. بريد barid

mail v. يبعت بالبريد yeb'at
belbarid

main adj. رئيسي ra'ysi

main n. الرئيسي elra'esi

mainly adv. بشكل رئيسي
beshakel ra'esi

mainstay n. عماد emad

maintain v. يعمل صيانة ye'mel
syaneh

maintenance n. صيانة syaneh

maize n. ذرة zurah

majestic adj. ملكي malaki

majesty n. سمو sumwwu

major adj. أساسي asasi

major n. تخصّص takhassus

major n. رائد ra'ed

majority n. أغلبيّة aghlabeyyeh

make v. يعمل ye'mel

make n. صنع sune'

maker n. صانع sane'

mal adjustment n. سوء توازن
su' twazun

mal administration n. سوء
إدارة su' edarah

malady *n.* داء da'
malaria *n.* ملاريا malarya
malaise *n.* وعكة wa'ekeh
malcontent *adj.* ناقم naqem
malcontent *n.* الناقم elnaqem
male *adj.* ذكوري zukuri
male *n.* ذكَر zakar
malediction *n.* لعنة la'neh
malefactor *n.* مذنب muzneb
maleficent *adj.* خبيث khabith
malice *n.* خبث khubth
malicious *adj.* خبيث khabith
malign *v.* يفتري yefteri
malign *adj.* مفتري mefteri
malignancy *n.* خباثة khabatheh
malignant *adj.* خبيث khabith
malignity *n.* بغض bughd
malleable *adj.* مرن merin
malnutrition *n.* سوء تغذية su' taghzeyeh
malpractice *n.* سوء تصرّف su' tasarruf
malt *n.* شعير البيرا sh'ir byrah
mal-treatment *n.* سوء معاملة su'e mu'amaleh
mamma *n.* ماما mama
mammal *n.* ثدي thadi
mammary *adj.* ثديي thadyy
mammon *n.* حبّ المصاري hubb elmasari
mammoth *n.* ماموث mamuth
mammoth *adj.* ضخم dakhm
man *n.* رجّال rejjal
man *v.* يبعتله رجال yeb'atluh rejal
manage *v.* يدير yedir

manageable *adj.* بيندار beyndar
management *n.* إدارة edarah
manager *n.* مدير mudir
managerial *adj.* إداري edari
mandate *n.* إنتداب intidab
mandatory *adj.* إلزامي elzami
manes *n.* أرواح الموتى arwah elmawtah
manful *adj.* شجاع shuja'
manganese *n.* منغنيز manganiz
manger *n.* معلف ma'laf
mangle *v.* يمثّل بالجثّة yemaththil bel jeththeh
mango *n.* مانجو manjo
manhandle *v.* يحرّك يدوياً yeharrek yadaweyyen
manhole *n.* غرفة تفتيش gherfet taftish
manhood *n.* رجولة rujuleh
mania *n.* هوس hawas
maniac *n.* مهووس mahwwus
manicure *n.* مانيكير manakir
manifest *adj.* واضح wadeh
manifest *v.* يبيّن yebayyen
manifestation *n.* تبيين tabyyin
manifesto *n.* البيان العام elbayan el'aam
manifold *adj.* متشعّب metsha'eb
manipulate *v.* يتلاعب بالأسعار yetla'ab bel as'ar
manipulation *n.* تلاعب بالأسعار tala'ub bel as'ar
mankind *n.* بشر bashar

manlike *adj.* رجولي rujuli	**marauder** *n.* حرامي harami
manliness *n.* رجولة rujuleh	**marble** *n.* مرمر marmar
manly *adj.* رجالي rejjali	**march** *n.* مشية mashyeh
manna *n.* المَنّ elmann	**March** *n.* آذار adar
mannequin *n.* مانيكان manikan	**march** *v.* يمشي yemshi
manner *n.* طريقة tariqah	**mare** *n.* فرس faras
mannerism *n.* تصنّع tasannu'	**margarine** *n.* سمن نباتي samen nabati
mannerly *adj.* مهذب muhazzab	**margin** *n.* هامش hamesh
manoeuvre *n.* مُناوَرة munawarah	**marginal** *adj.* هامشي hameshi
manoeuvre *v.* يناور yenawer	**marigold** *n.* زهر مخملي zahr mukhmali
manor *n.* مزرعة mazra'ah	**marine** *adj.* بحري bahri
manorial *adj.* إقطاعي eqta'ei	**mariner** *n.* بحّار bahhar
mansion *n.* قصر qasr	**marionette** *n.* دمية متحركة demyeh meteharkeh
mantle *n.* حجاب hijab	**marital** *adj.* زوجي zawji
mantle *v.* يتحجّب yetehajjab	**maritime** *adj.* تجاري-بحري tejari - bahri
manual *adj.* يدوي yadawi	**mark** *n.* علامة alameh
manual *n.* كتيّب kutayyeb	**mark** *v.* يعلّم ye'allem
manufacture *v.* يصنع yesanne'	**marker** *n.* قلم تحديد qalam tahdid
manufacture *n.* تصنيع tasne'	**market** *n.* سوق suq
manufacturer *n.* منتج muntij	**market** *v.* يسوّق yesawweq
manumission *n.* إعتاق e'taq	**marketable** *adj.* رايج rayij
manumit *v.* يعتق ye'teq	**marksman** *n.* هدّاف haddaf
manure *n.* سماد عضوي samad udwi	**marl** *n.* تراب كلسي trab klsi
manure *v.* يسمّد yesammed	**marmalade** *n.* مربى البرتقال mrabba elburtuqal
manuscript *n.* مخطوطة makhtutah	**maroon** *n.* اللون الكستنائي ellun elkastanae'i
many *adj.* كتير ktir	**maroon** *adj.* كستنائي kastanae'i
map *n.* خريطة kharitah	**marriage** *n.* زواج zwaj
map *v.* يحدّد عالخريطة yehadded alkharitah	**marriageable** *adj.* صالح للزواج saleh lelzwaj
mar *v.* يشوّه yeshawweh	
marathon *n.* ماراتون maratun	
maraud *v.* ينهب yenhab	

marrow n. نخاع العظام nukha'
elezam

marry v. يتزوّج yetzawwaj

Mars n. المرّيخ elmarrikh

marsh n. مستنقع mustanqa'

marshal n. مشير mushir

marshal v.t ينسّق yenasseq

marshy adj. مستنقعى
mustanqa'i

marsupial n. حيوان جرابى
haywan jurabi

mart n. سوق suq

marten n. سمّور sammur

martial adj. عسكري askari

martyr n. شهيد shahid

martyrdom n. إسْتشْهاد
istishhad

marvel n. مُعجِزة mu'jezeh

marvel v. يتعجب yet'ajjab

marvellous adj. خارق khareq

mascot n. جالب الحظّ jaleb
elhazz

masculine adj. ذكّرى zakari

mash n. بطاطا مهروسة batatah
mahruseh

mash v. يهرس yehrus

mask n. قناع qina'

mask v. يلبس قناع yelbes qina'

mason n. بنّى bannah

masonry n. ماسونيّة
masuneyyeh

masquerade n. حفلة تنكريّة
hafleh tanakureyyeh

mass n. كتلة ketleh

mass v. يكتّل yekattel

massacre n. مجزرة majzarah

massacre v. يدبح yedbah

massage n. مسّاج massaj

massage v. يعمل مسّاج ye'mil
massaj

masseur n. مدلّك medallek

massive adj. عملاق emlaq

massy adj. ضخم dakhem

mast n. برج تلفزيون burj
telfzyun

master n. قبطان kubtan

master n. الماجستير elmajestir

master n. سيد sayyed

master v. يغلب yeghleb

masterly adj. ببراعة bebara'ah

masterpiece n. تحفة فنّية tehfeh
fanneyyeh

mastery n. رَبَاعَة bara'ah

masticate v. يمضغ yemdagh

masturbate v. يعمل العادة السرية
ye'mel el'adeh elserreyyeh

mat n. سجّادة sejjadeh

matador n. مصارع ثيران
musare' thiran

match n. مطابقة mutabaqah

match v. يطابق yetabeq

match n. عود كبريت ud kebrit

match n. مباراة mubarah

matchless adj. مايشبه حدا ma
beyshbah hada

matchmaker n. خطّابة
khattabeh

mate n. شريك shrik

mate v. يرتبط yertebet

mate n. متّة matteh

mate v. يرافق yerafeq

material adj. مادّي maddi

material n. مادّة maddeh

materialism *n.* ماديّة maddeyyeh

materialize *v.* يتحقّق yetehaqqaq

materialize *v.* يجسّد yejassed

maternal *adj.* أمومي umumi

maternity *n.* أمومة umumeh

mathematical *adj.* رياضي riyadi

mathematician *n.* عالم رياضيّات a'lem ryaddeyyat

mathematics *n.* رياضيّات ryaddeyyat

matinee *n.* ماتينيه matineh

matricide *n.* قتل الإمّ qatl elemm

matriculate *v.* يقبل في الجامعة yeqbal beljam'ah

matriculation *n.* امتحان القبول في جامعة imtihan elqubul beljam'ah

matrimonial *adj.* زَوَاجي zawaji

matrimony *n.* نكَاح nikah

matrix *n.* مصّفوفة masfufeh

matron *n.* رئيسة الممرّضات ra'est elmumarredat

matter *n.* مسْألة mas'aleh

matter *n.* موضوع mawdu'

matter *v.* يهم yehemm

mattock *n.* جاروف jaruf

mattress *n.* فرشة farsheh

mature *adj.* مستوَي mestwei

mature *v.* يستوي yestwi

maturity *n.* إسْتواء estiwa'

maudlin *adj.* سكْران sakran

maul *n.* مدق madaqq

maul *v.* يدقّ بالمدق yedeqq belmadaqq

maulstick *n.* مسطرة الدهان mastaret eldehan

maunder *v.* يهذي yehzi

mausoleum *n.* ضريح darih

mawkish *adj.* بيلي النفس beyl'i elnafs

maxilla *n.* عظم الفك azem elfakk

maxim *n.* حكمة hikmeh

maximize *v.* يرفع لأقصى حدّ yerfa' la'qsa hadd

maximum *adj.* أقصى حدّ aqsa hadd

maximum *n.* الحد الأقصى elhadd elaqsa

May *n.* أيّار ayyar

may *v.* يجوز yejuz

mayor *n.* عمدة umdeh

maze *n.* حَيرة hireh

me *pron.* إليّ eli

meadow *n.* مرْج marj

meagre *adj.* نحيف nahif

meal *n.* وجبة wajbeh

mealy *adj.* مرشوش طحين marshush tehin

mean *adj.* ساقط saqt

mean *n.* معنى ma'nah

mean *v.* يعني ye'ni

meander *v.* يلفّ yeleff

meaning *n.* معنى ma'nah

meaningful *adj.* إله معنى elu ma'nah

meaningless *adj.* ماله معنى malu ma'nah

meanness *n.* دناءة dana'ah

means *n.* وسيلة wasileh
meanwhile *adv.* وبهالوقت w
behal waqt
measles *n.* حَصبة hasbeh
measurable *adj.* بينقاس
beynqas
measure *n.* مكيال mekyal
measure *v.* يقيس yeqis
measureless *adj.* مابينقاس ma
beynqas
measurement *n.* قياس qyas
meat *n.* لحم lahm
mechanic *n.* ميكانيك mikanik
mechanical *adj.* ميكانيكي
mikaniki
mechanics *n.* علم الميكانيك elm
elmikanik
mechanism *n.* حركيّة
harakeyyeh
medal *n.* مداليّة medaleyyeh
medallist *n.* مصمّم أوسمة
mesammem awsemeh
meddle *v.* يتطفّل yettaffal
medieval *adj.* من القرون الوسطى
mn elqurun elwestah
median *adj.* وسيط wasit
mediate *v.* يتوسّط yetwassat
mediation *n.* وساطة wasatah
mediator *n.* وسيط wasit
medic *n.* دكتور daktur
medical *adj.* طبّي tebbi
medicament *n.* دوا dawa
medicinal *adj.* دوائي dawa'e
medicine *n.* طبّ tebb
mediocre *adj.* وسط wasat
mediocrity *n.* توسّط tawassut
meditate *v.* يتأمّل yet'ammal

meditation *n.* تأمّل ta'ammul
meditative *adj.* تأمّلي
ta'ammuli
medium *n.* وسيط روحاني wasit
ruhani
medium *adj.* متوسّط
metwasset
meek *adj.* وديع wade'
meet *n.* تلبية talbeyeh
meet *n.* تقابل taqabul
meet *v.* يلبّي yelabbi
meet *v.* يقابل yeqabel
meeting *n.* مقابلة muqabaleh
megaphone *n.* بوق buq
melancholia *n.* سوداويّة
sawdaweyyeh
melancholic *adj.* سوْداوي
sawdawy
melancholy *n.* سوْداويّة
sawdaweyyeh
melancholy *adj.* سوْداوي
sawdawy
melee *n.* قتيلة kteleh
meliorate *v.* يحسّن yehassen
mellow *adj.* لين lyn
melodious *adj.* بيطرب beytrib
melodrama *n.* ميلودراما
miludrama
melodramatic *adj.* ميلوْدرامي
miludrami
melody *n.* لحن lahn
melon *n.* بطيخ أصفر batteikh
ahmar
melt *v.* يدوب yedub
member *n.* عضو udu
membership *n.* عضويّة
udwevyeh

membrane *n.* غِشَاء ghisha'

memento *n.* تَذْكَار tizkar

memoir *n.* مُذَكَّرَة muzakkarah

memorable *adj.* بَارِز barez

memorandum *n.* مُذَكَّرَة muzakkarah

memorial *n.* نصب تذكاري nasb tizkari

memorial *adj.* تذكاري tizkari

memory *n.* ذَاكِرَة zakrah

menace *n.* تَهْدِيد tahdid

menace *v.* يَهَدِّد yehadded

mend *v.* يُرَمِّم yerammem

mendacious *adj.* كَذَّاب kazzab

menial *adj.* سَافِل safil

menial *n.* سَافِل safil

meningitis *n.* التهاب سحايا eltihab essahayah

menopause *n.* سن اليأس senn elya's

menses *n.* دورة شهريّة dawrah shahreyyeh

menstrual *adj.* يَخُصّ الدورة الشهريّة bekhuss eldawrah elshahreyyeh

menstruation *n.* إستحاضة estihadah

mental *adj.* عَقْلِي aqli

mentality *n.* عَقْلِيّة aqleyyeh

mention *n.* ذَكْر zekr

mention *v.* يَذْكُر yezkur

mentor *n.* موجه mwajjeh

menu *n.* قائمة أكل qa'emet akel

mercantile *adj.* تِجاري tijari

mercenary *adj.* مِرْتَزِق murtazaq

merchandise *n.* تِجَارَة tijarah

merchant *n.* تاجِر tajer

merciful *adj.* رحيم rahim

merciless *adj.* بلا رَحْمَة bla rahmeh

mercurial *adj.* زِئْبَقِي ze'baqi

mercury *n.* زِئْبَق ze'baq

mercy *n.* رَحْمَة rahmeh

mere *adj.* بَحَتَ baht

merge *v.* يدمج yedmuj

merger *n.* اندماج indimaj

meridian *n.* خطّ التنصيف khatt eltansif

merit *n.* فَضِيلَة fadyleh

merit *v.* يَتَطَلَّب yetallab

meritorious *adj.* صالِح salih

mermaid *n.* حورية البحر hureyyet elbaher

merman *n.* رجل حورية البحر rajul hureyyet elbaher

merriment *n.* فَرَح farah

merry *a* فَرْحان farhan

mesh *n.* خيوط الشبكة khuyut elshabakeh

mesh *v.* يِشَبِّك yeshabbek

mesmerism *n.* تنويم مغناطيسى tanwim maghnatisi

mesmerize *v.* يِنَوِّم مغنطيسيا yenawwem maghnatiseyyan

mess *n.* لبكة labakeh

mess *v.* يِلَبِّك yelabbek

message *n.* رسالة risaleh

messenger *n.* رسول rasul

messiah *n.* يِسُوع yasu'

Messrs *n.* جناب janab

metabolism *n.* استقلاب isteqlab

metal *n.* معدن ma'dan

metallic *adj.* معدني ma'dani

metallurgy *n.* علم المعادن elm elma'den

metamorphosis *n.* اِنْسِلاخ insilakh

metaphor *n.* إِسْتِعَارَة esti'arah

metaphysical *adj.* مِيتَافِيزِيقي metafiziqi

metaphysics *n.* مِيتَافِيزِيقيا metafiziqya

mete *v.* يعطي حصة ye'ti hessah

meteor *n.* شهَاب shihab

meteoric *adj.* شهابي shihabi

meteorologist *n.* عالم أرصاد جوِّيّة a'lem arsad jawweyyeh

meteorology *n.* الارصاد الجوِّيّة elarsad eljawweyyeh

meter *n.* مقياس meqyas

method *n.* طريقة tareqah

methodical *adj.* نِظامي nizami

metre *n.* متر metr

metric *adj.* متري metri

metrical *adj.* متري metri

metropolis *n.* عاصمة a'semeh

metropolitan *adj.* مطراني mutrani

metropolitan *n.* مناطق حضريّة manateq hadareyyeh

mettle *n.* همّة hemmeh

mew *v.* ينوّي yenawwi

mew *n.* تنوِاية tenwayeh

mezzanine *n.* طابق وسط tabeq wasat

mica *n.* ميكا mika

microfilm *n.* فيلم مصغّر film musaghghar

micrometer *n.* ميكرومتر mikrometr

microphone *n.* ميكروفون mikrufun

microscope *n.* مجهَر majhar

microscopic *adj.* مجهري majhari

microwave *n.* ميكروويف mykruwyf

mid *adj.* وسط wasat

midday *n.* ظهر zuher

middle *adj.* وسط wasat

middle *n.* الوسط elwasat

middleman *n.* دَلّال dallal

middling *adj.* ماشي حاله mashi halu

midget *n.* قزم qazam

midnight *n.* نصّ الليل ness ellil

midriff *n.* الحجاب الحَاجز elhijab elhajez

midst *n.* نصّ ness

midsummer *n.* نصّ الصيف ness elsif

midwife *n.* الدايَة eldayeh

might *n.* قدرة qedrah

mighty *adj.* قوي qawi

migraine *n.* شُقِيقة shaqiqah

migrant *n.* مغتَرب mughtarib

migrate *v.* يهَاجر yehajer

migration *n.* جمرة hejrah

milch *adj.* حلوب halub

mild *adj.* مو حدّ mu hadd

mildew *n.* عفن afan

mile *n.* ميل myl

mileage *n.* المَسافة بالميل elmasafeh belmyl

milestone *n.* مَعلَم ma'lam

milieu *n.* جَوّ jaww

militant *n.* مقاتل muqatel

military *adj.* عِسْكَري askari

military *n.* قوّات مسلَحة quwwat musallaha

militate *v.* يناضل yenadel

militia *n.* ميليشيا milyshya

milk *n.* حليب halib

milk *v.* يحلب yehlub

milky *adj.* حليبي halibi

mill *n.* طاحونة tahuneh

mill *v.* يطحن yetehan

millennium *n.* ألفيّة alfeyyeh

miller *n.* طحّان tahhan

millet *n.* ذرة بيضا zurah bydah

milliner *n.* مصمّم القبّوعات النسواني musammem elqabbu'at elniswani

millinery *n.* بيع القبّوعات النسواني be' elqabbu'at elniswani

million *n.* مليون mlyun

millionaire *n.* مليونير malyunir

millipede *n.* أم أربعة وأربعين emm arba' wu arb'yn

mime *n.* بهلول bahlul

mime *v.* يقلّد yeqalled

mimesis *n.* تقليد taqlid

mimic *adj.* تقليد taqlid

mimic *n.* تقليد taqlid

mimic *v.* يقلّد yeqallid

mimicry *n.* تمويه tamwih

minaret *n.* مئذنة me'zaneh

mince *v.* يفرم yefrum

mind *n.* عقل aqel

mind *v.t.* يمانع yemane'

mindful *adj.* واعي wa'i

mindless *adj.* أبله ablah

mine *pron.* إليّ eli

mine *n.* منجم manjam

miner *n.* عامل منجم amel manjam

mineral *n.* معدن ma'dan

mineral *adj.* معدني ma'dani

mineralogist *n.* متخصّص بالمعادن metkhasses belma'den

mineralogy *n.* علم المعادن elm elma'den

mingle *v.* يخلط yekhlut

miniature *n.* صورة صغيرة surah sghereh

miniature *adj.* منمنم menamnam

minim *n.* قطْرَة qatrah

minimal *adj.* أقلّ a'qll

minimize *v.* يقلّل yeqallel

minimum *n.* الحدّ الأدنى elhadd eladna

minimum *adj.* يقلّل لأدنى حدّ yeqallel lelhadd eladna

minion *n.* محبّ muhebb

minister *n.* وزير wazir

ministrant *adj.* خادم khadem

ministry *n.* وزارة wazarah

minor *adj.* صغير saghir

minor *n.* قاصر qaser

minority *n.* أقليّة aqalleyyeh

minster *n.* كاتدرائية katedra'eyyeh

mint *n.* نعناع na'na'

mint *n.* طبع العملة tabe' el'emleh

mint *v.t.* يطبع العملة yetba' el'emleh

minus *adj.* ناقص naqes

minus *n.* إشارة - esharet -

minuscule *adj.* حرف صغير harf sghir

minute *adj.* دقيق daqiq

minute *n.* دقيقة daqiqah

minutely *adv.* بدقّة bedeqqah

miracle *n.* أُعجوبة u'jubeh

miraculous *adj.* عجيب ajib

mirage *n.* سراب sarab

mire *n.* طين tyn

mire *v.* يغطّ بالطين yeghutt beltyn

mirror *n.* مراية mrayeh

mirror *v.* يعكس صورة ye'kus suret

misadventure *n.* مكْرُوه makruh

misanthrope *n.* عدوّ للبشر addu lelbashar

misapplication *n.* سوء استعمال su' iste'mal

misapprehend *v.* يفهم غلط yefham ghalat

misapprehension *n.* سوء فهم su'e fahm

misappropriate *v.* يختلس yekhteles

misappropriation *n.* اختلاس ikhtilas

misbehave *v.* يتصرّف غلط yetsarraf ghalat

misbehaviour *n.* تصرّف غلط tasarruf ghalat

misbelief *n.* رأي غلط ra'e ghalat

miscalculate *v.* يحسب غلط yehsub ghalat

miscalculation *n.* حساب غلط hisab ghalat

miscall *v.* يتّصل غلط yettesel ghalat

miscarriage *n.* إجْهاض ijhad

miscarry *v.* تجْهِض tujhjd

miscellaneous *adj.* منوّع menawwa'

miscellany *n.* مُنوّعات munawwa'at

mischance *n.* حظ سيء hazz saye'

mischief *n.* أذى azah

mischievous *adj.* مأذي me'zi

misconceive *v.* يفهم غلط yefham ghalat

misconception *n.* سوء فهم su'e fahm

misconduct *n.* سوء تصرُّف su'e tasarruf

misconstrue *v.* يفسّر غلط yefasser ghalat

miscreant *n.* لئيم la'ym

misdeed *n.* ذنْب zanb

misdemeanour *n.* جنحة jenha

misdirect *v.* يتوه yetuh

misdirection *n.* توهان tawahan

miser *n.* بخيل bakhil

miserable *adj.* تعيس ta'is

miserly *adj.* بخيل bakhil

misery *n.* شقا shaqah

misfit *n.* سوء تغذية su'e taghzeyeh

misfortune *n.* مصيبة musibeh

misgive *v.* يشكّك yeshakkek

misgiving n. شَكّ shakk

misguide v. يتوّه yetawweh

mishap n. حظّ سيّء hazz saye'

misjudge v. يحكّم غلط yehkum ghalat

mislead v. يغلّط yeghallet

mismanagement n. سوء إدارة su'e idarah

mismatch v. لخبطة lakhbatah

misnomer n. اسم غلط esm ghalat

misplace v. يحط شي بالمكان الغلط yehett shi belmakan elghalat

misprint n. خطأ مطبعي khata' matba'e

misprint v. يغلط بالطباعة yeghlat belteba'ah

misrepresent v. يحرّف yeharref

misrule n. فوضى fawda

miss n. آنسة aniseh

miss n. خطأ khata'

miss v. يستفقد yestafqed

missile n. صاروخ sarukh

mission n. بعثة be'theh

missionary n. تبشيري tabshiri

missis, missus n. سيّدة sayyedeh

missive n. خطاب khitab

mist n. سحاب sahab

mistake n. غلط ghalat

mistake v. يغلط yeghlat

mister n. سيّد sayyed

mistreat v. يعامل بطريقة سيئة ye'amel betariqah saye'ah

mistress n. عشيقة ashiqah

mistrust n. شَكّ shakk

mistrust v. يشكّك yeshakkek

misty adj. ضبابي dababi

misunderstand v. يفهم غلط yefham ghalat

misunderstanding n. سوء فهم su'e fahm

misuse n. يستخدم غلط yestakhdem ghalat

misuse v. استخدام غلط istikhdam ghalat

mite n. سوسة suseh

mite n. عتّ ett

mitigate v. يسكّن yesakken

mitigation n. تسكين taskin

mix v. يخلط yekhlut

mixture n. خليط khalit

mnemonic adj. مساعد للذاكرة musa'ed lelzakerah

mnemonic n. رموز مختصرة rumuz mukhtasarah

moan v. يئنّ ye'en

moan n. آه ahh

moat n. خندق khandaq

moat v. يحفر خندق yehfur khandaq

mob n. رعاع ru'a'

mob v. يتجمّع الناس yetjamma' ennas

mobile adj. موبايل mubyl

mobility n. تنقلية tanaquleyyeh

mobilize v. يحرّك yeharrik

mock v. يقلّد yeqalled

mock adj. مزوّر mezawwar

mockery n. مهزلة mahzaleh

modality n. نمط namat

mode n. وضع wade'

model n. نوع nu'

model v. يصيغ yesigh
moderate adj. مُعتدِل me'tedel
moderate v. يُخَفِّف yekhaffef
moderation n. تَخْفِيف takhfif
modern adj. حَدِيث hadith
modernity n. حَداثة hadatheh
modernize v. يُجَدِّد yejadded
modernization n. تَجْدِيد tajdid
modest adj. مُتواضِع metwade'
modesty n. تَواضُع tawadu'
modicum n. جزء صغير jez' seghir
modification n. تَعْدِيل ta'dil
modify v. يعدّل ye'addel
module n. وحَدَة wehdeh
moil v. يكدح yekdah
moist adj. نَدْيان nadyan
moisten v. يندّي yenaddi
moisture n. نَداوَة nadaweh
molar n. ضِرْس ders
molar adj. طَاحِن tahin
molasses n. دِبس debs
mole n. شامة shameh
molecular adj. جزيئي juzy'e
molecule n. جزيء juzay'
molest v. يعاكس ye'akes
molestation n. مُعاكسة mu'akaseh
molten adj. مُمَيَّع mumayye'
mollusc n. رخوي rakhawi
moment n. لحْظَة lahzah
momentary adj. وقتي waqti
momentous adj. مصيري masiri
momentum n. عَزْم azm
monarch n. عاهِل a'hel

monarchy n. مَلَكِيَّة malakeyyeh
monastery n. صومعة suma'ah
monasticism n. رهبانية ruhbaneyyeh
Monday n. الأحَد elahad
monetary adj. نقّدي naqdi
money n. مصاري masari
monger n. بيّاع bayya'
mongoose n. نِمس nems
mongrel adj. هجين hajin
monitor n. شَاشة shasheh
monitor v. يراقب yeraqeb
monitory adj. تحذيري tahziri
monk n. راهب rahib
monkey n. قِرْد qerd
monochromatic adj. وحيد اللون wahid ellun
monocle n. نضّارة لعين وحدة naddarah la'eyn wehdeh
monocular adj. بعين وحدة be'yn wehdeh
monogamy n. الزواج بوحدة ezzwaj bewehdeh
monograph n. دِراسة diraseh
monogynous adj. متزوج وحدة metzawwej wehdeh
monologue n. مونولوج munuluj
monopolist n. محتكر mehteker
monopolize v. يحتكر yehteker
monopoly n. احتكار ihtikar
monotheism n. توحيد tawhid
monotheist n. موحد muwwahad
monotonous adj. روتيني rutini
monotony n. رتابة ratabeh

monsoon n. ريح موسميّة rih musemeyyeh

monster n. وحش wahsh

monstrous adj. متوحّش metwahhesh

monoestrous n. أحادي uhadi

month n. شهر shaher

monthly adj. شهري shahri

monthly adv. كل شهر kel shahr

monthly n. مجلّة شهريّة majalleh shahreyyeh

monument n. نصب تذكاري nasb tizkari

monumental adj. تذكاري tizkari

mood n. مزاج mazaj

moody adj. مزاجي mazaji

moon n. قمر qamar

moor n. سبخة sabkha

moor v. يربط السفينة بالحبل yerbut elsafineh belhabl

moorings n. مراسي السفن marasi elsufun

moot n. جذر jazr

mop n. مسح الأراضي maseh elaradi

mop v. يمسح الأراضي yemsah elaradi

mope v. يفكّر كتير yefakker ktir

moral adj. أخلاقي akhlaqi

morale n. معنويّات ma'naweyyat

moralist n. أستاذ أخلاق estaz akhlaq

morality n. أخلاقيّة akhlaqeyyeh

moralize v. يرفع معنويّات yerfa' ma'naweyyat

morbid adj. مرضي maradi

morbidity n. حالات مرضيّة halat maradeyyeh

more adj. أكتر aktar

more adv. وأكتر waktar

moreover adv. وأكتر من هيك waktar mn hik

morgue n. مشرحة mashraha

moribund adj. عم يحتضر am yehtudir

morning n. الصبح elsubh

moron n. مأفون ma'fun

morose adj. عابس a'bes

morphia n. مورفين murfin

morphine n. مورفين murfin

morphology n. صرف sarf

morrow n. بكرا bukrah

morse n. مورس murs

morsel n. فتفوتة fatfuteh

mortal adj. فتّاك fattak

mortal adj. بيموت beymut

mortal n. انسان insan

mortality n. عدد الوفيات adad elwafyyat

mortality n. وفاة wafat

mortar v. هاون hawn

mortgage n. رهن rahn

mortgage v. يرهن yerhun

mortgagee n. مانح الرهن manih elrahn

mortgagor n. صاحب الرهن sahib elrahn

mortify v. يصيب بالغنغرينا yesib belgangarina

mortuary *n.* مستودع الجثث mestawda' eljethath

mosaic *n.* موزاييك muzayyik

mosque *n.* مسجد masjid

mosquito *n.* بعوض ba'ud

moss *n.* طحلب tuhlub

most *adj.* أغلب aghlab

most *adv.* عالأغلب al'aghlab

most *n.* الأكثر elaktar

motel *n.* فندق صغير fenduq seghir

moth *n.* عتّ ett

mother *n.* إمّ emm

mother *v.* تولد tulad

motherhood *n.* أمومة umumeh

motherlike *adj.* متل الأمّ metl elemm

motherly *adj.* أمومي umumi

motif *n.* حافز hafez

motion *n.* حركة harakeh

motion *n.* تأشير ta'shir

motion *v.* يحرك yeharrik

motionless *adj.* ساكن saken

motivate *v.* يحفز yehaffez

motivation *n.* تحفيز tahfiz

motive *n.* دافع dafe'

motley *adj.* متنافر metnafir

motor *n.* موتور mutur

motor *v.* يسوق الموتور yesuq elmutur

motorist *n.* سائق الموتور sa'eq mutur

motto *n.* شعار she'ar

mould *n.* قالب qalib

mould *v.* يقولب yequlib

mould *n.* عفن afan

mouldy *adj.* معفّن me'affen

moult *v.* يبدلّ الريش yebaddel elrish

mound *n.* ساتر satir

mount *n.* ركبة rekbeh

mount *v.* يركب yerkab

mount *n.* منصب mansab

mountain *n.* جبل jabal

mountaineer *n.* تسلّق الجبال tasalluq eljabal

mountainous *adj.* جبلي jabali

mourn *v.* ينوح yenuh

mourner *n.* نواح nwah

mournful *n.* حزنان haznan

mourning *n.* حداد hidad

mouse *n.* فارة farah

moustache *n.* شوارب shawarib

mouth *n.* تمّ temm

mouth *v.* يحرّك شفايفه yeharrik shafayef

mouthful *n.* شرقة sharqah

movable *adj.* منقول manqul

movables *n.* أملاك منقولة amlak manquleh

move *n.* حركة harakeh

move *v.* يتحرّك yeteharrak

movement *n.* حركة harakeh

mover *n.* متحرّك meteharrek

movies *n.* أفلام aflam

mow *v.* يجزّ yejezz

much *a* كتير ktir

much *adv.* كتير ktir

mucilage *n.* صمغ samgh

muck *n.* زبل zabal

mucous *adj.* مخاطي mukhati

mucus *n.* مخطة makhtah

mud *n.* طين tyn

muddle *n.* تَشوُّش tashawwush

muddle *v.* يتشوش yetshawwash

muffle *v.* يحطّ خمار yehutt khimar

muffler *n.* خمار khimar

mug *n.* مغ القهوة mag elqahweh

muggy *adj.* مغمّ meghemm

mulberry *n.* توت tut

mule *n.* بابوج babuj

mulish *adj.* عنيد anid

mull *n.* تفكّر tafakkur

mull *v.* يتفكّر yetfakkar

mullah *n.* ملّا mullah

multifarious *adj.* متنوّع metnawwe'

multiform *n.* تعدّد الأشكال ta'addud elashkal

multilateral *adj.* متعدّد الأطراف met'added elatraf

multiple *adj.* مضاعف muda'af

multiple *n.* ضعف de'f

multiplex *adj.* تعددي ta'adudi

multiplicand *n.* مضروب ب madrub bi

multiplication *n.* عملية الضرب amaleyyt eldarb

multiplicity *n.* تعدديّة ta'addudeyyeh

multiply *v.* يضرب بالرياضيّات yedrub belryadeyyat

multitude *n.* جماهير jamahir

mum *n.* ماما mama

mumble *v.* يغمغم yeghamghem

mummy *n.* مامي mami

mummy *n.* مومياء mumya'

mumps *n.* أبو كعب abu ka'eb

munch *v.* ياكل بصوت yakul bsut

mundane *adj.* دنيوي denyawi

municipal *adj.* يخصّ البلديّة bykhuss elbaladeyyeh

municipality *n.* بلديّة baladeyyeh

munificent *adj.* سخي sakhi

munitions *n.* ذخيرة zakhirah

mural *adj.* جداري jidari

mural *n.* جداريّة jidareyyeh

murder *n.* جريمة قتل jarimet qatel

murder *v.* يقتل yeqtul

murderer *n.* قاتل qatil

murderous *adj.* سفّاح saffah

murmur *n.* خرير kharir

murmur *v.* يخرخر yekharkher

muscle *n.* عضلة adaleh

muscovite *n.* نخّار fakhkhar

muscular *adj.* عضلي adali

muse *v.* يوحي yuhi

muse *n.* وحي wahi

museum *n.* متحف metehaf

mush *n.* عصيدة asideh

mushroom *n.* فطر fetr

music *n.* موسيقا musiqa

musical *adj.* موسيقي musiqi

musician *n.* موسيقي musiqi

musk *n.* مسك misk

musket *n.* بارودة قصيرة barudeh seghireh

musketeer *n.* عسكري مسلّح askari mesallah

muslim *adj.* مسلم meslim

muslin *n.* موسلين muslin

must v. يلزم yelzam
must n. لزوم luzum
mustache n. شوارب shawarib
mustang n. حصان وحشى hisan wahshi
mustard n. خردَل khardal
muster v. يفصل yefsul
muster n. فصل fasel
musty adj. زنخ zenekh
mutation n. طفرة وراثيّة tefrah weratheyyeh
mutative adj. متحوّل metehawwel
mute adj. مكتوم maktum
mute n. كتم katm
mutilate v. يبتر yebtur
mutilation n. بتر batr
mutinous adj. عاصي a'si
mutiny n. عصيان عسكري esyan askari
mutiny v. يعصي ye'si
mutter v. يغمغم yeghamghem
mutton n. لحم غنم lahm ghanam
mutual adj. مشترك mushtarak
muzzle n. تكميم takmim
muzzle v. يحطّ كمّامة yehutt kammameh
my adj. إلى eli
myalgia n. وجع عضلات waja' adalat
myopia n. ضعف نظر de'f nazr
myopic adj. ضعيف النظر da'ef elnazar
myosis n. تضيّق الحدقة tadayyuq elhadaqah
myriad n. عدد كبير adad kbir

myriad adj. مابعدّ ma beyn'add
myrrh n. المرّ elmurr
myrtle n. آس aas
myself pron. لحالى lahali
mysterious adj. غامض ghamed
mystery n. غموض ghumud
mystic adj. متصوف metsawwef
mystic n. صوفيّ sufi
mysticism n. تصوّف tasawwuf
mystify v. يحيّر yehayyer
myth n. خُرافة khurafeh
mythical adj. خُرافي khurafi
mythological adj. أسطوري usturi
mythology n. علم الأساطير elm elasatir

N

nab v. يعتقل ye'teqel
nacre n. عرق اللولو erq elulu
nadir n. نظير nazir
nag n. قى naqq
nag v. ينق yenuqq
nagging adj. نقّاق naqqqaq
nagging n. قى naqq
nail n. أضفر udfur
nail n. مسمار mesmar
nail v. يثبّت بالمسمار yethabbet bel mesmar

naive adj. بَسيط basit
naivete n. بَساطة basatah
naivety n. بَراءَة bara'ah
naked adj. مكشِف mekashshif
name n. اسِم esm
name v. يسمّي yesammi
namely adv. بالاسم bel'ism
namesake n. تَسميَه ع اسم حدا tasmeyeh a ism hada
nanny n. مربيّة الولاد murabeyyet elwulad
nano n. نانو nanu
nanobiology n. علم النانو elm elnanu
nanochip n. رقاقة نانو ruqaqet elnanu
nanocircuitry n. دائرة النانو de'ret elnanu
nanoengineer n. مهندس النانو muhandes elnanu
nanohertz n. نانو هرتز nanu hertz
nanomechanics n. ميكانيك النانو mikanik elnanu
nanoparticle n. جزيئات النانو juzay'at elnanu
nanoplasma n. بلازما النانو blazma elnanu
nanotransistor n. مقاوم النانو muqawem elnanu
nap v. يرقُد yerqud
nap n. رقدِة raqdeh
nap n. زغبُر zughbur
nape n. قفا qafa
napkin n. محرمة mahrameh
narcissism n. نرجِسيّة narjeseyyeh

narcissus n. نرجِس narjes
narcosis n. تخدِير takhdir
narcotic n. بنج banj
narrate v. يروي قصّة yerwi qessah
narration n. رواية القصّة rewayet elqessah
narrative n. حِكاية hekayeh
narrative adj. روائي riwa'e
narrator n. راوي القَصّة rawi elqussah
narrow adj. ديِّق dayyeq
narrow v. يديِّق yedayyeq
nasal adj. أنفي anfi
nascent adj. حديث الولادة hadith elweladeh
nasty adj. بَذيء baze'
natal adj. خَلقِي khuluqi
natant adj. طافي tafi
nation n. أمّة ummeh
national adj. وطني watani
nationalism n. الوطنيّة elwataneyyeh
nationalist n. الوطني elwatani
nationality n. جنسيّة jinseyyeh
nationalization n. تأميم ta'mim
nationalize v. يأمِّم ya'ammem
native adj. محلّي mahalli
native n. أهل البلد ahel elbalad
nativity n. ميلاد milad
natural adj. طبيعي tabe'i
naturalist n. عالم الطبيعة a'lam eltabe'ah
naturalize v. يجنّس yejannes
naturally adv. أكيَد akid
nature n. طبيعة tabe'ah

naughty *adj.* مشاغب mushaghib

nausea *n.* لعية النفس la'yet elnafs

nautic(al) *adj.* بحري bahri

naval *adj.* بحري bahri

nave *n.* ساحة المسجد sahet elmasjid

navigable *adj.* ملاحي melahi

navigate *v.* يبحر yebhir

navigation *n.* إبحار ebhar

navigator *n.* بحّار bahhar

navy *n.* أسطول ustul

nay *adv.* لا ولو la wlu

near *adj.* قريب qarib

near *prep.* ناحك nahak

near *adv.* لناحك lanahak

near *v.* يقرّب yeqarreb

nearly *adv.* تقريباً taqryban

neat *adj.* أنيق aniq

nebula *n.* غمامة ghamameh

necessary *adj.* ضروري daruri

necessitate *v.* يتطلّب beyttallab

necessity *n.* ضرورة darurah

neck *n.* رقبة ruqyeh

necklace *n.* طوق tuq

necklet *n.* طوق tuq

necromancer *n.* عرّاف arraf

necropolis *n.* مدينة أموات madinet amwat

nectar *n.* رحيق rahiq

need *n.* حاجة hajeh

need *v.* يحتاج yehtaq

needful *adj.* لازم lazm

needle *n.* إبرة ibreh

needless *adj.* مو لازم mu lazm

needs *adv.* لوازم lawazm

needy *adj.* محتاج mehtaj

negate *v.* ينفي yenfi

nefarious *adj.* شرير sherrir

negation *n.* نفي nafi

negative *adj.* سلبي salbi

negative *n.* سالب salib

neglect *v.* يهمل yehmil

neglect *n.* إهمال ihmal

negligence *n.* سهو sahu

negligent *adj.* مهمل muhmil

negligible *adj.* مهمل muhmal

negotiable *adj.* يقبل التفاوض beyqbal eltafawud

negotiate *v.* يفاوض yefawed

nagotiation *n.* مفاوضة mufawadah

negotiator *n.* مفاوض mufawed

negress *n.* زنجيّة zenjeyyeh

negro *n.* زنجي zenji

neigh *v.* يصهل الحصان yesehal elhsan

neigh *n.* صهيل الحصان sahil elhasn

neighbour *n.* جار jar

neighbourhood *n.* جيرة jireh

neighbourly *adj.* ودّي weddi

neither *conj.* ولا wla

nemesis *n.* ثأر tha'r

neolithic *adj.* عتيق atiq

neon *n.* نيون nyun

nephew *n.* إبن أخ ibn akhkh

nepotism *n.* محسوبية mahsubeyyeh

Neptune *n.* نبتون nibtun

nerve *n.* عصب asab

nerve *n.* شجاعة shaja'ah

nerveless *adj.* خاير khayer

nervous *adj.* عصبي asabi

nescience *n.* جهل jahl

nest *n.* عش ushsh

nest *v.* يبني عش yebni ushsh

nether *adj.* سفلى sifli

nestle *v.* يحضن yehdun

nestling *n.* كتكوت katkut

net *n.* صافي safi

net *n.* شبكة shabakeh

net *v.* يصطاد بالشبكة yestad belshabakeh

net *adj.* صافي safi

nettle *n.* قُرّاص qurras

nettle *v.* يقرص yeqrus

network *n.* شبكة shabakeh

neurologist *n.* دكتور أعصاب duktur a'sab

neurology *n.* طب الأمراض العصبية tebb elamrad elmusta'seyeh

neurosis *n.* اضطراب عصبي ittirab asabi

neuter *adj.* محايد muhayd

neuter *n.* محايد muhayd

neutral *adj.* حيادي hyadi

neutralize *v.* يحيّد yehid

neutron *n.* نيوترون nyutrun

never *adv.* أبداً abadan

nevertheless *conj.* ومع هيك w ma' hik

new *adj.* جديد jdid

news *n.* أخبار akhbar

next *adj.* بعدا ba'da

next *adv.* ولبعدا wlaba'da

nib *n.* راس ras

nibble *v.* يعضّ ye'add

nibble *n.* عضّة addah

nice *adj.* لطيف latif

nicely *adv.* برقّة bereqqah

nicety *n.* إتقان itqan

niche *n.* محراب mehrab

nick *n.* فرضة fardah

nickel *n.* نيكل nikl

nickname *n.* لقب laqab

nickname *v.* يلقّب yelaqqeb

nicotine *n.* نيكوتين nikutin

niece *n.* بنت أخ bent akhkh

niggard *n.* بخيل bakhil

niggardly *adj.* بخيل bakhil

nigger *n.* زنجي zenji

nigh *adv.* تقريباً taqriban

nigh *prep.* عالتقريبي altaqribi

night *n.* ليل lyl

nightingale *n.* عندليب andalib

nightly *adv.* بالليل bellyl

nightmare *n.* كابوس kabus

nightie *n.* ليلة سعيدة leleh sa'ydeh

nihilism *n.* عَدَمية adameyyeh

nil *n.* صفر sefer

nimble *adj.* رشيق rashiq

nimbus *n.* غيم مطري ghim matari

nine *n.* الرقم 9 elraqm 9

nineteen *n.* الرقم 19 elraqm 19

nineteenth *adj.* التاسع عشر eltase' ashar

ninetieth *adj.* التسعينات eltis'yneyyat

ninth *adj.* التاسع eltase'

ninety *n.* الرقم 90 elraqm 90

nip *v.* يقرص yeqrus

nipple *n.* حلمة helmeh
nitrogen *n.* نتروجين nitrujin
no *n.* لا la
nobility *n.* النبلاء elnubala'
noble *adj.* نبيل nabil
noble *n.* ابن الحسب ibn elhasab
nobleman *n.* ابن الحسب ibn elhasab
nobody *pron.* ولا حدا wla hada
nocturnal *adj.* ليلي layli
nod *v.* يهز براسه yehezz brasuh
nod *n.* هز الرأس hazz elras
node *n.* عقدة uqdeh
noise *n.* عجقة ajqah
noisy *adj.* معجوق ma'juq
nomad *n.* بدوي badawi
nomadic *adj.* بدوي badawi
nomenclature *n.* تسمية tasmeyeh
nominal *adj.* إسمي esmi
nominate *v.* يرشح yerashsheh
nomination *n.* ترشيح tarshih
nominee *n.* مرشح merashshah
non-alignment *n.* عدم انحياز adam inhyaz
nonchalance *n.* فتور futur
nonchalant *adj.* فاتر fater
none *pron.* ولا حدا wla hada
none *adv.* لولا حدا la wla hada
nonentity *n.* عدم adam
nonetheless *adv.* ومع هيك w ma' hik
nonpareil *adj.* فريد farid
nonpareil *n.* فريد farid
nonplus *v.* يحير yehayyer
nonsense *n.* تفاهة tafahah

nonsensical *adj.* ماله معنى malu ma'nah
nook *n.* ركن rukn
noon *n.* ظهر zaher
noose *n.* عقدة حبل u'qdet habel
noose *v.* يعقد الحبل ye'qud elhabl
nor *conj.* ولا wla
norm *n.* عادة a'deh
normal *adj.* عادي a'di
normalcy *n.* وضع طبيعي wade' tabe'i
normalize *v.* يطبّع yetabbe'
normalization *n.* تطبيع tatbe'
north *n.* شمال shmal
north *adj.* شمالي shmali
north *adv.* عالشمال alshmal
northerly *adj.* شمالي shmali
northerly *adv.* عالشمال alshmal
northern *adj.* شمالي shmali
nose *n.* إنف enf
nose *v.* يحشر أنفه yehshur enfu
nosegay *n.* باقة صغيرة baqah seghireh
nosey *adj.* فضولي fuduli
nosy *adj.* فضولي fuduli
nostalgia *n.* حنين hanin
nostril *n.* منخار menkhar
nostrum *n.* دوا سري dwa serri
not *adv.* لا la
notability *n.* وجاهة wajaha
notable *adj.* من الأعيان mn ela'yan
notary *n.* كاتب عدل kateb adel
notation *n.* تسجيل tasjil

note n. ملاحظة mulahaza

note v. يلاحظ yelahez

noteworthy adj. يذكر yuzkar

nothing n. ولا شي wla shi

nothing adv. لولا شي la wla shi

notice n. بلاغ blagh

notice v. ينتبه yentebeh

notification n. تبليغ tabligh

notify v. يبلّغ yeballegh

notion n. انطباع شخصي inteba' shakhsi

notional adj. افتراضي iftiradi

notoriety n. سمعة سيّئة sem'ah sy'ah

notorious adj. مفضوح mafduh

notwithstanding prep. مع هيك ma' hik

notwithstanding adv. ومع هيك w ma' hik

nought n. صفر sefer

noun n. اسم esm

nourish v. يغذّي yeghazzi

nourishment n. تغذية taghzeyeh

novel adj. جديد jdid

novel n. رواية rwayeh

novelette n. قصّة قصيرة qessah qaserah

novelist n. روائي rewa'i

novelty n. جدّية jeddeyeh

November n. تشرين التاني tishrin ettani

novice n. مستجد mustajjed

now adv. حالا halan

nowhere adv. ولا مكان wla makan

noxious adj. مُضرّ muderr

nozzle n. بَزبوز bazbuz

nuance n. فرق صغير farq seghir

nubile adj. بالغ balegh

nuclear adj. نووي nawawi

nucleus n. نواة nawat

nude adj. عريان aryan

nude n. عرّي uri

nudity n. عرّي uri

nudge v. ينكز yenkuz

nugget n. نغيت nagit

nuisance n. مضايقة mudayakah

null adj. ملغي melghi

nullification n. إلغاء elgha'

nullify v. يلغي yelghi

numb adj. منمّل menammel

number n. رقم raqm

number v. يرقّم yeraqqem

numberless adj. مابينعدّ ma beyn'add

numeral adj. عددي adadi

numerator n. بسط bast

numerical adj. عددي adadi

numerous adj. كتير ktir

nun n. راهبة rahbeh

nunnery n. دير الراهبات dir elrahbat

nuptial adj. زواجي zawaji

nuptials n. عرس urs

nurse n. ممرضة mumareddah

nurse v. يمرّض yemarred

nursery n. حضانة hadaneh

nursery n. مشتَل mashtal

nurture n. حضانة hadaneh

nurture v. ياخد حضانة yakhud hadanet

nut n. جوزة juzeh

nut *v.* الجوز يجمع yejma' juz
nutmeg *n.* الطيب جوزة juzet eltib
nutrient *n.* أكل akel
nutrition *n.* تغذية taghzeyeh
nutritious *adj.* مغذي mughazzi
nutritive *adj.* مغذي mughazzi
nutty *adj.* بالبندق belbeduq
nuzzle *v.* إنفه يحك yehekk enfu
nylon *n.* نايلون naylun
nymph *n.* حورية hurreyyeh

O

oaf *n.* الخلقة مشوّه طفل tefl meshawwah elkhulqah
oak *n.* بلّوط ballut
oaktree *n.* البلّوط شجر shajar elballut
oar *n.* مجداف mejdaf
oarsman *n.* مجدّف mejaddef
oasis *n.* واحة wahah
oat *n.* شوفان shufan
oath *n.* يمين yamin
oatmeal *n.* الشوفان طحين tehin shufan
oatmeal *adj.* مطحون شوفان shufan matehun
obduction *n.* الجثّة تشريح tashrih eljeththeh
obduracy *n.* عناد enad
obdurate *adj.* عنيد anid

obedience *n.* طاعة ta'ah
obedient *adj.* مطيع mute'
obeisance *n.* سجود sejud
obesity *n.* سمنة semneh
obey *v.* يطيع yet'e
obituary *n.* نعوة na'weh
object *n.* شي shi
object *v.* يعارض ye'ared
objection *n.* اعتراض e'tirad
objectionable *adj.* مرفوض marfud
objective *n.* هدف hadaf
objective *adj.* موضوعي mawdu'e
oblation *n.* دبيحة dbiha
obligation *n.* إلتزام eltizam
obligatory *adj.* إلزامي elzami
oblige *v.* يلزم yelzm
oblique *adj.* مايل mayl
obliterate *v.* يطمس yetmus
obliteration *n.* طمس tams
oblivion *n.* نسيان nsyan
oblivious *adj.* النسيان كتير ktir elnsyan
oblong *adj.* مستطيلي mustatili
oblong *n.* مستطيل mustatil
obnoxious *adj.* كريه karih
obscene *adj.* فاجر fajer
obscenity *n.* فجور fujur
obscure *adj.* مستور mastur
obscure *v.* على يتستر yetsattar ala
obscurity *n.* تستّر tasattur
observance *n.* تقيّد taqyyed
observant *adj.* متقيّد metqayyed

observation *n.* مراقبة muraqabeh

observatory *n.* مَرْصَد marsad

observe *v.* يرصد yersud

obsess *v.* يِنهوِس yenhwes

obsession *n.* هوس hawas

obsolete *adj.* بليان balyan

obstacle *n.* عقبة aqabeh

obstetric *adj.* ولادي welladi

obstetrician *n.* دكتور توليدَ duktur tawlid

obstinacy *n.* مكابَرة mukabarah

obstinate *adj.* مكابِر mukaber

obstruct *v.* يصدّ yesudd

obstruction *n.* صدّ sadd

obstructive *adj.* مسدود masdud

obtain *v.* ياخد yakhud

obtainable *adj.* متوَفّر metwaffer

obvious *adj.* واضح wadeh

obviously *adv.* بوضوح bewuduh

occasion *n.* مناسِبة munasabeh

occasion *v.* يعمل مناسِبة ye'mul munasabeh

occasional *adj.* عرَضي aradi

occasionally *adv.* أحيانًا ahyanan

occident *n.* الغرب elgharb

occidental *adj.* غرْبي gharbi

occipital *n.* عظم القفا azem elqafa

occlude *v.* يِحبِس yehbus

occlusive *adj.* يِسدّ beysedd

occult *v.* يخفي yekhfi

occult *adj.* مخفي mekhfi

occupancy *n.* إشْغال eshghal

occupant *n.* ساكِن saken

occupation *n.* إشْغالَ eshghal

occupation *n.* مِهنة mehneh

occupier *n.* محتَلّ muhtall

occupy *v.* يحتلّ yehtall

occur *v.* يصير yesir

occurrence *n.* حدَث hadath

ocean *n.* محيط muhit

oceanic *adj.* محيطي muhiti

oceanographer n أخصائي محيطات akhussa'i muhitat

oceanology *n.* علم المحيطات elm elmuhitat

octagon *n.* متمَّن metamman

octangular *adj.* من 8 زوايا mn 8 zawayah

October *n.* تشْرين الأوَّل tishrin elawwal

octogenarian *n.* ثمانيني temanini

octogenarian *adj.* ثمانيني temanini

octopus *n.* أخطبوط akhtabut

octuple *adj.* تمان أضعاف tman ad'af

octuple *n.* تمان أضعاف tman ad'af

octuple *v.* يزيد 8 مرَّات yezid 8 marrat

ocular *adj.* بصَري basari

oculist *n.* دكتور عيون dektur eyun

odd *adj.* غريب gharib

odd *adj.* فرْدي fardi

oddity *n.* غرَابَة gharabeh

odds *n.* إحتِمال ihtimal

odious *adj.* مقرِف meqref

odium *n.* بُغْض bughed

odometer *n.* عدّاد السرعة addad elsur'ah

odontologist *n.* دكتور أسنان dektur asnan

odontology *n.* طبّ الأسنان tebb elasnan

odorous *adj.* ريحته طيّبة rehtu taybeh

odour *n.* عطر uter

offence *n.* ذنب zanb

offend *v.* يجرح بالحكي yejrah belhaki

offender *n.* مُذْنب muzneb

offensive *adj.* جارح jareh

offensive *adj.* هجومي hujumi

offensive *n.,* هجوم hujum

offer *v.* يعرض ye'rud

offer *n.* عرض ared

offering *n.* ضحيّة daheyyeh

office *n.* مكتب maktab

officer *n.* مسؤول mas'ul

official *adj.* رسمي rasmi

official *n.* موظف رسمي muwazzaf rasmi

officially *adv.* رسمياً rasmeyyan

officious *adj.* فضولي fuduli

offing *n.* يقرب yeqarreb

offset *v.* يوازن yewazen

offset *n.* موازنة muwazaneh

offshoot *n.* شعبة shu'beh

offspring *n.* سلالة sulaleh

often *adv.* عالغالب alghaleb

ogle *v.* يتطلّع تطليعة غراميّة yettala' tatle'ah gharameyyeh

ogle *n.* تطليعة غراميّة tatle'ah gharameyyeh

oil *n.* زيت zit

oil *n.* نفط neft

oil *v.* زيّت yezayyet

oilrig *n.* آلة تنقيب alet tanqib

oily *adj.* زيتي ziti

ointment *n.* مرْهم marham

okay *adj.* تمام tamam

okra *n.* بامية bamyeh

old *n.* كبير بالعمر kbir bel'umer

old *adj.* قديم qadim

oleaginous *adj.* زيتي ziti

olfactory *adj.* شمّي shammi

oligarchy *n.* حكم الأقليّة hekm elaqaleyyeh

olive *n.* زيت زيتون zit zitun

olympiad *n.* أولمبياد ulmbyad

omega *n.* أوميغا umega

omelette *n.* بيض مقلي beid meqli

omen *n.* نذير nazir

ominous *adj.* منحوس manhus

omission *n.* حذف hazef

omission *n.* سهو sahu

omit *v.* يحذف yehzuf

omnibus *n.* سيرفيس servis

omnipotent *adj.* قدير qadir

omnipresent *adj.* موجود في كل مكان mawjud fi kel makan

omniscient *adj.* العليم el'alim

on *prep.* على ala

once *adv.* أول ما awwal ma

oncogene n جين ورمي jiin warami

oncogenic *adj.* ورمي warami

oncologist n. أخصائي أورام
akhessa'ei awram

oncology n. علم الأورام elm
elawram

one n. الرقم 1 elraqm 1

one pron. أحادي uhadi

oneness n. وَحْدانِيَّة
wehdaneyyeh

onerous adj. مُتعب mut'ab

onion n. بصل basal

on-looker n. مشاهد mushahed

only adj. بس bas

only adv. وبس w bas

onomatology n. علم الأسماء elm
elasma'

onomatopoeia n. تقليد صوت
taqlid sut

onrush n. إنْطلاق intilaq

onset n. بداية bedayeh

onslaught n. كَرّ garr

ontogeny n. تطوّر الانسان
tatawur elinsan

ontological adj. وجودي wujudi

ontology n. علم الوجود elm
elwujud

onus n. حمْل heml

onward adj. قدّام qeddam

onwards adv. لقدّام laqeddam

ooze n. ترشيح tarshih

ooze v. يرشح yerashsheh

opacity n. كمدة kamdeh

opal n. عقيق aqiq

opaque adj. كامد kamed

open adj. مفتوح maftuh

open v. يفتح yeftah

opening n. فتحة fateha

openly adv. صراحة sarahah

opera n. أوبرا ubrah

operable adj. بينعملّه عمل جراحي
beyn'emellu amal jirahi

operate v. يعمل عمل جراحي
ye'mul amal jirahi

operation n. عمل جراحي amal
jirhai

operative adj. جراحي jirahi

operator n. مشغّل
mushaghghel

operetta n. أوبريت ubrit

opiate adj. منوّم menawwem

opiate n. دوا منوّم dwa
menawwem

opiate v. ينوّم yenawwem

opine v. يعبّر عن رأيه ye'abber an
ra'eyu

opinion n. رأي ra'i

opinionate v. يعاند ye'aned

opinionated adj. مستبدّ برأيه
mestabedd bera'yu

opinionless adj. ماله رأي malu
ra'i

opium n. أفيون afyun

opponent n. عدو adu

opportune adj. وقته waqtuh

opportunism n. وصوليّة
wusuleyyeh

opportunity n. فرصة fersah

oppose v. يعادي ye'adi

opposite adj. معاكس mu'akes

opposition n. تضارب tadarub

oppress v. يقمع yeqma'

oppression n. قمع qame'

oppressive adj. قمعي qame'i

oppressor n. طاغية tagheyh

opt v. يختار yekhtar

optic *adj.* بصري basari

optician *n.* نظاراتي nazarrati

optimism *n.* تفاؤُل tafa'ul

optimist *n.* متفائل metfa'el

optimistic *adj.* تفاؤُلي tafa'uli

optimum *n.* الأفضَل elafdal

optimum *adj.* أفضَل afdal

option *n.* خيار kheyar

optional *adj.* اختياري ikhtyari

opulence *n.* بحبوحة bahbuhah

opulent *adj.* ميسور maysur

oracle *n.* وحي wahi

oracular *adj.* نبوئي nebu'i

oral *adj.* شفهي shafahi

oral *adj.* فموي famwi

orally *adv.* شفهيا shafahyyan

orange *n.* برتقالة burtuqaleh

orange *adj.* لون برتقالي lun burtuqali

oration *n.* خطبة khutbeh

orator *n.* خطيب khatib

oratorical *adj.* خطابي khetabi

oratory *n.* مصلّى mesallah

orb *n.* مَدَار madar

orbit *n.* مَدَار madar

orbital *adj.* مَدَاري madari

orca *n.* الحوت القاتل elhut elqatel

orchard *n.* كرْم karam

orchestra *n.* أوركسترا urkestrah

orchestral *adj.* أوركِسْتِري urkestri

ordain *v.* يوجِب yujib

ordained *adj.* مَفروض mafrud

ordeal *n.* مصيبة musibeh

order *n.* أمر amer

order *v.* يأمُر ye'mur

orderly *adj.* مرَتّب merattab

orderly *n.* مساعد ممرض musa'ed mumarred

ordinance *n.* أمر إداري amer idari

ordinarily *adv.* بالعادة bel'adeh

ordinary *adj.* عادي a'di

ordnance *n.* مدفع حربي medfa' harbi

ore *n.* خام kham

organ *n.* عضو udu

organic *adj.* عضوي udwi

organism *n.* كائِن حي ka'en hayy

organization *n.* منظَّمة munazzameh

organize *v.* ينظِّم yenazzem

organza *n.* أوركانزا urkanzah

orgasm *n.* رجفة الجماع rajfet eljima'

orgasmic *adj.* لذّة الجماع lezzet eljima'

orgy *n.* عرْبَدة arbadeh

orient *n.* الشّرق elsharq

orient *v.* يوجّه yewajjeh

oriental *adj.* شرْقي sharqi

oriental *n.* الشرقي elsharqi

orientate *v.* يتوجه للشرق yetwajjah lelshareq

orientational *adj.* توجهي tawajjuhi

oriented *adj.* مُوجّه muwajjah

orifice *n.* فتحة fateha

origami *n.* أوريغامي urigami

origin *n.* منشأ mansha'

original *adj.* أصلي asli
original *n.* أصل asel
originality *n.* أصالة asaleh
originate *v.* يبتكر yebtekr
originator *n.* مبتكر mebteker
ornament *n.* زخرفة zakhrafeh
ornament *v.* يزخرف yezakhref
ornamental *adj.* مزخرف mezakhraf
ornamentation *n.* زينة zyneh
ornithologist *n.* عالم طيور a'lem tyur
ornithology *n.* علم الطيور elm eltyur
orphan *n.* يتيم yatim
orphan *v.* ييتم yeyattim
orphanage *n.* يتم yetem
orthodox *adj.* أرثوذكس arthuzuks
orthodoxy *n.* أرثوذكسية arthuzukseyyeh
orthograph *n.* تعامدية ta'amudeyyeh
orthographic *adj.* متعامد muta'amed
orthopaedics *n.* جراحة عظمية jiraha azmeyyeh
oscillate *v.* يذبذب yezabzeb
oscillation *n.* ذبذبة zabzabeh
oscillograph *n.* جهاز تسجيل الذبذبات jihaz tasjil elzabzat
oscillometric *adj.* ذبذبي zabzabi
oscilloscope *n.* رسّام الذبذبات rassam elzabzabat
osculant *adj.* لمسي lamsi
osculate *v.* يبوّس yebawwes

osmosis *n.* إرتشاح irtishah
osmose *v.* يرتشح yertesheh
ossify *v.* يتحوّل لعظم yetehawwal la'azm
ostensibility *n.* تكلّف takalluf
ostensible *adj.* متكلّف metekallef
ostensibly *adv.* بتكلّف betakalluf
ostension *n.* تأشير ta'shir
ostentation *n.* نفخة fakhfakhah
ostentatious *adj.* مبهرج mebahraj
ostracize *v.* يطرد yetrud
ostrich *n.* نعامة na'ameh
other *adj.* تاني tani
otherwise *adv.* وغير هيك w ghir hik
otherwise *conj.* والّا w ella
otherworld *n.* الغيب elghib
otherworldliness *n.* الغيبية elghebeyyeh
otoscope *n.* منظار الأذن menzar elezen
otter *n.* حيوان haywan
ottoman *n.* مسند masnad
ouch *int.* آخ aakh
ouch *n.* جوهرة jwharah
ought *v.* بيلزمه beylzamuh
ounce *n.* وقية weqeyyeh
our *pron.* إلنا elna
oust *v.* يخلع yekhla'
out *adv.* لبرّا labarrah
out *adj.* برّا barrah
out *prep.* من mn
outage *n.* عطل etel

outback n. منطقة نائية manteqa na'yeh

out-balance v. يرجّح yerajjeh

outbid v. يزايد بالمزاد yezayed belmazad

outbreak n. ثَوْرَة thawrah

outburst n. هيجان hayajan

outcast n. المَنبوذ elmanbuz

outcast adj. منبوذ manbuz

outcome n. مآل ma'al

outcry n. صياح syah

outdated adj. بطلان betlan

outdo v. يتغلّب yetghallab

outdoor adj. برّات البيت barrat elbit

outer adj. خارجي kharji

outfit n. لبس lebs

outfit v. يلبِّس yelabbes

outgrow v. يكبَر أكثر yekbar aktar

outhouse n. مرحاض خارجي merhad kharji

outing n. سفرَة safrah

outlandish adj. غَريب gharib

outlaw n. ملاحق mulahaq

outlaw v. يلاحِق yelaheq

outline n. تلخيص talkhis

outline v. يلخّص yelakhkhes

outlive v. يِعمِّر ye'ammer

outlook n. منظر manzr

outmoded adj. بطلان betlan

outnumber v. يزيد بالعدد yezid beladad

outpatient n. مَريض خارجي marid kharji

outpost n. مركز حدود markaz hdud

output n. مَردُود mardud

outrage n. فظاعة faza'ah

outrage v. يفظّع yefazze'

outright adv. بالتّمام beltamam

outright adj. تامّ tamm

outrun v. يتجنّب yetjannab

outset n. بداية bedayeh

outshine v. يغطّي على yeghatti ala

outside adj. برّاني barrani

outside n. سطح sateh

outside adv. لبرّا labarrah

outsider n. غَريب gharib

outsize adj. شاذّ shazz

outskirts n.pl. مشارف masharef

outspoken adj. صريح sarih

outstanding adj. معلّق me'allaq

outward adj. برّاني barrani

outward adv. لبرّا labarrah

outwards adv. لبرّا labarrah

outweigh v. يتقِل yetaqqel

outwit v. يغشّ yegheshsh

oval adj. بيضوي baydawi

ovary n. مبيض mabyad

ovation n. ترحيب tarhib

oven n. فرن fern

over prep. على ala

over adv. طول tul

over n. مفروغ منّه mafrugh mennu

overact v. يتصنّع yetsanna'

overall n. لبس الشغل lebs elsughul

overall adj. شامل shamel

overawe v. يخوّف yekhawwef

overboard *adv.* ع جنب a
janab

overburden *v.* يحمّله فوق طاقته
yehammluh fuq taqtuh

overcast *adj.* مغيّم meghayyem

overcharge *v.* يغلي سعر yeghalli
else'r

overcharge *n.* تغلاية سعر
teghlayt se'r

overcoat *n.* مانطو mantu

overcome *v.* يهزم yehzem

overdo *v.* يتجاوز الحدّ yetjawaz
elhadd

overdose *n.* جرعة زايدة jer'ah
zaydeh

overdose *v.* يعطي جرعة زايدة
ye'ti jer'ah zaydeh

overdraft *n.* سحب عالمكشوف
saheb almakshuf

overdraw *v.* يسحب عالمكشوف
yesehab almakshuf

overdue *adj.* متأخّر
met'akhkher

overhaul *v.* يرمّم yerammem

overhaul *n.* ترميم tarmim

overhear *v.* يسمع بالصدفة yesma'
belsudefeh

overjoyed *adj.* طاير من الفرح
tayer mn elfarah

overlap *v.* يتداخل yetdakhal

overlap *n.* تداخل tadakhul

overleaf *adv.* ع ظهر الصفحة a
zahr elsafha

overload *v.* يحمّل زيادة
yehammel zyadeh

overload *n.* تحميل زيادة tahmil
zyadeh

overlook *v.* يتغاضى yetghadah

overnight *adv.* طول الليل tul
ellil

overnight *adj.* ليلي layli

overrate *v.* يبالغ بتقدير yebalegh
betaqdir

overrule *v.* يفسخ yefsakh

overrun *v.t* يغزي yeghzi

oversee *v.* يراقب yeraqb

overseer *n.* مراقب muraqb

overshadow *v.* يحجب نور
yehjub nur

oversight *n.* مراقبة muraqabeh

overt *adj.* علني alani

overtake *v.* يتخطّى yetkhattah

overthrow *v.* ينقلب على
yenqeleb ala

overthrow *n.* انقلاب inqelab

overtime *adj.* إضافي edafi

overtime *n.* أجر إضافي ajer edafi

overture *n.* مفاتحة بالكلام
mufataha belkalam

overwhelm *v.* يستولي على
yestawli ala

overwork *v.* يتعب yet'eb

overwork *n.* ضغط شغل
daghet sughl

oviferous *adj.* بينتج بيض
beyntej beid

ovular *adj.* بيضي beidi

ovulate *v.* يبيّض yebeid

ovum *n.* بويضة buwaydah

owe *v.t* يصير مديون ل yesir
madyun la

owl *n.* بومة bumeh

own *adj.* إلنا elna

own *v.* يملك yemlik

owner *n.* مالك malik

ownership *n.* ملكيّة melkeyyeh

ox *n.* تور tur

oxcart *n.* عربایة بجرّها تور arabayeh bejerrha tur

oxidant *n.* مؤكسد mu'aksad

oxidate *v.* يأكسد ye'aksed

oxidation *n.* تأكسد ta'aksud

oxide *n.* صدأ sada'

oxyacid *n.* حمض أكسجيني hamd uksijini

oxygen *n.* أكسجين uksijin

oxygenate *v.* يأكسج ye'aksij

oxygenated *adj.* مأكسج me'aksaj

oxygenation *n.* أكْسَجة aksajeh

oyster *n.* محَارة maharah

oyster *adj.* صدفي sadafi

ozonation *n.* أوزنة uzaneh

ozone *n.* أوزون uzun

ozone layer *n.* طبقة الأوزون tabaqet eluzun

P

pace *n.* مشية mashyeh

pace *n.* إيقاع iqa'e

pace *v.* يتمشى yetmashshah

pacemaker *n.* قدوة qudweh

pacific *adj.* سلمي silmi

pacific *adj.* هادي hadi

pacifier *n.* المحيط الهادي elmuhit elhadi

pacifism *n.* سلميّة selmeyyeh

pacifist *n.* سلمي selmi

pacify *v.* يسايِر yesayer

pack *n.* حزمة hezmeh

pack *v.* يحزم yehzum

package *n.* حزمة hezmeh

package *n.* طرد tard

packet *n.* باكيت bakit

packing *n.* تعليب ta'lib

pact *n.* حلف helf

pad *n.* حشوة hashweh

pad *v.* يحشي yehshi

padding *n.* بطانة betaneh

paddle *v.* يجدّف yejaddef

paddle *n.* مجداف mejdaf

paddy *n.* رز مو مقشور rezz mu maqshur

paedologist *n.* أخصائي تربية akhessa'i tarbeyeh

paedology *n.* علم التربية elm eltarbeyeh

paedophiles *n.* شاذّ للأطفال shazz lelatfal

paedophilia *n.* الشذوذ للأطفال elshuzuz lelatfal

paedophiliac *n.* شذوذي للأطفال shuzuzi lelatfal

pagan *n.* الوثني elwathani

pagan *adj.* وثني wathani

paganism *n.* وثنية wathaneyyeh

page *n.* صفحة safha

page *n.* وصيف wasif

page *v.* يرقّم صفحات yeraqqim safhat

page *v.* يخدم yekhdum

pageant *n.* مَوْكِب mawkib
pageantry *n.* مهرجان mahrajan
pagoda *n.* معبد بطوابق ma'bad betawabeq
pail *n.* سِطل satel
pain *n.* وجع waja'
pain *v.* يوجع yewajje'
painful *adj.* بيوجع beywajje'
painstaking *adj.* مجتهد mejtehid
paint *n.* دهان dhan
paint *v.* يدهن yedhan
painter *n.* دهان dahhan
painting *n.* تدهين tadhin
painting *n.* رسم rasm
pair *n.* زوج zug
pair *v.* يجمع 2 سوا yejma' 2 sawa
pal *n.* صاحب sahib
palace *n.* قصر qasr
palanquin *n.* هودج hudaj
palatable *adj.* بيشهي beyshahhi
palatal *adj.* حنكي hanaki
palate *n.* حنك hanak
palatial *adj.* فخم fakhem
pale *n.* وتد watad
pale *adj.* باهت bahet
pale *v.* يبهت yebhat
paleness *n.* شحوب shuhub
palette *n.* لوحة ألوان lawhet alwan
palm *n.* كَفّ kaff
palm *n.* نخلة nakhleh
palm *v.* يخفي بكفه yekhfi bekaffuh
palmist *n.* قاري الكف qare' elkaff

palmistry *n.* قراية الكفّ qerayet elkaff
palpable *adj.* ملموس malmus
palpitate *v.* ينبض بسرعة yenbud beser'ah
palpitation *n.* نبض nabd
palsy *n.* شَلَل shalal
paltry *adj.* تافه tafeh
pamper *v.* يدلّع yedalle'
pamphlet *n.* منشور manshur
pamphleteer *n.* مؤلّف منشورات mu'allef manshurat
panacea *n.* دوا لكل الأمراض dwa lakel elamrad
pandemonium *n.* ضجّة dajjeh
pane *n.* لوح luh
panegyric *n.* مدح madh
panel *n.* لوحة luhah
panel *v.* يكسي بالألواح yeksi belalwah
pang *n.* غصّة ghassah
panic *n.* فزع faza'
panic *v.* يفزع yefazze'
panorama *n.* بانوراما banurama
pant *v.* يلهت yelhat
pant *n.* لهتة lahteh
pantaloon *n.* بنطلون bantalun
panther *n.* نمر nemer
pantomime *n.* ممثل صامت mumaththel samet
pantry *n.* بيت المونة beit elmuneh
papacy *n.* بابوية babaweyyeh
papal *adj.* بابوي babawi
paper *n.* ورقة waraqah
par *n.* معدّل me'addal

parable *n.* حكاية رمزيّة hekayeh ramzeyyeh

parachute *n.* باراشوت barashut

parachutist *n.* ظَلِّي mezalli

parade *n.* عرض عَسكري ard askari

parade *v.* يعمل عرض عسكري ye'mel ard askari

paradise *n.* جنّة janneh

paradox *n.* تَناقض tanaqud

paradoxical *adj.* متناقض metnaqed

paraffin *n.* كَاز kaz

paragon *n.* قِدْوة qudweh

paragraph *n.* فقرَة faqarah

parallel *adj.* متوازي metwazi

parallel *v.* يوازي yewazi

parallelism *n.* موازاة muwazat

parallelogram *n.* متوازي أضلاع metwazi eladla'

paralyse *v.* يِشِلّ yeshell

paralysis *n.* شلل shalal

paralytic *adj.* مَشلُول mashlul

paramount *n.* متفوِّق metfawweq

paramour *n.* عَشيق ashiq

paraphernalia *n. pl* جهيز jehiz

paraphrase *n.* شرح بطريقة تانية shareh betreqah tanyeh

paraphrase *v.* يشرح بطريقة تانية yeshrah betreqah tanyeh

parasite *n.* طفيلي tufayli

parcel *n.* طَرد tard

parcel *v.* يحطّ بالطرد yehutt beltard

parch *v.* يموت عطش yemut atash

pardon *v.* يصفَح yesfah

pardon *n.* صفَح safeh

pardonable *adj.* ممكن ينغفر mumken yenghefer

parent *n.* إب وأم abb w emm

parentage *n.* أبوة ubuwweh

parental *adj.* أبوي abawi

parenthesis *n.* قوسين qusin

parish *n.* أبرَشيّة abrasheyyeh

parity *n.* تَساوي tasawi

park *n.* حديقة hadiqah

park *v.* يصفّ سيارة yesuff sayyarah

parlance *n.* لهجة lahjeh

parley *n.* مؤتمر تفاوض mu'tamar tafawud

parley *v.* يتفاوض yetfawad

parliament *n.* مجلس الشعب majles elsha'eb

parliamentarian *n.* عضو مجلس الشعب udu majles elsha'eb

parliamentary *adj.* برلماني barlamani

parlour *n.* صالة الإستقبال salet elistiqbal

parole *n.* إخلاء سبيل بشروط ikhla' sabil beshrut

parole *v.* يخلي سبيل بشروط yekhli sabil beshrut

parricide *n.* قتل الأبّ qatl elabb

parrot *n.* ببغاء babagha'

parry *v.* يتفادى yetfadah

parry *n.* تفادي tafadi

parsley *n.* بقدونس baqdunes

parson *n.* كاهن kahen

part *n.* جزء jeze'

part *v.* يقسّم أجزاء yeqassem ajza'
partake *v.* يتقاسم yetqasm
partial *adj.* جزئي jeze'i
partial *adj.* متحيز metehayyez
partiality *n.* تحيز tahayyuz
participate *v.* يشارك yesharek
participant *n.* مشارك musharek
participation *n.* مُشاركة musharakeh
particle *n.* جزيئة juzay'ah
particular *adj.* تفصيلي tafsili
particular *n.* تفصيل tafsil
particularly *adv.* عالأخَص alakhass
partisan *n.* حزبي hizbi
partisan *adj.* حزبي hizbi
partition *n.* تقسيم taqsim
partition *v.* يقسم yeqassem
partner *n.* شريك shrik
partnership *n.* شراكة sharakeh
party *n.* حزب hezb
pass *v.* ينجح yenjah
pass *n.* نجاح najah
passage *n.* ممر mamarr
passenger *n.* مسافر mesafer
passion *n.* عاطفة a'tefeh
passionate *adj.* عاطفي a'tefi
passive *adj.* سلبي salbi
passport *n.* جواز سفر jawaz safar
past *adj.* مضى mada
past *n.* ماضي madi
paste *n.* معجون ma'jun
paste *n.* لزق lazq

paste *v.* يلزق yelzuq
pastel *adj.* ناعم na'em
pastel *n.* باستيل bastil
pastime *n.* تسلية tasleyeh
pastoral *adj.* ريفي rifi
pasture *n.* مرعى mar'ah
pasture *v.* يرعى بالمرعى yer'ah belmar'ah
patch *v.* يرقّع yeraqqe'
patch *n.* رقعة req'ah
patent *adj.* مسجل mesajjal
patent *n.* براءة إختراع bara'et ikhtera'
patent *v.* يسجّل براءة إختراع yesajjel bara'et ikhtera'
paternal *adj.* أبوي abawi
path *n.* طريق tariq
pathetic *adj.* بينشفق عليه beynshefeq aleh
pathos *n.* شَفقَة shafaqah
patience *n.* صبر sabr
patient *adj.* صبور sabur
patient *n.* مريض marid
patricide *n.* قتل الأب qatel elabb
patrimony *n.* ورثة werteh
patriot *n.* وطني watani
patriotic *adj.* وطني watani
partiotism *n.* وطنية wataneyyeh
patrol *v.* يدور بدورية yedur bedawreyyeh
patrol *n.* دورية dawreyyeh
patron *n.* راعي ra'i
patronage *n.* رعاية re'ayet
patronize *v.* يرعى yer'ah
pattern *n.* نموذج namuzaj

paucity *n.* قِلّة qelleh

pauper *n.* مُعدَم mu'dam

pause *n.* وقفة زغيرة waqfeh zeghereh

pause *v.* يوقّف شوي yewaqqef shway

pave *v.* يزفّت الطريق yezaffet eltariq

pavement *n.* تزفيت الطريق tazfit eltariq

pavilion *n.* جناح في معرض jnah fi ma'rad

paw *n.* مخلَب makhlab

paw *v.* يخرمش بالمخالب yekharmesh belmakhaleb

pay *v.* يدفع yedfa'

pay *n.* دفع dafe'

payable *adj.* لازم يندفع lazm yendefe'

payee *n.* مدفوع إله madfu' elu

payment *n.* دفعة daf'ah

pea *n.* بازلّا bazellah

peace *n.* سلام salam

peaceable *adj.* سلمي selmi

peaceful *adj.* مسالِم msalem

peach *n.* خوخ khukh

peacock *n.* طاووس tawwus

peahen *n.* طاووسة tawwuseh

peak *n.* قِمّة qemmeh

pear *n.* أجاص ajas

pearl *n.* لولو lulu

peasant *n.* فلّاح fallah

peasantry *n.* طبقة الفلاحين tabaqt elfallahin

pebble *n.* حصى hasah

peck *n.* مكيال mekyal

peck *v.* ينقر بمنقاره yenqur bemenqaruh

peculiar *adj.* مميَّز mumayyaz

peculiarity *n.* تميّز tamayyuz

pecuniary *adj.* نقدي naqdi

pedagogue *n.* مدرّس mudarres

pedagogy *n.* تربية tarbeyeh

pedal *n.* دوّاسة dawwaseh

pedal *v.* يدوس yedawwes

pedant *n.* متفلسف metfalsef

pedantic *n.* تفلسف tafalsuf

pedestal *n.* ركيزة rkizeh

pedestrian *n.* شخص ماشي shakhes mashi

pedigree *n.* أصيل asil

peel *v.* يقشر yeqshur

peel *n.* قشرة keshreh

peep *v.* يبصبص yebasbes

peep *n.* بصبصة basbasah

peer *n.* مثيل mathil

peerless *adj.* مالو مثيل malu mathil

peg *n.* وتَد watad

peg *v.* يثبّت سعر yethabbit se'er

peg *v.* يربط yerbut

pelf *n.* ثروة tharweh

pell-mell *adv.* بطيش betysh

pen *n.* قلم qalam

pen *n.* زريبة zrebeh

pen *v.* يكتب بالقلم yektub belqalam

penal *adj.* جنائي jina'i

penalize *v.* يعاقب ye'aqeb

penalty *n.* عقوبة uqubeh

pencil *n.* قلم رصاص qalam rsas

pencil v. يكتب بقلم رصاص
yektub beqalam rsas

pending adj. موقوف mawquf

pendulum n. رقّاص الساعة
raqqas elsa'ah

penetrate v. يخترق yekhteriq

penetration n. إختراق
ikhteraq

penis n. ذكره zakaruh

penniless adj. مُعْدم mu'dam

penny n. قرش qersh

pension n. راتب التقاعد ratib
eltaqa'ud

pension v. يحيل عالتقاعد yehil
leltaqa'ud

pensioner n. متقَاعد metqa'ed

pensive adj. مفَكّر mufakker

pentagon n. بيتاغون bentagun

peon n. حاجب hajeb

people n. ناس nas

people v. يجمع الناس yejma' nas

pepper n. بهار bhar

pepper v. يبهّر yebahher

per prep. حسب hasab

perambulator n. عربية الولاد
arabeyyt elwlad

perceive v. يحسّ yehess

perceive v. يفهم yefham

perceptible adj. محسوس mahsus

per cent adv. بالمية belmeyyeh

percentage n. نسبة مئويّة
nesbeh me'aweyyeh

perception n. حسّ hess

perceptive adj. فهيم fahim

perch n. سمك الفرخ samak
elfarkh

perennial adj. معمّر m'ammer

perennial n. نبات معمّر nabat
m'ammer

perfect adj. ممتاز mumtaz

perfect v. يتقن yetqn

perfection n. كمال kamal

perfidy n. غدر ghadr

perforate v. يخزّق yekhazzeq

perforce adv. بحكم الضرورة
behekm eldarurah

perform v. يأدّي ye'addi

performance n. أداء ada'

performer n. عازف azef

perfume n. برفان barfan

perfume v. يتبرفن yetbarfan

perhaps adv. بجوز bejuz

peril n. مجازفة mujazafeh

peril v. يجازف yejazef

perilous adj. مخطر mukhter

period n. فترة fatrah

periodical n. مجلّة دوريّة
majalleh dawreyyeh

periodical adj. دوري dawri

periphery n. محيط muhit

perish v. يفنى yefna

perishable adj. فاني fani

perjure v. يحلف كذب yehlef
kezb

perjury n. حلفان كذب helfan
kezb

permanence n. ديمومة
demumeh

permanent adj. دائم da'em

permissible adj. مسموح
masmuh

permission n. إذن ezn

permit v. يسمح yesmah

permit v. يأذن ye'zan

permit *n.* تَصْرِيح tasrih

permutation *n.* مبادلة mubadaleh

pernicious *adj.* خبيث khabith

perpendicular *adj.* عمودي amudi

perpendicular *n.* خط عمودي khatt amudi

perpetual *adj.* خالد khalid

perpetuate *v.* يُخَلِّد yekhalled

perplex *v.* يحيِّر yehayyer

perplexity *n.* حيرة hereh

persecute *v.* يجور على yejur ala

persecution *n.* ظلم zulm

perseverance *n.* مواظبة mwazabeh

persevere *v.* يواظب yewazeb

persist *v.* يلح yelehh

persist *n.* إلحاح elhah

persist *n.* دوام dawam

persistence *n.* إلحاح elhah

persistent *adj.* ضروري daruri

persistent *adj.* دايم daym

person *n.* شخص shakhes

personage *n.* شخصيّة بارزة shakhseyyeh barzeh

personal *adj.* شَخْصي shakhsi

personality *n.* شخصيّة shakhseyyeh

personification *n.* تجسيد tajsid

personify *v.* يجسّد yejassid

personnel *n.* شؤون الموظفين shu'un elmuwazafin

perspective *n.* مَنْظُور manzur

perspiration *n.* عَرَق araq

perspire *v.* يعرق ye'raq

persuade *v.* يقنع yeqne'

persuasion *n.* إقناع iqna'

pertain *v.* يخص yekhuss

pertinent *adj.* مربوط mazbut

perturb *v.* يشوّش yeshawwesh

perusal *n.* تَمَعُّن tama'un

peruse *v.* يتمعّن yetma'an

pervade *v.* ينتشر yentesher

perverse *adj.* منحرف menherf

perversion *n.* إنحراف inheraf

perversity *n.* شذوذ shuzuz

pervert *v.* ينحرف yenherif

pessimism *n.* تَشاؤم tasha'um

pessimist *n.* متشائم metsha'em

pessimistic *adj.* تشاؤمي tasha'umi

pest *n.* حشرة hasharah

pesticide *n.* مبيد حشرات mubid hasharat

pestilence *n.* وباء waba'

pet *n.* حيوان أليف haywan alif

pet *v.* يربّي حيوان أليف yerabbi haywan alif

petal *n.* بتلة bateleh

petition *n.* معروض ma'rud

petition *v.* يقدم معروض yeqaddem ma'rud

petitioner *n.* مقدّم المعروض muqaddem elma'rud

petrol *n.* بترول betrul

petroleum *n.* نفط naft

petticoat *n.* تنورة داخليّة tannurah dakhleyyeh

petty *adj.* طفيف tafif

petulance *n.* نَكَد nakad

petulant *adj.* نكدي nekadi

phalange *n.* عضمة الأصابع admet elasabe'

phalanx *n.* عضم الأصابع adem elasabe'

phallic *adj.* قضيبي qadibi

phallus *n.* قَضيب qadib

phantasmagoria *n.* أوهام awham

phantasmal *adj.* وهمي wahmi

phantom *n.* وهم wahm

pharmaceutic *adj.* صَيْدَلاني saydalani

pharmaceutical *adj.* صَيْدَلي saydali

pharmaceutist *n.* صَيْدَلاني saydalani

pharmacist *n.* صَيْدَلاني saydalani

pharmacy *n.* صيدليّة saydaleyyeh

phase *n.* مَرْحلة marhaleh

phenomenal *adj.* استثنائي istethna'i

phenomenon *n.* ظاهرة zaherah

phial *n.* قنّينة qanneneh

philander *n.* غزل ghazal

philander *v.* يغازل yeghazel

philanderer *n.* عاشق a'sheq

philanthropy *n.* إنْسانيّة insaneyyeh

philosopher *n.* فيلسوف faylasuf

philosophical *adj.* فلسفي falsafi

philosophy *n.* فلسفة falsafeh

phone *n.* تلفون telefun

phonetic *adj.* صوتي sawti

phonetics *n.* علم الصوتيّات elm elsawteyyet

phosphate *n.* فوسفات fusfat

phosphorus *n.* فوسفور fusfur

photo *n.* صورة surah

photograph *v.* صورة surah

photograph *n.* يلقط صورة yelqut surah

photographer *n.* مصوّر mesawwer

photographic *adj.* تصويري taswiri

photography *n.* تصويري taswiri

phrase *n.* عبارة ebarah

phrase *v.* يعبر ye'abber

phraseology *n.* صياغة syaghah

physic *n.* مسهل mesahhel

physic *v.* يعالج ye'alej

physical *adj.* جسدي jasadi

physical *adj.* محسوس mahsus

physician *n.* معالج mu'alej

physicist *n.* فيزيائي fizya'i

physics *n.* فَيزيا fizyah

physiognomy *n.* سحنة sehneh

physique *n.* كسم kasm

pianist *n.* عازف بيانو azef byanu

piano *n.* بيانو byanu

pick *v.* ينقّي yenaqqi

pick *n.* قطف qatf

picket *n.* اعتصام e'tisam

picket *v.* يعتصم ye'tesm

pickle *n.* مخلل mekhallal

pickle *v.* يخلل yekhallel

picnic *n.* سيران siran

picnic *v.* يتسيرن yetseran

pictorial *adj.* مصور mesawwer

picture *n.* صورة surah

185

picture v. يصوِّر yesawwer
picturesque adj. تصويري taswiri
piece n. قطعة qet'ah
piece v. يركِّب yerakkeb
pierce v. يثقُب yethqub
piercing n. ثقب thuqb
piercing adj. مخترق mekhterq
piety n. تقى tuqah
pig n. خنزير khinzir
pigeon n. حمامة hamameh
pigmy n. قزم qazam
pile n. كومة kumeh
pile v. يكوِّم yekawwem
piles n. بواسير bwasir
pilfer v. ينشل yenshul
pilgrim n. حجِّي hajji
pilgrimage n. حجّ hajj
pill n. حبّ habb
pillar n. عمود amud
pillow n. مخدّة mekhaddeh
pillow v. ينام عالمخدّة yenam almekhaddeh
pilot n. طيَّار tayyar
pilot v. يطيِّر yetayyer
pimple n. حبَّاية صغيرة habbayeh seghereh
pin n. دبوس dabbus
pin v. يشكّ بادبوس yeshekk bedabbus
pinch v. يقرص yeqrus
pine n. صنوبر sanubar
pine v. يضمر yedmur
pineapple n. أناناس ananas
pink n. لون وردي lun wardi
pink adj. وردي wardi
pinnacle n. ذروة zarweh

pioneer n. رائد rayed
pioneer v. يقود مجموعة yequd majmu'ah
pious adj. متديِّن metdayyen
pipe n. أنبوب unbub
pipe n. بربيج barbij
pipe n. غليون ghulyun
piquant adj. حدّ hadd
piracy n. قرصنة qarsaneh
pirate n. قرصان qursan
pirate v. يقرصن yeqarsen
pistol n. مسدّس musaddas
piston n. مكبس makbas
pit n. حفرة hufrah
pit v. يحفر yehfur
pitch n. زفت zeft
pitch v. يزفّت yezaffet
pitcher n. إبريق ebriq
pitcher n. كوز kuz
piteous adj. بستحقّ الشفقة beysteheqq elshafakah
pitfall n. مأزق ma'zeq
pitiable adj. بستحقّ الشفقة beysteheqq elshafakah
pitiful adj. تعيس ta'is
pitiless adj. عنيف afif
pitman n. عامل منجم a'mel manjam
pittance n. زيادة صغيرة zyadeh seghereh
pity n. شفقَة shafaqah
pity v. يشفق على yeshfuq ala
pivot n. مدار madar
pivot v. يدور حولى yedur hula
pixel n. بكسل bekasal
pizza n. بيتزا bitzah

pizzeria *n.* مطعم بيتزا mat'am betzah

placable *adj.* غَفُور ghafur

placate *v.* يسترضى yestardi

place *n.* مكان makan

place *v.* يحطّ بمكان yehutt bemakan

placebo *n.* دوا وهمي dwa wahmi

placement *n.* تحديد مستوى tahdid mestawah

placenta *n.* مشيمة mashimeh

placid *adj.* رَايق rayq

plague *adj.* منصاب بالطاعون mensab belta'un

plague *v.* طاعون ta'un

plain *adj.* صريح sarih

plain *n.* سهل sahl

plaintiff *n.* مدّعي medda'i

plan *n.* خطّة khuttah

plan *v.* يخطط yekhattet

plane *n.* سطح sateh

plane *v.* يسطّح yesatteh

plane *adj.* مسطّح msattah

plane *n.* طيارة tayyarah

planet *n.* كوكب kawkab

planetary *adj.* كوكبي kawkabi

plank *n.* لوح خشب luh khashab

plant *n.* زرعة zar'ah

plant *v.* يزرع yezra'

plantation *n.* زريعة zre'ah

plastic *n.* بلاستيك blastik

plastic *adj.* بلاستيكي blastiki

plaster *n.* لزقة جرح lazqet jerh

plaster *v.* يحطّ لزقة جرح yehutt lazqet jerh

plate *n.* صفيحة safiha

plate *n.* صحن sahn

plate *v.* يصفّح yesaffeh

plateau *n.* هضبة hadabeh

platinum *n.* البلاتين elblatin

platinum *adj.* بلاتيني blatini

platform *n.* منصّة manassah

platonic *adj.* عُذري uzri

platoon *n.* مفرزة mafrazeh

play *n.* مسرحيّة masraheyyeh

play *v.* يلعب yel'ab

playback *n.* إعادة e'adeh

playcard *n.* كرت اللعب kart le'b

player *n.* لاعب la'eb

playfield *n.* ملعب mal'ab

playful *adj.* لعوب la'ub

playground *n.* ملعب mal'ab

playhouse *n.* مسرح masrah

plea *n.* مرافعة murafa'ah

plead *v.* يترافع yetrafa'

pleader *n.* مرافع murafe'

pleasant *adj.* مفرِح mufreh

pleasantry *n.* مزحة mazhah

please *v.* يترجّى yetrajjah

please *adv.* رجاءً raja'

pleasure *n.* بسط bast

plebiscite *n.* إستفتاء istefta'

pledge *n.* رهن rahn

pledge *v.* يرهن yerhun

plenty *n.* كترة ketreh

plight *n.* محنة mehneh

plot *n.* حبكة habkeh

plot *v.* يحبك yehbuk

plough *n.* محراث mehrath

plough *v.* يحرث yehruth

ploughman *n.* حرّاث harrath

pluck *v.* ينتف yentuf

pluck *n.* نتف natf
plug *n.* قابِس qabes
plug *v.* يوصِل yewassel
plum *n.* خوخ khukh
plumber *n.* عامل صحّية a'mel seheyyeh
plunder *v.* ينهب yenhab
plunder *n.* نهب nahb
plunge *v.* يغمس yeghmus
plunge *n.* غمس ghams
plural *adj.* جمع jame'
plurality *n.* كثرة ketreh
plus *adj.* زِيادة zyadeh
plus *n.* زِيادة zyadeh
plush *adj.* مخملي mekhmali
plush *n.* مخمل mekhmal
plutonic *adj.* باطِني batni
plutonium *n.* بلوتونيوم blutunyum
pluvial *adj.* مطري matari
pluvial *n.* مطر غزير matar ghazir
pluviometer *n.* مقياس المطر meqyas elmatar
ply *v.* يجدِّل yejaddel
ply *n.* جدولة jadduleh
plyer *n.* جديلة jadeleh
pneuma *n.* روح ruh
pneumatic *adj.* روحي ruhi
pneumogastric *adj.* رئوي معدي re'awi ma'edi
pneumonia *n.* التهاب رئوي eltihab me'awi
pneumonic *adj.* رئوي re'awi
poach *v.* يسلق البيضة yesluq elbidah

poacher *n.* صيّاد بلا رخصة sayyad bla rukhsah
pocket *n.* جيب jib
pod *n.* قطيع qate'
podcast *n.* تدوين صوتي tadwin suwti
podcast *v.* يدوّن صوتيًّا yedawwen sutyyan
podcaster *n.* مدوِّن صوتي mdawwen sawti
podgy *adj.* قصير مدعبل qasir meda'bal
podium *n.* دكّة dekkeh
poem *n.* قصيدة qasideh
poesy *n.* شعر sha'er
poet *n.* شاعِر sha'er
poetaster *n.* ناظم أشعار nazem elasha'ar
poetess *n.* شاعِرة sha'erah
poetic *adj.* شعري she'ri
poetics *n.* شاعِرية sha'ereyyeh
poetry *n.* شعر she'ri
poignant *adj.* لادع lade'
point *n.* نقطة nuqtah
point *v.t.* يصوِّب yesawweb
pointed *adj.* مسنن msannan
pointedly *adv.* بشكل موجه beshaql mwajjah
pointedness n شكل مسنن beshakel msannan
pointless *adj.* تافه tafeh
poise *v.* يوازِن yewazin
poise *n.* توازن tawazun
poison *n.* سم samm
poison *v.* يسمِّم yesammem
poisonous *adj.* مسمِّم musammem

poke *v.* ينكز yenkuz

poke *n.* نكزة nakzeh

poker *n.* بوكر buker

polar *adj.* قطبي qetbi

polarity *n.* قطبية qetbeyyeh

polarize *v.* يستقطب yestaqteb

pole *n.* قطب qutb

polecat *n.* ابن عرس ibn ers

police *n.* شرطة shurtah

police *v.* يتطوّع بالشرطة yettawwa' belshurtah

policeman *n.* شرطي shurti

policy *n.* سياسة siyaseh

polish *v.* يلمّع yelamme'

polish *n.* تلميع talme'

polite *adj.* مأدّب me'addab

politeness *n.* أدب adab

politic *adj.* سياسي syasi

political *adj.* سياسي syasi

politician *n.* السياسي elsiyasi

politics *n.* علوم سياسية ulum siyaseyyeh

polity *n.* نظام حكم nizam hukm

poll *n.* إقتراع iqtera'

poll *v.* يقترع yeqtere'

pollen *n.* غبار الطلع ghubar eltal'

pollute *v.* يلوّث yelawweth

pollution *n.* تلوّث talawwuth

polo *n.* رياضة البولو riyadet elbulu

polyandry *n.* تعدّد الأزواج ta'addud elazwaj

polybutene *n.* بوليبتين bulebtin

polycentric *adj.* مراكزه كتيرة marakzuh ktireh

polycentrism *n.* كترة المراكز ketret elmarakez

polychrome *adj.* ألوانه كتيرة alwanuh ktireh

polyene *n.* بوليين bulyyin

polygamous *adj.* عنده أكتر من مرا andu akter mn marah

polygamy *n.* تعدّد الزوجات ta'addud elzawjat

polyglot *n.* تعدّد اللغات ta'addud ellughat

polyglot *adj.* لغاته كتيره lughatuh ktireh

polymath *n.* واسع المعرفة wase' elma'refeh

polymer *n.* بوليمر bulimer

polymerize *v.* يبلمر yebalmer

polytheism *n.* شرك sherk

polytheist *n.* مشرك meshrek

polytheistic *adj.* شركي sherki

pomp *n.* فخفخة fakhfakhah

pomposity *n.* نخامة fakhameh

pompous *adj.* متنطن metantan

pond *n.* بحرة bahrah

ponder *v.* يتأمل yet'ammal

pony *n.* حصان سباق hesan sibaq

poor *adj.* فقير faqir

pop *v.* يفرقع yefarqe'

pop *n.* فرقعة farqa'ah

pope *n.* البابا elbaba

poplar *n.* شجرة الحور shajaret elhur

poplin *n.* بوبلين bublyn

populace *n.* رعاع ru'a'

popular *adj.* مشهور mashehur

popularity *n.* شهرة shuhrah

popularize *v.* يشهر yeshehur

populate *v.* يسكّن yesakken

populate *v.* يأهّل ye'ahhel

population *n.* سكّان sukkan

populous *adj.* مسكون maskun

porcelain *n.* بورسلين bursalin

porch *n.* رواق rawaq

pore *n.* مسامة masameh

pork *n.* لحم خنزير lahm khanzir

porridge *n.* ثريد tharid

port *n.* مينا mina

portable *adj.* محمول mahmul

portage *n.* حمل heml

portal *n.* بوابة الكترونية bawabbéh elketruneyyeh

portend *v.* يبشّر yebashsher

porter *n.* حمّال hammal

portfolio *n.* إضبارة edbarah

portico *n.* رواق rawaq

portion *n.* حصّة hessah

portion *v.* يتحاصص yethasas

portrait *n.* رسمة شخص rasmet shakhes

portraiture *n.* فنّ رسم الأشخاص fann rasm elashkhas

portray *v.* يرسم بالكلام yersum belkalam

portrayal *n.* رسم بالكلام rasm belkalam

pose *v.* يعرض سؤال yer'ud su'al

pose *v.* يطرح موضوع yetrah mawdu'

pose *n.* وضعيّة wade'yyeh

position *n.* مكان makan

position *v.* يحطّ بمكان yehutt bemakan

positive *adj.* إيجابي ijabi

possess *v.* يملك yemluk

possession *n.* ملك melk

possibility *n.* إمكانيّة imkaneyyeh

possible *adj.* ممكن mumken

post *n.* بريد barid

post *v.* يبعت بالبريد yeb'at belbarid

post *n.* مكتب بريد maktab brid

post *n.* منصب mansib

post *adv.* بعداً ba'da

postage *n.* طوابع بريديّة tawabe' barideyyeh

postal *adj.* بريدي baridi

post-date *v.* يأخّر تاريخ ye'akhkher tarikh

poster *n.* لافتة lafteh

posterity *n.* ذريّة zareyyeh

postman *n.* ساعي البريد sa'i elbarid

postmaster *n.* مدير مكتب البريد mudir maktab elbarid

post-mortem *adj.* بعد الموت ba'ed elmut

post-mortem *n.* تشريح الجثّة tashrih eljiththeh

post-office *n.* مكتب البريد maktab brid

postpone *v.* يأجّل ye'ajjel

postponement *n.* تأجيل ta'jil

postscript *n.* تذييل tazyyil

posture *n.* قعدة qa'deh

pot *n.* نونيّة nuneyyeh

pot *v.* يقعد عالنونيّة yeq'ud al nuneyyeh

potash *n.* بوتاس butas

potassium *n.* بوتاسيوم
butasyum

potato *n.* بطاطا batata

potency *n.* فحُولِيَّة fhuleyyeh

potent *adj.* فحْل fahl

potential *adj.* محتمل
muhtamal

potential *n.* إحتماليّة
ihtimaleyyeh

potentiality *n.* إحتماليّة
ihtimaleyyeh

potter *n.* صانع الفخّار sane'
elfakhkhar

pottery *n.* صناعة الفخّار sina'et
elfakhkhar

pouch *n.* كِيس kis

poultry *n.* داجِن dajen

pounce *v.* ينقَضّ عَلى yenqadd
ala

pounce *n.* إنْقِضاض inqidad

pound *n.* لِيرة lirah

pound *v.* يدفِش yedfush

pour *v.* يصبّ yesubb

poverty *n.* فقر faqr

powder *n.* بودرة budrah

powder *v.* يطحن بودرة yetehan
budrah

power *n.* قوّة quwweh

powerful *adj.* قوي qawi

practicability *n.* عمليّة
amaleyyeh

practicable *adj.* عملي amali

practical *adj.* عملي amali

practically *adv.* بعمليّة
be'amaleyyeh

practice *n.* تمرين tamrin

practise *v.* يتمرّن yetmarran

practitioner *n.* متمرّن
metmarren

pragmatic *adj.* براغماتي
bragmati

pragmatism *n.* راغماتيّة
bragmateyyeh

praise *n.* مدح madh

praise *v.* يمدَح yemdah

praiseworthy *adj.* بيستاهل مدح
beystahel madh

pram *n.* عربيّة ولاد arabeyyt
wlad

prank *n.* مَقْلَب maqlab

prattle *v.* يبعبِع yeba'be'

prattle *n.* بعبعة ba'ba'ah

pray *v.* يصلّي yesalli

prayer *n.* صلاة salah

preach *v.* ينصح yensah

preacher *n.* ناصِح naseh

preamble *n.* تمهيد tamhid

precaution *n.* تحذير tahzir

precautionary *adj.* تحذيري
tahziri

precede *v.* يسبق yesbuq

precedence *n.* أسبقيّة
asbaqeyyeh

precedent *n.* أسْبَق asbaq

precept *n.* أمر amr

preceptor *n.* معلّم me'allem

precious *adj.* تقيل tqil

precis *n.* خلاصة khulasah

precise *n.* متقَن mutqan

precision *n.* إتقان itqan

preclude *v.* يحرم yehrum

precursor *n.* باكورة bakurah

predecessor *n.* سلف salaf

predestination *n.* القضاء والقدر
elqada' welqadar

predetermine *v.* يكتُب الله عليه
yektub Allah alyh

predicament *n.* طبقة tabaqah

predict *v.* يتنبّأ yetnabba'

prediction *n.* تنبّؤ tanabu'

predominance *n.* هيمنة
haymaneh

predominant *adj.* مهيمن
mehaymn

predominate *v.* يهيمن
yehaymn

pre-eminence *n.* تفوُّق
tafawwuq

pre-eminent *adj.* متفوِّق
metfawweq

preemptive *adj.* وقائي weqa'i

preen *n.* بروش brush

preen *v.* يفتخر ب yeftekher bi

preface *n.* ديباجة debajeh

preface *v.* يفتتح yefteteh

prefect *n.* تمام tamam

prefer *v.* يفضِّل yefaddel

preference *n.* تفضيل tafdil

preferential *adj.* مفضَّل
mufaddal

prefix *n.* سابقة sabqah

prefix *v.* يسبق بـ yesbuq bi

pregnancy *n.* حمل haml

pregnant *adj.* حامل hamil

prejudice *n.* تعصُّب ta'assub

prelate *n.* أسقُف usquf

preliminary *adj.* تمهيدي
tamhidi

prelude *n.* تمهيد tamhid

prelude *v.* يمهِّد yemahhed

premarital *adj.* قبل الزواج qabl
elzawaj

premature *adj.* بكِّير bakkir

premeditate *v.* يتأنّى yet'anna

premeditation *n.* تأنّي ta'ani

premier *adj.* أوّل awwal

premier *n.* رئيس الوزرا ra'is
elwuzarah

premiere *n.* عرض أوّل ared
awwal

premium *n.* إكراميّة
ikrameyyeh

premonition *n.* هاجس hajes

preoccupation *n.* إنْشغال
inshighal

preoccupy *v.* ينشغل yensheghel

preparation *n.* تجهيز tajhiz

preparatory *adj.* تجهيزي tajhizi

prepare *v.* يجهِّز yejahhiz

preponderance *n.* أرْجَحيّة
arjaheyyeh

preponderate *v.* يرجِّح yerajjeh

preposition *n.* حرف جر harf
jarr

prerequisite *adj.* ضرُوري
daruri

prerequisite *n.* شرْط shart

prerogative *n.* إمْتِياز imtyaz

prescience *n.* بصيرة basirah

prescribe *v.* يوصف علاج yusef
ilaj

prescription *n.* وصفة طبيّة
wasfeh tebeyyeh

presence *n.* حضور hudur

present *adj.* حاضر hader

present *n.* حاضر hader

present *n.* فعل مضارع fe'l mudare'

present *v.* يحضر yehdar

presentation *n.* عرض ared

presently *adv.* حاليًا halyan

preservation *n.* حفظ hefz

preservative *n.* مادّة حافظة maddeh hafzah

preservative *adj.* حافظ hafez

preserve *v.* يحفظ yehfaz

preserve *n.* كونسروة kunsurwah

preside *v.* يترأس yetra'as

president *n.* رئيس ra'is

presidential *adj.* رئاسي re'asi

press *v.* يضغط yedghat

press *n.* صحافة sahafeh

pressure *n.* ضغط daghet

pressurize *v.* يعدل الضغط ye'addel eldaghet

prestige *n.* برستيج bristij

prestigious *adj.* برستيجي bristiji

presume *v.* يتكبّر yetkabbar

presumption *n.* تكبّر takabbur

presuppose *v.* يفترض جدلا yefterd jadalan

presupposition *n.* إفتراض جدلي iftirad jadali

pretence *n.* تظاهر tazahur

pretend *v.* يتظاهر yetzahar

pretension *n.* حجّة hejjeh

pretentious *adj.* مغرور maghrur

pretext *n.* حجّة hejjeh

prettiness *n.* حلاوة halaweh

pretty *adj.* حلو helu

prevail *v.* ينتشر yentesher

prevalence *n.* إنتشار intishar

prevalent *adj.* منتشر mentesher

prevent *v.* يمنع yemna'

prevention *n.* منع mane'

preventive *adj.* وقائي weqa'i

previous *adj.* سابق sabeq

prey *n.* فريسة faryseh

prey *v.* يفترس yefteres

price *n.* سعر se'r

price *v.* يسعر yesa'er

prick *n.* شكّة shakkeh

prick *v.* يشكّ yeshekk

pride *n.* إعتزاز e'tizaz

pride *v.* يعتزّ ب ye'tazz bi

priest *n.* قسيس qassis

priestess *n.* قسيسة qassiseh

priesthood *n.* قسيسية qassiseyyeh

prima facie *adv.* بأوّل إنطباع be'awwal intiba'

primarily *adv.* بشكل أوّلي beshakel awwali

primary *adj.* أوّلي awwali

prime *v.* يملي yemalli

prime *adj.* أوّلي awwali

prime *n.* بداية bedayeh

primer *n.* فتيل ftil

primeval *adj.* بدائي beda'i

primitive *adj.* بدائي beda'i

prince *n.* أمير amir

princely *adj.* أميري amiri

princess *n.* أميرة amirah

principal *n.* مدير المدرسة mudir madraseh

principal *adj.* أصيل asil

principle *n.* مَبْدَأ mabda'

print *v.* يطبع yetba'

print *n.* طبع tabe'

printer *n.* طابعة tabe'ah

prior *adj.* ماضي madi

prior *n.* رئيس دير ra'is dir

prioress *n.* رئيسية دير ra'eset dir

priority *n.* أوْلوية awlaweyyeh

prison *n.* حبس habs

prisoner *n.* محبوس mahbus

privacy *n.* خصوصية khususeyyeh

private *adj.* خاص khass

privation *n.* حِرْمان hirman

privilege *n.* إمتياز imtyaz

prize *n.* جائزة ja'ezeh

prize *v.* يقدّر yeqadder

probability *n.* إمكانية imkaneyyeh

probable *adj.* ممكن mumken

probably *adv.* ممكن mumken

probation *n.* إختبار ikhtibar

probationer *n.* متمرّن metmarren

probe *v.* يجسّ yejess

probe *n.* جس jass

problem *n.* مشكلة meshkleh

problematic *adj.* مشكلجي meshkalji

procedure *n.* إجراء ijra'

proceed *v.* يكمّل yekammel

proceeding *n.* مرافعة murafa'ah

proceeds *n.* علَّات a'edat

process *n.* عملية amalyyeh

procession *n.* موْكب mawkeb

proclaim *v.* يصرّح yesarreh

proclamation *n.* تصريح tasrih

proclivity *n.* ميول myul

procrastinate *v.* يماطل yematel

procrastination *n.* مماطلة mumataleh

proctor *n.* مُراقب muraqb

proctor *v.* يراقب yeraqb

procure *v.* يدبّر yedabber

procurement *n.* تدبير tadbir

prodigal *adj.* صرِّيف sarrif

prodigality *n.* تبذير tabzir

produce *v.* يُنتِج yentej

produce *n.* مدْخول madkhul

product *n.* منتج muntaj

production *n.* إنتاج intaj

productive *adj.* إنتاجي intaji

productivity *n.* إنتاجية intajeyyeh

profane *adj.* مدنّس medannas

profane *v.* يدنّس yedannes

profess *v.* يعْتنق ye'teneq

profession *n.* مهنة mehneh

professional *adj.* مهني mehani

professor *n.* بروفسور brufesur

proficiency *n.* شطارة shatarah

proficient *adj.* شاطر shater

profile *n.* بروفايل brufyl

profit *n.* ربح rebh

profit *v.* يربح yerbah

profitable *adj.* ربحي rebhi

profiteer *n.* إستغْلالي isteghlali

profiteer *v.* يستغْل yesteghghel

profligacy *n.* إباحية ibaheyyeh

profligate *adj.* إباحي ibahi

profound *adj.* عميق amiq

profundity *n.* عمق umq

profuse *adj.* غزير ghazir

profusion *n.* غَزَارَة ghazarah

progeny *n.* نَسل nasl

programme *n.* برنامج bernamej

programme *v.* يبرمج yebarmej

progress *n.* إسْتِمرار istimrar

progress *v.* يستمر yestemerr

progressive *adj.* مستمر mestmerr

prohibit *v.* يحرّم yeharrem

prohibition *n.* تحريم tahrim

prohibitive *adj.* رادِع rade'

prohibitory *adj.* محرّم meharram

project *n.* مشروع mashru'

project *v.* يبرز yebruz

projectile *n.* قذيفة qazefeh

projectile *adj.* مقذوف maqzuf

projection *n.* إبراز ibraz

projector *n.* جهاز عرض jihaz ared

proliferate *v.* يتوالد yetwalad

proliferation *n.* توالد twalud

prolific *adj.* ولود walud

prolong *v.* مطوّل metawwal

prolongation *n.* تطويل tatwil

prominence *n.* بروز buruz

prominent *adj.* بارز barez

promise *n.* وعد wa'd

promise *v.* يوعد yu'id

promissory *adj.* إذني izni

promote *v.* يروّج yerawwej

promote *v.* يحفّز yehaffez

promotion *n.* ترويج إعلامي tarwij i'lami

promotion *n.* تحفيز tahfiz

prompt *adj.* سريع sari'

prompt *v.* يستدعي yested'i

prompter *n.* ملقّن mulaqqen

prone *adj.* منبطح menbeteh

pronoun *n.* ضمير damir

pronounce *v.* يلفظ yelfuz

pronunciation *n.* لفظ lafz

proof *n.* إثبات ithbat

proof *adj.* واقٍ waqi

prop *n.* داعِم da'em

prop *v.* يدعم yed'am

propaganda *n.* حرب دعائيّة harb de'aeyyeh

propagandist *n.* داعية da'eyh

propagate *v.* ينتشر yenteshr

propagation *n.* إنتشار intishar

propel *v.* يسيّر yesayyer

proper *adj.* مناسب munaseb

property *n.* عِقار aqar

prophecy *n.* نبوّة nebuwweh

prophesy *v.* يتكهّن yetkahhan

prophet *n.* نبي nabi

prophetic *adj.* نبوي nabawi

proportion *n.* تناسب tanasub

proportion *v.* يتناسب yetnasab

proportional *adj.* متناسب metnaseb

proportionate *adj.* متناسب metnaseb

proposal *n.* عرْض ared

propose *v.* يقترح yeqterh

proposition *n.* إقتراح iqterah

proprietary *adj.* مملوك mamluk

proprietor *n.* مالك malik

propriety *n.* ملك melk

prorogue *v.* يأجّل ye'ajjel

prose *n.* نثر nathr

prosecute *v.* يدّعي على yedde'i ala

prosecution *n.* الادّعاء eledde'a

prosecutor *n.* المدّعي العام
elmedde'i el'am

prosody *n.* عَرُوض arud

prospect *n.* تقْدِير taqdir

prospective *adj.* مُنتظَر
muntazar

prospectus *n.* نشرة اكتتاب
nashret iktitab

prosper *v.* يفلَح yeflah

prosperity *n.* رَفَاهِية
rafaheyyeh

prosperous *adj.* مَرْزُوق marzuq

prostitute *n.* قَحْبة qahbeh

prostitute *v.* يَزْني yezni

prostitution *n.* دعَارة da'arah

prostrate *adj.* مُتَسطّح
metsatteh

prostrate *v.* يَتسطَّح yetsattah

prostration *n.* سجُود sujud

protagonist *n.* بطَل batal

protect *v.* يحمي yehmi

protection *n.* حماية himayeh

protective *adj.* واقِ waqi

protector *n.* حَامي hami

protein *n.* بروتين brutin

protest *n.* إحتِجاج ihtijaj

protest *v.* يحتجّ yehtajj

protestation *n.* إحتِجاج ihtijaj

prototype *n.* نموذج أصلي
namuzaj asli

proud *adj.* فَخور fakhur

prove *v.* يبرهن yebarhn

proverb *n.* متَل matal

provide *v.* يقدّم yeqaddem

providence *n.* عناية enayeh

provident *adj.* مقتَصِد meqtesd

providential *adj.* محظوظ
mahzuz

province *n.* مُحَافَظَة muhafazah

provincial *adj.* إقليمي iqlimi

provincialism *n.* ريف rif

provision *n.* بَد band

provisional *adj.* مَشْروط
mashrut

proviso *n.* بند شرطي band
sharti

provocation *n.* إسْتِفْزَاز istefzaz

provocative *adj.* مستفز
mestefezz

provoke *v.* يسْتفزّ yestfezz

prowess *n.* شَجاعة shaja'ah

proximate *adj.* متقارب
metqareb

proximity *n.* تقَارب taqarub

proxy *n.* بروكسي bruksi

prude *n.* مُحتَشم mehteshm

prudence *n.* وقاية weqayh

prudent *adj.* متّزِن mettezn

prudential *adj.* وقائي weqa'i

prune *v.* يشذّب yeshazzeb

pry *v.* يتدخّل بشي مَابيخصّه
yetdakhkhal bshi ma
beykhussuh

pseudonym *n.* اسم مستعار ism
musta'ar

psyche *n.* نَفْس nafs

psychiatrist *n.* دكتور نفسي
dektur nafsi

psychiatry *n.* طب نفسي tebb
nafsi

psychic *adj.* نَفْسِي nafsi

psychologist *n.* دكتور نفسي
dektur nafsi

psychology n. علم النفس elm elnafs

psychopath n. مريض نفسي marid nafsi

psychosis n. مرض عقلي marad aqli

psychotherapy n. علاج نفسي elaj nafsi

puberty n. إحْتلام ihtilam

public adj. علني alani

public n. النّاس elnas

publication n. نشر nashr

publicity n. ترويج إعلامي tarwij l'ilami

publicize v. يعمّم ye'ammem

publish v. يَنْشر yenshur

publisher n. ناشر nasher

pudding n. بودينغ buding

puddle n. وحل wahl

puddle v. يعبّي وحل ye'abbi wahl

puerile adj. صبياني sibyani

puff n. قطع النَّفس qate' elnafas

puff v. ينقَطع نفسه yenqete' nafasuh

pull v. يسحب yesehab

pull n. سحب sahb

pulley n. بكَرة bakarah

pullover n. بلوزة صوف bluzeh suf

pulp n. لبّ lebb

pulp v. يشيل لبّ yeshil lebb

pulpit adj. منبر manbar

pulpy adj. لبّي lebbi

pulsate v. يخفُق yekhfuq

pulsation n. نبضة nabdah

pulse n. نبض nabd

pulse v. ينبض yenbud

pump n. ضخّ dakhkh

pump v. يضخ yedukhkh

pumpkin n. يقطين yaqtin

punch n. مبوكسة mbukaseh

punch v. يبوكس yebukes

punctual adj. دقيق بالوقت daqiq belwaqt

punctuality n. دقّة بالوقت deqqah belwaqt

punctuate v. يرقّم yeraqqem

punctuation n. ترقيم tarqim

puncture n. ثقب thuqb

puncture v. يثقب yethqub

pungency n. حدودية hududeyyeh

pungent adj. حدّ hadd

punish v. يعاقب ye'aqib

punishment n. عقوبة uqubeh

punitive adj. تأديبي ta'dibi

puny adj. قليل qalil

pupil n. طالب talib

puppet n. لعبة بالخيوطَ le'beh belkhyut

puppy n. جرو jaru

purblind n. ضعيف النظر da'ef nazar

purchase n. شري shereh

purchase v. يشتري yeshtri

pure a نقي naqi

purgation n. تطهير tatehir

purgative n. مسهِل musahhel

purgative adj. مسهِل musahhel

purge v. يسهِل الأمعاء yesahhel elam'a

purification n. تنقية tanqeyh

purify v. ينقّي yenaqqi

purist *n.* أصولي usuli
puritan *n.* بروتستانتي
  brutestanti
puritan *n.* متشدّد metshadded
puritanical *adj.* متشدّد
  metshadded
purity *n.* نقاوة naqaweh
purple *adj./n.* بنفسجي banafsaji
purport *n.* مضمون madmun
purport *v.* يدّعي yedde'i
purpose *n.* قصد qasd
purpose *v.* يقصد yeqsud
purposely *adv.* عن قصد an
  qasd
purr *n.* خَرْخَرَة kharkharah
purr *v.* يخرخر yekharkher
purse *n.* جزدان jezdan
pursuance *n.* متابعة metaba'ah
pursue *v.* يتّبع yettaba'
pursuit *n.* قضيّة مدنيّة qadeyyeh
  madaneyyeh
purview *n.* مدى madah
pus *n.* قيح qih
push *v.* يدفش yedfush
push *n.* دفشة dafsheh
put *v.* يحطّ yehutt
put *n.* حطّ hatt
puzzle *n.* تحزورة tahzurah
puzzle *v.* يحزر yehzur
pygmy *n.* قزم qazam
pyramid *n.* هرم haram
pyre *n.* محرقة mahraqah

quack *n.* بَطْبَطَة batbatah
quackery *n.* دجل dajal
quadrangle *n.* رباعي الزوايا
  ruba'i elzawaya
quadrangular *adj.* رباعي الزوايا
  ruba'i elzawaya
quadrilateral *n.* رباعي الأضلاع
  ruba'i eladla'
quadrilateral *adj.* رباعي
  الأضلاع ruba'i eladla'
quadruped *n.* حَيَوان haywan
quadruple *adj.* رباعي ruba'i
quadruple *v.* يزيد 4 مرّات yezid
  4 marrat
quail *n.* جبن jben
quaint *adj.* غريب gharib
quake *v.* يهتز yehtazz
quake *n.* هزّة hazzeh
qualification *n.* مؤهلات
  mu'ahelat
qualify *v.* يأهّل ye'ahhel
qualitative *adj.* نوعي naw'e
quality *n.* جودة judeh
quandary *n.* ورطة wartah
quantitative *adj.* كمّي kammi
quantity *n.* كمّيّة kameyyeh
quantum *n.* كمّ kamm
quarrel *n.* مشاكلة mshakaleh
quarrel *v.* يتشاكل yetshakal
quarrelsome *adj.* شرس sheres
quarry *n.* مقلع حجارة maqla'
  hajar

quarry v. يقلع حجارة yeqla' hajar

quarter n. ربع rebe'

quarter v. يقسم لرباع yeqassem larba'

quarterly adj. مرَّات 4 بالسنة belseneh 4 marrat

queen n. ملكة malikeh

queer adj. لوطي luti

queer v. يفسد yefsed

queer n. لوطي luti

quell v. يقمع yeqma'

quench v. يروي yerwi

query n. تساؤل tasa'ul

query v. يتساءل yetsa'al

quest n. طلب talab

quest v.t. يطلب yetelub

question n. سؤال su'al

question v. يستجوب yestajweb

questionable adj. مشبوه mashbuh

questionnaire n. إستطلاع istitla'

queue n. وقوف عالدور wuquf aldur

queue v. يقف بالدور yeqaf beldur

quibble n. فوغلة mzughaleh

quibble v. يزوغَل yezughel

quick adj. سريع sari'

quicksand n. ورطة wartah

quicksilver n. زئبق ze'baq

quiet adj. هادي hadi

quiet n. هدوء hudu'

quiet v.t. يسكّت yesakket

quilt n. لحيف lhef

quinine n. الكينين elkinin

quintessence n. خلاصة khulasah

quit v. يتروك yetruk

quite adv. كله kulluh

quiver n. رجفة rajfeh

quiver v. يرجف yerjuf

quixotic adj. خيالي khayali

quiz n. مذاكرة صغيرة muzakarah seghereh

quiz v. يعمل مذاكرة صغيرة ye'mel muzakarah seghereh

quorum n. نصاب قانوني nisab qanuni

quota n. حصّة hessah

quotation n. عرض سعر ared se'r

quote v. يعطي عرض سعر ye'ti ared se'r

quotient n. حصّة hessah

R

rabbi n. حبر يهودي hebr yahudi

rabbit n. أرنب arnab

rabble n. هج hamaj

rabies n. كلَب kalb

race n. سباق sibaq

race v. يتسابق yetsabaq

racial adj. عنصري unsuri

racialism n. عنصرية unsureyyeh

racism n. عنصرية unsureyyeh

racket n. بلص bals

racket *n.* مِضْرَب madrab

radiance *n.* رونق runaq

radiant *adj.* مشع mushe'

radiate *v.* يشع yeshe'

radiation *n.* إشْعَاع ish'a'

radical *adj.* متطرف metarref

radio *n.* راديو radyu

radiogram *n.* صورة أشعّة suret ashe'ah

radiography *n.* تَصْوِير بِالأَشعَّة taswir belashe'ah

radiolocation *n.* تحديد الموقع بالرادار tahdid mawqe' belradar

radiology *n.* علم الأشعّة elm elashe'a

radion *n.* راديون radyun

radiophone *n.* تلفون لاسلكي telfun lasilki

radish *n.* فجل fejl

radium *n.* راديوم radyum

radius *n.* شعَاع shu'a'

rag *n.* مساحة massahah

rag *v.* يمسح yemsah

raid *n.* غارة gharah

raid *v.* يغير yeghir

rail *n.* سكّة حديد sekkeh hadid

rail *v.* يسبّ yeṣebb

railing *n.* درابزون drabzun

railway *n.* سكّة حديد sekkeh hadid

rain *v.* تمطّر tematter

rain *n.* مطر matar

rainy *adj.* ممطر mumter

raise *v.* يربّي yerabbi

raisin *n.* زبيب zbib

rampant *adj.* مسْتَفْحِل mestafhel

rampant *adj.* متفشّي metfashshi

rampart *n.* ساتر sater

ranch *n.* مزْرعة mazra'ah

rancid *adj.* زنخ zenekh

rancidify *v.* يزنخ yezannekh

rancour *n.* حقد heqd

random *adj.* عشوائي ashwa'e

range *n.* نطاق netaq

rank *n.* درجة darajeh

ransack *v.* يفتّش yefattesh

ransom *n.* فدية fedyh

ransom *v.* يدفعَ فدية yedfa' fedyh

rape *n.* إغتصاب ightisab

rape *v.* يغتصب yeghteseb

rapid *adj.* سريع sari'

rapidity *n.* سرعة sur'ah

rapport *n.* علاقة حميمة alaqah hamimeyyeh

rare *adj.* نادر nader

rarefy *v.* يتخلخل yetkhalkhal

rarely *adv.* بالنادر belnader

rareness *n.* ندرة nedrah

rarity *n.* ندرة nedrah

rascal *n.* سافل safil

rash *adj.* نزق nezq

rash *n.* طفح جلدي tafah jeldi

rasp *n.* مبرد mebrad

rasp *v.* يبرد yebrud

raspberry *n.* توت احمر tut ahmar

raspy *adj.* خشن kheshn

rat *v.* يخلف بوعده yekhlef bewa'duh

rat *n.* جردون jardun

rate *v.* يثمّن yetammen

rate *n.* معدّل me'addal

ratify *v.* يصادق yesadeq

ratio *n.* نسبة nesbeh

ration *n.* تقتير taqtir

rational *adj.* عقلاني aqlani

rationale *n.* سبب جوهري sabab juhari

rationality *n.* عقلانيّة aqlaneyyeh

rationalize *v.* يبرّر yebarrer

ravage *n.* دمار damar

ravage *v.* يدمّر yedammer

rave *v.* يخرّف yekharref

raw *adj.* خام khamm

ray *n.* بصيص basis

razor *n.* شفرة حلاقة shafret hlaqah

reach *v.* يوصل yusel

react *v.* يتفاعل yetfa'al

reaction *n.* تفاعل tafa'ul

reactionary *adj.* تفاعلي tafa'uli

reactionist *n.* متفاعل metfa'el

reactivate *v.* ينشّط yenashshet

reactivation *n.* تنشيط tanshit

reactive *adj.* متفاعل metfa'el

reactor *n.* مفاعل mufa'el

read *v.t.* يَقرا yeqrah

reader *n.* قاري qari

readiness *n.* جهوزيّة juhuzeyyeh

ready *adj.* جاهز jahez

real *adj.* حقيقي haqiqi

reality *n.* حقيقة haqiqah

realization *n.* تحقيق tahqiq

realize *v.* يدرك yudrek

really *adv.* عنجد anjad

realtor *n.* دلّال dallal

realty *n.* عقار aqar

ream *n.* قعورة الكوسا qa'waret elkusah

ream *v.* يقعور الكوسا yeqa'wer elkusah

reamer *n.* مقوَرة meqwarah

reap *n.* حصاد hasad

reap *v.* يحصد yehsud

reaper *n.* حصّادة hassadeh

rear *adj.* خلفي khalfi

reason *n.* سبب sabab

reason *v.* يسبّب yesabbeb

reasonable *adj.* معقول ma'qul

rebate *n.* تخفيض takhfid

rebel *v.* يتمرّد yetmarrad

rebel *n.* متمرّد metmarred

rebellion *n.* تمرّد tamarrud

rebellious *adj.* متمرّد metmarred

recede *v.* ينتكس yentekes

receipt *n.* إستلام istelam

receive *v.* يستلم yestelm

receiver *n.* مستلم mestelm

recent *adj.* حالي hali

recently *adv.* حاليًا halyan

reception *n.* استقبال istiqbal

recess *n.* إستراحة istiraha

recession *n.* إنتكاس intikas

recipe *n.* وصفة wasfeh

recipient *n.* مستلم mestelm

reciprocal *adj.* متبادل mutbadal

reciprocate *v.* يتبادل yetbadal

recital *n.* تلاوة telaweh

recitation *n.* تلاوة telaweh

reckon v. يعدّ ye'edd	redemption n. استرجاع isterja'
reclaim v. يستصلح yestasleh	redouble v. يضاعف yeda'ef
reclamation n. إستصلاح istislah	redress v. يتلافى yetlafa
reclamation n. استرداد esterdad	redress n. تلافي talafi
recluse n. معتكف me'tekef	reduce v. يقلّل yeqallel
recognition n. إدراك idrak	reduction n. تقليل taqlil
recognize v. يدرك yedrek	redundance n. كثرة ketreh
recommend v. ينصح yensah	redundant adj. كثير ktir
recommendation n. نصائح nasa'eh	reel n. وشيعة washe'ah
recompense v. يكافي yekafi	reel v. يشغّل yeshaghghel
recompense n. مكافأة mukafa'ah	reel v. يلفّ yeleff
record v. يسجّل yesajjel	refer v. يؤشّر ye'ashsher
record n. سجلّ sejell	referee n. حكم hakam
recorder n. مسجّلة mesajjleh	reference n. إحالة ihaleh
recover v. يستردّ yestredd	referendum n. إستفتاء istefta'
recover v. يتعافى yet'afah	refine v. ينقّي yenaqqi
recovery n. إسترداد isterdad	refinement n. تنقية tanqyh
recruit n. توظيف tawzif	refinery n. مصفاية mesfayeh
recruit v. يوظّف yewazzef	reflect v. يعكس ye'kus
rectangle n. مستطيل mustatil	reflection n. إنعكاس in'ekas
rectangular adj. مستطيلي mustatili	reflective adj. إنعكاسي in'ekasi
rectification n. تصحيح tasehih	reflector n. عاكس a'kes
rectify v. يصحّح yesahheh	reflex n. منعكس mun'akas
rectum n. المستقيم elmustaqim	reflex adj. منعكس mun'akas
recur v. يكرّر yekarrer	reflexive adj. إنعكاسي in'ekasi
recurrence n. تكرار tekrar	reform v. يصلح yesalleh
recurrent adj. مكرّر mukarrar	reform n. إصلاح islah
red adj. أحمر ahmar	reformation n. تصحيح tasehih
red n. لون أحمر lun ahmar	reformatory n. سجن أحداث sejn ahdath
redden v. يحمّر yehammer	reformatory adj. تصحيحي tasehihi
reddish adj. محمر mehmarr	reformer n. مُصلح musleh
redeem v. يسترجع yestarje'	refrain v. يتجنّب yetjannab
	refrain n. تجنّب tajannub
	refresh v. ينعش yen'esh
	refreshment n. إنعاش in'ash

refrigerate v. يجمّد yejammed
refrigeration n. تجميد tajmid
refrigerator n. فريزر frizar
refuge n. ملجأ malja'
refugee n. لاجئ laje'
refulgence n. لمعة lam'ah
refulgent adj. لميع lamme'
refund v. يرجّع المصاري yerjje' elmasari
refund n. ترجيع المصاري tarje' elmasari
refusal n. رفض rafd
refuse v. يرفض yerfud
refutation n. تجريح tajrih
refute v. يجرّح yejarreh
regal adj. ملكي malaki
regard v. يعتبر ye'tebr
regard n. إعتبار e'tibar
regenerate v. يجدّد yejadded
regeneration n. تجديد tajdid
regicide n. قتل الملك qatl elmalik
regime n. نظام الحكم nizam elhukm
regiment n. فوج fuj
region n. إقليم eqlim
regional adj. إقليمي eqlimi
register n. سجلّ sejell
register v. يسجّل yesajjel
registrar n. أمين السجلّات amin elsejellat
registration n. تسجيل tasjil
registry n. السجلّات elsejellat
regret v. يندم yendam
regret n. ندم nadam
regular adj. نظامي nizami
regularity n. إنْتظام intizam

regulate v. ينظّم yenazzem
regulation n. إنظيمة anzemeh
regulator n. منظّم munazzam
rehabilitate v. يردّ إعتبار yerudd e'tibar
rehabilitation n. رد الإعتبار radd ele'tibar
rehearsal n. بروفة brufah
rehearse v. يعمل بروفة ye'mel brufah
reign v. يتحكّم yetehakkam
reign n. حكم hukm
reimburse v. يسدّ yesedd
reimbursement n. سداد sadad
rein n. رسن rasan
reinforce v. يعزّز ye'azzez
reinforcement n. تعزيز ta'ziz
reinstate v. يرجّع لمنصب سابق yerajje' lamanseb sabeq
reinstatement n. ترجيع لمنصب سابق tarje' lamanseb sabeq
reiterate v. يكرّر yekarrer
reiteration n. تكرار tekrar
reject v. يرفض yerfud
rejection n. رفض rafd
rejoinder n. رد سريع radd sari'
rejuvenate v. يرجّع شباب yerja' shabab
rejuvenation n. تجديد tajdid
relapse v. ينتكس yentekes
relapse n. نكسة nakseh
relation n. علاقة alaqah
relative adj. نسبي nisbi'
relax v. يرتاح yertah
relaxation n. راحة rahah
release v. يحرّر yeharrer
release n. تحرير tahrir

relent v. يحنّ على yehenn ala
relentless adj. عنيد anid
reliable adj. موثوق mawthuq
reliance n. ثقة theqah
relic n. بقايا الجثّة baqayah eljeththeh
relief n. تَسكين taskin
relief n. نجَدة najdeh
relieve v. يسكّنَ yesakken
religion n. دين din
religious adj. ديّن dayyen
relinquish v. يترك yetruk
relish v. يتمتّع ب yetmatta' bi
relish n. تمتّع ب tamattu' bi
reluctance n. نفور nufur
reluctant adj. نافر nafer
rely v. يعتمد على ye'temed ala
remain v. يبقى yebqa
remainder n. فضلة fadleh
remains n. آثار athar
remark n. إشارة esharah
remark v. يؤشر ye'ashsher
remarkable adj. ملحوظ malhuz
remedial adj. علاجي elaji
remedy n. دوا dwa
remedy v. يداوي yedawi
remember v. يتذكّر yetzakkar
remembrance n. غشاء ghisha'
remind v. يذكّر yezakker
reminder n. تنبيه tanbih
remission n. إعفاء e'fa'
remit v. يعفي ye'fi
remit v. يبعت حوالة yeb'at hwaleh
remittance n. تَحويل tahwil
remorse n. عتاب etab

remote adj. بعيد be'yd
removable adj. متحرّك meteharrek
removal n. تحريك tahrik
remove v. يحرّك yeharrek
remunerate v. يعوّض ye'awwed
remuneration n. تعويض ta'wid
remunerative adj. تعويضي ta'widi
renaissance n. نهَضة nahdah
render v. يحيل yehil
rendezvous n. مجلس majles
renew v. يجدّد yejadded
renewal n. تجديد tajdid
renounce v. يرتدّ yertadd
renown n. صيت sit
renowned adj. اجار a'jar
rent n. أجار a'jar
rent v. يستأجر yesta'jer
renunciation n. إنكار inkar
repair v. يصلح yesalleh
repair n. تصليح taslih
repairable adj. بيتصلّح beytsallah
repartee n. سرعة بديهة ser'et badiha
repay v. يسدّ yesedd
repayment n. سداد sadad
repeal v. يفسخ yefsakh
repeal n. فسخ faskh
repeat v. يعيد ye'id
repel v. يتمرّد yetmarrad
repellent adj. متمرّد metmarred
repellent n. متمرّد metmarred
repent v. يتوب yetub

repentance *n.* توبة tubeh

repentant *adj.* نَدْمَان nadman

repercussion *n.* مضاعفات muda'afat

repetition *n.* تكرار tekrar

replace *v.* يَستبدل yestabdel

replacement *n.* استبدال istebdal

replenish *v.* يستكمل yestakmil

replete *adj.* طفحان tafhan

replica *n.* نسخة طبق الأصل neskhah tebq elasel

reply *v.* يرد yerdd

reply *n.* رد radd

report *v.* يبلغ yeballegh

report *n.* تقرير taqrir

reporter *n.* مراسل murasel

repository *n.* مخزن makhzan

repress *v.* يقمع yeqma'

repression *n.* قمع qame'

reprimand *n.* لوم lum

reprimand *v.* يلوم yelum

reproduce *v.* يولد yulad

reproduce *v.* ينسخ yensakh

reproduction *n.* ولادة weladeh

reproduction *n.* نسخ nasekh

reptile *n.* زواحف zwahef

republic *n.* جمهورية jemhureyyeh

republican *adj.* جمهوري jemhuri

republican *n.* جمهوري jemhuri

repudiate *v.* يتبرا yetbarrah

repudiation *n.* تبري tabarri

repugnance *n.* مقت maqt

repugnant *adj.* كريه karih

repulse *v.* يصد yesudd

repulse *n.* صد sadd

repulsion *n.* اشمئزاز ishme'zaz

repulsive *adj.* مقرف muqref

reputation *n.* شهرة shuhrah

repute *v.* يشتهر yeshteher

repute *n.* شهرة shuhrah

request *v.* يطلب yetlub

request *n.* طلب talab

requiem *n.* قداس qaddas

require *v.* يتطلب yetallab

requirement *n.* شرط shart

rescue *v.* ينقذ yenqez

rescue *n.* إنقاذ inqaz

research *v.* يبحث yebhath

research *n.* بحث bahth

resemblance *n.* تشابه tashabuh

resemble *v.* يشبه yeshbah

resent *v.* يتدايق yetdayaq

resentment *n.* مدايقة medayaqah

reservation *n.* حفظ hefz

reserve *v.* يحفظ yehfaz

reservoir *n.* صهريج sahrij

reside *v.* يسكن yeskun

residence *n.* سكن sakan

resident *adj.* ساكن sakin

resident *n.* ساكن sakin

residual *adj.* زايد zayd

residue *n.* تفل tefl

resign *v.* يستقيل yestqil

resignation *n.* إستقالة estiqaleh

resist *v.* يقاوم yeqawm

resistance *n.* مقاومة muqawameh

resistant *adj.* مقاومة muqawameh

resolute *adj.* رايد rayd

resolution *n.* قرار qarar

resolve *v.* يقرّر yeqarrer

resonance *n.* رنين ranin

resonant *adj.* رنّان rannan

resort *v.* يلجأ yelja'

resort *n.* ملجئ malja'

resound *v.* يدوي yadawi

resource *n.* مورد mawred

resourceful *adj.* داهية dahyh

respect *v.* يحترم yehterm

respect *n.* إحترام ihteram

respectful *adj.* محترم muhtaram

respective *adj.* خصوصي khususi

respiration *n.* تنفّس tanaffus

respire *v.* يتنفّس yetnaffas

resplendent *adj.* نيّر nayyer

respond *v.* يجاوب yejaweb

respondent *n.* مدّعى عليه mudda'ah alih

response *n.* جواب jawab

responsibility *n.* مسؤولية mas'uleyyeh

responsible *adj.* مسؤول mas'ul

rest *v.* يرتاح yertah

rest *n.* راحة rahah

restaurant *n.* مطعم mat'am

restoration *n.* ترميم tarmim

restoration *n.* استرجاع esterja'

restore *v.* يرمّم yerammem

restore *v.* يسترجع yestarje'

restrain *v.* يردع yerda'

restrict *v.* يقيّد yeqayyed

restriction *n.* تقييد taqyyed

restrictive *adj.* مقيّد meqayyad

result *v.* ينتج yentij

result *n.* نتيجة natijeh

resume *v.* يكمّل yekammel

resume *n.* سيرة ذاتية sireh zateyyeh

resumption *n.* إكمال ikmal

resurgence *n.* نهضة nahdah

retail *v.* يبيع بالمفرق yebe' belmefarraq

retail *n.* بيع مفرق be' belmefarraq

retail *adv.* بالمفرق belmefarraq

retail *adj.* مفرّق mefarraq

retailer *n.* بيّاع مفرق byya' mefarraq

retain *v.* يحتفظ yehtefez

retaliate *v.* ياخد بالتّار yakhud beltar

retaliation *n.* أخذ بالتّار akhed beltar

retard *v.* يبطّئ yebatte'

retardation *n.* تبطيئ tabte'

retention *n.* حبس habs

retentive *adj.* احتفاظي ihtifazi

reticence *n.* تكتّم takattum

reticent *adj.* كتوم katum

retina *n.* شبكية العين shabakeyyet eleyn

retinue *n.* حاشية hashyh

retire *v.* يتقاعد yetqa'ad

retirement *n.* تقاعد taqa'ud

retouch *v.* ينقّح yenaqqeh

retrace *v.* يرجع من محل ماأجى yerja' mn mahal ma eja

retreat *v.* ينسحب yenseheb

retrench *v.* يحفر خندق yehfur khandaq

retrenchment n. حفر خندق hafr khandaq

retrieve v. يسترجع yestarje'

return v. يرجع من محل ماأجى yerja' mn mahal ma eja

return n. رجعة raj'ah

revelation n. إفْشاء ifsha'

revelry n. عرْبدة arbadeh

revenge v. ينتقم yentqem

revenge n. إنتقام intiqam

revengeful adj. إنتقامي intiqami

revenue n. عائدات a'eddat

revere v. يحترم yehterm

reverence n. إجْتِرام ehtiram

reverend adj. محترم muhtaram

reverent adj. صالح salih

reverie n. حلْم يقظة helm yaqazah

reversal n. عكْس akes

reverse adj. عكْسي aksi

reverse n. عكْس akes

reverse v. يعكس ye'kus

reversible adj. قلّاب qallab

revert v. يتراجع yetraja'

review v. يراجع yeraje'

review n. مراجعة muraja'ah

revise v. يفحص yefhas

revise v. يغيِر yeghayyer

revision n. فحص fahs

revision n. تغيِير taghyyer

revival n. بعث ba'th

revive v. يبعث yeb'ath

revocable adj. قابل للنقض qabl lelnaqd

revocation n. نقض naqd

revoke v. ينقّض yenqud

revolt v. يثور على yethur ala

revolt n. ثوْرة thawrah

revolution n. ثوْرة thawrah

revolutionary adj. ثوري thawri

revolutionary n. ثوْري thawri

revolve v. يدور yedur

revolver n. مسدّس musaddas

reward n. مكافأة mukafa'ah

reward v. يكافي yekafi

rheumatic adj. رُوماتِزْمي rumatizmi

rheumatism n. روماتيزم rumatizm

rhinoceros n. وحيد القرن wahid elqarn

rib n. ضلْع del'

ribbon n. ريبان rubyan

rice n. رزّ rezz

rich adj. غني ghani

riches n. غِنى ghinah

richness n. غِنى ghinah

rick n. كومة kumeh

rickets n. كساح kusah

rickety adj. كسيح kasih

rid v. يخلّص yekhalles

riddle n. غرْبال gherbal

riddle v. يغربل yegharbel

ride v. يركب yerkab

ride n. دورة durah

rider n. سوّاق swwaq

ridge n. حرف harf

ridicule v. يستهزء yestahze'

ridicule n. إستهْزاء istehza'

ridiculous adj. سخيف sakhif

rifle v. ينهب yenhab

rifle n. نهب nahb

rift n. مَفْلُوع maflu'

right adj. يمين yamin

right n. حق haqq

righteous adj. حقّاني haqqani

rigid adj. صلب salb

rim n. حافة haffeh

ring n. يطوّقَ yetawweq

ring v. خاتم khatem

ringlet n. حَلْقَة halaqah

ringworm n. تعلِية ta'labeh

rinse v. يغسّل بالمي yeghassel belmay

riot n. شغب shaghab

riot v. يعمل شغب ye'mel shaghab

rip v. يشرم yeshrum

ripe adj. مستوي mestwi

ripen v. يسوي yesawwi

ripple n. تموّج tamawwuj

ripple v. يتّموج yetmawwaj

rise v. يرتفع yertefe'

rise n. إرتفاع irtifa'

risk v. يخاطر yekhater

risk n. خطر khatar

risky adj. خطير khatir

rite n. شعيرة sha'irah

ritual adj. شعائري sha'ayri

rival n. غَريم gharim

rival v. يتبَارى yetbarah

rivalry n. مُنَافسة munafaseh

river n. نهر nahr

rivulet n. ساقية saqyh

road n. طَريق tariq

roadblock n. عائق a'eq

roadblock v. يعيق ye'iq

roadhouse n. استراحة طريق isteraht tariq

roam v. يسوح yesuh

rob v. يشلّح yeshalleh

robber n. حرامي harami

robbery n. سرقة serqah

robe n. حبل habl

robe v. يربط بالحبل yerbut belhabl

robot n. روبوت rubut

robust adj. قوي qawi

rock v. يتهزهز yetehazhaz

rock n. صخر sakher

rocker n. مرجوحة marjuha

rocket n. صاروخ sarukh

rocketeer n. كابتن صاروخ kaptin sarukh

rocking adj. هزّاز hazzaz

rod n. عود ud

rodent n. قَوَارض qawared

rogue n. خسيس khasis

roguery n. حيلة hyleh

roguish adj. خبيث khabith

role n. دور dur

roll n. لفة laffeh

roll v. يتدحرج yetdahraj

roller n. بكرة bakarah

romance n. رومانس rumans

romantic adj. رومانسي rumansi

rood n. صليب salib

roof n. سقف saqf

roof v. يسقّف yesaqqef

room n. غرفة ghurfeh

roomy adj. واسع wase'

root n. جِذر jazr

rope n. حبل habl

rope v. يربط بالحبل yerbut belhabl

rosary n. مسبَحَة masbaha

rose *n.* زهرة zahrah
roseate *adj.* وردي wardi
rostrum *n.* منقار menqar
rosy *adj.* وردي wardi
rot *n.* عفن afan
rot *v.* يعفن ye'affen
rotary *adj.* مدوّر medawwar
rotate *v.* يدور yedawwer
rotation *n.* دوران dawaran
rote *n.* حفظ بصمّ hefz basmm
rouble *n.* روبل rwil
rough *adj.* خشن kheshn
round *adj.* مدوّر medawwar
rouse *v.* يصحّي من النوم yesahhi mn elnum
rout *v.* يهزم yehzum
rout *n.* هزيمة hazemeh
route *n.* طريق tariq
routine *n.* روتين rutin
routine *adj.* روتيني rutini
rover *n.* رحّال rahhal
row *n.* صفّ saff
rowdy *adj.* فظّ fazz
royal *adj.* ملكي malaki
royalty *n.* ملكيّة malakeyyeh
royalty *n.* العائلة المالكة ela'yleh elmalkeh
rub *v.* يحكّ yehekk
rubber *n.* محاية mahayyeh
rubbing *n.* حكّ hakk
rubbish *n.* زبالة zebaleh
rubble *n.* أنقاض anqad
rubeola *n.* حصبة hasbeh
rubric *n.* سنّة sunneh
ruby *n.* ياقوت yaqut
ruck *n.* تني tani
ruck *v.* يتني yetni

rucksack *n.* شنتاية ظهر shantayt daher
rudder *n.* دفّة daqqah
ruddy *adj.* محمرّ mehmarr
rude *adj.* وقح weqh
ruin *n.* خراب kharab
ruin *v.* يخرّب yekharreb
rule *n.* حكم hukm
rule *v.* يحكم yehkum
ruler *n.* حاكم hakim
ruling *n.* حكم hukm
rumour *n.* إشاعة isha'ah
rumour *v.* يروّج إشاعة yerawwej isha'ah
run *v.* يركض yerkud
run *n.* ركض rakd
run *v.* يدير yedir
run *n.* إدارة edarah
runabout *n.* رحّالة rahhaleh
runaway *n.* هروب hurub
rundown *n.* خلاصة khulasah
runner *n.* عدّاء adda'
rupee *n.* روبيّة rubeyyeh
rupture *n.* فتق fetq
rupture *v.* ينفتق yenfetq
rural *adj.* ريفي rifi
ruse *n.* حيلة hyleh
rush *n.* ركض سريع rakd sare'
rush *v.* يركض بسرعة yerkud beser'ah
rush *n.* إنقضاض inqidad
rust *n.* صدأ sada'
rust *v.* يصدّي yesaddi
rustic *adj.* ريفي rifi
rustic *n.* ريفي rifi
rusticity *n.* بساطة basatah
rusty *adj.* متأكسد met'aksed

ruthless *adj.* متحجّر metehajjer

S

sack *n.* كيس kis
sack *v.* يعبّي بكياس ye'abbi belkis
sacrament *n.* القربان المقدس elqurban elmuqaddas
sacred *adj.* مقدّس muqaddas
sacrifice *n.* تضحية tadheyeh
sacrifice *v.* يضحّي yedahhi
sacrilege *n.* تدنيس tadnis
sacrilegious *adj.* مدنّس medannas
sad *adj.* زعلان za'lan
sadden *v.* يزعل yeza'el
saddle *n.* سرج sarj
saddle *v.* يحطّ السرج yehutt elsarj
sadism *n.* ساديّة sadeyyeh
sadist *n.* ساديّة sadeyyeh
sadness *n.* زعل za'al
safe *adj.* أمن amen
safe-deposit *n.* خزينة حديدية khazeneh hadedeyyeh
safeguard *n.* حماية himayeh
safeguard *v.* يحمي yehmi
safehouse *n.* مخبأ سرّي makhba' serri
safekeeping *n.* ذمّة zemmeh
safely *adv.* بأمان be'aman
safety *n.* سلامة salameh
saffron *n.* زعفران za'faran

saffron *adj.* زعفراني za'farani
sag *n.* ارتخاء irtikha'
sag *v.* يرتخي yertekhi
sahib *n.* صاحب sahib
sail *n.* شراع shera'
sail *v.* يسافر بالبحر yesafer belbahr
sailboat *n.* مركب شراعي markeb shera'i
sailing *n.* إبحار ibhar
sailor *n.* بحّار bahhar
saint *n.* قديس qeddis
saintly *adj.* قديسي qeddisi
sake *n.* خاطر khater
salable *adj.* رايج rayj
salad *n.* سلطة salatah
salamander *n.* سمندر samandar
salary *n.* راتب ratib
sale *n.* بيع be'
salesman *n.* بيّاع bayya'
salient *adj.* واضح wadeh
saline *adj.* ملحي melhi
salinity *n.* ملوحة mluhah
saliva *n.* ريق riq
sally *n.* نزوة nazweh
saloon *n.* صالون salun
salt *n.* ملح melh
salt *v.* يملّح yemalleh
salty *adj.* مالح malih
salutary *adj.* مفيد mufid
salutation *n.* سلام salam
salute *v.* يسلّم على yesallem ala
salute *n.* سلام salam
salvage *n.* إسعاف es'af
salvage *v.* يسعف yes'ef
salvation *n.* إسعاف es'af
samaritan *n.* سامري samri

samba *n.* سامبا samba

samba *v.* يرقص سامبا yerqus elsamba

same *adj.* نفس nafs

sample *n.* عيّنة ayyeneh

sample *v.* ياخد عيّنة yakhud ayyeneh

sampling *n.* أخذ عينات akhed elayyenat

samsonite *n.* سامسونايت samsunyt

samurai *n.* سِامُوراي samurai

sanatorium *n.* مصحّة masahhah

sanctification *n.* تطهير tatehir

sanctify *v.* يطهِّر yetahher

sanction *n.* عقوبة uqubeh

sanction *v.* يعاقب ye'aqeb

sanctity *n.* قدِسية qudseyyeh

sanctuary *n.* حرَم haram

sand *n.* رمل raml

sand *adj.* رملي ramli

sandal *n.* صندل sandal

sandalwood *n.* خشب الصندل khashab elsandal

sandbank *n.* شاطئ رملي shate' ramli

sandbox *n.* صندوق رمل sanduq raml

sandcastle *n.* قلعة رمل qal'et raml

sandhill *n.* تلّ رملي tall ramli

sandpaper *n.* ورق قَزاز waraq qzaz

sandpaper *v.* يحفّ بورق قزاز yeheff bewaraq qzaz

sandstorm *n.* عاصفة رمليِّة asfeh ramleyyeh

sandwich *n.* صندويشة sindwisheh

sandwich *v.* يلفّ صندويش yeleff sindwesheh

sandy *adj.* رملي ramli

sane *adj.* عاقِل a'qel

sanguine *adj.* دمَوي damawi

sanitary *adj.* صحّي sehhi

sanity *n.* سلامةَ العقل salamet ela'qel

satan *n.* شَيطان shitan

satanic *adj.* شَيطاني shitani

satchel *n.* شنتة shantah

satellite *n.* ستالايت satalyt

satiable *adj.* قابل للإشباع qabel leleshba'

satiate *v.* بِشيع yeshbe'

satiety *n.* تشبع tashabbu'

satin *n.* ساتان satan

satin *adj.* ساتاني satani

satire *n.* هِجاء heja'

satirical *adj.* هِجائي heja'i

satisfaction *n.* إرضاء irda'

satisfactory *adj.* مرضي merdi

satisfy *v.* يرضي yerdi

saturate *v.* يشرِب yesharreb

saturation *n.* تشريب tashrib

Saturday *n.* السبت elsabt

sauce *n.* مرقة marqah

saucer *n.* طبق الفنجان tabaq elfenjan

saucy *adj.* مرِق mereq

sauna *n.* ساونا sawnah

sauna *v.* يعمل ساونا ye'mul sawnah

saunter v. يَتَمَشّى yetmashshah

saunter n. تَمَشَايَة temshayh

sausage n. قديد qadid

saute n. سوتيه sutih

savage adj. وحشي wahshi

savage n. هَمَج hamaj

savagery n. هَمَجِيّة hamajeyyeh

savant n. علامة allameh

save v. يِنقذ yenqez

save v. يحفظ yehfaz

saviour n. مُنقذ munqez

savour n. طعم ta'm

savour v. يتذوّق yetzawwaq

saw n. منشار menshar

saw v. يِنشر بالمنشار yenshur belmenshar

saw n. حِكْمَة hikmeh

sawbones n. دكتور جرّاح dektur jarrah

sawbuck n. عشرة دولار ashra dular

sawdust n. نشارة الخشب nesharet khashab

sawfish n. سمك المنشار samak elmenshar

sawhorse n. حصان خشب hesan khashab

sawmill n. مَنْشَرِه manshar

sawn n. منشور manshur

sawyer n. نشار nashshar

say v. يقول yequl

say n. قول qul

scab n. قشرة الجرح qeshret eljerh

scabies n. جَرَب jarab

scaffold n. مشنقة mashnaqah

scale n. ميزان mizan

scan v. يفحص yefhas

scan n. فَحْص fahs

scandal n. فضيحة fdyha

scandalize v. يفضح yefdah

scandalous adj. فضايحي fadayhi

scandalously adv. بفضيحة befdyha

scant v. يقتّر على yeqatter ala

scant n. تقتير taqtir

scapegoat v. يخلّيه كبش الفدا yekhalleyh kabsh elfeda

scapegoat n. كبش الفدا kabsh elfeda

scapula n. لوح الكتف luh elketf

scapular adj. كتفي ketfi

scar n. ندبة nadbeh

scar v. يعمل ندبة ye'mul nadbeh

scarce adj. قليل qalil

scarcity n. قَلّة qelleh

scare n. رعب ru'eb

scare v. يرعب yer'eb

scarf n. لفحة lafha

scatter v. يشتّت yeshattet

scatterbrain n. مشتّت الذهن meshattat elzehn

scatterbrained adj. ذهنه مشتّت zehnuh meshattat

scattered adj. مشتّت meshattat

scattergun n. بدقيّة bendqeyyeh

scavenge v. يكنس yekannes

scavenger n. زَبّال zabbal

scenario n. سيناريو sinaryu

scenarist n. سيناريست sinarest

scene n. مَشْهد mashhad

scenery n. مَشْهد mashhad

scenic *adj.* مَسْرَحِي masrahi

scent *n.* عطر uter

scent *v.* يعطّر ye'atter

scent *v.* شَمّ shamm

sceptic *n.* شكّاك shakkak

sceptical *adj.* شكّاك shakkak

scepticism *n.* شكّ shakk

sceptre *n.* صولجان sulajan

schedule *n.* جدول jadwal

schedule *v.* يجدول yejadwel

schematic *adj.* تخطيطي takhtiti

scheme *n.* تخطّط mekhattat

scheme *v.* يتآمر yet'amr

schemer *n.* متآمر met'amer

schism *n.* انشقاق inshiqaq

schyzophrenia *n.* إنفصام شخصيّة infesam shakhseyyeh

scholar *n.* باحث bahith

scholarly *adj.* علمي elmi

scholarship *n.* منحة دراسيّة menha daraseyyeh

scholarship *n.* علم elm

scholastic *adj.* دراسيّ derasi

school *n.* مدرسة madraseh

school *v.* يدرّس yedarres

schoolhouse *n.* مبنى المدرسة mabna elmadraseh

schoolmaster *n.* مدرّس medarres

schoolmate *n.* رفيق الدراسة refiq elderaseh

schoolteacher *n.* مدرّس medarres

sciatic *adj.* ورْكي werki

sciatica *n.* عرق النّسا erq elnesa

science *n.* علم elm

scientific *adj.* علمي elmi

scientist *n.* عالِم a'lem

scissors *n.* مقصّ meqass

scoff *n.* اِستهزاء estihza'

scoff *v.* يستهزء yestahze'

scooter *n.* سكوتر skuter

scope *n.* نطاق netaq

scorch *v.* يشوّط yeshawwet

scorch *n.* تشويط tashwit

score *n.* هدف hadaf

score *v.* يسدّد هدف yesadded hadaf

scoreboard *n.* لوحة الأهداف luhet elahdaf

scorecard *n.* بطاقة النتائج betaqet elnata'ej

scorekeeper *n.* مراقب النتيجة muraqeb elnatijeh

scorekeeping *n.* مراقبة النتيجة muraqabet elnatijeh

scorer *n.* هدّاف haddaf

scorn *n.* إحتقار ihtiqar

scorn *v.* يحتقر yehteqer

scorpion *n.* عقرب aqrab

scot *n.* ضريبة daribeh

scot-free *adj.* معفى من الضريبة me'fa mn eldaribeh

scoundrel *n.* ندل nadel

scourge *n.* جلد jeld

scourge *v.* يجلد yejalled

scout *n.* إسْتكشاف istekshaf

scout *v.* يستكشف yestakshef

scowl *v.* يعبّس ye'bus

scowl *n.* عبسة abseh

scraggy *adj.* نحيل nahil

scramble *v.* يدفش yedfush

scramble *n.* دفش dafsh

scrambled *adj.* مخلوط makhlut

scambling *n.* كدح kadh

scrap *n.* خردة khurdeh

scrape *n.* تقشير taqshir

scrape *v.* يقشر yeqashsher

scraper *n.* مبشرة mabsharah

scratch *n.* يخرمش yekharmesh

scratch *v.* خرمشة kharmasheh

scratched *adj.* مخرمش mekharmesh

scratchy *adj.* مشوّك meshawwek

scrawl *v.* يشخبط yeshakhbet

scrawl *n.* شخبطة shakhbatah

scream *v.* يصرخ yesrakh

scream *n.* صرخة sarkhah

screen *n.* شاشة shasheh

screen *v.* يصوّر بالشاشة yesawwer belshasheh

screen name *n.* إسم الشاشة esm elshasheh

screensaver *n.* شاشة التوقّف shashet twaqquf

screenshot *n.* لقطة شاشة laqtet shasheh

screw *n.* برغي berghi

screw *v.* يشدّ البرغي yeshedd elberghi

script *n.* نصّ برمجي nass barmaji

scripture *n.* كتاب مقدّس kitab muqaddas

scroll *n.* لفّ laff

scrooge *n.* بخيل bakhil

scrotum *n.* صفن safan

scrub *n.* حفّ haff

scrub *v.* يحفّ yeheff

scruffiness *n.* قذارة qazarah

scrumptious *adj.* رائع ra'e'

scruple *n.* وسواس wuswas

scruple *v.* يوسوس yewaswes

scrupulous *adj.* موسوس muwaswas

scrutinize *v.* يدقّق yedaqeq

scrutiny *n.* تدقيق tadqiq

sculpt *v.* ينحت yenhat

sculptor *n.* نحّات nahhat

sculptural *adj.* نحتي nahti

sculpture *n.* نحتي nahti

sculpture *n.* تمثال temthal

scum *n.* رغوة raghweh

scum *v.* يرغي yerghi

scuttle *n.* زنبيل zanbil

scythe *n.* منجل menjal

scythe *v.* يقصّ بالمنجل yequss belmenjal

sea *n.* بحر bahr

seafloor *n.* قاع البحر qa'e elbahr

seafoam *n.* زبد البحر zabad elbahr

seafood *n.* أكل بحري akel bahri

seagull *n.* نورس nawras

seal *n.* ختم khetm

seal *n.* فقمة faqmeh

seal *v.* يختم yekhtum

sealant *n.* مانع تسرب mane' tasarrub

sealed *adj.* مختوم makhtum

seam *n.* درزة darzeh

seam *v.* يدرز yedruz

seamy *adj.* بشع beshe'

sear *n.* حرق harq

sear *v.* يحرق yehruq

search *n.* بحث bahth

search *v.* يبحث yebhath

searching *adj.* بحث bahth

searchlight *n.* ضوّ كشّاف daww kashshaf

search warrant *n.* مذكرة بحث muzakkaret bahth

seared *adj.* محروق mahruq

seashore *n.* ساحل sahil

season *n.* فصل fasl

season *v.* يتبّل yetabbel

seasonable *adj.* موسمي musmi

seasonal *adj.* موسمي musmi

seat *n.* مقعد maq'ad

seat *v.* يقعّد yeqa'ed

secede *v.* ينفصل yenfesl

secession *n.* إنفصال infesal

secessionist *n.* إنفصالي infesali

seclude *v.* يعزل ye'zul

secluded *adj.* معزول ma'zul

seclusion *n.* عزل azel

second *adj.* تاني tani

second *n.* ثانية thanyh

secondary *adj.* ثانوي thanawi

seconder *n.* مؤيّد mu'ayyed

secrecy *n.* سرّية serreyyeh

secret *adj.* سرّي serry

secret *n.* سرّ serr

secretary *n.* سكرتير sekrtir

secrete *v.* يفرز yefruz

secretion *n.* إفراز efraz

secretive *adj.* إفرازي efrazi

sect *n.* مذهب mazhab

sectarian *adj.* مذهبي mazhabi

section *n.* قسم qesm

sector *n.* قطّاع qetta'

secure *adj.* مأمّن me'amman

secure *v.* يأمّن ye'ammen

security *n.* أمن amen

sedan *n.* هودج hudaj

sedate *adj.* رزين razin

sedative *adj.* مسكّن musakken

sedative *n.* مسكّن musakken

sedentary *adj.* مقيم muqim

sediment *n.* عكر akar

sedition *n.* شغب shaghab

seditious *adj.* مشاغب mushaghib

seduce *v.* يغري yeghri

seduction *n.* إغراء eghra'

seductive *adj.* إغرائي eghra'i

see *v.* يشوف yeshuf

seed *n.* بذرة bezreh

seed *v.* يبذور yebzur

seek *v.* يسعى yes'a

seem *v.* يبان bayan

seep *v.* يقطّر yeqatter

seer *n.* مشاهد mushahed

seethe *v.* يفور yefur

segment *n.* جزء jeze'

segment *v.* يجزّء yejazze'

segregate *v.* يعزل ye'zul

segregation *n.* عزل azel

seismic *adj.* زلزالي zelzali

seismogram *n.* تسجيل الزلزال tasjil elzelzal

seismograph *n.* مقياس زلزال meqyas zelzal

seismoscope *n.* كاشف زلازل kashef zelzal

seize *v.* يحجز yehjuz

seizure *n.* حجز hajz

seldom *adv.* بالنادر belnader

select *v.* يختار yekhtar

selection *n.* إختيار ikhtyar

selective *adj.* إختياري ikhtyari

self *n.* نفس nafs
self-abuse *n.* إستمناء estimna'
self-centered *adj.* أناني anani
self-confident *adj.* واثق بنفسه watheq benafsuh
self-conscious *adj.* مستحي mestehi
self-control *n.* ضبط النفس dabt elnafs
self-doubt *n.* عدم الثقة بالنفس adam theqa belnafs
selfie *n.* سلفي selfi
selfish *adj.* أناني anani
selfless *adj.* مو أناني mu anani
sell *v.* يبيع yebe'
seller *n.* بيّاع bayya'
semblance *n.* شاكلة shakleh
semen *n.* مني mani
semester *n.* فصل دراسي fasl derasi
semicircle *n.* نصف دائرة nesf da'erah
seminal *adj.* منوي manawi
seminar *n.* حلقة بحث halqet bahth
senate *n.* مجلس الشيوخ majles elshyukh
senator *n.* سناتور sinatur
senatorial *adj.* سناتوري sinaturi
send *v.* يبعت yeb'at
senile *adj.* شيخوخي shikhukhi
senility *n.* شيخوخة shikhukhah
senior *adj.* أكبر akbar
senior *n.* سيد sayyed
seniority *n.* أسبقية asbaqeyyeh
sensation *n.* شعور shu'ur

sensational *adj.* شعوري shu'uri
sense *n.* إحساس eshsas
sense *v.* يحس yehess
senseless *adj.* عديم حس adim hass
sensibility *n.* حساسيّة hasaseyyeh
sensible *adj.* حسّاس hassas
sensitive *adj.* حساس hassas
sensual *adj.* شهواني shahwani
sensualist *n.* شهواني shahwani
sensuality *n.* شهوانيّة shahwaneyyeh
sensuous *adj.* حسي hessi
sentence *n.* جملة jumleh
sentence *n.* حكم المحكمة hekm elmahkameh
sentence *v.* يحكم yehkum
sentience *n.* إحساس ehsas
sentient *adj.* حسّاس hassas
sentiment *n.* شعور shu'ur
sentimental *adj.* عاطفي a'tifi
sentinel *n.* حارس hares
sentry *n.* حارس hares
separable *adj.* مفصول mafsul
separate *v.* يفصل yefsel
separate *adj.* منفصل menfesl
separation *n.* إنفصال infesal
sepsis *n.* تقيّح taqayyuh
September *n.* أيلول aylul
septic *adj.* متعفّن met'affen
sepulchre *n.* قبر qabr
sepulture *n.* قبر qabr
sequel *n.* نتيجة natijeh
sequence *n.* تسلسل tasalsul
sequester *v.* يحجز yehjuz
serene *adj.* رايق rayeq

serendipitous *adj.* عَرَضي aradi
serendipity *n.* صدفة sedfeh
serenity *n.* رَواق rawaq
serf *n.* عَبْد abd
sergeant *n.* رَقيب raqib
serial *adj.* مُتَسَلسل metsalsel
serial *n.* رقم مُتَسَلسل raqm metsalsel
series *n.* مسلسل musalsal
serious *adj.* خطير khatir
sermon *n.* مَوعظة maw'ezah
sermonize *v.* يوعظ yu'ez
serpent *n.* حية hayyeh
serpentine *n.* ثُعباني thu'ebani
servant *n.* خادم khadem
serve *v.* يَخدُم yekhdum
service *n.* خدمة khedmeh
service *v.* يصون yesun
serviceable *adj.* نافع nafe'
servile *adj.* خُنوع khunu'
servility *n.* خُنوع khunu'
servitude *n.* عبودية ubudeyyeh
sesame *n.* سمسم semsem
session *n.* جَلسة jalseh
set *v.* يجهز yejahhez
set *adj.* ثابت thabit
set *n.* مجموعة majmu'ah
setback *n.* نكسة nakseh
settee *n.* كَنبة kanabeh
settle *v.* يسوّي yesawwi
settle *v.* يستوطن yestawten
settlement *n.* تسوية tasweyeh
settlement *n.* إستيطان estitan
settler *n.* مستوطن mestawten
seven *n.* الرقم 7 elraqm 7
seven *adj.* سبعة sab'ah

seventeen *n., a* الرقم 17 elraqm 17
seventeenth *adj.* الصبطاعش elsabata'sh
seventh *adj.* السابع elsabe'
seventieth *adj.* السبعينيات elsab'eyneyyat
seventy *n., a* الرقم 70 elraqm 70
sever *v.* يبتر yebtur
several *adj.* كتير ktir
severance *n.* بتر batr
severe *adj.* عنيف anif
severity *n.* عنف unf
sew *v.* يخيّط yekhayyet
sewage *n.* صرف صحي sarf sehhi
sewer *n.* بالوعة balu'ah
sewer *n.* مجرور majrur
sewerage *n.* شبكة المجاري shabaket elmajari
sex *v.* يمارس الجنس yemares eljins
sex *n.* جنس jins
sexual *adj.* جنسي jinsi
sexuality *n.* غريزة جنسية gharezeh jinseyyeh
sexy *adj.* سكسي seksi
shabby *adj.* مهري mehri
shack *n.* كوخ kukh
shackle *n.* كبل kabl
shackle *v.* يربط yerbut
shade *n.* ظلّ zell
shade *v.* يظلل yezallel
shadow *n.* خيال khayal
shadow *v.* يظلل yezallel
shadowy *adj.* ظليل zalil

shaft *n.* عَمُود amud

shake *v.* يتخضخض yetkhadkhad

shake *n.* خَضّة khaddah

shaky *adj.* مهزوز mahzuz

shallow *adj.* سطحي satehi

sham *v.* يرائي yer'i

sham *n.* رياء rya'

sham *n.* تصنع tasannu'

sham *adj.* مصطنَع mestana'

shamble *v.* يتمايل yetmayal

shambles *n.* مسلخ maslakh

shame *n.* عيب eyb

shame *v.* يُخجِل yekhjal

shameful *adj.* يُخجِل beykhajjel

shameless *adj.* وقِح weqh

shampoo *n.* شامبو shambu

shampoo *v.* يتحمّم بالشامبو yetehammam belshambu

shape *n.* شكل shakel

shape *v.* يشكّل yeshakkel

shapely *adj.* وسيم wasim

shapeup *n.* إختيار الموظّفين ikhtyar elmuwazzafin

shard n شِقفة sheqfeh

share *v.* يشارك yesharek

share *v.* يساهم yesahem

share *n.* مشاركة musharakeh

share *n.* حصة hessah

sharebroker *n.* سمسار أسهم semsar asehum

shareholder *n.* حامل السهم hamel elsahm

shareholding *n.* إمتلاك الأسهم imtilak elasehum

shark *n.* قِرش qersh

sharp *adj.* مسنون masnun

sharp *adj.* جارح jarih

sharp *adj.* موجع muje'

sharpen *v.* يسن yesenn

sharpener *n.* مسن masann

sharper *n.* برايةٍ barrayeh

shatter *v.* يتكسّر yetkassar

shave *v.* يحلق yehliq

shave *n.* حلاقة hlaqah

shaven *adj.* محلوق mahluq

shavings *n.* ورية baryh

shawarma *n.* شاورما shawrma

shawl *n.* شال shal

she *pron.* هيّة heyyeh

sheaf *n.* حزمة hezmeh

shear *v.* يحزم yehzum

shears *n. pl.* مجز mejazz

sheathe *v.* يغلّف yeghallef

shed *v.* يَسكب yeskub

shed *n.* سكب sakb

sheep *n.* خِروف kharuf

sheepish *adj.* أهبل ahbal

sheer *adj.* بحتٍ baht

sheet *n.* ورقة waraqah

sheet *n.* صفيحة safiha

shelf *n.* رفّ raff

shell *n.* صدفة sedfeh

shell *n.* قنبلة qunbleh

shell *v.* يزتّ قنابل yezett qanabel

shelter *n.* مأوى ma'wa

shelter *v.* يؤوي ye'wi

shelve *v.* يحطّ عالرفّ yehutt alraff

shepherd *n.* راعي ra'i

shield *n.* تُرس ters

shield *v.* يحمي yehmi

shift *v.* ينتقل yenteql

shift *n.* مناوبة munawabeh

shifty *adj.* موارب muwareb

shilling *n.* شلن shelen

shilly-shally *v.* يتردّد yetraddad

shilly-shally *n.* تردّد taraddud

shin *n.* ساق saq

shine *v.* يشعشع yesha'she'

shine *n.* ضوّ الشمس daww elshams

shiny *adj.* مشعشع mesha'she'

ship *n.* سفينة safeneh

ship *v.* يشحن yeshhan

shipboard *n.* ظهر السفينة dahr elsafineh

shipbuilder *n.* صانعُ السُفُن sane' elsufun

shipload *n.* حمولة السفينة humulet elsafineh

shipmaster *n.* قبطان kuptan

shipment *n.* شحنة shehneh

shipowner *n.* مالك السفينة malek elsafineh

shipped *adj.* مشحون mashhun

shipping *n.* شحن shahn

shipshape *adj.* مرتّب merattab

shipwreck *n.* حطام سفينة hutam elsafineh

shipwreck *v.* يغرق سفينة yegharreq safineh

shipyard *n.* ترسانة بحرية tersaneh bahreyyeh

shire *n.* ناحية nahyeh

shirk *v.* يتملّص yetmallas

shirker *n.* متملّص metmalles

shirt *n.* قميص qamis

shive *n.* شظية shazeyyh

shiver *v.* يتشظّى yetshazzah

shoal *n.* فوج fuj

shock *n.* صدمة sadmeh

shock *v.* يصدم yesdum

shoe *n.* حذاء hiza'

shoe *v.* يحطّ نعل yehutt na'el

shoot *v.* يضرب بالمسدّس yedrub belmusaddas

shoot *v.* يقنص yeqnus

shoot *v.* يوجّه yewajjeh

shoot *n.* قنص qans

shoot *n.* صيد syd

shop *n.* دكّانة dekkaneh

shop *v.* يتسوّق yetsawwaq

shopaholic *n.* مدمن تسوّق medmen tasawwuq

shopkeeper *n.* صاحب الدكّانة saheb eldekkaneh

shoplift *v.* يسرق من الدكّان yesruq mn eldekkan

shoplifter *n.* حرامي الدكّان harami eldekkan

shopowner *n.* صاحب الدكّانة sahib eldekkanh

shore *n.* ساحل sahil

shore *v.* يدعم yed'am

shoreline *n.* حافّة الشّاطئ haffet elshate'

short *n.* تنبل tanbal

short *adj.* قصير qasir

shortbread *n.* الغريّبة elgharbeyyeh

shortcake *n.* الغريّبة elgharbeyyeh

shortcoming *n.* عيْب eyb

shorten *v.* يقصر yeqasser

shortening *n.* تقصير taqsir

shortfall *n.* عجز ajez

shorthand *n.* إختزال ikhtizal

shortish *adj.* مايل للقصير mayl lelqasir

shortly *adv.* قريباً qareban

shorts *n. pl.* شورت shurt

shot *n.* لَقطة laqtah

shotgun *n.* بارودِة barudeh

should *v.* يتوجب yetwajjab

shoulder *n.* كتف ketf

shoulder *v.* يتولى yetwallah

shout *n.* صريخ srikh

shout *v.* يصرخ yesarrekh

shove *v.* يدِس yedess

shove *n.* دس dass

shovel *n.* جاروف jaruf

shovel *v.* يجرف yejruf

show *v.* يفرجي yefarji

show *n.* فرجة ferjeh

shower *n.* دوش dush

shower *v.* يتحمم yetehammam

showery *adj.* ممطِر mumter

showoff *n.* تباهي tabahi

showpiece *n.* تحفة tehfeh

shred *n.* نتفة netfeh

shred *v.* ينتف yentuf

shrew *n.* ناشز nashez

shrewd *adj.* فهيم fahim

shriek *n.* زَعيق ze'iq

shriek *v.* يزعق yez'aq

shrill *n.* زلغوطة zalghutah

shrine *n.* مقام maqam

shrink *v.* ينكمش yenkemesh

shrinkage *n.* إنكماش inkimash

shroud *n.* كفن kafan

shroud *v.* يكفِن yekaffen

shrub *n.* شجيرة shujayrah

shrug *v.* يهزّ الكتاف yehezz elktaf

shrug *n.* هزّ الكتاف hazz elktaf

shudder *v.* يقشعر yeqash'er

shudder *n.* قشعريرة qash'arerah

shuffle *v.* يراوغ yerawegh

shuffle *v.* يخلط yekhlut

shuffle *n.* مراوغة murawaghah

shuffle *n.* خلط khalt

shun *v.* يتحاشى yetehasha

shut *v.* يسكِر yesakker

shutter *n.* درفة darfeh

shuttle *n.* مكوك makkuk

shuttle *v.* يتحرّك متل المكوك yeteharrak mtel elmakkuk

shy *n.* نجول khajul

shy *v.* يخجل yekhajjel

siamese *adj.* سيامي syami

sick *adj.* مريض marid

sickbed *n.* تخت المريض takht elmarid

sicken *v.* يمرّض yemarred

sickle *n.* منجل manjal

sickly *adj.* مرضان mardan

sickness *n.* مرَض marad

side *n.* جنب janb

side *v.* يجي ع جنب yeji a janb

sidearm *n.* سلاح slah

sidearm *v.* يسلّح yesalleh

sidearm *adj.* مسلح mesallah

sideband *n.* نطاق جانبي nitaq janbi

sidebar *n.* عمود جانبي amud janbi

sideboard *n.* مقصف maqsaf

sidecar *n.* سيّارة مسحوبة sayyarah masehubeh

220

sideline *n.* خَطّ جانِبي khatt janbi

sidereal *adj.* فلكي falaki

sidesaddle *n.* سَرج جانِبي sarj janbi

sideshow *n.* عرض جانبي ard janbi

sidetrack *n.* خط جانبي khatt janbi

sidewalk *n.* رَصيف rasif

sidewall *n.* حيط hit

sideway *adj.* جانِبي janbi

siege *n.* حِصار hesar

siege *v.* يُحاصِر yehaser

siesta *n.* قيلولةَ qeluleh

sieve *n.* غِرْبال gherbal

sieve *v.* يغربِل yegharbel

sift *v.* يَخُل yenkhul

sigh *n.* تَنهيدةٍ tanhydeh

sigh *v.* يتَنَهَد yetnahhad

sight *n.* رؤيا ru'ya

sight *v.* يشوف yeshuf

sign *n.* توقيع tawqi'

sign *v.* يوَقِع yewaqqe'

signal *n.* إشارة esharah

signal *adj.* إشاراتي esharati

signal *v.* يبثّ إشارة yebethth esharah

signatory *n.* صاحِب التوقيع sahib eltawqi'

signature *n.* توقيع tawqi'

significance *n.* أهميِة ahameyyeh

significant *adj.* مهمّ mehmm

signification *n.* قصد qasd

signify *v.* يقصد yeqsud

silence *n.* سكوت skut

silence *v.* يسكّت yesakket

silencer *n.* كاتِم صوتَ katem sut

silent *adj.* صِامت samit

silhouette *n.* صورة مظللة surah mezalleleh

silicon *n.* سيليكُون silikun

silk *n.* حرير harir

silken *adj.* حِريري hariri

silky *adj.* حريري hariri

silly *adj.* سَخيف sakhif

silver *n.* فِضة feddah

silver *adj.* فضِّي feddi

silver *v.* يلبِّس فِضَّة yelabbes feddah

similar *adj.* بيشبهه beyshbahu

similarity *n.* تَشابُه tashabuh

simile *n.* تَشْبيه tashbih

similitude *n.* تَشابُه tashabuh

simmer *v.* يغلي عالبطيء yeghli a'lbati'

simmer *v.* يبقبق yebaqbeq

simple *adj.* بسيط basit

simplicity *n.* بساطة basatah

simplification *n.* تبسيط tabsit

simplify *v.* يبسَط yebasset

simultaneous *adj.* مع بعض ma' ba'd

sin *n.* ذنب zanb

sin *v.* يذنب yeznib

since *prep.* من وقت mn waqt

sincere *adj.* مخلِص mukhles

sincerity *n.* إخْلاَص ikhlas

sinful *adj.* مذنِب muznib

sing *v.* يغني yeghanni

singe *v.* يشوِط yeshawwet

singe *n.* تَشويط tashwit

singer n. مطرب mutrib

single adj. عازب azib

single adj. مفرد mefred

single adj. وحيد wahid

single v. يفرد yefred

singular adj. مفرد mufrad

singularity n. إفرادية efradeyyeh

singularly adv. لحاله lahalu

sinister adj. منحوس manhus

sink v. يغرق yeghraq

sink n. مجلى majla

sinner n. مذنب muznib

sinuous adj. منحني menheni

sip v. يشرق yeshruq

sip n. شرقة sharqah

sir n. سيّد sayyed

siren n. صفارة إنذار saffaret inzar

sister n. أخت ukhkht

sisterhood n. أخوّة ukhuwweh

sit v. يقعد yeq'ud

site n. موقع mawqe'

situation n. موقف mawqef

six n., a الرقم 6 elraqm 6

sixteen n., adj. الرقم 16 elraqm 16

sixteenth adj. الصطّاعش elsitta'esh

sixth adj. السادس elsades

sixtieth adj. الستينيّات elsetineyyat

sixty n., adj. الرقم 60 elraqm 60

sizable adj. ضخم dakhm

size n. قياس qyas

size v. يقيس yeqis

sizzle v. نيشّ yeneshsh

sizzle n. نشّ nashsh

skate n. زلّاجة zallajeh

skate v. يتزلّج yetzallaj

skein n. شلّة shelleh

skeleton n. هيكل عظمي haykal azmi

sketch n. سكتْش skitsh

sketch v. يرسم yersum

sketchy adj. مخطّط له mukhattat elu

skid v. يتزحلق yetzahlaq

skid n. زحلوقة zahluqah

skilful adj. ماهر mahr

skill n. مهارة maharah

skin n. جلد jeld

skin v. يجلّد yejalled

skip v. يطفّ yetuff

skip v. يطّ yenutt

skip n. طفّة taffeh

skip n. نطّة nattah

skirmish n. مناوشة menawasheh

skirmish v. يناوش yenawesh

skirt n. تنورة tannurah

skirt v. يحاذي yehazi

skit n. مونولوج munuluj

skull n. جمجمة jemjmeh

sky n. سما sama

slab n. بلاطة blatah

slack adj. رخو rakhu

slacken v. يرتخي yertekhi

slacks n. بنطلون bantalun

slake v. يروي yerwi

slam v. يخبط الباب yekhbut elbab

slam n. خبط الباب khabt elbab

slander *n.* تشويه سمعة tashweh sem'ah

slander *v.* يشوّه سمعة yeshwweh sem'ah

slanderous *adj.* تَشْهِيري tashhiri

slang *n.* العاميّة elammeyyeh

slant *v.* ينحَدر yenheder

slant *n.* انحِدار inhidar

slap *n.* ضربة كفّ darbet kaff

slap *v.* يضرب كفّ yedrub kaff

slash *v.* يشطّب yeshatteb

slash *n.* تشطيب tashtib

slate *n.* لوح luh

slattern *n.* الوسخ elwesekh

slaughter *n.* دبح dabh

slaughter *v.* يدبح yedbah

slave *n.* إستعباد este'bad

slave *v.* يستعبد yesta'bed

slavery *n.* عبودية ubudeyyeh

slavish *adj.* خنوع khunu'

slay *v.* يدبح yedbah

sleek *adj.* مصقول masqul

sleep *v.* ينام yenam

sleep *n.* نوم num

sleeper *n.* نايم naym

sleepy *adj.* نعسان na'san

sleeve *n.* كمّ kemm

sleight *n.* خفّة إيد kheffet eyd

slender *n.* نحيف nahif

slice *n.* شرحة sharha

slice *v.* يشرّح yesharreh

slick *adj.* أملس amlas

slide *v.* يقع yeqa'

slide *n.* وقوع wuqu'

slight *adj.* شوي shwayy

slim *adj.* رشيق rashiq

slim *v.* يخفّ yenhaf

slime *n.* طين tyn

slimy *adj.* لزج lezj

sling *n.* حمّالة hammaleh

sling *n.* معلاق me'laq

slip *v.* يزلّ yezell

slip *n.* زلّة zelleh

slipper *n.* مشّاية mashayyeh

slipshod *adj.* مقصّر meqasser

slit *n.* تقطيع بالطول taqte' beltul

slit *v.* يقطّع بالطول yeqatte' beltul

slogan *n.* شعار she'ar

slope *n.* منحدر munhader

slope *v.* ينحدر yenheder

sloth *n.* كسل kasal

slothful *n.* بليد balid

slough *n.* إنسلاخ insilakh

slough *n.* مستنقع mustanqa'

slough *v.* ينسلخ yenselekh

slovenly *adj.* قذر qazr

slow *adj.* بطيء bate'

slow *v.* يتباطأ yetbata'

slowly *adv.* ببطء bebute'

slowness *n.* بلادة baladeh

sluggard *n.* كسلان kaslan

sluggish *adj.* نتبل tanbal

sluice *n.* سكر الميّ sakar elmay

slum *n.* شارع فقير share' faqir

slumber *v.* يغفى yeghfa

slumber *n.* غفوة ghafweh

slump *n.* ركود rukud

slump *v.* يركد yerkud

slur *n.* لطخة latkhah

slush *n.* تلج دايب talj dayb

slushy *adj.* مطيّن metayyen

slut *n.* كلبة kalbeh

sly *adj.* خبيث khabith

smack *n.* تمطّق tamattuq

smack *v.* يَتمَطَّق yetmattaq	snarl *v.* يزمجر yezamjer
small *adj.* صغير seghir	snatch *v.* ينتش yentush
smallpox *n.* جدري jadari	snatch *n.* نتش natsh
smart *adj.* ذكي zaki	sneak *v.* ينسل yensall
smart *n.* شاطر shater	sneak *n.* إنسِلال insilal
smash *v.* يكسِّر yekasser	sneer *v.* يهزّ إنفه yehezz enfuh
smash *n.* تكسير taksir	sneer *n.* هزّ الإنف hazz elenf
smear *v.* يلطخ yelattekh	sneeze *v.* يعطس ye'tus
smear *n.* لطخ latkh	sneeze *n.* عطسة atseh
smell *n.* ريحة riha	sniff *v.* يستنشق yestansheq
smell *v.* يشم yeshemm	sniff *n.* إستنشاق estenshaq
smelt *v.* يدوب yedawweb	snob *n.* شايف حاله shayf haluh
smile *n.* إبتسامة ibtesameh	snobbery *n.* شوفة الحال shufet
smile *v.* يبتسم yebtesm	elhal
smith *n.* حداد haddad	snore *v.* يشخر yeshkhur
smog *n.* ضباب dabab	snore *n.* شخير shekhir
smoke *n.* دخان dukhkhan	snout *n.* بزبوز bazbuz
smoke *v.* يدخن yedakhkhen	snow *n.* تلج دايب talj dayb
smoky *adj.* مدخّن	snow *v.* تلج tetallej
medakhkhen	snowy *adj.* متلّج metallej
smooth *adj.* ناعم na'em	snuff *n.* فتيل الشمعة ftil
smooth *v.* ينعم yena'em	elsham'ah
smother *v.* يخنق yekhnuq	snug *adj.* مكنكن mkankan
smoulder *v.* يطفي yetaffi	so *adv.* كتير ktir
smug *adj.* نضيف nedif	so *conj.* مشان هيك mshan hik
smuggle *v.* يهرب yeharreb	soak *v.* ينقع بالمي yenqa' belmay
smuggler *n.* مهرب meharreb	soak *n.* نقع بالمي naqe' belmay
snack *n.* أكل خفيف akl khafif	soap *n.* صابون sabun
snag *n.* جذع jeze'	soap *v.* يصوبن yesuben
snail *n.* حلزون halazun	soapy *adj.* صابوني sabuni
snake *n.* حية hayyeh	soar *v.* يعلي ye'alli
snap *v.* يلقط yelqutt	sob *v.* يشهق yeshhaq
snap *n.* لقطة laqtah	sob *n.* شهيق shahiq
snare *n.* فخ fakhkh	sober *adj.* رزين razin
snare *v.* يوقع بالفخ yewaqqe'	sobriety *n.* رزانة razaneh
belfakhkh	sociability *n.* إجتماعية
snarl *n.* زمجرة zamjarah	ijtema'eyyeh

sociable *adj.* إجْتِمَاعي ijtima'ey

socialism *n.* إشْتِراكِيّة ishtirakeyyeh

socialist *n,a* إِشْتِراكي ishtiraki

society *n.* مَجتمع mejtama'

sociology *n.* علم الإجتماع elm elejtima'

sock *n.* جراب jrab

socket *n.* مقبس maqbas

sod *n.* مْرج marj

sodomite *n.* لُوطي luti

sodomy *n.* لَوَاطة lwatah

sofa *n.* صوفاية sufayeh

soft *n.* طري tari

soften *v.* يطري yetarri

soil *n.* تُراب trab

soil *v.* يوسّخ yewassekh

sojourn *v.* يقعد فترة مؤقّتة yeq'ud fatrah mu'aqqateh

sojourn *n.* إقامة مؤقّتة eqameh mu'aqqateh

solace *v.* يعزّي ye'azzi

solace *n.* عَزَا azah

solar *adj.* شمسي shamsi

solder *n.* لحام leham

solder *v.* يلحم yelhum

soldier *n.* عسكري askari

sole *n.* وَحيد wahid

sole *n.* مفرد mufred

sole *adj.* وَحيد wahid

solemn *adj.* إلو هيبة elu hybeh

solemnity *n.* هيبة hybeh

solicit *v.* يتوسّل yetwassal

solicitation *n.* توسّل tawassul

solicitor *n.* محامي muhami

solicitous *adj.* غَيْران ghayran

solicitude *n.* غَيْران ghayran

solid *adj.* صلب salb

solid *n.* جماد jamad

solidarity *n.* تَماسُك tamasuk

solitary *adj.* معتزل me'tezl

solitude *n.* إنعزال en'ezal

solo *n.* عزف منفرد azef menfered

solo *adj.* فردي fardi

solo *adv.* لوحده lwahduh

soloist *n.* عازف منفرد azef menfered

solubility *n.* دوبان dwaban

soluble *adj.* بيدوب beydub

solution *n.* محلول mahlul

solution *n.* حلّ hall

solve *v.* يحلّ yehell

solvency *n.* قُدْرَة ع الدفع qudrah a eldafe'

solvent *adj.* قادر يدفع qader yedfa'

solvent *n.* مُذيب muzib

sombre *adj.* معتّم me'tem

some *adj.* شوَيّة shwayyeh

somebody *pron.* واحد wahed

somebody *n.* شخص shakhes

somehow *adv.* بطريقة ما betareqah ma

someone *pron.* شخص shakhes

somersault *n.* شقلبة shaqlabeh

somersault *v.* يتشقلَب yetshaqlab

somnambulism *n.* مشي أثناء النوم mashi athna' elnum

somnambulist *n.* ماشي بنومه mashi benumuh

somnolence *n.* نعَس na'as

somnolent *n.* نَعْسان na'san

son *n.* إِبن ebn

song *n.* غِنِيّة ghenneyh

songster *n.* مُطْرِب mutreb

sonic *adj.* صَوتي suwti

sonnet *n.* سوناتة sunatah

sonority *n.* جَهورِية jahureyyeh

soon *adv.* قَرِيبا qariban

soot *n.* سُخام sakhkham

soot *v.* يُسخِم yesakhkhem

soothe *v.* يرفّه عن yeraffeh an

sophism *n.* سفسطائِية safusta'eyyeh

sophist *n.* سفسطائي safusta'ei

sophisticate *v.* يعقّد ye'aqqed

sophisticated *adj.* معقّد mu'aqqad

sophistication *n.* تعقيد ta'qid

sorcerer *n.* مشعْوِذ mesha'wez

sorcery *n.* شَعوَذة sha'wazeh

sordid *adj.* خَسِيس khasis

sore *adj.* متقرّح metqarreh

sore *n.* قُرحة qarhah

sorrow *n.* حزن hezn

sorrow *v.* يحزن yehzan

sorry *adj.* آسف asef

sort *n.* نوع nu'

sort *v.* يصنّف yesannef

soul *n.* روح ruh

sound *adj.* عميق amiq

sound *v.* يبان yeban

sound *n.* صوتِ suwt

soup *n.* شوربا shurba

sour *adj.* حامض hamud

sour *v.* يحمّض yehammed

source *n.* مصْدِر masdar

south *n.* جنوب janub

south *adj.* جنوبي janubi

south *adv.* للجنوب leljanub

southern *adj.* جنوبي janubi

souvenir *n.* تذكار tezkar

sovereign *n.* عاهِل a'hel

sovereign *adj.* عنده سِيادة anduh seyadeh

sovereignty *n.* سيادة الدولة syadet eldawleh

sow *v.* يزرع yezra'

sow *n.* خنزيرة khanzereh

space *n.* فضا fadah

space *v.* يوسّع yewasse'

spacious *adj.* فسيح fasih

spade *n.* جاروف jaruf

spade *v.* يحفر yehfur

span *n.* شبر sheber

span *v.* يقيس بالشبر yeqis belsheber

Spaniard *n.* إسْباني esbani

Spanish *adj.* إسْباني esbani

spanner *n.* مَفَك mefakk

spare *v.* يحتاط yehtat

spare *adj.* متروك matruk

spare *n.* إحتِياطي ehtyati

spark *n.* شَرَارة shararah

spark *v.* يطلّع شرارة yetalle' shararah

sparkle *v.* يلمَع yelma'

sparkle *n.* لمَعان lama'an

sparrow *n.* عصفور الدوري asfur elduri

sparse *adj.* خفيف khafif

spasm *n.* تَشنّج tashannuj

spasmodic *adj.* تشنّجي tashannuji

spate *n.* سيل syl

spatial *adj.* فضائي fada'ei

spawn *n.* بيض السمك beid elsamak

spawn *v.* يبيض السمك yebeid elsamak

speak *v.* يحكي yehki

speaker *n.* متحدّث metehaddeth

spear *n.* رمح remh

spear *v.* يطعن برمح yet'an beremeh

spearhead *n.* راس الرمح ras elremh

special *adj.* مميز mumayyaz

specialist *n.* مختصّ mekhtass

speciality *n.* إختصاص ekhtisas

specialization *n.* تخصّص takhassus

specialize *v.* يتخصّص yetkhassas

species *n.* أنواع anwa'

specific *adj.* محدّد mehaddad

specification *n.* تحديد tahdid

specify *v.* يحدّد yehadded

specimen *n.* عيّنة ayyenh

speck *n.* بقعة buq'ah

spectacle *n.* منظر manzar

spectacular *adj.* إستعراضي este'radi

spectator *n.* مُشاهد mushahed

spectre *n.* هاجس hajes

speculate *v.* يضارب yedareb

speculation *n.* مضاربة mudarabeh

speech *n.* حديث hadith

speed *n.* سرعة sur'ah

speed *v.* يسرّع yesarre'

speedily *adv.* بسرعة bser'ah

speedy *adj.* سريع sare'

spell *n.* تهجاية tehjayh

spell *v.* يهجّي yehajji

spell *n.* رقية ruqyh

spend *v.* يمضي yemaddi

spend *v.* يصرف yesruf

spendthrift *n.* سفيه safih

sperm *n.* سائل منوي sa'el manawi

sphere *n.* نطاق nitaq

spherical *adj.* كروي kurawi

spice *n.* بهار behar

spice *v.* يبهّر yebahher

spicy *adj.* متبّل metabbal

spider *n.* عنكبوت ankabut

spike *n.* مسمار mesmar

spike *v.* يثبّت بمسمار yethabbit bemesmar

spill *v.* يسفح yesfah

spill *n.* سفح safh

spin *v.* يغزل yeghzul

spin *n.* غزل ghazl

spinach *n.* سبانخ sabanekh

spinal *adj.* نخاعي nukha'i

spindle *n.* مغزل maghzal

spine *n.* عمود فقري amud faqari

spinner *n.* غزّال ghazzal

spinster *n.* عانس anis

spiral *n.* لولب lulab

spiral *adj.* لولبي lulabi

spirit *n.* روح ruh

spirited *adj.* حرك herk

spiritual *adj.* روحي ruhi

spiritualism *n.* روحانية ruhaneyyeh

spiritualist *n.* روحاني ruhani	**sport** *v.* يعمل رياضة ye'mel ryadah
spirituality *n.* روحانيّة ruhaneyyeh	**sportive** *adj.* رياضي ryadi
spit *v.* يبزق yebzuq	**sportsman** *n.* رياضي ryadi
spit *n.* بزقة bazqah	**spot** *n.* بقعة buq'ah
spite *n.* نكاية nikayeh	**spot** *v.* يبقّع yebaqqe'
spittle *n.* ريق riq	**spotless** *adj.* نضيف nedif
spittoon *n.* مبزقة mabzaqah	**spouse** *n.* زوج zuj
splash *v.* يرشّ بالمي yerushsh belmay	**sprain** *n.* فكشة faksheh
splash *n.* رشّ المي rashsh elmay	**sprain** *v.* ينفكش yenfekesh
spleen *n.* طحال tehal	**spray** *n.* سبراي sepray
splendid *adj.* باهر baher	**spray** *v.* يرشّ سبراي yerushsh sepray
splendour *n.* روعة ru'ah	**spread** *v.* ينتشر yentesher
splinter *n.* شظيّة shazeyyeh	**spread** *v.* يفشي yefshi
splinter *v.* يتشظّى yeshazzi	**spread** *n.* إنتشار intishar
split *v.* يقسم yeqsum	**spree** *n.* فورة furah
split *n.* قسم qesm	**sprig** *n.* غصن صغير ghesn segher
spoil *v.* ينزع من الدلال yenza' mn eldalal	**sprightly** *adj.* ورش weresh
spoil *v.* يفسد yefsed	**spring** *v.* ينبع yenba'
spoil *n.* غنيمة ghanimeh	**spring** *n.* الربيع elrabie'
spokesman *n.* ناطق nateq	**sprinkle** *v.* يرشّ yerushsh
sponge *n.* سفنجة sfenjeh	**sprint** *v.* يركض بسرعة yerkud beser'ah
sponge *v.* يمسح بالسفنجة yemsah belsfenjeh	**sprint** *n.* ركض سريع rakd sare'
sponsor *n.* كفيل kafil	**sprout** *v.* يبرعم yebare'm
sponsor *v.* يكفل yekfal	**sprout** *n.* برعم bur'um
spontaneity *n.* عفويّة afaweyyeh	**spur** *n.* حافز hafez
spontaneous *adj.* عفوي afawi	**spur** *v.* يحفّز yehaffez
spoon *n.* معلقة ma'laqah	**spurious** *adj.* مزوّر mezawwar
spoonful *n.* ملات المعلقة malat elma'laqah	**spurn** *v.* يتأبّى عن yet'abbah an
sporadic *adj.* متقطّع metqatte'	**spurt** *v.* يتدفّق yetdaffaq
sport *n.* رياضة ryadah	**spurt** *n.* تدفق tadaffuq
	sputnik *n.* سبوتنيك sputnik
	sputum *n.* بلغم balgham
	spy *n.* تجسس tajassus

spy v. يتجسّس yetjassas

squad n. مفرزة mafrazeh

squadron n. أسْطول ustul

squalid adj. وسخ wesekh

squander v. يبدّر yebazzer

square n. باحة bahah

square n. مربّع murabba'

square adj. مربّع murabba'

square v. يربّع yerabbe'

squash v. يهرس yehrus

squash n. مهروس mahrus

squat v. يقرفص yeqarfes

squeak n. صرير sarir

squeeze v. يعصر ye'sur

squint v. يحوِل yehwil

squint n. أحوَل ahwal

squire n. نسونجي neswanji

squirrel n. سنجاب senjab

stab v. يطعن yet'an

stab n. طعنة te'neh

stability n. إسْتِتْباب estitbab

stabilization n. إسْتِقْرار estiqrar

stabilize v. يستقرّ yesteqrr

stable adj. مستقرّ mestaqerr

stable n. إسَطبل establ

stadium n. إسْتاد estad

staff n. كادر kader

staff n. غراض ghrad

staff v. يجيب كادر yejib kader

stag n. مضارب بالبورصة mudareb belbursah

stage n. تدريب tadrib

stage v. يعمل تدريب ye'mel tadrib

stagger v. يترنّح yetrannah

stagger n. ترنّح tarannuh

stagnant adj. كاسد kased

stagnate v. يكسد yeksud

stagnation n. كساد kasad

staid adj. رزين razin

stain n. بقعة buq'ah

stain v. يبقّع yebaqqe'

stainless adj. نضيف nedif

stair n. درج daraj

stake n. رهان rehan

stake n. خازوق khazuq

stake v. يراهن yerahn

stale adj. بايت bayt

stale v. يبات yebat

stalemate n. جمود jumud

stalk n. ساق saq

stall n. كشك keshk

stall n. معلف ma'laf

stall v. يماطل yematel

stallion n. فحل fahl

stalwart adj. قوي qawi

stamina n. تحمّل tahammul

stammer v. يتأتِئ yeta'te'

stammer n. تأتأة ta'ta'ah

stamp n. طابع tabe'

stamp v. يختم yekhtum

stampede n. فرار جماعي frar jama'i

stampede v. يتفرّق yetfarraq

stand v. يقف yeqaf

stand n. ستاند stand

standard n. معيار me'yar

standard adj. عادي adi

standardization n. معياريّة me'yareyyeh

standardize v. يعاير ye'ayer

standing n. وقوف wuquf

standpoint n. وجهة wejha

standstill *n.* توقُّف tawaqquf

stanza *n.* مقطع شعر maqta' she'er

staple *n.* تيلة tileh

staple *n.* دبوس dabbus

staple *v.* يحطّ دبوس yehutt dabbus

star *n.* نجم najm

star *v.* يبدى yebda

starch *n.* نشا nasha

stare *v.* يحلق yebahleq

stare *n.* بحلقة bahlaqah

stark *adj.* تامّ tamm

starry *adj.* نجمي najmi

start *v.* يبدى yebda

start *n.* بداية bedayeh

startle *v.* يجفل yejfal

starvation *n.* مجاعة maja'ah

starve *v.* يموت جوع yemut ju'

state *n.* دولة dawleh

state *v.* يقول yequl

stateliness *n.* مهابة mahabeh

stately *adj.* فخم fakhm

statement *n.* مقولة maquleh

statesman *n.* رجل دولة rajul dawleh

static *n.* ساكن saken

static *adj.* ساكن saken

station *n.* محطّة mahattah

station *v.* يركّز yerakkez

stationary *adj.* جامد jamed

stationer *n.* بيّاع القرطاسية bayya' elqurtaseyyeh

stationery *n.* قرطاسيّة qurtaseyyeh

statistical *adj.* إحْصائي ehsa'i

statistician *n.* إحْصائي ehsa'i

statistics *n.* الإحصاء elehsa'

statue *n.* تمثال temthal

stature *n.* مكانة makaneh

status *n.* وضع wade'

statute *n.* تشريع tashri'

statutory *adj.* قانوني qanuni

staunch *adj.* صامد samed

stay *v.* يبقى yebqah

stay *n.* إقامة eqameh

steadfast *adj.* ثابت thabit

steadiness *n.* ثبات thabat

steady *adj.* ثابت thabit

steady *v.* يثبّت yethabbet

steal *v.* يسرق yesruq

stealthily *adv.* بالسر belserr

steam *n.* بخار bukhar

steam *v.* يتبخّر yetbakhkhar

steamer *n.* باخرة bakhrah

steed *n.* حصانٌ سريع hesan sare'

steel *n.* بولاد bulad

steep *adj.* مغطوط maghtut

steep *v.* يغطّ yeghutt

steeple *n.* سباق حرّ sebaq herr

steer *v.* يوجّه yewajjeh

stellar *adj.* نجمي najmi

stem *n.* جذر jazr

stem *v.* ينمو yenmu

stench *n.* صنة sanneh

stencil *n.* ورق حرير waraq harir

step *n.* خطوة khetweh

step *v.* يخطو خطوة yekhtu khetweh

steppe *n.* بادية badeyh

stereotype *n.* قالب qalib

stereotype *v.* يقولب yequlib

stereotyped adj. مُقُوْلَب mequlab

sterile adj. عَقيم aqim

sterility n. عقم uqm

sterilization n. تعقيم ta'qim

sterilize v. يعقّم ye'aqqem

sterling adj. إسترليني esterlini

sterling n. جنيه إسترليني jnih esterlini

stern adj. كالح kaleh

stethoscope n. سمّاعة الدكتور sammaటet eldektur

stew n. لخنة lakhanah

stew v. يطبخ ع نار واطية yetbukh a nar wateyh

steward n. مضيف mudif

stick n. عصاية asayeh

stick v. يلزق yelzuq

sticker n. لصاقة lusaqah

stickler n. مكابر mekaber

sticky adj. دبِق debq

stiff adj. ميبّس meyabbas

stiffen v. يبِّس yeyabbes

stifle v. يخنق yekhnuq

stigma n. وصمة wasmeh

still adj. ثابت thabit

still adv. بثبات bethabat

still v. يهدّي yehaddi

stillness n. ثبات thabat

stimulant n. منبّه munabbeh

stimulate v. ينبّه yenabbeh

stimulus n. حافز hafez

sting v. يَقرص yeqrus

sting n. قرصة qarsah

stingy adj. قرّاص qarras

stipend n. معاش ma'ash

stipulate v. يشترط yeshteret

stipulation n. شرط shart

stir v. يحرّك yeharrek

stirrup n. سوار sewar

stitch n. لفقة lafqah

stitch v. يلفق yelfuq

stock n. مخزون makhzun

stock n. سهم sahm

stock v. يخزّن yekhazzen

stocking n. جورب jawrab

stoke v. يشعل النار yesh'ul nar

stomach n. معدة me'deh

stomach v. يطيق yetiq

stone n. حجر hajar

stone v. يضرب بالحجر yedrub belhajar

stony adj. حجري hajari

stool n. براز buraz

stoop v. يطاطي yetati

stoop n. مطاطاة matatah

stop v. يوقّف yewaqqef

stop n. موقف mawqef

stoppage n. توقيف tawqif

storage n. تخزين takhzin

store n. مخزن makhzan

store v. يخزّن yekhazzen

storey n. طابق tabeq

stork n. لقلق laqlaq

storm n. عاصفة asfeh

storm v. يعصف ye'suf

stormy adj. عاصف a'sef

story n. قصة qessah

stout adj. سمين smin

stove n. وجاق wujaq

stow v. يحزم yehzum

straggle v. يتسكّع yetsakka'

straggler n. متشرّد metsharred

straight adj. مستقيم mustaqim

straighten v. يِجلّس yejalles

straightforward adj. حقّاني haqqani

straightway adv. فَوْراً fawran

strain v. يِتعب yet'ab

strain n. إرهاق erhaq

strain n. تعب ta'ab

strait n. ممر ديّق mamar dayyeq

straiten v. يدَيِّق yedayyeq

strand v. يضفِر yedaffer

strand n. ضَفْرة dafrah

strange adj. غريب gharib

stranger n. غريب gharib

strangle v. يخنُق yekhnuq

strangulation n. إختناق ekhtinaq

strap n. ربّاط rabbat

strap v. يربط yerbut

stratagem n. حيلة hileh

strategic adj. ستراتيجي stratiji

strategist n. ستراتيجي stratiji

strategy n. ستراتيجيّة stratejeyyeh

stratum n. طبَقة tabaqah

straw n. قشّ qashsh

strawberry n. فريز friz

stray v. يِنحرف yenherf

stray adj. طايش taysh

stray n. طايش taysh

stream n. جدْول jadwal

stream v. يِنساب yensab

streamlet n. جدْول jadwal

street n. شارع share'

strength n. طول tul

strengthen v. إيطوّل yetawwel

strenuous adj. صعب sa'eb

stress n. توتّر tawattur

stress n. جهد jehd

stress v. يشدّد على yeshadded ala

stress v. يأكّد على ye'akked ala

stretch v. يتمطمط yetmatmat

stretch n. مطمطة matmatah

stretcher n. نقّالة naqqaleh

strew v. يرشّ yerushsh

strict adj. متشدّد metshadded

stricture n. تضيق tadyyeq

stride v. يمشي بسرعة yemshi bser'ah

stride n. مشية سريعة mashyh share'ah

strident adj. عالي a'li

strife n. خصومة khusumeh

strike v. يضرب yedrub

strike n. ضربة darbeh

striker n. ضارب darib

stringency n. قسوة qasweh

stringent adj. قاسي qasi

strip n. شريط shrit

strip v. يبلص yeblus

stripe n. تَسطير tastir

stripe v. يسطّر yesatter

strive v. يكافح yekafeh

stroke n. سكتة دماغيّة sakteh demagheyyeh

stroke v. يمسّد yemassed

stroke n. خفّقة khafqah

stroke n. شوط shut

stroll v. يدور yedur

stroll n. دورة durah

strong adj. قوي qawi

stronghold n. حصن hesn

structural adj. هيكلي haykali

structure n. هيكل haykal

struggle v. يكافح yekafeh

struggle *n.* مكافحة mukafahah

strumpet *n.* مومس mumes

strut *v.* ينفخ حاله yenfukh haluh

strut *n.* نفخ الحال nafekh elhal

stub *n.* عقب aqeb

stubborn *adj.* عنيد anid

stud *n.* مسمار براس mesmar bras

student *n.* طالب taleb

studio *n.* ستوديو studyu

studious *adj.* مدروس madrus

study *v.* يدرس yedrus

study *n.* دراسة deraseh

study *n.* بحث bahth

stuff *n.* حشوة hashweh

stuff *v.* يحشي yehshi

stuffy *adj.* مسدود masdud

stumble *v.* يقع yeqa'

stumble *n.* وقعة waq'ah

stump *n.* بتر batr

stump *v.* يبتر yebtur

stun *v.* يدوخ yadawwekh

stunt *v.* يقزم yeqazzem

stunt *n.* تقزيم taqzim

stupendous *adj.* مُدهش mudhesh

stupid *adj.* غبي ghabi

stupidity *n.* غباء ghaba'

sturdy *adj.* متين matin

sty *n.* زريبة الخنازير zrebet elkhanazir

style *n.* أسلوب uslub

subdue *v.* يكبت yekbut

subject *n.* موضوع mawdu'

subject *v.* يطوّع yetawwe'

subjection *n.* خضوع khudu'

subjective *adj.* ذاتي zati

subjugate *v.* يروّض yerawwed

subjugation *n.* ترويض tarwid

sublet *v.* يأجر من آجار ye'ajjer mn ajar

sublimate *v.* يبخّر yebakhkher

sublime *adj.* راقي raqi

sublimity *n.* سمو sumwwu

submarine *n.* غوّاصة ghawwasah

submarine *adj.* تحت المي taht elmay

submerge *v.* يغطس yeghtus

submission *n.* تقديم taqdim

submissive *adj.* تقديمي taqdimi

submit *v.* يقدّم yeqaddem

subordinate *adj.* تابع tabe'

subordinate *n.* مرؤوس mar'us

subordinate *v.* يتبع yetba'

subordination *n.* تبعية taba'eyyh

subscribe *v.* يشارك yesharek

subscription *n.* إشتراك eshtirak

subsequent *adj.* لاحق lahiq

subservience *n.* خنوع khunu'

subservient *adj.* خانع khane'

subside *v.* يرسب yersab

subsidiary *adj.* فرعي far'i

subsidize *v.* يدعم yeda'am

subsidy *n.* دعم حكومي da'em hukumi

subsist *v.* يعيش ye'ysh

subsistence *n.* عيشة eysheh

substance *n.* مادّة maddeh

substantial *adj.* أساسي asasi

substantially *adv.* بشكل أساسي beshakl asasi	**sufficiency** *n.* كفاية kefayeh
substantiate *v.* يجسّم yejassem	**sufficient** *adj.* يكفّي beykaffi
substantiation *n.* تجسيم tajsim	**suffix** *n.* لاحقة laheqah
substitute *n.* بديل badil	**suffocate** *v.* يخنق yekhnuq
substitute *v.* يستبدل yestabdel	**suffocation** *n.* خنق khanq
substitution *n.* إستبدال estebdal	**suffrage** *n.* تصويت taswit
subterranean *adj.* جوفي jufi	**sugar** *n.* سكّر sekkar
subtle *n.* بارع bare'	**sugar** *v.* يحلّي بالسكّر yehalli belsekkar
subtlety *n.* براعة bara'ah	**suggest** *v.* يقترح yeqterh
subtract *v.* ينقص yenaqqes	**suggestion** *n.* إقتراح iqterah
subtraction *n.* تنقيص tanqis	**suggestive** *adj.* إقتراحي iqterahi
suburb *n.* ضاحية dahyh	**suicidal** *adj.* إنتحاري intihari
suburban *adj.* ضواحي dawahi	**suicide** *n.* إنتحار intihari
subversion *n.* تهديم tahdim	**suit** *n.* بدلة badleh
subversive *adj.* تهديمي tahdimi	**suit** *v.* يرفع قضية yerfa' qadeyyeh
subvert *v.* يهدم yehdum	**suitability** *n.* تناسب tnasub
succeed *v.* ينجح yenjah	**suitable** *adj.* مناسب munaseb
success *n.* نجاح najah	**suite** *n.* جناح janah
successful *a* ناجح najeh	**suitor** *n.* خطيب khatib
succession *n.* تسلسل tasalsul	**sullen** *adj.* عبوس abus
successive *adj.* تسلسلي tasalsuli	**sulphur** *n.* كبريت kebrit
successor *n.* وريث warith	**sulphuric** *adj.* كبريتي kebriti
succour *n.* إسعاف es'af	**sultry** *adj.* خانق khaneq
succour *v.* يسعف yes'ef	**sum** *n.* مجموع majmu'
succumb *v.* يستسلم yestaslim	**sum** *v.* يجمع yejma'
such *adj.* مثل matal	**summarize** *v.* يلخّص yelakhkhes
suck *v.* يمصّ yemuss	**summary** *n.* تلخيص talkhis
suck *n.* مصّ mass	**summary** *adj.* ملخّص mulakhkhas
suckle *v.* يرضع yeradde'	**summer** *n.* صيف syf
suckling *n.* رضاعة reda'ah	**summit** *n.* قمّة qemmeh
sudden *n.* فجائي fuja'i	**summon** *v.* يستدعي yestad'i
suddenly *adv.* فجأة faj'ah	**summons** *n.* استدعا ested'a
sue *v.* يقاضي yeqadi	**sumptuous** *adj.* فاخر fakher
suffer *v.* يعاني ye'ani	**sun** *n.* شمس shams
suffice *v.* يكفي yekaffi	

sun *v.* يشمّس yeshammes

Sunday *n.* الأحَد elahad

sunder *v.* يقسم yeqsum

sunny *adj.* مشمس meshmes

sup *v.* يمصّ yemuss

sup *n.* مصّ mass

superabundance *n.* طفح tafah

superabundant *adj.* طفحان tafhan

superb *adj.* رائع ra'e'

superficial *adj.* سطحي satehi

superficiality *n.* سطحيّة sateheyyeh

superfine *adj.* فاخر fakher

superfluity *n.* غزارة ghazarah

superfluous *adj.* غزير ghazir

superhuman *adj.* جبّار jabbar

superintend *v.* يراقب yeraqib

superintendence *n.* مراقبة muraqabeh

superintendent *n.* مُراقِب muraqib

superior *adj.* أعْظَم a'zam

superiority *n.* تفَوّق tafawwuq

superman *n.* سوبرمان superman

supernatural *adj.* خارق khareq

supersede *v.* يحلّ محل yehell mahall

supersonic *adj.* أسرع من الصوت asra' mn elsut

superstition *n.* خرافة khurafeh

superstitious *adj.* خرافي khurafi

supertax *n.* ضريبة زيادة darebeh zyadeh

supervise *v.* يشرف على yeshref ala

supervision *n.* إشراف eshraf

supervisor *n.* مشرف meshref

supper *n.* عشا asha

supple *adj.* لين lyn

supplement *n.* كمالة kamaleh

supplement *v.* يكمّل yekammel

supplementary *adj.* تكميلي takmili

supplier *n.* مورّد mwarred

supply *v.* يورّد yewarred

supply *n.* مونة muneh

support *v.* يدعم yed'am

support *n.* دعم da'em

suppose *v.* يفترض yeftered

supposition *n.* إفتراض efterad

suppress *v.* يكبح yekbah

suppression *n.* كبح kabh

supremacy *n.* سيطرة saytarah

supreme *adj.* أعلى a'la

surcharge *n.* رسم زيادة rasm zyadeh

surcharge *v.* يفرُض رسم زيادة yefrud rasm zyadeh

sure *adj.* أكيد akid

surely *adv.* عالأكيد al'akid

surety *n.* تأمين ta'min

surf *n.* تصفّح النت tasaffuh elnet

surf *v.* يتصفّح النت yetsaffah elnet

surface *n.* سطح sateh

surface *v.* يسطّح yesatteh

surfeit *n.* عوالة awaleh

surge *n.* غليان ghalayan

surge *n.* فورة furah

surge *v.* يغلي yeghli	swallow *v.* يبلع yebla'
surgeon *n.* جراح jarrah	swallow *n.* بلع bale'
surgery *n.* جراحة jirahah	swallow *n.* جرعة jur'ah
surmise *n.* ظن zann	swamp *n.* سبخة sabkha
surmise *v.* يظن yezunn	swamp *v.* يغمر yeghmur
surmount *v.* يتغلب yetghallab	swan *n.* بجعة baja'ah
surname *n.* كنية kenyeh	swarm *n.* سرب serb
surpass *v.* يجاوز yetjawaz	swarm *v.* يتجمع yetjamma'
surplus *n.* فائض fa'ed	swarthy *adj.* أسمر asmar
surprise *n.* مفاجأة mufaja'ah	sway *v.* يحرك yeharrek
surprise *v.* يفاجئ yefaje'	sway *v.* يهز yehezz
surrender *v.* يستسلم yestaslem	sway *n.* تحريك tahrik
surrender *n.* إستسلام estislam	sway *n.* هز hazz
surround *v.* يحاوط yehawet	swear *v.* يحلف yehlif
surroundings *n.* بيئة be'ah	sweat *n.* عرق araq
surtax *n.* ضريبة زيادة darebeh zyadeh	sweat *v.* يتعرق yet'arraq
surveillance *n.* مراقبة muraqabeh	sweater *n.* بلوزة صوف bluzeh suf
survey *n.* مسح maseh	sweep *v.* يكنس yeknus
survey *v.* يعمل مسح ye'mel maseh	sweep *n.* كنس kans
survival *n.* عيشة eysheh	sweeper *n.* مكنسة meknseh
survive *v.* يعيش ye'ysh	sweet *adj.* حلو helu
suspect *v.* يشتبه ب yeshtebeh bi	sweet *n.* حلو helu
suspect *adj.* مشبوه mashbuh	sweeten *v.* يحلّي yehalli
suspect *n.* إشتباه eshtibah	sweetmeat *n.* حلويات helweyyat
suspend *v.* يوقف yuqef	sweetness *n.* حلاوة halaweh
suspense *n.* قلق qalaq	swell *v.* ينتفخ yentefekh
suspension *n.* تعطيل ta'attul	swell *n.* إنتفاخ intifakh
suspicion *n.* إشتباه eshtibah	swift *adj.* سريع sare'
suspicious *adj.* مشبوه mashbuh	swim *v.* يسبح yesbah
sustain *v.* يعيل ye'yl	swim *n.* سباحة sbaha
sustenance *n.* إعالة e'aleh	swimmer *n.* سبّاح sabbah
swagger *v.* يتباهى yetbaha	swindle *v.* ينصب yensub
swagger *n.* تباهي tabahi	swindle *n.* نصب nasb
	swindler *n.* نصّاب nassab

swine *n.* مربّي الخنازير mrabbi
khanazir

swing *v.* يتراوح yetrawah

swing *n.* تراوح tarawuh

Swiss *n.* سويسري swisri

Swiss *adj.* سويسري swisri

switch *n.* زر كهرباً zrr
kahrabah

switch *v.* يحوّل yehawwel

swoon *n.* إغماء eghma'

swoon *v.* يغمى عليه yughma'
alyh

swoop *v.* ينقضّ على yenqadd
ala

swoop *n.* إنقضاض inqidad

sword *n.* سيف sif

sycophancy *n.* تمسيح جوخ
tamsih jukh

sycophant *n.* مسيّح جوخ
massyh jukh

syllable *n.* مَقْطَع meqatta'

syllabus *n.* منهج دراسي manhaj
derasi

symbiosis *n.* تَكَافُل takaful

symbol *n.* رمز ramz

symbolic *adj.* رمزي ramzi

symbolism *n.* رمزِيّة
ramzeyyeh

symbolize *v.* يرمز yermuz

symmetrical *adj.* مَتَطَابِق
mettabeq

symmetry *n.* تطابق tatabuq

sympathetic *adj.* حسّاس
hassas

sympathize *v.* يتعاطف مع
yet'ataf ma

sympathy *n.* تعاطُف ta'atuf

symphony *n.* سمفونيّة
semfuneyyeh

symposium *n.* ندوة nadweh

symptom *n.* عرَض arad

symptomatic *adj.* عرَضي aradi

synergy *n.* تعاون ta'awun

synonym *n.* مُرَادف muradef

synopsis *n.* خُلَاصة khulasah

syntax *n.* إعْراب e'rab

synthesis *n.* تَرْكِيب tarkib

syringe *n.* سيرنغ serang

syringe *v.* يضرب إبرة yedrub
ebreh

syrup *n.* سيروب sirub

system *n.* نظام nizam

systematic *adj.* نظامي nizami

T

table *n.* طاولة tawleh

table *n.* جدول jadwal

tablet *n.* لوح luh

tablet *n.* حبّة دوا habbet dawa

tabloid *n.* جريدة jaredeh

taboo *n.* محظُور mahzur

taboo *adj.* محظُور mahzur

taboo *v.* يمنع yemna'

tabular *adj.* مسطّح mesattah

tabulate *v.* يصنّف yesannef

tabulation *n.* تصنيف tasnif

tacit *adj.* سكوني skuti

taciturn *adj.* كتُوم katum

tack *n.* درزة darzeh

tack *v.* يدرز yedruz

tackle *n.* نقاش neqash

tackle *v.* يناقش yenaqesh

tact *n.* لباقة labaqah

tactful *adj.* لبق labeq

tactician *n.* خبير تكتيك khabir taktik

tactics *n.* تكتيك taktik

tactile *adj.* لمسي lamsi

tag *n.* علامة alameh

tag *v.* بطاقة سعر betaqet se'r

tail *n.* دنب danab

tail *v.* يضم yedumm

tailor *n.* خَيَّاط khayyat

tailor *v.* يخيط yekhayyet

taint *n.* عيب ayb

taint *v.* يعيب ye'ib

take *v.* ياخد yakhud

takeaway *adj.* سفري safari

takeaway *n.* أكل سفري akel safari

taken *adj.* مَأخُود ma'khud

takeoff *n.* طيران tayaran

takeout *adj.* مسحوب masehub

takeout n إزاحة ezaha

takeover *n.* إستيلاء estila'

taker *n.* آخذ a'khed

tale *n.* حكاية hekayeh

talebearer *n.* نمّام nammam

talebearing *n.* نميمة namimeh

talent *n.* موهبة mawhebeh

talisman *n.* حجاب hijab

talk *v.* يحكي yehki

talk *n.* حكي haki

talkative *adj.* ملسن melsen

talkativeness *n.* كرّ kerr

tall *adj.* طويل tawil

tallow *n.* شحم shahm

tally *n.* أرشيف arshif

tally *v.* ينسجم yensijm

talon *n.* مخلب makhlab

taloned *adj.* إلو مخالب elu makhlab

tamarind *n.* تمر هندي tamr hendi

tame *adj.* أليف alif

tame *v.* يروّض yerawwed

tamper *v.* يدكّ yedekk

tamper *n.* مدكّ medakk

tampon *n.* سدّادة saddadeh

tampon *v.* يسدّ yesedd

tan *v.* يسمّر yesammer

tan *n.* تسمير tasmir

tan *adj.* مسمر mesmarr

tandem *n.* مقطورة maqturah

tandoor *n.* تنور tannur

tang *n.* يعزّ ye'ezz

tang *v.* أزيز aziz

tangent *n.* ظلّ zell

tangible *adj.* ملموس malmus

tangle *n.* إرتباك ertibak

tangle *v.* يرتبك yertebk

tango *n.* رقصة التانغو raqset tangu

tango *v.* يرقص تانغو yerqus tangu

tank *n.* صهريج sahrij

tank *n.* دبابة dabbabeh

tankard *n.* كوز kuz

tanker *n.* ناقلة نفط naqelt naft

tanner *n.* دبّاغ dabbagh

tannery *n.* مدبغة madbaghah

tantamount *adj.* معادل me'adel

tantamount *v.* يعادل ye'adel
tap *n.* حَنَفِيّة hanafeyyeh
tap *n.* طَرْقة tarqah
tap *v.* يدقّ yeduqq
tap *v.* ينتفع yentefe'
tape *n.* شريط shrit
tape *v.* يسجّل ع شريط yesajjel a shrit
tape player *n.* مسجلة msajjleh
taper *v.* يبري yebri
tar *n.* قَطْرانّ qutran
tar *v.* يزفّت yezaffit
tarantism *n.* رقْصة raqwasah
tardiness *n.* تأخير ta'khir
tardy *adj.* بطىء bate'
target *n.* هدف hadaf
tariff *n.* تعرفة جمركيّة ta'rufeh jumrukeyyeh
task *n.* مهمّة mahammeh
taste *n.* طعمة ta'meh
taste *v.* يستطعم yestate'em
tasteful *adj.* طيّب tayyeb
tasty *adj.* بيشهّي beyshahhi
tatter *n.* خِرْقة kherqah
tatter *v.* يشقّ yeshuqq
tattoo *n.* وشم washm
tattoo *v.* يعمل وشم ye'mul washm
taunt *v.* يعيّر ye'ayyer
taunt *n.* تعيير ta'yyer
taut *adj.* متوتّر metwatter
tavern *n.* خمّارة khammarah
taw *v.* يدبغ yedbugh
taw n دبغ dabegh
tawer *n.* دبّاغ dabbagh
tax *n.* ضريبة darebeh

tax *v.* يفرض ضريبة yefrud darebeh
taxable *adj.* يخضع للضريبة beykhda' leldarebeh
taxation *n.* فرض الضرايب fard eldarayb
taxi *n.* تكسي taksi
taxicab *n.* تكسي taksi
taxidermy *n.* تحنيط tahnit
tea *n.* شاي shay
teabag *n.* كيس شاي kis shay
teach *v.* يدرّس yedarres
teacher *n.* مدرّس mudarres
teachings *n.* وصايا wasaya
teacup *n.* فنجان شاي fenjan shay
team *v.* يجتمع بفريق yejteme' befariq
team *n.* فريق fariq
teammate *n.* عضو بفريق udu befariq
teamwork *n.* عمل جماعي amal jama'i
teapot *n.* برّاد الشاي barrad elshay
tear *v.* يشقّ yeshuqq
tear *n.* شقّ shaqq
tear *n.* دمعة dam'ah
tearful *adj.* ببكي bebakki
tease *v.* يدايق yedayq
tease *n.* مدايقة mudayaqah
teaser *n.* سعر مغري se'r meghri
teat *n.* حلمة helmeh
technical *adj.* تقني teqani
technicality *n.* تقنيّة teqaneyyeh
technician *n.* تقني teqani

technique *n.* طَريقَة tareqah

technological *adj.* تكنولوجي teknuluji

technology *n.* تكنولوجيا teknulujia

tectonic *adj.* بنائي bena'i

tedious *adj.* بَيملَّل beymallel

tedium *n.* مَلَل malal

teem *v.* يعجق ye'juq

teenager *n.* مراهق muraheq

teens *n. pl.* مراهقة murahaqah

teethe *v.* يسنّن yesannen

teetotaller *n.* موقِف شرب mwaqqef sherb

telecast *n.* تلفزة talfazeh

telecast *v.* يتلفز yetalfez

telecommunications *n.* إتصالات سلكيّة ولاسلكيّة ettisalat selkeyyeh wla selkeyyeh

teleconference *n.* إجتماع هاتفي ejtima' hatefi

telecourse *n.* درس تلفزيوني dars telfezyuni

telegraph *n.* فاكس faks

telegraph *v.* يبعت فاكس yeb'at faks

telekinesis *n.* تحريك ذهني tahrik zehni

telemarket *v.* يسوّق بالهاتف yesawweq belhatef

telemarketing *n.* تسويق بالهاتف taswiq belhatef

telemetry *n.* قياس عن بعد qyas an bu'd

telepathic *adj.* تخاطري takhaturi

telepathist *n.* متخاطِر metkhater

telepathy *n.* تخاطُر takhatur

telephone *n.* تلفون telifun

telephone *v.* يتلفِن yetalfn

telescope *n.* مجهر mejhar

telescopic *adj.* مجهري mejhari

televise *v.* يتلفز yetalfez

television *n.* تلفزيون telfezyun

tell *v.* يخبِّر yekhabber

teller *n.* أمين صندوق amin sanduq

telling *n.* إخبار ekhbar

telltale *n.* نمّام nammam

temeritous *adj.* متهوِّر metehawwer

temerity *n.* تهوُّر tahawwur

temper *n.* طبع tabe'

temper *v.* يليِّن yelayyn

temperament *n.* مزاج mazaj

temperamental *adj.* مزاجي mazaji

temperance *n.* عفّة effeh

temperate *adj.* عفيف afif

temperature *n.* درجة الحرارة darajet elhararah

tempest *n.* عاصفة a'sfeh

tempestuous *adj.* عاصف a'sef

template *v.* يقولب yequleb

template *n.* قالب qalib

temple *n.* هيكل haykal

temporal *adj.* مؤقَّت mu'aqqat

temporary *adj.* بشكل مؤقّت beshakel mu'aqqat

tempt *v.* يغري yeghri

temptation *n.* إغراء eghra'

tempter *n.* شيطان shitan

ten *n., a* الرقم 10 elraqm 10

tenacious *adj.* متماسك metmasek

tenacity *n.* تَمَاسُك tamasuk

tenant *n.* خيمة khemeh

tend *v.* يميل yemil

tendency *n.* ميل myl

tender *n.* مناقصة munaqasah

tender *v.* يدخل مناقصة yedkhul munaqasah

tender *adj.* غَضّ ghadd

tenderhearted *adj.* حنون hanun

tenderize *v.* يطرّي yetarri

tenderness *n.* طراوة taraweh

tendinitis *n.* إلتهاب وتر eltihab watar

tenebrous *adj.* غامق ghameq

tenet *n.* مذهب mazhab

tenfold *adj.* عشر أضعاف asher ad'aaf

tenfold *adv.* بعشر أضعاف be'asher ad'aaf

tennis *n.* تنس tenis

tenor *n.* أجل ajal

tense *adj.* مشدود mashdud

tense *adj.* موتّر mwattar

tense *n.* زمن zaman

tense *v.* يشدّ yeshedd

tensile *adj.* يمطّ beymutt

tension *n.* ضغط الدم daghet eldamm

tension *v.* يوتّر yewatter

tensioned *adj.* متوتّر metwatter

tensor *n.* عضلة موتّرة adaleh mwattrah

tensor *adj.* مُوتّر mwatter

tent *n.* خيمة khemeh

tentative *adj.* مؤقّت mu'aqqat

tenth *adj.* العاشر elasher

tentmaker *n.* خَيّام khayyam

tenuous *adj.* ضعيف da'ef

tenuously *adv.* بضعف beda'ef

tenure *v.* يتثبت بوظيفة yethabbet bewazefeh

tenure *n.* تثبيت وظيفي tathbit wazifi

tepid *adj.* فاتر fater

tepidity *n.* فتور futur

terabit *n.* تيرابت tirabet

terabyte *n.* تيرابايت tirabyt

term *n.* كلمة klmeh

term *n.* شرط shart

term *n.* بند band

term *v.* يسمّي yesammi

terminable *adj.* بقبل الفسخ beqbal elfasekh

terminal *adj.* نهائي niha'i

terminal *n.* محطة النهاية mahattet elnihayeh

terminate *v.* ينهي yenhi

termination *n.* إنهاء enha'

terminology *n.* علم المصطلحات elm elmustalahat

terminus *n.* غاية ghayh

termite *n.* نمل أبيض naml abyad

terrace *n.* بلكون balkun

terrain *n.* أرض ard

terrestrial *adj.* برّي barri

terrible *adj.* سيء saye'

terrier *n.* سجل عقاري sejell aqari

terrific *adj.* يخوّف beykhawwef

terrify *v.* يخوّف yekhawwef

territorial *adj.* إقليمي eqlimi

territory *n.* إقليم eqlim

terror *n.* إرهاب erhab

terrorism *n.* الإرهاب elerhab

terrorist *n.* إرهابي erhabi

terrorize *v.* يرهب yerheb

terse *adj.* موجز mujaz

tertian *adj.* ثلاثي thulathi

tertiary *n.* التالت eltalet

tertiary *adj.* تالت talet

test *v.* يختبر yekhteber

test *n.* إختبار ikhtibar

testament *n.* وصيّة waseyyeh

testicle *n.* بيضة الرجال bedet elrejjal

testify *v.* يشهّد yeshhad

testimonial *n.* شهادة shahadeh

testimony *n.* شهادة shahadeh

testosterone *n.* هرمون ذكري harmun zakari

tete-a-tete *n.* وجها لوجه wajhan lawajeh

tetra *n.* رباعي ruba'i

text *n.* نص ness

textbook *n.* دفتر daftar

textile *adj.* منسوج mansuj

textile *n.* نسيج nasij

texture *n.* تركيب tarkib

thank *v.* يشكر yeshkur

thanks *n.* شكراً shukran

thankful *adj.* شاكر shaker

thankless *adj.* ناكر للجميل naker leljamil

thatch *n.* قش qashsh

thatch *v.* يسقف بالقش yesquf belqashsh

thaw *v.* يدوّب yedawweb

thaw *n.* تدويب tadwib

theatre *n.* مسرح masrah

theatrical *adj.* مسرحي masrahi

theft *n.* سرقة serqah

theism *n.* توحيد tawhid

theist *n.* موحّد mwahhed

thematic *adj.* موضوعي mawdu'i

theme *n.* موضوع mawdu'

then *adv.* وبعدا wba'da

thence *adv.* وبعدا wba'da

theocracy *n.* حكومة دينية hukumeh deneyyeh

theologian *n.* عالم ديني a'lem dini

theology *n.* لاهوت lahut

theorem *n.* نظري nazari

theorist *n.* صاحب نظريّة sahib nazareyyeh

theorize *v.* يحطّ نظريّة yehutt nazareyyeh

theory *n.* نظريّة nazareyyeh

therapy *n.* علاج elaj

there *adv.* هونيك hunik

thereabouts *adv.* تقريباً taqriban

thereafter *adv.* وبعدا wba'da

therefore *adv.* مشان هيك mshan hik

thermal *adj.* حراري hrari

thermometer *n.* مقياس حرارة meqyas hrarah

thermos (flask) *n.* ترمس termus

thesis *n.* أُطْروحَة utruhah

thick *adj.* سميك smik

thick *n.* سماكة samakeh

thicken *v.* يسمّك yesammek

thicket *n.* أَدْغال adghal

thief *n.* حَرامي harami

thigh *n.* فَخْذ fakhd

thimble *n.* كشتبان keshteban

thin *adj.* نحيف nhif

thin *adj.* رفيع rafe'

thin *v.* يضعف yed'af

thing *n.* شي shi

think *v.* يفكّر yefakker

thinker *n.* مفكّر mefakker

third *adj.* ثالت talit

third *n.* التالت eltalit

thirst *n.* عطش atash

thirst *v.* يعطش ye'tash

thirsty *adj.* عطشان atshan

thirteen *n.* الرقم 13 elraqm 13

thirteenth *n.* التلاطعاش eltalta'sh

thirtieth *n.* الثلاثينيات eltlatineyyat

thirty *n.* الرقم 30 elraqm 30

thistle *n.* شوك shuk

thorax *n.* صَدْر sadr

thorn *n.* حَسَك hasak

thorny *adj.* محسّك mehassek

thoroughfare *n.* مرور murur

thought *n.* فكْرة fekrah

thoughtful *adj.* كتير التفكير ktir eltafkir

thousand *n.* الرقم 1000 elraqm 1000

thrall *n.* عَبْد abd

thralldom *n.* إسْتعْباد este'bad

thrash *v.* يجلد yejlud

thread *n.* خيط khit

thread *v.* يدخّل الخيط بالإبرة yedakhkhel el'ebreh belkhit

threat *n.* تهديد tahdid

threaten *v.* يهدّد yehadded

three *n.* الرقم 3 elraqm 30

thresh *v.* يطحن yetehan

threshold *n.* عتبة atabeh

thrice *adv.* تلات أضعاف tlat ad'af

thrift *n.* توْفير tawfir

thrifty *adj.* حريص haris

thrill *n.* رعشة ra'sheh

thrill *v.* يرتعش yerte'sh

thrive *v.* يترعرع yetra'ra'

throat *n.* حلْق halq

throaty *adj.* مبحوح mabhuh

throb *v.* يخفق yekhfuq

throb *n.* خفقان khafaqan

throe *n.* مخاض makhad

throne *n.* عرْش arsh

throne *v.* يقعد عالعرش yeq'ud al'arsh

throng *n.* زحِمة zahmeh

throng *v.* تزحِم tezhum

throw *v.* زتّ yezett

throw *n.* زتّ zatt

thrust *v.* يدفش yedfush

thrust *n.* دفش dafsh

thud *n.* خبطة khabtah

thud *v.* يخبط yekhbut

thug *n.* سفّاح saffah

thumb *n.* إبْهام ibham

thumb *v.* يقلب بإبهامه yeqlub bi'ibhamuh

thunder *n.* رعْد ra'ed

thunder *v.* ترعِد ter'ud

thunderous *adj.* رَعْدي ra'di

Thursday *n.* الخميس elkhamis

thus *adv.* فـ fa

thwart *v.* يعجز ye'ajjez

tick *n.* تكة takkeh

tick *v.* يتكّ yetekk

ticket *n.* بطاقة betaqah

tickle *v.* يغرغر yeghargher

ticklish *adj.* حساس hassas

tide *n.* مد وجزر madd w jazr

tidings *n. pl.* أخبار akhbar

tidiness *n.* ترتيب tartib

tidy *adj.* مرتب mrattab

tidy *v.* يرتّب yeratteb

tie *v.* يربط كرافة yerbut krafeh

tie *n.* كرافة krafeh

tier *n.* صفّ saff

tiger *n.* نمر nemr

tight *adj.* ديّق dayyeq

tighten *v.* يديّق yedayyeq

tigress *n.* نمرة nemrah

timber *n.* خشب khashab

time *n.* وقت waqt

timely *adj.* بوقته bwaqtuh

timid *adj.* جبان jaban

timidity *n.* جبن jebn

timorous *adj.* جبان jaban

tin *n.* تنكة tanakeh

tin *n.* قصدير qasdir

tin *v.* يبيّض الطناجر yebayyed eltanajer

tincture *n.* صبغة sabghah

tincture *v.* يصبغ yesbugh

tinsel *n.* زينة zyneh

tint *n.* صبغة sabghah

tint *v.* يصبغ yesbugh

tiny *adj.* صغير seghir

tip *n.* بخشيش bakhshish

tip *v.* يلقّم yelaqqim

tip *n.* سنّ senn

tip (off) *v.* يحذّر yehzar

tipsy *adj.* سكران sakran

tire *v.* يتعب yet'eb

tire *n.* دولاب dulab

tiresome *adj.* متعب met'ab

tissue *n.* محرمة mahrameh

titanic *adj.* تيتانيك titanik

tithe *n.* ضريبة العشر darebet elusher

title *n.* عقد aqed

title *n.* سند ملكيّة sanad mulkeyyeh

title *v.* يلقّب yelaqqeb

titular *adj.* نخري fakhri

toast *n.* نخب nakhb

toast *v.* يشرب نخب yeshrab nakhb

tobacco *n.* تبغ tabegh

today *n.* اليوم elyum

toe *n.* إصبع الرجل esba' rejl

toffee *n.* توفي tufi

together *adv.* مع بعض ma ba'ed

toil *n.* إرهاق erhaq

toil *v.* يتعب yet'ab

toilet *n.* تواليت twalit

token *n.* رمز ramz

tolerable *adj.* محتمل muhtamal

tolerance *n.* تسامح tasamuh

tolerant *adj.* متسامح metsameh

tolerate *v.* يسامح yesameh

toleration *n.* تسامح tasamuh

toll *n.* رسم مرور rasm murur

tomato *n.* بندورة bandurah

tomb n. قبر qabr

tome n. مجلد mujallad

tomorrow n. بكرا bukrah

ton n. طن tenn

tone n. رنة ranneh

tongs n. pl. ملقط menaqqat

tongue n. لسان lsan

tonic adj. منعش mun'esh

tonight n. الليلة ellyleh

tonsil n. لوزة luzeh

tonsure n. حلاقة hlaqah

too adv. كمان kaman

tool n. أداة adat

tooth n. سن senn

toothache n. وجع سنين waja' snen

top n. سطح sateh

topaz n. ياقوت أصفر yaqut asfar

topic n. موضوع mawdu'

topography n. طبوغرافيا tubughrafya

topple v. ينقلب على yenqelib ala

topsy turvy adj. بالمقلوب belmaqlub

topsy turvy adv. فوقاني تحتاني fuqani tehtani

torch n. فانوس fanus

torment n. وجع waja'

torment v. يوجع yewajje'

tornado n. إعصار e'sar

torpedo n. طوربيد turbid

torpedo v. ينسف yensuf

torrent n. سيل syl

torrid adj. سخن sekhn

tortoise n. سلحفة selhfeh

torture n. تعذيب ta'zib

torture v. يعذب ye'azzeb

toss v. يرمي yermi

toss n. رماية rmayeh

total adj. إجمالي ejmali

total n. الإجمالي el'ejmali

touch v. يلمس yelmus

touch n. لمسة lamseh

tough adj. خشن kheshen

toughen v. يخشن yekhashshen

tour n. جولة jawleh

tour v. يعمل جولة ye'mel jawleh

tourism n. سياحة syahah

tourist n. سايح sayh

tournament n. بطولة butuleh

tow n. سحب sahb

tow v. يسحب yesehab

towards prep. ناح nah

towboat n. قاطرة qatrah

towel n. منشفة manshafeh

towel v. ينشف yenashshef

tower n. برج berj

town n. قرية qaryeh

toxemia n. تسمم الدم tasammum eldamm

toxic adj. يسمم beysammem

toxicity n. سمية semmeyyeh

toxicology n. علم السموم elm elsumum

toxin n. ذيفان zyfan

toy n. لعبة le'beh

trace n. أثر athar

trace v. يتتبع yettabba'

trachea n. قصبة هوائية qasabeh hawa'eyyeh

tracheoscopy *n.* تنظير القصبة الهوائية tanzir elqasabeh elhawa'eyyeh

tract *n.* مَسلك maslak

traction *n.* سحب sahb

tractor *n.* تراكتور traktur

trade *n.* تِجارة tejarah

trade *v.* يتاجر yetajer

trader *n.* تاجر tajer

tradition *n.* تقليد taqlid

traditional *adj.* تقليدي taqlidi

traffic *n.* عُجّة سير aje'et sir

traffic *v.* يتاجر yetajer

tragedy *n.* تراجيديا trajidya

tragic *adj.* تراجيدي trajidi

trail *n.* سبيل sabil

trail *v.* يجرجر yejarjer

trailer *n.* مقطورة maqturah

train *n.* قطار qetar

trainee *n.* متدرب mettedarreb

training *n.* تدريب tadrib

traitor *n.* خائِن khayn

tram *n.* ترام tram

trample *v.* يدوس yedus

trance *n.* غيبوبة ghaybubeh

tranquil *adj.* رايق rayq

tranquility *n.* روقان rawaqan

tranquillize *v.* يروق yerawweq

transact *v.* يعمل صفقة ye'mel safqah

transaction *n.* صفقة safqah

transcend *v.* يتفوق yetfawwaq

transcendent *adj.* متفوق metfawweq

transcribe *v.* ينسخ yensakh

transcriber *n.* ناسخ nasekh

transcription *n.* نسخ naskh

transfer *n.* نقل ملكيّة naql melkeyyeh

transfer *v.* ينقل ملكيّة yenqul melkeyyeh

transferable *adj.* بينتقل beynteqel

transform *v.* يتحوّل yetehawwal

transformation *n.* تحوّل tahawwul

transgress *v.* يتخطّى yetkhattah

transgression *n.* تخطّي takhatti

transit *n.* ترانزيت tranzit

transition *n.* إنتقال intiqal

transitive *n.* إنتقالي intiqali

transitory *adj.* مرْحلي marhali

translate *v.* يترجم yetarjem

translation *n.* ترجمة tarjameh

transmigration *n.* تقمص أرواح taqammus arwah

transmission *n.* بثّ bathth

transmit *v.* يبثّ yebethth

transmitter *n.* جهاز إرسال jihaz ersal

transparent *adj.* شفّاف shaffaf

transplant *v.* يزرع عضو yerra' udu

transplantation *n.* زراعة عضو zera'et udu

transport *v.* ينقل yenqul

transportation *n.* نقل naql

trap *n.* مصيدة masyadeh

trap *v.* يقع بالمصيدة yeqa' belmasyadeh

trapezoid *n.* شِبه مُنْحَرِف shebh menheref

trash *n.* زبالة zbaleh

trashed *adj.* مكسَّر mekassar

trauma *n.* رض redd

traumatic *adj.* رضّي reddi

traumatism *n.* رضّة raddah

travel *v.* يسافر yesafer

travel *n.* سفر safar

traveller *n.* مسافر mesafer

traverse *v.* يتنهّل yetnassal

traverse *n.* تنصل tanassul

tray *n.* صينيّة seneyyeh

treacherous *adj.* غدّار ghaddar

treachery *n.* غدر ghadr

tread *v.* يدعس yed'as

tread *n.* دعس da'es

treadmill *n.* طاحونة tahuneh

treason *n.* خيانة kheyaneh

treasure *n.* ثروة tharweh

treasurer *n.* أمين خزينة amin khazyneh

treasury *n.* خزينة khazyneh

treatment *n.* معاملة mu'amaleh

treaty *n.* معاهدة mu'ahadeh

tree *n.* شجرة shajarah

tremble *v.* يرجف yerjuf

trench *n.* خندق khandaq

trench *v.* يحفر خندق yehfur khandaq

trend *n.* موضة mudah

trespass *v.* يتطاول yettawal

trespass *n.* مطاولة metawaleh

trial *n.* تجربة tajrubeh

triangle *n.* مثلث muthallath

tribal *adj.* عشايري ashayri

tribe *n.* عشيرة ashireh

tribulation *n.* محنة mehneh

tribunal *n.* محكمة mahkameh

tributary *adj.* فرعي fare'i

tribute *n.* أتاوة ataweh

trickster *n.* غشّاش ghashshash

tricky *adj.* محتال mehtal

tricolour *adj.* ثلاثي الألوان thulathi elalwan

trigger *n.* قواس qwas

trigger *v.* يقوّس yeqawwes

trim *n.* قص qass

trim *v.* يقص yequss

trinity *n.* الثالوث المقدّس elthaluth elmuqaddas

trip *v.* يطلع رحلة yetla' rehleh

trip *n.* رحلة rehleh

triple *adj.* ثلاثي thulathi

triple *v.t.,* يضرب ب 3 yedrub bi 3

tripod *n.* منصب mansab

triumph *n.* نصر nasr

triumph *v.* ينتصر yentesr

triumphant *adj.* منتصر menteser

trivial *adj.* تافه tafeh

troop *n.* قوّات quwwat

troop *v.* يجمّع yejamme'

tropic *n.* مدار madar

tropical *adj.* مداري madari

trouble *n.* مشكلة meshkleh

trouble *v.* يعمل مشكلة ye'mul meshkleh

troublesome *adj.* مشكلجي meshkalji

trousers *n. pl* بنطلون bantalun

truce *n.* هدنة hedneh

truck *n.* شاحنة shahneh

True *adj.* صح sahh

trumpet *n.* بوق buq

trumpet *v.* ينفخ بالبوق yenfukh belbuq

trunk *n.* جِذع jeze'

trust *n.* ثقة theqah

trust *v.* يوثق yewaththeq

trustee *n.* وصي wasi

trustful *adj.* بنوثق فيه beynwetheq fih

trusty *n.* موثوق mawthuq

truth *n.* صدق sedq

truthful *adj.* صادق sadeq

try *v.* يحاول yehawel

try *n.* محاولة muhawaleh

tryst *n.* موعِد maw'ed

tub *n.* بانيو banyu

tube *n.* أنبوب unbub

tuberculosis *n.* سلّ sell

tubular *adj.* أنابيبي anabibi

tuition *n.* تعليم ta'lim

tumble *v.* يوقع yuqa'

tumbler *n.* بهلوان bahlwan

tumbler *n.* طاسة taseh

tumour *n.* ورم waram

tumult *n.* هوشة husheh

tunnel *n.* نفق nafaq

turban *n.* عمامة amameh

turbine *n.* طوربين turbin

turbulence *n.* شغب shaghab

turbulent *adj.* مشاغب mushagheb

turf *n.* حلبة halabeh

turkey *n.* تركيّا terkeyyah

turmeric *n.* كركم kurkum

turmoil *n.* هيجان hyajan

turn *v.* يقلب yeqlib

turn *v.* يدور yedur

turn *n.* دور dur

turn *n.* دوران dawaran

turner *n.* خرّاط kharrat

turnip *n.* لفت left

turtle *n.* سلحفة selhfeh

tusk *n.* ناب الفيل nab elfil

tussle *n.* صراع sera'

tutor *n.* معلّم me'allem

tutorial *adj.* تعليمي ta'limi

tutorial *n.* درس خصوصى dars khsusi

twelfth *adj.* الطناعش eltna'esh

twentieth *n.* العشرينيات eleshreneyyat

twenty *n.* الرقم 20 elraqm 20

twice *adv.* مرتين martin

twilight *n.* شفق shafaq

twin *n.* توأم taw'am

twin *adj.* توأم taw'am

twinkle *v.* يلمع yelma'

twist *v.* يبرم yebrum

twist *n.* برم barm

two *n.* الرقم 2 elraqm 2

twofold *adj.* ضِعفين de'fin

type *n.* أسلوب uslub

type *v.* يطبع yetba'

typhoid *n.* تيفوئيد tefu'yd

typhus *n.* حمى التيفوس hemmah eltifus

typical *adj.* نمطي namati

tyranny *n.* بطش batsh

tyrant *n.* طاغي taghi

tyre *n.* إطار الدولاب etar eldulab

U

udder *n.* ثدي thadi

ufo *n.* طبق طاير tabaq tayer

ugly *adj.* بشع beshe'

ulcer *n.* قرحة qarha

ulcerous *adj.* متقرح metqarreh

ultimate *adj.* مطلق mutlaq

ultimatum *n.* إنذار نهائي enzar niha'iy

ultrasonic *adj.* أسرع من الصوت asra' mn elsut

ultraviolet *adj.* فوق البنفسجي fuq elbanafsaji

umbrella *n.* شمسية shamseyyeh

umpire *n.* حكم hakam

umpire *v.t.,* يحكم yehkum

unabashed *adj.* ما بخجل ma beykhjal

unable *adj.* مو قادر mu qader

unabridged *adj.* كامل kamel

uncle *n.* عم amm

under *prep.* تحت taht

undercurrent *n.* تيّار تحتي tayyar tahti

underdog *n.* خاسر khaser

undergo *v.* يدوق yeduq

undergraduate *n.* طالب جامعي taleb jame'y

underhand *adj.* سرّي serri

underline *v.* يحطّ خطّ تحته yehutt khatt tahtuh

undermine *v.* يحجّم yehajjem

underneath *prep.* تحت taht

understand *v.* يفهم yefham

undertake *v.* يتعهّد yet'ahhad

undertone *n.* نغمة خفيفة naghmeh khafifeh

underwear *n.* لبس داخلي lebs dakhli

undo *v.* يتراجع yetraja'

undue *adj.* مو مستحق mu mesteheqq

undulate *v.* يتموّج yetmawwaj

undulation *n.* تمويج tamwij

unearth *v.* ينبش yenbush

unfold *v.* يفتح yeftah

unfortunate *adj.* تعيس ta'is

unification *n.* لمّ الشمل lamm elshaml

union *n.* إتّحاد ittihad

unionist *n.* نقابي naqabi

unique *adj.* فريد frid

unison *n.* إئتلاف e'etilaf

unit *n.* وحدة wehdeh

unite *v.* يوحّد yewahhed

unity *n.* وحدة wehdeh

universal *adj.* عالمي a'lami

universality *n.* عالمية a'lameyyeh

universe *n.* الكون elkun

university *n.* جامعة jam'ah

unless *conj.* إلّا ella

until *prep.* لوقت lawaqt

up *adv.* لفوق lafuq

up *prep.* فوق fuq

upbraid *v.* يلوم yelum

upheaval *n.* فوران fawaran

upon *prep.* وقت waqt

upper *adj.* فوقاني fuqani

upright *adj.* حقّاني haqqani

uprising *n.* إنتفاضة intifadah

uproar *n.* معمعة ma'ma'ah

uproot *v.* يقلع yeqla'

upset *v.* يدايق yedayeq

upshot *n.* زبدة zbdeh

upstart *n.* حديث النعمة hadith elne'meh

up-to-date *adj.* حديث hadith

upward *adj.* فوقاني fuqani

upwards *adv.* لفوق lafuq

urban *adj.* مدني madani

urbane *adj.* أنيس anis

urbanity *n.* أُنس uns

urchin *n.* قنفذ qunfuz

urge *v.* يلح yelehh

urge *n.* إلحاح elhah

urgency *n.* إضطرار ittirar

urgent *adj.* مستعجل mesta'jil

urinal *n.* نونية nuneyyeh

urinary *adj.* بولي buli

urinate *v.* يبوّل yebawwel

urination *n.* تبويل tabwil

urine *n.* بول bul

urn *n.* جرّة jarrah

usage *n.* إستخدام estikhdam

use *n.* إستخدام estikhdam

use *v.* يستخدم yestakhdem

useful *adj.* مفيد mufid

usual *adj.* عادي adi

usually *adv.* عادةً adeh

usurer *n.* مرابي mrabi

utensil *n.* كلّة keleh

uterus *n.* رحم rahm

utility *n.* منفعة manfa'ah

utilization *n.* إنتفاع intifa'

utilize *v.* ينتفع yentefe'

utopia *n.* مدينة فاضلة madineh fadeleh

utterance *n.* كلام klam

vacancy *n.* فَضَا fada

vacant *adj.* فاضي fadi

vacate *v.* يخلي yekhli

vacation *n.* إخلاء ekhla'

vaccinate *v.* يطعّم yeta'em

vaccination *n.* تطعيم tat'eym

vaccine *n.* لقاح luqah

vacillate *v.* يتذبذب yetzabzab

vacuum *n.* مكنسة كهربا meknseh kahruba'eyyeh

vacuum *v.* يكنس بالمكنسة yeknus belmeknseh

vagabond *adj.* نوري nawari

vagary *n.* نزوة nazweh

vagina *n.* مهبل mahbal

vague *adj.* غامض ghamed

vagueness *n.* غموض ghumud

vainglory *n.* تكبّر takabbur

vale *n.* وادي wadi

valiant *adj.* جريء jare'

valid *adj.* صالح saleh

validity *n.* تاريخ الصلاحية tarikh elsalaheyyeh

valley *n.* وادي wadi

valour *n.* شجاعة shaja'ah

valuation *n.* تقييم taq'yym

value n. قيمة qemeh
value v. يقيّم yeqayym
valve n. صمّام sammam
van n. مروحة marwaha
vanish v. يتبخّر yetbakhkhar
vanity n. بطلان butlan
vanquish v. يهزم yehzum
vaporize v. يبخّر yebakhkher
vaporous adj. بخاري bukhari
vapour n. بخار bukhar
variable adj. مشكّل mshakkal
variety n. تشكيلة tashkeleh
varnish n. ورنيش warnish
varnish v. يورنش yewarnesh
vary v. يغيّر yeghayyer
vase n. مزهريّة mazhareyyeh
vaseline n. فازلين fazlin
vast adj. واسع wase'
vault n. قبو qabu
vault n. خزنة khazneh
vault v. يحني yehni
vegan n. نباتي nabati
vegan adj. نباتي nabati
vegetable n. خضرا khedrah
vegetarian n. نباتي nabati
vehemence n. عنف unf
vehement adj. عنيف anif
vehicle n. سيّارة sayyarah
veil n. إيشارب eysharb
veil v. يحجّب yehajjeb
vein n. وريد warid
velocity n. سرعة sur'ah
velvet n. مخمل mukhmal
velvety adj. مخملي mukhmali
venal adj. مرتشي merteshi
venality n. رشوة rashweh
vendor n. بيّاع bayya'

vengeance n. تار tar
venial adj. طفيف tafif
venom n. سمّ semm
venomous adj. حقود haqud
vent n. مخرج mukhrej
ventilate v. يهوّي yehawwi
ventilation n. تهوية tahweyeh
ventilator n. جهاز تهوية jihaz tahweyeh
venture n. مغامرة mughamarah
venture v. يغامر yeghamer
venturesome adj. مغامر mughamer
venturous adj. مخاطر mukhater
venue n. مكان makan
veracity n. ثبات thabat
verb n. فعل fe'l
verbal adj. فعلي fe'li
verbatim adj. حرفي harfi
verbatim adv. بالحرف belharf
verdant adj. مورق mwarraq
verdict n. قرار محكمة qarar mahkameh
verge n. طرف taraf
verification n. تحقّق tahaqquq
verify v. يتحقّق yetehaqqaq
verisimilitude n. احتماليّة ihtimaleyyeh
veritable adj. حقيقي haqiqi
vernacular n. اللغة العاميّة ellughah elameyyeh
vernacular adj. دارج darij
vernal adj. ربيعي rabe'iy
versatile adj. متعدد الاستعمال met'added eleste'mal

versatility *n.* تعدُّد الاستعمال ta'ddud eleste'mal

verse *n.* شعر she'r

version *n.* نسخة neskhah

vertical *adj.* عمودي amudi

verve *n.* حيوية hayaweyyeh

very *adj.* كتير ktir

vessel *n.* زورق zuraq

vest *n.* صدرية sedreyyeh

vest *v.* يفوّض yefawwed

vested *adj.* مفوّض mfawwad

vestige *n.* أثر athrr

veteran *n.* محنّك mehannak

veteran *adj.* محنّك mehannak

veterinary *adj.* بيطري bytari

veto *n.* فيتو vitu

veto *v.* يستخدم الفيتو yestakhdem elvitu

vex *v.* ينغّص yenaghghes

vexation *n.* تنغيص tanghis

via *prep.* ب bi

viable *adj.* صالح salih

vial *n.* قنّينة qannineh

vibrate *v.* يهزّ yehezz

vibration *n.* إهتزاز ihtizaz

vicar *n.* نائب na'eb

vicarious *adj.* مفوّض mefawwad

vice *n.* رذيلة razyleh

vice *n.* نائب na'eb

viceroy *n.* نائب ملك na'eb malek

vice-versa *adv.* والعكس صحيح wel'aks sahih

vicinity *n.* جوار jewar

vicious *adj.* سافل safil

victim *n.* ضحيّة daheyyeh

victimize *v.* يضحّي ب yedahhi bi

victor *n.* منصور mansur

victorious *adj.* منتصر menteser

victory *n.* نصر nasr

victuals *n. pl* مونة muneh

video *n.* فيديو vidyu

video *v.* يصوّر فيديو yesawwer vidyu

view *n.* فرجة ferjeh

view *v.* يتفرّج yetfarraj

vigil *n.* وقفة العيد waqfet el'eyd

vigilance *n.* إنتباه intibah

vigilant *adj.* منتبه mentebeh

vigorous *adj.* قوي qawi

vile *adj.* خسيس khasis

vilify *v.* يشوه سمعة yeshawweh sem'et

villa *n.* فيلّا villa

village *n.* ضيعة de'ah

villager *n.* ضيعجي de'aji

villain *n.* حقير haqir

vindicate *v.* يبرّي yebarri

vindication *n.* تبرية tabreyeh

vine *n.* كرم karm

vinegar *n.* خلّ khall

violate *v.* يغتصب yeghteseb

violation *n.* إغتصاب ightisab

violence *n.* عنف unf

violent *adj.* عنيف anif

violet *n.* بنفسج banafsag

violin *n.* كمان kaman

violinist *n.* عازف كمان azef kaman

virgin *n.* بكر bekr

virgin *adj.* بكر bekr

virginity *n.* بكارة bakarah

virile *adj.* فَحْل fahl

virility *n.* رجولة rjuleh

virtual *adj.* إفتراضي eftiradi

virtue *n.* عفة effeh

virtuous *adj.* عفيف afif

virus *n.* فيروس virus

visibility *n.* رؤية ru'yeh

visible *adj.* مرئي mar'i

vision *n.* نظر nazar

visit *n.* زيارة zyarah

visit *v.* يزور yezur

visitor *n.* زائر zayer

vital *adj.* حيوي hayawi

vitality *n.* حيوية hayaweyyeh

vitalize *v.* ينشط yenashshet

vitamin *n.* فيتامين vitamin

vitiate *v.* يتلف yetlef

vivacious *adj.* نشيط nashit

vivacity *n.* نشاط nashat

viva voce *n.* فحص شفهي fahs shafahi

viva voce *adj.* يعمل فحص شفهي ye'mel fahes shafahi

vivid *adj.* فاقع faqe'

vixen *n.* ثعلبة tha'labeh

vocabulary *n.* مصطلح mustalah

vocal *adj.* صوتي sawti

vogue *n.* صرعة sar'ah

voice *n.* صوت sut

voice *v.* يلفظ yelfuz

void *adj.* فاضي fadi

void *v.* يقضي yefaddi

volcanic *adj.* بركاني burkani

volcano *n.* بركان burkan

volition *n.* مشيئة mashy'ah

volley *n.* تهديد tahdid

volley *v.* يهدّد yehadded

volt *n.* فولت vult

voltage *n.* جهد jehd

volume *n.* حجم hajm

voluminous *adj.* ضخم dakhem

voluntarily *adv.* طواعية tawa'eyyeh

voluntary *adj.* طوعي tu'i

volunteer *n.* متطوّع mutatawwe'

volunteer *v.* يتطوّع yettawwa'

voluptuary *n.* شهواني shahwani

voluptuous *adj.* شهواني shahwani

vomit *v.* يستفرغ yestafregh

vomit *n.* إستفراغ istfragh

voracious *adj.* جَعان faj'an

vortex *n.* زوبعة zuba'ah

votary *n.* مؤيد mu'ayyed

vote *n.* صوت sut

vote *v.* يصوّت yesawwet

voter *n.* مصوّت mesawwet

vouch *v.* يكفل yekfal

voucher *n.* إيصال iysal

voyage *n.* سفر بحري safar bahri

voyage *v.* يسافر بالبحر yesafer belbahr

voyager *n.* مسافر msafer

voyeur *n.* مبصبص mbasbes

voyeurism *n.* بصبصة basbasah

vulgar *adj.* بلدي baladi

vulgarity *n.* سوقية suqeyyeh

vulnerable *adj.* قابل للعطب qabel lel'atab

vulnerable *adj.* سريع الكسر sarei' elkaser

vulture n. جشع jeshe'

waddle v. يتهادى yetehadah

waft v. يهوج yehuj

waft n. هوجة hujeh

wag v. يهتز yehtazz

wag n. هزة hazzeh

wage n. معاش ma'ash

wager n. رهان rehan

wager v. يراهن yerahin

wagon n. شاحنة نقل shahenet naql

wail v. يولول yewalwel

wail n. ولولة walwaleh

wain n. نجم الدبّ الأكبر najm eldebb elakbar

waist n. خصر khasr

waistband n. ربطة خصر rabtet khasr

waistcoat n. صدّارة saddarah

wait v. يستنّى yestannah

wait n. إنتظار intizar

waiter n. كرسون karsun

waitress n. كرسونة karsuneh

waive v. يتنازل yetnazal

waiver n. تنازل tanazul

wake v. يسهر yesehar

wake n. سهر sahar

wake n. فيقة feqah

wakeful adj. فايق fayeq

walk v. يمشي yemshi

walk n. مشي mashi

wall n. حيط hit

wall v. يعلق عالحيط ye'alleq al hit

wallet n. جزدان jezdan

wallop v. يبوكس yebukes

wallow v. يتمرّغ yetmarragh

walnut n. جوز juz

wan adj. مصفر mesfarr

wand n. عصاية الساحر asayet elsaher

wander v. يمتشّى yetmashshah

wane v. ينتاقص yetnaqas

waney adj. متناقص metnaqes

want n. حاجة hajeh

want v. يريد yrid

wanton adj. فلتان faltan

war n. حرب harb

war v. يحارب yehareb

warble n. تغريدة taghredeh

warble v. يغرد yegharred

warbler n. مطرب mutreb

warden n. وصي wasi

warder n. سجّان sajjan

wardrobe n. خزانة khzaneh

wardship n. وصاية wesayeh

ware n. بضاعة beda'ah

warehouse n. مستودع mestawda'

warm adj. دافي dafi

warm v. يدفّي yedaffi

warmth n. دفا dafa

warn v. يحذّر yehazzer

warning n. تحذير tahzir

warrant n. ضمانة damaneh

warrant v. يضمن yedman

warrantee n. مكفول makful

warrantor n. كفيل kafil

warranty n. كفالة kafaleh

warrior n. محارب mhareb

wart n. تالولة taluleh

wary adj. منتبه mentebeh

wash v. يغسل yeghsul

wash n. غسل ghasl

washable adj. بنغسل beynghesel

washer n. غسّالة ghassaleh

wasp n. زنبوط zanbut

wastage n. هدر hadr

wastage n. تبذير tabzir

waste adj. مهدور mahdur

waste n. زبالة zbaleh

waste v. يهدر yehdur

waste v. يبذّر yebazzer

watch v. يتفرّج yetfarraj

watch n. ساعة sa'ah

water n. مي may

water v. يسقي yesqi

waterfall n. شلال shallal

water-melon n. بطيخ أحمر battikh ahmar

waterproof adj. مضاد للمي mudad lelmay

watery adj. مخفّف mekhaffaf

watt n. واط wat

wave n. موجة mujeh

wave v. يلوّح بإيده yelawweh be'yduh

waver v. يترنّح yetrannah

wavy adj. مطعّج meta'aj

wax n. شمع shame'

wax v. يشيل بالشمع yeshil belshame'

way n. طريق tariq

weak adj. ضعيف de'if

weaken v.t. & i ضعّف yedae'f

weakness n. ضعف de'f

weal n. رخا rakha

wealth n. غنى ghenah

wealthy adj. غني ghani

wean v. يفطم yeftum

weapon n. سلاح slah

wear v. يلبس yelbes

weary adj. مللّ bymallel

weary v. يملّل yemallel

weather n. طقس taqs

weave v. يحبك yehbuk

weaver n. حبّاك habbak

web n. شبكة shabakeh

wed v. يتزوّج yetzawwaj

wedding n. عرس ers

wedge n. وتد watad

wedge v. يدقّ وتد yeduqq watad

Wednesday n. الأربعاء elarbe'a

weed n. حشيش hashish

weed v. يشيل الحشيش yeshil elhashish

week n. أسبوع esbu'

weekly adj. إسبوعي esbu'ey

weekly adv. بالإسبوع bel'usbue'

weekly n. جريدة إسبوعية jaredeh esbu'eyyeh

weep v. ينوح yenuh

weevil n. سوسة suseh

weigh v. يوزن yuzen

weight n. وزن wazn

weighty adj. وزن wezen

weir n. سدّ صغير sadd segher

weird adj. مسحور masehur

welcome n. ترحيب tarhib

welcome v. يرحّب yerahheb

weld v. يلحُم yelhum
weld n. لحام leham
welfare n. مصلحة maslaha
well adj. منيح mnih
well n. بير bir
well v. يحفر بير yehfur bir
well-known adj. معروف ma'ruf
west n. غرب gharb
west adv. بالغرب belgharb
western adj. غربي gharbi
wet adj. نديان nadyan
wet v. يندّي yenaddi
wetness n. نداوة nadaweh
whale n. حوت hut
wheat n. قمح qamh
wheel n. دولاب dulab
wheel v. يركّب دولاب yerakkeb dulab
whip v. يضرُب بالكرباج yedrub belkerbaj
whip n. كرباج kerbaj
whirl v. يبرم yebrum
whisk v. يخفق yekhfuq
whisk n. خفق khafq
whisker n. شوارب shwareb
whisky n. ويسكي wiski
whisper v. يهمس yehmus
whisper n. همس hams
whistle v. يصفر yesaffer
whistle n. تصفير tasfir
white adj. أبيض abyad
white n. الأبيض elabyad
whiten v. يبيّض yebayyed
whole adj. كامل kamel
wholesale n. بيع جملة bei' jumleh

wholesaler n. بيّاع جملة bayya' jumleh
wholly adv. بالكامل belkamel
wide adj. عريض arid
wide adv. بالعرض bel'ard
widen v. يعرّض ye'arred
widespread adj. منتشر mentesher
widow n. أرملة armaleh
widow v. يترمّل yetrammal
widower n. أرمل armal
wife n. مرت mart
wild adj. بري barri
will n. وصيّة waseyyeh
will n. إرادة eradeh
willing adj. رايد rayd
win v. يربح yerbah
win n. ربح rebh
wind n. هوا hwa
windmill n. طاحونة tahuneh
window n. شبّاك shebbak
windy adj. عاصف asef
wine n. خمر khamr
wing n. جناح janah
winner n. رابح rabeh
winter n. شتي sheteh
winter v. يشتّي yeshatti
wipe v. يمسح yemsah
wipe n. مسح maseh
wire n. سلك selk
wireless adj. لا سلكي la selki
wiring n. تمديد الأسلاك tamdid elaslak
wisdom n. حكمة hikmeh
wisdom-tooth n. ضرس العقل ders elaqel
wise adj. حكيم hakim

wish n. أمنيةٍ umneyeh

wish v. يَتَمَنَّى yetmannah

wit n. فطنة fetneh

witch n. ساحرة sahrah

with prep. مع ma

withdraw v. ينسحب yensehb

withdrawal n. إنسحاب ensihab

within prep. جوّات juwwat

without adv. من دون mn dun

withstand v. يتحمل yetehammal

witness n. شاهد shahed

witness v. يشهد yeshhad

wolf n. ديب dib

woman n. مرا mrah

womanhood n. أنوثة unutheh

womb n. رحم rahm

wonder n. أعجوبة u'jubeh

wonder v. يتعجب yet'ajjab

wood n. خشب khashab

woods n. غابة ghabeh

wooden adj. خشبي khashabi

wool n. صوف suf

woollen adj. مصوّف mesawwaf

word n. كلمة klmeh

work n. شغل shughul

work v. يشتغل yeshteghel

worker n. عامل a'mel

workshop n. ورشة عمل warshet amal

world n. عالم a'lam

worm n. دودة dudeh

worn adj. مهري mehri

worry n. قلق qalaq

worry v. يقلق yeqlaq

worsen v. يسوء yesawwe'

worship n. عبادة ebadeh

worship v. يعبد ye'bud

worshipper n. عابد a'bed

worth adj. بيسوى byswah

worthless adj. ما بيسوى ma byswah

wound n. جرح jerh

wound v. يجرح yejrah

wrap v. يلف الهدية yeleff elhadeyyeh

wrap n. لفّ الهدية laff elhadeyyeh

wrapper n. لفّة الهدية laffet elhadeyyeh

wreck n. حطام hutam

write v. يكتب yektub

writer n. كاتب katib

wrong adj. غلط ghalat

xenomania n. هوس hawas

xenophobe n. خوف من الأجانب khuf mn elajaneb

x-ray n. أشعة سينيّة ashe'a sineyyeh

x-ray v. يعمل أشعة سينيّة ye'mel ashe'ah sineyyeh

Y

Z

yacht *n.* يخت yakht
yard *n.* يارد yard
yawn *v.* يتثاوب yettawab
year *n.* سنة seneh
yearly *adj.* سنوي sanawi
yeast *n.* خميرة khamireh
yellow *adj.* أصفر asfar
yellow *n.* الأصفر elasfar
yellowish *adj.* مصفرّ mesfarr
yes *adv.* إي eyh
yesterday *n.* مبارحة embarhah
yield *v.* يصرخ yesarrekh
yoga *n.* يوغا yuga
yogurt *n.* لبن laban
yolk *n.* صفار البيض safar elbeid
young *n.* شب shabb
youth *n.* شباب shabab

zebra *n.* حمار الوحش hemar elwahsh
zero *n.* صفر sefr
zest *n.* قشر الليمون qeshr limon
zinc *n.* زنك zink
zip code *n.* رمز المنطقة ramz elmantiqah
zip up *v.* يزرّ السحاب yezerr elsahhab
zipper *n.* سحّاب sahhab
zone *n.* منطقة manteqah
zoo *n.* حديقة حيوان hadeqt haywan
zoom *n.* تقريب taqrib
zoom in *v.* يكبّر الصورة yekabber elsurah
zoom out *v.* يصغّر الصورة yesaghgher elsurah

Levantine Arabic-English

أ

father *n* abb أبّ

August *n* aab آب

parent *n* abb w emm أبّ وإمّ

lewd *adj* ebahi إبَاحِي

profligate *adj* ibahi إبَاحِي

profligacy *n* ibaheyyeh إبَاحِيّة

elementary *adj* ibteda'i إبْتِدَائِي

amputee *n* abtar أبْتَر

blackmail *n* ibtizaz ابتزاز

graft *n* ibtizaz ابتزاز

smile *n* ibtesameh إبتسامة

innovation *n* ibtikar ابتكار

exult *v* ibtihaj ابتهاج

alphabet *n* abjadiyeh أبجديّة

navigation *n* ebhar إبحار

sailing *n* ibhar إبحار

ever *adv* abdan أبدا

never *adv* abadan أبداً

creation *n* 'ibda إبداع

eternity *n* abadeyyeh أبديّة

acupuncture *n* ebr siniyeh إبر صينية

projection *n* ibraz إبْراز

needle *n* ibreh إبرة

geranium *n* ebret elra'e ابرة الراعى

diocese *n* abrasheyyeh أبرَشيّة

parish *n* abrasheyyeh أبرَشيّة

leper *n* abras أبرَص

leprous *adj* abras أبرَص

pitcher *n* ebriq إبريق

jug *n* ibreq إبريق

kettle *n* ibriq إبريق

abolition *v* ibtal إبْطال

abolishment *n* ibtal إبْطال

abolitionism *n* ibtaleyyeh إبْطاليّة

dimension *n* aba'ad أبعاد

denunciation *n* iblagh ابلاغ

dense *adj* ablah أبله

dumb *adj* ablah أبله

idiot *n* ablah أبلَه

mindless *adj* ablah أبلَه

fiend *n* eblis إبليس

son *n* ebn إبن

nephew *n* ibn akhkh إبن أخّ

noble *n* ibn elhasab ابن الحسب

nobleman *n* ibn elhasab ابن الحسب

bantling *n* ibn haram ابن حرام

bastard *n* ibn haram ابن حرام

polecat *n* ibn ers ابن عرس

cousin *n* ibn amm ابن عمّ

thumb *n* ibham إبهام

jaundice *n* abu safar أبو صفار

mumps *n* abu ka'eb أبو كعب

parentage *n* ubuwweh أبوّة

irritation *n* etharrah إثارة	parental *adj* abawi أبوي
n etharah jenseyyeh إثارة جنسيّة	paternal *adj* abawi أبَوِي
eroticism	white *n* elabyad الأبيض
demonstration *n* ithbat إثبات	blank *adj* abyad أبيض
proof *n* ithbat إثبات	white *adj* abyad أبيض
trace *n* athar أثر	tribute *n* ataweh أتاوة
vestige *n* athrr أثرّ	direction *n* ittijah اتّجاه
impact *n* athar أثَر	bent *n* itijah إتجاه
antiquarian *adj* athari أثَرِي	union *n* ittihad إتّحاد
n athqal reyadeyyeh أثقال رياضيّة	atropine *n* artobin أتروبين
dumbbell	call *n* ittisal اتّصال
as *pron* 'athnaa أثناء	calling *n* ittisal اتّصال
asleep *adv* athnaa' ehnum أثناء النوم	إتّصالات سلكيّة ولاسلكيّة ettisalat
ether *n* athir أثير	*n* selkeyyeh wla selkeyyeh
renowned *adj* a'jar اجار	telecommunications
rent *n* a'jar أجار	assent *n* itifaq إتّفاق
leave *n* ejazeh إجازة	agreement *n* ettifaqyeh اتفاقيّة
pear *n* ajas أجاص	precision *n* itqan إتقان
compulsion *n* ijbar إجبار	nicety *n* itqan إتْقان
compulsory *adj* ijbari إجباري	dependence *n* ittikal إتّكال
coven *n* ijtima' saharah اجتماع سَحَرَة	dependent *adj* ittikali إتّكالي
n ejtima' hatefi إجتماع هاتفي	impeachment *n* ettiham إتّهام
teleconference	indictment *n* ittiham إتّهام
sociable *adj* ijtima'ey إجْتِمَاعِي	charge *n* ittiham إتّهام
sociability *n* ijtema'eyyeh إجْتِمَاعِيّة	*n* itiham muakis اتّهام معاكِس
diligence *n* ijtihad إجْتِهاد	countercharge
overtime *n* ajer edafi أجْر إضافي	etiquette *n* etikit اتيكيت
foreleg *n* ejr amameyyeh أجر أماميّة	remains *n* athar آثار

reverence *n* ehtiram إحترام

retentive *adj* ihtifazi احتفاظي

celebration *n* ihtifal احتفال

gala *n* ihtifal احتفال

festive *adj* ehtifali إحْتِفَالي

festivity *n* ehtifalyyeh احتفاليّة

scorn *n* ihtiqar إحْتِقار

derogatory *adj* ihtiqari احتقاري

monopoly *n* ihtikar احتكار

friction *n* ihtikak إحْتِكاك

puberty *n* ihtilam إحْتِلام

contingency *n* ihtimal إحْتِمال

odds *n* ihtimal إحْتِمال

n ihtimaleyyeh احتماليّة

verisimilitude

potential *n* ihtimaleyyeh إحْتِماليّة

n ihtimaleyyeh إحْتِماليّة

potentiality

inclusion *n* 'ihtiwa احتواء

containment *n* 'ihtiwa إحْتِواء

backup *n* ihtiyati احتياطي

spare *n* ehtyati إحْتِيَاطي

cheat *n* ihteyal احتيال

knavery *n* ihtyal إحتيال

deception *n* ihtyal إحْتِيال

Monday *n* elahad الأحـد

Sunday *n* elahad الأحـد

embarrassment *n* ihraj إحراج

procedure *n* 'ijra إجراء

criminal *adj* ijrami إجرامي

hire *n* ejrah إجرَة

n ejret elmuwasalt أجرة المواصلات

fare

cartage *n* ejret naqel أجرة نقل

tenor *n* ajal أجَل

consensus *n* 'ijmaa إجْماع

gross *n* elejmali الإجمالي

total *n* el'ejmali الإجمالي

gross *adj* ejmali إجمالي

total *adj* ejmali إجمالي

foreign *adj* ajnabi أجْنَبي

abortion *n* ijhad إجهاض

miscarriage *n* ijhad إجْهاض

abortive *adj* ijhadi إجهاضي

monoestrous *n* uhadi أحادي

one *pron* uhadi أُحَادي

n ihatah belsawael إحاطة بالسوائل

circumfluence

reference *n* ihaleh إحالة

frustration *n* ihbat إحباط

depression *n* ihbat إحبَاط

protest *n* ihtijaj إحتجاج

protestation *n* ihtijaj إحتجاج

hold *n* ihtejaz احتِجاز

combustion *n* ihtiraq إحتِراق

respect *n* ihteram إحْتِرام

informative *adj* ikhbari إخباري	abashing *n* ehraj إحْراج
sister *n* ukhkht أخْت	initial *n* ahruf ula أحرف أُولى
approbation *n* ikhtibar اختِبار	sentience *n* ehsas إحساس
experiment *n* ikhteyar اختِبار	sense *n* eshsas إحْساس
probation *n* ikhtibar إختبار	better *adj* ahsan أحسن
test *n* ikhtibar إختبار	statistics *n* 'elehsa الإحصاء
invention *n* 'ikhtera اخْتراع	computation *n* 'ihsa إحصاء
inventive *adj* ikhtera'i اخْتراعي	*adj* ihsaa' hayawi إحصاء حيوي
penetration *n* ikhteraq إخْتراق	biometric
shorthand *n* ikhtizal إخْتزال	statistical *adj* ehsa'i إحْصائي
brevity *n* ikhtisar اختِصار	statistician *n* ehsa'i إحْصائي
abbreviation *n* ikhtisar إختصار	red *adj* ahmar أحمر
speciality *n* ekhtisas إختصاص	*adj* ahmar ramadi أحمر رمادي
abduction *n* ikhtitaf إخْتطاف	damask
abscondence *n* 'ekhtifa اختفاء	cinnabar *n* 'ahmar lammei أحمر لمّيع
disappearance *n* 'ikhtifa اخْتفاء	flush *n* ihmirar إحمرار
convulsion *n* ikhtilaj اخْتلاج	glow *n* ihmirar إحمرار
n ikhtilas اختلاس	ihmirar men elkhajal إحمرار من الخجل
misappropriation	blushing *n*
difference *n* ikhtelaf اختلاف	squint *n* ahwal أحول
disagreement *n* ikhtilaf إخْتلاف	*n* ihya' zikra إحياء ذكرى
fermentation *n* ikhtimar اخْتمار	commemoration
asphyxia *n* ikhtinaq اختناق	occasionally *adv* ahyanan أحياناً
strangulation *n* ekhtinaq إختناق	brother *n* akhkh أخّ
selection *n* ikhtyar إختيار	ouch *int* aakh آخ
ikhtyar إختيار الموظفين	telling *n* ekhbar إخْبار
shapeup *n* elmuwazzafin	news *n* akhbar أخبار
alternative *adj* ikhtiari اختياري	tidings *n* akhbar أخبار

discharge n 'ikhla إخلاء

evacuation n 'ekhla إخلاء

vacation n 'ekhla إخلاء

ikhla' sabil إخلاء سبيل بشروط

parole n beshrut

sincerity n ikhlas إخْلاص

loyalty n ikhlas إخْلاص

n elakhlaq elwajbeh الأخلاق الواجبة

deontology

adj akhlaquh say'ah أخلاقه سيئة

incorrigible

ethical adj akhlaqi أخْلاقي

moral adj akhlaqi أخْلاقي

ethos n akhlaqyyat أخْلاقيات

morality n akhlaqeyyeh أخْلاقيّة

brotherhood n ukhkhuweh أخوة

sisterhood n ukhuwweh أخوّة

fraternal adj akhawi أخَوِي

confraternity n akhaweyyeh أخوِيّة

fraternity n akhaweyyeh أخوِيّة

performance n 'ada أداء

ethics n aadab آدَاب

gizmo n adat أداة

instrument n adat أداة

tool n adat أداة

gadget n adat أداة

n adat este'sal أداة استئصال

eradicator

optional adj ikhtyari اختياري

selective adj ikhtyari إختياري

n akhed beltar أخد بالثأر

retaliation

adj akhad bilhusban أخد بالحسبان

alert

doctored adj aakhid elaj آخِذ علاج

groove n akhdud أخدود

taker n a'khed آخذ

n akhed elayyenat أخذ عينات

sampling

last adj akher آخر

asexuality n 'ikhsaa إخصَاء

fecundation n ikhsab إخْصاب

n akhessa'ei awram أخصائي أورام

oncologist

n akhessa'i tarbeyeh أخصائي تربية

paedologist

n akhessa'e jinat أخصائي جينات

geneticist

n akhussa'i muhitat أخصَائي محيطات

oceanographer

green adj aghdar أخضر

octopus n akhtabut أخطبوط

less adj akhaff أخفّ

n ekhfaae' elesim إخفاء الاسم

anonymity

failure n ekhfaq إخفاق

March n adar آذار	an art adat ta'rif أداة تعريف
broadcast n izaei إذاعي	administration n iedara إدارة
humiliation n izlal إذلال	management n edarah إدارة
permission n ezn إذن	run n edarah إدارة
promissory adj izni إذني	administrative adj iedari إداري
harm n aza أذى	managerial adj edari إداري
mischief n azah أذى	condemnation n idaneh إدانة
will n eradeh إرادة	conviction n idaneh إدَانة
disquiet n irbak إرْباك	politeness n adab أدب
Wednesday n elarbe'a الأربعاء	literature n adab أدب
interdependence n ertibat ارتباط	courtesy n addab أدَب
tangle n ertibak إرْتِبَاك	literary adj adabi أدبي
sag n 'irtikha إرْتِخاء	input n idkhal إدخال
osmosis n irtishah إرتشاح	insertion n edkhal إدخال
altitude n ertifae ارتفاع	n idkhal hadf إدخال هدف
rise n 'irtifa إرتفاع	goalscoring
orthodox adj arthuzuks أُرْثُوذُكس	n adraj khalfeyeh أدراج خلفيّة
n arthuzukseyyeh أُرْثُوذُكسيّة	backstairs
orthodoxy	recognition n idrak إدراك
likely adj arjah أرْجَح	adrenaline n adrynalyn ادرينالين
n arjaheyyeh أرْجَحيّة	claim n iddea'a إدعاء
preponderance	prosecution n eledde'a الادّعاء
least adv arkhas أرخص	thicket n adghal أدغال
consignment n irsaleyyeh إرسالِيّة	elision n edgham إدغام
n arustuqrateyeh ارستقراطيّة	addiction n edmaan إدمان
aristocracy	cutis n adamet el-jeld أدمة الجلد
n arusteqrateyyeh ارستقراطيّة	ear n eden إدن
gentry	litterateur n adib أُديب

hare *n* arnab barri أرنب برّي	chancery *n* arshif أرشيف
terrorism *n* elerhab الإرهاب	tally *n* arshif أرْشِيف
terror *n* erhab إرهاب	elarsad eljawweyyeh الارصاد الجوِّية
n irhab bi'e إرهاب بيئي	meteorology *n*
ecoterrorism	earth *n* elared الأرض
terrorist *n* erhabi إرهابي	ground *n* ard أرض
strain *n* erhaq إرْهاق	land *n* ard أرض
toil *n* erhaq إرْهاق	floor *n* ard أرض
n arwah elmawtah أرواح الموتى	terrain *n* ard أرْض
manes	*n* ard elmarsah أرض المرسى
takeout *n* ezaha إزَاحَة	dockyard
n izalet summum إزالة التسمُّم	*n* ared elmaarakeh أرض المعركة
detoxication	battleground
n ezalet elshshuhum إزالة الشحوم	coppice *n* ared deghleh أرض دغلة
delipidation	*n* ared mustanqaat أرض مستنقعات
n ezalet elkles إزالة الكلس	bogland
decalcification	*n* ard mesttahah أرض مسطَّحة
n ezalet elnamash إزالة النمَش	flatland
emaculation	satisfaction *n* 'irda إرْضاء
boom *n* izdihar ازدهار	earthly *adj* ardi أرْضِي
blue *adj* azraq أزرق	artichoke *n* ardi shawki أرضي شوكي
annoyance *n* ezaaj إزعاج	fanatic *n* elar'an الأرْعَن
discomfort *n* izaaj إزْعاج	frivolous *adj* ar'an أرْعَن
dacoit *n* az'ar أزْعَر	indiscreet *adj* ar'an أرْعَن
crisis *n* azmeh أزِمة	fanatic *adj* ar'an أرْعَن
chisel *n* izmil إزْميل	widower *n* armal أرْمَل
azote *n* a'zut آزوت	widow *n* armaleh أرملة
tang *v* aziz أزيز	rabbit *n* arnab أرنب

268

exponent n uss أُسّ

myrtle n aas آس

ground n asas أساس

basis n asas أساس

basic adj asasi أساسي

chief adj asasi أساسي

fundamental adj asasi أساسي

major adj asasi أساسي

substantial adj asasi أَساسِي

Spaniard n esbani إسْبانِي

Spanish adj esbani إسْبانِي

precedent n asbaq أسْبَق

precedence n asbaqeyyeh أسْبَقِيّة

seniority n asbaqeyyeh أسْبَقِيّة

week n 'esbu أسبوع

weekly adj esbu'ey إسبوعي

fort-night n esbu'en أسبوعين

stadium n estad إسْتَاد

n estaz akhlaq أستاذ أخلاق

moralist

autocracy n istibeddad استبداد

replacement n istebdal استبدال

substitution n estebdal إسْتِبدال

stability n estitbab إسْتِتْباب

investment n istithmar استثمار

exception n 'estethna استثناء

phenomenal adj istethna'i استثنائى

exceptional adj estethna'e استثنائي

extraordinary adj estithna'e إستثنائي

n estijabeh sawteyeh استجابة صوتيّة

antiphony

interrogation n istijwab استجواب

inquest n estijwab إسْتِجْواب

inquisition n estijwab إسْتِجْواب

interrogative adj istijwabi استجوابي

menstruation n estihadah إستحاضة

impossibility n estihaleh استحالة

impracticability n estihaleh استحالة

disdain n istehqar استحقار

n estikhbarat استخبارات

intelligence

usage n estikhdam إستخدام

use n estikhdam إستخدام

n istikhdam aljinas استخدام الجناس

alliteration

v istikhdam ghalat استخدام غلط

misuse

n istikhlas elglutin استخلاص الغلوتين

deglutination

decoy n istidraj استدراج

draw n istedraj استدراج

summons n ested'a استدعا

call n istida'a استدعَا

break n istiraha استراحة

breaktime n istiraha استراحة

recess n istiraha إسْتِراحَة

plebiscite *n* 'istefta إِسْتِفْتَاء	interlude *n* estirahah إِسْتِرَاحَة
referendum *n* 'istefta إِسْتِفْتَاء	*n* isteraht tariq استراحة طريق
aggravation *n* istifhal استفحال	roadhouse
aggravate *v* istafhal استفحل	anamnesis *n* 'esterjaa استرجاع
vomit *n* istfragh إِسْتِفْرَاغ	redemption *n* 'isterja استرجاع
provocation *n* istefzaz إِسْتِفْزَاز	restoration *n* 'esterja استرجاع
abdication *n* istiqaleh إِسْتِقَالَة	reclamation *n* esterdad استرداد
resignation *n* estiqaleh إِسْتِقَالَة	recovery *n* isterdad إِسْتِرْدَاد
reception *n* istiqbal استقبال	*n* esterdad melkeyyet استرداد ملكِيَّة
stabilization *n* estiqrar إِسْتِقْرَار	eviction
metabolism *n* isteqlab استقلاب	sterling *adj* esterlini إِسْتِرْلِينِي
independence *n* istiqlal استقلال	estrogen *n* estrojin إِسْتُرُوجِين
scout *n* istekshaf إِسْتِكْشَاف	edema *n* istisqah استسقا
receipt *n* istelam إِسْتِلَام	surrender *n* estislam إِسْتِسْلَام
alaistimae الاستماع بكل الحواس	consultation *n* istisharah استشارة
allness *n* bikull alhawas	counsel *n* istisharah استشارة
progress *n* istimrar إِسْتِمْرَار	martyrdom *n* istishhad إِسْتِشْهَاد
continuation *n* istimrar إِسْتِمْرَار	reclamation *n* istislah إِسْتِصْلَاح
continuity *n* istimrareyeh إِسْتِمْرَارِية	questionnaire *n* 'istitla إِسْتِطْلَاع
self-abuse *n* 'estimna إِسْتِمْنَاء	metaphor *n* esti'arah إِسْتِعَارَة
sniff *n* estenshaq إِسْتِنْشَاق	bondage *n* iste'bad استعبَاد
depletion *n* istinfaz إِسْتِنْفَاد	slave *n* este'bad إِسْتِعْبَاد
abomination *n* estinkar إِسْتِنْكَار	thralldom *n* este'bad إِسْتِعْبَاد
ridicule *n* 'istehza إِسْتِهْزَاء	spectacular *adj* este'radi إِسْتِعْرَاضِي
scoff *n* 'estihza إِسْتِهْزَاء	colony *n* iste'mar استعمار
consumption *n* istihlak استهلاك	colonial *adj* iste'mari إِسْتِعْمَارِي
maturity *n* 'estiwa إِسْتِوَاء	exploit *n* estighlal استغلال
lease *n* este'jar استئجار	profiteer *n* isteghlali إِسْتِغْلَالِي

squadron *n* ustul أَسْطُول	import *n* estirad استيراد
ambulance *n* isa'af إسعاف	eradication *n* este'sal استئصال
succour *n* es'af إسعاف	settlement *n* estitan إِسْتِيطان
salvage *n* es'af إسْعاف	apprehension *n* istiaab استيعاب
salvation *n* es'af إسْعاف	comprehension *n* isti'ab استيعاب
sorry *adj* asef آسِف	appropriation *n* 'istillae استيلاء
apostle *n* asquf أَسْقُف	capture *n* 'istilaa استيلاء
prelate *n* usquf أُسْقُف	takeover *n* 'estila إِسْتِيلاء
cobbler *n* iskafi إسكافي	lion *n* asad أسد
style *n* uslub أُسلوب	leonine *adj* asadi أُسدي
diction *n* uslub أُسْلُوب	captivity *n* aser أسر
type *n* uslub أُسْلُوب	*n* usrah hakmeh أُسرَةٌ حاكِمَة
lifestyle *n* eslub hayat أسلوب حياة	dynasty
locution *n* eslub klam أسلوب كلام	*adj* asra' mn elsut أسرع من الصوت
name *n* esm اسم	supersonic
noun *n* esm اسم	*adj* asra' mn elsut أسرع من الصوت
screen *n* esm elshasheh إسم الشاشة	ultrasonic
name	barn *n* istabel إسطبل
misnomer *n* esm ghalat اسم غلط	stable *n* establ إسطبل
alias *n* ism musta'ar اسم مستعار	astrolabe *n* asterlaab أسطرلاب
n ism musta'ar اسم مستعار	cylinder *n* istwaneh اسطوانة
pseudonym	cylindrical *adj* istwani اسطواني
swarthy *adj* asmar أَسْمَر	legend *n* usturah أسطورة
cement *n* ismant إسمنت	legendary *adj* usturi أسطوري
nominal *adj* esmi إسْمِي	mythological *adj* usturi أسطوري
diarrhea *n* ishal إسهال	armada *n* istul أسطول
catharsis *n* ishal shadid إسهال شديد	fleet *n* ustul أسطول
contribution *n* iseham إسهام	navy *n* ustul أُسْطُول

occupancy *n* eshghal إشْغَال	armlet *adj* eswara اسوارة
repulsion *n* ishme'zaz اشْمِئْزاز	bangle *n* eswara اسوارة
abhorrence *n* eshme'zaz إشْمِئْزاز	black *adj* aswad أَسْود
aversion *n* ishme'zaz إشْمِئْزاز	acetone *n* aciton أَسيتون
originality *n* asaleh أصَالة	captive *n* asir أَسير
finger *n* 'esba أصْبع	signal *adj* esharati إشاراتي
toe *n* esba' rejl إصبع الرجل	beck *n* isharah إشارة
issue *n* isdar إصدار	remark *n* esharah إشارة
determination *n* israr إصرار	signal *n* esharah إشارة
insistence *n* esrar إصرار	gesture *n* isharah إشارَة
jostle *n* istidam اصْطِدام	minus *n* - esharet - إشارة
idiomatic *adj* istilahi إصطلاحي	rumour *n* isha.ah إشاعة
artificial *adj* istinaei إصطناعي	bruit *n* isha'a إشاعَة
junior *adj* asghar أصْغر	canard *n* isha'a kizib إشاعة كذِب
yellow *n* elasfar الأصفر	gratification *n* 'eshba إشْباع
yellow *adj* asfar أصْفر	combat *n* ishtibak إشْتِباك
buff *n* asfar burtuqli أصفر برتقالي	suspect *n* eshtibah إشْتِباه
original *n* asel أصْل	suspicion *n* eshtibah إشْتِباه
descent *n* asel أصْل	subscription *n* eshtirak إشْتِراك
reform *n* islah إصلاح	socialist *n,a* ishtiraki اِشْتِرا كي
bald *adj* 'aslaa أصْلع	socialism *n* ishtirakeyyeh إشْتِرا كيّة
bonafide *adj* asli أصْلي	inflammation *n* eshti'al إشْتِعال
original *adj* asli أصْلي	etymology *n* eshtiqaq اشتقاق
purist *n* usuli أصولي	supervision *n* eshraf إشراف
genuine *adj* asil أصيل	radiation *n* 'ish'a إشْعاع
principal *adj* asil أصيل	x-ray *n* ashe'a sineyyeh أشعَّة سينِيّة
pedigree *n* asil أصِيل	gamma *n* ashe'et gamma أشعَّة غامًّا
lightening *n* eda'ah إضاءة	occupation *n* eshghal إشْغال

إعتَام عَدَسِة العين ietam adaset elein
cataract n

regard n e'tibar إعتَبار

consideration n i'tibar إعْتِبار

assault n 'ietidaa إعتِداء

الاعتدال الربيعي ele'tedal elrabe'i n
equinox

apology n e'tizaar اعتِذار

interception n e'terad اعتراض

demur n ietirad اعتِراض

objection n e'tirad اعتراض

acknowledgement n eteraaf اعتراف

admission n ietiraff اعتراف

confession n ietiraf اعتراف

pride n e'tizaz إعتزاز

picket n e'tisam اعتصام

belief n ie'tikaad اعتِقاد

arrest n i'tiqal اعتقال

accreditation n e'temad اعتماد

credential n ietimad اعتِماد

credential adj ietimadi اعتِمادي

admiration n i'ejab إعجاب

like n e'jab إعجاب

enamourment n e'jab إعجاب

liking n e'jab إعجاب

wonder n u'jubeh أعجوبة

miracle n u'jubeh أعجوبة

config n e'dad إعداد

إضاءة خلفيّة ida'a khalfeyeh n
backlight

إضَافي overtime adj edafi

إضْبارَة portfolio n edbarah

إضبارة file n edbarah

إضْطِراب disorder n ittirab

اضطراب عصبي ittirab asabi n
neurosis

إضْطِرار urgency n ittirar

إضعَاف debilitation n id'af

أضفر nail n udfur

إطار الدولاب tyre n etar eldulab

أطرش deaf adj atrash

أُطْروحَة thesis n utruhah

إطفاء الحريق firefight n itfa' hariq

إطفائي firefighter n itfa'e

إطفائيّة firehouse n itfa'eyyeh

إطلاع acquaintance n 'etela

إطلاق darting n itlaq

إطلاق emittance n itlaq

أطلس atlas n atlas

أظفر fingernail n uzfur

إعادة playback n e'adeh

إعاقَة disability n iaqah

إعاقَة handicap n ey'aqah

إعَالة sustenance n e'aleh

إعْتاق manumission n e'taq

lure *n* 'eghra إغراء

seduction *n* 'eghra إغراء

temptation *n* 'eghra إغراء

seductive *adj* eghra'i إغرائي

close *n* ighlaq إغلاق

most *adj* aghlab أغلب

majority *n* aghlabeyyeh أغلبيّة

swoon *n* 'eghma إغْماء

blight *n* a'afeh آفة

launch *n* iftitah إفتتاح

inaugural *adj* iftitahyeh إفْتتَاحي

editorial *n* iftitaheyyeh إفْتتاحِيّة

adoration *n* ifttan افتتان

assumption *n* iftiraad اقتراض

supposition *n* efterad إقتراض

n iftirad jadali إقتراض جدلي

presupposition

notional *adj* iftiradi اقتراضي

virtual *adj* eftiradi إقتراضي

hypothetical *adj* ifteradi إفْتِراضي

concoction *n* ifti'al إفتعال

singularity *n* efradeyyeh إفراديّة

secretion *n* efraz إفراز

secretive *adj* efrazi إفرازي

revelation *n* 'ifsha إفْشاء

optimum *n* elafdal الأفْضَل

optimum *adj* afdal أفْضَل

boa *n* afaa kibireh أفعى كبيرة

execution *n* e'dam إعدام

n e'dam belkahraba إعدام بالكهربا

electrocution

n e'dam khanqan إعدام خنقا

garrotte

syntax *n* e'rab إعراب

gimp *adj* a'raj أعرج

celibate *adj* a'zab أعزَب

defenceless *adj* a'zal أعزَل

tornado *n* e'sar إعصار

cyclone *n* iesar إعْصار

ela'da' الأعضاء التناسليّة

genitalia *n* ettanasuleyyeh

superior *adj* a'zam أعْظَم

acquittal *n* 'e'faa إعفاء

remission *n* 'e'fa إعفاء

advertisement *n* i'elan إعلان

announcement *n* eilan إعلان

n e'lan yadawi إعلان يدوي

handbill

supreme *adj* a'la أعْلَى

n a'maal tijareyeh أعمال تجاريّة

business

blind *adj* a'ama أعمى

rape *n* ightisab إغتصاب

violation *n* ightisab إغتصاب

assassination *n* ighteyal اغتيال

allurement *n* 'ighraa إغراء

least *adj* aqall أَقَلّ	horizon *n* ufuq أفق
less *adv* aqall أَقَلّ	bankruptcy *n* iflaas إفلاس
minimal *adj* a'aqll أَقَلّ	insolvency *n* iflas إفْلاس
minority *n* aqalleyyeh أَقَلِّية	movies *n* aflam أفلام
region *n* eqlim إقليم	*n* aflam jenseyyeh أفلام جنسيّة
territory *n* eqlim إقليم	erotica
provincial *adj* iqlimi إقليمي	cartoon *n* aflam kartun أفلام كرتون
regional *adj* eqlimi إقليمي	opium *n* afyun أفْيُون
territorial *adj* eqlimi إقليمي	stay *n* eqameh إقامة
persuasion *n* 'iqna إقناع	*n* eqameh mu'aqqateh إقامة مؤقتة
hearsay *n* aqwal ennas أقوال الناس	sojourn
elder *adj* akbar أكبر	excerpt *n* iqtebas اقتباس
senior *adj* akbar أَكْبَر	intrusion *n* iqtiham اقتحام
most *n* elaktar الأكتر	irruption *n* iqtiham اقتحام
more *adj* aktar أكتر	proposition *n* iqterah إقتراح
discovery *n* iktishaf اكتشاف	suggestion *n* iqterah إقتراح
ectoplasm *n* aktublazm اكتوبلازم	suggestive *adj* iqterahi إقتراحي
premium *n* ikrameyyeh إكْرامِيّة	poll *n* 'iqtera إقتراع
acrylic *adj* acrilik اكريليك	conjunction *n* iqtiran إقتران
eczema *n* akzimah أكزيما	economy *n* iqtisadi اقتصاد
oxygenation *n* aksajeh أَكْسَجة	economic *adj* iqtisadi اقتصادي
oxygen *n* uksijin أُكسجين	economical *adj* iqtisadi اقتصادي
accessory *n* ikseswar اكسسوار	daisy *n* uqhuwan الخُوان
ikseswarat اكسسوارات معدن	maximum *adj* aqsa hadd أقصى حدّ
bling *n* maadan	*n* iqtaa' lelkaniseh إقطاعة للكنيسة
elixir *n* iksir إكْسِير	benefice
aliment *n* akl أَكل	manorial *adj* eqta'ei إقطاعي
eatable *n* akl أَكل	feudal *adj* eqta'e إقْطاعي

album *n* album ألبوم

n alet taswir waraq آلة تصوير ورق
copier

oilrig *n* alet tanqib آلة تنقيب

calculator *n* aleh hasebeh آلة حاسِبة

hoist *v* aleh raf'a آلة رافعة

n alet qyas elwaqt آلة قياس الوقت
chronograph

obligation *n* eltizam إلتزام

abid *n* eltizam إلِتزَام

tendinitis *n* eltihab watar إلتهاب وتر

persist *n* elhah إلحاح

persistence *n* elhah إلحاح

urge *n* elhah إلحاح

disbelief *n* ilhad إلحاد

mandatory *adj* elzami إلزامي

obligatory *adj* elzami إلزامي

forcible *adj* elzami إلزامي

imperative *adj* elzami إلزامي

n alaab nareyyeh ألعاب ناريّة
fireworks

abrogation *n* elgha'a إلغاء

cessation *n* 'elghaa إلغاء

nullification *n* 'elgha إلغاء

cancellation *n* 'elghaa إلغَاء

elimination *n* 'elgha إلغَاء

n elgha'e ettajzy'a إلغاء التجزئة
defragmentation

food *n* akel أكل

nutrient *n* akel أكل

seafood *n* akel bahri أكل بحري

snack *n* akl khafif أكل خفيف

takeaway *n* akel safari أكل سفري

n akel sha'el nar أكل شاعِل نار
flambé

dainty *n* akel tayyeb أكل طيِّب

n aakel luhum آكل لحوم
carnivore

akel luhum elbashar أكل لحوم البشَر
cannibalism *n*

aakel luhum el آكل لحوم البشَر

androphagi *n* bashar

aakel luhum آكل لحوم البشَر

cannibal *n* elbashar

coronet *n* iklil إكليل

garland *n* iklil إكْليل

resumption *n* ikmal إكمال

absolute *adj* akeed أكيد

certain *adj* akid أكيد

downright *adj* akid أكيد

naturally *adv* akid أكيد

sure *adj* akid أكيد

indisputable *adj* akid أكيد

but *prep* ella إلّا

unless *conj* ella إلّا

machinery *n* alat آلات

أﻟﻮاﻧﻪ كتيرة adj alwanuh ktireh	eliminatory adj elgha'ei إﻟﻐﺎﺋﻲ
polychrome	chiliad n alif seneh أﻟﻒ ﺳﻨﺔ
divinity n uluheyyeh أُﻟﻮﻫِﻴّﺔ	alfa n alfaa أﻟﻔﺎ
me pron eli إﻟﻲ	millennium n alfeyyeh أﻟﻔِﻴّﺔ
mine pron eli إﻟﻲ	diamond n almas أﻟﻤﺎس
my adj eli إﻟﻲ	our pron elna إﻟﻨﺎ
automatic adj aali آﻟﻲ	own adj elna إﻟﻨﺎ
أﻟﻴﺎف زﺟﺎﺟﻴّﺔ n alyaf zujajeyyeh	god n elah إﻟﻪ
fiberglass	Cupid n elah elhub إﻟﻪ اﻟﺤُﺐ
tame adj alif أﻟِﻴﻒ	meaningful adj elu ma'nah إﻟﻪ ﻣﻌﻨﻰ
mother n emm إمّ	her pron elha إﻟﻬﺎ
أم أربع وأربعين em arba' wu arbeyin	inspiration n elham إﻟﻬﺎم
centipede n	goddess n aleha إﻟﻬَﺔ
أم أربعة وأربعين emm arba' wu	divine adj elahi إﻟﻬِﻲّ
millipede n arb'yn	him pron elu إﻟﻮ
either adv emma إمّﺎ	his pron elu إﻟﻮ
front adj amami أﻣﺎﻣﻲ	إﻟﻮ أطراف ﺻﻨﺎﻋﻴّﺔ elu atraaf sinaeyeh
forward adj amami أﻣَﺎﻣﻲ	bionic adj
fidelity n amaneh أﻣﺎﻧﺔ	biantennary adj elu antilin إﻟﻮ اﻧﺘِﻴﻠﻴﻦ
emperor n embratur اﻣﺒﺮاطﻮر	bicellular adj elu khalitin إﻟﻮ ﺧﻠﻴﺘﻴﻦ
empress n embraturah إﻣﺒﺮاطﻮرة	dread adj elu rahbeh إﻟﻮ رﻫِﺒﺔ
empire n embratureyyeh إﻣْﺒَﺮاطُﻮرِﻳّﺔ	biangular adj elu zawitin إﻟﻮ زاوِﻳﺘﻴﻦ
n emberyaleyyeh إﻣْﺒِﺮْﻳﺎﻟِﻴّﺔ	binocular adj elu eyntin إﻟﻮ ﻋﻴﻨﺘﻴﻦ
imperialism	bipolar adj elu ketbin إﻟﻮ ﻗﻄﺒﻴﻦ
amberite n ambrit أﻣﺒﺮﻳﺖ	biaxial adj elu mehwarin إﻟﻮ ﻣﺤﻮرﻳﻦ
ampere n ampir أﻣﺒﻴﺮ	taloned adj elu makhlab إﻟﻮ ﻣﺨﺎﻟﺐ
nation n ummeh أمّﺔ	solemn adj elu hybeh إﻟﻮ ﻫﻴﺒﺔ
examination n emtihan اﻣﺘﺤﺎن	bifacial adj elu wajhin إﻟﻮ وﺟﻬﻴﻦ

bowel *n* 'amaa أمْعَاء

intestine *n* am'ae أمْعاء

possibility *n* imkaneyyeh إمكانيّة

probability *n* imkaneyyeh إمكانيّة

hope *n* amal أمل

estate *n* amlak أملاك

n amlak manquleh أملاك منقولة

movables

slick *adj* amlas أمْلَس

cosmopolitan *adj* umami أُمَمِي

security *n* amen أمن

safe *adj* amen آمن

adj aamen alatfal آمن عالأطفال

babyproof

wish *n* umneyeh أمنية

maternity *n* umumeh أمومة

motherhood *n* umumeh أمومة

motherly *adj* umumi أمومي

maternal *adj* umumi أُمُومي

illiterate *adj* ummy أمّي

illiteracy *n* ummeyyeh أمّيّة

prince *n* amir أمير

princess *n* amirah أميرة

princely *adj* amiri أميري

amen .*interj* amin آمين

n amin elsejellat أمين السجلّات

registrar

امتحان القبول فى جامعة imtihan

n elqubul beljam'ah

matriculation

absorptivity *n* alemtisas الامتصاص

امتصاص حيوي imtisas hayawi *n*

bioabsorption

fullness *n* imtila'e إمتلاء

n imtilak elasehum إمتلاك الأسهم

shareholding

abstinence *n* 'emtina امتناع

imtina' am ezzawaj امتناع عن الزواج

celibacy *n*

gratitude *n* imtinan إمتنان

concession *n* imteyaz إمتياز

franchise *n* imtyaz إمْتِياز

prerogative *n* imtyaz إمْتِياز

privilege *n* imtyaz إمْتِياز

command *n* amr أمر

order *n* amer أمر

precept *n* amr أمر

ordinance *n* amer idari أمر إداري

habeas *n* amr qada'i أمر قضائي

corpus

n amraad elqaleb أمراض القلب

cardiology

amriki men أمريكي من أصل أوربي

creole *n* asel urubi

constipation *n* imsaak إمسَاك

attention *n* intibaah انتباه

heed *n* intibah انتباه

vigilance *n* intibah إِنْتباه

suicide *n* intihari إنتحار

kamikaze *n* intihari إنتحاري

suicidal *adj* intihari إنتحاري

n entihal shakhseyyet انتحال شخصيّة

impersonation

election *n* intikhab انتخاب

n intikhabat fareyyeh انتخابات فرعيّة

by-election

mandate *n* intidab إنتداب

accession *n* entisab انتساب

affiliation *n* intisab انتساب

entry *n* intisab إنْتِسَاب

prevalence *n* intishar إنتشار

propagation *n* intishar إنتشار

spread *n* intishar إنتشار

erection *n* intisab انتصاب

erectile *adj* intisabi انتصابي

wait *n* intizar إنتظار

regularity *n* intizam إِنتظام

swell *n* intifakh إنتفاخ

inflation *n* intifakh إِنْتفاخ

intifakh elbatn انتفاخ البطن بالغازات

flatulence *n* belghazat

uprising *n* intifadah إنتفاضة

utilization *n* 'intifa إنتفاع

n amin khazyneh أمين خزينة

treasurer

keeper *n* amin sanduq أمين صندوق

teller *n* amin sanduq أمين صندوق

cashier *n* amin sanduq أمين صندُوق

n amin elmaktabeh أمين مكتبة

librarian

if .*conj* enn إن

ego *n* el'anna الأنا

I *pron* ana أنا

deputation *n* inabeh إنابة

deputy *n* inabeh إنابة

tubular *adj* anabibi أنابيبي

n anaqah zaydeh أناقة زايدة

falmboyance

pineapple *n* ananas أناناس

selfish *adj* anani أناني

egocentric *adj* anani أنَاني

self-centered *adj* anani أنَاني

egotism *n* ananeyyeh أنانيّة

emission *n* inbe'ath انبعاث

dazzle *n* inbihar انبهار

tube *n* unbub أنبوب

pipe *n* unbub أنْبوب

capillary *n* inbub sha'ri أنبوب شَعري

production *n* intaj إنتاج

productive *adj* intaji إنتاجي

productivity *n* intajeyyeh إنتاجيّة

decay n inhilal إنحلال

breakout n 'indilaa اندلاع

adhesion n endimag اندماج

merger n indimaj اندماج

n enzar niha'iy إنذار نهائي
ultimatum

glide n inzilaq ازلاق

enzyme n enzym اززيم

enzymic adj enzymi اززيي

urbanity n uns أُنس

mortal n insan انسان

humane adj ensani إنساني

humanity n ensanyyeh إنسانيّة

philanthropy n insaneyyeh إنْسَانيّة

damsel n aniseh آنسة

miss n aniseh آنسة

chime n insijam انسجام

concord n insijam انسجام

consistency n insijam إنسجَام

withdrawal n ensihab إنسحاب

slough n insilakh إنسلاخ

metamorphosis n insilakh اِنْسِلاخ

sneak n insilal إنسلال

inch n insh إنش

preoccupation n inshighal إنْشغال

schism n inshiqaq انشقاق

discipline n indibat إنضبَاط

censorious adj intiqadi انتقادي

transition n intiqal إنتقال

transitive n intiqali إنتقالي

revenge n intiqam إنتقام

revengeful adj intiqami إنتقامي

eclectic adj intiqa'i انتقائي

recession n intikas إنْتِكَاس

belonging n 'intimaa انتماء

accomplishment n 'entihaa انتهاء

antique adj antika انتيكا

aerial n antil انتيل

antennae n antil hawaei أنتيل هوائي

female n untha أنثى

achievement n enjaz إنجاز

fulfilment n injaz إنجاز

bible n injil إنجيل

evangel n enjil إنجيل

evangelic adj enjili إنجيلي

decline n inhidar انحدار

slant n inhidar انحدار

anamorphosis adj enhiraf انحراف

deviation n inhiraf انحراف

aberrance n inhiraf إنحراف

perversion n inheraf إنحراف

inhiraf an انحراف عن الموضوع
digression n elmawdu'e

depression n inhisar إنحسار

degenerate n inhitat إنحطاط

rubble *n* anqad أنْقاض

breakup *n* inqisam إنقِسام

swoop *n* inqidad إنقضاض

pounce *n* inqidad إنْقِضاض

rush *n* inqidad إنْقِضاض

breakoff *n* 'inqitaa انقطاع

n enqitae elddawra انقطاع الدورة

amenorrhoea

n enqetaa' elnafas انقطاع النفس

apnoea

overthrow *n* inqelab انقلاب

coup *n* inqilab إنقِلاب

denial *n* inkar إنكار

renunciation *n* inkar إنْكار

shrinkage *n* inkimash إنْكِماش

completion *n* 'inha إنهاء

termination *n* 'enha إنهاء

n inha' eliste'mar إنهاء الاستعمار

decolonization

escapist *n* inhizami إنهِزامي

downfall *n* inhyar انهِيار

species *n* 'anwa أنواع

womanhood *n* unutheh أنوثة

anorak *n* anorak أنوراك

bland *adj* anis أنيس

urbane *adj* anis أنِيس

chic *adj* aniq أنيق

genteel *adj* anik أنيق

n inteba' shakhsi انطباع شخصي

notion

inertia *n* 'intifa إنطفاء

blastoff *n* intilaq انطلاق

onrush *n* intilaq إنْطِلاق

regulation *n* anzemeh أنظمة

refreshment *n* in'ash إنعاش

solitude *n* en'ezal إنْعِزال

reflection *n* in'ekas إنعكاس

n enekas eldaww انعكاس الضوّ

anaclasis

reflective *adj* in'ekasi إنعكاسي

reflexive *adj* in'ekasi إنْعِكَاسِي

nose *n* enf إنف

blowout *n* infijar انفِجار

explosion *n* enfijar انفِجار

n infijar elburkan انفجار البركان

eruption

secession *n* infesal إنفِصال

separation *n* infesal إنفِصال

secessionist *n* infesali إنفِصالي

infesam shakhseyyeh إنفِصام شخصيّة

schyzophrenia *n*

cold *n* influwanza انفلونزا

influenza *n* influwanza انفلونزا

nasal *adj* anfi أنفِي

rescue *n* inqaz إنقاذ

debris *n* anqad أنْقاض

ozone *n* uzun أوزون	handsome *adj* aniq أنيق
below *prep* awtaa أوطى	neat *adj* aniq أنيق
beneath *prep* awtaa أوطى	moan *n* ahh آه
eucalypt *n* elukalebtus الاوكالبتوس	groan *n* aahat آهات
alpha *n* awwal أوّل	affront *n* ihaneh إهانة
first *n* elawwal الأوّل	dishonour *n* ihaneh إهانة
first *adj* awwal أوّل	loggerhead *n* ahbal أهبَل
premier *adj* awwal أوّل	asinine *adj* ahbal أهبَل
once *adv* awwal ma أوّل ما	daft *adj* ahbal أهْبَل
olympiad *n* ulmbyad أولمبياد	sheepish *adj* ahbal أهْبَل
priority *n* awlaweyyeh أوْلَوِيّة	vibration *n* ihtizaz إهتزاز
initial *adj* awwali أوّلي	concern *n* ihtimam اهتمام
primary *adj* awwali أوّلي	dedicatory *n* 'ihda إهداء
prime *adj* awwali أوّلي	kin *n* ahel أهْل
omega *n* umega أوميغا	native *n* ahel elbalad أهل البلد
phantasmagoria *n* awham أوهام	foremost *adj* ahamm أهَمّ
yes *adv* eyh إي	disregard *n* ihmal إهمال
any *adj* ayy أيّ	ignorance *n* ihmal إهمال
anyone *pron* ayy shakhes أي شخص	neglect *n* ihmal إهْمال
anywho *adv* ayy shakhes أي شخص	importance *n* ahameyyeh أهميّة
anything *pron* ayy shi أي شي	significance *n* ahameyyeh أهميّة
anyplace *pron* ayy makan أي مكان	opera *n* ubrah أوبرا
anywhere *adv* ayy makan أي مكان	operetta *n* ubrit أوبريت
anytime *adv* ayy waet أي وقت	organza *n* urkanzah أوركانزا
anywhen *adv* ayy wa'et أي وقت	orchestra *n* urkestrah أوركسترا
May *n* ayyar أيّار	orchestral *adj* urkestri أُورْكِسْتِري
coalition *n* ietilaf إئتلاف	origami *n* urigami أوريغامي
unison *n* e'etilaf إئتلاف	ozonation *n* uzaneh أوزنة

altruistic *adj* ithari إيثاري

affirmative *adj* ijabi إيجابي

positive *adj* ijabi إيجابي

hand *n* eyd إيد

deposit *n* iyda' belbank إيداع بالبنك

Irish *adj* erlandi ايرلندي

Irish *n* erlandi ايرلندي

aerobics *n* irobik ايروبيك

veil *n* eysharb إيشارب

voucher *n* iysal إيصال

Italian *n* elitali الإيطالي

Italian *adj* itali إيطالي

injunction *n* ey'az إيعاز

cadence *n* 'iqaa إيقاع

pace *n* iqa'e إيقاع

icon *n* ayquneh أيقونة

iconic *adj* ayquni أيقوني

September *n* aylul أيلول

belief *n* iman إيمان

faith *n* eyman إيمان

eleyman الايمان بالقضاء والقدر

fatalism *n* belqada' welqadar

ب

by *prep* bi بـ

via *prep* bi ب

---

door *n* bab باب

pope *n* elbaba البابا

dad *n* baba بابا

daddy *n* baba بابا

mule *n* babuj بابوج

papal *adj* babawi بابوي

papacy *n* babaweyyeh بابويّة

square *n* bahah باحة

n bahit elkeniseh باحة الكنيسة
churchyard

scholar *n* bahith باحث

steamer *n* bakhrah باخرة

steppe *n* badeyh بادية

aubergine *n* bazenjaan باذنجان

brinjal *n* banjan باذنجان

bar *n* bar بار

parachute *n* barashut باراشوت

cold *adj* bared بارد

cool *adj* bared بارد

frigid *adj* bared بارد

prominent *adj* barez بارز

conspicuous *adj* barez بارز

memorable *adj* barez بارز

subtle *n* 'bare بارع

carbine *n* barudeh بارودة

shotgun *n* barudeh بارودة

n barudeh seghireh بارودة قصيرة
musket

abed *adv* beltakhet بالتخت	baron *n* baron بارون
bilttartib el'abjadi بالترتيب الأبجدي	barium *n* barium باريوم
alphabetical *adj*	bazaar *n* bazar بازار
alike *adv* blttasawi بالتساوي	pea *n* bazellah بازلًّا
evenly *adv* beltasawi بالتساوي	pastel *n* bastil باستيل
adv beltasalsul بالتَّسَلسُل	by *adv* bi'esm باسم
consecutively	bus *n* bas باص
allusive *adj* bilttalmih بالتلميح	armpit *n* bat باط
outright *adv* beltamam بالتّمام	invalid *adj* batel باطِل
downright *adv* beltamam بالتّمَام	inside *n* baten باطن
verbatim *adv* belharf بالحرف	plutonic *adj* batni بَاطِني
justly *adv* belhaqq بالحَقّ	concrete *n* batun باطُون
stealthily *adv* belserr بالسرّ	*adv* be'tiraf elkll باعتراف الكل
belseneh 4 marrat بالسنة 4 مرَّات	admittedly
quarterly *adj*	*n* baqah seghireh باقة صغيرة
aright *adv* beldabt بالضبط	nosegay
ordinarily *adv* bel'adeh بالعادة	*adv* be'aqrab makan بأقرب مكان
wide *adv* bel'ard بالعرض	hereabouts
adult *n* baligh بالغ	cudgel *n* bakurah باكُورَة
nubile *adj* balegh بالـغ	precursor *n* bakurah باكُورَة
west *adv* belgharb بالغرب	packet *n* bakit باكيت
full *adv* belkamel بالكامل	last *adv* belakher بالآخر
fully *adv* belkamel بالكامل	weekly *adv* 'bel'usbue بالإسبوع
wholly *adv* belkamel بالكامل	namely *adv* bel'ism بالاسم
entirely *adv* belkamel بالكامِل	first *adv* belawwal بالأوَّل
nightly *adv* bellyl بالليل	nutty *adj* belbeduq بالبندق
likewise *adv* belmetl بالمثل	certainly *adv* betta'kid بالتأكيد
retail *adv* belmefarraq بالمفرّق	adoptive *adj* bltbny بالتبنّي

gladly *adv* bebst يبسط	backward *adv* belmaklub بالمقلوب
slowly *adv* 'bebute بطء	topsy turvy *adj* belmaqlub بالمقلوب
parrot *n* 'babagha ببغاء	per cent *adv* belmeyyeh بالمِيِّة
lamentable *adj* bebakki بيكي	rarely *adv* belnader بالنادر
tearful *adj* bebakki بيكي	seldom *adv* belnader بالنادر
beastly *adj* bebahameh ببهامة	aerial *adj* blhwa بالهوا
delightedly *adv* bibahjeh ببهجة	cesspool *n* balua'a بالوعَة
ex-parte *adv* betahayyuz بتحيزُ	sewer *n* balu'ah بالوعَة
decreasingly *adv* betakhfid بتخفيض	balloon *n* baluneh بالونة
amputation *n* bater بتر	ballet *sn* baleh باليه
stump *n* batr بتر	safely *adv* be'aman بأمان
mutilation *n* batr بَتّر	okra *n* bamyeh بامية
severance *n* batr بَتّر	banjo *n* banjo بانجو
petrol *n* betrul بترول	astir *adv* beinfea'al بإنفعال
darkly *adv* beta'tim بتعتيم	panorama *n* banurama بانوراما
billable *adj* betfutar بتفوتَر	tub *n* banyu بانيو
ostensibly *adv* betakalluf بتكلُّف	lacklustre *adj* bahet باهت
petal *n* bateleh بتلة	pale *adj* bahet باهت
adj 'betwafuq elara بتوافق الآراء	coclourless *adj* bahet باهِت
consensual	splendid *adj* baher باهر
anxiously *adv* bitawatur بتوتَر	*adv* 'be'awwal intiba بأوَّل إنطباع
heritable *adj* betwarrath بتورَّث	prima facie
transmission *n* bathth بثّ	anyway *adv* beayy tariqa بأي طريقة
still *adv* bethabat بثبات	byte *n* bayt بايت
boldly *adv* bejura'a بِجُرْئَة	stale *adj* bayt بايت
swan *n* baja'ah بجعة	agaze *adv* bibahalaqa ببحلقة
perhaps *adv* bejuz بجوز	masterly *adj* bebara'ah ببراعة
navigator *n* bahhar بحّار	rationalize *v* yebarrer ببرِّر

tip *n* bakhshish بَخْشيش	boatman *n* bahhar بَحّار
after *.conj* bkhsws بخصوص	sailor *n* bahhar بَحّار
incense *n* bakhur بخور	mariner *n* bahhar بَحّار
dreamily *adv* bekhayalleyyeh بخياليّة	opulence *n* bahbuhah بَحبوحَة
scrooge *n* bakhil بَخيل	ease *n* bahbuha بَحبوحَة
frugal *adj* bakhil بَخيل	sheer *adj* baht بحت
miser *n* bakhil بَخيل	mere *adj* baht بَحْت
miserly *adj* bakhil بَخيل	research *n* bahth بحث
niggard *n* bakhil بَخيل	search *n* bahth بحث
niggardly *adj* bakhil بَخيل	searching *adj* bahth بحث
foreknowledge *n* badaha بَداهَة	study *n* bahth بَحْث
beginning *n* bedayeh بداية	sea *n* bahr بحر
commencement *n* bidayeh بداية	pond *n* bahrah بَحْرَة
prime *n* bedayeh بداية	(nautic(al *adj* bahri بحري
start *n* bedayeh بداية	naval *adj* bahri بحري
inception *n* bedayeh بداية	marine *adj* bahri بَحْري
outset *n* bedayeh بِدَاية	abominably *adv* beheqed بحقد
onset *n* bedayeh بِدَايَة	*adv* behekm eldarurah بحكم الضرورة
anabolic *adj* bedaey بدائي	perforce
primeval *adj* beda'i بِدَائي	stare *n* bahlaqah بحلقة
primitive *adj* beda'i بِدَائي	lagoon *n* buhayrah بُحَيرة
fad *n* bed'a بدعة	lake *n* buhayrah بُحَيرة
defensive *adv* 'bidifa بدفاع	steam *n* bukhar بخار
exactly *adv* bedeqqah بدقّة	vapour *n* bukhar بُخار
minutely *adv* bedeqqah بدقّة	vaporous *adj* bukhari بُخاري
suit *n* badleh بدلة	abrasively *adv* bekhushuneh بخشونة
costume *n* badleh بدلة	bluntly *adv* bekhushuneh بخشونة
buff *n* badleh askareyeh بدلة عسكريّة	gratuity *n* bakhshish بَخْشيش

adj barrat elqanun برّات القانون extrajuducial	corporal *adj* badani بَدَنِّ
fridge *n* barrad برّاد	agape, *adv* bdahsheh بدهشة
teapot *n* barrad elshay برّاد الشاي	*adj* bidun 'akhlaq بدون أخلاق amoral
stool *n* buraz براز	nomad *n* badawi بَدَوِي
feces *n* buraz بُرَاز	nomadic *adj* badawi بَدَوِي
fecal *adj* burazi بُرَازِي	alternate *adj* badil بديل
subtlety *n* bara'ah براعة	lieu *n* badyl بديل
mastery *n* bara'ah بَرَاعَة	substitute *n* badil بَديل
pragmatic *adj* bragmati براغماتي	intuition *n* badihah بَديهة
n bragmateyyeh براغماتيّة pragmatism	intuitive *adj* badihi بَديهي
	impropriety *n* baza'a بَذَاءَة
outside *adj* barrani برّاني	filth *n* baza'a بَذَاءَة
outward *adj* barrani برّاني	seed *n* bezreh بذرة
sharper *n* barrayeh برّاية	brazen *adj* 'bazei بَذيء
gibber *n* barbarah بربرة	improper *adj* 'baze بَذيء
babble *n* barbarah بربَرَة	nasty *adj* 'baze بَذيء
barbarous *adj* barbari بَرْبَري	filthy *adj* 'baze بَذيء
barbarity *n* barbareyeh بَرْبَرِيَّة	fealty *n* berr بِرّ
pipe *n* barbij بربيج	out *adj* barrah برّا
orange *n* burtuqaleh برتقالة	*adj* brra eitar ezzawaj برّا إطار الزواج extramarital
asterism *n* berj برج	
tower *n* berj برج	brra elkurah برّا الكرة الأرضيّة
Leo *n* berj elasad برج الأسد	extraterrestrial *adj* elardeyyeh
Capricorn *n* berj eljadi برج الجدي	innocence *n* bra'ah براءة
Gemini *n* 'burj eljawza برج الجوزاء	naivety *n* bara'ah بَرَاءَة
aries *n* berj elhamal برج الحمل	patent *n* 'bara'et ikhtera براءة إختراع
aquarius *n* berj eldalu برج الدلو	outdoor *adj* barrat elbit برّات البيت

barrel *n* barmil برميل

cask *n* barmil khasab برميل خشب

programme *n* bernamej برنامج

n brnamej watheiqi برنامج وَثائقي

documentary

frame *n* brwaz برواز

puritan *n* brutestanti بروتستانتي

protein *n* brutin بروتين

prominence *n* buruz بروز

preen *n* brush بروش

boast *n* barwazah بَروظَة

profile *n* brufyl بروفايل

rehearsal *n* brufah بروفَة

professor *n* brufesur بروفسور

bureaucrat *n* beruqrati بروقراطي

n beruqrateyeh بروقراطية

Bureacuracy

proxy *n* bruksi بروكسي

broccoli *n* brukuli بروكولي

bromite *n* bromit بروميت

bronze *n* bronz برونز

bronze *adj* bronzi برونزي

leisurely *adv* beraweyyeh بروية

wild *adj* barri بَري

terrestrial *adj* barri بَري

innocent *adj* 'bare بري•

shavings *n* baryh برية

mail *n* barid بريد

mast *n* burj telfzyun برج تلفزيون

bourgeoise *n* burjwazi برجوازي

bourgeois *adj* burjwazeyeh برجوازيّة

cold *n* bard برد

dew *n* barad بَرَد

drape *n* bardayeh برداية

curtain *n* berdayeh بردابة

prestige *n* bristij برستيج

prestigious *adj* bristiji برستيجي

brochure *n* brushur برشور

leprosy *n* baras بَرَص

sprout *n* bur'um برعم

bud *n* burumeh برعمة

although .*conj* berrghm بِرَغم

flea *n* barghut برغوت

screw *n* berghi برغي

perfume *n* barfan برفان

glitter *n* barq بَرق

benignly *adv* bereqqa بِرقّة

nicely *adv* bereqqah بِرقّة

hurricane *n* burkan بركان

volcano *n* burkan بركان

volcanic *adj* burkani بركاني

benediction *n* barakeh بَرَكة

benison *n* barakeh بَرَكة

parliamentary *adj* barlamani برلماني

twist *n* barm برم

amphibious *adj* barmaei برمائي

speedily *adv* bser'ah بسرعة

enjoyment *n* bast بسط

numerator *n* bast بَسْط

pleasure *n* bast بَسْط

biscuit *n* biskwit بسكويت

n biskwit rqiq بسكويت رقيق
cracker

simple *adj* basit بسيط

naive *adj* basit بَسِيط

gospel *n* bsharah بِشارَة

joviality *n* bashasheh بشاشة

forerunner *n* bashayer بشاير

adj 'beshbah el waja بشبه الوجع
achelike

abnormally *adv* beshuzuz بشذوذ

grate *n* bashr بشر

mankind *n* bashar بشَر

human *adj* bashari بشري

awful *adj* 'beshe بشع

heinous *adj* 'beshe بشع

seamy *adj* 'beshe بشع

ugly *adj* 'beshe بشع

adj beshakel uzun بشكل أذن
auriform

adv beshakel asasi بشكل أساسي
basically

adv beshakl asasi بشكل أساسي
substantially

post *n* barid بَرِيد

n 'elbarid essare البريد السريع
express

n barid elketroni بريد الكتروني
email

courier *n* barid sari'e بريد سريع

postal *adj* baridi بريدي

british *adj* britani بريطاني

snout *n* bazbuz بزبوز

nozzle *n* bazbuz بَزْبُوز

linseed *n* bezer elkettan بزر الكتَّان

spit *n* bazqah بزقة

extra *adv* bezyadeh بزيادة

just *adj* bas بس

only *adj* bas بس

however .*conj* bas بس

but .*conj* bas بَس

naivete *n* basatah بساطة

rusticity *n* basatah بساطة

simplicity *n* basatah بساطة

gardener *n* bestani بستاني

beysteheqq elshafakah بستحقّ الشفقة
piteous *adj*

beysteheqq elshafakah بستحقّ الشفقة
pitiable *adj*

horticulture *n* bastaneh بستنة

apace *adv* beser'aa بسرعة

fast *adv* bser'a بسرعة

glimmer *n* basis بصيص	*adv* beshakel awwali بشكل أوّلي
ray *n* basis بصيص	primarily
ware *n* beda'ah بضاعة	*adv* beshakel ra'esi بشكل رئيسي
tenuously *adv* beda'ef بضَعْف	mainly
astray, *adv* 'bidayaa بضياع	*adv* beshakel mubher بشكل مُبهِر
battery *n* batareyeh بطاريَة	dazzlingly
potato *n* batata بطاطا	*adv* beshaql mwajjah بشكل موجَّه
n batatah mahruseh بطاطا مهروسة	pointedly
mash	*adj* beshakel mu'aqqat بشكل مؤقَّت
ticket *n* betaqah بِطاقَة	temporary
n betaqet elnata'ej بطاقة النتائج	gloatingly *adv* beshamteh بشماتة
scorecard	elate *adj* bashush بشوش
betaqet zakrah بطاقة ذاكرة مدمجة	jovial *adj* bashush بشوش
flashcard *n* mudmajeh	voyeurism *n* basbasah بصبصة
tag *v* betaqet se'r بطاقة سعر	peep *n* basbasah بصبصة
padding *n* betaneh بطانة	bonafide *adv* bisahtik بصحتك
comforter *n* bataneyyeh بطّانيّة	*adj* yesruf nazar بصرف النظر
quack *n* batbatah بَطْبَطَة	irrespective
duck *n* battah بطّة	optic *adj* basari بصري
flask *n* bateha بَطْحَة	ocular *adj* basari بَصَري
affluence *n* btr بطر	hard *adv* besu'ubeh بصعوبة
affluent *adj* btran بطران	onion *n* basal بصل
adv 'betaraqa sayea بطريقة سيئة	bulb *n* basaleh بَصَلة
badly	impression *n* basmeh بَصْمة
ill *adv* betareqah say'a بطريقة سيئَة	aloud *adv* bisawt ali بصوت عالي
adv bitariqa ghalat بطريقة غلط	cognizance *n* basirah بصيرة
amiss	insight *n* basirah بَصيرة
	prescience *n* basirah بَصيرة

water- *n* battikh ahmar بطيخ أحمر
melon

n batteikh ahmar بطيخ أصفر
melon

headlong *adv* betish بطيش

pell-mell *adv* betysh بطيش

prattle *n* ba'ba'ah بعبعة

revival *n* ba'th بَعث

expedition *n* be'theh بعثة

mission *n* be'theh بعثة

after *prep* ba'd بعد

post- *adj* ba'ed elmut بعد الموت
mortem

baed fawwat بعد فوات الأوان
afterthought *n* al'awan

after *adv* baed ma بعد ما

next *adj* ba'da بعدا

post *adv* ba'da بعدا

dung *n* baer بَعر

adv be'aradeyyeh بعَرضيّة
extrinsically

adv be'asher ad'aaf بعشر أضعاف
tenfold

deeply *adv* beumeq بعمق

practically *adv* be'amaleyyeh بعمليّة

mosquito *n* ba'ud بعوض

distant *adj* beid بعيد

far *adj* beyed بعيد

adv betareqa kafeyeh بطريقة كافية
enough

adv betareqah ma بطريقة ما
somehow

betareqa mu'akeseh بطريقة معاكسة
appositely *adv*

betariqah hammyyeh بطريقة هدميّة
deconstructively *adv*

tyranny *n* batsh بَطْش

hero *n* batl بطل

protagonist *n* batal بَطَل

outdated *adj* betlan بطلان

outmoded *adj* betlan بطلان

vanity *n* butlan بُطْلان

heroine *n* bataleh بطلة

avidly *adv* 'betamaa بطمع

abdomen *n* batn بطن

belly *n* baten بطن

abdominal *adj* batni بطني

tournament *n* butuleh بطولة

champion *n* butuleh بطولة

chivalry *n* butuleh بُطولة

heroic *adj* butuli بطولي

chivalrous *adj* butuli بُطولي

heroism *n* butulyyeh بطوليّة

laggard *n* 'betu بطئ

slow *adj* 'bate بطيء

tardy *adj* 'bate بطيء

galore *adv* bketreh بكثرة

bacteria *n* bakteria بكتريا

maiden *n* bekr بكر

virgin *n* bekr بكر

virgin *adj* bekr بكر

morrow *n* bukrah بكرا

tomorrow *n* bukrah بكرا

pulley *n* bakarah بَكَرَة

roller *n* bakarah بَكَرَة

pixel *n* bekasal بكسل

bekul ma ta'nehi بكل ماتعنيه الكلمة

arrant *n* elkalemeh

buckle *n* biklet shaer بِكلة شعر

aheap *adv* bekumeh بكومة

cry *n* beke بكي

early *adj* bakkir بكّير

premature *adj* bakkir بكّير

bikini *n* bekini بكيني

deoxy *adj* bla uksijin بلا أكسجين

adv bla hudud بلا حدود

abandonedly

acephalous *adj* bla ras بلا راس

merciless *adj* bla rahmeh بلا رحمة

boneless *adj* bla adem بلا عضم

bare *adj* bla lebes بلا لبس

achromatic *adj* bla loon بلا لون

platinum *n* elblatin البلاتين

platinum *adj* blatini بلاتيني

remote *adj* be'yd بعيد

adj be'yn wehdeh بعين وحدة

monocular

dimly *adv* 'bighaba بغباء

mad *adv* 'beghaba بَغباء

odium *n* bughed بغّض

malignity *n* bughd بغض

adv beghumud بغموض

enigmatically

comatose *adj* beghaybubeh بغيبوبة

gleefully *adv* befarah بفرح

scandalously *adv* befdyha بفضيحة

chaotic *adv* befawdaweyeh بفوضوية

bug *n* baqq بقّ

n baqayah eljeththeh بقايا الجثّة

relic

adj beqbal elfasekh بقبل الفسخ

terminable

parsley *n* baqdunes بقدونس

cow *n* baqarah بقرة

speck *n* buq'ah بقعة

spot *n* buq'ah بقّعة

stain *n* buq'ah بقّعة

eyespot *n* buq'et eleyn بقعة العين

dreadfully *adv* beqwweh بقوّة

virginity *n* bakarah بكارة

baccalaureate *n* bakaluria بكالوريا

all *adv* bikamel بكامل

agog *adj* blahfeh بلهفة

ill *n* balweh بلوِة

plutonium *n* blutunyum بلوتونيوم

glass *n* ballur بلُّور

glazier *n* ballurji بلُّورجي

blouse *n* bluzeh بلوزة

pullover *n* bluzeh suf بلوزة صوف

sweater *n* bluzeh suf بلوزة صوف

acorn *n* baloot بلوَط

oak *n* ballut بلُّوط

obsolete *adj* balyan بليان

dopey *adj* balid بليد

slothful *n* balid بَليد

billion *n* bilyon بليون

billionaire *n* bilyunir بليونير

considering *prep* bima ennu بِما إنّو

apt *adj* bemahaluh بمحله

aloof *adv* bimaezil aan بمعزل عن

weary *adj* bymallel بملِّل

build *n* 'binaa بناء

construction *n* 'bina بِناء

girlish *adj* bennati بنّاتي

building *n* binayeh بناية

edifice *n* benayrh kbireh بناية كبيرة

tectonic *adj* bena'i بنائي

daughter *n* bent بنت

girl *n* bent بنت

niece *n* bent akhkh بنت أخّ

slowness *n* baladeh بلادة

n blazma elnanu بلازما النانو

nanoplasma

plastic *n* blastik بلاستيك

plastic *adj* blastiki بلاستيكي

floor *n* blat بلاط

slab *n* blatah بلاطة

notice *n* blagh بلاغ

n balagh rasmi بلاغ رسمي

communiqué

agitation *n* balbaleh بلبلة

jumble *n* balbaleh بلبلة

country *n* balad بلد

borough *n* baldeh بَلدة

vulgar *adj* baladi بلدي

indigenous *adj* baladi بَلدي

commune *n* baladeyyeh بلَديّة

municipality *n* baladeyyeh بلَديّة

adjacent *adj* blzq بلزق

balm *n* balsam بَلسَم

racket *n* bals بلص

kindly *adv* belutf بلطف

swallow *n* 'bale بلع

esophageal *adj* bal'umi بلعومى

guttural *adj* bal'umi بلعومي

sputum *n* balgham بلغَم

terrace *n* balkun بَلكُون

balcony *n* balkuneh بلكونة

adj benmesek beleyd بَخسك بالإيد handy

adj beynwetheq fih بنوثق فيه trustful

mason n bannah بَنّى

brown adj benni بَنّي

pepper n bhar بهار

spice n behar بَهار

astonishment n bahteh بَهتة

flabbergast n bahteh بَهتة

delight n bajeh بهجة

gaiety n bahjeh بَهجة

tumbler n bahlwan بَهلوان

buffoon n bahlul بهلول

mime n bahlul بَهلول

beast n bahiim بهيم

gate n bawwabeh بوابة

bawabbeh بواّبة الكترونيّة

portal n elketruneyyeh

piles n bwasir بَواسير

poplin n bublyn بوبلين

potash n butas بوتاس

potassium n butasyum بوتاسيوم

powder n budrah بودرة

pudding n buding بودينغ

china n bursalan بورسلان

porcelain n bursalin بورسلين

focal adj bu'eri بؤري

chit n bent weqha بنت وقَحة

narcotic n banj بَنج

clausula n band بند

term n band بند

provision n band بَند

proviso n band sharti بند شرطي

band n band lelshaer بَند للشعر

scattergun n bendqeyyeh بندقيّة

tomato n bandurah بندورة

downward adv benzul بنزول

benzidine n benzydin بِنزيدين

benzene n benzyn بِنزين

gasoline n bnzin بِنزين

bnshereh bekam بنشرح بكم كلمة

effable adj klmeh

pantaloon n bantalun بنطلون

slacks n bantalun بنطلون

trousers n pl bantalun بنطلون

n bantalun lelrekbeh بنطلون للركبة

breeches

clean adv benazafeh بنظافة

washable adj beynghesel بنغسل

violet n banafsag بنفسَج

purple adj/n banafsaji بنفسجي

bank n bank بنك

n bank elma'lumat بنك المعلومات

databank

monger n 'bayya بيّاع

salesman n 'bayya بيّاع

seller n 'bayya بيّاع

vendor n 'bayya بيّاع

bayya' elqurtaseyyeh بيّاع القرطاسيّة

stationer n

n bayya' jumleh بيّاع جملة

wholesaler

hawker n bayya' jawwal بيّاع جوّال

book- n bayaa' ketub بيّاع كتب

seller

retailer n byya' mefarraq بيّاع مفرّق

n elbayan el'aam البيان العام

manifesto

data n bayanat بيانات

piano n byanu بيانو

enjoyable adj beybset بيبسط

accommodation n beit بيت

apartment n beit بيت

flat n beit بيت

house n beit بيت

n beit elhares بيت الحارس

gatehouse

n beit elankabut بيت العنكبوت

cobweb

doghouse n beit elkalb بيت الكلب

kennel n beit elkalb بيت الكلب

pantry n beit elmuneh بيت المونة

kiss n buseh بوسة

compass n busleh بوصلة

clearly adv bewuduh بوضوح

legibly adv bewuduh بوضوح

obviously adv bewuduh بوضوح

boot n buwt بوط

bugle n buq بوق

clarion n buq بوق

cornet n buq بوق

megaphone n buq بوق

trumpet n buq بوق

abusively adv bwqaha بوقاحة

timely adj bwaqtuh بوقته

poker n buker بوكر

bouquet n buqeyh بوكيه

urine n bul بوّل

steel n bulad بولاد

urinary adj buli بولي

polybutene n bulebtin بوليتين

bolero n buliru بوليرو

detective adj bulisi بوليسي

polymer n bulimer بوليمر

polyene n bulyyin بولين

owl n bumeh بومة

bohemian adj buhimi بوهيمي

ovum n buwaydah بويضة

affect v by'athr ala بيأثر على

blank n bayad بياض

يخصّ الدورة الشهريّة bekhuss
adj eldawrah elshahreyyeh
menstrual

adj bekhuss elqaleb يخصّ القلب
cardio

adj bekhuss elkilab يخصّ الكلاب
canine

adj bekhuss elnughbeh يخص النخبة
elite

adj bekhuss elnasab يخصّ النسب
genealogical

beykhda' leldarebeh يخضع للضريبة
taxable *adj*

terrific *adj* beykhawwef يخوّف
bawn *n* 'baydae بيدق
soluble *adj* beydub بيدوب
well *n* bir بير
ale *n* bayra بيرة
beer *n* bira بيرة
berajje' ezzekrayat يرجّع الذكريات
evocative *adj*
ghastly *adj* bera'eb يرعّب
foamy *adj* byerghi يرغي
flapping *adj* berafref يرفرف
beryllium *n* berylyum بيريليوم
deplorable *adj* beyza'el يزعّل
grievous *adj* byza'el يزعّل

duplex *n* beit btabqin يت بطابقين
glasshouse *n* beit balluri يت بلُّوري
brothel *n* bit da'ara يت دعارَة
bungalow *n* beit qashsh يت قَش
beta *n* betta بيتّا
pentagon *n* bentagun بيتاغون
eatable *adj* beyttakal بيتاكَل
blackmail *v* yebtazz بيتزّ
pizza *n* bitzah بيتزا
creditable *adj* beytsaddaq يتصدّق
repairable *adj* beytsallah يتصلّح
necessitate *v* beyttallab يتطلّب
curable *adj* beyta'alaj يتعالَج
beyharrek elmasha'er يحرّك المشاعر
emotive *adj*
enthusiastic *adj* byhammes يحمّس
ashamed *adj* bikhajjil يخجّل
shameful *adj* beykhajjel يخجّل
بخصّ الأخلاق الواجبة bekhuss
adj elakhalq elwajbeh
deontological
bykhuss elbaladeyyeh يخصّ البلديّة
municipal *adj*
adj bekhuss elhubub يخصّ الحبوب
cereal
adj bekhus eldanab يخصّ الدَّنَب
caudal

بيع sale *n* 'be

بيع القبُّعات النسواني be' elqabbu'at

millinery *n* elniswani

بيع بالمفرَّق *n* bei' belmfarraq

dealership

بيع جملة wholesale *n* bei' jumleh

بيع مفرَّق retail *n* be' belmefarraq

يعطي أمل hopeful *adj* yeya'ti amal

beyqbal eltafawud يقبل التفاوض

negotiable *adj*

adj beyqder yetjannabuh يقدر يتجنَّبه

escapable

بيقلِّل من قدر شخص beqallel mn

depreciatory *adj* qadr shakhes

يكفِّي sufficient *adj* beykaffi

بيلزمه ought *v* beylzamuh

adj beyl'i elnafs بيلي النفس

mawkish

بيلياردو billiard *n* bilyardu

بيمارِستان madhouse *n* bymarstan

بيمطّ tensile *adj* beymutt

بيملِّل humdrum *adj* beymallel

بيملِّل tedious *adj* beymallel

بيوّت deadly *adj* bymawwet

بيوّت deathly *adj* bymawwet

بيوّت mortal *adj* beymut

بين amid *prep* bayn

بين among *prep* bein

adj beystahel madh يستاهل مدح

praiseworthy

occlusive *adj* beysedd يسدّ

intoxicant *n* beystul يسطُل

toxic *adj* beysammem يسمِّم

worth *adj* byswah يسوى

adj beyshbah elbashar يشبه البشر

anthropoid

adj beyshbah ejjebneh يشبَه الجبنة

cheesy

similar *adj* beyshbahu يشبهه

delicious *adj* byshahhi يشهِّي

dainty *adj* byshahhi يشهِّي

palatable *adj* beyshahhi يشهِّي

tasty *adj* beyshahhi يشهِّي

spawn *n* beid elsamak بيض السمك

omelette *n* beid meqli بيض مقلي

elliptic *adj* baydawi بيضاوي

egg *n* bedah بيضة

testicle *n* bedet elrejjal بيضة الرجَّال

humorous *adj* bydahhek بيضحّك

laughable *adj* beydahhek بيضحّك

debilitating *adj* byd'af بيضعف

oval *adj* baydawi بيَضَوي

ovular *adj* beidi بيضي

melodious *adj* beytrib بيطرب

deafening *adj* beyutrush بيطرُش

veterinary *adj* bytari بيطري

ت

follower n 'tabe تابع

subordinate adj 'tabe تابع

henchman n tabe' amin تابع أمين

ark n tabout تابوت

coffer n tabut تابوت

stammer n ta'ta'ah تأتأة

effect n ta'thir تأثير

influence n ta'thir تأثير

n taa'thir hayawi تأثير حيوي
bioactivity

crown n taj تاج

merchant n tajer تاجر

trader n tajer تاجر

jobber n tajer jumleh تاجر جملة

draper n tajer jukh تاجر جوخ

n tajer kutub atiqa تاجر كتب عتيقة
antiquarian

adjournment n ta'jil تأجيل

postponement n ta'jil تأجيل

delay n ta'ekhir تأخير

tardiness n ta'khir تأخير

punitive adj ta'dibi تأديبي

vengeance n tar تار

annals npl tarikh تاريخ

date n tarikh تاريخ

amongst prep bein بين

between prep bein بين

betwixt prep bein بين

adj beyntej beid ينتج بيض
oviferous

transferable adj beynteqel ينتقل

deletable adj bynhezef ينحذف

endurable adj beynhemel ينحمل

manageable adj beyndar يندار

adj beynazzil qimet ينزّل قيمة
depreciating

adj beynshefeq aleh ينشفق عليه
pathetic

adj yenesh elqalib ينعش القلب
cordial

doable adj ben'emil ينعمل

beyn'emellu ينعمله عمل جراحي
operable adj amal jirahi

measurable adj beynqas ينقاس

as .conj baynama ينما

maddening adj beyhaster بهستر

interesting adj beyhemm بهم

painful adj 'beywajje بوجّع

generable adj bywalled بولّد

environment n be'aa بيئة

surroundings n be'ah بيئة

ecological adj be'i بيئي

environmental adj be'ei بيئي

oxidation *n* ta'aksud تَأَكْسُد	*n* tarikh elsalaheyyeh تاريخ الصلاحيّة
ablation *n* ta'akul تآكُل	expiry
erosion *n* ta'akul تآكُل	*n* tarikh elsalaheyyeh تاريخ الصلاحيّة
fret *n* ta'akul تآكُل	validity
ablative *adj* ta'akuli تآكُلي	*n* tarikh elweladeh تاريخ الولادة
erosive *adj* ta'akuli تآكُلي	birthdate
affirmation *n* ta'kid تأكيد	historical *adj* tarikhi تاريخي
confirmation *n* ta'kid تأكيد	history *n* traikhi تاريخي
emphasis *n* ta'kid تأكيد	historic . *a* ta'rikhi تأريخي
tertiary *n* eltalet الثالت	fresh *adj* tazah تازه
third *n* eltalit الثالت	ninth *adj* 'eltase التاسع
tertiary *adj* talet تالت	*adj* eltase' ashar التاسع عشر
glare *n* ta'alluq تألّق	nineteenth
wart *n* taluleh تالولة	establishment *n* ta'sis تأسيس
n ta'lif qwamis تأليف القواميس	constituent *adj* ta'sisi تأسيسي
lexicography	corroborative *adj* ta'sisi تأسيسي
even *adj* tamm تامّ	indication *n* ta'shir تأشير
outright *adj* tamm تامّ	motion *n* ta'shir تأشير
stark *adj* tamm تامّ	ostension *n* ta'shir تأشير
collusion *n* ta'amur تآمُر	indicative *adj* ta'shiri تأشيري
contemplation *n* ta'ammul تأمُّل	discontent *n* ta'affuf تأفّف
meditation *n* ta'ammul تأمُّل	absurd *adj* taafeh تافه
meditative *adj* ta'ammuli تأمُّلي	paltry *adj* tafeh تافه
nationalization *n* ta'mim تأميم	banal *adj* tafeh تافه
insurance *n* ta'min تأمين	pointless *adj* tafeh تافه
surety *n* ta'min تأمين	trivial *adj* tafeh تافه
another *adj* tani تاني	inferior *adj* tafeh تافه
else *adj* tani تاني	adaptation *n* ta'qlum تأقلُم

adoption n tbnni تَبنّي	other adj tani تَاني
urination n tabwil تبويل	second adj tani تَاني
lay v tabyyid تبييض	premeditation n ta'ani تَأنّي
manifestation n tabyyin تَبيين	n ta'nib damir تأنيب الضمير
v tetfattah elwardeh تتفتَّح الوردة	compunction
bloom	interchange n tabadul تَبادُل
snow v tetallej تتلّج	n tabadul itlaq nar تَبادُل إطلاق نار
coronation n tatwij تتويج	crossfire
n tathbit wazifi تثبيت وظيفي	brag n tabahi تَباهي
tenure	swagger n tabahi تَباهي
gravitation n tajazub تَجَاذُب	showoff n tabahi تَباهي
commerce n tijarah تجارة	extravagance n tabzir تبذير
trade n tejarah تجارة	prodigality n tabzir تبذير
merchandise n tijarah تِجَارَة	wastage n tabzir تبذير
adj tejaret eljukh تجارة الجوخ	donation n 'tabarru تبرّع
drapery	repudiation n tabarri تبرّي
tejarah تجارة الكترونيّة	absolution n tabriyeh تبرية
e-commerce n elketruneyyeh	vindication n tabreyeh تبرية
mercantile adj tijari تجارى	justification n tabrir تبرير
adj tejari - bahri تجارى-بحرى	tabrir ghiab fi تبرير غياب في الجرايم
maritime	alibi n aljarayim
commercial adj tijari تجاري	simplification n tabsit تبسيط
before prep tijah تجاه	missionary n tabshiri تَبشيري
regeneration n tajdid تجديد	lining n tabtin تبطين
rejuvenation n tajdid تجديد	retardation n 'tabte تبطّئ
renewal n tajdid تجديد	subordination n taba'eyyh تبعيّة
modernization n tajdid تَجْديد	tobacco n tabegh تَبغ
experience n tajrubeh تجرُبة	notification n tabligh تبليغ

n tajyyr elshik تجيير الشيك
endorsement

n iltiham malati التحام ملاطي
concrescence

endearment n tahbib تحبيب

below prep tahit تحت

beneath prep tahet تحت

down prep tahet تحت

under prep taht تحت

underneath prep taht تحت

submarine adj taht elmay تحت المي

downstairs adj tehtani تحتاني

challenge n tahaddi تحدّي

contour n tahdid تحديد

specification n tahdid تحديد

n tahdid elhudud تحديد الحدود
delimitation

n tahdid elhudud تحديد الحدود
demarcation

tahdid mawqe' تحديد الموقع بالرادار
radiolocation n belradar

n tahdid mestawah تحديد مستوى
placement

gaze n tahdiq تحديق

caution n tahzir تحذير

precaution n tahzir تحذير

warning n tahzir تحذير

monitory adj tahziri تحذيري

trial n tajrubeh تجربة

bargain n tajraa تجرة

empiricist n eltajribi التجريبي

empirical adj tajribi تجريبي

empiricism n tajrebeyyeh تجريبية

refutation n tajrih تجريح

libel n tajrih تجريح

spy n tajassus تجسس

personification n tajsid تجسيد

incarnation n tajseem تجسيم

embodiment n tajsim تجسيم

substantiation n tajsim تجسيم

belch n 'tajashu تجشؤ

burp n 'tajashue تجشؤ

crimp n tajeydeh تجعيدة

curl n tajeydeh تجعيدة

refrigeration n tajmid تجميد

compilation n 'tajmei تجميع

facelift n tajmil wajeh تجميل وجه

aesthetic adj tajmili تجميلي

cosmetic adj tajmili تجميلي

avoidance n tajannub تجنّب

eschewment n tajannub تجنّب

refrain n tajannub تجنّب

abort v tujhed تجهض

miscarry v tujhid تجهض

preparation n tajhiz تجهيز

preparatory adj tajhizi تجهيزي

showpiece n tehfeh تحفة

n tehfeh fanneyyeh تحفة فنيّة

masterpiece

caution n tahaffuz تَحَفُّظ

motivation n tahfiz تحفيز

promotion n tahfiz تحفيز

verification n tahaqquq تحقُّق

abasement n tahkir تحقير

contempt n tahqir تحقير

realization n tahqiq تَحْقيق

control n tahakkum تحكُّم

arbitration n tahkimi تحكيم

arbitrary adj tahkimi تحكيمي

n tahalul hayawi تحلُّل حيوي

biodegradation

analysis n tahlil تحليل

analytical adj tahlili تحليلي

endurance n tahammul تحمُّل

stamina n tahammul تحمُّل

n tahmil zyadeh تحميل زيادة

overload

embalming n tahnit تحنيط

taxidermy n tahnit تحنيط

transformation n tahawwul تحوُّل

conversion n tahwil تَحْويل

convert n tahwil تَحْويل

remittance n tahwil تَحْويل

precautionary adj tahziri تحذيري

liberty n taharrur تَحَرُّر

harassment n taharrush تحرُّش

ferret n taharri تحرِّي

inspection n taharri تحرِّي

investigation n taharri تحرِّي

edition n tahrir تحرير

release n tahrir تحرير

liberation n tahrir تَحْرير

editorial adj tahriri تحريري

abetment n tahrid تحريض

inducement n tahrid تحريض

instigation n tahrid تحريض

animation n tahrik تحريك

removal n tahrik تحريك

sway n tahrik تحريك

n tahrik zehni تحريك ذهني

telekinesis

prohibition n tahrim تحريم

puzzle n tahzurah تحزورة

alertness n thssb تَحَسُّب

advancement n thssun تَحَسُّن

betterment n tahsiin تحسين

enhancement n tahsin تحسين

improvement n tahsin تحسين

collection n tahsil تحصيل

entrenchment n tahsin تحصين

crash n tahattum تحطُّم

rebate *n* takhfid تَخْفِيض

moderation *n* takhfif تَخْفِيف

n takhfif essur'a تخفيف السرعة

deceleration

abandon *v* takhallah تخلّى

acetifier *n* takhlil تخليل

glut *n* tekhmeh تُخمة

guess *n* takhmin تخمين

intimidation *n* takhwif تخويف

envision *v* takhayyul تَخيّل

imagery *n* takhayyulat تخيّلات

overlap *n* tadakhul تداخل

procurement *n* tadbir تدبير

inference *n* tadakhkhul تدخُّل

gradation *n* tadarruj تدرُّج

stage *n* tadrib تدريب

training *n* tadrib تدريب

gradual *adj* tadriji تدريجي

inauguration *n* tadshin تدشين

influx *n* tadaffuq تدفّق

spurt *n* tadaffuq تدفُّق

scrutiny *n* tadqiq تَدْقيق

n tadqiq hesabat تدقيق حسابات

audit

droop *n* tedlayeh تدلاية

lop *n* tadalli تدلّي

annihilation *n* tadmir تدمير

sacrilege *n* tadnis تَدْنيس

n tahwil laghaz تحويل لغاز

gasification

bow *n* taheyyet ihtiram تحيّة احترام

bias *n* tahayyuz تحيّز

partiality *n* tahayyuz تحيّز

telepathy *n* takhatur تخاطُر

telepathic *adj* takhaturi تخاطري

hide *n* tekhbyeh تخباية

blundering *n* takhabbut تخبُّط

bed *n* takhit تخت

cot *n* takhet eltifil تخت الطفل

crib *n* takhit eltefel تخت الطفل

n takht elmarid تخت المريض

sickbed

curd *n* takhaththur تخثُّر

anaesthesia *n* takhdir تخدير

narcosis *n* takhdir تخدير

storage *n* takhzin تخزين

major *n* takhassus تخصُّص

specialization *n* takhassus تخصُّص

allocation *n* takhsis تخصيص

devotion *n* takhsis تخصيص

تخصيص مصاري لتسديد دين

n takhasses masari litasdid din

amortization

transgression *n* takhatti تخطّي

schematic *adj* takhtiti تخطيطي

decrease *n* takhfid تخفيض

تربية النحل tarbeit elnahel *n*
apiculture

التربية الوطنيّة eltarbeyeh
civics *n* elwataneyeh

ترتبط tertebet *adj* interdependent

ترتيب tartib *n* tidiness

ترتيبات tartibat *n* arrangement

ترتيلة tartyleh *n* hymn

ترجمة tarjameh *n* translation

ترجي tarraji *n* adjuration

ترجّي tarajji *n* appeal

ترجّي tarajji *n* entreaty

ترجيح tarjih *n* likelihood

ترجيع الذكريات tarje' ezzekrayat *n*
evocation

ترجيع المصاري tarje' elmasari *n*
refund

تَرجيع قطع الماكينة لورا tarje' kita'
elmakina lawara
backlash *n*

ترجيع لمنصب سابق tarje' lamanseb
sabeq *n* reinstatement

ترحيب tarhib *n* hail

ترحيب tarhib *n* ovation

ترحيب tarhib *n* welcome

ترحيل tarhil *n* expulsion

تردُّد taraddud *n* frequency

تردُّد taraddud *n* shilly-shally

تَردُّد taraddud *n* indecision

تدهين painting *n* tadhin

تدويب thaw *n* tadwib

تدوين صوتي podcast *n* tadwin suwti

تذكار memento *n* tizkar

تذكار souvenir *n* tezkar

تذكار keepsake *n* tizkar

تذكاري memorial *adj* tizkari

تذكاري monumental *adj* tizkari

تذكّر anamnesis *n* tazakkur

التذوُّق degustation *n* ettazawwuq

تذييل postscript *n* tazyyil

تراب clod *n* turab

تراب soil *n* trab

تراب كلسي marl *n* trab klsi

ترابُط correlation *n* tarabut

تراجُع عن الموقف tarajue' an
elmawkif
backtrack *n*

تراجيدي tragic *adj* trajidi

تراجيديا tragedy *n* trajidya

تراخي languor *n* tarakhi

ترأُّس heading *n* tara'us

تراكتور tractor *n* traktur

تراكُم accumulation *n* trakum

ترام tram *n* tram

ترانزيت transit *n* tranzit

تراوح swing *n* tarawuh

تَربية pedagogy *n* tarbeyeh

n tarwij i'lami ترويج إعلامي promotion	gear n tres ترس
n tarwij I'ilami ترويج إعلامي publicity	shield n ters ترس
subjugation n tarwid ترويض	arsenal n tirsaneh ترسانة
fallow n taryyeh elard تريح الأرض	n tersaneh bahreyyeh ترسانة بحرية shipyard
commitment n iltizam التزام	candidacy n tarshih ترشيح
budge n tazahzuh تزحزح	nomination n tarshih ترشيح
throng v tezhum تزحم	ooze n tarshih ترشيح
insecurity n 'taza'zu تزعزع	amends npl tardiyeh ترضية
n tazfit eltariq تزفيت الطريق pavement	thunder v ter'ud ترعد
blossom v tuzhir تزهر	punctuation n tarqim ترقيم
fake n tazwir تزوير	n tark edderaseh ترك الدراسة dropout
forge n tazwir تزوير	heritage n terkeh تركة
forgery n tazwir تزوير	turkey n terkeyyah تركيا
falsification n tazyyif تزييف	installation n tarkib تركيب
garnishment n tazyyin تزيين	texture n tarkib تركيب
tolerance n tasamuh تسامح	synthesis n tarkib تركيب
toleration n tasamuh تسامح	concentration n tarkiz تركيز
forbearance n tasamuh تسامح	focalization n tarkiz تركيز
inquiry n tasa'ul تساؤل	focusing adj tarkizi تركيزي
query n tasa'ul تساؤل	(thermos (flask n termus ترمس
adj 'tasawi eladla تساوى الاضلاع equilateral	coding n tarmiz ترميز
equal n tasawi تساوي	overhaul n tarmim ترميم
parity n tasawi تساوي	restoration n tarmim ترميم
obscurity n tasattur تستّر	stagger n tarannuh ترنّح
	carol n tarnemeh ترنيمة

entertainment *n* tasleyeh تَسلية

pastime *n* tasleyeh تَسلية

delivery *n* taslim تَسليم

n tasammum eldamm تَسَمُّم الدَّم

toxemia

denomination *n* tasmeyeh تَسميّة

nomenclature *n* tasmeyeh تَسْمِيَة

tasmeyeh a ism تَسمية ع اسم حدا

namesake *n* hada

tan *n* tasmir تَسمير

cadge *n* tasawwul تَسَوُّل

compromise *n* tasweyeh تَسوية

settlement *n* tasweyeh تَسوية

n taswiq belhatef تَسويق بالهاتف

telemarketing

similarity *n* tashabuh تَشابه

resemblance *n* tashabuh تَشَابُه

similitude *n* tashabuh تَشَابُه

pessimism *n* tasha'um تَشَاؤُم

pessimistic *adj* tasha'umi تَشاؤُمي

satiety *n* 'tashabbu تَشَبُّع

assimilation *n* tashbeeh تَشبيه

likeness *n* tashbih تَشبيه

simile *n* tashbih تَشْبِيه

deflection *n* tashtit تَشتيت

lubrication *n* tashehim تَشحيم

diagnosis *n* tashekhiss تَشخيص

absorption *n* tashroub تَشَرُب

registration *n* tasjil تَسجيل

notation *n* tasjil تَسْجيل

n tasjil elahdath تَسجيل الأحداث

chronicle

n tasjil elzelzal تَسجيل الزّلزال

seismogram

leak *n* tasarrub تَسرُّب

leakage *n* tasrib تَسْريب

discharge *n* tasrih تَسريح

n tasrih elasaker تَسريح العساكر

demobilization

coif *n* tasrihit shaer تَسريحة شعر

acceleration *n* 'tasree تَسريع

stripe *n* tastir تَسطير

ablegation *n* tasfir تَسفير

mitigation *n* taskin تَسكين

relief *n* taskin تَسْكين

n 'taskin alwaja تَسكين الوجع

alleviation

sequence *n* tasalsul تَسَلْسُل

succession *n* tasalsul تَسَلْسُل

n tasalsul zamani تَسَلسُل زمني

chronology

successive *adj* tasalsuli تَسلسلي

climb *n* tasalluq تَسَلُق

n tasalluq eljabal تَسَلُق الجبال

mountaineer

amusement *n* tasliyeh تَسلية

defamatory *adj* tashehiri تشهيري

slanderous *adj* tashhiri تَشْهيري

muddle *n* tashawwush تشوّش

confusion *n* tashwish تشويش

scorch *n* tashwit تشويط

singe *n* tashwit تشويط

deformity *n* tashwih تشويه

n tashweh sem'ah تشويه سمعة

slander

n 'tashwih simaa تشويه سمعة

calumny

intersection *n* tasalub تصالب

crossing *n* tasalub تَصَالُب

correction *n* tashih تصحيح

rectification *n* tasehih تَصْحيح

reformation *n* tasehih تَصحيح

reformatory *adj* tasehihi تصحيحي

defiance *n* tasaddi تصدّي

export *n* tasdir تصدير

act *n* tsaroof تصرف

behaviour *n* tasarruf تصرّف

n tasarruf ghalat تصرّف غلط

misbehaviour

declaration *n* tasrih تصريح

proclamation *n* tasrih تصريح

permit *n* tasrih تَصْريح

n tasrif emleh تصريف عملة

exchange

saturation *n* tashrib تشريب

anatomy *n* tashrih تشريح

dissection *n* tashrih تشريح

n tashrih eljeththeh تشريح الجثّة

obduction

n tashrih eljiththeh تشريح الجثّة

post-mortem

legislation *n* tashre'e تشريع

statute *n* 'tashri تَشْريع

legislative *adj* tashre'i تشريعي

n tishrin elawwal تشرين الأوّل

October

n tishrin ettani تشرين الثاني

November

slash *n* tashtib تشطيب

ignition *n* tash'il تشعيل

encryption *n* tashfir تشفير

formation *n* tashkil تشكيل

variety *n* tashkeleh تشكيلة

n tashammu' elkabed تشمُّع الكبَد

cirrhosis

spasm *n* tashannuj تشنّج

contraction *n* tashannuj تشنّج

tashannuj athna' تشنّج أثناء الحمل

eclampsia *n* elhamel

spasmodic *adj* tashannuji تشنّجي

defamation *n* tashehir تشهير

invective *n* tashehir تَشْهير

sacrifice *n* tadheyeh تضحية

stricture *n* tadyyeq تضييق

n tadayyuq elhadaqah تضيُّق الحدقة

myosis

analogy *n* tatabuq تطابق

symmetry *n* tatabuq تطابق

biformity *n* tatabuq تطابُق

congruency *n* tatabuq تطابُق

indentification *n* tatabuq تطابُق

emanation *n* tatayur تطاير

normalization *n* 'tatbe تطبيع

application *n* tatbiq تطبيق

extremity *n* tatarruf تطرُّف

extreme *adj* tatarrufi تطرُّفي

beadwork *n* tatriiz تطريز

brocade *n* tateriz تطريز

embroidery *n* tatriz تَطْرِيز

vaccination *n* tat'eym تطعيم

intervention *n* tatafful تطفُّل

n tatli'e ahsha'a تطليع الأحشاء

evisceration

tatle'ah gharameyyeh تطليعَة غراميّة

ogle *n*

sanctification *n* tatehir تطهير

purgation *n* tatehir تَطْهِير

folding *n* tetwayeh تطواية

evolution *n* tatawwur تطوُّر

disposal *n* tasrifeh تَصْريفة

browse *n* tasaffuh تصفُّح

exploration *n* tasaffuh تصفُّح

surf *n* tasaffuh elnet تصفُّح النت

liquidation *n* tasfeyeh تصفية

whistle *n* tasfir تصفير

acclamation *n* tsfiq تصفيق

applause *n* tasfiq تصفيق

clap *n* tasfiq تصفيق

amelioration *n* taslih تصليح

repair *n* taslih تصليح

design *n* tasmim تصميم

affectation *n* 'tsnue تصنُّع

mannerism *n* 'tasannu تصنُّع

sham *n* 'tasannu تصنُّع

manufacture *n* 'tasne تصنيع

classification *n* tasnif تصنيف

tabulation *n* tasnif تَصْنيف

conception *n* tasawwur تصوُّر

mysticism *n* tasawwuf تصوُّف

ballot *n* taswiit تصويت

suffrage *n* taswit تصويت

n taswir belashe'ah تَصْوير بالأشِعَّة

radiography

photographic *adj* taswiri تصويري

photography *n* taswiri تصويري

picturesque *adj* taswiri تَصْويري

opposition *n* tadarub تَضَارُب

exclamation *n* ta'ajjub تعجُّب	تطوُّر الانسان tatawur elinsan *n*
impassable *adj* ta'jizi تعجيزي	ontogeny
insurmountable *adj* ta'jizi تعجيزي	evolutionary *adv* tatawwuri تطوُّري
census *n* te'dad sukkani تعدَاد سكَاني	development *n* tatwir تطوير
تعدُّد الأزواج ta'addud elazwaj *n*	induction *n* 'tatwe تطويع
polyandry	draft *n* 'tatwe تَطويع
تعدُّد الاستعمال ta'ddud eleste'mal *n*	prolongation *n* tatwil تطويل
versatility	pretence *n* tazahur تظاهُر
تعدُّد الأشكال ta'addud elashkal *n*	conflict *n* taarud تعارُض
multiform	contradiction *n* taarud تعارُض
تعدد الزوجات taadud elzawjat *n*	affection *n* ta'atuf تعاطُف
bigamy	sympathy *n* ta'atuf تعاطُف
تعدُّد الزوجات ta'addud elzawjat *n*	contrast *n* taakus تَعَاكُس
polygamy	orthograph *n* ta'amudeyyeh تعامديّة
تعدُّد اللغات ta'addud ellughat *n*	handle *n* ta'amul تعامل
polyglot	conduct *n* ta'amul تعامُل
multiplex *adj* ta'adudi تعدُّدي	dealings *n* ta'amulat تعامُلات
تعددِيّة ta'addudeyyeh *n*	cooperation *n* ta'awun تعاون
multiplicity	collaboration *n* ta'awun تعاوُن
breach *n* ta'addi تعدِّي	synergy *n* ta'awun تَعَاوُن
amendment *n* ta'dil تعديل	cooperative *adj* ta'awuni تعاوُني
modification *n* ta'dil تعديِل	coexistence *n* ta'ayush تعايُش
torture *n* ta'zib تعذيب	fatigue *n* ta'ab تعب
تعرفة جمركيّة ta'rufeh jumrukeyyeh *n*	strain *n* ta'ab تعب
tariff	alamort *adj* ta'ban ktir تعبان كتير
definition *n* ta'rif تعريف	expression *n* ta'bir تعبير
condolence *n* te'zayeh تعزاية	expressive *adj* ta'biri تعبيري
consolation *n* te'zayeh تعزاية	dimness *n* ta'tim تعتيم

immersion *n* ta'mid تَعْمِيد

longevity *n* ta'mir تَعْمِير

circular *n* ta'mim تعميم

circulation *n* ta'mim تعميم

bark *n* te'wayeh تعواية

compensation *n* ta'wid تعويض

indemnity *n* ta'wid تعويض

remuneration *n* ta'wid تعويض

remunerative *adj* ta'widi تعويضي

unfortunate *adj* ta'is تعيس

miserable *adj* ta'is تعِيس

pitiful *adj* ta'is تعِيس

calibration *n* ta'yyir تعيير

gibe *n* ta'yyir تعيير

taunt *n* ta'yyer تعيير

appointment *n* ta'eyyin تعيين

connivance *n* taghadi تغاضي

nourishment *n* taghzeyeh تغذية

nutrition *n* taghzeyeh تغذية

chirp *n* taghrid تغريد

warble *n* taghredeh تغريدة

enticement *n* taghrir تغرير

n teghlayt se'r تغلاية سعر

overcharge

envelopment *n* taghlif تغليف

coating *n* taghlifeh تغليفة

alteration *n* taghyir تغيير

change *n* taghyyir تغيير

reinforcement *n* ta'ziz تعزيز

injustice *n* ta'assuf تعسّف

ninetieth *adj* eltis'yneyyat التعسينات

antitheism *n* taessub تعصّب

bigot *n* taassub تعصّب

prejudice *n* ta'assub تعصّب

n ta'assub qawmi تعصّب قومي

chauvinism

ire *n* ta'sib تعصيب

breakdown *n* ta'attul تعطّل

suspension *n* ta'attul تعطّل

deactivation *n* ta'til تعطيل

complication *n* ta'qid تعقيد

sophistication *n* ta'qid تعقيد

sterilization *n* ta'qim تعقيم

bile *n* taakkur elmizaj تعكّر المزاج

ringworm *n* ta'labeh تعلبة

packing *n* ta'lib تعليب

comment *n* ta'liq تعليق

education *n* ta'lim تعليم

learning *n* ta'lim تعليم

tuition *n* ta'lim تعليم

n ta'lim mukhtalat تعليم مختلط

coeducation

instruction *n* ta'limat تعليمات

didactic *adj* ta'limi تعليمي

tutorial *adj* ta'limi تعليمي

baptism *n* ta'amiid تعميد

brood *n* tafqis elbid نفقيس البيض	revision *n* taghyyer تغيير
brood *adj* tafqisi تفقيسي	abruption *n* 'tfaja تفاجئ
mull *n* tafakkur تفكُّر	apple *n* teffaha تفاحة
brood *n* tafkir ktir تفكير كتير	parry *n* tafadi تفادي
decomposition *n* tafkik تفكيك	reaction *n* tafa'ul تفاعل
residue *n* tefl تفل	interplay *n* tafa'ul تَفَاعُل
pedantic *n* tafalsuf تفلسُف	reactionary *adj* tafa'uli تفاعلي
fie *interj* tfeh alik تفه عليك	absurdity *n* tfaha تفاهة
excellence *n* tafawwuq تفوُّق	insipidity *n* tafaha تفاهة
pre-eminence *n* tafawwuq تفوُّق	nonsense *n* tafahah تفاهَة
superiority *n* tafawwuq تَفوّق	disparity *n* tafawut تَفَاوُت
delegacy *n* tafwid تفويض	optimism *n* tafa'ul تَفَاؤُل
delegate *n* tafwid تفويض	optimistic *adj* tafa'uli تفاؤلي
delegation *n* tafwid تفويض	*n* tafattuh elwardeh تَفَتُّح الوردة
n eltiqa' ennahrin التقاء نهرين	bloom
confluence	dilaceration *n* taftit تفتيت
meet *n* taqabul تقابُل	blast *n* tafjir تفجير
lapse *n* taqadm تقادم	burst *n* tafjir تفجير
proximity *n* taqarub تقارب	explosive *adj* tafjiri تفجيري
retirement *n* taqa'ud تقاعد	bifurcation *n* 'tafarru تفرُّع
ration *n* taqtir تقتير	germination *n* tafrikh تفريخ
scant *n* taqtir تقتير	detail *n* tafsil تفصيل
n taqtir belnafakah تقتير بالنفقَة	particular *n* tafsil تفصيل
husbandry	elaborate *adj* tafsili تفصيلي
appreciation *n* taqdir تقدير	particular *adj* tafsili تفصيلي
discretion *n* taqdir تقدير	tifdayeh men elhawa تفضاية من الهوا
esteem *n* taqdir تقدير	deflation *n*
prospect *n* taqdir تَقْدِير	preference *n* tafdil تفضيل

mimic n taqlid تقليد	n taqdir bel'estedlal تقدير بالاستدلال
tradition n taqlid تقليد	extrapolation
mimesis n taqlid تقّليد	submission n taqdim تقديم
n taqlid sut تقليد صوت	introductory adj taqdimi تقديمي
onomatopoeia	submissive adj taqdimi تقديمي
traditional adj taqlidi تقليدي	zoom n taqrib تقريب
conventional adj taqlidi تقّليدي	almost adv taqriban تقريبا
reduction n taqlil تقليل	nearly adv taqryban تقريباً
empathy n eltaqammus التقمّص	nigh adv taqriban تقريباً
n taqammus arwah تقمّص أرواح	thereabouts adv taqriban تقريباً
transmigration	approximate adj taqribi تقريبي
empathic adj taqmmusi تقمّصي	report n taqrir تقرير
technician n teqani تقني	stunt n taqzim تقزم
technical adj teqani تقني	allotment n taqsim تقسيم
technicality n teqaneyyeh تقنية	partition n taqsim تقّسيم
insularity n 'taququ تقوقع	n taksim ledawa'r تقسيم لدوائر
piety n tuqah تقى	departmentalization
godly adj taqi تقّي	n taqsim lmajmua'at تقسيم لمجموعات
sepsis n taqayyuh تقيّح	aggroupment
observance n taqyyed تقّيد	scrape n taqshir تقشير
precious adj tqil تقيل	default n taqsir تقصير
restriction n taqyyed تقييد	shortening n taqsir تقصير
assessment n taqyyem تقييم	incapacity n taqsir تقّصير
estimate n taqyyem تقييم	distillery n taqtir تقطير
estimation n taqyyem تقييم	slit n taqte' beltul تقطيع بالطول
valuation n taq'yym تقييم	emulation n taqlid تقليد
estimative adj taqyyimi تقييمي	imitation n taqlid تقليد
symbiosis n takaful تكافل	mimic adj taqlid تقليد

thrice *adv* tlat ad'af تلات أضعاف

thirteenth *n* eltalta'sh التلاطعاش

fraud *n* talaub تَلاعُب

n tala'ub bel as'ar تلاعب بالأسعار

manipulation

redress *n* talafi تلافي

recital *n* telaweh تلاوة

recitation *n* telaweh تلاوِة

meet *n* talbeyeh تلبية

casing *n* talbis تلبيس

slush *n* talj dayb تلج دايب

snow *n* talj dayb تلج دايب

abstraction *n* tlkhees تلخيص

summary *n* talkhis تلخيص

outline *n* talkhis تلخيص

decay *n* talaf تلَف

telecast *n* talfazeh تلفزة

television *n* telfezyun تلفزيون

phone *n* telefun تلفون

telephone *n* telifun تلفون

n telfun lasilki تلفون لاسلكي

radiophone

fabrication *n* talfiq تلفيق

figment *n* talfiq تلفيق

inoculation *n* talqih تلقيح

allusion *n* talmih تلميح

inkling *n* tamlih تلميح

hint *n* talmih تلميح

presumption *n* takabbur تكبُّر

vainglory *n* takabbur تكبّر

amplification *n* takbir تكبير

tick *n* takkeh تكّة

reticence *n* takattum تكتّم

tactics *n* taktik تكتيك

condensate *n* takthiif تكثيف

recurrence *n* tekrar تكرار

reiteration *n* tekrar تكرار

repetition *n* tekrar تكرار

dedication *n* takris تكريس

cab *n* taksi تكسي

taxi *n* taksi تكسي

taxicab *n* taksi تكسي

breaking *n* taksir تكسير

smash *n* taksir تكسير

cubical *adj* takeybi تكعيبي

atonement *n* takfiir an تكفير عن

ostensibility *n* takalluf تكلُّف

cost *n* taklifeh تكلفة

supplementary *adj* takmili تكميلي

muzzle *n* takmim تكميم

adj teknuluji تكنولوجي

technological

technology *n* teknulujia تكنولوجيا

conglomerate *n* takawwur تكوُّر

dune *n* tall raml تلّ رمل

sandhill *n* tall ramli تلّ رملي

insubordination *n* tamarrud تَمَرّد

exercise *n* tamrin تمرين

practice *n* tamrin تمرين

crocodile *n* timsah تمساح

n temsah 'amriki تمساح أمريكي
alligator

n tmsih eljwkh تمسيح الجوخ
adulation

n tamsih jukh تمسيح جوخ
sycophancy

saunter *n* temshayh تمشاية

n temshayeh khassah تمشاية خاصّة
bywalk

rain *v* tematter تَمطّر

smack *n* tamattuq تمطّق

perusal *n* tama'un تَمعّن

evasion *n* tamallus تَملّص

acquisition *n* tmalook تَملَك

fidget *n* tmulmul تَملُل

preamble *n* tamhid تَمهيد

prelude *n* tamhid تَمهيد

preliminary *adj* tamhidi تمهيدي

ripple *n* tamawwuj تَموّج

undulation *n* tamwij تَمويج

finance *n* tamwil تمويل

camouflage *n* tammwih تَمويه

mimicry *n* tamwih تَمويه

peculiarity *n* tamayyuz تَميّز

finish *n* 'talme تلميع

polish *n* 'talme تلميع

pollution *n* talawwuth تلوّث

fibrosis *n* talayyuf تليّف

fibrosity *n* talayyuf تليّف

mouth *n* temm تمّ

consistency *n* tamasuk تماسُك

solidarity *n* tamasuk تَماسُك

tenacity *n* tamasuk تَماسُك

okay *adj* tamam تمام

prefect *n* tamam تمام

even *adv* tamaman تماما

octuple *adj* tman ad'af ثمان أضعاف

octuple *n* tman ad'af ثمان أضعاف

relish *n* tamattu' bi تَمتّع ب

consolidation *n* tamtin تمتين

effigy *n* temthal تمثال

sculpture *n* temthal تمثال

statue *n* temthal تمثال

acting *n* tamtheel تمثيل

tamtheleyeh tahzurat تمثيليّة تحزورات
charade *n*

apotheosis *n* tamjid تمجيد

glorification *n* tamjid تمجيد

n tamdid elaslak تمديد الأسلاك
wiring

tamarind *n* tamr hendi تمر هندي

rebellion *n* tamarrud تَمرّد

traverse n tanassul تنصُّل	discrimination n tamyyiz تمييز
induction n tansib تنصيب	distinction n tamyyiz تمييز
tanzir elqasabeh تنظير القصبة الهوائيّة	tamyyez تمييز العلامة التجاريّة
tracheoscopy n elhawa'eyyeh	branding n elalameh eltijareyeh
endoscopic adj tanziri تنظيري	abnegation n tanazul تنازل
endoscopy n tanziri تنظيري	waiver n tanazul تنازل
vexation n tanghis تنغيص	suitability n tnasub تناسب
hum n tanghym تنغيم	proportion n tanasub تَنَاسُب
respiration n tanaffus تنفّس	genital adj tanasuli تناسلي
adj tnfusi elwy تنفسي علوي	consonance n tanaghum تناغم
aerodigestive	ambivalence n tanaqud تناقض
refinement n tanqyh تنقية	paradox n tanaqud تناقض
implement n tanfiz تنفيذ	antinomy n tanaqudh تناقُض
mobility n tanaquleyyeh تنقليّة	antithesis n tanaqudh تناقُض
purification n tanqeyh تنقية	short n tanbal تنْبَل
subtraction n tanqis تنقيص	sluggish adj tanbal تنْبَل
dictation n tanqil تنقيل	forecast n tanabbu'e تنبُّؤ
tin n tanakeh تنكة	prediction n 'tanabu تنبُّؤ
disguise n tanakkur تنكُّر	reminder n tanbih تنبيه
sigh n tanhydeh تنهيدة	astrology n tanjiim تنجيم
mew n tenwayeh تنوايّة	damp n tandeyeh تندية
tandoor n tannur تنُّور	tennis n tenis تنس
furnace n tannur تنّور	n tinis elrisheh تنِس الرّيشة
kiln n tannur تنّور	badminton
skirt n tannurah تنُّورة	coordination n tansiq تنسيق
n tannurah be kasrat تنّورة بكسرات	reactivation n tanshit تنشيط
kilt	dehydration n tanshif تنشيف
	eavesdrop n tanassut تنصُّت

elusion *n* taharrub تَهرُّب

eltaharrub mn التهرُّب من الواقع

escapism *n* 'elwaqe

acrobatics *n* tehreej تهريج

acrobatic *adj* tehreji تهريجي

accusation *n* tehmeh تهمة

congratulation *n* tahne'a تهنئة

temerity *n* tahawwur تهوُّر

ventilation *n* tahweyeh تهوية

irritation *n* tahayyuj تهيُّج

configuration *n* tahye'a تهيئة

poise *n* tawazun توازن

balance *n* tawazun توازُن

tawazn elhwa توازن الهوا والغاز

aerostatics *n* wlghaz

communication *n* tawasul تواصل

contact *n* tawasul تواصل

modesty *n* 'tawadu تواضُع

accordancy *n* twafq توافق

harmony *n* tawafuq توافق

proliferation *n* twalud توالد

toilet *n* twalit تواليت

twin *n* taw'am توأم

twin *adj* taw'am توأم

repentance *n* tubeh توبة

berry *n* tut توت

mulberry *n* tut توت

raspberry *n* tut ahmar توت احمر

n tannurah dakhleyyeh تَنّورة داخليّة
petticoat

illumination *n* tanwir تنوير

n tanwim maghnatisi تنويم مغناطيسى
mesmerism

n tanwim maghnatisi تنويم مغنطيسي
hypnotism

intimation *n* tanwih تنويه

ruck *n* tani تني

both *pron* eltenin التنين

duo *n* tenin تنين

dragon *n* tennin تِنّين

eltihab التهاب الزائِدة الدوديّة

n elzaedeh eldudeyeh
appendicitis

n eltihab me'awi التهاب رئوي
pneumonia

n eltihab essahayah التهاب سحايا
meningitis

inflammatory *adj* eltihabi الْتِهابي

felicitations *int* tahani تهاني

spell *n* tehjayh تهجاية

threat *n* tahdid تهديد

volley *n* tahdid تهديد

menace *n* tahdid تَهديد

subversion *n* tahdim تَهديم

subversive *adj* tahdimi تَهديمي

edification *n* tahzib تهذيب

foresight *n* 'tawaqqu توقُّع

anticipation *n* tawaque تَوَقُّع

die *n* tawaqquf توقُّف

standstill *n* tawaqquf توقُّف

sign *n* 'tawqi توقيع

signature *n* 'tawqi توقيع

n tawqi'e belfakh توقيع بالفخّ
entrapment

stoppage *n* tawqif توقيف

beget *v* tulad تولَد

mother *v* tulad تولَد

v tulad elhaywanat تولد الحيوانات
litter

foal *v* twlad elmuhr تولَد مُهر

garlic *n* tum توم

misdirection *n* tawahan توهان

current *n* tayyar تيّار

n tayyar tahti تيّار تحتي
undercurrent

draught *n* tayyar hawa تيّار هوا

titanic *adj* titanik تيتانيك

terabyte *n* tirabyt تيرابايت

terabit *n* tirabet تيرابت

goat *n* tys تيس

typhoid *n* tefu'yd تيفوئيد

staple *n* tileh تيلة

stress *n* tawattur توتُّر

anxiety *n* tawatur تَوَتُّر

echinid *adj* tutya'ei توتيائي

orientational *adj* tawajjuhi توجُّهي

monotheism *n* tawhid توحيد

theism *n* tawhid تَوحيد

courtship *n* tawaddud تَوَدُّد

adieu *n* 'twdie توديع

ox *n* tur تور

blush *n* tawarrud تورُّد

flush *n* tawarrud تورُّد

implication *n* tawrit تَوْريط

foliation *n* tawwriq تَوْريق

distribution *n* tawzi'e توزيع

mediocrity *n* tawassut تَوسُّط

beseech *n* tawassul توسُّل

beseeching *n* tawassal توسُّل

solicitation *n* tawassul تَوَسُّل

expansion *n* 'tawse توسيع

descriptive *adj* tawsifi توصيفي

carriage *n* tawsil توصيل

connection *n* tawsil توصيل

clarification *n* tawdih توضيح

employment *n* tawzif توظيف

recruit *n* tawzif توظيف

toffee *n* tufi توفي

thrift *n* tawfir تَوْفير

expectation *n* tawaqqu'e توقُّع

fig *n* tin تين

ث

constant *adj* thabit ثابِت

set *adj* thabit ثابِت

steadfast *adj* thabit ثابِت

steady *adj* thabit ثابِت

firm *adj* thabit ثابِت

still *adj* thabit ثابِت

nemesis *n* tha'r ثَأْر

third *adj* talit ثالِت

elthaluth el'moqaddas الثالوث المقدَّس

trinity *n* elmuqaddas

secondary *adj* thanawi ثانوي

beta *adj* thani ثاني

dioxide *n* thani uksid ثاني أكسيد

second *n* thanyh ثانِية

steadiness *n* thabat ثبَات

stillness *n* thabat ثبَات

veracity *n* thabat ثبَات

firmness *n* thabat ثبَات

breast *n* thadi ثدي

mammal *n* thadi ثدي

udder *n* thadi ثدي

bosom *n* thadi ثَدي

mammary *adj* thadyy ثديي

treasure *n* tharweh ثروة

pelf *n* tharweh ثَروة

fortune *n* tharweh ثَروة

n tharweh a'mmeh ثروة عامّة

commonwealth

porridge *n* tharid ثريد

serpentine *n* thu'ebani ثُعباني

fox *n* tha'lab ثعلب

vixen *n* tha'labeh ثعلبة

auger *n* thaqqabeh ثقَّابة

culture *n* thaqafeh ثقافة

cultural *adj* thaqafi ثقافي

hollow *n* thuqb ثقب

piercing *n* thuqb ثقب

puncture *n* thuqb ثقب

aperture *n* thuqub ثقُب

bore *v* thuqub ثقُب

n thuqb el meftah ثقب المفتاح

keyhole

trust *n* theqah ثقة

confidence *n* thiqa ثقَة

reliance *n* theqah ثقَة

barrack *n* thakaneh ثكنة

n thaqaneh askareyeh ثكنة عسكريّة

cantonment

n thakaneh askareyyeh ثكنة عسكريّة

casern

tertian *adj* thulathi ثلاثي

triple *adj* thulathi ثلاثي

جار neighbour *n* jar	ثلاثي الألوان *adj* thulathi elalwan
جارح offensive *adj* jareh	tricolour
جارِح sharp *adj* jarih	الثلاثينيات thirtieth *n* eltlatineyyat
جارح injurious *adj* jareh	ثمانيني octogenarian *n* temanini
جارور drawer *n* jarur	ثمانيني octogenarian *adj* temanini
جاروف shovel *n* jaruf	ثُنائي bilateral *adj* thunaei
جاروف spade *n* jaruf	ثُنَائي dual *adj* thunaei
جاروف mattock *n* jaruf	ثنائي الأبعاد *adj* thunaei elabaad
جاري current *adj* jari	bidimensional
جاكيت jacket *n* jakit	ثنائي اللغة *adj* thunaei ellugha
جاكيت طويل garment *n* jakit twil	bilingual
جالبُ الحظّ mascot *n* jaleb elhazz	ثُنَائِيّة duality *n* thunaeyyeh
جَالَيري gallery *n* galiri	ثور bull *n* thur
جامد stationary *adj* jamed	ثور أمريكي bison *n* thawr amriki
جامد immovable *adj* jamid	ثَوْرَة outbreak *n* thawrah
جامع compositor *n* 'jame	ثَوْرَة revolt *n* thawrah
جامعة university *n* jam'ah	ثَوْرَة revolution *n* thawrah
جامعة league *n* jam'ah	ثوري revolutionary *adj* thawri
جامعي academic *adj* jamei	ثَوْري revolutionary *n* thawri
جاموس buffalo *n* jamus	
جان fairy *n* jan	
جانِب facet *n* janib	ج
جانبي flank *adj* janbi	
جانبي sideway *adj* janbi	
جانّ جنونه beserk *adj* janen jununu	جابي collector *n* jabi
الجاني culprit *n* eljani	جاجِة hen *n* jajeh
جاني delinquent *n* jani	جادّة avenue *n* jaddeh
جاهز ready *adj* jahez	جاذبية glamour *n* jazbeyyeh
	جاذبية gravity *n* jazbeyyeh

cheddar *n* jebneh shidar جبنة شيدر	imprudent *adj* jahel جاهل
bloc *n* jabha جبهة	*adj* jay men erein جاي من عرقين
cast *n* jbireh جبيرة	biracial
brow *n* jebin جبين	*n* jay mn nasab جاي من نَسَب
forehead *n* jbin جبين	descendant
corpse *n* jiththeh جثّة	prize *n* ja'ezeh جائزة
body *n* jeththeh جثّة	superhuman *adj* jabbar جبّار
cadaver *n* jeththeh جثّة	alp *n* jibal el'alb جبال الألب
ancestor *n* jadd جدّ	chicken *adj* jaban جبَان
forefather *n* jadd جدّ	coward *n* jaban جبَان
competence *n* jadarah جدَارة	fearful *adj* jaban جبَان
eligibility *n* jadarah جدَارة	timid *adj* jaban جبَان
mural *adj* jidari جداري	timorous *adj* jaban جبَان
mural *n* jidareyyeh جدارية	cemetery *n* jabbaneh جبّانة
gawky *adj* jadbeh جدبة	levy *n* jibayeh جبَاية
gawk *n* eljadbeh الجدبة	algebra *n* aljabr الجبر
dupe *n* jadbeh جدبة	absolutism *n* jbarout جبروت
idiocy *n* jadbaneh جدبنة	grandeur *n* jabarut جبَروت
smallpox *n* jadari جدري	jibril aleh esalam جبريل عليه السلام
argument *n* jadal جدَل	archangel *n*
debate *n* jadal جدَل	daub *n* jabsin جبصين
schedule *n* jadwal جدول	mountain *n* jabal جبل
table *n* jadwal جدول	iceberg *n* jabl talj جبل تلج
chart *n* jadwal جدوَل	mountainous *adj* jabali جبَلي
stream *n* jadwal جدوَل	quail *n* jben جبن
streamlet *n* jadwal جدوَل	timidity *n* jebn جبن
agenda *n* jdwal a'mal جدول عمل	cowardice *n* jubin جبن
bayou *n* jadwal mai جدوَل مي	cheese *n* jebneh جبنة

creek n jadwal mai جَدْوَل مي	n jiraha azmeyyeh جراحة عظميّة
ply n jadduleh جدُّولة	orthopaedics
earnest adj jaddi جدّي	operative adj jirahi جراحي
novelty n jeddeyeh جدِّية	scabies n jarab جَرَب
new adj jdid جديد	gale n jarab جَرَب
novel adj jdid جديد	urn n jarrah جرّة
eligible adj jadir جدير	germ n jrthumeh جرثومة
plyer n jadeleh جديلة	gash n jreh جرح
glam adj jazzab جذّاب	gashing adj jreh جرح
engaging adj jazzab جَذّاب	hurt n jreh جرح
moot n jazr جذر	injury n jerh جرح
root n jazr جذر	wound n jerh جرح
stem n jazr جَذْر	lizard n jardun جردون
n jazer elshawandar جذر الشوندر	rat n jardun جردون
beetroot	bell n jaras جرس
snag n 'jeze جذع	gong n jaras جَرَس
trunk n 'jeze جذع	doorbell n jaras elbab جرس الباب
drag n jarr جرّ	dosage n jar'a جرعَة
draw n jarr جرّ	dose n jar'a جرعَة
hosiery n jrab جراب	swallow n jur'ah جرعَة
sock n jrab جراب	n jer'ah zaydeh جرعة زايدة
dare n jur'a جرأة	overdose
daring n jur'a جرأة	puppy n jaru جرو
boldness n jura'a جُرأة	cub n jaru جَرْو
intrepidity n jur'ah جُرأة	bold adj jari'e جريء
surgeon n jarrah جرّاح	daring adj 'jare جريء
surgery n jirahah جراحة	defiant adj jari'e جريء
	valiant adj 'jare جرِيء

probe *n* jass جَسّ	intrepid *adj* 'jare جَرِيء
carnal *adj* jasadi جَسَدي	gazette *n* jarideh جَريدة
physical *adj* jasadi جَسَدي	tabloid *n* jaredeh جَريدة
bridge *n* jiser جسر	*n* jaredeh esbu'eyyeh جَريدة إسبوعيّة
n jser meteharrek جسر متحرّك	weekly
drawbridge	crime *n* jarimeh جَريمة
body *n* jesem جسم	jarimeh جَريمة الكترونيّة
vulture *n* 'jeshe جِشع	cybercrime *n* elktruneyyeh
avarice *n* 'jashaa جَشَع	murder *n* jarimet qatel جَريمة قتل
ado *n* jaja'a جعجعة	fragment *n* 'jeze جزء
crease *n* ja'lakeh جعلكة	part *n* 'jeze جزء
geographical *adj* jughrafi جغرافي	segment *n* 'jeze جزء
adj jughrafi syasi جغرافي سياسي	modicum *n* jez' seghir جزء صغير
geopolitical	purse *n* jezdan جزدان
geography *n* jughrafya جغرافيا	wallet *n* jezdan جزدان
antipathy *n* jafa جَفا	ebb *n* jazr جزر
arefaction *n* jafaf جفاف	carrot *n* jazarah جزرة
drought *n* jafaf جَفاف	log *n* jeze' shajarah جزع شجرة
eyelid *n* jfn eleyn جفن العين	molecule *n* 'juzay جُزَيء
lid *n* jefn eleyn جفن العين	island *n* jazireh جزيرة
gel *n* jill جلّ	isle *n* jazireh sghireh جزيرة صغيرة
executioner *n* jallad جلّاد	jazereh merjaneyyeh جزيرة مَرجانيّة
leather *n* jeld جلد	atoll *n*
scourge *n* jeld جلد	partial *adj* jeze'i جزئي
skin *n* jeld جلد	*n* juzay'at elnanu جزيئات النانو
fortitude *n* jalad جَلَد	nanoparticle
doeskin *n* jld naem جلد ناعم	particle *n* juzay'ah جزيئة
dermic *adj* jildi جلدي	molecular *adj* juzy'e جُزَيئي

camel *n* jamal جَمَل	session *n* jalseh جَلْسة
sentence *n* jumleh جملة	clot *n* jaltah جلطة
audience *n* jumhur جمهور	*n* jelfanometer جلفانوميتر
republican *n* jemhuri جمهوري	galvanometer
republican *adj* jemhuri جمهوري	eljulus ma' elatfal الجلوس مع الأطفال
republic *n* jemhureyyeh جمهورِيّة	babysitting *n*
stalemate *n* jumud جُمُود	frost *n* jalid جليد
all *n* aljamie الجميع	ice *n* jalid جليد
Messrs *n* janab جَنَاب	icy *adj* jalidi جليدي
fringe *n* janah جناح	lordly *adj* jalil جَليل
suite *n* janah جَنَاح	solid *n* jamad جَمَاد
wing *n* janah جَنَاح	inanimate *adj* jamad جَمَاد
n jnah fi ma'rad جناح في معرض	intercourse *n* 'jema جِماع
pavilion	collective *adj* jamaei جماعي
funeral *n* jnazeh جنازة	beauty *n* jamal جمال
felony *n* jenayeh جناية	multitude *n* jamahir جَمَاهير
penal *adj* jina'i جِنَائي	abreast *adv* jamb ba'ed جمب بعض
along *prep* janb جنب	gymnastics *n* eljmbaz الجباز
side *n* janb جنب	gymnast *n* jmbazi جمبازي
by *prep* janb جَنب	gymnastic *adj* jmbazi جمبازي
heaven *n* janneh جنّة	crevette *n* jambari جمبري
paradise *n* janneh جنّة	skull *n* jemjmeh جمجمة
gentle *adj* jentil جنتل	cobblestone *n* jamrah جمرة
gentleman *n* jentil جنتل	plural *adj* 'jame جمع
misdemeanour *n* jenha جنحة	*v* jame' elaswat جمع الأصوات
delinquency *n* jinha جنحة	canvass
gondola *n* jandul جندول	Friday *n* eljum'a الجمعة
chain *n* janzir جَنزير	assembly *n* jam'eyeh جمعيّة

projector *n* jihaz ared جهاز عرض

jihaz ared جهاز عرض سينمائي

bioscope *n* sinamaei

jihaz fakk elrumuz جهاز فكّ الرموز

decoder *n*

effort *n* hjhed جهد

stress *n* jehd جهد

voltage *n* jehd جهد

imprudence *n* jahl جهل

nescience *n* jahl جَهْل

folly *n* jahl جَهْل

hell *n* jehannam جهنَّم

sonority *n* jahureyyeh جهوريّة

readiness *n* juhuzeyyeh جهوزيّة

paraphernalia *n pl* jehiz جهيز

atmosphere *n* jaww جَوّ

milieu *n* jaww جَوّ

indoors *adv* jwwah جوًّا

inside *adj* jawwah جوًّا

answer *n* jawab جواب

response *n* jawab جواب

inside *prep* jwwat جوَّات

within *prep* juwwat جوَّات

vicinity *n* jewar جوار

passport *n* jawaz safar جواز سفر

guava *n* jawwafeh جوَّافة

gasket *n* jwan جُوان

indoor *adj* jwwani جُوَّاني

gender *n* jens جنس

sex *n* jins جنس

erotic *adj* jensi جنسي

sexual *adj* jinsi جنسي

nationality *n* jinseyyeh جنسيّة

south *n* janub جَنُوب

south *adj* janubi جَنُوبي

southern *adj* janubi جَنُوبي

amuck *adv* junun جنون

berserk *n* junun جنون

insanity *n* jnun جنون

lunacy *n* jnun جنون

frenzy *n* jnun جُنُون

madness *n* jnun جنُون

genie *n* jenni جنّي

embryo *n* janin جَنِين

embryonic *adj* janini جنيني

fetal *adj* janini جنيني

n jnih esterlini جنيه إسترليني

sterling

device *n* jihaz جهاز

appliance *n* jihaz جهاز

n jihaz ersal جهاز إرسال

transmitter

jihaz tasjil جهاز تسجيل الذبذبات

oscillograph *n* elzabzat

n jihaz tahweyeh جهاز تهوية

ventilator

gigabit n jigabet جيغابت

generation n jil جيل

gelatin n jilatin جيلاتين

jelly n jelyh جيليه

oncogene n jiin warami جين ورمي

gene n jeneh جينة

genome n jinum جينوم

genetic adj jini جيني

geological adj jiuluji جيولوجي

ح

peon n hajeb حاجِب

eyebrow n hajeb eleyn حاجب العين

n hajib elmalek حاجِب الملك

chamberlain

want n hajeh حاجِة

need n hajeh حاجِة

hurdle n hajez حاجِز

barricade n hajiz حاجِز

n hajiz taftish حاجز تفتيش

checkpoint

accident n hadith حادث

guard n hares حارِس

sentinel n hares حارِس

sentry n hares حارِس

quality n judeh جودة

stocking n jawrab جَورَب

walnut n juz جوز

coconut n juz hind جوز هند

nut n juzeh جَوزة

nutmeg n juzet eltib جوزة الطيب

hunger n ju'e جوع

hungry adj ju'aan جوعان

subterranean adj jufi جوفي

chorus n juqa جَوقَة

joker n juker جوكَر

innings n jawlat جولات

tour n jawleh جولة

cist n jawhar جوهَر

essence n jawhr جوهَر

gem n juharah جوهرة

ouch n jwharah جوهرة

jewel n juharah جَوْهَرَة

cardinal adj jawhari جوهري

essential adj jawhari جوهري

airy adj jawwi جوّي

atmospheric adj jawwi جوّي

pocket n jib جيب

advent n jyeh جية

lime n jir جير

neighbourhood n jireh جيرة

army n jish جيش

gigabyte n jigabayt جيغابايت

armature *n* hafiza حافظة	*n* hares elghabeh حارس الغابة
lush *adj* hafil حافل	forester
commandant *n* hakim حاكم	*n* hares marmah حارس المَرْمَى
ruler *n* hakim حاكم	goalkeeper
forthwith *adv* halan حالا	bouncer *n* haris bar حارس بار
now *adv* halan حالا	certain *adj* hazim حازم
n halat maradeyyeh حالات مرضيّة	hiccup *n* hazuqah حازوقة
morbidity	cogent *adj* hasim حاسم
condition *n* haleh حالة	decisive *adj* hasim حاسم
recent *adj* hali حالي	computer *n* hasub حاسوب
recently *adv* halyan حاليًا	computeracy *n* hasub حاسوب
presently *adv* halyan حاليًا	retinue *n* hashyh حاشية
acidic *adj* hamod حامض	aftereffect *n* elhasil الحاصل
lime *n* hamud حامض	present *adj* hader حاضر
sour *adj* hamud حامُض	present *n* hader حاضر
pregnant *adj* hamil حامل	attendant *n* hadir حاضر
hamil ijazeh حامل إجازة جامعيّة	brink *n* haffeh حافّة
bachelor *n* jameyeh	fringe *n* haffeh حافّة
lancer *n* hamel elremeh حامل الرمح	rim *n* haffeh حافّة
n hamel elsahm حامل السهم	*n* 'haffet elshate حافّة الشّاطئ
shareholder	shoreline
protector *n* hami حامي	hoof *n* hafez حَافِر
garrisson *n* hamyeh حامية	motif *n* hafez حافز
pill *n* habb حَبّ	drive *n* hafiz حافز
love *n* hubb حُبّ	spur *n* hafez حافِز
hubb elkheyr حُبّ الخير للناس	stimulus *n* hafez حافز
altruism *n* lilnnas	incentive *n* hafez حافز
acne *n* hab eshabab حب الشباب	preservative *adj* hafez حافظ

lover n habib حبِّيب

n habibeh seryyeh حبيبة سريِّة

concubine

darling adj habibi حبيبي

decidedness n hatmeyyeh حتميِّة

evitability n hatmeyyeh حتميِّة

albeit .conj hatta law حتى لو

junk n huthaleh حُثَالة

pilgrimage n hajj حج

amulet n hejab حِجَاب

fetish n hijab حِجَاب

talisman n hijab حِجَاب

mantle n hijab حِجَاب

n elhijab elhajez الحِجَاب الحَاجِز

midriff

kerchief n hijab elmarah حِجَاب المرا

allegation n hejjeh حِجَّة

pretension n hejjeh حِجَّة

pretext n hejjeh حِجَّة

argument n hijjeh حِجَّة

stone n hajar حجر

n hajar elmaghnatis حجر المغنطيس

loadstone

cameo n hajar karim حَجَر كريم

stony adj hajari حجري

seizure n hajz حجز

volume n hajm حجم

pilgrim n hajji حجِّي

affluenza n hubb elmal حب المال

n hubb elmasari حبّ المصاري

mammon

agape n hubb uzri حب عذري

weaver n habbak حَبَّاك

bleb n habbayeh حبَّاية

blister n habbayeh حبَّاية

n habbayeh seghereh حبَّاية صغيرة

pimple

bead n habbeh حبَّة

grain n hayyeh حبِّة

tablet n habbet dawa حبَّة دوا

ink n hebr حبر

rabbi n hebr yahudi حبر يهودي

confinement n habes حبس

prison n habs حبس

retention n habs حَبْس

clasp n habseh حَبِسة

clip n habseh حَبِسة

basil n 'habae حَبَق

plot n habkeh حبكة

robe n habl حبل

cord n habel حَبْل

rope n habl حَبْل

festoon n habel zyneh حبل زينة

bungee n habel mattati حبل مطَّاطي

beloved n habib حبيب

darling n habib حبيب

conversation *n* hadith حديث

modern *adj* hadith حديث

speech *n* hadith حديث

up-to-date *adj* hadith حديث

n hadith elne'meh حديث النعمة

upstart

adj hadith elweladeh حديث الولادة

nascent

n hadith muhimm حَديث مهمّ

discourse

iron *n* hadid حديد

cast-iron *adj* hadid sabb حَديد صَبّ

garden *n* hadiqah حديقة

park *n* hadiqah حديقة

zoo *n* hadeqt haywan حديقة حيوان

shoe *n* 'hiza حذَاء

cautious *adj* hazar حَذِر

omission *n* hazef حَذْف

ploughman *n* harrath حرّاث

calorific *adj* harari حراري

thermal *adj* hrari حراري

escort *n* hiraseh حِراسة

inviolable *adj* haram حَرَام

blanket *n* heram حِرَام

abactor *n* harami حرامي

marauder *n* harami حرامي

robber *n* harami حرامي

burglar *n* harami حَرامي

acrid *adj* hadd حَدّ

limit *n* hadd حَدّ

piquant *adj* hadd حَدّ

pungent *adj* hadd حَدّ

frontier *n* hadd حَدّ

border *n* hadd حَدّ

boundary *n* hadd حَدّ

hot *adj* hadd حَدّ

n elhadd eladna الحَدّ الأدنى

minimum

n elhadd elaqsa الحَد الأقصى

maximum

either *pron* hada mn حدا من

modernity *n* hadatheh حداثة

blacksmith *n* haddad حدّاد

smith *n* haddad حدّاد

mourning *n* hidad حِداد

curvature *n* hadbeh حدبة

hunch *n* hadbeh حدبة

event *n* hadath حدث

occurrence *n* hadath حدَث

juvenile *adj* hadath حدَث

incident *n* hadath حدَث

conjecture *n* hades حدَس

happening *n* huduth حدوث

limitation *n* hdud حدود

acrimony *n* hdodiye حدودية

pungency *n* hududeyyeh حدوديّة

dynamic *adj* hirik حِرِك

spirited *adj* herk حِرِك

motion *n* harakeh حَرَكة

move *n* harakeh حَرَكة

movement *n* harakeh حَرَكة

n haraket elrejlin حركة الرجلين

footwork

hitch *n* harakeh sare'a حركة سَريعة

kinetic *adj* haraki حَرَكي

mechanism *n* harakeyyeh حركيّة

sanctuary *n* haram حَرَم

campus *n* 'haram jamei حَرَم جامعي

hardship *n* herman حِرمان

privation *n* hirman حِرْمان

freedom *n* hureyyeh حريّة

silk *n* harir حرير

asbestos *n* harir sakhri حرير صخري

silken *adj* hariri حَريري

silky *adj* hariri حَريري

keen *adj* haris حريص

thrifty *adj* haris حَريص

blaze *n* hariq حريق

fire *n* hareq حريق

n hariq muta'mmad حريق مُتعمَّد

arson

girdle *n* hizam حِزَام

party *n* hezb حزب

partisan *n* hizbi حِزْبي

thief *n* harami حَرَامي

n harami eldekkan حرامي الدكّان

shoplifter

war *n* harb حرب

n harb de'aeyyeh حرب دعائيّة

propaganda

bayonet *n* herbeh حَربة

lance *n* harbeh حَربة

belligerent *adj* harbi حربي

keenness *n* hers حرص

edge *n* harf حرف

ridge *n* harf حرف

preposition *n* harf jarr حَرْف جَر

n haref saken حرف ساكِن

consonant

adj harf sghir حرف صغير

minuscule

brim *n* herif finjan حِرف فنجان

capital *n* haref kbir حرف كبير

literal *adj* harfi حرفي

verbatim *adj* harfi حرفي

craftsman *n* hirafi حِرَفي

artisan *n* hirafi حِرَفي

burn *n* herq حرق

sear *n* harq حَرْق

n hareq eljuthath حرق الجثث

cremation

agile *adj* hrik حرِك

allergy *n* hasasya حساسية	partisan *adj* hizbi حِزْبي
sensibility *n* hasaseyyeh حَسَّاسيّة	determination *n* hazm حزم
per *prep* hasab حسَب	sheaf *n* hezmeh حزْمة
ancestry *n* hasab حَسَب	bale *n* hezmeh حزْمة
as .*conj* hasab حَسَب	pack *n* hezmeh حزْمة
duly *adv* hasab elusul حسب الأصول	package *n* hezmeh حزْمة
aleatory *adj* hsb alhazz حسب الحظ	*n* hezmet elhatab حزمة الحطب
adj hasab eltalab حسب الطلب	faggot
bespoken	sorrow *n* hezn حزْن
envy *n* hasad حَسَد	dolorous *adj* haznan حَزْنان
anguish *n* hasra حسرة	mournful *n* haznan حَزْنان
thorn *n* hasak حَسَك	perception *n* hess حسّ
deduction *n* hasim حسم	arithmetic *n* elhisab الحساب
discount *n* hasm حسم	account *n* hsab حساب
alms *n* hasaneh حَسَنة	calculation *n* hisab حسَاب
benefaction *n* hasaneh حَسَنة	escrow *n* hesab daman حساب ضمان
envious *adj* hasud حَسُود	*n* hisab ghalat حساب غلط
sensuous *adj* hessi حسّي	miscalculation
congregation *n* hashed حشد	arithmetical *adj* hesabi حسابي
insect *n* hasharah حشرة	enumerative *adj* hesabi حسابي
pest *n* hasharah حَشَرَة	begrudging *adj* hessad حسَّاد
interference *n* heshreyyeh حشريّة	sympathetic *adj* hassas حسَّاس
stuff *n* hashweh حشوة	sensible *adj* hassas حسَّاس
pad *n* hashweh حَشْوة	sensitive *adj* hassas حسَّاس
hashweh حشوة معدنيّة بتَمنع التسرُّب	sentient *adj* hassas حسَّاس
ettasarrub 'ma'daneyyeh btmna	ticklish *adj* hassas حسَّاس
flashing *n*	*adj* hassas ktir حسَّاس كتير
weed *n* hashish حَشيش	exquisite

cobble *n* hasweh حَصوِة	cultivation *n* hasad حصاد
acquirement *n* husool حصول	harvest *n* hasad حصاد
attainment *n* elhusul ala الحصول على	reap *n* hasad حصاد
pebble *n* hasah حَصَى	harvester *n* hasad حصّاد
civilization *n* hadarah حضارة	reaper *n* hassadeh حَصّادة
kindergarten *n* hadaneh حضانة	blockade *n* hisar حِصار
nurture *n* hadaneh حِضَانة	siege *n* hesar حِصَار
nursery *n* hadaneh حضانه	horse *n* hisan حصان
embrace *n* heden حضن	*n* hsan khashab حصان خشب
cuddle *n* hudun حُضُن	hobbyhorse
lap *n* heden حِضْن	*n* hesan khashab حصان خشب
attendance *n* hudur حضور	sawhorse
presence *n* hudur حضور	pony *n* hesan sibaq حصان سباق
hudur elshakhseyeh حُضُور الشخصية	steed *n* 'hesan sare حصان سريع
charisma *n*	*n* hisan wahshi حصان وحشى
put *n* hatt حطّ	mustang
wreck *n* hutam حُطام	impunity *n* hasaneh حصانة
n hutam elsafineh حطام سفينة	rubeola *n* hasbeh حصبِة
shipwreck	measles *n* hasbeh حَصْبِة
luck *n* hazz حظّ	share *n* hessah حصّة
mischance *n* 'hazz saye حظ سيء	portion *n* hessah حصّة
mishap *n* 'hazz saye حظّ سيء	quota *n* hessah حصّة
ban *n* hazer حَظَر	quotient *n* hessah حصّة
block *n* hazur حَظر	exclusive *adj* hasri حصري
embargo *n* hazer حَظَر	bulwark *n* hesun حصن
curfew *n* hazer tijwal حظر تجوّل	stronghold *n* hesn حصن
cote *n* hazirah حَظيرة	fort *n* hsen حصن
scrub *n* haff حَفّ	bastion *n* hesen حصِن

insignificance *n* haqarah حَقَارَة	drill *n* haffarah حَفَّارَة
equitable *adj* haqqani حَقَّانِي	dig *n* hafr حفر
righteous *adj* haqqani حَقَّانِي	excavation *n* hafr حفر
impartial *adj* haqqani حَقَّانِي	*n* hafr khandaq حفر خندق
straightforward *adj* haqqani حَقَّانِي	retrenchment
upright *adj* haqqani حَقَّانِي	etching *n* hafr klisheh حفر كليشيه
baggage *n* haqaeb حقائب	gap *n* hufrah حفرة
animosity *n* heqed حقد	hole *n* hefrah حفرة
grudge *n* heqd حقد	pit *n* hufrah حفرَة
rancour *n* heqd حقد	hufret el'udhn حفرة الأذن الخارجية
abase *v* haqqar حقّر	alveary *n* elkharijiyeh
field *n* hakl حقل	*n* hufrit elinfijar حفرة الانفجار
croft *n* haqel seghir حقل صغير	crater
agrarian *adj* haqly حقلي	firepit *n* hifret elhariq حفرة الحريق
despiteful *adj* haqud حقود	preservation *n* hefz حفظ
venomous *adj* haqud حَقُود	conservation *n* hefez حفظ
n haqibeh alzaher حقيبة عالظهر	reservation *n* hefz حفظ
backpack	rote *n* hefz basmm حفظ بصم
abject *adj* haqir حقير	*n* hafleh tanakureyyeh حفلة تنكرِيّة
bastard *adj* hakiir حقير	masquerade
villain *n* haqir حقير	binge *v* haflet sukr حفلة سكر
insignificant *adj* haqir حَقير	*n* hafleh musiqeyyeh حفلة موسيقيّة
fact *n* haqeqah حقيقة	concert
reality *n* haqiqah حقيقة	diaper *n* haffudah حفُّوضة
real *adj* haqiqi حقيقي	barefoot *adj* hafyan حفيان
veritable *adj* haqiqi حقيقي	right *n* haqq حق
intrinsic *adj* haqiqi حَقيقي	abjection *n* haqarah حَقَارَة
abrasion *n* hakk حَكّ	lowliness *n* haqarah حَقَارَة

n hukumeh deneyyeh حكومة دينيّة
theocracy

talk n haki حكي

blab n haki fadi حكي فاضي

blether n haki fadi حكي فاضي

bollocks n haki fadi حكي فاضي

bunk n haki fadi حكي فاضي

wise adj hakim حكيم

solution n hall حلّ

barber n hallaq حلّاق

shave n hlaqah حلاقة

tonsure n hlaqah حلاقة

sweetness n halaweh حلاوة

prettiness n halaweh حلاوة

arena n halabeh حَلَبة

turf n halabeh حَلَبة

escargot n halazun حلزون

snail n halazun حَلَزُون

alliance n helf حلف

pact n helf حلف

ally n helf حِلف

perjury n helfan kezb حلفان كذب

gorge n halq حلق

throat n halq حلق

episode n halaqah حَلَقة

ringlet n halaqah حَلَقة

seminar n halqet bahth حلقة بحث

abrasiveness n hakk حَكّ

rubbing n hakk حَكّ

n hakk eljeld حَكّ الجلد
dermabrasion

tale n hekayeh حكاية

narrative n hekayeh حِكاية

fiction n hkayeh حِكَاية

n hekayeh ramzeyyeh حكاية رمزيّة
parable

itch n hakkeh حكّة

judgement n hekm حكم

governance n hukm حكم

ruling n hukm حكم

arbiter n hakam حكم

referee n hakam حكم

umpire n hakam حكم

reign n hukm حكم

rule n hukm حكم

n hekm elaqaleyyeh حكم الأقليّة
oligarchy

n hekm elmahkameh حكم المحكمة
sentence

doom n hkem rabna حكم ربنا

maxim n hikmeh حكمة

wisdom n hikmeh حكمة

aphorism n hekmeh حكمة

saw n hikmeh حِكمة

government n hukumeh حكومة

enthusiasm *n* hamas حماس	*n* halakah seghireh حلقة صغيرة
fervour *n* hamaseh حماسة	annulet
arduous *adj* hamasi حماسي	dream *n* hlem حلم
carrier *n* hammal حمّال	leniency *n* helm حلم
porter *n* hammal حمّال	*n* helim yaqazah حلم يقظة
sling *n* hammaleh حمّالة	daydream
braces *n* hammaleh حمّالة	reverie *n* helm yaqazah حلم يقظة
bath *n* hammam حمّام	nipple *n* helmeh حلمة
lavatory *n* hammam حمّام	teat *n* helmeh حلمة
pigeon *n* hamameh حمامة	beautiful *adj* helu حلو
dove *n* hamameh حمَامة	good *adj* helu حلو
protection *n* himayeh حماية	pretty *adj* helu حلو
safeguard *n* himayeh حماية	sweet *adj* helu حلو
acid *n* hamdh حمض	sweet *n* helu حلو
n hamd uksijini حمض أكسجيني	confectioner *n* helwani حلواني
oxyacid	milch *adj* halub حَلوب
acid *adj* hamdhi حمضي	candy *n* helweyat حلويّات
citric *adj* hamdi حمضي	confectionery *n* helweyyat حلويّات
citrus *n* hamdi حمضي	dessert *n* helweyyat حلويّات
load *n* heml حمل	sweetmeat *n* helweyyat حلوَيَات
pregnancy *n* haml حمل	milk *n* halib حليب
bearing *n* hamel حَمل	milky *adj* halibi حليبي
lamb *n* hamal حَمَل	indulgent *adj* halim حَليم
portage *n* heml حَمل	lenient *adj* halim حَليم
burden *n* hemel حِمل	donkey *n* hmar حمار
onus *n* heml حِمْل	*n* hemar elwahsh حمار الوحش
campaign *n* hamleh حملة	zebra
	ardour *n* hamas حماس

dialogue *n* hiwar حوار

disciple *n* hiwari حَوَارِي

about *prep* hawali حوالي

around *adv* hawali حَوَالي

whale *n* hut حوت

n elhut elabyad الحوت الأبيض
beluga

orca *n* elhut elqatel الحوت القاتل

nymph *n* hurreyyeh حوريّة

n hureyyet elbaher حورية البحر
mermaid

courtyard *n* hush حوش

n huwdh samak حوض سمك
aquarium

ambient *adj* hewlna حولنا

around *prep* hawalin حَولِين

district *n* hayy حَيّ

ghetto *n* hayy elyahud حيّ اليهود

life *n* hayat حياة

n elhayat elnabateyyeh الحياة النباتيّة
flora

neutral *adj* hyadi حيادي

serpent *n* hayyeh حَيّة

snake *n* hayyeh حَيّة

hesitant *adj* hyran حيران

bewilderment *n* hireh حيرة

perplexity *n* hereh حيرة

dismay *n* hireh حيرة

n hamleh salibeyyeh حملة صليبيّة
crusade

n hemam burkaneyyeh حمم بركانية
lava

n hemam burkaneyyeh حمم بركانيّة
magma

acidity *n* hmoodhaa حموضة

cargo *n* hmuleh حمولة

carriage *n* humuleh حمولة

n humulet elsafineh حمولة السفينة
shipload

fever *n* hummah حمّى

n hemmah eltifus حمّى التيفوس
typhus

n humma eddank حمّى الضنك
dengue

febrile *adj* hemmi حمّي

benign *adj* hamid حميد

cereal *n* hentah حنطة

tap *n* hanafeyyeh حَنَفيّة

jaw *n* hanak حَنَك

palate *n* hanak حَنَك

palatal *adj* hanaki حنكي

affectionate *adj* hnun حنون

tenderhearted *adj* hanun حنون

fondler *n* hanun حنون

bend *v* hanyeh حَنية

nostalgia *n* hanin حَنين

خ

ring *v* khatem خاتم

ministrant *adj* khadem خادم

servant *n* khadem خادم

external *adj* kharji خارجي

outer *adj* kharji خارجي

supernatural *adj* khareq خارق

inimitable *adj* khareq خارق

marvellous *adj* khareq خَارق

stake *n* khazuq خازوق

underdog *n* khaser خاسر

private *adj* khass خاصّ

sake *n* khater خاطر

bye-bye *interj*. khaterkum خاطركُم

abductor *n* khatif خاطف

imperishable *adj* khalid خالد

eternal *adj* khaled خالد

perpetual *adj* khalid خَالد

immortal *adj* khalid خَالد

accomplished *adj* khales خالص

crude *adj* kham خام

ore *n* kham خام

raw *adj* khamm خَام

immature *adj* kham خَام

idle *adj* khamil خامل

inn *n* khan خان

hesitation *n* hireh حيرة

maze *n* hireh حيرة

sidewall *n* hit حيط

wall *n* hit حيط

gimmickry *n* hyal حِيَل

stratagem *n* hileh حيلة

roguery *n* hyleh حِيلة

ruse *n* hyleh حِيلة

hoax *n* hyleh حِيلة

animal *n* haywan حيوان

brute *n* hayawan حيوَان

otter *n* hayawan حَيَوان

quadruped *n* hayawan حَيَوان

n 'haywan eljarbue حيوان الجربوع

badger

pet *n* haywan alif حيوان أليف

heywan bemshi حيوان بمشي عرجلتين

biped *n* arejltin

n haywan jurabi حيوان جرابي

marsupial

haywanat حَيَوانَات المنْطِقَة

fauna *n* elmantiqah

brutish *adj* hayawani حَيَواني

animate *adj* hayawi حيوي

vital *adj* hayawi حيوي

vitality *n* hayaweyyeh حيوِيّة

verve *n* hayaweyyeh حَيَويّة

coy *n* khajal خَجَل

abash *v* khajjal خَجَّل

bashful *adj* khajul خَجُول

shy *n* khajul خَجُول

gull *n* 'khida خِدَاع

footman *n* khaddam خَدَّام

beguiling *adj* khedaa خَدعَة

service *n* khedmeh خدمة

cheek *n* khudud خدود

ruin *n* kharab خراب

havoc *n* kharab خَرَاب

turner *n* kharrat خَرَّاط

superstition *n* khurafeh خرافة

myth *n* khurafeh خُرَافة

superstitious *adj* khurafi خرافي

fabulous *adj* khurafi خُرَافي

fictitious *adj* khurafi خُرَافي

mythical *adj* khurafi خُرَافي

purr *n* kharkharah خَرْخَرَة

scrap *n* khurdeh خردة

mustard *n* khardal خَرْدَل

hose *n* khartum خرطوم

tatter *n* kherqah خِرْقَة

scratch *v* kharmasheh خرمشة

locust *n* kharnub خرنوب

checkout *n* khuruj خروج

sheep *n* kharuf خروف

graduate *n* kherrij خِرِّيج

subservient *adj* 'khane خَانِع

sultry *adj* khaneq خَانِق

nerveless *adj* khayer خَايِر

apprehensive *adj* khayef خَايِف

traitor *n* khayn خَايِن

malignancy *n* khabatheh خَبَاثة

malice *n* khubth خُبْث

bread *n* khebez خبز

slam *n* khabt elbab خبط الباب

thud *n* khabtah خَبْطة

bash *n* khabtah خَبْطَة

foul *n* elkhabith الخبيث

maleficent *adj* khabith خبيث

pernicious *adj* khabith خبيث

roguish *adj* khabith خبيث

foul *adj* khabith خَبِيث

sly *adj* khabith خَبِيث

malicious *adj* khabith خَبِيث

malignant *adj* khabith خَبِيث

expert *n* elkhabir الخبير

adept *n* khabeer خبير

expert *adj* khabir خبير

antiquary *n* khabir athar خبير آثار

n khabir taktik خبير تكتيك

tactician

financier *n* khabir mali خبير مالي

epilogue *n* khetam ختام

seal *n* khetm ختم

lath *n* khashabeh خَشَبة	alumna *n* khirrij jama'a خريج جامعة
wooden *adj* khashabi خشبي	murmur *n* kharir خرير
jingle *n* khashkhasheh خشخشة	map *n* kharitah خريطة
clatter *n* khashekhasheh خشخَشة	autumn *n* khariif خريف
abrasive *adj* kheshen خشن	wardrobe *n* khzaneh خزانة
raspy *adj* kheshn خشن	closet *n* khizaneh خزانة
tough *adj* kheshen خشن	*n* khizaneh elha rfuf خزانة إلها رفوف
blunt *adj* kheshen خشن	cupboard
coarse *adj* kheshin خشن	*n* khezaneh beqefl خزانة بقفل
rough *adj* kheshn خشن	locker
fertile *adj* kheseb خصب	fable *n* khuza'balat خُزَعْبَلات
waist *n* khasr خصر	biopsy *n* khuza'a خُزعَة
flank *n* khasr خَصر	vault *n* khazneh خزنة
forelock *n* kheslet sha'er خصلة شعر	treasury *n* khazyneh خزينة
litigant *n* khasm خَصم	khazeneh hadedeyyeh خزينة حديدية
fertility *n* khusubeh خصوبة	safe-deposit *n*
especial *adj* khususi خصوصي	casualty *n* khasaer خسائر
respective *adj* khususi خصوصي	eclipse *n* khusuf خُسُوف
privacy *n* khususeyyeh خصوصية	sordid *adj* khasis خسيس
litigation *n* khusumeh خصومة	despicable *adj* khasis خَسِيس
strife *n* khusumeh خُصُومة	rogue *n* khasis خَسِيس
controversy *n* khusumeh خُصُومة	vile *adj* khasis خَسِيس
jolt *n* khadd خَضّ	timber *n* khashab خشب
shake *n* khaddah خَضّة	wood *n* khashab خشب
vegetable *n* khedrah خضرا	*n* khashab elabanus خشب الابنوس
acquiescence *n* 'khodhoe خضوع	ebony
subjection *n* 'khudu خُضُوع	*n* khashab elsandal خشب الصندل
font *n* khatt خط	sandalwood

jeopardy *n* khatar خَطَر	*n* khatt elistewa'e خط الأستواء
step *n* khetweh خطوة	equator
addresser *n* khatib خطيب	*n* khatt eleyed خط الإيد
betrothed *adj* khatib خطيب	calligraphy
fiancé *n* khatib خطيب	*n* khatt eltansif خطّ التنصيف
orator *n* khatib خَطِيب	meridian
suitor *n* khatib خَطِيب	longitude *n* khatt ettul خط الطول
dangerous *adj* khatir خطير	italics *n* elkhatt elmayl الخطّ المايل
risky *adj* khatir خطير	sidetrack *n* khatt janbi خط جانبي
serious *adj* khatir خطير	sideline *n* khatt janbi خطّ جانبي
critical *adj* khatir خَطِير	latitude *n* khatt arid خط عرض
bat *n* khaffash خَفّاش	*n* khatt amudi خط عمودي
agility *n* khffeh خفّة	perpendicular
humour *n* kheffet damm خِفّة الدم	error *n* 'ghata خطأ
sleight *n* kheffet eyd خِفّة إيد	miss *n* 'khata خطأ
whisk *n* khafq خفق	blunder *n* khata' kebir خطأ كبير
churn *n* khafeq ellaban خفق اللبن	*n* khata' matba'e خطأ مطبعى
throb *n* khafaqan خفقان	misprint
flapping *n* khafaqan خفقان	missive *n* khitab خِطَاب
stroke *n* khafqah خَفْقَة	matchmaker *n* khattabeh خطّابة
impulse *n* khafqah خَفْقَة	elocution *n* khatabeh خَطَابة
implicit *adj* khafi خَفِي	oratorical *adj* khetabi خطابي
bland *adj* khafif خفيف	betrothal *n* khutbeh خطبة
light *adj* khafif خفيف	engagement *n* khutbeh خطبة
sparse *adj* khafif خفيف	oration *n* khutbeh خطبة
acetate *n* khall خل	plan *n* khuttah خطّة
vinegar *n* khall خلّ	risk *n* khatar خطر
alegar *n* khal alshaeir خل الشعير	danger *n* khatar خطَر

blend n khalit خَليط	rundown n khulasah خَلاصة
mixture n khalit خَليط	extract n khulasah خُلاصة
n khalit maedan خَليط معدن	precis n khulasah خُلاصة
amalgam	synopsis n khulasah خُلاصة
immoral adj 'khale خَليع	digest n khulasah خُلاصة
cellular adj khalyawi خَلِيَوي	quintessence n khulasah خُلاصة
muffler n khimar خِمار	immorality n khala'ah خَلاعة
tavern n khammarah خَمّارة	contention n khilaf خِلاف
wine n khamr خَمر	discord n khilaf خِلاف
liquor n khamr خَمر	creator n khallaq خَلّاق
idleness n khumul خُمول	during prep khilal خِلال
lethargy n khumul خُمُول	adv khilal el ayyam خِلال الأيام
yeast n khamireh خَميرة	adays
Thursday n elkhamis الخَميس	anklet n khelkhal خَلخال
dagger n khanjar خَنْجَر	shuffle n khalt خَلط
moat n khandaq خَندق	n khalt elma'adin خَلط المَعادن
ditch n khandaq خَنْدَق	amalgamation
trench n khandaq خَنْدَق	hotchpotch n khaltah خَلْطة
pig n khinzir خِنزير	behind adj khalfi خَلفي
boar n khinzir barri خِنزير بَرّي	rear adj khalfi خَلفي
sow n khanzereh خِنزيرة	back adj khalfi خَلفي
beetle n khenifseh خِنفسة	natal adj khuluqi خِلْقي
suffocation n khanq خَنق	immortality n khulud خُلود
servile adj 'khunu خُنُوع	cell n khaleyyeh خَلِيّة
slavish adj 'khunu خُنُوع	n khaleyyet elnahil خَلِيّة النحل
servility n 'khunu خُنُوع	beehive
subservience n 'khunu خُنُوع	hive n khaleyyeh nahl خَلِيّة نحل
bellowing n khiwar خِوار	gulf n khalij خَليج

treason *n* kheyaneh خيانة

dishonesty *n* kheyaneh خيانة

fiasco *n* khybeh خيبة

benefic *adj* khayri خيري

charitable *adj* khiri خيري

bamboo *n* khizaran خيزُران

cane *n* khizaraneh خيزرانة

hemp *n* khish خيش

jute *n* khish خيش

filament *n* khit خيط

thread *n* khit خيط

filamented *adj* khyti خيطي

tenant *n* khemeh خيمة

tent *n* khemeh خيمة

filamentation *n* khyut خيوط

n khuyut elshabakeh خيوط الشبكة
mesh

د

malady *n* 'da داء

poultry *n* dajen داجن

interior *adj* dakhli داخلي

inward *adj* dakhli داخلي

inner *adj* dakhli داخلي

inland *adj* dakhli داخلي

internal *adj* dakhli داخلي

peach *n* khukh خوخ

plum *n* khukh خوخ

helmet *n* khuzeh خوذة

dale *n* khur خَوْر

fear *n* khuf خوف

khuf mn elajaneb خوف من الأجانب
xenophobe *n*

elkhwf mn elfadda الخوف من الفضا
agoraphobia *n*

afraid *adj* khwfaan خوفان

alternative *n* khiar خيار

option *n* kheyar خيار

cucumber *n* khyar خيَار

choice *n* khayar خَيَار

tailor *n* khayyat خَيَّاط

faction *n* khayal خيال

fancy *n* khayal خيال

imagination *n* khayal خيال

shadow *n* khayal خيال

fictional *adj* khalali خيالى

dreamy *adj* khayali خيالي

factious *adj* khayali خيالي

fanciful *adj* khayali خيالي

fancy *adj* khayali خيالي

imaginative *adj* khayali خيالي

quixotic *adj* khayali خيالي

tentmaker *n* khayyam خَيَّام

betrayal *n* kheyaneh خيانة

adj da'emet elkhudrah دائمة الخضرة evergreen	interior *n* eddakhleyyeh الداخليّة
creditor *n* da'n دائن	circuit *n* daret kahrabah دارة كهربا
bear *n* debb دبّ	vernacular *adj* darij دارج
tank *n* dabbabeh دبّابة	backup *adj* da'em داعِم
tanner *n* dabbagh دبّاغ	prop *n* da'em داعِم
tawer *n* dabbagh دبّاغ	*n* 'daei lelijtima داعي لاجتماع convener
fly *n* debbaneh دبّانة	propagandist *n* da'eyh داعِية
n debbanet elhsan دبّانة الحصان gadfly	catalyst *n* 'dafe دافِع
n debbanet mayo دبّانة مايو ephemera	drive *n* 'dafe دافِع
slaughter *n* dabh دبح	motive *n* 'dafe دافِع
clutch *n* deberyaj دبرِياج	warm *adj* dafi دافي
molasses *n* debs دِبس	resourceful *adj* dahyh داهِية
taw *n* dabegh دبغ	crafty *adj* dahyeh داهِيّة
clingy *adj* debeq دبِق	cunning *adj* dahyeh داهِية
gelatinous *adj* dayyeq دبِق	artful *adj* daheyeh داهِية
sticky *adj* debq دبق	midwife *n* eldayeh الدّاية
birdlime *n* dabaq دبَق	giddy *adj* daykh دايخ
dub *n* dablajeh دبلجة	dazed *adj* dayekh دايخ
diploma *n* diploma دبلوما	circle *n* daera دائرة
diplomatic *adj* diplumasi دبلوماسي	*n* de'ret elnanu دائرة النانو nanocircuitry
diplomat *n* diplumasi دبلوماسي	*n* daera intikhabeyeh دائرة انتخابيّة constituency
n diplomaseyyeh دبلوماسِيّة diplomacy	persistent *adj* daym دايم
hornet *n* dabbur دبّور	permanent *adj* da'em دائم
pin *n* dabbus دبّوس	everlasting *adj* da'em دائم
	lasting *adj* da'em دائم

n deraset elnabat دراسة النبات	staple n dabbus دبّوس
botany	oblation n dbiha دبيحة
deraset دراسة طبقات الأرض	discourteous adj dajj دجّ
geology n tabaqat elard	chicken n dajajeh دجاجة
scholastic adj derasi دِرَاسِي	quackery n dajal دجل
drama n drama دراما	imposture n dajl دجل
latch n derbas دِرْباس	smoke n dukhkhan دخّان
bolt n derbas elbab درباس الباب	income n dakhl دخل
drum n derbakkeh دربكّة	entrance n dukhul دخول
ace n darra درّة	accessibility n dkholiyeh دخولية
stair n daraj دَرَج	dropzone n drabzun درابزون
n daraj meteharrek درج متحرِّك	railing n drabzun دَرَابْزُون
escalator	bannister n darabzun دَرَابْزون
class n darajeh درجة	study n deraseh دراسة
degree n darajeh درجة	monograph n diraseh دِرَاسة
extent n darajeh درجة	deraset el'athar دراسة الآثار القديمة
grade n darajeh درجة	archaeology n elqademeh
rank n darajeh دَرَجة	deraset دراسة الأمراض المستوطنة
n darajet elhararah درجة الحرارة	n elamrad elmestawteneh
temperature	endemiology
n darajeh quswa درجة قصوى	n diraset elburaz دراسة البُراز
extreme	coprology
adj darajeh meawweyyeh دَرَجة مئويّة	n diraset eltturbeh دراسة التربة
centigrade	agrology
chat n dardasheh دردَشة	n diraset elharakeh دراسة الحركة
seam n darzeh درزة	dynamics
tack n darzeh درزة	n deraset elqazaef دراسة القَذائِف
lesson n dars دَرْس	ballistics

warmth *n* dafa دفا

defence *n* 'fifa دفاع

bonfire *n* daffayeh دفَّاية

hearth *n* daffayeh دفَّاية

rudder *n* daqqah دَقّة

helm *n* daffet elqareb دفّة القارب

textbook *n* daftar دفتَر

booklet *n* daftar دفتَر

ledger *n* daftar elistaz دفتر الأستاذ

scramble *n* dafsh دفش

thrust *n* dafsh دفش

curt *adj* difish دفِش

harsh *adj* dfesh دفِش

push *n* dafsheh دفشة

pay *n* 'dafe دفع

payment *n* daf'ah دفعة

burial *n* dafen دَفِن

accuracy *n* deqqa دقة

bang *n* da'a دقّة

n deqqah belwaqt دقّة بالوقت

punctuality

barb *n* da'en دقن

beard *n* da'en دقن

chin *n* daqen دقن

bib *n* daquneh دقّونة

accurate *adj* daqiq دقيق

exact *adj* daqiq دقيق

minute *adj* daqiq دقيق

n dars telfezyuni درس تلفزيوني

telecourse

n dars khsusi درس خصوصى

tutorial

armature *n* 'dere درع

armour *n* 'dere درع

blindage *n* 'dere درع

n dere' muzarkash درع مزركش

blazon

shutter *n* darfeh درفة

dram *n* drham درهَم

dozen *n* dazzineh دزِّينة

shove *n* dass دسّ

constitution *n* dastur دَسْتور

invocation *n* du'a دُعاء

debauchery *n* da'arah دَعَارَة

prostitution *n* da'arah دَعَارَة

hold *n* di'ameh دِعَامة

tread *n* da'es دعس

advocacy *n* daem دعم

boost *n* da'em دعم

support *n* da'em دعم

n da'em hukumi دعم حكومي

subsidy

advocacy *n* daeweh دعوة

invitation *n* da'weh دعوة

n da'eweh leijtima'a دعوة لاجتماع

convocation

middleman n dallal دَلّال

realtor n dallal دَلّال

delta n delta دلتا

indulgence n 'dala دلع

dolphin n delfin دلفين

clue n dalil دليل

conductor n dalil دليل

directory n dalil دليل

evidence n dalil دليل

guidance n dalil دليل

guide n dalil دليل

n dalil essyyah دليل السيّاح
handbook

blood n damm دمّ

destruction n damar دمار

ravage n damar دمار

brain n dimakh دماغ

cerebral adj demaghi دماغي

growl n damdmeh دمدمة

tear n dam'ah دمعة

cachet n damgha دمغَة

imprint n dam'ah دَمْغَة

n damghet eddahab دمغة الدهب
hallmark

abscess n dummaleh دملة

bloody adj damawi دَموي

sanguine adj damawi دَمَوي

adj daqiq belwaqt دقيق بالوقت
punctual

minute n daqiqah دَقيقة

shop n dekkaneh دكّانة

podium n dekkeh دكّة

dictator n diktatur دكّاتور

doctor n diktur دكتور

medic n daktur دكتور

dentist n dektur asnan دكتور أسنان

n dektur asnan دكتور أسنان
odontologist

n duktur a'sab دكتور أعصاب
neurologist

n duktur tawlid دكتور توليد
obstetrician

n dektur jarrah دكتور جرّاح
sawbones

n duktor jeldeyyeh دكتور جلديّة
dermatologist

oculist n dektur eyun دكتور عيون

intern n diktur muqim دكتور مقيم

n dektur nafsi دكتور نفسي
psychiatrist

n dektur nafsi دكتور نفسي
psychologist

doctorate n dikturah دكتوراه

fondling n dalal دلال

broker n dallal دلّال

laxative *n* dwa mesahhel دوا مسهِّل	*n* demyeh meteharkeh دمية متحركة
opiate *n* dwa menawwem دوا منوِّم	marionette
placebo *n* dwa wahmi دوا وهمي	hideous *adj* damim دَميم
fowl *n* dwajen دواجن	meanness *n* dana'ah دناءة
pedal *n* dawwaseh دَوّاسة	tail *n* danab دنب
persist *n* dawam دوام	lace *n* dantil دَنتيل
medicinal *adj* dawa'e دَوائي	crooning *n* dandaneh دندنة
solubility *n* dwaban دوبان	base *adj* 'danie دنيء
daziness *n* eddukha الدوخَة	earthen *adj* denyawi دنيوى
daze *n* dukha دوخَة	mundane *adj* denyawi دنيوي
drizzle *n* dukhah دوخَة	paint *n* dhan دهان
worm *n* dudeh دودة	painter *n* dahhan دهَّان
caterpillar *n* dudeh دودة	gold *n* dahab دهب
role *n* dur دور	golden *adj* dahabi دهبي
turn *n* dur دور	eon *n* dahr دَهْر
rotation *n* dawaran دوران	amazement *n* dahsheh دهشة
turn *n* dawaran دوران	cellar *n* dahliz دهليز
circuit *n* dawra دورَة	lobby *n* dahliz دِهْليز
course *n* dawrah دورَة	anoint *v* dahen دهن
stroll *n* durah دورَة	lard *n* dehn elkhanzir دهن الخَنزير
ride *n* durah دوْرَة	fat *n* dehun دهون
cycle *n* dawrah دوْرَة	drug *n* dawah دوا
n dawrah shahreyyeh دورَة شهريّة	remedy *n* dwa دوا
menses	medicament *n* dawa دَوَا
periodical *adj* dawri دوري	nostrum *n* dwa serri دوا سرّي
patrol *n* dawreyyeh دَوْريّة	dwa lakel elamrad دوا لكل الأمراض
shower *n* dush دوش	panacea *n*
duke *n* duq دُوق	antidote *n* dawa lelsamm دوا للسمّ

tight *adj* dayyeq ديّق

cock *n* dik ديك

decor *n* dikur ديكور

decoration *n* dikur ديكور

decorative *adj* dikuri ديكوري

adj dimukrati ديموقراطي

democratic

n dimukrateyyeh ديموقراطيّة

democracy

permanence *n* demumeh ديمومة

debt *n* din دين

religion *n* din دين

religious *adj* dayyen ديّن

dynamite *n* dinamit ديناميت

chaise *n* diwaneh ديوانة

couch *n* diwaneh ديوانة

deodorant *n* diuduran ديودوران

ذ

subjective *adj* zati ذاتي

memory *n* zakrah ذاكرة

oscillation *n* zabzabeh ذبذبة

oscillometric *adj* zabzabi ذبذبي

ammunition *n* dhakhira ذخيرة

munitions *n* zakhirah ذخيرة

cubit *n* zira'a ذراع

duchess *n* duqah دوقة

ducat *n* elduqeyyeh الدوقيّة

wheel *n* dulab دولاب

tire *n* dulab دُولاب

n dulab msannan دولاب مسنّن

gearwheel

buck *n* dular دولار

dollar *n* dular دولار

state *n* dawleh دولة

international *adj* duwali دولي

always *adv* dawman دوما

domino *n* dumino دومينو

doughnut *n* dunat دونات

abase *adv* duni دوني

inferiority *n* duneyyeh دُونيّة

duet *n* duwitto دويتو

wolf *n* dib ديب

facade *n* dibajeh ديباجة

preface *n* debajeh ديْباجة

cloister *n* dir دير

convent *n* dir دير

hermitage *n* dir دير

abbey *n* dir elrahbat دير الراهبات

nunnery *n* dir elrahbat دير الراهبات

diesel *n* dizel ديزِل

decibel *n* disibil ديسيبيل

decillion *n* disilyyun ديسيليون

narrow *adj* dayyeq ديّق

sin n zanb ذنب

misdeed n zanb ذَنْب

adj zehnuh meshattat ذهنه مشتّت

scatterbrained

connaisseur n zawwaq ذوّاق

epicure n zawwaq ذَوّاق

decorum n zuq ذوق

toxin n zyfan ذيفان

ر

winner n rabeh رابح

annectent adj rabit رابِط

link n rabit رابِط

association n rabita رابِطة

hillock n rabyeh رابية

salary n ratib راتب

n ratib eltaqa'ud راتب التقاعُد

pension

annuity n ratin sanawi راتب سنوي

comfort n raha راحة

relaxation n rahah راحة

convenience n raha راحَة

rest n rahah راحَة

leisure n raha راحَة

prohibitive adj 'rade رادِع

radio n radyu راديو

maize n zurah ذرة

atom n zarra ذرّة

corn n zurah ذُرة

millet n zurah bydah ذرة بيضا

climax n zarweh ذروة

heyday n zarweh ذروة

pinnacle n zarweh ذروة

atomic adj zarri ذرّي

posterity n zareyyeh ذريّة

intelligence n 'zaka ذكاء

male n zakar ذكَر

mention n zekr ذِكْر

penis n zakaruh ذكَرُه

n zikra meaweyyeh ذكرى مِئويِّة

centenary

n zikra meaweyyeh ذكرى مِئويِّة

centennial

zikra meaweyeh ذكرى مئوية تانية

bicentenary adj taneyeh

masculine adj zakari ذكَري

male adj zukuri ذُكُوري

brilliant adj zaki ذكي

clever adj zaki ذكي

intelligent adj zaki ذكي

smart adj zaki ذكي

safekeeping n zemmeh ذِمّة

guilt n zanb ذنب

offence n zanb ذنب

n rawi elqussah راوي القصّة narrator	radium n radyum راديوم
opinion n ra'i رأي	radion n radyun راديون
misbelief n ra'e ghalat رأي غلط	apex n ras راس
banner n rayeh راية	head n ras راس
marketable adj rayij رايج	nib n ras راس
salable adj rayj رايج	cape n ras رأس
resolute adj rayd رايد	spearhead n ras elremh راس الرمح
willing adj rayd رايد	capital n ras mal رأس مال
major n ra'ed رائد	cephaloid adj ra'seyeh رأسيّة
pioneer n rayed رائد	adult adj rashid راشد
astronaut n 'raed fadaa رائد فضاء	complacent adj radi راضي
fantastic adj ra'e رائع	content adj radi راضي
great adj ra'e رائع	herdsman n ra'ey راعي
scrumptious adj 'ra'e رائع	patron n ra'i راعي
superb adj 'ra'e رائع	shepherd n ra'i راعي
gorgeous adj ra'e رَائع	confluent adj rafid رافد
placid adj rayq رايق	crane n rafe'ah رافعَة
serene adj rayeq رايق	crowbar n rafe'ah رافعَة
tranquil adj rayq رايق	derrick n raf'a رافعَة
deity n rabb رَبّ	jack n raf'ah رافعَة
strap n rabbat ربَّاط	dancing adj raqes راقص
lace n 'rabbat elhiza رباط الحذاء	sublime adj raqi راقٍ
garter n rabbatah ربَّاطة	n rakeb elmisklit راكب المسكليت cyclist
n 'ruba'i eladla رباعي الأضلاع quadrilateral	archer n rami elsiham رامي السهام
adj 'ruba'i eladla رباعى الأضلاع quadrilateral	clergy n rahib راهب
	monk n rahib راهِب
	nun n rahbeh راهِبة

quiver n rajfeh رجفة

orgasm n 'rajfet eljima رجفة الجِمَاع

n rajul a'maal رجل أعمَال

businessman

rajul hureyyet رجل حورية البحر

merman n elbaher

n rajul dawleh رجل دولة

statesman

n mjel mesttahah رجل مسطَّحة

flatfoot

manliness n rujuleh رجولة

virility n rjuleh رجولة

manhood n rujuleh رُجُولة

manlike adj rujuli رجولي

damnable adj rajim رَجِيم

backpacker n rahhal رحَّال

rover n rahhal رَحَّال

runabout n rahhaleh رَحَّالة

trip n rehleh رحلة

excursion n rehleh رحلة

journey n rehleh رحلة

n rihleh blttayara رحلة بالطيارة

airlift

uterus n rahm رحم

womb n rahm رحم

mercy n rahmeh رحمة

nectar n rahiq رَحِيق

department n rahil رحيل

n ruba'i elzawaya رباعى الزوايا

quadrangle

adj ruba'i elzawaya رباعى الزوايا

quadrangular

quadruple adj ruba'i رباعي

tetra n ruba'i رباعي

deist n rabbani رَبَّاني

dame n rabbeh ربّة

gain n rebh ربح

profit n rebh ربح

win n rebh ربح

lucre n rebeh رِبْح

profitable adj rebhi ربحي

n rabtet khasr ربطة خصر

waistband

quarter n 'rebe ربع

asthma n rabu ربو

godhead n rebubeyyeh ربوبيّة

deism n rbubeyyeh رُبُوبيّة

spring n 'elrabie الربيع

vernal adj rabe'iy ربيعي

monotony n ratabeh رَتَابة

please adv 'raja رجاءً

man n rejjal رجَّال

manly adj rejjali رجَّالي

return n raj'ah رجعة

bigotry n rajeyeh رجعيّة

jerk n rajfeh رجفة

sober *adj* razin رزين	merciful *adj* rahim رحيم
staid *adj* razin رزين	weal *n* rakha رخا
grave *adj* razin رَزين	alabaster *adj* rukhami رخامي
letter *n* risaleh رسالة	elasticity *n* rakhaweh رخاوة
message *n* risaleh رسالة	licence *n* rekhsah رخصة
draftsman *adj* rassam رسّام	elastic *adj* rakhu رَخْو
n rassam elzabzabat رسّام الذبذبات	slack *adj* rakhu رَخْو
oscilloscope	mollusc *n* rakhawi رَخْوِي
n rassam kharyet رسّام خرايط	cheap *adj* rekhis رخيص
cartographer	gross *adj* rkhis رخيص
n rassam kartun رسّام كرتون	inexpensive *adj* rkhis رَخيص
cartoonist	reply *n* radd ردّ
carpal *adj* resghi رسغي	*n* radd ele'tibar رد الإعتبار
drawing *n* rasm رسم	rehabilitation
fee *n* rasm رسم	rejoinder *n* 'radd sari رد سريع
painting *n* rasm رسم	inhibition *n* 'rade رَدْع
figure *n* rasm رَسْم	buttock *n* redef ردف
n rasm belkalam رسم بالكلام	dribble *n* razaz رَذَاذ
portrayal	vice *n* razyleh رَذيلة
graph *n* rasm byani رسم بياني	rice *n* rezz رزّ
n rasm zyadeh رسم زيادة	*n* rezz mu maqshur رز مو مقشور
surcharge	paddy
toll *n* rasm murur رسم مرور	composure *n* razaneh رزانة
capital *adj* rasmali رسمالي	sobriety *n* razaneh رَزَانة
n rasmet shakhes رسمة شخص	livelihood *n* rezq رِزْق
portrait	bunch *n* ruzmeh رزمة
ceremonious *adj* rasmi رسمي	almanac *n* roznama رُزنامة
formal *adj* rasmi رسمي	sedate *adj* razin رزين

humidity *n* rutubeh رطوبة

dank *n* rutubeh kbireh رطوبة كبيرة

mob *n* 'ru'a رُعاع

populace *n* 'ru'a رُعَاع

care *n* reayeh رعاية

patronage *n* re'ayet رعاية

n re'ayet elmawashi رعاية المواشي

graze

horror *n* ru'b رعب

scare *n* ru'eb رعب

thunder *n* ra'ed رَعْد

thunderous *adj* ra'di رَعْدي

thrill *n* ra'sheh رعشة

flutter *n* ra'sheh رعشة

indiscretion *n* ru'uneh رعُونة

bent *n* raghbeh رغبة

desire *n* raghbeh رغبة

scum *n* raghweh رغوة

foam *n* raghweh رغوة

n raghwet elsabun رغوة الصابون

lather

loaf *n* rghif رغيف

shelf *n* raff رَفّ

luxury *n* rafaheyyeh رَفاهِيّة

prosperity *n* rafaheyyeh رَفاهِيّة

fling *v* rafs رفس

kick *v* rafseh رفسة

disapproval *n* rafd رفض

official *adj* rasmi رسمي

officially *adv* rasmeyyan رسمياً

rein *n* rasan رَسَن

messenger *n* rasul رسول

splash *n* rashsh elmay رشّ المي

n rashashet tawabel رشّاشة التوابل

caster

bribe *n* rashweh رشوة

venality *n* rashweh رشوة

brisk *adj* rashiq رشيق

slim *adj* rashiq رشيق

limber *adj* rashiq رَشيق

limber *n* rashiq رَشيق

nimble *adj* rashiq رَشيق

lead *n* rsas رصاص

bullet *n* resasa رصاصَة

leaden *adj* rsasi رَصَاصِي

rased masari leshi رصد مصاري لشي

appropriation *n*

sidewalk *n* rasif رَصِيف

contusion *n* radd رضّ

trauma *n* redd رضّ

suckling *n* reda'ah رضاعَة

traumatism *n* raddah رضّة

content *n* rida رضى

consent *n* rida رضى

traumatic *adj* reddi رَضّي

humid *adj* retb رطب

ten *n, a* elraqm 10 **10** الرقم	refusal *n* rafd رفض
hundred *n* elraqm 100 **100** الرقم	rejection *n* rafd رفض
n elraqm 1000 **1000** الرقم	elevation *n* 'rafe رفع
thousand	comrade *n* rifqa رفقَة
eleven *n* elraqm 11 **11** الرقم	thin *adj* 'rafe رفيع
thirteen *n* elraqm 13 **13** الرقم	friend *n* rfiq رفيق
fourteen *n* elraqm 14 **14** الرقم	*n* refiq elderaseh رفيق الدراسة
fifteen *n* elraqm 15 **15** الرقم	schoolmate
sixteen *n, adj* elraqm 16 **16** الرقم	*n* rfiq musa'ed رفيق مساعِد
seventeen *n, a* elraqm 17 **17** الرقم	helpmate
eighteen *adj* elraqam 18 **18** الرقم	*n* raqqas elsa'ah رقَّاص الساعة
nineteen *n* elraqm 19 **19** الرقم	pendulum
two *n* elraqm 2 **2** الرقم	dancer *n* raqqasah رقَّاصَة
twenty *n* elraqm 20 **20** الرقم	flake *n* ruqaqah رقاقَة
three *n* elraqm 30 **3** الرقم	chip *n* ruqaqah رُقاقَة
thirty *n* elraqm 30 **30** الرقم	*n* ruqaqet elnanu رقاقة نانو
four *n* elraqm 4 **4** الرقم	nanochip
forty *n* elraqm 40 **40** الرقم	neck *n* ruqyeh رقبِة
five *n* elraqm 5 **5** الرقم	cervical *adj* raqabi رقبي
fifty *n* elraqm 50 **50** الرقم	gentility *n* reqqah رقَّة
six *n, a* elraqm 6 **6** الرقم	nap *n* raqdeh رقدة
sixty *n, adj* elraqm 60 **60** الرقم	dance *n* raqsah رقصَة
seven *n* elraqm 7 **7** الرقم	tango *n* raqset tangu رقصة التانغو
seventy *n, a* elraqm 70 **70** الرقم	patch *n* req'ah رقعة
eight *n* elraqam 8 **8** الرقم	digit *n* raqam رقم
eighty *n* elraqam 80 **80** الرقم	figure *n* raqm رقم
nine *n* elraqm 9 **9** الرقم	number *n* raqm رقم
ninety *n* elraqm 90 **90** الرقم	one *n* elraqm 1 **1** الرقم

code *n* ramz رمز

symbol *n* ramz رمز

token *n* ramz رمز

zip *n* ramz elmantiqah رمز المنطقة
code

symbolic *adj* ramzi رمزي

symbolism *n* ramzeyyeh رمزِيّة

sand *n* raml رمل

sand *adj* ramli رملي

sandy *adj* ramli رملي

n rumuz ta'bereyyeh رموز تعبيريّة
emoji

n rumuz mukhtasarah رموز مختصرة
mnemonic

eyelash *n* rumush eleyn رموش العين

n ramyeh mwaffaqa رمية موفّقة
bull's eye

resonant *adj* rannan رنّان

tone *n* ranneh رنّة

resonance *n* ranin رنين

stake *n* rehan رهان

bet *n* rihan رِهان

wager *n* rehan رِهان

monasticism *n* ruhbaneyyeh رهبانيّة

dread *v* rahbeh رهبِة

mortgage *n* rahn رهن

lien *n* rahn رَهْن

pledge *n* rahn رَهْن

n raqm metsalsel رقم متَسلسل
serial

digital *adj* raqami رقمي

tarantism *n* raqwasah رَقْوَصَة

sergeant *n* raqib رَقيب

spell *n* ruqyh رقْية

leg *n* rekbeh ركبة

knee *n* rekbeh ركبِة

mount *n* rekbeh ركبِة

gallop *n* raked ركض

run *n* rakd ركض

jog *v* raked رْكض

rush *n* 'rakd sare ركض سريع

sprint *n* 'rakd sare ركض سريع

nook *n* rukn رُكْن

slump *n* rukud ركود

pedestal *n* rkizeh ركيزة

n rakizeh ma'dan ركيزة معدَن
corbel

flimsy *adj* rakik ركيك

ash *n* ramad رماد

grey *adj* rmadi رمادي

toss *n* rmayeh رماية

n rimayet elsiham رماية السهام
archery

javelin *n* remh رمح

spear *n* remh رمح

lancet *adj* remhi رمحي

spiritualism *n* ruhaneyyeh روحانِيَّة	awesome *adj* rahib رهيب
spirituality *n* ruhaneyyeh روحانِيَّة	hostage *n* rahineh رهينة
dear *adj* ruhi روحي	portico *n* rawaq رواق
pneumatic *adj* ruhi روحي	serenity *n* rawaq رواق
spiritual *adj* ruhi روحي	eave *n* rawaq روَاق
immaterial *adj* ruhi رُوحي	porch *n* rawaq روَاق
calendar *n* ruznameh روزنامة	novel *n* rwayeh رواية
splendour *n* ru'ah روعة	*n* rewayet elqessah رواية القصَّة
tranquility *n* rawaqan روقان	narration
rheumatic *adj* rumatizmi رُوماتِزمِي	novelist *n* rewa'i روائي
arthritis *n* rumatizem روماتيزم	narrative *adj* riwa'e رِوَائي
rheumatism *n* rumatizm روماتيزم	dress *n* rub روب
romance *n* rumans رومانس	rouble *n* rwil رُوبِل
romantic *adj* rumansi رومانسي	droid *n* rubut روبوت
lustre *n* runaq رونق	robot *n* rubut روبوت
radiance *n* runaq روَنَق	lobster *n* rubyan روبيان
sight *n* ru'ya رؤيا	crayfish *n* rubyan رُوبيَان
visibility *n* ru'yeh رؤية	rupee *n* rubeyyeh رُوبِيَّة
forethought *n* raweyyeh روَيَّة	routine *n* rutin روتين
drool *n* rewel رويل	*n* rutin elshughel روتين الشغل
sham *n* 'rya رياء	harness
hypocrisy *n* 'rya رِيَاء	routine *adj* rutini روتيني
captaincy *n* riyaseh رئاسة	monotonous *adj* rutini رُوتِيني
presidential *adj* re'asi رئاسي	spirit *n* ruh روح
sport *n* ryadah رياضة	pneuma *n* ruh رُوح
polo *n* riyadet elbulu رياضة البولو	soul *n* ruh رُوح
reyyadet alaab رياضة ألعاب القوى	jollity *n* ruh mrhah روح مرحَة
athletics *n* elqewa	spiritualist *n* ruhani رُوحاني

رثوي معدي re'awi ma'edi *adj*
pneumogastric

رئيس raeyis *n* chairman

رئيس ra'is *n* president

رئيس العمال ra'es elummal *n*
foreman

رئيس الوزرا ra'is elwuzarah *n*
premier

رئيس دير ra'es dir *n* abbot

رئيس دير ra'is dir *n* prior

رئَيسة المُمَرِّضات ra'est elmumarredat
matron *n*

رئيسة دير ra'eset dir *n* prioress

الرئيسي elra'esi *n* main

رئيسي raeysi *adj* capital

رئيسي ra'isi *adj* key

رئيسي ra'ysi *adj* main

ز

زاحِف zahif *adj* creepy

زاهِد zahid *n* ascetic

زاهي zahi *adj* aglare

زاوية zawyeh *n* angle

زاوية zawyeh *n* corner

زايد zayid *adj* adscititious

زايد zayd *adj* residual

رياضة الكريكت riyadet elkrikit *n*
cricket

رياضي riyadi *adj* mathematical

رياضي ryadi *adj* sportive

رياضي ryadi *n* sportsman

رياضيّ reyyaddi *adj* athletic

رياضيّات ryaddeyyat *n*
mathematics

ريائي rya'i *adj* hypocritical

ريبان rubyan *n* ribbon

رئة re'ah *n* lung

ريجيم rijim *n* diet

ريح موسميّة rih musemeyyeh *n*
monsoon

ريحة riha *n* aroma

ريحة riha *n* smell

ريحته طيّبة rehtu taybeh *adj*
odorous

ريشة risheh *n* feather

ريف rif *n* provincialism

ريفي rifi *adj* rural

ريفي rifi *adj* rustic

ريفي rifi *n* rustic

ريفي rifi *adj* pastoral

ريق riq *n* spittle

ريْق riq *n* saliva

رئوي re'awi *adj* pneumonic

n zera'et elghabat زراعة الغابات
forestry

adj zira'a blhwa زراعة بالهوا
aeroponic

n zera'et udu زراعة عضو
transplantation

agricultural adj zira'ei زراعي

giraffe n zarafeh زرافة

plant n zar'ah زَرعَة

arsenic n zarnikh زرنيخ

byre n zribeh زريبة

pen n zrebeh زريبة

n zrebet elkhanazir زرية الخنازير
sty

plantation n zre'ah زَرِيعَة

dacoity n zaeraneh زعرَنة

hawthorn n za'rur زَعرور

n zaezaet elistiqrar زعزعة الاستقرار
destabilization

saffron n za'faran زَعْفَران

saffron adj za'farani زعفراني

grief n za'al زعل

sadness n za'al زعل

sad adj za'lan زعلان

fin n ze'enfeh زعنفة

shriek n ze'iq زعيق

acclamation n zaghareed زغاريد

lanugo n zaghab زَغَب

appendix n zaeydeh زائدة

visitor n zayer زائر

scavenger n zabbal زَبّال

waste n zbaleh زبالة

garbage n zbaleh زبالة

trash n zbaleh زبالة

rubbish n zebaleh زبَالة

seafoam n zabad elbahr زبد البحر

upshot n zbdeh زبدة

butter n zebdeh زبدة

bowl n zebdeyeh زبديّة

cuvette n zebdeyyeh زبديّةِ

muck n zabal زبل

customer n zbun زبون

currant n zbib زبيب

raisin n zbib زبيب

throw n zatt زَتّ

cast n zatt زَتّ

dysentery n zuhar زُحَار

crowd n zham زحام

crawl n zahef زَحْف

skid n zahluqah زُحْلُوقَة

throng n zahmeh زحمة

crowded adj zahmeh زحمة

ornament n zakhrafeh زَخْرَفة

button n zerr زرّ

switch n zrr kahrabah زر كهربا

agriculture n zira'a زراعة

forearm *n* znd زند

dungeon *n* zinzaneh زنزانة

cell *n* zinzaneh زنزانة

zinc *n* zink زنك

dice *n* zaher eltawleh زهر الطاولة

n zahr mukhmali زهر مخملي

marigold

blossom *n* zahra زهرة

rose *n* zahrah زهرة

marriage *n* zwaj زواج

n ezzwaj bewehdeh الزواج بوحدة

monogamy

nuptial *adj* zawaji زواجي

matrimonial *adj* zawaji زَوَاجِي

reptile *n* zwahef زَوَاحِف

n zawal zukuret زوال الذكورة

demasculinization

n madeyyet zawal زوال المادّة

dematerialisation

vortex *n* zuba'ah زوبعة

husband *n* zuj زوج

pair *n* zug زوج

spouse *n* zuj زَوْج

couple *n* zuj men زوج من

couplet *n* zuj men زوج من

marital *adj* zawji زوجى

binary *adj* zawji زوجي

conjugal *adj* zawji زوجي

nap *n* zughbur زغبر

pitch *n* zeft زفت

cheer *n* zaqzaqah زقزقة

crepe *n* zelabeyeh زلابية

skate *n* zallajeh زلّاجة

albumen *n* zulal albid زُلال البيض

slip *n* zelleh زلّة

seismic *adj* zelzali زلزالي

shrill *n* zalghutah زلغوطة

gaffe *n* zelleyeh زلّة

snarl *n* zamjarah زمجرة

emerald *n* zumurrud زمرُّد

tense *n* zaman زمن

epoch *n* zaman زَمَن

buddy *n* zamil زميل

colleague *n* zamil زميل

fellow *n* zamil زميل

adultery *n* zinna زنا

lily *n* zanbaq زنبق

wasp *n* zanbut زنبوط

scuttle *n* zanbil زَنبِيل

frail *adj* zanbil زَنبِيل

ginger *n* zanjabil زَنجَبِيل

negro *n* zenji زِنجِي

nigger *n* zenji زِنجِي

negress *n* zenjeyyeh زِنجِيّة

musty *adj* zenekh زنخ

rancid *adj* zenekh زنخ

سابع 'elsabe *adj* seventh السابع

antecedent *n* sabeq سابق

former *adj* sabeq سابق

previous *adj* sabeq سابق

prefix *n* sabqah سابِقة

satin *n* satan ساتان

satin *adj* satani ساتاني

barrier *n* satir ساتِر

mound *n* satir ساتِر

rampart *n* sater ساتِر

nave *n* sahet elmasjid ساحة المَسجِد

bewitching *adj* saher ساحِر

magician *n* saher ساحِر

witch *n* sahrah ساحِرة

coast *n* sahil ساحِل

seashore *n* sahil ساحِل

shore *n* sahil ساحِل

coastal *adj* sahli ساحِلي

littoral *adj* sahli ساحِلي

sixth *adj* elsades السادس

sadism *n* sadeyyeh ساديّة

sadist *n* sadeyyeh ساديّة

artless *adj* sazaj ساذج

credulous *adj* sazaj ساذج

hour *n* sa'ah ساعة

falsehood *n* zur زُور

vessel *n* zuraq زورق

barge *n* zawra'a زورَق

boat *n* zawraq زورَق

addition *n* el zeyadeh الزيادة

additional *adj* zeyadeh زيادة

augmentation *n* zeyadeh زيادة

further *adj* zyadeh زيادة

increase *n* zyadeh زيادة

plus *adj* zyadeh زيادة

plus *n* zyadeh زيادة

double *adj* zyadeh زيادة

extra *adj* zydeh زيادة

n zyadeh seghereh زيادة صغيرة pittance

visit *n* zyarah زيارة

mercury *n* ze'baq زِئبَق

quicksilver *n* ze'baq زِئبَق

mercurial *adj* ze'baqi زِئبَقي

oil *n* zit زيت

castor oil *n* 'zit khuwe زيت خروَع

olive *n* zit zitun زيت زيتون

oily *adj* ziti زيتي

oleaginous *adj* ziti زيتي

aberration *n* zayaghan زيغان

garnish *n* zineh زينة

ornamentation *n* zyneh زينة

tinsel *n* zyneh زينة

watch *n* sa'ah ساعة	*adj* samm udweyan سامّ عضوياً
clock *n* sa'ah ساعَة	biohazardous
postman *n* sa'i elbarid ساعي البريد	samba *n* samba سامبا
low *adj* safel سافِل	samaritan *n* samri سامري
menial *adj* safil سافِل	samsonite *n* samsunyt سامسونايت
menial *n* safil سافِل	samurai *n* samurai ساموراي
rascal *n* safil سافِل	sauna *n* sawnah ساونا
vicious *adj* safil سافِل	tourist *n* sayh سايح
indecent *adj* safil سافِل	motorist *n* sa'eq mutur سائق الموتور
shin *n* saq ساق	cabby *n* saeq taksi سائق تكسي
stalk *n* saq ساق	fluid *n* sa'el سائل
fallen *n* elsaqet الساقط	liquid *n* sa'el سائل
fallen *adj* saqet ساقط	sperm *n* sa'el manawi سائل منوي
mean *adj* saqt ساقِط	forefinger *n* sabbabeh سَبّابَة
rivulet *n* saqyh ساقية	*n* sbat shatwi سبات شتوي
motionless *adj* saken ساكن	hibernation
resident *adj* sakin ساكن	swimmer *n* sabbah سبّاح
resident *n* sakin ساكن	swim *n* sbaha سباحة
static *n* saken ساكن	race *n* sibaq سباق
static *adj* saken ساكن	steeple *n* sebaq herr سباق حرّ
domiciled *adj* saken ساكِن	spinach *n* sabanekh سبانخ
habitat *n* saken ساكِن	reason *n* sabab سبب
occupant *n* saken ساكِن	cause *n* sabab سبَب
inhabitant *n* saken ساكن	*n* sabab juhari سبب جوهري
adj saken asli ساكن أصلي	rationale
aboriginal	causal *adj* sababi سَبَي
negative *n* salib سالِب	causality *n* sababeyyeh سَبَبِيّة
	Saturday *n* elsabt السبت

registry n elsejellat السِّجلَّات	moor n sabkha سبخة
archives npl sijillat سجلَات	bog n sabkha سَبخَة
jail n sejn سجن	swamp n sabkha سَبْخَة
n sejn ahdath سجن أحداث	spray n sepray سبراي
reformatory	seven adj sab'ah سبعة
obeisance n sejud سجود	adj elsab'eyneyyat السبعينيات
prostration n sujud سجود	seventieth
zipper n sahhab سحَّاب	before .conj sabaq سبق
mist n sahab سَحَاب	antecedent adj sabaq سبَق
draw n saheb سحب	sputnik n sputnik سبوتنيك
pull n sahb سحب	trail n sabil سَبِيل
tow n sahb سحب	satellite n satalyt ستلايت
traction n sahb سحب	stand n stand ستاند
draft n saheb سَحْب	strategic adj stratiji ستراتيجي
n saheb almakshuf سحب عالمكشوف	strategist n stratiji ستراتيجي
overdraft	strategy n stratejeyyeh ستراتيجيّة
charm n seher سحر	citrine n sitrin سترين
magic n sehr سِحْر	studio n studyu ستوديو
magical adj sehri سحري	bodice n sityaneh ستيانة
physiognomy n sehneh سحنة	sixtieth adj elsetineyyat الستينيَّات
complexion n sihneh سحنة	mat n sejjadeh سجَّادَة
bounty n sakha سَخَا	carpet n sijjadeh سجَّادَة
liberality n 'sakha سَخَاء	jailer n sajjan سجَّان
soot n sakhkham سخَّام	warder n sajjan سجَّان
geyser n sakhkhan سخَّان	record n sejell سجلّ
torrid adj sekhn سخن	register n sejell سجلّ
heat n skhuneh سخونة	terrier n sejell aqari سجل عَقَارِي
bountiful adj sakhi سخي	log n sejell yumi سجلّ يومي

esoteric *adj* serri سِرّي	munificent *adj* sakhi سَخِي
secret *adj* serry سِرّي	silly *adj* sakhif سَخِيف
underhand *adj* serri سِرّي	ridiculous *adj* sakhif سَخِيف
esoterism *n* serreyyeh سِرِّيّة	barrage *n* sadd سَدّ
brigade *n* sareyyeh سَرِيّة	dam *n* sadd سَدّ
secrecy *n* serreyyeh سِرِّيّة	embankment *n* sadd سَدّ
clinical *adj* sariri سريري	weir *n* sadd segher سَدّ صغير
cursory *adj* sari'e سريع	reimbursement *n* sadad سداد
express *adj* 'sare سريع	repayment *n* sadad سداد
fast *adj* sari'e سريع	tampon *n* saddadeh سدَّادة
prompt *adj* 'sari سريع	cork *n* saddadeh سدَّادة
quick *adj* 'sari سريع	credulity *n* sazajeh سذاجة
rapid *adj* 'sari سريع	secret *n* serr سِرّ
speedy *adj* 'sare سريع	mirage *n* sarab سَراب
instant *adj* 'sari سريع	swarm *n* serb سِرْب
swift *adj* 'sare سريع	saddle *n* sarj سَرْج
adj sare' eleshti'al سريع الاشتعال	sidesaddle *n* sarj janbi سَرْج جانِبي
inflammable	fern *n* sarkhas سرخس
adj sarei' elkaser سريع الكسر	cancer *n* saratan سرطان
vulnerable	rapidity *n* sur'ah سرعة
deck *n* sateh سطح	speed *n* sur'ah سرعة
plane *n* sateh سطح	velocity *n* sur'ah سُرْعَة
surface *n* sateh سطح	repartee *n* ser'et badiha سرعة بديهَة
top *n* sateh سطح	abaction *n* serqah سرقة
outside *n* sateh سَطْح	robbery *n* serqah سرقة
n sateh elmastabeh سطح المصطبة	theft *n* serqah سرقة
benchtop	burglary *n* serqa سرقَة
	confidential *adj* serri سِرّي

takeaway *adj* safari سَفَري

sophist *n* safusta'ei سفسطائي

sophism *n* safusta'eyyeh سفسطائيّة

bloodshed *n* safek damm سفك دمّ

bottom *n* sefel سفل

nether *adj* sifli سفلى

sponge *n* sfenjeh سفنجة

ambassador *n* safir سفير

ark *n* safineh سفينة

ship *n* safeneh سفينة

n safineh harbeyyeh سفينة حربيّة

cruiser

n safineh kbereh سفينة كبيرة

carrack

spendthrift *n* safih سَفيه

impertinent *adj* safih سَفيه

bottler *n* saqqa سَقّا

barman *n* saqqa elbar سَقّا البار

catch *n* saqqatah سَقّاطة

n saqqatet elbab سَقّاطة الباب

doorknob

irrigation *n* sqayeh سقاية

ceiling *n* saqf سقف

roof *n* saqf سقف

hut *n* sqifeh سقيفة

loft *n* sqefeh سقيفة

sakk elemleh سكّ العملة المعدنيّة

coinage *n* elma'daneyyeh

n sateh elmaktab سطح المكتب

desktop

facet *n* sateh sghur سطح صغير

superficial *adj* satehi سطحي

shallow *adj* satehi سَطْحي

superficiality *n* sateheyyeh سطحيّة

bucket *n* satel سطل

pail *n* satel سَطْل

leverage *n* satweh سَطْوة

happiness *n* sa'adeh سعادة

capacity *n* sia'a سعة

felicity *n* sa'd سَعْد

price *n* se'r سعر

teaser *n* se'r meghri سعر مغري

cough *n* saelih سعلة

happy *adj* sa'ed سعيد

thug *n* saffah سفّاح

murderous *adj* saffah سَفّاح

hooligan *n* saffah سَفّاح

embassy *n* safarah سفارة

indecency *n* safaleh سَفَالة

impertinence *n* safaha سَفَاهَة

spill *n* safh سفح

travel *n* safar سفر

voyage *n* safar bahri سفر بحري

outing *n* safrah سفرَة

v safrah bahreyyeh سفرة بحرية

cruise

scooter *n* skuter سكوتر	habitation *n* sukkan سكّان
tacit *adj* skuti سكُوتي	population *n* sukkan سكّان
bacchanal *n* sekkir سكّير	*n* sukkan buhimia سكان بُوهيميا
bacchanal *adj* sekkir سكّير	bohemian
drunkard *n* sakkir سكّير	shed *n* sakb سكب
knife *n* sekkyneh سكّينة	lane *n* sekkeh سكّة
tuberculosis *n* sell سلّ	*n* sikket elmihrath سكّة المحراث
armament *n* silah سلاح	colter
sidearm *n* slah سلاح	rail *n* sekkeh hadid سكّة حديد
weapon *n* slah سلاح	railway *n* sekkeh hadid سكّة حديد
n silah al ketef سلاح عالكتف	*n* sakteh demagheyyeh سكتة دماغيّة
bazooka	stroke
breed *n* sulaleh سُلالة	sketch *n* skitsh سكتش
offspring *n* sulaleh سُلالة	sugar *n* sekkar سكّر
peace *n* salam سلام	glucose *n* sekkar elenib سكّر العنب
salute *n* salam سَلام	sluice *n* sakar elmay سكر المي
salutation *n* salam سَلاَم	drunk *adj* sakran سكران
safety *n* salameh سلامة	maudlin *adj* sakran سكّران
n salamet ela'qel سلامة العقل	tipsy *adj* sakran سكّران
sanity	intoxication *n* sakrah سكرة
negative *adj* salbi سلبي	secretary *n* sekrtir سكرتير
passive *adj* salbi سلبي	alcoholic *n* sekarji سكرجي
basket *n* salleh سَلّة	sexy *adj* seksi سكسي
n sallet elmuhmalat سلّة المهملات	residence *n* sakan سكن
dumpster	dwelling *n* sakan سَكَن
tortoise *n* selhfeh سلحفة	doghole *n* sakan wesekh سكن وسخ
turtle *n* selhfeh سلحفة	hush *n* skut سكوت
docile *adj* seles سلس	silence *n* skut سكوت

allowance *n* samah سماح

elssamah blddukhul السماح بالدخول

admittance *n*

fertilizer *n* samad سماد

compost *n* samad سَمَاد

manure *n* samad udwi سماد عضوي

samma طسماعة الدكتور *n* et eldektur

stethoscope

thick *n* samakeh سماكة

density *n* samakeh سماكة

intensity *n* samakeh سماكة

grocer *n* samman سمّان

grocery *n* smaneh سمانة

celestial *adj* samawi سماوي

cyan *adj* samawi سماوي

azure *n* samawi سَماوي

commissioner *n* simsar سمسار

n semsar asehum سمسار أسهم

sharebroker

sesame *n* semsem سِمْسِم

fame *n* sim'ah سمعة

notoriety *n* sem'ah sy'ah سمعة سيّئة

disrepute *n* sem'a say'a سمعة سيّئة

auditive *adj* samei سمعي

symphony *n* semfuneyyeh سمفونيّة

bleak *n* samak abyad سمك ابيض

eel *n* samak elanklis سمك الانكليس

catfish *n* samak elsallur سمك السلّور

n silseleh muttesleh سلسلة متّصلة

continuum

authority *n* sulta سلطة

salad *n* salatah سلطة

command *n* sulta سُلطَة

elsultah السّلْطَةُ التّشْرِيعيّة

legislature *n* eltashre'eyyeh

n sultah qada'eyyeh سلطة قضائيّة

judiciary

crab *n* saltaun سلطعون

commodity *n* sila'a سلعة

predecessor *n* salaf سَلَف

advance *n* slfeh سلفة

selfie *n* selfi سلفي

chord *n* silk سلك

wire *n* selk سلك

ladder *n* sullam سُلَّم

amicable *adj* silmi سلمي

pacifist *n* selmi سلمي

pacific *adj* silmi سِلْمِي

peaceable *adj* selmi سِلْمِي

pacifism *n* selmeyyeh سلميّة

intact *adj* salim سليم

poison *n* samm سم

venom *n* semm سم

bane *n* samm mumiit سم مُميت

firmament *n* sama سما

sky *n* sama سما

tip *n* senn سِنّ

cog *n* sann eddulab سنّ الدولاب

menopause *n* senn elya's سن اليأس

senator *n* sinatur سِناتُور

senatorial *adj* sinaturi سناتوري

abutment *n* sannadeh سنادة

year *n* seneh سنة

rubric *n* sunneh سُنّة

cent *n* sint سِنت

squirrel *n* senjab سنجاب

title *n* sanad mulkeyyeh سند ملكيّة

bonds *n* sanadat سَنَدات

anvil *n* sanadan سَندان

annual *adj* sanawi سنوي

yearly *adj* sanawi سنوي

wake *n* sahar سهر

easy *adj* sahl سهل

plain *n* sahl سهل

dart *n* sahem سهم

stock *n* sahm سهم

arrow *n* sahem سَهم

omission *n* sahu سهو

negligence *n* sahu سَهو

inattentive *adj* sahyan سهيان

mal *n* su' edarah سوء إدارة

administration

n su'e idarah سوء إدارة

mismanagement

perch *n* samak elfarkh سمك الفرخ

cod *n* samak elqedd سمك القُدّ

n samak elmenshar سمك المنشار

sawfish

carp *n* samak shabbut سمك شبّوط

bonefish *n* samak azmi سمك عظمي

n samak memallah سمك مملَّح

herring

fish *n* samakeh سمكة

n samen nabati سمن نباتي

margarine

adiposity *n* smneh سمنة

obesity *n* semneh سِمنة

salamander *n* samandar سمندر

Highness *n* sumwu سمّو

eminence *n* sumuu سمو

sublimity *n* sumwwu سمو

majesty *n* sumwwu سمو

marten *n* sammur سمّور

toxicity *n* semmeyyeh سمّيّة

intense *adj* smik سميك

intensive *adj* smik سميك

thick *adj* smik سميك

beefy *adj* samiin سمين

fat *adj* smin سمين

stout *adj* smin سمين

elephantine *adj* smin سمين

tooth *n* senn سنّ

n sawaq elmesklit سوّاق المسكليت
biker

n sawwaq arabeh سوّاق عربة
coachman

drive n sawwaqah سواقة

question n su'al سؤأل

superman n superman سوبرمان

saute n sutih سوتيه

melancholic adj sawdawy سَوْداوي

melancholy adj sawdawy سَوْداوي

n sawdaweyyeh سَوْداويّة
melancholia

n sawdaweyyeh سَوْداويّة
melancholy

fence n sur سور

n sur elu fatehat سور إله فتحات
battlement

weevil n suseh سوسة

mite n suseh سُوسة

market n suq سوق

mart n suq سُوق

domestic n suq mahalli سوق محلّي

vulgarity n suqeyyeh سوقية

sonnet n sunatah سوناتة

Swiss n swisri سويسري

Swiss adj swisri سويسري

bad adj 'saye سيء

terrible adj 'saye سيء

n su' iste'mal سوء استعمال
misapplication

infamy n su'e essem'a سُوء السُّمْعَة

n su' tasarruf سوء تصرُّف
malpractice

n su'e tasarruf سوء تصرُّف
misconduct

n su' taghzeyeh سوء تغذية
malnutrition

misfit n su'e taghzeyeh سوء تغذية

mal n su' twazun سوء توازن
adjustment

n su'e fahm سوء فهم
misapprehension

n su'e fahm سوء فهم
misconception

n su'e fahm سوء فهم
misunderstanding

mal- n su'e mu'amaleh سوء معاملة
treatment

both adj sawa سوا

jointly adv sawa سوا

stirrup n sewar سِوار

bracelet n swara سوارة

driver n sawwaqah سوّاق

rider n swwaq سوّاق

mahout n swwaq elfil سوّاق الفيل

sir *n* sayyed سَيِّد

mister *n* sayyed سَيِّد

v sayyed elle'beh سَيِّد اللعبة
gamemaster

missis, missus .*n* sayyedeh سَيِّدة

lady *n* sayyedeh سَيِّدة

ceramics *n* seramik سيراميك

picnic *n* siran سيران

resume *n* sireh zateyyeh سيرة ذاتيّة

omnibus *n* servis سيرفيس

circus *n* sirk سيرك

syringe *n* serang سيرنغ

syrup *n* sirub سيروب

supremacy *n* saytarah سَيطَرة

sword *n* sif سيف

cigarette *n* sikarah سيكارة

spate *n* syl سيل

torrent *n* syl سيل

flow *n* syalan سيلان

silicon *n* silikun سيليكون

scenarist *n* sinarest سيناريست

scenario *n* sinaryu سيناريو

cinema *n* sinamah سينما

adj saye' essem'a سيئ السمعة
infamous

enclosure *n* syaj سِياج

hedge *n* syaj shajr سياج شجر

tourism *n* syahah سياحة

dominion *n* siyadeh سِيادَة

lordship *n* syadeh سِيادة

n syadet eldawleh سيادة الدولة
sovereignty

automobile *n* sayyarah سيارة

car *n* sayyarah سيّارة

vehicle *n* sayyarah سيّارة

n 'sayyaret itfa سيّارة إطفاء
firetruck

n sayyara kashef سيّارة كشف
convertible

sayyarah masehubeh سيّارة مسحوبة
sidecar *n*

policy *n* siyaseh سياسة

politician *n* elsiyasi السياسي

politic *adj* syasi سياسي

political *adj* syasi سياسي

context *n* seyaq سِياق

siamese *adj* syami سيامي

cyanide *n* syanid سيانيد

cetylic *adj* sitili سيتيلي

cetin *n* sitin سيتين

cigar *n* sijar سيجار

master *n* sayyed سيِّد

senior *n* sayyed سَيِّد

adept *adj* shater شاطِر	ش
proficient *adj* shater شاطِر	
smart *n* shater شاطِر	ashen *adj* shahib شاحِب
beach *n* 'shate شاطِئ	drab *adj* shahib شاحِب
sandbank *n* shate' ramli شاطئ رملي	charger *n* shahen شاحِن
poet *n* sha'er شاعِر	truck *n* shahneh شاحنة
lyricist *n* sha'er ghena'e شاعِر غنائي	lorry *n* shahneh شَاحنة
bard *n* shaiir malahim شاعَر ملاحِم	*n* shahneh musattaha شاحنة مسطَّحة
poetess *n* sha'erah شاعِرة	flatbed
poetics *n* sha'ereyyeh شاعِريّة	wagon *n* shahenet naql شاحنة نقل
ablaze *adv* sha'el شاعِل	abnormal *adj* shazz شاذّ
aflame *adv* shael nnar شاعِل نار	anomalous *adj* shaaz شاذّ
flambé *adj* sha'el nar شاعِل نار	atypic *adj* shazz شاذّ
thankful *adj* shaker شاكر	bizarre *adj* shazz شاذّ
semblance *n* shakleh شاكِلة	freak *adj* shazz شاذّ
crutch *n* shakush شاكوش	outsize *adj* shazz شاذّ
hammer *n* shakush شاكوش	*n* shazz lelatfal شاذّ للأطفال
shawl *n* shal شال	paedophiles
n elshryan elabhar شالشريان الأبهر	emblem *n* sharah شارَة
aorta	street *n* 'share شارع
cabana *n* shaleh شاليه	bypass *n* share' farei شارع فرعي
shampoo *n* shambu شامبو	byway *n* share' farei شارع فرعي
mole *n* shameh شامة	slum *n* share' faqir شارع فقير
overall *adj* shamel شامِل	monitor *n* shasheh شاشة
comprehensive *adj* shamil شامِل	screen *n* shasheh شاشة
inclusive *adj* shamil شامِل	*n* shashet twaqquf شاشة التوقّف
witness *n* shahed شاهد	screensaver

courageous *adj* shuja'e شُجَاع

manful *adj* 'shuja شُجَاع

courage *n* shaja'a شجَاعة

hardihood *n* shaja'a شجَاعة

nerve *n* shaja'ah شجَاعة

valour *n* shaja'ah شجَاعة

bravery *n* shaja'a شجَاعة

prowess *n* shaja'ah شجَاعَة

oaktree *n* shajar elballut شجر البَلُّوط

shajar ettiin elhindi شجر التين الهندي

banyan *n*

shajr da'em شجر دائم الخَضرة

evergreen *n* elkhudrah

beech *n* shajar zaan شجر زَان

tree *n* shajarah شجرة

cedar *n* shajaret elarz شجرة الأرز

poplar *n* shajaret elhur شجرة الحور

cypress *n* shajaret essaru شجرة السرو

shrub *n* shujayrah شُجَيْرَة

beggar *n* shahhad شَحَّاد

canter *n* shahhad شَحَّاد

grease *n* shahm شحم

tallow *n* shahm شَحَم

lobe *n* shahmet elezen شحمة الأذن

shipping *n* shahn شحن

freight *n* shahen شَحْن

shipment *n* shehneh شِحْنة

paleness *n* shuhub شحوب

n shahid muhallaf شاهِد مُحلَّف

deponent

shawarma *n* shawrma شاورما

tea *n* shay شاي

snob *n* shayf haluh شايف حالَه

barbed *adj* sha'ek شائك

junior *n* shabb شبّ

young *n* shabb شبّ

youth *n* shabab شباب

February *n* shebat شباط

window *n* shebbak شبَّاك

ghost *n* shabah شبح

span *n* sheber شبر

net *n* shabakeh شبكة

network *n* shabakeh شبكة

web *n* shabakeh شبكة

n shabaket elmajari شبكة المجاري

sewerage

shabakeh kharejeyyeh شبكة خارجيّة

extranet *n*

n shabakeyyet eleyn شبكيّة العين

retina

n shebh menheref شِبْه مُنْحَرِف

trapezoid

akin *adj* shbih شبيه

double *n* shabih شَبِيه

winter *n* sheteh شتي

brave *adj* 'shujaa شُجَاع

n shakhes a'mmi شخص عامِّي

commoner

n shakhes ghabi شخص غبي

bonehead

n shakhes klasiki شخص كلاسيكي

classic

n shakhes mashi شخص ماشي

pedestrian

n shakhes metanniq شخص مُتَأنِّق

dandy

shakhes شخص متزوج تنتين

bigamist n metzawwej tentiin

shakhes شخص متعِّصب قوميًّا

n muta'assib qawmeyyan

chauvinist

n shakhes metfahhim شخص متفهِّم

bottler

n shakhes muhafez شخص محافظ

conservative

n shakhes mustabbed شخص مستبّد

autocrat

n shakhes mashehur شخص مشهور

celebrity

shakhes شخص مهووس كتُب

bookish n mahwwus ketub

n shakhes wahmi شخص وهمي

dummy

personal adj shakhsi شَخْصِي

scrawl n shakhbatah شخبطة

somebody n shakhes شخص

someone pron shakhes شخص

person n shakhes شخص

shakhes شخص ارستقراطي

aristocrat n arustuqrati

n elshakhes elarabi الشخص العربي

Arab

n elshakhes elmayyet الشخص الميِّت

dead

shakhs شخص بشتغل بالإيدتين سوا

n beshteghel bil'idteyn suwa

ambidexter

adder n sakhs byzeed شخص يزيد

n 'shakhes tabe شخص تابع

dependant

shakhes janen شخص جانن جنونه

beserker n jununu

barnacle n 'shakhes debe شخص دبق

n shakhes rasmali شخص رأسمالي

capitalist

n shakhes rakhu شخص رخُو

butterfingers

n shakhes reyaddi شخص رياضيّ

athlete

n shakhes tamuh شخص طَموح

aspirant

caption *n* shareh شرح

commentary *n* shareh شرح

explanation *n* shareh شرح

illustration *n* sharh شرح

n sharh belsuwar شرح بالصور

depiction

shareh betreqah شرح بطريقة تانية

paraphrase *n* tanyeh

slice *n* sharha شرحَة

haggard *adj* sheres شرِس

quarrelsome *adj* sheres شَرِس

ferocious *adj* shares شَرِس

condition *n* shart شرط

term *n* shart شرط

prerequisite *n* shart شَرْط

requirement *n* shart شَرْط

stipulation *n* shart شَرْط

police *n* shurtah شرطَة

policeman *n* shurti شرطي

conditional *adj* sharti شَرطي

legal *adj* shar'i شرعي

legitimate *adj* shar'ei شَرْعي

legitimacy *n* shar'eyyeh شَرْعيّة

legality *n* shar'eyyeh شَرْعيّة

grace *n* sharaf شرَف

honour *n* sharaf شرَف

east *n* sharq شرق

east *adj* sharq شرق

character *n* shakhseyyeh شخصيّة

personality *n* shakhseyyeh شخصيّة

n shakhseyyeh barzeh شخصيّة بارزة

personage

n shakhseyyeh kbireh شخصيّة كبيرة

magnate

snore *n* shekhir شخير

intensity *n* sheddeh شدّة

abnormalcy *n* shuzuz شذوذ

abnormality *n* shuzuz شذوذ

anomaly *n* shuzuz شذوذ

irregularity *n* shuzuz شُذُوذ

perversity *n* shuzuz شُذُوذ

n elshuzuz lelatfal الشذوذ للأطفال

paedophilia

n shuzuzi lelatfal شذوذي للأطفال

paedophiliac

evil *n* sharr شرّ

buyer *n* sharra شَرَأ

drink *n* shrab شراب

spark *n* shararah شرارة

bedding *n* sharshif شراشف

sail *n* 'shera شِرَاع

partnership *n* sharakeh شراكة

n shrb alkhamr شرب الخمر

alcoholism

anus *n* sharj شرج

anal *adj* sharji شرجي

partner n shrik شريك	orient n elsharq الشَّرق
n shrik mutadamin شريك متضامن	mouthful n sharqah شرقَة
copartner	sip n sharqah شرقَة
adj shatt elbaher شط البحر	oriental n elsharqi الشرقي
beachside	eastern adj sharqi شرقي
proficiency n shatarah شطارة	oriental adj sharqi شَرقي
bidet n shattafeh شطّافة	agnosticism n sherk شرك
chess n shatranj شطرنج	polytheism n sherk شرك
shive n shazeyyh شظيّة	company n sharikeh شركة
splinter n shazeyyeh شظيّة	firm n sherkeh شركة
motto n she'ar شعار	carrier n sherkit naqel شركة نقل
slogan n she'ar شعار	polytheistic adj sherki شركي
beam n 'shuaa شُعاع	bitch n sharmuta شرموطة
radius n 'shu'a شُعَاع	courtesan n sharmutah شرموطة
ritual adj sha'ayri شعائري	chrysalis n sharnaqah شرنقَة
liturgical adj sha'yri شَعَائري	bulimia n sharah شرَه
folk n sha'b شعب	abstraction n shrood شرود
offshoot n shu'beh شعبة	purchase n shereh شري
folk adj sha'bi شعبي	artery n sheryan شريان
hair n sha'er شعر	bibber n sharriib شرّيب
poesy n sha'er شعْر	evil adj sherrir شرير
poetry n she'ri شعْر	nefarious adj sherrir شريّر
verse n she'r شعْر	strip n shrit شريط
shaer kasir khishin شعر قصير خشن	tape n shrit شريط
bristle n	lacy adj shariti شريطى
n shaer mejaddal شعر مجدَّل	honest adj sharif شريف
dreadlock	associate n sharik شريك
poetic adj she'ri شعري	mate n shrik شريك

lip n sheffeh شِفَة	capillary adj sha'ri شَعري
blade n shafra شَفرة	lattice n sa'reyyeh شَعريّة
razor n shafret hlaqah شفرة حلاقة	sorcery n sha'wazeh شَعوَذة
twilight n shafaq شفق	feeling n shu'ur شعور
pathos n shafaqah شَفَقَة	sensation n shu'ur شُعور
pity n shafaqah شَفَقَة	sentiment n shu'ur شُعور
labial adj shafahi شفهي	sensational adj shu'uri شعوري
oral adj shafahi شفهي	barley n sha'ir شعير
orally adv shafahyyan شفهياً	malt n sh'ir byrah شعير البيرا
cleft n seqq شقّ	rite n sha'irah شعيرة
tear n shaqq شقّ	fray n shaghab شغب
fissure n sheqq شقّ	riot n shaghab شغب
misery n shaqah شقا	turbulence n shaghab شغب
shard n sheqfeh شقفة	sedition n shaghab شَغَب
adv shiqfeh shiqfeh شقفة شقفة	function n shughl شغل
asunder	job n sheghl شغل
somersault n shaqlabeh شقلبة	labour n sheghl شغل
migraine n shaqiqah شَقيقَة	work n shughul شغل
doubt n shakk شك	handicraft n shughl eyd شغل إيد
scepticism n shakk شك	handiwork n shughl eyd شغل إيد
misgiving n shakk شَك	shughul ghir qanuni شغل غير قانوني
mistrust n shakk شَك	crookery n
sceptic n shakkak شكّاك	sheghul men شغل من قفا الكيف
sceptical adj shakkak شكّاك	bungle n qafa elkif
prick n shakkeh شكّة	labourer n shaghghil شغيل
thanks n shukran شكراً	functionary n shaghghil شَغّيل
form n shakel شكل	transparent adj shaffaf شفّاف
look n shakl شكل	lucent adj shaffaf شفّاف

umbrella *n* shamseyyeh شمسيّة	shape *n* shakel شكل
wax *n* 'shame شمع	*n* shakel baydawi شكل بيضاوي
candle *n* 'shama شمعة	ellipse
crone *n* shimmeqrin شمقرين	*n* beshakel msannan شكل مسنّن
olfactory *adj* shammi شمّي	pointedness
n shanati elsafar شناتي السفر	shakluh metel شكلُه متل المكعّب
luggage	cubiform *adj* elmuka'ab
case *n* shanta شنتَا	complaint *n* shakweh شكوِة
n shantayt daher شنتاية ظهر	cascade *n* shallal شلّال
rucksack	waterfall *n* shallal شلّال
satchel *n* shantah شنتة	falls *n* shallal شَلّال
meteor *n* shihab شهَاب	skein *n* shelleh شلّة
meteoric *adj* shihabi شهابي	palsy *n* shalal شَلَل
affidavit *n* shahadeh شهادة	paralysis *n* shalal شَلَل
certificate *n* shahadeh شهادة	shilling *n* shelen شلِن
testimonial *n* shahadeh شهادة	scent *v* shamm شَمّ
testimony *n* shahadeh شهادة	gloat *n* shamateh شماتة
n shahd elasal شهد العسل	*n* shammas elkaniseh شمّاس الكنيسة
honeycomb	beadle
month *n* shaher شهر	*n* shammas elkniseh شمّاس الكنيسة
n shahr elasal شهر العسل	deacon
honeymoon	north *n* shmal شمال
repute *n* shuhrah شهرة	north *adj* shmali شمالي
popularity *n* shuhrah شهرَة	northerly *adj* shmali شمالي
reputation *n* shuhrah شُهْرَة	northern *adj* shmali شمالي
monthly *adj* shahri شهري	chimpanzee *n* shambanzi شبانزي
magnanimous *adj* shahem شَهْم	sun *n* shams شمس
appetent *adj* shahwani شهواني	solar *adj* shamsi شمسي

craving n shuq شُوق	lustful adj shahwani شهواني
thistle n shuk شوك	lusty adj shahwani شهواني
chocolate n shukula شوكولا	voluptuary n shahwani شهواني
beet n shawandar شوندر	voluptuous adj shahwani شهواني
shu'un elmuwazafin شؤون الموظفين	sensual adj shahwani شَهْواني
personnel n	sensualist n shahwani شَهْواني
few adj shway شوي	sensuality n shahwaneyyeh شَهْوانِيّة
lightly adv shwai شوي	appetence n shahweh شهوة
slight adj shwayy شويّ	lust n shahweh شهوة
some adj shwayyeh شويّة	n shahweh jinseyyeh شهوة جنسِيّة
little adv shwayyeh شويّة	fetishism
object n shi شي	appetite n shayyeh شهِيّة
thing n shi شي	martyr n shahid شهِيد
n shi belfet ennazar شي بلفت النظر	sob n shahiq شهِيق
eyecatcher	whisker n shwareb شوارب
cheater n shi mezayyaf شي مزيَّف	moustache n shawarib شوارِب
exhibit n shi ma'rud شي معروض	mustache n shawarib شَوَارِب
gnarl n shi ma'kud شي معقود	soup n shurba شُورَبَا
n sheikh qabeleh شيخ قَبيلِة	n shurabah desmeh شوربة دسمة
chieftain	bisque
senility n shikhukhah شَيْخُوخَة	shorts n pl shurt شورت
senile adj shikhukhi شيخوخي	stroke n shut شوط
devil n shitan شيطان	oat n shufan شوفان
tempter n shitan شيْطان	adj shufan matehun شوفان مطحون
satan n shitan شَيْطان	oatmeal
infernal adj shitani شيْطاني	snobbery n shufet elhal شوفة الحال
satanic adj shitani شَيْطاني	chauffeur n shufir شوفير
chef n shifra شيف	longing n shuq شَوْق

n sahib eldekkanh صاحب الدكّانة

shopowner

n sahib elrukhsah صاحب الرخصة

licensee

n sahib elrahn صاحب الرهن

mortgagor

n saheb elsa'adeh صاحب السعادة

excellency

n saheb elshughul صاحب الشغل

employer

banker n sahib bank صاحب بنك

dreamer n sahin hlem صاحب حلم

n saheb mehneh صاحب مهنة

apprentice

n sahib nazareyyeh صاحب نظريّة

theorist

adj sahi men enum صاحي من النوم

awake

truthful adj sadeq صادق

rocket n sarukh صاروخ

missile n sarukh صاروخ

clear adj safi صافي

net n safi صافي

net adj safi صافي

auditorium n saleh صالة

hall n saleh صالة

n salet elistiqbal صالة الإستقبال

parlour

cypher n shifra شيفرة

cipher n shifra شيفرَة

cheque n shik شيك

n shil eluksijin شيل الأكسجين

deoxidation

shil men شيل من قائمة المجرمين

n qaement elmejrmin

decriminalization

communist n shiuei شيوعي

communism n shiueyeh شيوعيّة

ص

soap n sabun صابون

soapy adj sabuni صابُوني

sahib n sahib صاحب

pal n sahib صاحِب

bawd n sahib صاحِب

intimate adj sahib صاحِب

n saheb elemtihan صاحب الامتحان

examiner

n sahin enjaz صاحب الانجاز

achiever

n 'sahib eltawqi صاحب التوقيع

signatory

n saheb eldekkaneh صاحب الدكّانة

shopkeeper

morning *n* elsubh الصبح

patience *n* sabr صبر

adj elsabata'sh الصبطاعش
seventeenth

tincture *n* sabghah صَبْغَة

tint *n* sabghah صَبْغَة

patient *adj* sabur صبور

boy *n* sabi صبي

brat *n* sabi صبي

lad *n* sabi صَبي

boyish *adj* sibyani صبيانيّ

puerile *adj* sibyani صبياني

lass *n* sabeyyeh صَبيّة

correct *adj* sahh صحّ

True *adj* sahh صحّ

journalism *n* sahafeh صحافة

press *n* sahafeh صحافة

companion *n* suhbeh صُحبة

health *n* sahhah صحة

desert *n* sahrah صحرا

journalist *n* sahafi صحفي

dish *n* sahn صحن

plate *n* sahn صحن

healthy *adj* sihhi صحّي

sanitary *adj* sehhi صحّي

hygienic *adj* sihhi صحّي

n sahayan men enum صحيان من النوم
awakening

valid *adj* saleh صالح

viable *adj* salih صالح

meritorious *adj* salih صالح

reverent *adj* salih صالح

edible *adj* saleh lelakel صالح للأكل

adj saleh lelzera'a صالح للزراعة
arable

adj saleh lelzwaj صالح للزواج
marriageable

adj saleh lelsakan صالح للسكن
inhabitable

saloon *n* salun صالون

silent *adj* samit صامت

staunch *adj* samed صامد

maker *n* 'sane صانع

n sane' elsufun صانع السُّفُن
shipbuilder

n sane' elfakhkhar صانع الفخّار
potter

glassmaker *n* sane' ballur صانع بلّور

advisable *adj* sayib صايب

goldsmith *n* sayegh صايغ

jeweller *n* sayegh صايغ

foundry *n* sabb صبّ

boyhood *n* siba صبا

cactus *n* sabbar صبّار

dye *n* sbagh صبَاغ

am *abbr* elssubh الصبح

echo n sadah صدى

chum n sadiq hamim صديق حميم

openly adv sarahah صراحةً

candour n saraha صَراحة

tussle n 'sera صِراع

bundle n serrah صرّة

scream n sarkhah صرخة

cockroach n sarsur صرصور

cicada n sarsur ellil صرصور الليل

cricket n sarsur ellil صرصور الليل

epilepsy n 'sara صَرْع

din n sar'a صرعَة

craze n sar'ah صَرْعَة

vogue n sar'ah صَرْعَة

morphology n sarf صرْف

sewage n sarf sehhi صرف صحي

drainage n sarf sehhi صرف صحّي

explicit adj sarih صريح

frank adj sarih صريح

plain adj sarih صريح

candid adj sarih صَريح

outspoken adj sarih صَريح

shout n srikh صريخ

squeak n sarir صرير

creak n sarir صَرير

prodigal adj sarrif صرّيف

sixteenth adj elsitta'esh الصطّاعش

difficult adj saeb صعب

n sahifeh yumeyyeh صحيفة يوميّة daily

rock n sakher صخر

boulder n sakher kbir صخر كبير

obstruction n sadd صدّ

repulse n sadd صدّ

rust n 'sada صدأ

oxide n 'sada صدأ

beforehand adv sadarah صدارة

waistcoat n saddarah صدّارة

amity n sadaqa صداقة

chest n sader صدر

thorax n sadr صَدْر

vest n sedreyyeh صدريّة

crack n 'sade صدع

fracture n 'sade صَدْع

cotemporal adj sidghi صدغي

serendipity n sedfeh صدفة

conch n sadafeh صَدَفة

shell n sedfeh صَدَفة

n sedfeh helweh صدفة حلوة godsend

oyster adj sadafi صدفي

honesty n sedq صدق

truth n sedq صدق

benevolence n sadaqa صَدَقة

dole n sadaqah صَدَقَة

shock n sadmeh صدمة

transaction n safqah صفقة

deal n safaqah صفقَة

buy n 'safqet shiraa صفقة شراء

scrotum n safan صَفَن

plate n safiha صفيحة

sheet n safiha صَفِيحة

falcon n saqr صَقْر

hawk n saqr صَقْر

accipitral adj saqri صقري

deed n sakk صكّ

prayer n salah صلاة

goodness n salah صَلاَح

jurisdiction n salaheyyeh صَلاَحِيّة

concrete adj selb صلب

solid adj salb صلب

rigid adj salb صلْب

backbone n solb صُلب

bond n silah صِلَة

liaison n silah صِلَة

clay n silsal صلصال

crucifix n salib صَلِيب

rood n salib صَلِيب

valve n sammam صمّام

clam n samt صمت

acacia n samgh صمغ

mucilage n samgh صمغ

n simlakh eleden صملاخ الإدن

cerumen

hard adj sa'eb صعب

strenuous adj sa'eb صَعْب

adj saeb tahamulu صعب تحمُّله

burdensome

difficulty n su'ubeh صعوبة

ascent n suood صُعُود

minor adj saghir صغير

small adj seghir صغير

tiny adj seghir صغير

grade n saff صفّ

line n saff صفّ

tier n saff صفّ

array n saff صَفّ

class n saff صَفّ

row n saff صَفّ

lucidity n 'safa صفاء

yolk n safar elbeid صفار البيض

siren n inzar saffaret صفّارِة إنذار

adjective n sifa صفة

n sifa mumayazeh صفة مميزة

attribute

pardon n safeh صفح

page n safha صَفْحة

safhet صفحة مؤلفات الكاتب

bibliography n mualafat elkatib

nil n sefer صفر

nought n sefer صفر

zero n sefr صفر

sound *n* suwt صوت	صُمون طويل sammoun tawil *n*
voice *n* sut صوت	baguette
hoot *n* sut elbum صوت البوم	core *n* samim صميم
bleat *n* sut elkharuf صوت الخروف	hook *n* sinnarah صنّارة
grunt *n* sut elkhenzir صوت الخنزير	gig *n* sinnaret sid صنّارة صيد
gobble *n* sut eddik صوت الديك	industry *n* sina'ah صناعة
drumbeat *n* sut eltabl صوت الطبل	صناعة الفَخّار sina'et elfakhkhar *n*
sut elkitroni aali صوت الكتروني عالي	pottery
blip *n*	industrial *adj* sina'e صناعي
baritone *n* saut jahuri صوت جَهوري	stench *n* sanneh صِنّة
falsetto *n* sut ali صوت عالي	sandal *n* sandal صندَل
acoustic *adj* sawtti صوتي	box *n* sinduq صندوق
phonetic *adj* sawti صوتي	case *n* sanduq صندوق
sonic *adj* suwti صوتي	crate *n* sinduq صندوق
vocal *adj* sawti صوتي	صندوق رمل sanduq raml *n*
acoustics *n* sawteyat صوتيات	sandbox
image *n* surah صورة	cubby *n* sinduq seghir صندوق صغير
photo *n* surah صورة	sandwich *n* sindwisheh صندويشة
picture *n* surah صورة	make *n* 'sune صُنْع
photograph *v* surah صورة	category *n* senef صنف
صُورةُ أَشِعّة suret ashe'ah *n*	pine *n* sanubar صنوبر
radiogram	fusion *n* sahr صَهر
surah sghereh *n* صورة صغيرة	cistern *n* sahrij صهريج
miniature	reservoir *n* sahrij صهريج
surah tebq elasel صورة طبق الأصل	tank *n* sahrij صهريج
fac-simile *n*	neigh *n* sahil elhasn صهيل الحصان
sura falakeyeh *n* صورة فلكيّة	advisability *n* swab صواب
constellation	vote *n* sut صوت

shoot n syd صيد

dib n sid belsinnarah صيد بالصنّارة

adj saydalani صَيْدَلاني
pharmaceutic

pharmaceutist n saydalani صَيْدَلاني

pharmacist n saydalani صَيْدَلاني

druggist n saydali صيدلي

pharmaceutical adj saydali صَيْدَلي

pharmacy n saydaleyyeh صيدليّة

form n sheghah صيغة

formula n sheghah صِيغَة

n sighet ta'ajjub صيغَةُ تعجّب
interjection

summer n syf صيف

aestival adj syfi صيفي

China n elsin الصين

tray n seneyyeh صينيّة

ض

suburb n dahyh ضاحِيَة

striker n darib ضارب

n darib elmadrab ضارب المضرب
batsman

fog n dabab ضباب

smog n dabab ضَبَاب

foggy adj dababi ضبابي

n surah lilaweyeh صورة للأوعية
angiogram

n surah mezalleleh صورة مظلّلة
silhouette

chick n sus صوص

wool n suf صوف

fleece n suf elkharuf صوف الخروف

sofa n sufayeh صوفاية

mystic n sufi صوفيّ

mace n sulajan صولجان

sceptre n sulajan صولجان

monastery n suma'ah صومعة

bawl v siyah صياح

outcry n syah صِياح

huntsman n essayyad الصيّاد

fisherman n sayyad صيّاد

sayyad bla rukhsah صيّاد بلا رخصة
poacher n

fowler n sayyad asafir صيّاد عصافير

n sayyad klab صيّاد كلاب
dogcatcher

phraseology n syaghah صِياغَة

fast n syam صيام

maintenance n syaneh صيانة

celebrity n sit صيت

renown n sit صِيت

hunt n syd صيد

hunter n syd صيد

mammoth *adj* dakhm ضَخْم

bulky *adj* dakhem ضخم

adj dedd elhariq ضدّ الحريق

fireproof

antipodes *n* dhuddin ضدّين

n dareb ibreh ضرب الإبرة

injection

eldareb belkhizaran الضرب بالخيزران

caning *n*

hit *n* darbeh ضربة

strike *n* darbeh ضربة

darbeh biqafa eleyed ضربة بقفا الإيد

backhand *n*

n darbeh qadeyeh ضربة قاضية

deathblow

slap *n* darbet kaff ضربة كفّ

damage *n* darar ضَرَر

disadvantage *n* darar ضَرَر

molar *n* ders ضِرْس

wisdom- *n* ders elaqel ضرس العقل

tooth

necessity *n* darurah ضرورة

necessary *adj* daruri ضروري

persistent *adj* daruri ضروري

prerequisite *adj* daruri ضَرُورِي

excise *n* darebeh ضريبة

tax *n* darebeh ضريبة

scot *n* daribeh ضَرِيبَة

misty *adj* dababi ضَبَابِي

adjustment *n* dabt ضبط

self- *n* dabt elnafs ضبط النفس

control

hyaena, hyena *n* 'dabe ضَبُع

babel *n* dajjeh ضجّة

clamour *n* dajjeh ضجّة

pandemonium *n* dajjeh ضجّة

fuss *n* dajjeh ضجّة

displeasure *n* dajar ضَجَر

laugh *n* dehkeh ضحكة

laughter *n* dehkeh ضحكة

forenoon *n* dahweh ضَحْوة

victim *n* daheyyeh ضحيّة

offering *n* daheyyeh ضحيّة

pump *n* dakhkh ضخّ

giantess *n* dakhameh ضخامة

bulk *n* dakhameh ضخامة

immensity *n* dakhmeh ضخامة

magnitude *n* dakhameh ضخامة

n dakhamet elras ضخامة الراس

bighead

enormous *adj* dakhem ضخم

huge *adj* dakhem ضخم

sizable *adj* dakhm ضخم

voluminous *adj* dakhem ضخم

massy *adj* dakhem ضخم

immense *adj* dakhm ضَخْم

strand *n* dafrah ضفرة

braid *n* dafra ضفرَة

cue *n* dafrah ضفرَة

rib *n* 'del ضِلع

costal *adj* dilei ضلعي

annexation *n* damm ضَم

assurance *n* daman ضمان

guarantee *n* daman ضمان

warrant *n* damaneh ضَمانة

atrophy *n* dumur ضُمور

conscience *n* damir ضمير

pronoun *n* damir ضَمير

light *n* daww ضوّ

n daww ettakhit ضوّ التخت

bedlamp

shine *n* daww elshams ضوّ الشمس

n daww elkamirah ضوّ الكاميرا

flashbulb

n daww elmasrah ضوّ المسرح

limelight

daylight *n* daww ennehar ضوّ النهار

gleam *n* daww da'ef ضوّ ضعيف

n daww kashshaf ضوّ كشّاف

searchlight

suburban *adj* dawahi ضواحي

hubbub *n* dujeh ضوجِة

loss *n* 'daya ضياع

hospitality *n* dyafeh ضيافة

tithe *n* darebet elusher ضريبة العشر

n darebeh zyadeh ضريبة زيادة

supertax

n darebeh zyadeh ضريبة زيادة

surtax

mausoleum *n* darih ضريح

multiple *n* de'f ضعف

weakness *n* de'f ضعف

debility *n* daef ضَعف

double *n* de'f ضَعف

impotence *n* de'f jinsi ضَعْفٌ جِنْسِي

myopia *n* de'f nazr ضعف نظر

twofold *adj* de'fin ضعفين

debile *adj* da'if ضعيف

feeble *adj* da'ef ضعيف

tenuous *adj* da'ef ضعيف

weak *adj* de'if ضعيف

adj da'ef elnazar ضعيف النظر

myopic

purblind *n* da'ef nazar ضعيف النظر

depression *n* daghet ضغط

pressure *n* daghet ضغط

n daghet eldamm ضغط الدمّ

tension

n daghet sughl ضغط شغل

overwork

bank *n* diffeh ضِفّة

frog *n* 'defda ضفدع

tyrant *n* taghi طاغي

despot *n* tagheyeh طاغِيَة

oppressor *n* tagheyh طاغِيَة

natant *adj* tafi طافي

crew *n* taqim طاقِم

aigrette *n* taqyeh طاقَة

hood *n* taqeyyeh طاقِيَة

ta'eh suf طاقية صوف للراس والرقبة

balaclava *n* lelras welraqabeh

leghorn *n* taqeyyeh qash طاقِيَة قش

student *n* taleb طالَب

pupil *n* talib طالِب

n taleb jame'y طالِب جامعي

undergraduate

table *n* tawleh طاوِلة

peacock *n* tawwus طاوُوس

peahen *n* tawwuseh طاووسة

cormorant *n* taer elghaq طائر الغاق

aloft *adv* tayir bil aali طاير بالعالي

adj tayer mn elfarah طاير من الفرح

overjoyed

clumsy *adj* tayesh طايِش

daredevil *adj* tayesh طايِش

impetuous *adj* tayesh طايِش

injudicious *adj* tayesh طايِش

stray *adj* taysh طايش

stray *n* taysh طايش

medicine *n* tebb طبّ

village *n* de'ah ضيعة

hamlet *n* de'a ضيعَة

villager *n* de'aji ضيعجي

guest *n* dif ضيف

angina *n* dhiq tanaffus ضيق النَفَس

distress *n* diqah ضيقَة

ط

ball *n* tabeh طابة

football *n* tabeh طابة

stamp *n* 'tabe طابَع

printer *n* tabe'ah طابعة

storey *n* tabeq طابِق

n tabeq wasat طابِق وسط

mezzanine

file *n* tabur طابُور

molar *adj* tahin طاحن

windmill *n* tahuneh طاحونة

grinder *n* tahuneh طاحونة

mill *n* tahuneh طاحُونة

treadmill *n* tahuneh طاحُونة

tumbler *n* taseh طاسِة

adherence *n* ta'a طاعة

obedience *n* ta'ah طاعة

compliance *n* ta'a طاعَة

plague *v* ta'un طاعون

natural *adj* tabe'i طبيعي

spleen *n* tehal طِحَال

alga *n* tahalib طحالب

miller *n* tahhan طَحّان

moss *n* tuhlub طُحْلُب

crunch *n* tahen طَحْن

flour *n* tehin طحين

n tehin shufan طحين الشوفان

oatmeal

tenderness *n* taraweh طَرَاوة

glee *n* tarab طَرَب

estragon *n* tarkhun طرخون

dismissal *n* tard طرد

package *n* tard طَرْد

parcel *n* tard طَرْد

adj tard markazi طرد مركزي

centrifugal

verge *n* taraf طَرَف

collision *n* tarqa طرقَة

beat *n* tarqa طَرقَة

tap *n* tarqah طَرْقَة

knock *v* tarqah طَرْقَة

soft *n* tari طري

approach *n* tariq طريق

path *n* tariq طريق

road *n* tariq طريق

route *n* tariq طريق

way *n* tariq طريق

n tebb elasnan طبّ الأسنان

odontology

tebb elamrad طب الأمراض العصبيّة

neurology *n* elmusta'seyeh

psychiatry *n* tebb nafsi طب نفسي

cook *n* tabbakh طَبّاخ

chalk *n* tabshurah طبشورَة

print *n* 'tabe طبع

temper *n* 'tabe طَبْع

mint *n* tabe' el'emleh طبع العملة

n tabaq elfenjan طبق الفنجان

saucer

ufo *n* tabaq tayer طبق طاير

predicament *n* tabaqah طبقة

layer *n* tabaqah طبقة

stratum *n* tabaqah طَبَقة

n tabaqah ejtimaeyeh طبقة اجتماعيّة

caste

n tabaqet eluzun طبقة الأوزون

ozone layer

n tabaqt elfallahin طبقة الفلاحين

peasantry

drumfish *n* tableh طبلة

bulldog *n* tabanjeh طبنجة

n tubughrafya طبوغرافيا

topography

medical *adj* tebbi طبّي

nature *n* tabe'ah طبيعة

n tefrah weratheyyeh طفرة وراثيّة mutation	alley n tariq khalfi طريق خلفي
infant n tefl طفل	highway n 'tariq sare طريق سريع
kid n tefl طفل	dead- n tariq masdud طريق مسدود end
child n tefil طفل	n tariq masdud طريق مسدود impasse
cherub n 'tefil bare طفل بريء	
bantling n tefel zeghir طفل زغير	n tariq mumahhad طريق معبَّد causeway
tefl meshawwah طفل مشوَّه الخلقة oaf n elkhulqah	manner n tariqah طريقة
childhood n tufuleh طفولة	method n tareqah طريقة
infancy n tufuleh طُفُولة	technique n tareqah طريقَة
childish adj tufuli طفولي	tariqet bril طريقة بريل للقراءة braille n lelqera'a
infantile adj tufuli طفولي	
venial adj tafif طفيف	basin n tesht طشت
petty adj tafif طَفِيف	savour n ta'm طعم
crasher n tufayli طُفَيلي	graft n tu'em طُعم
parasite n tufayli طُفَيلي	n tuem lelmasyadeh طُعم للمصيدة bait
crepitation n taqq طَقّ	
weather n taqs طقس	taste n ta'meh طعمة
clack n taqtaqah طقطَقَة	stab n te'neh طعنة
n taqm elttayara طقم الطيارة aircrew	lunge n ta'neh طَعْنة
	skip n taffeh طقّة
divorce n talaq طلاق	superabundance n tafah طفح
quest n talab طلب	rash n tafah jeldi طفح جلدي
request n talab طلب	replete adj tafhan طفحان
application n talab طَلَب	superabundant adj tafhan طفحان
demand n talab طَلَب	averse adj tafraan طفران

torpedo *n* turbid طُورْبيد	*n* tulue' elfajer طلوع الفجر
turbine *n* turbin طوربين	breakneck
voluntary *adj* tu'i طوعي	dawnlight *n* tulue elfajr طلوع الفجر
flood *n* tufan طوفان	*n* tlu'e an essekkeh طلوع عن السكّة
cataclysm *n* tufan طوفَان	derailment
necklace *n* tuq طوق	fluent *adj* taliq طليق
necklet *n* tuq طوق	avid *adj* 'tammaa طمّاع
tuq men eshshurtah طوق من الشرطة	greedy *adj* 'tamma طمّاع
cordon *n*	desirous *adj* tamma'e طَمّاع
height *n* tul طول	obliteration *n* tams طمس
length *n* tul طول	greed *n* 'tama طمع
over *adv* tul طول	avidity *adv* 'tamaa طَمَع
strength *n* tul طول	cupidity *n* tama'e طَمَع
overnight *adv* tul ellil طول الليل	ambitious *adj* tamuh طموح
fold *n* taweyeh طوية	ambition *n* tumuh طُموح
foldup *adj* tawyeh طوية	aspiration *n* tumuh طُموح
tall *adj* tawil طويل	ton *n* tenn طنّ
pilot *n* tayyar طيّار	twelfth *adj* eltna'esh الطناعش
aviator *n* tayyar طيّار	cart *n* tunbur طُنبُر
aircraft *n* tayara طيارة	buzz *n* tantaneh طَنْطَنة
aeroplane *n* tyyara طيّارة	drone *n* tantaneh طَنْطَنة
aerocraft *n* tyyara طيّارة	clink *n* tanin طنين
plane *n* tayyarah طيَّارة	*n* tawabe' barideyyeh طوابع بريديّة
airbus *n* tayara ayrbas طيارة ايرباص	postage
tyyara bdun tayyar طيّارة بدون طيّار	emergency *n* 'taware طوارئ
aerobot *n*	voluntarily *adv* tawa'eyyeh طواعيّة
jet *n* tayyarah nafatheh طيَّارة نفَّاثة	adobe *n* tubeh طوبة
kite *n* tayyarah waraq طيّارة ورق	brick *n* tubeh طوبِة

circumstance *n* zaref ظرف

envelope *n* zarf ظرف

adverbial *adj* zrffi ظرفي

circumstantial *adj* zarfi ظرفي

gallant *n* elzarif الظريف

elegant *adj* zarif ظريف

gallant *adj* zarif ظريف

shade *n* zell ظلّ

tangent *n* zell ظلّ

persecution *n* zulm ظلم

shadowy *adj* zalil ظليل

surmise *n* zann ظنّ

distrust *n* zann ظَنّ

back *n* zaher ظهر

midday *n* zuher ظهر

noon *n* zaher ظهر

n dahr elsafineh ظهر السفينة

shipboard

dorsal *adj* zahri ظهري

zuhur la awwal marrah ظهور لأوّل مرّة

debutant *n* marrah

ع

overboard *adv* a janab ع جنب

adj a shakil qalib ع شكل قلب

cordate

daredevil *n* tayasheh طياشة

bighearted *adj* tayyeb طيّب

tasteful *adj* tayyeb طيّب

luscious *adj* tayyeb طيّب

dodo *n* tir eldudu طير الدودو

aviation *n* tayaran طيران

flight *n* tayaran طيران

takeoff *n* tayaran طيّران

ass *n* teyz طيز

impetuosity *n* tish طيش

argil *n* teyn طين

mire *n* tyn طين

slime *n* tyn طين

mud *n* tyn طين

lute *n* tyn طين

ظ

brutal *adj* zalim ظالم

distinct *adj* zaher ظاهر

phenomenon *n* zaherah ظاهرة

antelope *n* zabi ظبي

deer *n* zabi ظبي

elk *n* zabi ظبي

doe *n* zabyeh ظبية

elegance *n* zarafeh ظرافة

adverb *n* zrf ظرف

عارضة ضخمة n a'redah dakhmeh	ع ظهر الصفحة a zahr elsafha adv
crossbeam	overleaf
عازب single adj azib	عابد worshipper n a'bed
عازبة bachelorette n a'azebeh	عابر ephemeral adj a'ber
عازِف performer n azef	عابِر ephemeric adj a'ber
عازِف instrumentalist n azef	عابِس morose adj a'bes
عازف المزمار n aazif mezmaar	عاج ivory n aaj
bagpiper	عاجِز cripple n ajiz
عازف بيانو pianist n azef byanu	عاجِز helpless adj aajiz
عازف كمان violinist n azef kaman	عاجِز incapable adj ajez
عازف منفرد n azef menfered	عاجِز infirm adj a'jez
soloist	عاجِز invalid n ajez
عازِل insulator n azel	عاجز جنسياً adj a'jez jinseyyan
العاشر tenth adj elasher	impotent
عاشِق philanderer n a'sheq	عادةً usually adv adeh
عاصِف windy adj asef	عادة habit n adeh
عاصِف boisterous adj aasif	عادة norm n a'deh
عاصِف stormy adj a'sef	عادِل fair adj adel
عاصِف tempestuous adj a'sef	عادي normal adj a'di
عاصفة storm n asfeh	عادي ordinary adj a'di
عاصفة tempest n a'sfeh	عادي usual adj adi
عاصفة ثلجِيّة n asefeh thaljeyyeh	عادي standard adj adi
blizzard	عار discredit v aar
عاصفة رملِيّة n asfeh ramleyyeh	عارِض casual adj ared
sandstorm	عارضة girder n ardah
عاصِمة metropolis n a'semeh	عارضة goalpost n ardah
عاصِمة capital n asemeh	عارِضة crossbar n a'redah
عاصِي mutinous adj a'si	

ecologist *n* aalim bi'a عالم بيئة

theologian *n* a'lem dini عالم ديني

n a'lem ryaddeyyat عالم رياضيَّات

mathematician

alem tabaqat عالم طبقات الأرض

geologist *n* elard

ornithologist *n* a'lem tyur عالم طيور

astronomer *n* aalem falak عالم فَلَك

n aalem ketub عالم كتب

bibliographer

logician *n* alem mateq عالم منطق

fashionable *adj* almudah عالموضة

ecumenic *adj* aalami عالمي

ecumenical *adj* aalami عالمي

global *adj* aalami عالمي

universal *adj* a'lami عالمي

universality *n* a'lameyyeh عالميّة

high *adj* aali عالي

lofty *adj* a'li عالي

loud *adj* a'li عالي

strident *adj* a'li عالي

alto *n* aali عالي

argute *adj* aali esut عالي الصوت

alpine *adj* ali ketir عالي كتير

general *adj* aamm عامّ

common *adj* a'm عامّ

factor *n* aamel عامل

worker *n* a'mel عامل

compassion *n* a'tifeh عاطفة

emotion *n* a'tefeh عاطفة

passion *n* a'tefeh عاطفة

emotional *adj* a'tefi عاطفي

passionate *adj* a'tefi عاطفي

sentimental *adj* a'tifi عاطفي

disloyal *adj* aaqq عاقّ

sane *adj* a'qel عاقل

reflector *n* a'kes عاكس

particularly *adv* alakhass عالأخصّ

most *adv* al'aghlab عالأغلب

absolutely *adv* al akeed عالأكيد

affirmatively *adv* al'akid عالأكيد

surely *adv* al'akid عالأكيد

nigh *prep* altaqribi عالتقريبي

ashore *adv* 'alshatie عالشاطئ

north *adv* alshmal عالشمال

northerly *adv* alshmal عالشمال

often *adv* alghaleb عالغالب

globe *n* elaalm العالم

world *n* a'lam عالم

scientist *n* a'lem عالم

a'lem arsad عالم أرصاد جويِّة

meteorologist *n* jawweyyeh

n alam elahlam عالم الأحلام

dreamworld

n a'lam eltabe'ah عالم الطبيعة

naturalist

family n ayleh عائلة	n aamel elfunduq عامل الفندق
n ela'yleh elmalkeh العائلة المالكة	bellboy
royalty	n aamel elfuduq عامل الفندق
worship n ebadeh عبادة	bellhop
cult n ibadeh عِبَادة	n aamel elmarsah عامل المرسى
clause n ebarah عبارة	dockworker
phrase n ebarah عِبَارَة	catalyzer n amel tahfiz عامل تحفيز
cloak n abayeh عباية	n aamel hayawi عامل حيوي
frock n abayeh عباية	bioagent
gown n abayeh عباية	n a'mel seheyyeh عامل صحيّة
serf n abd عَبْد	plumber
thrall n abd عَبْد	miner n amel manjam عامل منجم
across adv abr عبر	pitman n a'mel manjam عامل منجم
frown n abseh عبسة	colloquial adj aammi عامّي
scowl n abseh عبسة	colloquialism n aameyyeh عاميّة
genius n elabkari العبقري	slang n elammeyyeh العاميّة
genial adj abkari عبقري	spinster n anis عانِس
geniality n abkareyyeh عبقريّة	monarch n a'hel عاهِل
early adv abakkir عبكّير	sovereign n a'hel عاهِل
slavery n ubudeyyeh عبوديّة	revenue n a'eddat عائدات
servitude n ubudeyyeh عُبُوديّة	proceeds n a'edat عائدَات
sullen adj abus عبوس	alive adj aysh عايش
mite n ett عتّ	live adj ayesh عايش
moth n ett عتّ	n ayesh belmukhayyam عايش بالمخيّم
admonition n itab عتاب	camper
remorse n etab عتاب	roadblock n a'eq عائق
admonisher n atban عتبان	impediment n a'eiq عائق
threshold n atabeh عتبة	host n ayel عائل

عدّاد السرعة n addad elsur'ah
odometer

عدّادة counter n addadeh

عدالة justice n adaleh

عداوة antagonism n a'daweh

عداوة enmity n adaweh

عداوة feud n adaweh

عدّة kit n eddeh

عدّة apparatus n uddeh

عدد الوفيات n adad elwafyyat
mortality

عدد كبير myriad n adad kbir

عددي numeral adj adadi

عددي numerical adj adadi

عدس lentil n ades

عدسة lens n adaseh

عدَم nonentity n adam

عدم استقرار n adam isteqrar
instability

عدم الثقة بالنفس adam theqa belnafs
self-doubt n

عدم الوضوح n adam elwuduh
illegibility

عدم انحياز non- n adam inhyaz
alignment

عدم أهليّة n adam ahleyyeh
disqualification

عتبة الباب lintel n atabet elbab

عتق emancipation n eteq

عتلة الرافعة lever n 'atalet elrafe

العتمة darkness n elutmeh

عتمة dark n utmeh

عتيق antiquated adj atiq

عتيق neolithic adj atiq

عجرفة insolence n ajrafeh

عجز shortfall n ajez

عجز inability n ajez

عجز infirmity n ajez

عجقة noise n ajqah

عجقة سير traffic n aje'et sir

عجل calf n ejel

عجل bullock n ejel

عجلة haste n ajaleh

عجلة hurry n ajaleh

عجلة celerity n ajaleh

عجنب aside adv ajanab

عجنة batch n ajneh

عجول fast adj ajul

عجيب miraculous adj ajib

عجين dough n ajin

عدّ count n a'dd

عدّ تنازلي n a'dd tanazuli
countdown

عدّ وصفّ altercation n a'd wesaff

عدّاء runner n 'adda

maiden *adj* uzri عُذْرِي	*n* adam tahammul عدم تَحمُّل
platonic *adj* uzri عُذْرِي	intolerance
necromancer *n* arraf عرّاف	*n* adam zekir elesim عدم ذكر الاسم
hag *n* arrafeh عرّافة	anonymosity
cart *n* arabayeh عربايةة	*n* adam ridah عدم رضى
arabayeh bejerrha عربايةة بجرّها تور	dissatisfaction
oxcart *n* tur	*n* adam nuduj عدم نضوج
arabeh yejerra عربة يجرّ حصان	immaturity
barouche *n* hesaan	*n* adm wjood ras عدم وجود راس
chariot *n* arabet khil عربة خيل	acephaly
revelry *n* arbadeh عَرْبَدة	nihilism *n* adameyyeh عَدَمِيّة
orgy *n* arbadeh عَرْبَدة	antagonist *n* adu عدو
Arabic *adj* arabi عربي	enemy *n* adu عدو
n arabeyyt elwlad عربيّة الولاد	opponent *n* adu عَدُو
perambulator	*n* addu lelbashar عدوّ للبشر
pram *n* arabeyyt wlad عربيّة ولاد	misanthrope
nuptials *n* urs عرس	bellicose *adj* edwani عدواني
wedding *n* ers عرس	hostile *adj* edwani عدواني
throne *n* arsh عَرْش	aggressive *adj* edwani عدواني
breadth *n* ared عرض	inimical *adj* udwani عُدْواني
display *n* ared عرض	aggression *n* edwanieh عدوانية
offer *n* ared عرض	hostility *n* edwaneyyeh عدوانيّة
presentation *n* ared عرض	infection *n* adweh عدوة
symptom *n* arad عَرَض	senseless *adj* adim hass عديم حسّ
proposal *n* ared عَرْض	*n* azab jahanam عذاب جهنم
premiere *n* ared awwal عرض أوّل	damnation
sideshow *n* ard janbi عرض جانبي	excuse *n* uzer عذر
quotation *n* ared se'r عرض سعر	maiden *adj* azra'e عَذْراء

lair *n* arin عرين

solace *n* azah عَزَا

solo *n* azef menfered عزف منفرد

insulation *n* azl عزل

isolation *n* azel عزل

seclusion *n* azel عزل

segregation *n* azel عزل

n ezleh jamaeyyeh عزلة اجتماعيّة
desocialization

momentum *n* azm عَزْم

celibacy *n* uzubeyeh عزوبيّة

martial *adj* askari عسكري

soldier *n* askari عسكري

military *adj* askari عَسْكَرِي

n askari fi fylaq عسكري في فيلق
legionary

n askari mesallah عسكري مسلَّح
musketeer

honey *n* asal عسل

nest *n* ushsh عشّ

dinner *n* asha عشا

supper *n* asha عَشَا

adj ashate' khalij عشاطئ خليج
bayside

tribal *adj* ashayri عشايري

grass *n* esheb عشب

herb *n* eshbeh عشبة

tenfold *adj* asher ad'aaf عشر أضعاف

parade *n* ard askari عرض عسكري

symptomatic *adj* aradi عرَضي

extrinsic *adj* aradi عرَضي

incidental *adj* aradi عرَضي

occasional *adj* aradi عرَضي

serendipitous *adj* aradi عرَضي

arrowroot *n* ararut عرَعروط

custom *n* urf عُرْف

crest *n* urf eddik عرف الدّيك

conversant *adj* arfan عرَفَان

customary *adj* urfi عُرْفي

sweat *n* araq عرق

perspiration *n* araq عَرَق

nacre *n* erq elulu عرق اللولو

sciatica *n* erq elnesa عرق النسا

ethnicity *n* erqeyyeh عرقيّة

eyelet *n* erwayeh عروابة

loop *n* urweh عُرْوة

bride *n* arus عروس

prosody *n* arud عَرُوض

nude *n* uri عُرْي

nudity *n* uri عُرْي

nude *adj* aryan عريان

groom *n* aris عريس

bridegroom *n* arris عرّيس

bower *n* arisheh عرَيشة

broad *adj* ariid عريض

wide *adj* arid عريض

n asfur elduri عصفور الدوري
sparrow

crane n asfur elkirki عصفور الكركي

indiscipline n esyan عصيان

insurrection n esyan عِصْيان

n esyan askari عصيان عسكري
mutiny

mush n asideh عصيدة

crowdy adj asideh عصيدة

juice n asir عصير

cider n asir tiffah عصير تفّاح

incurable adj udal عُضَال

bit n adda عضّة

nibble n addah عضّة

muscle n adaleh عضلة

biceps n adaleh brasin عضلة براسين

n adaleh daleyyeh عضلة دالِّية
deltoid

n adaleh mwattrah عضلة موتّرة
tensor

muscular adj adali عَضَلي

n 'adem elasabe عضم الأصابع
phalanx

bone n admeh عضمة

n 'admet elasabe عضمة الأصابع
phalange

member n udu عضو

organ n udu عضو

n elushur elmitri العشر المتري
decimetre

decade n asher snin عشر سنين

decennary n asher snin عشر سنين

sawbuck n ashra dular عشرة دولار

decimal adj ushri عُشْري

n eleshreneyyat العشرينيات
twentieth

indiscriminate adj ashwa'e عشوائي

random adj ashwa'e عشوائي

tribe n ashireh عشيرة

paramour n ashiq عَشيق

mistress n ashiqah عَشيقة

gang n asayeh عِصابة

baton n asayeh عصابة

clave n asayeh عصابة

stick n asayeh عصابة

birch n asayet taa'dib عصابة التأديب

crook adj asayet erraei عصابة الراعي

wand n asayet elsaher عصابة الساحر

nerve n asab عَصَب

n aseb eluyun عصب العيون
blindfold

nervous adj asabi عصبي

irritable adj asabi عصبي

brainstorm n asef zihni عصف ذهني

bird n asfur عصفور

occipital *n* azem elqafa عظم القفا

femur *n* azmet elfalhd عظمة الفَخد

azmet hanak عظمة حَنك الحوت

baleen *n* elhut

magnificent *adj* azim عَظِيم

chastity *n* effeh عِفّة

temperance *n* effeh عِفّة

virtue *n* effeh عِفّة

demon *n* afrit عفريت

elf *n* afrit عفْريت

mould *n* afan عفن

rot *n* afan عفن

mildew *n* afan عَفَن

amnesty *n* afw عفو

condonation *n* afu عفُو

spontaneous *adj* afawi عفوي

impulsive *adj* afwi عَفْوِي

spontaneity *n* afaweyyeh عفوِيّة

chaste *adj* afif عفيف

incorruptible *adj* afif عفيف

temperate *adj* afif عفيف

virtuous *adj* afif عَفِيف

property *n* aqar عقار

realty *n* aqar عَقَار

dogmatic *adj* aqaeidi عَقَائِدي

stub *n* aqeb عَقَب

obstacle *n* aqabeh عقبة

compact *n* aqed عقد

limb *n* udu عُضْو

teammate *n* udu befariq عضو بفريق

edu be naqabet elmuhamin عضو بنقابة المحامين

bencher *n* elmuhamin

n udu fi elmajlis عضو في المجلس

councillor

udu fi lejnet عضو في لجنة محلّفين

juryman *n* muhallafin

udu majles عضو مجلس الشعب

parliamentarian *n* elsha'eb

udu muhayd عُضْو محايد في برلمان

crossbench *adj* filbarlaman

organic *adj* udwi عضوي

membership *n* udweyyeh عضوِيّة

abeyance *n* ataleh عطالة

fragrance *n* uter عطر

odour *n* uter عطر

scent *n* uter عطر

sneeze *n* atseh عطسة

thirst *n* atash عطش

athirst *adj* atshaan عطشان

thirsty *adj* atshan عطشان

outage *n* etel عطل

conge *n* eteleh عطلة

holiday *n* eteleh عطلة

loving *adj* atuf عَطُوف

along *adv* a'tul عطول

maxilla *n* azem elfakk عظم الفك

against *adj* aks عكس

apposite *adj* akes عكس

reverse *n* akes عكس

antonym *n* akes عكس

contra *.pref* akes عكْس

reversal *n* akes عكْس

reverse *adj* aksi عكْسِي

curve *n* akfeh عكفة

therapy *n* elaj عِلاج

n elelaj belrawayeh العلاج بالروايح

aromatherapy

n elaj nafsi علاج نفسي

psychotherapy

curative *adj* eilaji علاجي

cure *n* eilaji علاجي

remedial *adj* elaji عِلاجي

forager *n* allaf عَلّاف

relation *n* alaqah علاقَة

alaqah علاقة جنسيّة مو شرعيّة

n jinseyyeh mu shar'eyyeh

intimacy

n alaqah hamimeyyeh عَلاقَة حَميمة

rapport

n alaqa gharamiyh علاقة غرامية

affair

n alaqa gharamiyeh علاقة غرامية

amour

blabber *n* allak عَلّاك

contract *n* aqed عَقد

title *n* aqed عَقد

bight *n* uqdeh عقدة

knot *n* uqdeh عقدة

bow *n* uqdeh عُقدة

complex *n* uqdeh عُقدة

node *n* uqdeh عُقْدة

noose *n* u'qdet habel عقدة حبل

scorpion *n* aqrab عقرب

mind *n* aqel عقل

rational *adj* aqlani عقلاني

rationality *n* aqlaneyyeh عقلانيّة

mental *adj* aqli عَقْلي

mentality *n* aqleyyeh عقليّة

futility *n* uqm عقم

sterility *n* uqm عقم

sanction *n* uqubeh عقوبة

penalty *n* uqubeh عقوبة

punishment *n* uqubeh عقوبة

creed *n* aqideh عقيدة

dogma *n* aqideh عَقيدة

opal *n* aqiq عقيق

cabuncle *n* aqiq ahmar عقيق أحمر

barren *n* akiim عقيم

sterile *adj* aqim عَقيم

futile *adj* aqim عَقيم

sediment *n* akar عَكَر

lee *n* akar عَكَر

علم الأساطير elm elasatir *n* mythology	علامة alameh *n* mark
علم الأسماء elm elasma' *n* onomatology	علامة alameh *n* tag
علم الأشعَّة elm elashe'a *n* radiology	علَّامة allameh *n* savant
علم الأورام elm elawram *n* oncology	علامة الولادة alamet elweladeh *n* birthmark
علم البيئة elim elbi'a *n* ecology	علامة تجاريّة alameh tijareyeh *n* brand
علم البيئة elm elbe'aa *n* environmentalism	علاوة alweh *n* increment
علم التجميل e'lim elttjmil *npl* aesthetics	علاوة بالأرض alaweh beared *n* berm
علم التربية elm eltarbeyeh *n* paedology	علبة elbeh *n* can
علم الحشرات elm elhasharat *n* entomology	علبة تروس elbet trus *n* gearbox
علم السموم elm elsumum *n* toxicology	علبة صيغة elbet sigha *n* casket
علم الصحَّة elm essahhah *n* hygiene	علّة elleh *n* ailment
علم الصوتيّات elm elsawteyyet *n* phonetics	علّة elleh *n* drawback
علم الطيران e'lm elttayaran *npl* aeronautics	علف alaf *n* foraging
علم الطيور elm eltyur *n* ornithology	علَف alaf *n* feed
علم الفَلَك ilim elfalak *n* astronomy	علَف alaf *n* fodder
علم اللغة elm ellughah *n* linguistics	علَف alaf *n* forage
علم المحيطات elm elmuhitat *n* oceanology	علف الحصان alaf elhusan *n* livery
	علكة elkeh *n* gum
	علم elm *n* flag
	علم elm *n* science
	علِم elm *n* scholarship
	علم الإجتماع e'lm elejtima *n* sociology
	علم الأحياء e'lem elahyaa *n* biology

aboard *adv* almarkab على المركب

apart *adv* ala janab على جنب

adj ala shate' elbaher على شاطئ البحر
beachfront

dashing *adj* ala ajaleh على عجلة

adv ala mala wshshh على ملا وشّه
afloat

leisurely *adj* ala mahl على مهل

omniscient *adj* el'alim العليم

uncle *n* amm عمّ

adj am yehtudir عم يحتضر
moribund

mainstay *n* emad عِمَاد

turban *n* amameh عمامة

aunt *n* ammeh عمّة

mayor *n* umdeh عمدة

age *n* eumr عمر

n umru 100 sineh عمره 100 سنة
centenarian

depth *n* umq عمق

profundity *n* umq عمق

bottom *n* umuq عُمْق

action *n* mal3 عمل

feat *n* amal butuli عمل بطولي

operation *n* amal jirhai عمل جراحي

teamwork *n* amal jama'i عمل جماعي

charity *n* amal khir عمل خير

good *n* amal khir عمل خير

n elm elmustaqbal علم المستقبل
futurology

n elm elmustalahat علم المصطلحات
terminology

n elm elma'den علم المعادن
metallurgy

n elm elma'den علم المعادن
mineralogy

logic *n* elm elmateq علم المنطق

n elm elmikanik علم الميكانيك
mechanics

nanobiology *n* elm elnanu علم النانو

psychology *n* elm elnafs علم النفس

n e'lm elhawaeyiat علم الهوائيات
aerobiology

ontology *n* elm elwujud علم الوجود

lay *adj* elmani علْمَاني

layman *n* elmani علْمَاني

scientific *adj* elmi علْمي

scholarly *adj* elmi عِلْمِي

overt *adj* alani علني

public *adj* alani علني

n ulum iqtisadeyyeh علوم اقتصاديّة
economics

n ulum siyaseyyeh علوم سياسية
politics

on *prep* ala على

over *prep* ala على

perpendicular *adj* amudi عمودي

vertical *adj* amudi عمودي

commission *n* umuleh عمولة

generally *adv* umuman عموماً

ablepsy *n* amah عمى

amaurosis *n* a'ma عمى

blindness *n* ama عمى

dean *n* amid عميد

deep *adj* amiq عميق

inmost *adj* amiq عميق

profound *adj* amiq عميق

sound *adj* amiq عميق

client .*n* amil عميل

after *prep* a'n عن

indeed *adv* an haqq عن حقّ

deliberate *adj* an qasd عن قصد

intentional *adj* an qasd عن قصد

purposely *adv* an qasd عن قصد

obduracy *n* enad عناد

providence *n* enayeh عنَاية

grape *n* enb عنب

really *adv* anjad عنجد

adamant *n* e'nd عند

nightingale *n* andalib عندليب

andu akter mn عنده أكتر من مرا

polygamous *adj* marah

adj anduh seyadeh عنده سيادة

sovereign

giant *n* emlaq عملاق

gigantic *adj* emlaq عملاق

massive *adj* emlaq عملاق

emlaq bein wehdeh عملاق بعين وحدة

cyclops *n* wehdeh

currency *n* emleh عملة

n emleh ma'daneyyeh عملة معدَن

coin

n emleh ma'daneyeh عملة معدَنيّة

casting

feasible *adj* amali عملي

practicable *adj* amali عملي

practical *adj* amali عملي

practicability *n* amaleyyeh عمليّة

process *n* amalyyeh عمليّة

n amaleyyt eldarb عملية الضرب

multiplication

amaleyyeh hesabeyyeh عمليّة حسابيّة

equation *n*

amaleyeh kaysareyyeh عمليّة قيصريّة

cesarean *n*

pillar *n* amud عمود

column *n* amud عَمُود

shaft *n* amud عَمُود

sidebar *n* amud janbi عمود جانبي

n amud dawwar عمود دوّار

armature

spine *n* amud faqari عمود فقري

era *n* ahed عهد

covenant *n* ahed عهد

custody *n* uhdeh عهدة

surfeit *n* awaleh عوالة

buoy *n* awwameh عوّامة

rod *n* ud عُود

match *n* ud kebrit عود كبريت

loin *n* urah عَوْرة

buoyancy *n* uum عُوم

indistinct *adj* awes عَويص

clinic *n* eyadeh عيادة

defect *n* ayeb عيب

deficit *n* ayeb عيب

flaw *n* eyb عيب

taint *n* ayb عيب

shame *n* eyb عَيْب

shortcoming *n* eyb عَيْب

demerit *n* eybeh عِيبة

blemish *n* eybeh عِيبة

n eid alghattas عيد الغطاس

epiphany

anniversary *n* eid sanawi عيد سنوي

eid milad elmasyh عيد ميلاد المسيح

Christmas *n*

living *n* eysheh عِيشة

subsistence *n* eysheh عِيشة

survival *n* eysheh عيشة

eye *n* eyn عين

n eindh wahmmeh عنده وحمة

albino

element *n* ensur عنصر

racial *adj* unsuri عنصري

elemental *adj* unsuri عُنْصري

ethnic *adj* unsuri عُنْصري

racialism *n* unsureyyeh عنصريّة

racism *n* unsureyyeh عنصريّة

vehemence *n* unf عنف

violence *n* unf عنف

severity *n* unf عُنْف

cluster *n* anqud عنقُود

spider *n* ankabut عنكبوت

address *n* enwan عنوان

label *n* unwan عنوان

dour *adj* anid عنيد

headstrong *adj* anid عنيد

mulish *adj* anid عنيد

obdurate *adj* anid عنيد

stubborn *adj* anid عنيد

relentless *adj* anid عَنيد

inexorable *adj* anid عَنيد

forceful *adj* anif عنيف

vehement *adj* anif عنيف

violent *adj* anif عنيف

pitiless *adj* afif عَنيف

severe *adj* anif عَنيف

fierce *adj* anif عَنيف

absent *adj* ghayeb غايِب

terminus *n* ghayh غايَة

follies *n* 'ghaba غَباء

stupidity *n* 'ghaba غَباء

pollen *n* 'ghubar eltal غِبار الطلع

fallout *n* ghubar nawawi غُبار نووي

blur *n* ghabash غَباش

dust *n* ghabrah غِبرَا

n ghabret eltabashir غِبرة الطباشير
chalkdust

dumbo *n* elghabi الغبي

dunce *n* elghabi الغبي

fool *n* elghabi الغبي

boneheaded *adj* ghabi غبي

dorky *adj* ghabi غبي

foolish *adj* ghabi غبي

stupid *adj* ghabi غبي

ghathayan غثيان من حركة السيَّارة
n men haraket al sayyarah
carsickness

lunch *n* ghada غدا

treacherous *adj* ghaddar غدَّار

gland *n* ghuddeh غُدَة

n ghedad tanasuleyyeh غدد تناسليَّة
gonads

perfidy *n* ghadr غدر

treachery *n* ghadr غدر

babe *n* gherr غِرّ

specimen *n* ayyenh عِيّنة

sample *n* ayyeneh عِيّنة

jungle *n* ghabeh غابة

woods *n* ghabeh غابة

forest *n* ghayeh غابِة

raid *n* gharah غارة

invasion *n* gharah غارَة

foray *n* gharah غارَة

gas *n* ghaz غاز

cooker *n* ghaz ettabekh غاز الطبخ

conquerer *n* ghazi غازي

gasesous *adj* ghazi غازي

gassy *adj* ghazi غازِي

gallon *n* galun غالون

expensive *adj* ghali غالي

costly *adj* ghali غالي

ambiguous *adj* ghamid غامض

enigmatical *adj* ghamed غامِض

mysterious *adj* ghamed غامِض

vague *adj* ghamed غامِض

enigmatic *adj* ghamed غامِض

equivocal *adj* ghamed غامِض

tenebrous *adj* ghameq غامِق

absentee *n* el ghayib الغايب

cadet n ghirr غِرّ

crow n ghurab غُرَاب

oddity n gharabeh غَرَابة

staff n ghrad غراض

gramme n gram غرام

fine n gharameh غرامة

forfeit n gharameh غرامة

n gharamet ta'khir غرامة تأخير
demurrage

amorous adj gharami غرامي

occident n elgharb الغرب

west n gharb غرب

riddle n gherbal غِرْبال

sieve n gherbal غِرْبال

western adj gharbi غربي

occidental adj gharbi غَرْبي

gargle v gargarah غَرْغَرَة

room n ghurfeh غرفة

chamber n ghurfeh غرفة

compartment n ghurfeh غرفة

n ghurfet elrasm غرفة الرسم
drawing-room

n gherfet elqa'deh غرفة القعدة
lounge

n ghirfit ennum غرفة النوم
bedroom

n gherfet taftish غرفة تفتيش
manhole

n gherfeh zeghereh غرفة صغيرة
cabin

cell n gherfeh seghereh غرفة صغيرة

fond adj gharman غرمَان

dusk n ghurub غُرُوب

arrogance n ghurur غرور

conceit n ghurur غرور

glue n ghreh غري

alien adj ghryb غريب

antic n gharib غريب

grotesque adj ghrib غريب

odd adj gharib غريب

strange adj gharib غريب

stranger n gharib غريب

eerie adj gharib غَريب

outlandish adj gharib غَريب

outsider n gharib غَريب

quaint adj gharib غَريب

foreigner n gharib غَريب

adj gharib elatwar غريب الاطوار
eccentric

shortbread n elgharbeyyeh الغريّة

shortcake n elgharbeyyeh الغريّة

instinct n gharezeh غريزة

n gharezeh jinseyyeh غَريزَةٌ جِنْسيَّة
sexuality

inborn adj gharizi غريزي

instinctive adj gharizi غريزي

pang *n* ghassah غصّة	adversary *n* ghrim غريم
gulp *n* ghassah غصّة	rival *n* gharim غَرِيم
bough *n* ghesun غصن	foe *n* gharim غَرِيم
bush *n* ghusen غصن	superfluity *n* ghazarah غزارة
furrow *n* ghesn غصن	profusion *n* ghazarah غَزَارَة
sprig *n* ghesn segher غصن صغير	gazelle *n* ghazal غزال
tender *adj* ghadd غَضّ	spinner *n* ghazzal غَزَّال
juicy *adj* ghadd غَضّ	flirt *n* ghazl غزِل
anger *n* ghadab غضب	philander *n* ghazal غزِل
cartilage *n* ghudruf غضروف	compliment *n* ghazal غزِل
coif *n* ghata غطا	spin *n* ghazl غزِل
cover *n* ghata غطا	conquest *n* ghazweh غزوة
bonnet *n* ghata غَطا	superfluous *adj* ghazir غزِير
n ghata ettakhit غطا التخت	profuse *adj* ghazir غزِير
bedsheet	washer *n* ghassaleh غسّالة
coverlet *n* ghata ettakhit غطا التخت	laundress *n* ghassaleh غَسّالة
dip *n* ghates غطس	wash *n* ghasl غسل
doze *n* ghafweh غفوة	adulteration *n* ghshsh غشّ
slumber *n* ghafweh غفوة	bam *n* gheshsh غِشّ
placable *adj* ghafur غَفُور	bluff *n* ghesh غِشّ
boiler *n* ghallayeh غلّاية	cheat *n* ghishsh غِشّ
cauldron *n* ghallayeh غلّاية	deceit *n* ghishsh غِشّ
mistake *n* ghalat غلط	remembrance *n* 'ghisha غشاء
wrong *adj* ghalat غلط	membrane *n* 'ghisha غِشَاء
baulk *n* ghalat غَلَط	deceitful *adj* ghashshash غَشَّاش
incorrect *adj* ghalat غَلَط	dishonest *adj* ghashshash غَشَّاش
err *v* ghalat غَلَط	trickster *n* ghashshash غَشَّاش
faulty *adj* ghaltan غلطان	haze *n* ghashaewh غَشَاوِة

lullaby *n* ghennyt elnum غنيّة النوم

n gheneyeh turatheyeh غنيّة تراثيّة

ballad

spoil *n* ghanimeh غنيمة

booty *n* ghanimeh غَنيمة

loot *n* ghanimeh غَنيمَة

submarine *n* ghawwasah غوّاصة

gorilla *n* gurilla غوريللا

dive *n* ghus غوص

demagogue *n* ghawgha'ei غوغائي

demagogy *n* ghawgha'eyyeh غوغائيّة

ghoul *n* ghul غُول

golf *n* gulf غولف

ghoulish *adj* ghuli غولي

absence *n* ghiyab غياب

otherworld *n* elghib الغيب

gossip *n* ghybeh غيبة

backbite *v* ghibeh غيبة

coma *n* ghaybubeh غيبوبة

trance *n* ghaybubeh غيبوبة

n elghebeyyeh الغيبيّة

otherworldliness

guitar *n* gitar غيتار

acellular *adj* ghir khalawi غير خلوي

acentric *adj* ghir markazi غير مركزي

solicitous *adj* ghayran غَيّران

solicitude *n* ghayran غَيّران

jealousy *n* ghereh غيرة

goofy *adj* ghaltan غلطان

erroneous *adj* ghaltan غَلْطان

goof *v* ghaltah غلطة

fault *n* ghaltah غلطَة

boil *n* ghalayan غَلَيان

surge *n* ghalayan غَلَيان

glycerine *n* gliserin غليسيرين

churl *n* ghaliz غليظ

pipe *n* ghulyun غَلْيُون

flasher *n* ghammaz غمّاز

nebula *n* ghamameh غمامة

dunk *n* ghamr غمر

plunge *n* ghams غمس

mystery *n* ghumud غموض

ambiguity *n* ghumood غُموض

vagueness *n* ghumud غُموض

lyrical *adj* ghena'e غنائي

gangrene *n* gangarina غَنْغَرينا

riches *n* ghinah غِنى

richness *n* ghinah غِنى

wealth *n* ghenah غِنى

rich *adj* ghani غني

wealthy *adj* ghani غني

elghani sahib الغني صاحب النفوذ

affluential *n* elnnufuz

ghani sahib nufuz غني صاحب نفوذ

affluential *adj*

song *n* ghenneyh غنيّة

axe n fa's فأْس	fury n ghiz غيظ
hatchet n fas sghir فاس صغير	nimbus n ghim matari غيم مطري
corrupt adj fasid فاسد	cloud n ghemeh غيمة
depraved adj fased فاسد	jealous adj ghayyur غيُور
debauchee n fasiq فاسق	
interim n fasel فاصل	ف
categorical adj fasel فاصِل	
interval n fasel فاصِل	
book- n fasel kitab فاصِل كِتاب	thus adv fa ف
mark	lukewarm adj fater فاتِر
apostrophe n faseleh فاصِلة	nonchalant adj fater فاتِر
comma n fasleh فاصِلة	tepid adj fater فاتِر
flagrant adj fadeh فاضِح	bill n fatura فاتورة
blank adj fadi فاضي	invoice n faturah فاتورة
devoid adj fadi فاضي	chit n fatwret matam فاتورة مطعَم
empty adj fadi فاضي	obscene adj fajer فاجِر
vacant adj fadi فاضي	lascivious adj fajer فاجِر
void adj fadi فاضي	libertine n fajer فاجِر
doer n fael فاعِل	bereavement n fajiaa فاجِعة
adj faked elshaheyeh فاقد الشهية	atrocious adj fahish فاحِش
anorexic	superfine adj fakher فاخِر
vivid adj 'faqe فاقِع	sumptuous adj fakher فاخِر
fax n faks فاكس	fugitive n farr فارّ
telegraph n faks فاكس	mouse n farah فارة
fruit n fakha فاكهة	knight n fares فارس
auspice n faal فال	chevalier n faris فارِس
torch n fanus فانوس	vaseline n fazlin فازلين
lantern n fanus فانُوس	hack v fas فاس

snuff *n* ftil elsham'ah فتيل الشمعة

suddenly *adv* faj'ah فَجْأة

accidental *adj* fuja'i فَجائي

sudden *n* fuja'i فَجائي

dawn *n* elfajr الفجر

aurora *n* fajer فَجر

gluttony *n* 'faja فَجَع

glutton *n* fajaan فَجْعان

voracious *adj* faj'an فَجْعان

insatiable *adj* faj'an فَجْعان

radish *n* fejl فَجل

cavity *n* fajweh فَجوة

obscenity *n* fujur فَجور

check *n* fahes فَحص

revision *n* fahs فَحص

scan *n* fahs فَحص

n fahes hayawi فَحص حيوي

bioscopy

viva *n* fahs shafahi فَحص شفهي

voce

checkup *n* fahes tebbi فَحص طبّي

potent *adj* fahl فَحل

stallion *n* fahl فَحْل

virile *adj* fahl فَحْل

coal *n* fahim فَحم

potency *n* fhuleyyeh فَحُوليَّة

ambush *n* fakhkh فَخّ

snare *n* fakhkh فَخّ

perishable *adj* fani فاني

advantage *n* fayideh فايدة

good *n* faydeh فايدة

benefit *n* fa'edeh فائدة

ebullient *adj* fayer فاير

frantic *adj* fayr فاير

excess *n* fayed فايض

excess *adj* fayed فايض

surplus *n* fa'ed فائض

wakeful *adj* fayeq فايق

cracker *n* fattash nari فتّاش ناري

mortal *adj* fattak فتّاك

lethal *adj* fattak فتّاك

adorable *adj* fattan فتّان

enticing *adj* fattan فتّان

opening *n* fateha فتحة

orifice *n* fateha فتحة

lacuna *n* fatehah فتحَة

loop- *n* fateha lelrami فتحة للرمي

hole

period *n* fatrah فترة

morsel *n* fatfuteh فتفوتة

hernia *n* fetq فتق

rupture *n* fetq فتّق

fascination *n* fetneh فتنة

nonchalance *n* futur فُتور

tepidity *n* futur فُتور

primer *n* ftil فتيل

hilarity *n* farah kbir فرح كبير

elated *adj* farhan فرحان

hilarious *adj* farhan فرحان

merry *a* farhan فَرْحان

jolly *adj* farhan فَرْحان

jubilant *adj* farhan فَرْحان

bass *n* farkh فَرخ

flapper *n* farkh فَرْخ

individual *adj* fardi فردي

solo *adj* fardi فردي

odd *adj* fardi فَرْدي

individualism *n* fardeyyeh فرديّة

individuality *n* fardeyyeh فرديّة

mare *n* faras فَرَس

cavalry *n* fursan فُرسَان

furlong *n* farsakh فَرْسَخ

furniture *n* farsh فرش

brush *n* firshayeh فرشاية

mattress *n* farsheh فِرْشة

opportunity *n* fersah فرصة

chance *n* fursah فرْصَة

imposition *n* fard فرض

n fard eldarayb فرض الضرايب

taxation

nick *n* fardah فَرْضَة

hypothesis *n* faradeyyeh فَرْضيّة

branch *n* 'fare فرع

adjuvant *adj* farei فرعي

muscovite *n* fakhkhar نَقّار

crockery *n* fakhkharah نَقَّارَة

luxuriance *n* fakhmeh نَقامة

pomposity *n* fakhameh نَقَامَة

thigh *n* fakhd نفذ

honorary *adj* fakhri نفري

titular *adj* fakhri نفري

ostentation *n* fakhfakhah نَقْفَخة

pomp *n* fakhfakhah نَقْفَخة

august *adj* fakhem نفم

stately *adj* fakhm نفم

palatial *adj* fakhem نَقْم

luxuriant *adj* fakhm نَقْم

proud *adj* fakhur نفور

acre *n* faddan فدان

guerilla *n* fida'e فدائي

ransom *n* fedyh فدْية

stampede *n* frar jama'i فرار جماعي

escapee *n* frari فراري

n firash elmut فراش الموت

deathbed

butterfly *n* farasheh فراشة

baker *n* farran فرّان

view *n* ferjeh فرجة

show *n* ferjeh فرجة

merriment *n* farah فرح

elation *n* farah فَرَح

jubilation *n* farah فَرَح

capacious *adj* fasih فسيح	tributary *adj* fare'i فرعي
spacious *adj* fasih فَسِيح	subsidiary *adj* far'i فَرعي
fail *n* fashal فشل	deference *n* farq فرق
clove *n* fass فَصّ	nuance *n* farq seghir فرق صغير
eloquence *n* fasaha فَصَاحَة	pop *n* farqa'ah فرقعة
lucerne *n* fassah فصَّة	oven *n* fern فرن
easter *n* fseh فصح	French *adj* fransi فرنسي
chapter *n* fasel فصل	fur *n* faru فرو
muster *n* fasel فصل	unique *adj* frid فريد
season *n* fasl فصل	nonpareil *adj* farid فَرِيد
semester *n* fasl derasi فصل دراسي	nonpareil *n* farid فَريد
eloquent *adj* fasih فصيح	incomparable *adj* farid فَرِيد
lucid *adj* fasih فَصِيح	strawberry *n* friz فريز
blank *n* fada فضا	refrigerator *n* frizar فريزر
space *n* fadah فضا	prey *n* faryseh فريسة
vacancy *n* fada فَضَا	team *n* fariq فريق
scandalous *adj* fadayhi فضايحي	panic *n* 'faza فَزَع
spatial *adj* fada'ei فضائي	aghast *adj* fza'an فزعان
silver *n* feddah فضَّة	corruption *n* fasad فسَاد
remainder *n* fadleh فضلة	canary *adj* fassad فَسَّاد
curiosity *n* fudul فضُول	depravation *n* fasad فَسَاد
curious *adj* fuduli فضولي	jobbery *n* fasad idari فساد إداري
exquisitive *adj* fduli فضولي	*n* feseha belghabeh فسحَة بالغابة
nosey *adj* fuduli فضولي	glade
nosy *adj* fuduli فضولي	countermand *v* fasekh فسخ
officious *adj* fuduli فضولي	repeal *n* faskh فسخ
inquisitive *adj* fuduli فُضُولِي	annulment *n* fasekh فَسَخ
silver *adj* feddi فِضِّي	debauch *n* fesq فسق

n feqdan shakhes فقدان شخص bereavement	scandal n fdyha فضيحة
poverty n faqr فقر	merit n fadyleh فَضيلة
anaemia n fiker eldamm فقر الدم	ablactation n fitam فطام
paragraph n faqarah فقرة	fungus n fter فطر
seal n faqmeh فقمة	mushroom n fetr فطر
jurisprudence n feqh فقه	inherent adj fitri فطْري
doctrine n feqeh فقه	innate adj fitri فطْري
poor adj faqir فقير	acumen n fetneh فطنة
jurist n faqih فقيه	wit n fetneh فطنة
detachment n fakk فَكّ	breakfast n fetur فطور
n fakk ettashfir فَكّ التشفير decryption	rowdy adj fazz فظّ
n fakk eddaghet فَكّ الضغط decompression	outrage n faza'ah فَظَاعَة
decrypt n fakk tashfir فك تشفير	effective adj fa'al فَعّال
comic n fukaha فُكاهَة	efficiency n fa'aleyyeh فعّاليّة
comic adj fukahi فُكاهي	verb n fe'l فعل
intellect n feker فِكْر	auxiliary n feil musaed فعل مُساعد
idea n fekrah فكرة	present n 'fe'l mudare فعل مضارع
thought n fekrah فكرة	actually adv fe'ln فعلا
fallacy n fekrah ghalat فكرة خطأ	actual adj fe'li فعلي
sprain n faksheh فكشة	verbal adj fe'li فعلي
agriculturist n flaah فَلاّح	bubble n fuqa'a فقاعة
peasant n fallah فَلاّح	blob n fuqa'a فُقاعة
boor n fallah rifi فلاح ريفي	insensibility n fiqdan فقدان الحسّ
flash n flash فلاش	n feqdan elnutuq فقدان النطق aphasia
flannel n vanilya فلانيلّا	n fiqdan zhakira فقدان ذاكرة amnesia

perceptive *adj* fahim فهيم

shrewd *adj* fahim فَهِم

fragrant *adj* fawwah فَوَّاح

fizzy *adj* fawwar فَوَّار

n fawakeh mejaffafeh فوا كه مجفّفة

comfit

cohort *n* fuj فوج

shoal *n* fuj فوج

regiment *n* fuj فوج

anon *adv* fawran فورا

instantly *adv* fawran فورا

straightway *adv* fawran فَوْراً

fizz *n* fawaran فوران

upheaval *n* fawaran فَوَرَان

ebullience *n* furah فورة

spree *n* furah فورة

surge *n* furah فَوْرَة

format *n* furmat فورمات

instantaneous *adj* fawri فوري

phosphate *n* fusfat فوسفات

phosphorus *n* fusfur فوسفور

anarchist *n* fawdawi فوضوي

anarchism *n* fawdawiyeh فوضوية

anarchy *n* fawda فوضى

chaos *n* fawda فوضى

commotion *n* fawda فوضى

misrule *n* fawda فَوْضَى

above *prep* fuq فوق

wanton *adj* faltan فلتان

filter *n* feltr فلتر

philosophy *n* falsafeh فلسفة

philosophical *adj* falsafi فلسفي

folklore *n* flklur فلكلور

folkloric *adj* flkluri فلكلوري

sidereal *adj* falaki فلكي

film *n* felm فلم

chilli *n* filfleh فليفلة

n flifleh hamrah فليفلة حمرا

capsicum

cork *n* fallyneh فلّينة

oral *adj* famwi فموي

art *n* fann فنّ

gastronomy *n* fann ettahi فنّ الطهي

n fann elhurub فنّ الهروب

escapology

fann rasm فنّ رسم الأشخاص

portraiture *n* elashkhas

artist *n* fannan فنّان

cup *n* finjan فنجان

teacup *n* fenjan shay فنجان شاي

hotel *n* fenduq فندق

motel *n* fenduq seghir فندق صغير

artistic *adj* fanni فَنّي

leopard *n* fahd فهد

index *n* fahras فهرس

glossary *n* fehres فِهْرَس

elephant *n* fil فيل

villa *n* villa فيلَّا

philosopher *n* faylasuf فيلسوف

legion *n* faylaq فَيْلَق

n film musaghghar فيلم مصغَّر

microfilm

fillet *n* fileh فيليه

formerly *adv* fima mada فيما مضى

geeky *adj* fyyu khaddah فيُّو خضَّة

algal *adj* fiu tahalib فيو طحالب

fuel *n* fyul فيول

ق

plug *n* qabes قابس

adj 'qabel leleshba قابل للإشباع

satiable

adj qabel lelishti'al قابل للاشتعال

combustile

adj qabel lel'eltizam قابل للالتزام

abideable

adj qabel lel'atab قابل للعطب

vulnerable

qabil lilqsma قابل للقسمة دون كسور

aliquot *n* dun kusur

fragile *adj* qabel lelkasr قابل للكسر

up *prep* fuq فوق

adj fuq elbanafsaji فوق البنفسجي

ultraviolet

epidural *n* fuq eljafeyeh فوق الجافية

upper *adj* fuqani فوقاني

upward *adj* fuqani فوقاني

adv fuqani tehtani فوقاني تحتاني

topsy turvy

bean *n* ful فول

volt *n* vult فولت

folic *n* folik فوليك

fondant *n* fundan فوندان

gramophone *n* funugraf فونوغراف

at *prep* fi في

in *prep* fi في

n fe'ah muthaqqafeh فئة مثقَّفة

intelligentsia

vitamin *n* vitamin فيتامين

veto *n* vitu فِيتُو

federal *adj* fedrali فيدرالي

federation *n* fedraleyyeh فيدراليّة

video *n* vidyu فيديو

virus *n* virus فيروس

physics *n* fizyah فيزيا

fizya elhararah فيزيا الحرارة المتدنّية

cryogenics *n* elmutadaneyeh

physicist *n* fizya'i فيزيائي

wake *n* feqah فيقة

قاطع تذاكِر 'qate' tazaker n	قابل للنقض adj qabl lelnaqd
conductor	revocable
قاطع تيَّار 'qate' tayyar n fuse	قاتِل homicide n qatel
قاطع طريق 'qate' tariq gangster n	قاتِل murderer n qatil
قاطع طريق 'kate' tariie bandit n	قاتِل مأجور assassin n katil ma'jur
قاطع طريق 'qate' tariq brigand n	قادِر able adj qader
قاع البحر qa'e elbahr seafloor n	قادِر almighty adj qadir
قاعة جمباز qa'et jmbaz n	قادِر capable adj qader
gymnasium	قادِر يدفع 'solvent adj 'qader yedfa
قاعدة base n ka'edeh	قاذفة bomber n kazifah
قاعدة بيانات qaedit bayanat n	قارِب ferry n qareb
database	قارِب عبَّارة n qareb elabbarah
قاعِدي basal adj kaeydi	ferryboat
قاق jay n qaq	قارّة continent n qarrah
قالب stereotype n qalib	قارون croesus n qarun
قالب template n qalib	قاري reader n qari
قالِب briquet n qalib	قارّي continental adj qarri
قالِب die n qalib	قاري الكفّ 'palmist n qare' elkaff
قالِب mould n qalib	قاسي drastic n qasi
قاموس dictionary n qamus	قاسي hard adj qasi
قامُوس lexicon n qamus	قاسي stringent adj qasi
قانون law n qanun	قاسِي inflexible adj qasi
قانون canon n qanun	قاصِر minor n qaser
قانون داخلي bylaw n qanun dakhli	قاضي judge n qadi
قانوني lawful adj qanuni	قاضي magistrate n qadi
قانُوني statutory adj qanuni	قاطِرة towboat n qatrah
قائد leader n qa'ed	قَاطِرَة locomotive n qatrah
قائِد commander n qaed	

basement *n* abu قَبو

vault *n* qabu قَبو

hat *n* qabbu'a قُبُّوعة

cap *n* qabua'a قُبُّوعَة

admission *n* kubul قبول

horde *n* qabeleh قبيلة

dogfight *n* qital jawwi قتال جوّي

combative *adj* qitali قتالي

kill *n* qatl قتل

parricide *n* qatl elabb قتل الأبّ

patricide *n* qatel elabb قتل الأبّ

fratricide *n* qatl elakhkh قتل الأخّ

matricide *n* qatl elemm قتل الإمّ

n 'qatl elrade قَتل الرَّضيع

infanticide

regicide *n* qatl elmalik قتل الملك

clash *n* qtil قتيل

fight *n* qtel قتيل

catfight *n* ketil elqatat قتيل القطاط

affray *n* qtileh قتيلة

brawl *n* qetileh قتيلة

melee *n* kteleh قتيلة

drab *n* qahbeh قَحْبة

prostitute *n* qahbeh قَحْبة

lighter *n* qaddahah قدّاحَة

requiem *n* qaddas قدّاس

before *prep* kiddam قدّام

onward *adj* qeddam قدّام

admiral *n* ka'ed bhri قائد بحري

list *n* qa'emeh قائمة

menu *n* qa'emet akel قائمة أكل

n elqaemeh elsuda القائمة السودا

blacklist

n qaemet tahqiq قائمة تدقيق

checklist

alcove *n* qbbeh قبّة

canopy *n* qubbeh قُبِّة

dome *n* qebbeh قُبِّة

collar *n* qabbet qamis قَبِّة قَميص

grave *n* qabr قبر

tomb *n* qabr قبر

sepulchre *n* qabr قبر

sepulture *n* qabr قبر

dolmen *n* qaber qadim قَبر قَديم

grip *n* qabdah قبضَة

fist *n* qabdet eleyd قبضة الإيد

shipmaster *n* kuptan قبطان

master *n* kubtan قبطان

ago *adv* qbl قبل

before *adv* kabel قبل

adj kabel elzawaj قبل الزواج

antenuptial

adj qabl elzawaj قبل الزواج

premarital

adj kabel elweladeh قبل الولادة

antenatal

415

ejaculate n qazf elmani قذف المني	goblet n kadah قَدَح
ejaculatory adj qazfi قذفي	beaker n qadah kbir قَدَح كبير
fireball n qazefeh قذيفة	destiny n qadar قَدَر
grenade n kazifeh قذيفة	fate n qadar قَدَر
projectile n qazefeh قَذِيفة	ability n qudrah قدرة
kinship n qrabeh قرابة	capability n qudrah قُدْرَة
decision n qarar قرار	might n qedrah قُدْرَة
resolution n qarar قرار	n 'elqudra alddfe القدرة ع الدفع
n qarar mahkameh قرار محكمة	affordability
verdict	n 'qudrah a eldafe قُدْرَة ع الدفع
stingy adj qarras قرَّاص	solvency
nettle n qurras قُرَّاص	n elqudrah albast القدرة عالبسط
kith n qrayeb قرايب	enjoyability
n qerayet elkaff قراية الكفّ	sanctity n qudseyyeh قدسيّة
palmistry	foot n qadam قدَم
elqurban elmuqaddas القربان المقدس	antiquity n qidam قدَم
sacrament n	pacemaker n qudweh قُدْوة
ulcer n qarha قرحة	paragon n qudweh قُدْوة
sore n qarhah قَرْحَة	sausage n qadid قديد
n qarhet elfirash قرحة الفِراش	omnipotent adj qadir قدير
bedsore	saint n qeddis قدِّيس
ape n kerd قرد	saintly adj qeddisi قدِّيسي
monkey n qerd قرد	ancient adj kadim قديم
n kerd elmaymun قرد الميمون	old adj qadim قديم
baboon	immemorial adj qadim قَديم
penny n qersh قرش	scruffiness n qazarah قذارة
shark n qersh قرش	slovenly adj qazr قَذِر
disc n qrs قرص	ejaculation n elqazf القذف

pigmy *n* qazam قَزَم	pirate *n* qursan قرصان
pygmy *n* qazam قَزَم	sting *n* qarsah قرصة
instalment *n* qest قسط	piracy *n* qarsaneh قرصنة
division *n* qesm قسم	loan *n* qard قرض
section *n* qesm قسم	stationery *n* qurtaseyyeh قِرْطاسِيّة
split *n* qesm قسم	lot *n* qur'ah قُرْعَة
allot *v* qassam قَسَّم	cinnamon *n* qerfeh قِرفة
lot *n* qesm قِسْم	horn *n* qrn قرن
stringency *n* qasweh قسوة	antler *n* karen قَرن
bishop *n* kasis قسيس	century *n* karn قَرن
priest *n* qassis قسيس	cauliflower *n* karnabit قرنبيط
priestess *n* qassiseh قَسِّيسة	cornea *n* elqarneyeh القرنِيّة
priesthood *n* qassiseyyeh قَسِّيسِيّة	contiguous *adj* qarib قريب
hay *n* qashsh قَشّ	convergent *adj* qarib قريب
thatch *n* qashsh قَشّ	near *adj* qarib قريب
straw *n* qashsh قَشّ	forthcoming *adj* qarib قَريب
husk *n* qeshr قشر	qarib men قريب من الأرحام
zest *n* qeshr limon قشر الليمون	cognate *adj* elarham
peel *n* keshreh قِشرة	soon *adv* qariban قريبا
dandruff *n* qishreh قِشرة	shortly *adv* qareban قَريباً
crust *n* qishreh قِشْرة	town *n* qaryeh قرية
scab *n* qeshret eljerh قشرة الجرح	consort *n* qarin قرين
ague *n* qasharira قشعريرة	accomplice *n* 'areen esou قرين السوء
shudder *n* qash'arerah قشعريرة	gnome *n* qazam قزم
chill *n* qasharereh قشعَريَرَة	midget *n* qazam قزم
trim *n* qass قَصّ	bantam *n* kazam قَزَم
butcher *n* qassab قَصَّاب	dwarf *n* qazam قَزَم
	dwarf *adj* qazam قَزَم

phallus *n* qadib قَضيب	قصبة هوائيّة qasabeh hawa'eyyeh *n*
phallic *adj* qadibi قَضيبي	trachea
case *n* kadeyeh قضيّة	bronchial *adj* qasabi قصبي
cause *n* kadeyeh قضيّة	cut *n* qassah قصّة
issue *n* qadeyyeh قضيّة	story *n* qessah قصّة
قضيّة مدنيّة qadeyyeh madaneyyeh *n*	قصّة رمزيّة kessa razeyeh *n*
pursuit	apologue
train *n* qetar قطار	bob *n* qassa al qasir قصّة عالقصير
sector *n* 'qetta قطّاع	قصّة قصيرة qessah qaserah *n*
cutter *n* katta'a قطّاعة	novelette
pole *n* qutb قطب	intention *n* qasd قصد
keystone *n* qutub قُطْب	purpose *n* qasd قصد
القطب الشمالي elqutub elshamali *n*	signification *n* qasd قصد
Arctic	tin *n* qasdir قصدير
polar *adj* qetbi قطبي	palace *n* qasr قصر
قطبي جنوبي ketbi janubi *adj*	mansion *n* qasr قَصْر
antarctic	قَصف بالقنابل kasuf belkanabel *n*
polarity *n* qetbeyyeh قطبية	bombardment
cat *n* qettah قطّة	deficit *n* qusur قصور
kitten *n* qettah sghereh قطّة صغيرة	entropy *n* qusur harari قصور حراري
قطر الدائرة qeter eddaerah *n*	poem *n* qasideh قصيدة
diameter	short *adj* qasir قصير
tar *n* qutran قَطْرَان	قصير مدعبل qasir meda'bal *adj*
eyewash *n* qatrah قَطْرَة	podgy
minim *n* qatrah قَطْرَة	judicature *n* 'qada قَضَاء
قطع النَفَس qate' elnafas *n* puff	القضاء والقدر elqada' welqadar *n*
decidedly *adv* qat'an قطعًا	predestination
piece *n* qet'ah قطعة	judicial *adj* qada'e قضائي

n qellet ihtiram قلّة احترام	pick n qatf قطف
disrespect	cotton n qutun قطن
n qellet khebrah قلّة الخبرة	herd n 'qate قطيع
inexperience	flock n 'qate قَطيع
impatience n qellet sabr قلّة الصبر	pod n 'qate قَطيع
avulsion n 'qale قلع	posture n qa'deh قعدة
fortress n qal'ah قلعة	n qa'waret elkusah قعورة الكوسا
castle n kalaa قلعَة	ream
citadel n qala'a قلعَة	nape n qafa قفا
acropolis n kal'et athina قلعة أثينا	leap n qafzeh قفزة
sandcastle n qal'et raml قلعة رمل	cage n qafas قفص
worry n qalaq قلق	dock n qafas elittiham قفص الاتّهام
suspense n qalaq قَلَق	n kafas elasfur قفص العصفور
pen n qalam قلم	birdcage
marker n qalam tahdid قلم تحديد	aviary n qafas assafir قفص عصافير
ballpoint n kalam heber قلم حبر	closure n qefel قفل
pencil n qalam rsas قلم رصاص	lock n qefl قفل
beret n kelensuweh قلنسوة	n qufel mrakkab قفل مرّكب
alkaline adj qulawi قلوي	deadbolt
insufficient adj qalil قليل	reversible adj qallab قَلاّب
little adj qalil قليل	cardio n elqaleb القلب
puny adj qalil قليل	heart n qalb قلب
scarce adj qalil قَليل	hardy adj kabu qawi قلبه قوي
impatient adj qalil sabr قليل صبر	dauntless adj qalbu qawi قلبُه قوي
gamble n qmar قمار	cardiac adj kalbi قلبي
cloth n qmash قماش	dearth n qelleh قلّة
peak n qemmeh قمّة	scarcity n qelleh قلّة
summit n qemmeh قمّة	paucity n qelleh قلّة

wheat *n* qamh قمح	*n* kuwatt bhryeh قوات بحرية admiralty
moon *n* qamar قمر	*n* quwwat musallaha قوّاتُ مُسَلَّحة military
oppression *n* 'qame قمع	rodent *n* qawared قَوَارِض
repression *n* 'qame قمع	trigger *n* qwas قواس
oppressive *adj* qame'i قمعي	force *n* qwweh قوّة
louse *n* qamleh قَمْلِة	power *n* quwweh قوِّة
chemise *n* qamis قميص	brunt *n* qwet elsadmeh قوّة الصدمة
shirt *n* qamis قميص	arch *n* qaws قَوس
jersey *n* qamis suf قميص صوف	bracket *n* qusin قوسين
channel *n* kanat قناة	parenthesis *n* qusin قوسين
canal *n* kanah قناة	gothic *n* quti قوطي
mask *n* 'qina قناع	gothic *adj* quti قوطي
gasmask *n* qina' ghaz قناع غاز	krill *n* qawqa'ah قوقعة
contentment *n* qana'a قَنَاعَة	say *n* qul قول
shell *n* qunbleh قَنْبِلة	dictum *n* qul ma'thur قول مأثور
bomb *n* kunbula قُنبِلة	cast *n* qulabeh قولَبِة
flare *n* isharah qunblet قنبلة إشارة	colon *n* kulun قولون
beaver *n* qundus قُنْدُس	acute *adj* awi قوي
shoot *n* qans قَنّص	powerful *adj* qawi قوي
arcade *n* qantara قَنطرة	robust *adj* qawi قوي
urchin *n* qunfuz قنفذ	stalwart *adj* qawi قوي
phial *n* qanneneh قَنّينة	strong *adj* qawi قوي
vial *n* qannineh قَنّينة	mighty *adj* qawi قَوي
bottle *n* qannineh قَنّينة	vigorous *adj* qawi قَوي
coffee *n* kahweh قهوة	lead *n* qyadeh قيادة
n kahwet enternit قهوة انترنت cybercafé	leadership *n* qyadeh قيادة
troop *n* quwwat قوّات	

كاتب سحور kateb sehur n
bewitching

كاتب سيرة ذاتيّة katib elsireh
biographer n elzateyeh

كاتب عدل notary n kateb adel

كاتِب عَمود في جريدة katib amud fi
columnist n jarideh

كاتب مسرحي kateb masrahi n
dramatist

كاتب مقالات katb maqalat n
essayist

كاتدرائية minster n katedra'eyyeh

كاتدرائيّة cathedral n katedraeyeh

كاتم صوت silencer n katem sut

كاتو cake n kato

كاثوليكي catholic adj kathuliki

كاثوليكيّة n kathulikeyeh
catholicism

كاحل ankle n kahel

كادِح laborious adj kadeh

كادر staff n kader

كادميوم cadmium n kademyum

كاذب deceptive adj kazib

كارثة disaster n karitheh

كارِثة catastrophe n karetheh

كارثي disastrous adj karithi

كارِثي catastrophic adj karethi

كاردينال cardinal n kardinal

measurement n qyas قياس

size n qyas قياس

قياس عن بعد n qyas an bu'd
telemetry

harp n qitharah قيثارة

lyre n qitharah قيثارة

pus n qih قَيح

bound n qid قيد

carat n kirat قيراط

cesarean adj kaysari قيصري

siesta n qeluleh قيلولة

value n qemeh قيمة

ك

كَ as prep ka

dolman n kab كاب

cape n kab كَاب

dejection n ka'abeh كآبة

gloom n ka'abeh كآبة

captain n kaptin كابتن

كابتن صاروخ n kaptin sarukh
rocketeer

nightmare n kabus كابوس

writer n katib كاتب

كاتب باسم مستعار katb be'ism
ghostwriter n musta'ar

n kanun elawwal كانون الأول
december

January n kanun ettani كانون الثاني

druid n kahin كاهِن

parson n kahen كاهِن

clerical adj kahini كاهِني

caustic adj kawi كاوي

entity n ka'en كائِن

organism n ka'en hayy كائِن حَيّ

cabaret n kabareh كاريه

atrocity n kabair كابائر

suppression n kabh كبح

liver n kabed كَبِد

n kebr elras كبر الرأس
macrocephaly

sulphur n kebrit كبريت

sulphuric adj kebriti كبريتي

capsule n kapsuleh كبسولة

n kabsh elfeda كبش الفدا
scapegoat

clew n kabkubeh كبكوبة

cable n kabel كِبل

shackle n kabl كَبل

big adj kbir كبير

grand adj kbir كبير

macro adj kbir كبير

elder n elkbir belumer الكبير بالعمر

aged adj kbir bleumr كبير بالعمر

caricature n karikatir كاريكاتير

paraffin n kaz كاز

casino n kazino كازينو

chalice n kas كاس

chalice n kas elquddas كاس القدّاس

custard n kastard كاسترد

stagnant adj kased كاسد

cassette n kasit كاسيت

bright adj kashif كاشف

n kashef zelzal كاشف زلازل
seismoscope

atheist n kafir كافِر

camphor n kafur كافُور

adequate adj kaffi كافي

enough adj kafi كافي

caviar n kafiyar كافيار

cafe n kafeh كافِّه

kaki n kaki كاكي

stern adj kaleh كالح

calcite n kalsit كالسيت

calcium n kalsiyum كالسيوم

opaque adj kamed كامِد

unabridged adj kamel كامل

whole adj kamel كامل

entire adj kamil كامِل

integral adj kamel كامِل

camera n kamira كاميرا

shoulder n ketf كتف

scapular adj ketfi كتفي

nestling n katkut كتكوت

agglomerate n ktll كلّ

lump n ketleh كلة

mass n ketleh كلة

iceblock n ketlet talj كلة تلج

n keteleh hayaweyeh كلة حيويّة

biomass

mute n katm كتم

reticent adj katum كَتوم

taciturn adj katum كَتوم

manual n kutayyeb كُتيّب

battalion n katibeh كتيبة

corps n katibeh كتيبة

abundant adj kteer كتير

crass adj ktir كتير

many adj ktir كتير

much a ktir كتير

much adv ktir كتير

numerous adj ktir كتير

redundant adj ktir كتير

several adj ktir كتير

so adv ktir كتير

very adj ktir كتير

adj ktir eltafkir كتير التفكير

thoughtful

elderly adj kbir belumur كبير بالعمر

old n kbir bel'umer كبير بالعمر

n kabenet eltalifon كبّينة التلفون

booth

book n kitab كتاب

e- n ktab elketruni كتاب الكتروني

book

n kitab muqaddas كتاب مقدّس

scripture

kitabet elsireh elzateyeh كتابة السيرة الذاتيّة

biography n

n kitabeh meshaffarah كتابة مشفّرة

cryptography

catalogue n katalug كتالوج

linen n kettan كتّان

n kter elghalayan كتر الغليان

decrepitation

abundance n ktreh كترة

redundance n ketreh كترة

aboundance n ketreh كترة

plenty n ketreh كترة

plurality n ketreh كترة

n ketret elmarakez كترة المراكز

polycentrism

electron n elktron الكترون

cyber adj elktruni الكتروني

electronic adj elketroni الكتروني

ketchup n katshap كتشب

carbide *n* kerbid كربيد

basketball *n* kuret salleh كرة السلّة

card *n* kart كرت

playcard *n* kart le'b كرت اللعب

carton *n* kartun كرتون

cardboard *n* kartun كرتُون

n kartun muqawwa كرتون مقوّى
board

cherry *n* karaz كَرَز

cherry *adj* karazi كَرَزي

waiter *n* karsun كرسون

waitress *n* karsuneh كرسونة

craw *n* kerish كِرش

celery *n* krafs كَرَفس

curcumin *n* kurkum كُرْكُم

turmeric *n* kurkum كُرْكُم

vine *n* karm كرم

generosity *n* karam كَرَم

orchard *n* karam كَرْم

n krumuzum كروموزوم
chromosome

abhor *v* kurh كره

dislike *n* kereh كره

hate *n* kurh كره

lark *n* krawan كروان

crochet *n* krusheh كروشيه

chrome *n* krum كروم

spherical *adj* kurawi كروي

adj ktir elnsyan كتير النسيان
oblivious

chilly *adj* ktir bared كتير بارد

hefty *adj* ktir tqil كتير تقيل

adj ktir khas كتير خاص
extraspecial

dank *adj* ktir reteb كتير رطِب

adj ktir metanneq كتير متأنّق
falmboyant

angular *adj* ktir naheif كتير نحيف

impenetrable *adj* katim كَتِيم

consistence *n* kathafeh كَّافة

scambling *n* kadh كدح

bruise *n* kadmeh كدمة

liar *n* elkazzab الكذّاب

mendacious *adj* kazzab كذّاب

lie *n* kezbeh كذبة

talkativeness *n* kerr كَرّ

onslaught *n* garr كَرّ

leek *n* kurrat كرّات

karat *n* karatih كاراتيه

garage *n* karaj كَرَاج

tie *n* krafeh كرافة

animus *n* karaheyeh كراهيّة

whip *n* kerbaj كرباج

lash *n* kerbaj كِرْباج

carbonization *n* karbaneh كربَنة

carbon *n* karbun كربون

indolent *adj* kasul كَسُول	crystal *n* kristal كريستال
rickety *adj* kasih كَسِيح	cream *n* krym كريم
lame *adj* kasih كَسِيح	generous *adj* karim كريم
checkmate *n* kish malik كِش مَلِك	obnoxious *adj* karih كريه
thimble *n* keshteban كشتبان	repugnant *adj* karih كريه
stall *n* keshk كشك	abominable *adj* karih كَرِيه
frill *n* kashkash كَشْكَش	coriander *n* kezbarah كزبرة
gooseberry *n* kishmesh كشمش	rickets *n* kusah كساح
cashmere *n* kashmir كشمير	akinesia *n* kusah كُساح
heel *n* ka'eb كعب	depression *n* kasad كَساد
n kaeb elssafha كعب الصفحة	stagnation *n* kasad كَساد
affixation	cracker *n* kassarah كسَّارة
flap *n* kaff كَفّ	cullet *n* kasaret elballur كسَّارة بللور
biff *n* kaff كَفّ	chestnut *n* kastanah كستنَا
palm *n* kaff كَفّ	auburn *adj* kastana'ei كستنائي
efficacy *n* kafa'ah كفاءة	maroon *adj* kastanae'i كَسْتَنَائي
warranty *n* kafaleh كفالة	breakage *n* kaser كسر
bail *n* kafaleh كَفَالَة	fraction *n* kasr كسر
adequacy *n* kfayeh كفاية	*n* keser amami كسر أمامي
sufficiency *n* kefayeh كفاية	breakfront
atheism *n* kufur كُفر	casserole *n* kasruleh كسرولة
coffin *n* kafan كَفَن	laziness *n* kasal كسل
shroud *n* kafan كَفَن	sloth *n* kasal كَسَل
acceder *n* kafoo كفو	lazy *n* kaslan كسلان
efficient *adj* kufu'e كُفُؤ	sluggard *n* kaslan كَسْلان
gauntlet *n* kfuf كفوف	physique *n* kasm كسم
glove *n* kfuf كفوف	clothing *n* kisweh كِسوة
sponsor *n* kafil كفيل	eclipsis *n* elkusuf الكسُوف

n kalimat ughneyeh كلمات أغنية	warrantor *n* kafil كفيل
lyric	all *adj* kel كل
term *n* klmeh كلمة	each *adj* kell كلّ
word *n* klmeh كلمة	everybody *pron* kel hada كل حدا
n kelmeh asasyyeh كلمة أساسيّة	everyone *pron* kel hada كل حدا
keyword	monthly *adv* kel shahr كلّ شهر
all *pron* klna كلنا	*pron* kel makan كل مكان
bodily *adv* kulluh كلّه	everywhere
quite *adv* kulluh كلّه	*adj* kel nes shaher كل نص شهر
chlorine *n* klur كلور	bimonthly
chloroform *n* klurufurm كلوروفورم	everyday *adj* kel yum كل يوم
college *n* keliyyeh كلّيّة	classic *adj* klasiki كلاسيكي
faculty *n* kleyyeh كلّيّة	classical *adj* klasiki كلاسيكي
academy *n* kliyeh كليَة	utterance *n* klam كلام
kidney *n* klyeh كلية	*n* kalam ala infirad كلام على انفراد
cliché *n* klisheh كليشيه	aside
sleeve *n* kemm كمّ	*adj* klamuh mneh كلامه منيح
quantum *n* kamm كمّ	euphemistic
drib *n* kamm qalil كمّ قليل	every *adj* klamuh mnih كلامه منيح
perfection *n* kamal كمَال	dog *n* kalb كلب
integrity *n* kamal كمَال	rabies *n* kalb كلَب
supplement *n* kamaleh كمالة	greyhound *n* kleb syd كلب صيد
gag *n* kammameh كمّامة	hound *n* kleb syd كلب صيد
also *adv* kaman كمان	slut *n* kalbeh كلبة
besides *adv* kaman كمان	cuff *n* kalabshah كلبشة
else *adv* kaman كمان	fetter *n* klabshah كلبشة
too *adv* kaman كمان	handcuff *n* kalabshah كلبشة
violin *n* kaman كمان	everything *pron* klshi كلشي

tankard n kuz كُوز

ancon n 'kuwe كوع

elbow n ku'e كوع

cocaine n kukaen كوكائين

planet n kawkab كوكب

astral adj kawkabi كوكبي

planetary adj kawkabi كوكبي

colonel n kulunil كولونيل

cholera n kulira كوليرا

rick n kumeh كومة

pile n kumeh كومة

heap n kumeh كومة

comedian n kumidi كوميدي

comical adj kumidi كوميدي

comedy n kumidya كوميديا

universe n elkun الكَون

cosmos n elkun الكُون

countess n kuntissa كُونتيسًّا

preserve n kunsurwah كُونْسِرْوَة

congress n kungres كونغرس

cosmic adj kuni كُونِي

brandy n konyak كونياك

beamless adj kebi كيبي

artifice n kyd كَيد

cunning n kayd كِيْد

kerosene n kirusin كيروسين

bag n kees كيس

sack n kis كيس

opacity n kamdeh كُمدة

belt n kamar كَمَر

cello n kamanja كَمَنجة

fiddle n kamanjah كَمَنجة

quantitative adj kammi كُمّي

quantity n kameyyeh كُمِّية

ambuscade n kamin كَمِن

canary n kanari كاري

settee n kanabeh كَنَبّة

sweep n kans كنس

ecclesiastical adj kanasi كَنَسِي

kangaroo n kangaru كنغارو

surname n kenyeh كنية

church n keniseh كنيسة

n keniseh seghireh كنيسة صغيرة

chapel

electricity n kahrabah كهربا

electric adj kahrubae'i كهربائي

cave n kahef كهف

koala n kuala كوالا

cobalt n kubalt كوبالت

cobra n kubra كوبرا

coupon n kubun كوبون

cottage n kukh كوخ

shack n kukh كُوخ

igloo n kukh mqabbab كوخ مقبَّب

choir n kural كورال

pitcher n kuz كوز

not adv 'la أَلا	كِيس pouch n kis
cordless adj la silki لا سلكي	كيس شاي teabag n kis shay
wireless adj la selki لا سلكي	كيس هوا airbag n kys hwa
indifference n la mubalat لا مبالاة	كيف how adv keif
careless adj la mubali لا مبالي	كيف ما كان adv keif m kaan
indifferent adj la mubali لا مبالي	anyhow
blasé adj la mubali لا مُبالي	كيف ما كان adj kif ma kan
adj la markazi لا مركزي	haphazard
decentralized	canister n keleh كِلة
infinite adj la niha'e لا نهائي	utensil n keleh كُلّة
nay adv la wlu لا ولو	kilo n kilo كِلو
laptop n labtup لابتوب	kilogram n kilogram كيلوغرام
adj labes nazarat لابس نظارات	alchemy n kimia كيميا
bespectacled	chemistry n kimia كيميا
badly adv laabad hadd لأبعد حَدّ	adj kimia hayaweyeh كيميا حيويّة
refugee n 'laje لاجئ	biochemical
subsequent adj lahiq لاحق	alchemist n kimiaei كيميائي
suffix n laheqah لاحقة	chemical adj 'kimyae كيميائي
poignant adj 'lade لادع	chemist n 'kimyaei كيميائي
needful adj lazm لازم	existence n kenuneh كينونة
intransitive (adj (verb lazem لازِم	quinine n elkinin الكينين
indispensable adj lazem لازِم	bleak adj ka'eyb كئيب
adj 'lazm yendefe لازم يندفع	gloomy adj ka'ib كئيب
payable	
adhesive n laseq لاصق	
adhesive adj laseq لاصق	
gameplayer n la'eb لاعب	**ل**
player n la'eb لاعِب	no n la لا

n lebs dakhli لبس داخلي underwear	poster n lafteh لافتة
corduroy n lebes qutni لبس قطني	lavender n lavendar لافندر
lebes men wabar لبس من وبر الجمل camlet n eljamal	lactose n laktuz لاكتوز
beyond adv labaed لبعد	because .conj le'annu لأنّه
forth adv laba'din لبعدين	infinity n la niha'eyyeh لانهائيّه
hereafter adv laba'dyn لبعدين	theology n lahut لاهوت
afield adv lbeyd لبعيد	beneath adv la awta لأوطى
away adv labe'yed لبعيد	becoming adj layeq لايق
far adv labeyed لبعيد	decent adj layq لايق
tactful adj labeq لبِق	pulp n lebb لبّ
mess n labakeh لبكة	gist n lebb لُبّ
ivy n leblab لبلاب	crumb n lebb elsumen لبّ الصمن
yogurt n laban لبن	decency n labaqah لَبَاقَة
n laban mrawwab لبَن مروّب buttermilk	tact n labaqah لَبَاقَة
lioness n labweh لبوة	abroad adv labarrah لبرّا
pulpy adj lebbi لبّي	out adv labarrah لبرّا
knowledgeable adj labib لبيب	outside adv labarrah لبرّا
below adv latahit لتحت	outward adv labarrah لبرّا
beneath adv la tahit لتحت	outwards adv labarrah لبرّا
down adv latahet لتحت	attire n lebes لبس
litre n letr لتر	clothes n lebes لبس
curb n lijam elhusan لجام الحصان	dressing n lebes لبس
beside prep lejanab لجَنَب	outfit n lebs لبس
committee n lajneh لجنة	firesuit n lebs elitfa'e لبس الإطفائي
jury n lajnet tahlif لجنة التحليف	ferment n lebs elkhimar لبس الخمار
	overall n lebs elsughul لبس الشغل
	bedrobe n lebes ennum لبس النوم
	apparel n lebes khas لبس خاص

quilt *n* lhef لحيف

mismatch *v* lakhbatah لخبطة

stew *n* lakhanah لخنة

accordingly *adv* lza لذا

epicurean *adj* lazzati لذَّاقي

epicurean *n* lazzati لذَّاقي

delectability *n* lizzeh لذَّة

orgasmic *adj* 'lezzet eljima لذَّة الجماع

slimy *adj* lezj لزج

paste *n* lazq لزق

bandage *n* lazqet jerh لزقة جرح

plaster *n* lazqet jerh لزقة جرح

must *n* luzum لُزُوم

armlet *adj* lisan لسان

tongue *n* lsan لسان

sticker *n* lusaqah لصاقة

kindness *n* latafeh لطافة

smear *n* latkh لطخ

blot *n* latekha لطخَة

blur *n* latkha لطخَة

slur *n* latkhah لَطْخَة

besides *prep* letaraf لَطَرَف

amiability *n* lutf لُطف

affable *adj* ltif لطيف

amiable *adj* latif لطيف

gracious *adj* latif لطيف

kind *adj* latif لطيف

nice *adj* latif لطيف

below *adv* lajhannam لجهنم

asylum *n* 'lujouo لَجُوء

inwards *adv* lajuwwah لجوّاً

inside *adv* lajuwwah لجوّا

duvet *n* lhaf لحاف

singularly *adv* lahalu لحاله

myself *pron* lahali لحالي

weld *n* leham لحام

solder *n* leham لِحَام

fairly *adv* lahadd ma لحدّ ما

further *adv* lahdd ma لحدّ ما

lick *n* lahs لَحْس

fellatio *n* lahs elqadib لحس القَضيب

adv lahesn hazzuh لحسن حظُّه

luckily

awhile *adv* lahza لحظة

moment *n* lahzah لحظة

instant *n* lahzah لحظَة

flesh *n* lahm لحم

junction *n* lahm لحم

meat *n* lahm لحم

beef *n* lahem baqar لحم بقر

bacon *n* lahem khanzir لحم خنزير

pork *n* lahm khanzir لحم خنزير

mutton *n* lahm ghanam لحم غنم

epiglittis *n* lahmet elhaleq لحمة الحالق

melody *n* lahn لحن

about *adv* lahawali لحوالي

n ellugha elfaranseyyeh اللغة الفرنسيّة	abuser *n* la'aan لعّان
French	toy *n* le'beh لعبة
conundrum *n* lughez لغز	doll *n* lebeh لعبة
lingual *adj* lughawi لُغَوِي	game *n* le'beh لعبة
linguist *n* lughawi لُغَوِي	checkers *n* lebet eldama لعبة الداما
linguistic *adj* lughawi لُغَوِي	crambo *n* le'bet elqafyeh لعبة القافية
scroll *n* laff لفّ	*n* ellluebeh elly baed اللعبة اللي بعد
gift- *v* laff elhadayah لفّ الهدايا	aftergame
wrap	*n* le'beh belkhyut لعبة بالخيوط
wrap *n* laff elhadeyyeh لفّ الهديّة	puppet
roll *n* laffeh لفّة	curse *n* la'neh لعنة
n laffet elhadeyyeh لفّة الهديّة	damn *n* la'neh لعنة
wrapper	malediction *n* la'neh لَعْنَة
turnip *n* left لِفْت	playful *adj* la'ub لَعُوب
attraction *n* lafet intibah لفت انتباه	gambler *n* la'eyb qmar لعِيّب قمار
scarf *n* lafha لفحة	nausea *n* la'yet elnafs لعية النفس
pronunciation *n* lafz لفظ	*adj* lughatuh ktireh لغاته كتيره
stitch *n* lafqah لَفْقَة	polyglot
above *adv* lafuq لفوق	language *n* lughah لغة
highly *adv* lafuq لفوق	*n* lughah ajnabeyyeh لغة أجنبيّة
up *adv* lafuq لفوق	lingo
upwards *adv* lafuq لفوق	ellugha elinklizeyyeh اللغة الانكليزيّة
convergence *n* 'liqa لقاء	English *n*
vaccine *n* luqah لقاح	*n* ellughah elameyyeh اللغة العاميّة
clamp *n* laqqatah لَقّاطَة	vernacular
nickname *n* laqab لَقَب	*n* ellugha elarabeyeh اللغة العربية
ahead *adv* lqddam لقدام	Arabic
forward *adv* lqeddam لقدّام	

sparkle n lama'an لَمَعَان	onwards adv laqeddam لقدّام
glaze n laman eltalj لمعان التلج	snap n laqtah لقطَة
refulgence n lam'ah لمعة	shot n laqtah لَقْطَة
refulgent adj 'lamme لَمِع	n laqtet shasheh لقطة شاشة
aglow adv 'lmmye لَمِع	screenshot
lustrous adj 'lamme لَمِع	stork n laqlaq لقلق
near adv lanahak لَنَاحَك	bite n leqmeh لقمة
downwards adv lanzul لنزول	each adv lakell لكلّ
adieu .interj alla yehik الله يحميك	eternally adv lelabad للأبد
damn int allah yelanak الله يلعنَك	forever adv lelabad للأبد
her adj laha لها	better adv lelahsan للأحسن
flame n lahab لهَب	alas .interj lilasf للأسف
gasp n lahteh لهتة	bisexual adj leljensin للجنسين
pant n lahteh لهتة	south adv leljanub للجنوب
accent n lahjeh لهجة	east adv lelsharq للشرق
parlance n lahjeh لهجة	aback adv lelwaraa للورا
dialect n lahjeh لهجة	hitherto adv lelyum لليوم
hither adv lahun لهون	n lamm elshaml لَمُّ الشَّمْل
brigadier n 'liwae لِواء	unification
needs adv lawazm لَوَازِم	bulb n lamba لمبة
sodomy n lwatah لواطَة	lamp n lambah لمبَة
lotus n lutus لُوتُس	glance n lamha لَمْحَة
bar n luh لوح	n lamha ammeh لمْحَة عامّة
board n luh لوح	conspectus
slate n luh لوح	touch n lamseh لمسة
pane n luh لَوْح	osculant adj lamsi لمسي
tablet n luh لَوْح	tactile adj lamsi لَمْسِي
scapula n luh elketf لوح الكتف	gloss n lama'an لَمَعَان

until *prep* lawaqt لوقت	plank *n* luh khashab لوح خشب
long *adv* lwaqet tawil لوقت طويل	*n* lawh sibaha kasir لوح سباحَة قصير
none *adv* la wla hada لولا حدا	bodyboard
nothing *adv* la wla shi لولا شي	panel *n* luhah لَوْحَة
spiral *n* lulab لَوْلَب	*n* lawhit e'elanat لوحة إعلانات
spiral *adj* lulabi لَوْلَبي	billboard
pearl *n* lulu لولو	*n* luhet elahdaf لوحة الأهداف
reprimand *n* lum لوم	scoreboard
blame *n* luwm لَوم	*n* luhet elmafatih لوحة المفاتيح
censure *n* lum لَوم	keypad
colour *n* lun لون	palette *n* lawhet alwan لوحة ألوان
red *n* lun ahmar لون أحمر	canvas *n* lawha zeyteyeh لوحة زيتيّة
n lun ahmar ramadi لون أحمر رمادي	alone *adj* lawahduh لوحده
damask	solo *adv* lwahduh لوحده
blue *n* lun azraq لون أزرق	aft *adv* lwra لورا
green *n* ellun elakhdar اللون الأخضر	back *adv* lawara لَوَرا
n ellun elqurmuzi اللون القرمزي	behind *adv* lawara لَوَرا
crimson	lord *n* lurd لورد
n ellun elkastanae'i اللون الكَسْتَنَائي	almond *n* luz لَوَز
maroon	amygdala *n* luz لُوز
indigo *n* ellun elnili اللون النيلي	tonsil *n* luzeh لوزة
orange *adj* lun burtuqali لون برتقالي	lotion *n* lushen لوشن
brown *n* luwn benni لون بنّي	gay *n* elluti اللوطي
cyan *n* lun samawi لون سماوي	gay *adj* luti لوطي
pink *n* lun wardi لون وردي	queer *adj* luti لوطي
aptitude *n* layaqa لياقة	queer *n* luti لوطي
fit *n* layakah لياقة	sodomite *n* luti لُوطي
liberal *adj* liberali ليبرالي	logarithim *n* lugaritm لوغاريتم

unabashed *adj* ma beykhjal ما بِخجل

adj 'ma benseme ما بِنسمع

inaudible

adj ma bnqas ما بِنقاس

immeasurable

adj ma beynhedm ما بنهضِم

indigestible

adj ma beyntaq ما يِتطبَّق

inapplicable

adj me beystaradd ما يِستردّ

irrecoverable

worthless *adj* ma byswah ما يِسوى

dissimilar *adj* ma byshbah ما يِشبه

adj ma beynhasa ما يِنحصى

incalculable

countless *adj* ma beynad ما يِنعَدّ

except *prep* ma ada ما عدا

adj ma andu hess ما عنده حسّ

insensible

adj ma andu khebra ما عنده خبرة

callow

adj mafeyyu shakk ما فيو شكّ

doubtless

adj ma beytfassar مابتفسَّر

inexplicable

adj ma beynqsem مابتقسَّم

indivisible

liberalism *n* liberaleyyeh ليبراليّة

pound *n* lirah لِيرَة

fibre *n* lif ليف

coir *n* lif juz hind ليف جوز الهند

fibroid *adj* lifi لِيفي

fibrous *adj* lifi لِيفي

night *n* lyl ليل

tonight *n* ellyleh الليلة

nightie *n* leleh sa'ydeh ليلة سعيدة

lilac *n* lilak لَيلَك

nocturnal *adj* layli ليلي

overnight *adj* layli ليلي

lemon *n* limon ليمون

lemonade *n* limonadah ليمونادا

lenience *n* lyn لين

mellow *adj* lyn لَيّن

supple *adj* lyn لَيّن

laxity *n* lyn لِين

miscreant *n* la'ym لَئيم

ignoble *adj* la'ym لَئيم

م

adj ma beytbarrar ما بتبرَّر

indefensible

adj ma beynwesef ما بتنوصف

indescribable

goo n maddeh debqa مادّة دبقَة	adj ma beyntaq مابنطاق
alkali n maddeh qulawia مادة قلوية	insupportable
n madeh kimaweyyeh مادة كيماوية	intolerable adj ma beyntaq مابنطاق
chemical	myriad adj ma beyn'add مابعدّ
n madeh musa'edeh مادة مساعدة	adj ma beyngheleb مابنغلب
adjuvant	invincible
n madeh mutahhera مادة مطهّرة	limitless adj ma beynheser مايِحصر
antiseptic	adj ma beyshbah hada مابيشبه حدا
n maddeh mehayyjeh مادّة مهيّجة	matchless
irritant	insoluble n ma beynhall مابينحلّ
material adj maddi مادّي	adj ma beyn'add مابينعدّ
materialism n maddeyyeh مادية	innumerable
mischievous adj me'zi مأذي	adj ma beyn'add مابينعدّ
marathon n maratun ماراتون	numberless
pitfall n ma'zeq مأزق	adj ma beynqas مابينقاس
deadlock n ma'ziq مأزِق	measureless
dilemma n ma'ziq مأزِق	matinee n matineh ماتِنيه
captive adj ma'sur مأسور	master n elmajestir الماجستير
duct n masurah ماسُورَة	taken adj ma'khud مَأخُود
n masuret elsarf ماسورة الصرف	courteous adj meaddab مأدّب
drainpipe	polite adj me'addab مأدّب
masonry n masuneyyeh ماسُونيّة	material n maddeh مادّة
n mashi benumuh ماشي بنومه	substance n maddeh مادّة
somnambulist	item n maddeh مادّة
middling adj mashi halu ماشي حاله	elmadeh المادة الصفراوية
mashiyh el'umur ماشية الأمور تمام	bile n elsafraweyeh
afoot adv tamam	n maddeh hafzah مادّة حافظة
past n madi ماضي	preservative

peerless *adj* malu mathil مالو مثيل	prior *adj* madi ماضي
adj malu maf'ul مالو مفعول inoperative	moron *n* ma'fun مَأفُون
familiar *adj* ma'luf مألوف	mafia *n* mafya مافيا
financial *adj* mali مالي	feline *adj* maker ماكر
fiscal *adj* mali مالي	canny *adj* maker ماكِر
mamma *n* mama ماما	oxygenated *adj* me'aksaj مُأكسَج
mum *n* mama ماما	machine *n* makinah ماكِينة
secure *adj* me'amman مأمَّن	outcome *n* ma'al مآل
mammoth *n* mamuth مامُوث	salty *adj* malih مالح
mummy *n* mami مامي	proprietor *n* malik مالك
mango *n* manjo مانجو	owner *n* malik مالك
n manih elrahn مانع الرهن mortgagee	*n* malek elsafineh مالك السفينة shipowner
coat *n* mantu مانطو	*n* malek elqalaa مالك القلعة castellan
garb *n* mantu مانطو	beardless *adj* malu da'en ماله دقن
overcoat *n* mantu مانطو	opinionless *adj* malu ra'i ماله رأي
delayment *n* 'mane مانِع	baseless *adj* malu mubarir مالُه مُبرر
hindrance *n* 'mane مَانِع	*adj* malu ma'nah ماله معنى meaningless
sealant *n* mane' tasarrub مانع تسرُّب	*adj* malu ma'nah ماله معنى nonsensical
adj mane' haml مانع حمل contraceptive	ineffective *adj* malu athar مالو أثر
mannequin *n* manikan مانِيكان	insipid *adj* malu ta'meh مالو طعمة
manicure *n* manakir مانِيكير	*adj* malu alaqah مالو علاقة irrelevant
skilful *adj* mahr ماهر	*adj* malu kafu مالو كفؤ incompetent
haunt *n* ma'wa مأوى	
lodge *n* ma'wa مأوى	
shelter *n* ma'wa مأوى	

throaty *adj* mabhuh مَبْحوح

censer *n* mabkharah مِبْخَرَة

principle *n* 'mabda مَبْدَأ

extravagant *adj* mubazzer مِبَذَر

lavish *adj* mubazzer مِبَذَر

cooler *n* mubarred مُبَرِّد

rasp *n* mebrad مِبْرَد

justifiable *adj* mubarrar مُبَرَّر

spittoon *n* mabzaqah مِبْزَقَة

glad *adj* mabsut مبسوط

scraper *n* mabsharah مِبْشَرَة

grater *n* mabsharah مِبْشَرَة

voyeur *n* mbasbes مبصبص

abolisher *n* mubtil مبطل

emissary *n* mabuth مَبْعوث

maculate *adj* 'mebaqqe مُبَقَّع

amount *n* mablagh مبلغ

informer *n* muballegh مُبَلِّغ

debit *n* mablagh madin مبلغ مدين

n mabna elmadraseh مبنى المدرسة

schoolhouse

mabna ma مبنى مع إطلالة رائعة

belvedere *n* itlaleh rae'a

erect *adj* mabni مبني

delightful *adj* mubhij مبهج

dazzling *adj* mubher مبهِر

ostentatious *adj* mebahraj مبهرج

flabbergasted *adj* mabhut مبهوت

conductor *n* maystru مايسترو

fluid *adj* may'e مايع

liquid *adj* 'maye مايع

bent *adj* mayel مايل

italic *adj* mayl مايل

oblique *adj* mayl مايل

adj mayl lelqasir مايل للقصير

shortish

initiative *n* mubadarah مُبادرة

permutation *n* mubadaleh مبادلة

contest *n* mubarah مُبَارَاة

game *n* mubarah مُبَارَاة

match *n* mubarah مُبَارَاة

yesterday *n* embarhah مبارحة

duel *n* mubarazeh مبَارَزة

auspicious *adj* mubarak مُبَارَك

immediate *a* mubashr مباشر

direct *adj* mubashar مباشِر

live *adv* mubashar مباشِر

exaggeration *n* mubalaghah مبالغة

hyperbole *n* mubalaghah مُبَالَغَة

homage *n* mubaya'ah مُبَايَعَة

beginner *n* 'mubtade مبتدئ

blackmailer *n* mubtazz مُبْتَزّ

innovator *n* mebteker مبتكِر

originator *n* mebteker مبتكِر

exultant *adj* mebtehej مبتهج

hoarse *adj* mabhuh مَبْحوح

spicy *adj* metabbal مُتبَّل

mate *n* matteh مَتّة

continual *adj* 'mutatabe مُتتَابِع

adj mutajanis مُتجَانِس

homogeneous

ruthless *adj* metehajjer مُتحجِّر

speaker *n* metehaddeth مُتحدِّث

licentious *adj* mutaharrer مُتحرِّر

removable *adj* meteharrek مُتحرِّك

mover *n* meteharrek مُتحرِّك

adj mtaharrik blhwa مُتحرك بالهوا

aerodynamic

inspector *n* meteharri مُتحرِّي

museum *n* metehaf مُتحف

ardent *adj* mutahammes مُتحمِّس

eager *adj* metehammes مُتحمِّس

fervent *adj* metehammes مُتحمِّس

mutative *adj* metehawwel مُتحوِّل

biased *adj* metehayyez مُتحيِّز

ex-parte *adj* methayyez مُتحيِّز

partial *adj* metehayyez مُتحيِّز

telepathist *n* metkhater مُتخاطِر

metkhasses مُتخصِّص بالمعادن

mineralogist *n* belma'den

backward *adj* mutakhallef مُتخلِّف

blockhead *n* mutakhallef مُتخلِّف

gorge *adj* matkhum مُتخوم

imaginary *adj* mutakhayyal مُتخيَّل

punch *n* mbukaseh مبوكسة

n mubid hasharat مبيد حشرات

insecticide

n mubid hasharat مبيد حشرات

pesticide

n mubid leljarathim مبيد للجراثيم

germicide

ovary *n* mabyad مبيَض

bleach *n* mubayyed مُبيِّض

pursuance *n* metaba'ah متابعة

belated *adj* met'akhkher مُتأخِّر

late *adj* met'akhkher مُتأخِّر

overdue *adj* met'akhkher مُتأخِّر

arrears *npl* muta'akhkher مُتأخِّر

ingrained *adj* nmet'assel مُتأصِّل

rusty *adj* met'aksed مُتأكسِد

corrosive *adj* metaakil مُتآكِل

schemer *n* met'amer مُتآمِر

conspirator *n* mutaamer مُتآمِر

dapper *adj* metanniq مُتأنِّق

dude *n* metanneq مُتأنِّق

n elmetanneq zyadeh المتأنِّق زيادة

falmboyant

careful *adj* metanni مُتأنِّي

labyrinth *n* matahah مَتَاهة

reciprocal *adj* mutbadal مُتبادل

estranged *adj* metba'ed مُتباعِد

donor *n* 'metbarre مُتبرِّع

deadbeat *n* 'elmetsakke المتسكّع

dawdler *n* 'metsakke متسكّع

deadbeat *adj* 'metsakke متسكّع

loafer *n* 'metsakke مُتَسكّع

idler *n* 'metsakke مُتَسَكّع

consecutive *adj* mutasalsel مُتَسَلسِل

serial *adj* metsalsel مُتَسَلسِل

mutasalsil zamaneyyan مُتَسَلسِل زمنياً

chronological *n* zamaneyyan

authoritative *adj* mutasallet متسلّط

climber *n* mutasalleq متسلّق

mutasalliq jibal متسلّق جبال الألب

alpinist *n* el'alb

pessimist *n* metsha'em متشائم

puritan *n* metshadded متشدّد

puritanical *adj* metshadded مُتَشدّد

strict *adj* metshadded مُتَشَدّد

straggler *n* metsharred مُتَشرِّد

manifold *adj* metsha'eb مُتَشَعّب

cirrhotic *adj* 'metshamme متشمّع

cross *adj* mutasalib مُتَصَالب

benevolent *adj* mutasadeq مُتَصَدّق

browser *n* mutasaffeh مُتَصَفِّح

caller *n* muttasil مُتّصِل

mystic *adj* metsawwef مُتَصَوّف

adj metdareb متضارب

irreconcilable

congruent *adj* mutatabiq متطابق

trainee *n* mettedarreb مُتدرّب

effusive *adj* metdaffeq متدفّق

pious *adj* metdayyen مُتَدَيّن

metre *n* metr متر

coherent *adj* mutarabet مترابِط

inseparable *adj* metrabet مُتَرَابِط

n mtarjem shafahi مترجم شفهي

interpreter

dated *adj* mtarrakh مُتَرّخ

luxurious *adj* mutraf مُتْرَف

flabby *adj* metrahhel مُتَرَهّل

spare *adj* matruk مَتْروك

metric *adj* metri متري

metrical *adj* metri متري

insecure *adj* 'metza'ze مُتَزَعْزِع

austere *adj* mutazammit متزمّت

prudent *adj* mettezn متّزن

judicious *adj* mettezen متّزن

adj metzawwej tentiin متزوج تنتين

bigamous

adj metzawwej wehdeh متزوّج وحدة

monogynous

tolerant *adj* metsameh متسامح

alike *adj* mutasawi متساوي

equal *adj* metsawi متساوي

equivalent *adj* metsawi متساوي

even *adj* metsawi متساوي

prostrate *adj* metsatteh مُتَسَطّح

متعهّد حفلات haflat meahhed *n*
caterer

متعود على mt'awed ala *adj*
accustomed

متغاضي mutaghadi *adj* conniving

متفائل metfa'el *n* optimist

متفاعل metfa'el *n* reactionist

متفَاعل metfa'el *adj* reactive

متفتّت metfattet *adj* flaking

متفشّي metfashshi *adj* rampant

متفق عليه muttafaq a'lyh *adj*
agreeable

متفلسف metfalsef *n* pedant

متفهّم mutafahhem *adj* considerate

متفوّق mutafawwiq *adj* deft

متفوّق metfawweq *n* paramount

متفوّق metfawweq *adj* -pre
eminent

متفوّق metfawweq *adj*
transcendent

متقارب metqareb *adj* proximate

متقَاعد metqa'ed *n* pensioner

متقاعد mutakaed *n* annuitant

متقَاعس metqa'es *adj* listless

متقرّح metqarreh *adj* ulcerous

متقرّح metqarreh *adj* sore

متقرّحة أجريه metqarrha rejleh *adj*
footsore

متطابق mettabeq *adj* symmetrical

متطابق mutatabeq *adj* analogous

متطابقين metabqin *adj* identical

متطرّف mettarref *n* extremist

متطرّف metarref *adj* radical

متطفّل metataffel *n* leech

متطوّع mutatawwe' *n* volunteer

متعامد muta'amed *adj* orthographic

متعامل muta'amil *n* dealer

متعب met'ab *adj* tiresome

متعِب mut'ab *adj* onerous

متعِب mut'eb *adj* inconvenient

متعجرف met'ajref *adj* haughty

متعجرف met'ajref *adj* insolent

متعدد الاستعمال met'added
versatile *adj* eleste'mal

متعدّد الأطراف met'added elatraf
multilateral *adj*

متعرّج muta'rrej *adj* anfractuous

متعصّب mutaessib *n* antitheist

متعصّب met'assib *adj* intolerant

متعصّب قوميًا muta'assib
chauvinist *adj* qawmeyyan

متعفّن met'affen *adj* septic

متعلّم met'allem *n* learner

متعلّم met'allem *adj* literate

متعمّد mutaammad *adj* conscious

adj mtl ma nhka abl متل ما نحكا قبل
aforesaid

n matal maskharji مَتَل مسخرجي
epigram

snowy *adj* metallej متلّج

blotted *adj* metlattekh متلّطخ

after *adj* mtluh متله

tenacious *adj* metmasek متماسك

abet *v* metmadded متمدّد

adj metmarred متمرّد
insubordinate

rebel *n* metmarred متمرّد

rebellious *adj* metmarred متمرّد

repellent *adj* metmarred متمرّد

repellent *n* metmarred متمرّد

practitioner *n* metmarren متمرّن

probationer *n* metmarren متمرّن

shirker *n* metmalles متملّص

octagon *n* metamman متمّن

.dj mutanazil متنازل
condescending

assignee *n* mutanazal lahu متنازل له

proportional *adj* metnaseb متناسب

adj metnaseb متناسب
proportionate

incoherent *adj* metnafer متنافر

motley *adj* metnafir متنافر

waney *adj* metnaqes متناقص

ascetic *adj* mutaqashshif متقشّف

sporadic *adj* 'metqatte متقطّع

fitful *adj* 'metqatte متقطّع

capricious *adj* mutaqalleb متقلّب

jerky *adj* metqalleb متقلّب

n metqammes aatefi متقمّص عاطفي
empath

precise *n* mutqan مُتْقَن

observant *adj* metqayyed متقيّد

lethargic *adj* metkasel متكاسل

frequent *adj* metkarrer متكرّر

ostensible *adj* metekallef متكلّف

adage *n* matal متل

as *adv* metal متل

like *adj* matal متل

proverb *n* matal متل

such *adj* matal متل

ideal *n* matal a'la متل أعلى

adj metl elemm متل الإمّ
motherlike

adj metel elamwat متل الأموات
cadaverous

adj metel elbalsam متل البَلَسم
balmlike

apish *adj* metl elqerd متل القرد

adj mtl ma nhka abl متل ما نحكا قبل
aforementioned

متوحّش metwahhesh *adj*

monstrous

courtier *n* metwadded متودّد

medium *adj* metwasset متوسّط

available *adj* mutawaffir متوفّر

obtainable *adj* metwaffer متوفّر

garlicky *adj* mtawwam متوّم

coherent *adj* matin متين

durable *adj* matin متين

sturdy *adj* matin متين

example *n* methal مثال

instance *n* methal مثال

ideal *adj* methali مثالي

idealist *n* methali مثالي

idealistic *adj* methali مثالي

eutopia *n* elmethalyyeh المثاليّة

idealism *n* methalyyeh مثاليّة

bladder *n* mathaneh مثانة

fixer- *n* muthabbit ulwi مثبّت علوي

upper

jot *n* methqal zarrah مثقال ذرّة

intellectual *adj* muthaqqaf مثقّف

intellectual *n* muthaqqaf مثقّف

book-worm *n* muthaqqaf مثقّف

byword *n* mathal مَثَل

apotheosis *n* matal aala مثل أعلى

triangle *n* muthallath مثلّث

fruitful *adj* muthmir مثمر

ambivalent *adj* mutanaqid متناقض

paradoxical *adj* metnaqed متناقض

bully *n* mutanammer متنمّر

multifarious *adj* 'metnawwe متنوّع

diverse *adj* 'metnawwe متنوّع

elusive *adj* meteharrab متهرّب

accusator *n* mutahim متهم

accused *n* mutaham متهم

adventurous *adj* mthwur متهوّر

temeritous *adj* metehawwer متهوّر

adj metehawwer متهوّر

inconsiderate

ancestral *adj* mutawarath متوارث

mtawazn elhwa متوازن الهوا والغاز

aerostatic *adj* wlghaz

parallel *adj* metwazi متوازي

n 'metwazi eladla متوازي أضلاع

parallelogram

humble *adj* 'metwade متواضع

modest *adj* 'metwade متواضع

harmonious *adj* metwafeq متوافق

metwfeq beaqel متوافق بالعقل والروح

congenial *adj* welruh

anxious *adj* mutawater متوتّر

tensioned *adj* metwatter متوتّر

taut *adj* metwatter متوتّر

crowned *adj* mutawwaj متوّج

aqueduct *n* majra مجرى

galactic *adj* majarri مَجَرِّي

shears *n pl* mejazz مِجَزّ

carnage *n* majzarah مَجْزَرَة

massacre *n* majzarah مَجْزَرَة

incarnate *adj* mejassam مجسّم

curly *adj* muja'ad مجعّد

journal *n* majalleh مجلّة

magazine *n* majalleh مجلّة

n majalleh dawreyyeh مجلّة دوريّة

periodical

n majalleh rekhisah مجلّة رخيصة

dreadful

n majalleh shahreyyeh مجلّة شهريّة

monthly

tome *n* mujallad مُجلّد

board *n* majlis مجلس

council *n* majlis مجلس

rendezvous *n* majles مَجْلِس

n majles elsha'eb مجلس الشعب

parliament

n majles elshyukh مجلس الشيوخ

senate

n majles elwuzara مجلس الوزراء

cabinet

sink *n* majla مَجْلى

iced *adj* mejammad مجمّد

compound *n* 'mujamma مجمّع

peer *n* mathil مَثِيل

allegory *n* majaz مجاز

peril *n* mujazafeh مجازفة

allegorical *adj* majazi مجازي

figurative *adj* majazi مَجازي

famine *n* maja'a مجاعة

starvation *n* maja'ah مَجَاعَة

complaisant *adj* mujamil مُجامِل

complaisance *n* mujamaleh مُجامَلة

flattery *n* mujamaleh مُجامَلة

gratis *adv* majanan مجاناً

free *adj* majjani مجاني

juxtaposition *n* mejawarah مجاورة

community *n* 'mujtama مجتمع

society *n* 'mejtama مجتمع

painstaking *adj* mejtehid مجتهد

glory *n* majd مجد

diligent *adj* mujidd مُجِدّ

industrious *adj* mujedd مُجِدّ

paddle *n* mejdaf مِجداف

oar *n* mejdaf مِجْداف

oarsman *n* mejaddef مجدّف

galaxy *n* majarrah مجرّة

impersonal *adj* mjarrad مجرّد

mujrem mahkum aleh مجرم محكوم عليه

convict *n* aleh

sewer *n* majrur مجرور

drain *n* majrur مجرُور

accountancy n muhasabeh محاسبة	combination n 'majmu مجموع
lecturer n muhader محاضر	sum n 'majmu مجموع
docent n muhader مُحَاضِر	group n majmu'a مجموعة
lecture n muhadarah محاضرة	set n majmu'ah مَجْمُوعَة
conservative adj muhafez محافظ	n majmu'et trus مجموعة تروس
governor n muhafez مُحافظ	gearset
province n muhafazah مُحَافَظَة	aliferous adj mjnnh مجنّح
advocate n muhami محامي	brainless adj majnun مجنون
attorney n muhami محامي	crazy adj majnun مجنون
lawyer n muhami محامي	demented adj majnun مجنون
barrister n muhami مُحامي	insane adj majnun مجنون
solicitor n muhami مُحَامي	lunatic n majnun مجنون
attempt n muhawaleh محاولة	telescope n mejhar مجهر
try n muhawaleh محاولة	microscope n majhar مِجْهَر
endeavour n muhawaleh محاولة	telescopic adj mejhari مجهري
eraser n mahayyeh مَحايّة	microscopic adj majhari مِجْهَري
rubber n mahayyeh مَحَّاية	anonymous adj majhul مجهول
neuter adj muhayd مُحَايِد	hollow adj mjawwaf مُجَوَّف
neuter n muhayd مُحَايِد	airborne adj mjwqal مجوقَل
amatory adj muhheb محبّ	jewellery n mjawharat مجوهرات
minion n muhebb مُحَّب	glorious adj majid مجيد
muhebb lilkheyr محبّ للخير للناس	muhadatheh مُحادثة الكترونيّة
altruist n lilnnas	cyberchat n elktruneyyeh
cartridge n mahbarah محبَرة	warrior n mhareb محارب
favourite n elmahbub المحبوب	belligerent n muhareb مُحارب
beloved adj mahbub محبوب	oyster n maharah مَحَارَة
idol n mahbub محبوب	accountant n mhaseb محاسب
lovable adj mahbub محبوب	book-keeper n muhasib مُحاسِب

holocaust *n* mahraqah محرقة

crematorium *n* mihraqah مِحْرَقَة

pyre *n* mahraqah مَحْرَقَة

combustor *n* mehraqa محرقة

engine *n* muharrek محرّك

prohibitory *adj* meharram محرّم

tissue *n* mahrameh محرمة

handkerchief *n* mahrameh محرمة

napkin *n* mahrameh محرمة

escorted *adj* mahrus محروس

seared *adj* mahruq محروق

destitute *adj* mahrum محروم

thorny *adj* mehassek محسّك

benefactor *n* muhsen محسن

nepotism *n* mahsubeyyeh محسوبيّة

enviable *adj* mahsud محسود

perceptible *adj* mahsus محسوس

physical *adj* mahsus محسوس

indomitable *adj* muhassan محصّن

crop *n* mahsul محصول

n muhdir elmahkameh محضر المحكمة

bailiff

station *n* mahattah محطّة

n mahattet elnihayeh محطة النهاية

terminal

mahtut jmb محطوط جمب بعضه

juxtaposed *adj* ba'duh

taboo *n* mahzur محظور

lovely *adj* mahbub محبوب

prisoner *n* mahbus محبوس

adj mahbus belqafas محبوس بالقفص

caged

needy *adj* mehtaj محتاج

tricky *adj* mehtal محتال

knave *n* mehtal محتال

respectful *adj* muhtaram محترم

reverend *adj* muhtaram محترم

coy *adj* mehtishim محتشم

prude *n* mehteshm محتشم

contemptuous *adj* muhtaqer محتقر

monopolist *n* mehteker محتكر

occupier *n* muhtall محتلّ

potential *adj* muhtamal محتمل

tolerable *adj* muhtamal محتمل

inevitable *adj* mahtum محتوم

content *n* muhtawah محتوى

bent *adj* mohaddab محدّب

specific *adj* mehaddad محدّد

limited *adj* mahdud محدود

finite *adj* mahdud محدود

niche *n* mehrab محراب

plough *n* mehrath محراث

awkward *adj* muhrij محرج

embarrassing *adj* muhrej محرج

editor *n* muharrer محرّر

liberator *n* muharrer محرّر

reddish *adj* mehmarr محمرّ	taboo *adj* mahzur محظُور
ruddy *adj* mehmarr محمرّ	lucky *adj* mahzuz محظوظ
blushing *adj* muhmarr مُحمرّ	providential *adj* mahzuz محظوظ
laudable *adj* mahmud محمود	fortunate *adj* mahzuz محظُوظ
borne *adj* mahmul محمول	etched *adj* mahfur محفور
portable *adj* mahmul محمول	interrogative *n* muhaqqeq محقّق
n mahmul fi eljaww محمول في الجو	detective *n* muhaqqeq مُحقّق
airborne	arbitrator *n* mukakkem محكّم
feverish *adj* mahmum محموم	court *n* mahkameh محكمة
plight *n* mehneh محنة	tribunal *n* mahkameh محكمة
tribulation *n* mehneh محنة	*adj* mahkum aleh محكوم عليه
veteran *n* mehannak محنّك	doomed
veteran *adj* mehannak محنّك	debated *adj* mehki fih محكي فيه
axle *n* mehwar محور	locus *n* mahall محلّ
hub *n* mehwar محور	florist *n* mahl zhur محل زهور
axial *adj* mehwari محوري	gin *n* mahlaj kutn محلج قطن
adj mehawwal laghaz محوّل لغاز	juror *n* muhallaf محلّف
gasified	analyst *n* muhallil محلّل
baffling *adj* muhayyer محيّر	shaven *adj* mahluq محلوق
ocean *n* muhit محيط	solution *n* mahlul محلول
periphery *n* muhit محيط	*n* mahlul kahruba'i محلول كهربائي
n muhit eddaera محيط الدائرة	electrolyte
circumference	domestic *adj* mahalli محلّي
n elmuhit elhadi المحيط الهادي	domestical *adj* mahalli محلّي
pacifier	local *adj* mahalli محلّي
oceanic *adj* muhiti مُحيطي	native *adj* mahalli محلّي
throe *n* makhad مخاض	locality *n* mahaleyyeh محلية
addressee *n* mukhatab مُخاطب	ablush *adv* mehmarr محمر

dope *n* mukhadder مُخَدِّر

destroyer *n* mukharreb مُخَرِّب

exit *n* mukhrej مُخْرَج

vent *n* mukhrej مُخْرَج

director *n* mukhrij مُخْرِج

filmmaker *n* mukhrej مُخْرِج

lathe *n* makhratah مَخْرَطَة

scratched *adj* mekharmesh مُخَرْمَش

cone *n* makhrut مَخْروط

conical *adj* makhruti مَخْروطي

store *n* makhzan مَخْزَن

repository *n* makhzan مَخْزَن

n 'makhzan badaye مَخْزَن بَضَايع
godown

granary *n* makhzan kamh مَخْزَن قَمح

n makhzan waqud مَخْزَن مَحروقات
bunker

stock *n* makhzun مَخْزون

gelding *n* elmakhsi المَخْصي

gelded *adj* makhsi مَخْصي

eunuch *n* makhsi مَخْصي

mucus *n* makhtah مَخْطَة

perilous *adj* mukhter مُخْطِر

chart *n* mukhattat مُخَطَّط

diagram *n* mukhattat مُخَطَّط

scheme *n* mekhattat مُخَطَّط

mukhattat sadah مُخَطَّط صَدَى القَلب
echocardiogram *n* elqalb

venturous *adj* mukhater مُخاطِر

hazard *n* mukhatarah مُخاطَرَة

mucous *adj* mukhati مُخاطي

irregular *adj* mekhalef مُخالِف

infringement *n* mukhalafeh مُخالَفة

safehouse *n* makhba' serri مَخْبأ سِرّي

bakery *n* makhbaz مَخْبَز

laboratory *n* mukhtabar مُخْتَبَر

inventor *n* 'mukhtare مُخْتَرِع

piercing *adj* mekhterq مُخْتَرِق

specialist *n* mekhtass مُخْتَصّ

mkhts ebr siniyeh مُخْتَص الابر الصينية
acupuncturist *n*

mukhtas be'elem مُخْتَصّ بِعِلم الأحياء
biologist *n* 'elahyaa

n mekhtass be'aa مُخْتَصّ بِيئة
environmentalist

breviary *n* mukhtasar مُخْتَصَر

coot *n* mughtall مُخْتَلّ

n mukhtall aqleyan مُخْتَلّ عَقليًا
cretin

different *adj* mekhtelef مُخْتَلِف

sealed *adj* makhtum مَخْتوم

degrading *adj* mukhjil مُخْجِل

pillow *n* mekhaddeh مِخَدَّة

cushion *n* mekhaddeh مِخَدَّة

anaesthetic *n* elmukhadder المُخَدِّر

doped *adj* mukhadder مُخَدِّر

axis *n* madar مدار	sketchy *adj* mukhattat elu مُخَطَّطٌ لَهُ
orb *n* madar مَدَار	manuscript *n* makhtutah مَخْطُوطَة
orbit *n* madar مَدَار	abductee *n* makhtuf مخطوف
pivot *n* madar مَدَار	watery *adj* mekhaffaf مخفَّف
tropic *n* madar مَدَار	clandestine *adj* mekhfi مخفي
tropical *adj* madari مَدَاري	occult *adj* mekhfi مخفي
orbital *adj* madari مَدَاري	invisible *adj* mekhfi مخفي
mudafe' am مدافع عن حقوق الإنسان	talon *n* makhlab مخلَب
humanitarian *adj* huquq elensan	claw *n* makhlab مخلَب
medal *n* medaleyyeh مدَاليّة	paw *n* makhlab مخلَب
madam *n* madam مدام	sincere *adj* mukhles مخلِص
duration *n* mudawameh مُدَاوَمة	pickle *n* mekhallal مخلَّل
tease *n* mudayaqah مدايقة	scrambled *adj* makhlut مخلوط
resentment *n* medayaqah مدايَقَة	being *n* makhluuq مخلوق
botheration *n* mudayaqah مدايَقَة	creature *n* makhluq مخلوق
tannery *n* madbaghah مَدْبَغة	*n* makhluq fadae'i مخلوق فضائي
panegyric *n* madh مدح	extraterrestrial
praise *n* madh مدح	plush *n* mekhmal مخمل
gateway *n* madkhal مَدْخَل	velvet *n* mukhmal مخمَل
smoky *adj* medakhkhen مدخِّن	plush *adj* mekhmali مخملي
chimney *n* madkhaneh مدخَنة	velvety *adj* mukhmali مخملي
produce *n* madkhul مَدْخُول	bisexual *adj* mukhannath مخنَّث
coach *n* mydarreb مُدَرِّب	effeminate *adj* mekhannath مخنَّث
amphitheatre *n* mudarraj مُدَرَّج	horrible *adj* mukhif مخيف
instructor *n* mdarres مدرِّس	dire *adj* mukhif مخيف
teacher *n* mudarres مدرِّس	fantasy *n* mukhayyeleh مخيّلة
schoolmaster *n* medarres مدرِّس	camp *n* mukhayyam مخيّم
schoolteacher *n* medarres مدرِّس	tide *n* madd w jazr مد وجزر

civic *adj* madani مدني

civil *adj* madani مدني

urban *adj* madani مدني

gilt *adj* mdahhab مدهَّب

stupendous *adj* mudhesh مُدهِش

circular *adj* mudawwar مدوَّر

cyclic *adj* medawwar مدوَّر

rotary *adj* medawwar مدوَّر

round *adj* medawwar مدوَّر

adj mdukar zeyadeh مدوكً زيادة

baroque

n mdawwen sawti مدوِّن صوتي

podcaster

purview *n* madah مَدى

acclaim *n* mdih مديح

commendation *n* madih مديح

laud *n* madih مديح

long *adj* madid مديد

administrator *n* muddir مدير

boss *n* mudir مدير

manager *n* mudir مدير

n mudir madraseh مدير المدرسة

principal

n mudir elmarsah مدير المرسى

dockmaster

mudir maktab مدير مكتب البريد

postmaster *n* elbarid

debtor *n* madin مَدين

pedagogue *n* mudarres مُدرِّس

school *n* madraseh مدرسة

studious *adj* madrus مَدروس

n mudda'a alyh مدَّعى عليه

defendant

n mudda'ah alih مدَّعى عليه

respondent

plaintiff *n* medda'i مدَّعي

claimant *n* muddaei مُدَّعي

n elmedde'i el'am المدَّعي العام

prosecutor

cannon *n* 'medfae مَدفَع

n medfa' harbi مدفع حربي

ordnance

artillery *n* medfae'yeh مدفعيّة

payee *n* madfu' elu مدفوع إله

maul *n* madaqq مَدقّ

n mudaqeq hesabat مدقق حسابات

auditor

tamper *n* medakk مدكّ

dangling *adj* mdaldal مدلدَل

masseur *n* medallek مدلّك

droopy *adj* mdallah مدلَّى

addict *n* mudmn مدمن

n medmen tasawwuq مدمن تسوُّق

shopaholic

sacrilegious *adj* medannas مدنَّس

profane *adj* medannas مدنَّس

myrrh n elmurr المرّ

bitter adj murr مُرّ

woman n mrah مرا

n mara helweh ktir مَرَا حلوة كتير

belle

usurer n mrabi مرابي

review n muraja'ah مراجعة

synonym n muradef مُرادف

reporter n murasel مراسل

correspondent n murasil مُراسِل

n murasaleh مُراسلة

correspondence

ceremony n marasim مَراسِم

ceremonial adj marasmi مراسمي

n marasi elsufun مراسي السفن

moorings

pleader n 'murafe مُرافع

plea n murafa'ah مرافعة

proceeding n murafa'ah مرافعة

bodyguard n murafiq مُرافِق

accompaniment n murafaqa مرافقة

convoy n murafaqah مُرافَقَة

censor n muraqib مُراقِب

controller n muraqeb مُراقِب

overseer n muraqb مُراقِب

proctor n muraqb مُراقِب

superintendent n muraqib مُراقِب

city n madineh مدينة

n madinet amwat مدينة أموات

necropolis

n madineh fadeleh مدينة فاضلة .

utopia

indebted adj madyun مَدْيون

credit n madyuneyyeh مديونية

muzakarah seghereh مذاكرة صغيرة

quiz n

genocide n mazbaha مذبحة

n muzakkarat مُذَكّرات

autobiography

memoir n muzakkarah مذَكّرة

memorandum n muzakkarah مُذَكّرة

n muzakkaret bahth مذكرة بحث

search warrant

guilty adj muzneb مذنب

comet n muzannab مُذَنَّب

culpable adj muzneb مُذْنِب

delinquent adj muznib مُذْنِب

malefactor n muzneb مُذْنِب

offender n muzneb مُذْنِب

sinful adj muznib مُذْنِب

sinner n muznib مُذْنِب

sect n mazhab مذهب

tenet n mazhab مَذْهَب

sectarian adj mazhabi مذهبي

solvent n muzib مُذيب

gainful *adj* murbeh مُرْبِح	*n* muraqeb elnatijeh مراقب النتيجة
lucrative *adj* murbih مُرْبِح	scorekeeper
chubby *adj* merabrab مربَرب	muraqb emtihanat مراقب إمتحانات
square *n* 'murabba مُرَبَّع	invigilator *n*
square *adj* 'murabba مُرَبَّع	observation *n* muraqabeh مراقبة
joint *adj* marbut مربوط	*n* muraqabeh مراقبة
jam *n* mrabbah مربَّى	superintendence
n mrabba elburtuqal مربَّى البرتقال	surveillance *n* muraqabeh مراقبة
marmalade	censorship *n* muraqabeh مُراقَبة
n mrabbi khanazir مربِّي الخنازير	oversight *n* muraqabeh مُراقَبة
swine	muraqabet مراقبة الإمتحانات
n murabbi elnahil مُربِّي النحل	invigilation *n* elemtihanat
beekeeper	*n* muraqabet elnatijeh مراقبة النتيجة
n murabeyyet elwulad مربِّية الولاد	scorekeeping
nanny	*adj* marakzuh ktireh مراكزه كتيرة
afresh *adv* marra tanyeh مرة ثانية	polycentric
again *adv* marra tanyeh مرة ثانية	teenager *n* muraheq مراهق
anew *adv* mara tanyeh مرة ثانية	adolescent *adj* murahiq مراهق
adj marah kel sintin مرة كل سنتين	adolescence *n* murahaqa مراهقة
biennial	teens *n pl* murahaqah مراهقة
wife *n* mart مرت	bettor *n* murahin مُراهِن
n mart elmuhafez مرت المحافظ	betting *adj* murahaneh مُراهنة
governess	evasive *adj* mrawegh مراوغ
tidy *adj* mrattab مرتَّب	indirect *adj* mrawegh مُراوغ
orderly *adj* merattab مُرَتَّب	shuffle *n* murawaghah مراوغة
shipshape *adj* merattab مُرَتَّب	*n* murawagha مُراوغة
associate *adj* murtabit مُرتبط	circumvention
abjurer *n* murtadd مُرتدّ	mirror *n* mrayeh مراية

grapple *n* mersayeh مرساية

decree *n* marsum مرسوم

edict *n* marsum مرسوم

graphic *adj* marsum مَرْسُوم

berth *n* marsah مرسى

dock *n* marsah مرسى

nominee *n* merashshah مُرَشَّح

candidate *n* murashshah مُرَشَّح

adj marshush tehin مرشوش طحين

mealy

observatory *n* marsad مَرْصَد

illness *n* marad مرض

sickness *n* marad مَرَض

disease *n* maradh مَرَض

maradh eljamra elkhabitheh مرض الجمرة الخبيثة

anthrax *n*

n marad essikkari مرض السُّكَّري

diabetes

psychosis *n* marad aqli مرض عقلي

n marad mestawten مرض مستوطِن

endemic

indisposed *adj* mardan مرضان

sickly *adj* mardan مرضان

satisfactory *adj* merdi مرضي

morbid *adj* maradi مَرَضي

daunting *adj* mur'eb مُرعِب

dreadful *adj* mureb مُرعِب

lea *n* mar'e مرعى

mercenary *adj* murtazaq مرتزق

hireling *n* murtazaq مُرتَزَق

venal *adj* merteshi مرتشي

twice *adv* martin مرتين

adj 'martin belesbue مرتين بالأسبوع

bi-weekly

adj martin belsineh مرتين بالسنة

biannual

lawn *n* marj مَرْج

meadow *n* marj مَرْج

sod *n* marj مَرْج

coral *n* marjan مرجان

rocker *n* marjuha مرجوحة

fun *n* marah مرح

joy *n* marah مَرَح

joyful *n* merih مرِح

cabinet *n* merhad مرحاض

latrine *n* merhad مِرحاض

n merhad kharji مرحاض خارجي

outhouse

phase *n* marhaleh مَرْحَلة

n elmarhaleh eljay المرحلة الجاي

aftergrowth

transitory *adj* marhali مَرْحَلي

output *n* mardud مَرْدُود

prosperous *adj* marzuq مَرْزُوق

anchor *n* mersaat مرساة

errand *n* mersal مِرْسال

eminent *adj* marmuq مَرْموق

malleable *adj* merin مِرِن

flexible *adj* mren مِرِن

balsam *n* marham مَرهَم

ointment *n* marham مَرْهَم

balsamic *adj* marhami مَرهمي

van *n* marwaha مَروحة

fan *n* marwaha مَروحَة

thoroughfare *n* murur مرور

n elmrawwedh المروَّض

domesticator

subordinate *n* mar'us مَرؤوس

comfortable *adj* murih مريح

comfy *adj* murih مريح

cosy *adj* murih مريح

convenient *adj* murih مريح

Mars *n* elmarrikh المرّيخ

ill *adj* marid مريض

patient *n* marid مريض

sick *adj* marid مريض

n marid kharji مَريض خارِجي

outpatient

n marid nafsi مريض نفسي

psychopath

dilute *adj* mriq مريق

apron *n* maryuleh مَريولة

visible *adj* mar'i مرئي

mood *n* mazaj مزاج

pasture *n* mar'ah مرعى

desirable *adj* marghub مرغوب

harbour *n* 'mara مرفا

anchorage *n* 'marfaa مرفأ

attachment *n* morfak مرفق

objectionable *adj* marfud مرفوض

inadmissible *adj* marfud مَرْفوض

saucy *adj* mereq مرق

sauce *n* marqah مرقة

broth *n* maraqa مَرَقة

composition *n* murakkab مركَّب

compound *n* murakkab مركَّب

compound *adj* murakkab مركَّب

compounder *n* murakkab مركَّب

n markeb shera'i مركب شراعي

sailboat

n mrakkib qrun مركَّب قرون

cuckold

focused *adj* mrakkaz مركَّز

center *n* markaz مركَز

centre *n* markaz مركَز

markaz مركز الزلزال السطحي

epicentre *n* elzalazel elsatehi

outpost *n* markaz hdud مركز حدود

central *adj* markazi مركزي

centrical *adj* markazi مركزي

alabaster *n* mrmr مرمر

marble *n* marmar مَرْمَر

jocular *adj* mazuh مزوح	temperament *n* mazaj مزاج
spurious *adj* mezawwar مزوّر	moody *adj* mazaji مزاجي
mock *adj* mezawwar مزوّر	temperamental *adj* mazaji مزاجي
fake *adj* mzawwar مُزوّر	auction *n* mazad alani مزاد علني
quibble *n* mzughaleh مزوغلة	farmer *n* 'muzare مزارع
gaudy *adj* mezweq مزوق	grower *n* 'nmuzare مُزارع
alloy *n* mazij maadin مزيج معادن	dump *n* mazbaleh مزبلة
false *adj* mzayyaf مزيّف	pertinent *adj* mazbut مزبوط
bogus *adj* muzayyaf مُزيّف	funny *n* mazha مزحة
citrine *adj* muzayyaf مُزيّف	jest *n* mazha مزحة
eliminator *n* muzil مُزيل	pleasantry *n* mazhah مَزحَة
muzil awraq eshshajar مزيل أوراق الشجر	ornamental *adj* mezakhraf مزخرف
defoliant *n*	gutter *n* mzrab مزراب
adj muzil araq مزيل عرق	farm *n* mazra'a مزرعة
deodorant	ranch *n* mazra'ah مزرعة
adj muzil eshshuhum مزيل للشحوم	manor *n* mazra'ah مَزرَعَة
delipidate	blazoned *adj* muzarkash مزركش
adj muzil lelsha'er مزيل للشَعر	adverse *adj* muze'j مزعج
depilatory	alarming *adj* muzej مزعج
adorner *n* mzyyen مزيَن	annoying *adj* muzeij مُزعج
afternoon *n* elmassa المسا	alleged *adj* mazoum مزعوم
evening *n* msa مسا	lubricant *n* mezalleq مزلّق
massage *n* massaj مسّاج	glider *n* muzalleq مُزلّق
rag *n* massahah مسّاحَة	clarinet *n* mezmar مزمار
n massahit elrejlin مسّاحة الرجلين	bagpipe *n* mezmaar مزمار
doormat	flute *n* mezmar مُزمار
el masaha bl faddan المساحة بالفدان	chronic *adj* muzmin مُزمِن
acreage *n*	vase *n* mazhareyyeh مَزهَريّة

lessee *n* mesta'jer مستأجِر

autocratic *adj* mustabbed مُستَبِدّ

bossy *adj* mustabbed مُستَبِّد

adj mestabedd bera'yu مستَبِدّ برأيه

opinionated

novice *n* mustajjed مستجِدّ

fossil *n* mustahaththeh مُستَحَاثة

mustahdarat مستحضرات تجميل

cosmetic *n* tajmil

due *adj* mestahaqq مُستَحَقّ

due *n* elmustahaqqat المستحقَّات

emulsifier *n* mustahlab مُستَحْلِب

abashed *adj* mestehi مستحي

self-conscious *adj* mestehi مستحي

impossible *adj* mustahil مستحيل

adj mustahil مستحيل

impracticable

mestaredd مستردّ الملكِيّة

evictor *n* elmelkeyyeh

chancellor *n* mustashar مستشار

counsellor *n* mustashar مُستشار

hospital *n* mestashfah مستشفى

oblong *n* mustatil مستطيل

rectangle *n* mustatil مستطيل

oblong *adj* mustatili مستطيلي

rectangular *adj* mustatili مستطيلي

hasty *adj* mesta'jil مستعجِل

urgent *adj* mesta'jil مستعجِل

acolyte *n* musa'ed مساعد

helpful *adj* musa'ed مساعد

aide *n* musaed مُساعد

assistant *n* musaed مُساعد

auxiliary *adj* musaed مُساعد

musa'ed lelzakerah مساعد للذاكرة

mnemonic *adj*

n musa'ed mumarred مساعد ممرض

orderly

help *n* musa'adeh مساعدة

assistance *n* musaadeh مساعَدة

aid *n* musaed مُساعدة

distance *n* masafeh مسافة

espace *n* masafeh مسافة

n elmasafeh belmyl المَسَافة بالميل

mileage

traveller *n* mesafer مسافر

voyager *n* msafer مسافر

passenger *n* mesafer مسافِر

matter *n* mas'aleh مَسْألة

peaceful *adj* msalem مسالِم

pore *n* masameh مسامة

equality *n* musawat مساواة

causative *adj* musabbeb مُسَبِّب

abuse *n* msabeh مسبة

insult *n* mesabbeh مسبّة

rosary *n* masbaha مِسْبَحَة

beads *n* masbaha مِسْبَحة

depot n 'mestawda مستودع	intricate adj mesta'si مُسْتَعْصِي
warehouse n 'mestawda مستودع	rampant adj mestafhel مُسْتَفْحِل
n mestawda' asleha مستودع أسلحة	provocative adj mestefezz مستفزّ
armoury	hereafter n mestakbal مستقبل
n mestawda' eljethath مستودع الجثث	future n mustaqbal مستقبل
mortuary	future adj mustaqbalan مستقبلا
obscure adj mastur مَسْتُور	futuristic adj mustaqbali مستقبلي
dispensary n mestawsaf مُسْتَوْصَف	stable adj mestaqerr مُسْتَقَرّ
endemic adj mestawten مستوطِن	independent adj metaqell مستقلّ
settler n mestawten مستوطِن	autonomous adj mustaqqil مُسْتَقَلّ
adj mistaweb مستوعِب	straight adj mustaqim مستقيم
apprehensive	rectum n elmustaqim المُسْتَقِيم
level n mestawah مستوى	receiver n mestelm مستلم
mature adj mestwei مستوي	recipient n mestelm مستلم
ripe adj mestwi مستوي	abiding adj mestamerr مستمرّ
level adj mestwi مسْتَوِي	progressive adj mestmerr مستمرّ
mosque n masjid مسجد	ceaseless adj mustamerr مستمرّ
patent adj mesajjal مسجّل	continuous adj mustamerr مُسْتَمَرّ
tape player n msajjleh مسجلة	listener n 'mesteme مستمع
recorder n mesajjleh مسجلة	document n mustanad مستند
survey n maseh مسح	depleted adj mustanfiz مستنفذ
wipe n maseh مسح	slough n 'mustanqa مستنقع
mop n maseh elaradi مَسح الأَراضِي	marsh n 'mustanqa مستنقع
takeout adj masehub مسحوب	bog n mustanaqaa مُسْتَنْقَع
weird adj masehur مسحور	n mustanqa' sighir مُسْتَنْقَع صغير
bewitched adj masehur مسحور	boglet
irony n maskharah مسخرة	marshy adj mustanqa'i مستنقعى
cynic n maskharah مسخَرة	irresponsible adj mestahter مستهتر

book-keeping *n* masek dafater مسك الدفاتر	burlesque *adj* maskharah مسخَرَة
grasp *n* maskeh مَسكة	burlesque *n* maskharah مسخَرَة
bicycle *n* misklit مسكليت	cynical *adj* maskharji مسخرجي
bike *n* misklit مسكليت	ironical *adj* maskharji مسخرجي
abode *n* maskan مَسْكَن	pistol *n* musaddas مسدّس
domicile *n* maskan مَسْكَن	revolver *n* musaddas مسدّس
lodging *n* maskan مَسْكَن	gun *n* musaddas مسدّس
sedative *adj* musakken مُسَكِّن	dead-end *adj* masdud مسدود
sedative *n* musakken مُسَكِّن	obstructive *adj* masdud مسدود
calmative *adj* musakken مُسَكِّن	stuffy *adj* masdud مَسْدُود
habitable *adj* maskun مسكون	theatre *n* masrah مسرح
populous *adj* maskun مَسْكُون	playhouse *n* masrah مَسْرَح
sidearm *adj* mesallah مسلَّح	dramatic *adj* masrahi مسرحي
shambles *n* maslakh مَسْلَخ	theatrical *adj* masrahi مسرحي
series *n* musalsal مسلسل	scenic *adj* masrahi مسرَحي
tract *n* maslak مَسْلَك	play *n* masraheyyeh مسرحيّة
muslim *adj* meslim مسلِم	cancerogenic *adj* musartin مسرطن
nail *n* mesmar مسمار	accelerator *n* 'msarre مسرِع
spike *n* mesmar مسمار	flat *adj* musattah مسطَّح
stud *n* mesmar bras مسمار براس	flatbed *adj* musattah مسطَّح
tan *adj* mesmarr مسمرّ	plane *adj* msattah مسطَّح
poisonous *adj* musammem مسمِّم	tabular *adj* mesattah مسطَّح
permissible *adj* masmuh مَسْمُوح	*n* mastaret eldehan مسطرة الدهان maulstick
audible *adj* 'masmue مسموع	dumbfounded *adj* mastul مسطول
adj masmue' w marei مسموع ومرئي audiovisual	ambulant *adj* muse'f مُسعِف
sharpener *n* masann مَسَنّ	mad *adj* mas'ur مَسْعُور
	musk *n* misk مِسْك

n elmasyheyyeh المسيحيّة
Christianity

adj 'musil leldumu مسيل للدموع
lachrymose

infantry n elmushat المُشَاة

outskirts npl masharef مَشَارِف

participant n musharek مُشارِك

share n musharakeh مشاركة

n musharakeh مُشاركة
participation

communal adj 'masha مَشاع

turbulent adj mushagheb مشاغب

naughty adj mushaghib مشاغِب

seditious adj mushaghib مُشَاغِب

quarrel n mshakaleh مشاكلة

for prep mshan مشان

for .conj mshan مشان

ad hoc adj mshaan heik مشان هيك

so .conj mshan hik مشان هيك

adv mshan hik مشان هيك
therefore

on-looker n mushahed مشاهد

seer n mushahed مُشَاهِد

spectator n mushahed مُشَاهِد

slipper n mashayyeh مَشَّايِة

dubious adj mashbuh مشبوه

suspect adj mashbuh مشبوه

suspicious adj mashbuh مَشْبُوه

ottoman n masnad مسنَد

blunt adj mesannan مستّن

pointed adj msannan مسنّن

sharp adj masnun مَسْنُون

lax adj mesahhel مسهّل

physic n mesahhel مسهّل

cathartical adj musahhil مُسهّل

purgative n musahhel مُسهّل

purgative adj musahhel مُسهّل

draft n meswaddeh مسودّة

draught n meswaddeh مسودّة

answerable adj mas'ul مسؤول

liable adj mas'ul مسؤول

officer n mas'ul مسؤول

accountable adj mas'ool مسؤول

responsible adj mas'ul مسؤول

constable n masul amen مسؤول أمن

accountability n mas'oliyeh مسؤولية

n mas'uleyyeh مسؤوليّة
responsibility

Christ n welmasyh المسيح

n massih jukh مسيح جوخ
brownnoser

n massyh jukh مسيّح جوخ
sycophant

Christian n elmasyhi المسيحي

Christian adj masyhi مسيحي

project n 'mashru مشروع	questionable adj mashbuh مَشْبوه
comb n musht مُشط	scattered adj meshattat مشتَّت
n mashtur elnuss مشطور بالنُّص	n meshattat elzehn مشتَّت الذهن
crotch	scatterbrain
radiant adj 'mushe مُشِعّ	mutual adj mushtarak مشترك
luminous adj 'mushe مُشِعّ	mushtark بحملة صليبيّة مشترك
shiny adj 'mesha'she مشعشع	crusader n behamleh salibeyyeh
sorcerer n mesha'wez مشعوذ	jupiter n elmushtari المُشْتَري
juggler n musha'wez مُشَعوذ	blazing adj mushta'el مُشتَعِل
operator n mushaghghel مُشَغِّل	nursery n mashtal مَشْتَل
busy adj mashghul مشغول	greasy adj mshahham مشحَّم
laboured adj mashghul مشغول	fraught adj mashhun مشحون
encrypted adj meshaffer مشفَّر	shipped adj mashhun مشحون
variable adj mshakkal مشكَّل	tense adj mashdud مَشْدُود
problem n meshkleh مشكلة	adj mashdud belhibal مشدود بالحبال
trouble n meshkleh مشكلة	corded
problematic adj meshkalji مشكلجي	morgue n mashraha مَشْرَحَة
adj meshkalji مشكلجي	legislator n musharre'e مُشرِّع
troublesome	honourable adj musharref مشرِّف
doubtful adj mashkuk fi مشكوك فيه	supervisor n meshref مشرف
paralytic adj mashlul مَشلُول	caretaker n mushref مُشرِف
sunny adj meshmes مشمس	caretaker adj mushref مُشرِف
apricot n meshmush مشمش	polytheist n meshrek مُشرك
mack n 'meshamma مشمَّع	alcohol n mashrub مشروب
cerated adj 'meshamma مشمَّع	beverage n mashrub مشروب
loath adj mushma'ezz مُشْمَئِزّ	brew n mashrub bira مشروب بيرة
gallows . n mashnaqah مشنقة	provisional adj mashrut مَشْروط
scaffold n mashnaqah مشنقة	enterprise n mashru'e مشروع

مُصاب بغثيان من الحركة السيارة
musab beghathayan men haraket
carsick *adj* al sayyarah

forfeiture *n* msadarah مصادرة

confiscation *n* musadarh مُصادَرَة

gladiator *n* 'musare مُصارِع

n musare' thiran مصارع ثيران .
matador

fund *n* masari مصاري

money *n* masari مصاري

cash *n* masari naqdi مصاري نقدي

lollipop *n* masasah مصاصة

cross *n* musalabeh مُصالِبة

affinity *n* musahara مصاهرة

in-laws *n* musaharah مصاهَرة

n masabb ennaher مصبّ النهر
estuary

laundry *n* masbaghah مَصْبَغَة

sanatorium *n* masahhah مَصَحَّة

source *n* masdar مصدر

gerund *n* masdar مصدَر

insistent *adj* muserr مُصِرّ

entrails *n* musran مُصْران

culvert *n* masraf مَصْرَف

epileptic *adj* masru'e مَصْروع

epileptic *n* masru'e مَصْروع

expenditure *n* masrufat مصروفات

bench *n* mastabeh مصطبة

scene *n* mashhad مَشْهَد

scenery *n* mashhad مَشْهَد

landscape *n* mashhad مَشْهَد

mashhad udeh مشهد عودة للماضي

flashback *n* lelmadi

famous *adj* mashhur مشهور

popular *adj* mashehur مشهور

scratchy *adj* meshawwek مشوَّك

walk *n* mashi مشي

n mashi athna' elnum مشي أثناء النوم
somnambulism

dash *n* mashi beajaleh مشي بعجَلة

gait *n* mashyeh مشية

march *n* mashyeh مشية

pace *n* mashyeh مِشْية

n mashyh share'ah مشية سريعة
stride

marshal *n* mushir مُشير

placenta *n* mashimeh مَشيمة

n mashymet elein مَشيمة العين
choroid

volition *n* mashy'ah مشيئة

suck *n* mass مصّ

sup *n* mass مصّ

musab be ama مُصاب بعمى ألوان

colour-blind *adj* alwan

dairy n masna' alban مصنع ألبان

brewery n masna bira مصنع بيرة

n musanne' kenani مصنع قناني
bottler

voter n mesawwet مصوّت

constituent n musawwet مُصوّت

geographer n mesawwar مصوّر

photographer n mesawwer مصوّر

pictorial adj mesawwer مصوّر

woollen adj mesawwaf مصوّف

adversity n msibeh مصيبة

affliction n msibeh مصيبة

blow n musibeh مصيبة

misfortune n musibeh مصيبة

calamity n mesibeh مصيبة

ordeal n musibeh مصيبة

trap n masyadeh مصيدة

crucial adj masiri مصيري

momentous adj masiri مَصِيري

mudaa' men مُضاء من الخلف
backlit adj elkhalef

anti .pref muddad مضادّ

adj mudad humudah مُضاد حموضة
antacid

n muddad hayawi مضاد حيوي
antibiotic

adj muddad tayaran مضاد طيران
anti-aircraft

idiom n mustalah مصطلح

vocabulary n mustalah مصطلح

sham adj 'mestana مصطنع

elevator n mas'ad مصعد

lift n mes'ad مصعد

diminutive adj musaghghar مصغّر

refinery n mesfayeh مصفاية

yellowish adj mesfarr مصفرّ

wan adj mesfarr مصفرّ

mesafqin مصفقين بالمصاري
claque n belmasari

matrix n masfufeh مَصْفوفة

sleek adj masqul مَصْقول

reformer n musleh مُصلح

n msalleh muharekat مصلح محركات
fitter

welfare n maslaha مصلحة

interest n maslahah مصلحة

behalf n maslaha مصلَحَة

crucified adj maslub مَصْلوب

oratory n mesallah مصلّى

designer n musammem مصمّم

n 'musammem azya مصمم أزياء
dressmaker

musammem مصمّم القبوعات النسواني
milliner n elqabbu'at elniswani

mesammem awsemeh مصمّم أوسمة
medallist n

ago *adv* mdyo مضيو

match *n* mutabaqah مطابقة

conformity *n* mutabaqa مُطابَقَة

aerodrome *n* matar مطار

chase *n* mutaradeh مطاردة

stoop *n* matatah مطاطاة

trespass *n* metawaleh مطاولة

cuisine *n* matbakh مطبخ

kitchen *n* matbakh مطبخ

applicable *adj* mutabbaq مُطبّق

flatulent *adj* mtableh مطبلة

rain *n* matar مطر

downpour *n* matar ghazir مطر غزير

pluvial *n* matar ghazir مطر غزير

archbishop *n* mutraan مُطران

metropolitan *adj* mutrani مُطراني

singer *n* mutrib مطرب

warbler *n* mutreb مطرِب

songster *n* mutreb مُطرِب

jar *n* matraban مطربان

canteen *n* matarah مَطَرة

lay *n* matrah مَطْرَح

beady *adj* mutarraz مطرز

gleeful *adj* matrub مطروب

pluvial *adj* matari مطري

wavy *adj* meta'aj مطعّج

diner *n* mat'am مطعم

restaurant *n* mat'am مطعم

adj mudad lelmay مضاد للمي
waterproof

contrarian *n* mudareb مُضارِب

mudareb belbursah مضارب بالبورصة
stag *n*

speculation *n* mudarabeh مضاربة

multiple *adj* muda'af مضاعف

duplicate *adj* muda'af مضاعَف

geminate *adj* muda'af مضاعَف

n muda'afat مُضَاعَفات
repercussion

augment *v* mudaafeh مُضاعَفة

nuisance *n* mudayakah مضايقة

aerosol *adj* mdbdeb مضبضب

hazy *adj* medabdeb مضبضب

noxious *adj* muderr مُضرّ

bat *n* midrab مضرب

racket *n* madrab مضرَب

n madrub bi مَضْروب ب
multiplicand

debilitant *n* mud'ef مُضعف

compact *adj* madghut مضغوط

purport *n* madmun مضمون

gleaming *adj* mdawwi مضوّي

past *adj* mada مضى

hospitable *adj* medyaf مضياف

steward *n* mudif مُضيف

hostel *n* mudefeh مَضْيَفة

pizzeria *n* mat'am betzah مطعم بيتزا

inert *adj* metaffa مطفي

case *n* matelab مَطلَب

acquaint *v* 'mttele مطلع

learned *adj* mettele' ala مطّلع على

ultimate *adj* mutlaq مُطلَق

liability *n* matlub مطلوب

stretch *n* matmatah مطمطة

pompous *adj* metantan مطنطن

antiseptic *adj* mutahher مُطهِّر

prolong *v* metawwal مطوّل

lengthy *adj* metawwal مطوّل

interminable *adj* metawwel مطوَّل

adj metawwel da'enuh مطوّل دقنه

bearded

folding *adj* metawwah مطوّى

mtawwayeh zawayah مطويِّة زواياه

dogeared *adj*

obedient *adj* 'mute مطيع

amenable *adj* 'mutie مطيع

compliant *adj* 'mutei مطيع

dutiful *adj* 'mute مطيع

slushy *adj* metayyen مطيّن

grievance *n* mazlameh مَظلَمة

parachutist *n* mezalli مظلّي

appearance *n* mazhar مظهر

guise *n* mazhar مظهر

---

n muzahher elshik مظهّر الشيك

endorser

with *prep* ma مع

interj ma' essalameh مع السلامة،

good-bye

altogether *adv* mae ba'ad مع بعض

both *adv* m'a baad مع بعض

simultaneous *adj* ma' ba'd مع بعض

together *adv* ma ba'ed مع بعض

however *adv* ma' hik مع هيك

prep ma' hik مع هيك

notwithstanding

tantamount *adj* me'adel معادل

wage *n* ma'ash معاش

emolument *n* ma'ash مَعَاش

stipend *n* ma'ash مَعَاش

convalescent *adj* muaafa معافى

hale *adj* me'afah معافى

disabled *adj* muaaq مُعَاق

opposite *adj* mu'akes معاكس

contrary *adj* muakes مُعَاكس

cross *adj* mu'akes مُعَاكس

molestation *n* mu'akaseh مُعَاكَسة

physician *n* mu'alej مُعَالِج

coefficient *n* muaamel مُعَامِل

treatment *n* mu'amaleh معاملة

treaty *n* mu'ahadeh معاهدة

convention *n* mu'ahadeh مُعَاهَدة

mineral *adj* ma'dani معدني	*n* ma'bad betawabeq معبد بطوابق
countable *adj* maedud معدود	pagoda
infectious *adj* me'di معدي	moderate *adj* me'tedel معتدل
gastric *adj* me'di مَعِدي	aggressor *n* muetadi معتدي
contagious *adj* mu'di مُعْدي	solitary *adj* me'tezl معتزل
exhibition *n* ma'rad معرَض	recluse *n* me'tekef مُعْتَكِف
fair *n* ma'rad معرَض	dark *adj* muattem مُعْتِم
muarrad larih معرَّض لريح قويّة	sombre *adj* me'tem مُعْتِم
drafty *adj* qawweyyeh	dim *adj* m'attem مُعْتِم
adj mu'arrad lelkhatar معرَّض للخطر	idiotic *adj* ma'tuh مَعْتوه
endangered	admirer *n* mu'jab مُعْجَب
knowledge *n* ma'refeh معرفة	enamoured *adj* mu'jab مُعْجَب
n ma'reft elqira'ah معرفة القراءة	devotee *n* mujab مُعْجَب
literacy	fan *n* mu'jab مُعْجَب
n ma'refeh khassah معرفة خاصة	marvel *n* mu'jezeh مُعْجِزة
lore	noisy *adj* ma'juq معجوق
battle *n* maarakeh معركة	paste *n* ma'jun معجون
petition *n* ma'rud معروض	equipment *n* mu'eddat معدّات
favour *n* ma'ruf معروف	belly *n* me'deh معدة
well-known *adj* ma'ruf معروف	stomach *n* me'deh معدة
maroof kaman b معروف كمان ب	average *n* mu'addal معدَّل
alias *adv*	par *n* me'addal معدَّل
secluded *adj* ma'zul معزول	rate *n* me'addal معدَّل
convivial *adj* ma'sharani مَعْشَراني	pauper *n* mu'dam مُعْدَم
angry *adj* meassib معصّب	penniless *adj* mu'dam مُعْدَم
furious *adj* me'assib معصّب	metal *n* ma'dan معدن
irate *adj* me'assib معصّب	mineral *n* ma'dan معدن
infallible *adj* ma'sum مَعْصوم	metallic *adj* ma'dani معدني

uproar *n* ma'ma'ah مَعْمَعَة

factory *n* ma'mal معمل

adamant *adj* meanned مَعَنَّد

abstract *adj* ma'nawi معنوي

morale *n* ma'naweyyat معنويّات

mean *n* ma'nah معنى

meaning *n* ma'nah معنى

institute *n* ma'had مَعْهَد

intestinal *adj* me'awi مِعَوي

criterion *n* meyar معيار

standard *n* me'yar معيار

n me'yareyyeh معياريّة

standardization

designated *adj* muayyan مُعَيَّن

deficient *adj* ma'yub مَعيوب

mug *n* mag elqahweh مغّ القهوة

departure *n* mughadarah مغادرة

cavern *n* magharah مَغَارَة

argonaut *n* mughamir مُغَامِر

venturesome *adj* mughamer مُغَامِر

adventure *n* mughamara مغامرة

venture *n* mughamarah مغامرة

migrant *n* mughtarib مُغْتَرِب

nutritious *adj* mughazzi مغَذّي

nutritive *adj* mughazzi مغَذّي

ladle *n* maghrafeh مغرفة

arrogant *adj* maghrur مغرور

coky *adj* maghrur مغرور

enigma *n* mu'deleh مُعْضِلَة

deactivator *n* muattal معطّل

decadent *adj* meaffin معفّن

mouldy *adj* me'affen معفّن

addle *adj* meaffn معفّن

me'fa mn eldaribeh معفى من الضريبة

scot-free *adj*

exempt *adj* me'fi معفي

sophisticated *adj* mu'aqqad معقَّد

complex *adj* muaqqad مُعقَّد

crooked *adj* ma'quf مَعْقُوف

reasonable *adj* ma'qul معقول

dingy *adj* meakkar معكَّر

sling *n* me'laq مِعْلاَق

manger *n* ma'laf معلف

stall *n* ma'laf معلف

bunk *n* ma'laf مَعْلَف

abeyant *adj* me'allaq معلَّق

commentator *n* mualleq معلّق

outstanding *adj* me'allaq معلَّق

spoon *n* ma'laqah معلقة

preceptor *n* me'allem معلّم

tutor *n* me'allem معلّم

milestone *n* ma'lam مَعْلَم

information *n* ma'limat معلومات

n ma'lumat aameh معلومات عامّة

background

perennial *adj* m'ammer معمِّر

afflictive *adj* 'mufje مُفجِع	pretentious *adj* maghrur مَغْرُور
bereaved *adj* 'mafjue مُفجوع	enticer *n* mughri مُغْري
irrefutable *adj* mufhim مُفْحِم	spindle *n* maghzal مغزَل
joyous *n* mefreh مُفرِح	drift *n* maghza مغزى
cheerful *adj* mufrih مُفرِح	fuzzy *adj* meghashsha مغَشّى
pleasant *adj* mufreh مُفرِح	steep *adj* maghtut مَغْطُوط
single *adj* mefred مفرد	close *adj* mughlaq مُغْلَق
singular *adj* mufrad مُفرِد	muggy *adj* meghemm مغمّ
sole *n* mufred مُفرِد	faint *adj* mughma alyh مغمى عليه
platoon *n* mafrazeh مَفْرَزة	magnet *n* maghnatis مغنطيس
squad *n* mafrazeh مَفْرَزة	magnetic *adj* maghnatisi مغنطيسي
excessive *adj* mufret مُفرِط	*n* maghnateseyyeh مغْنَطيسِيّة
retail *adj* mefarraq مفرَّق	magnetism
ordained *adj* mafrud مَفْروض	cloudy *adj* meghayyim مغيّم
over *n* mafrugh mennu مفروغ مِنّه	overcast *adj* meghayyem مغيّم
joint *n* mefassal مفصِل	*n* mufataha belkalam مفاتحة بالكلام
n 'mefsal elusba مفصل الإصبع	overture
knuckle	surprise *n* mufaja'ah مفاجأة
separable *adj* mafsul مفصول	abrupt *adj* 'mufaje مفاجئ
fir *n* mafsul مَفْصُول	*n* mufaraka tarikhiyeh مفارقة تاريخية
favourite *adj* mudfaddal مفضَّل	anachronism
preferential *adj* mufaddal مُفضَّل	reactor *n* mufa'el مُفَاعِل
notorious *adj* mafduh مَفْضُوح	negotiator *n* mufawed مفاوِض
spanner *n* mefakk مفكّ	nagotiation *n* mufawadah مفاوَضة
thinker *n* mefakker مفكّر	key *n* meftah مفتاح
pensive *adj* mufakker مفكّر	malign *adj* mefteri مفتري
loose *adj* mafkuk مَفْكُوك	ajar *adv* maftuh مفتوح
insolvent *adj* mufles مُفلِس	open *adj* maftuh مفتوح

resistance *n* muqawameh مقاومة	rift *n* 'maflu مَفْلُوع
resistant *adj* muqawameh مقاومة	concept *n* mafhum مفهوم
barter *n* mukadadah مقايَضَة	intelligible *adj* mafhum مَفْهُوم
catacomb *n* maqbarah مقبَرَة	vicarious *adj* mefawwad مفوّض
socket *n* maqbas مقبس	delegator *n* mufawwad مفوَّض
appetizer *n* muqabelat مقبلات	vested *adj* mfawwad مفَوَّض
acceptable *adj* makbool مقبول	advantageous *adj* mufid مفيد
admissible *adj* mkbuol مقبول	useful *adj* mufid مفيد
repugnance *n* maqt مقت	salutary *adj* mufid مُفيد
conjunct *adj* muqtaren مقتَرِن	agamist *n* muqabl مقابل
provident *adj* meqtesd مقتصد	interview *n* muqabaleh مقابلة
anthology *n* muktatafat مقتطفات	meeting *n* muqabaleh مقابلة
meqdar kaff eleyd مقدار كف الإيد	against *prep* mqabyl مقابيل
handful *n*	militant *n* muqatel مقاتل
heavenly *adj* muqaddas مقدَّس	combatant *n* muqatil مُقاتِل
sacred *adj* muqaddas مقدَّس	*n* muqatel belsif مقاتل بالسيف
holy *adj* muqaddas مُقَدَّس	fencer
endowed *adj* muqaddam مقَدَّم	comparative *adj* muqaran مُقارَن
n muqaddem eltaen مقدم الطعن	comparison *n* muqaraneh مُقارَنة
appellant	interruption *n* maqata'ah مقاطَعَة
n mukaddem eltalab مقدم الطلب	boycott *n* muqata'a مُقاطَعَة
applicant	article *n* maqaleh مقالة
muqaddem elma'rud مقدِّم المعروض	essay *n* maqaleh مقالة
petitioner *n*	fry *n* maqali مقالي
n muqaddem emtihan مقدِّم امتحان	shrine *n* maqam مَقَام
examinee	contractor *n* muqawel مُقَاوِل
front *n* muqademeh مقدمة	*n* muqawem elnanu مقاوم النانو
introduction *n* muqademeh مقدِّمة	nanotransistor

eyeball n meqlet eleyn مقلة العين

counterfeit adj meqallad مقلّد

imitator n mqalled مقلّد

counterfeiter n meqallad مُقَلِّد

quarry n maqla' hajar مقلع حجارة

fickle adj mqa;qal مقلقل

reamer n meqwarah مقورة

arch adj muqawwas مُقَوّس

stereotyped adj mequlab مُقَوْلَب

statement n maquleh مقولة

meter n meqyas مقياس

gauge n meqyas مِقياس

n miqyas elertifae مقياس الارتفاع

altimeter

n meqyas elmatar مقياس المطر

pluviometer

n meqyas hrarah مقياس حرارة

thermometer

n meqyas zelzal مقياس زلزال

seismograph

mekyas sere't مقياس سرعة الهوا

anemometer n elhawwa

mekyas daghet مقياس ضغط الهوا

barometer n elhawa

meqyas kathafet مِقْياسُ كَثَافَةِ اللَّبَن

lactometer n ellaban

meqyas la umq مقياس لعمق المي

fathom n elmay

n muqademet ktab مقدمة الكتاب

foreword

projectile adj maqzuf مقذوف

cognitive adj muqarrab مُقَرّب

curriculum n muqarrar مقرّر

decided adj muqarrar مقرّر

disgusting adj muqref مقرف

odious adj meqref مقرف

repulsive adj muqref مُقْرِف

crisp adj meqarmesh مقرمش

legible adj 'maqrue مَقْروء

loathsome adj muqazzez مقزّز

callous adj muqassa مقسّى

scissors n meqass مقصّ

slipshod adj meqasser مقَصّر

sideboard n maqsaf مقصف

adj maqsur hararyyan مقصور حرارياً

entropic

n maqsuret ettayyar مقصورة الطيّار

cock-pit

syllable n 'meqatta مَقْطَع

stanza n maqta' she'er مقطع شعر

tandem n maqturah مقطورة

trailer n maqturah مقطورة

seat n maq'ad مقعد

concave adj muqa'ar مقعّر

frolic n maqlab مَقْلَب

prank n maqlab مَقْلَب

capsular *adj* mekabsan مكبسَنّ

bureau *n* maktab مكتب

desk *n* maktab مكتب

office *n* maktab مكتب

post- *n* maktab brid مكتب البريد

office

post *n* maktab brid مكتب بريد

library *n* maktabeh مكتبة

agglomerate *adj* mkttil مكتّل

latent *adj* maktum مكتوم

mute *adj* maktum مكتوم

felinity *n* makr مكر

recurrent *adj* mukarrar مكرّر

dedicatory *adj* mukarras مكرّس

disagreeable *adj* makruh مكروه

misadventure *n* makruh مكّروه

trashed *adj* mekassar مكسّر

naked *adj* mekashshif مكشّف

cube *n* muka'ab مكعّب

warrantee *n* makful مكفول

adj mkallal belghar مكلّل بالغار

laureate

adj mukammel مكمّل

complementary

broom *n* mekneseh مكنسة

sweeper *n* meknseh مكنسة

meknseh كهربا مكنسة

vacuum *n* kahruba'eyyeh

bound *adj* muqayyad مقيّد

restrictive *adj* meqayyad مقيّد

sedentary *adj* muqim مُقيم

brake *n* makabeh مكبح

stickler *n* mekaber مكَابِر

obstinate *adj* mukaber مُكَابر

obstinacy *n* mukabarah مكَابَرة

recompense *n* mukafa'ah مكافاة

award *n* mukafa'a مكافأة

reward *n* mukafa'ah مكافأة

bonus *n* mukafa'a مُكافأة

n mukafa'a fakhreyyeh مكافأة نخريّة

honorarium

struggle *n* mukafahah مكافحة

place *n* makan مكان

position *n* makan مكان

venue *n* makan مَكان

n makan elmukhayyam مكان المخيّم

campsite

makan saff مكان صَفّ الزوارق

boathouse *n* elzawareq

adj makan a'm مكان عامّ

commonplace

stature *n* makaneh مكانة

n mukbbah a'lhwa مكبح عالهوا

airbrake

amplifier *n* mukabber مكبّر

piston *n* makbas مكبَس

adjunct *n* mulhaq ملحق

appendage *n* mulhaq مُلحق

appendix *n* mulhaq مُلحق

appurtenance *n* mulhaq مُلحق

epic *n* malhameh ملحَمة

epical *adj* malhami مَلحَمي

remarkable *adj* malhuz مَلحُوظ

cohesive *adj* malhum ملحُوم

saline *adj* melhi ملحِي

summary *adj* mulakhkhas ملخَّص

abstract *n* mulakhkhas مُلخَّص

binding *adj* mulzim مُلزِم

imposing *adj* mulzem مُلزِم

talkative *adj* melsen ملسِن

cohesive *adj* malsuq ملصوق

playfield *n* mal'ab مَلعَب

playground *n* mal'ab مَلعَب

accursed *adj* mal'oon ملعون

damn *adj* mal'un ملعُون

damned *adj* mal'un ملعُون

null *adj* melghi ملغي

file *n* malaf ملف

folio *n* malaf ملف

adj mulfit lelintibah مُلفت للانتباه

attractive

adj mulft llnazar ملفت للنظر

admirable

cabbage *n* malfuf ملفُوف

snug *adj* mkankan مكنكن

shuttle *n* makkuk مكُّوك

component *adj* mukawwan مكوِّن

ingredient *n* mukawwenat مكونات

measure *n* mekyal مكيال

peck *n* mekyal مكيال

machination *n* makideh مكيدة

mullah *n* mullah مُلّا

n malat elma'laqah ملات المعلقة

spoonful

note *n* mulahaza ملاحظة

outlaw *n* mulahaq ملاحَق

fugitive *adj* mulaheq مُلاحَق

navigable *adj* melahi ملاحي

haven *n* malaz ملاذ

malaria *n* malarya ملاريا

lieutenant *n* mulazem مُلازِم

dispute *n* mlasaneh ملاسنة

angel *n* malak ملاك

boxing *n* mulakameh ملاكمة

countenance *n* malamih ملامح

encrusted *adj* mlabbas ملبَّس

n elmultahimeh المُلتَحِمة

conjunctiva

ablaze *adv* melteheb ملتهِب

refuge *n* 'malja مَلجأ

resort *n* 'malja ملجئ

salt *n* melh ملح

laxative *adj* mulayyen مُلَيِّن

million *n* mlyun مليون

millionaire *n* malyunir مليونير

n mumataleh مماطلة

procrastination

excellent *adj* mumtaz ممتاز

perfect *adj* mumtaz ممتاز

asset *n* mumtalakat ممتلكات

belongings *n* mumtalakat ممتلكات

actor *n* mumathel ممثل

n mumaththel samet ممثل صامت

pantomime

actress *n* mumatheleh ممثلة

acarpous *adj* mmhil ممحل

commendable *adj* mamduh ممدُوح

aisle *n* mamarr ممر

passage *n* mamarr ممر

corridor *n* mamarr ممّر

strait *n* mamar dayyeq ممر ضيق

nurse *n* mumareddah ممرضة

lunatic *adj* mamsus ممسُوس

rainy *adj* mumter ممطر

showery *adj* mumter ممطر

possible *adj* mumken ممكن

probable *adj* mumken ممكن

probably *adv* mumken ممكن

tongs *n pl* menaqqat ملقط

n mlaqat eljarrah ملقط الجرّاح

forceps

prompter *n* mulaqqen مُلَقِّن

king *n* malek ملك

possession *n* melk ملك

propriety *n* melk ملك

n melk yamin ملك يمين

concubinage

queen *n* malikeh ملكة

royal *adj* malaki ملكي

majestic *adj* malaki مَلَكي

regal *adj* malaki مَلَكي

ownership *n* melkeyyeh مِلكِيّة

royalty *n* malakeyyeh مَلَكِيّة

monarchy *n* malakeyyeh مَلَكِيّة

tedium *n* malal مَلَل

glossy *adj* 'mulamma ملمّع

palpable *adj* malmus ملموس

tangible *adj* malmus ملموس

charismatic *adj* mulhem مُلهِم

salinity *n* mluhah مُلُوحَة

imperial *adj* mluki مُلُوكي

colourful *adj* mulawwan مُلوّن

full *adj* malyan مليان

adj malyan metabbat مليان مطبّات

bumpy

comely *adj* melih مَليح

adv mn elyum wba'ed ومن اليوم وبعد	ممكن إطلاق سراحه بكفالة mumken
henceforward	*adj* itlaq sarahu bekafaleh
afar *adv* mn beid من بعيد	bailable
inland *adv* mn jwwah من جواً	*adj* mumken tahwelu ممكن تحويله
without *adv* mn dun من دون	convertible
prep mn traf ll tani من طرف للتاني	*adj* mumken yenghefer ممكن ينغفر
across	pardonable
prep men taraf latani من طرف للتاني	dull *adj* mumell مُمِلّ
athwart	irksome *adj* mumell مُمِلّ
adv mn fatrah qarebeh من فترة قريبة	castor *n* mamlaha مَمْلَحَة
lately	kingdom *n* mamlakeh مملكة
afore *prep* mn qbl من قبل	proprietary *adj* mamluk مملوك
former *pron* mn qabl من قبل	forbidden *adj* mamnu'e ممنوع
heartily *adv* mn qlbuh من قلبه	grateful *adj* mamnun ممنون
adv mn hallaq wray من هلق وراي	crisp *adj* mumawwaj مُمَوّج
henceforth	camouflaged *adj* mumawwah مُمَوّه
adv mn hum wray من هون وراي	fatal *adj* mumit مميت
hence	special *adj* mumayyaz مميز
adv mn hun wrayeh من هون ورايح	peculiar *adj* mumayyaz مُمَيّز
forth	molten *adj* 'mumayye مُمَيّع
adj men wara elzaher من ورا الظهر	from *prep* mn من
backstairs	out *prep* mn من
since *prep* mn waqt من وقت	manna *n* elmann المَنّ
lamentation *n* manahah مَنَاحَة	*adj* mn 8 zawayah من 8 زوايا
climate *n* manakh مناخ	octangular
n manakh hayawi مناخ حيوي	notable *adj* mn ela'yan من الأعيان
bioclimate	mn elqurun من القرون الوسطى
beacon *n* manara مَنَارة	medieval *adj* elwestah

pulpit *adj* manbar منبر	expedient *adj* munaseb مناسب
dais *n* menbar مَنْبَر	fit *adj* mnaseb مناسب
extrovert *n* menbeset منبسط	gainly *adj* munasib مناسب
prone *adj* menbeteh منْبطح	proper *adj* munaseb مناسب
alarm *n* mnbbh منبّه	suitable *adj* munaseb مناسب
stimulant *n* munabbeh منبّه	appropriate *adj* munasib مُناسِب
outcast *n* elmanbuz المَنْبوذ	apt *adj* munasib مُناسِب
outcast *adj* manbuz مَنْبوذ	condign *adj* munasib مُناسِب
wary *adj* mentebeh منتبه	occasion *n* munasabeh مناسبة
vigilant *adj* mentebeh منتبِه	manateq hadareyyeh مناطق حضريّة
circumspect *adj* mentebeh منتبِه	metropolitan *n*
product *n* muntaj مُنتَج	immunity *n* mana'ah مناعة
manufacturer *n* muntij مُنتِج	immune *adj* mana'e مُناعِي
by- *n* muntaj thanawi مُنتَج ثانوي	agonist *n* munafes مُنافِس
product	competitive *adj* munafes مُنافِس
prevalent *adj* mentesher منتشر	competition *n* munafaseh مُنافَسة
widespread *adj* mentesher منتشر	rivalry *n* munafaseh مُنافَسة
diffuse *adj* mentesher منتشِر	hypocrite *n* munafeq مُنافِق
ecstatic *adj* menteshi منتشي	insincere *adj* munafiq مُنافِق
victorious *adj* menteser منتصر	deliberation *n* munaqasheh مناقشة
triumphant *adj* menteser منتصِر	bidder *n* munaqis مُناقِص
prospective *adj* muntazar مُنتَظَر	bid *n* munaqasa مُناقَصَة
even *adj* mentezem منتظم	tender *n* munaqasah مُناقَصَة
complete *adj* mentihi منتهي	fingerpaint *n* manakir مناكير
sickle *n* manjal منْجَل	shift *n* munawabeh مناوبة
scythe *n* menjal منْجَل	gambit *n* mnawarah مناورة
mine *n* manjam منْجَم	manoeuvre *n* munawarah مُنَاوَرَة
astrologer *n* munajjim مُنجِّم	skirmish *n* menawasheh مُنَاوَشة

insurgent *n* menshaqq مُنْشَق

pamphlet *n* manshur منشور

sawn *n* manshur مَنْشُور

adj mensab belta'un منصاب بالطاعون
plague

brace *n* mansab منصَب

mount *n* mansab منصَب

tripod *n* mansab منصَب

chair *n* mansib منصِب

post *n* mansib منصِب

n manseb elqadi مَنْصِب القاضِي
magistrature

منصِب شمّاس الكنيسة mansib
deaconship *n* shammas elkniseh

platform *n* manassah منصَّة

menasset ared منصِّة عرض الأزياء
catwalk *n* 'elazya

victor *n* mansur منصور

area *n* metaqa منطقة

zone *n* manteqah منطقة

n metaet maarek منطقة المعارك
battlezone

n manteqa na'yeh منطقة نائية
outback

logical *adj* mateqi منطقي

n menzar elezen منظار الأذن
otoscope

outlook *n* manzr مَنْظَر

grant *n* menhah منحة

n menha deraseyyeh منحة دراسيّة
scholarship

declinous *adj* menheder منحَدِر

cliff *n* munhadar منحَدَر

slope *n* munhader مُنحَدِر

perverse *adj* menherf منحرف

apiary *n* manhaleh منحَلة

sinuous *adj* menheni منحَنِي

inauspicious *adj* manhus مَنْحُوس

luckless *adj* manhus مَنْحُوس

ominous *adj* manhus مَنْحُوس

sinister *adj* manhus مَنْحُوس

nostril *n* menkhar منخار

low *n* menkhefed منْخَفِض

conical *n* mankhal syni منخَل صيني

domiciliary *adj* manzli مَنْزِلِي

adj manzu'e essilah منزوع السلاح
demilitarized

consistent *adj* mensejim منسَجِم

coordinate *adj* munassiq مُنسِّق

textile *adj* mansuj منسوج

origin *n* 'mansha منشأ

facility *n* munsha'a منشأة

saw *n* menshar مِنْشار

sawmill *n* manshar مَنْشَر

towel *n* manshafeh منشفة

insurgent *adj* menshaqq مُنْشَق

enervated *adj* munhak مُنهَك	spectacle *n* manzar مَنظَر
miscellaneous *adj* 'menawwa مُنوّع	regulator *n* munazzam مُنَظّم
miscellany *n* munawwa'at مُنوّعات	munazzim elsafaqat منظّم الصفقات
opiate *adj* menawwem مُنوّم	dealmaker *n*
seminal *adj* manawi مَنَوي	*n* munazzameh مُنظّمة
semen *n* mani مَني	organization
fine *adj* mneh منيح	perspective *n* manzur مَنظُور
good *adj* mnih منيح	prevention *n* 'mane منع
well *adj* mnih منيح	contraception *n* mae' haml منع حمل
stateliness *n* mahabeh مهابة	tonic *adj* mun'esh مُنعِش
immigrant *n* muhajer مُهَاجِر	reflex *n* mun'akas مُنعَكَس
skill *n* maharah مهارة	reflex *adj* mun'akas مُنعَكَس
craft *n* maharah مهارَة	manganese *n* manganiz مَنغَنيز
humility *n* mahaneh مهانة	bellows *n* menfaakh منفَاخ
vagina *n* mahbal مَهبِل	separate *adj* menfesl منفصل
batter *n* mehteri مهتري	insular *adj* menfesl منفصل
interested *adj* mehtamm مهتَمّ	utility *n* manfa'ah منفعة
attentive *adj* muhtam مُهتَمّ	exile *n* manfi منفى
dormitory *n* 'mahja مهجع	beak *n* mena'ar منقار
abandonable *adj* mahjur مهجور	rostrum *n* menqar مِنقَار
anbandonee *n* mahjur مهجور	saviour *n* munqez منقذ
archaic *adj* mahjur مهجور	extinct *adj* menqured منقرض
desolate *adj* mahjur مهجُور	movable *adj* manqul منقول
lonesome *adj* mahjur مهجُور	humorist *n* mnakket منكّت
waste *adj* mahdur مهدور	numb *adj* menammel منمّل
edificant *adj* muhazzab مُهذّب	miniature *adj* menamnam مَنمَنم
mannerly *adj* muhazzab مُهذّب	*n* manhaj derasi منهج دراسي
dowery *n* mher مهر	syllabus

n muhandes memari معماري مهندس
architect

professional adj mehani مهني

geek n mahwwus مهووس

maniac n mahwwus مهووس

irritant adj mehayyej مهيج

dominant adj mehaymen مهيمن

predominant adj mehaymn مهيمن

selfless adj mu anani مو أناني

adj mu bemahalluh مو بمحله
inopportune

mild adj mu hadd مو حد

acritical adj mo khateer مو خطير

inaccurate adj mu daqiq مو دقيق

inexact adj mu daqiq مو دقيق

acyclical adj mo dawmn مو دوما

informal adj mu rasmi مو رسمي

illegitimate adj mu shar'e مو شرعي

unable adj mu qader مو قادر

illegal adj mu qanuni مو قانوني

lawless adj mu qanuni مو قانوني

needless adj mu lazm مو لازم

lifeless adj mu ma'hul مو مأهول

adj mu metnaseq مو متناسق
asymmetrical

adj mu mhaddad مو محدد
indefinite

---

foal n muhr مهر

smuggler n meharreb مهرب

acrobat n muharej مهرج

clown n muharrej مهرج

carnival n mahrajan مهرجان

pageantry n mahrajan مهرجان

festival n mahrajan مهرجان

squash n mahrus مهروس

shabby adj mehri مهري

worn adj mehri مهري

farce n mahzaleh مهزلة

mockery n mahzaleh مهزلة

shaky adj mahzuz مهزوز

important adj mehem مهم

significant adj mehmm مهم

considerable adj muhemm مهم

task n mahammeh مهمة

commission n mahammeh مهمة

forlorn adj mehmel مهمل

ignorant adj muhmel مهمل

negligible adj muhmal مهمل

negligent adj muhmil مهمل

occupation n mehneh مهنة

career n mehneh مهنة

profession n mehneh مهنة

engineer n muhandes مهندس

n muhandes elnanu النانو مهندس
nanoengineer

conspiracy *n* mu'amarah مؤامرة

intrigue *n* mu'amarah مُؤَامَرَة

mobile *adj* mubyl موبايل

endless *adj* mu'abbad مُؤَبَّد

lifelong *adj* mu'abbad مُؤَبَّد

demise *n* mut موت

death *n* muteh موتة

decease *n* muteh موتة

tense *adj* mwattar مُوَتَّر

tensor *adj* mwatter مُوَتَّر

conference *n* mu'tamar مؤتمر

n mu'tamar tafawud مؤتمر تفاوض

parley

confidant *n* mu'taman مُؤتَّمَن

motor *n* mutur مُوتُور

female *adj* mu'annath مُؤنَّث

impressive *adj* mu'athther مُؤثَّر

influential *adj* mu'athther مُؤثَّر

credible *adj* mawthuq موثوق

authentic *adj* mawthuq موثوق

reliable *adj* mawthuq مَوثُوق

trusty *n* mawthuq مَوثُوق

wave *n* mujeh موجة

n mawjeh aarmeh موجة عارمة

billow

lesser *adj* mu'ajjer مُؤجِّر

brief *adj* mujaz موجَز

concise *adj* mujaz موجَز

adj mu mesteheqq مو مستحقّ

undue

astatic *adj* mu mistaqer مو مستقّر

illicit *adj* mu mashru'e مو مشروع

incredible *adj* mu ma'qul مو معقول

adj mu malmus مو ملموس

intangible

illogical *adj* mu mantiqi مو منطقي

adj mu manteqi مو منطقي

irrational

illegible *adj* mu wadeh مو واضح

confrontation *n* muwajaha مواجهة

encounter *n* muwajaha مواجهة

n mawad metfajrah مواد متفجرة

explosive

shifty *adj* muwareb مُوَارِب

parallelism *n* muwazat مُوَازَاة

offset *n* muwazaneh موازنة

cattle *n* mawashi مواشي

citizen *n* muwatin مواطِن

civilian *n* muwaten مواطِن

citizenship *n* muwateneh مواطَنة

perseverance *n* mwazabeh مواظبة

acceptance *n* mwaka'a موافقة

approval *n* muwafaqa موافقة

n muwafaqa rasmeyeh موافقة رسمية

approbation

loyalist *n* mwali موالي

incorporate *adj* mu'asses مؤسَّس	abridged *adj* mujaz مُوجَز
founder *n* mu'asses مؤسِّس	abridgement *n* mujaz مُوجَز
corporate *adj* muassasati مؤسَّساتي	laconic *adj* mujaz مُوجَز
corporation *n* muassaseh مؤسَّسة	terse *adj* mujaz مُوجَز
foundation *n* mu'assaseh مؤسَّسة	sharp *adj* 'muje مُوجَع
incorporation *n* mu'assaseh مؤسَّسة	mentor *n* mwajjeh موجِّه
institution *n* mu'assaseh مُؤسَّسة	oriented *adj* muwajjah مُوجَّه
muslin *n* muslin مُوسلِين	mawjud fi kel موجود في كل مكان
seasonable *adj* musmi موسمي	omnipresent *adj* makan
seasonal *adj* musmi موسمي	theist *n* mwahhed موحِّد
scrupulous *adj* muwaswas مُوَسوِس	monotheist *n* muwwahad مُوَحَّد
encyclopaedia *n* mawsu'ah موسوعة	cheerless *adj* muwhish مُوحِش
music *n* musiqa موسيقا	behind *n* muakhkhera مُؤخِّرة
musical *adj* musiqi موسيقي	baleful *adj* muezi مؤذي
musician *n* musiqi موسيقي	annalist *n* muarrekh مُؤرِّخ
indicator *n* mu'ashsher مُؤشِّر	historian *n* mu'arrekh مُؤرِّخ
fashion *n* mudah موضة	resource *n* mawred مورِد
trend *n* mudah موضة	flowery *adj* mwarred مورِد
subject *n* 'mawdu موضوع	supplier *n* mwarred مورِّد
topic *n* 'mawdu موضوع	morse *n* murs مورس
theme *n* 'mawdu مَوْضوع	morphia *n* murfin مُورفِين
matter *n* 'mawdu مَوْضوع	morphine *n* murfin مُورفِين
objective *adj* mawdu'e موضوعي	leafy *adj* mwarreq مورِق
thematic *adj* mawdu'i موضوعي	foliate *adj* mwarreq مُوَرَّق
n mawte' qadam موطئ قدم	verdant *adj* mwarraq مُورِق
foothold	hereditary *adj* mawruth موروث
clerk *n* muwazzaf موظَّف	mosaic *n* muzayyik موزاييك
employee *n* muwazzaf موظَّف	banana *n* muzeh موزة

pageant *n* mawkib مَوْكِب

procession *n* mawkeb مَوْكِب

affirmative *adj* mw'akkd مؤَّكد

definite *adj* mu'akkad مؤَّكد

assertive *adj* muakkad مؤَّكد

emphatic *adj* mu'akkad مُؤَّكد

oxidant *n* mu'aksad مؤكسد

generator *n* muwalledeh مولِّدة

n muwalledet kahrabah مولِّدة كهربا

dynamo

author *n* muallef مؤلِّف

mu'allef manshurat مؤلِّف منشورات

pamphleteer *n*

babe *n* mawlud مولود

baby *n* mawlud مولود

mawlud men مولود من بيئة منحطّة

baseborn *adj* bea'a monhattah

strumpet *n* mumes مومس

faithful *adj* mu'men مؤمِن

mummy *n* 'mumya مُومِياء

victuals *n pl* muneh مونة

cache *n* muneh مونة

supply *n* muneh مونة

monologue *n* munuluj مُونُولُوج

skit *n* munuluj مُونُولُوج

talent *n* mawhebeh موهبة

competent *adj* mu'ahhal مؤهَّل

qualification *n* mu'ahelat مؤهلات

n muwazzaf rasmi موظَّف رسمي

official

muwazzaf fi safara موظَّف في سفارة

attache *n*

muwazzaf methabbat موظف مثبَّت

incumbent *n*

date *n* maw'ed موعد

tryst *n* maw'ed مَوْعد

n elmawed eniha'i الموعد النهائي

deadline

sermon *n* maw'ezah مَوْعظَة

apt *adj* muwaffaq موفق

tentative *adj* mu'aqqat مؤَّقت

contemporary *adj* muaqqat مؤَّقت

temporal *adj* mu'aqqat مُؤَّقت

formidable *adj* mwaqqar مُوَقَّر

location *n* 'mawqe موقع

site *n* 'mawqe موقع

locale *n* 'mawqe مَوْقع

attitude *n* mawqif موقف

stop *n* mawqef موقف

halt *n* mawqef موقف

situation *n* mawqef موقف

n mwaqqef sherb موقِف شرب

teetotaller

pending *adj* mawquf موقوف

inmate *n* mawquf مَوْقُوف

caravan *n* mawkib مَوْكِب

feature *n* mezeh ميزة

opulent *adj* maysur ميسور

mica *n* mika ميكا

machinist *n* mikanisyan ميكانسيان

mechanic *n* mikanik ميكانيك

n mikanik elnanu ميكانيك النانو

nanomechanics

mechanical *adj* mikaniki ميكَانِيكِي

microphone *n* mikrufun ميكروفون

micrometer *n* mikrometr ميكرومتر

microwave *n* mykruwyf ميكروويف

lean *n* myl ميل

mile *n* myl ميل

tendency *n* myl ميل

nativity *n* milad ميلاد

lurch *n* myalan ميلان

melodrama *n* miludrama ميلُودْرامَا

adj miludrami ميلُودْرامي

melodramatic

militia *n* milyshya ميليشيَا

port *n* mina مينَا

enamel *n* mina elsnin مينا السنين

inclination *n* myul ميول

proclivity *n* myul ميول

n almuyul liljinsin الميول للجنسين

ambissexuality

Celsius *adj* meawwi مِئَوي

gifted *adj* mawhub مَوْهُوب

deluded *adj* mawhum مَوْهُوم

favourable *adj* mu'ayyed مؤيد

seconder *n* mu'ayyed مُؤَيَّد

votary *n* mu'ayyed مُؤَيَّد

water *n* may مي

elmay ezzarqah المي الزرقا بالعين

glaucoma *n* beleyn

brine *n* mai malha مي مالحة

n mayal liljinsin ميال للجنسين

ambissexual

dried *adj* meyabbas مُيَّس

stiff *adj* meyabbas مُيَّس

adj & n meyyet de'f مية ضعف

centuple

dead *adj* mayyet ميِّت

deceased *adj* mayyet ميِّت

adj metafiziqi مِيتَافِيزِيقِي

metaphysical

n metafiziqya مِيتَافِيزِيقِيا

metaphysics

charter *n* mithaq ميثاق

compact *n* mithaq ميثاق

n midan elmaarakeh ميدان المعركة

battlefield

minaret *n* me'zaneh مئذنة

scale *n* mizan ميزان

budget *n* mizaneyeh ميزانيّة

activist *n* nashet ناشط

dry *adj* nashif ناشف

preacher *n* naseh ناصِح

spokesman *n* nateq ناطِق

gatekeeper *n* natur ناطُور

janitor *n* natur ناطُور

n nazem elasha'ar ناظم أشعار
poetaster

binoculars *n* nazur ناظور

smooth *adj* na'em ناعِم

cozy *adj* naem ناعِم

pastel *adj* na'em ناعِم

reluctant *adj* nafer نافِر

beneficial *adj* 'nafe نافِع

serviceable *adj* 'nafe نافِع

critic *n* naqid ناقِد

detractor *n* naqid ناقِد

incomplete . *a* naqes ناقِص

minus *adj* naqes ناقِص

imperfect *adj* naqes ناقِص

less *prep* naqes ناقِص

tanker *n* naqelt naft ناقلة نفط

malcontent *n* elnaqem الناقِم

indignant *adj* naqem ناقِم

malcontent *adj* naqem ناقِم

adj naker leljamil ناكر للجميل
thankless

nano *n* nanu نانو

ن

tusk *n* nab elfil ناب الفيل

consequent *adj* natij ناتِج

successful *a* najeh ناجِح

towards *prep* nah ناح

near *prep* nahak ناحَك

aspect *n* nahyeh ناحية

county *n* nahyeh ناحية

shire *n* nahyeh ناحية

electorate *n* nakhib ناخِب

rare *adj* nader نادِر

bartender *n* nadil fi bar نادِل في بار

club *n* nadi نادي

bistro *n* nadi layli نادي ليلي

n nar elmukhayyam نار المخيَّم
campfire

fiery *adj* nari ناري

downward *adj* nazil نازِل

public *n* elnas الناس

people *n* nas ناس

transcriber *n* nasekh ناسِخ

hermit *n* nasek ناسِك

blain *n* nasur ناسور

fistula *n* nasur ناسُور

publisher *n* nasher ناشِر

shrew *n* nashez ناشِز

prophetic *adj* nabawi نبوي	nanohertz *n* nanu hertz نانو هرتز
oracular *adj* nebu'i نبوئي	vice *n* na'eb نائب
prophet *n* nabi نبي	vicar *n* na'eb نَائب
noble *adj* nabil نبيل	viceroy *n* na'eb malek نائب ملك
nitrogen *n* nitrujin نتروجين	nylon *n* naylun نايْلُون
snatch *n* natsh نتش	sleeper *n* naym نايم
pluck *n* natf نتف	chia *n* nabat elshya نبات الشيا
shred *n* netfeh نتفة	*n* nabat mutasalleq نبات مَتسلَّق
conclusion *n* natijeh نتيجة	betel
result *n* natijeh نتيجة	*n* nabat mu'arresh نبات معرِّش
sequel *n* natijeh نتيجة	creeper
n natijeh salbeyeh نَتِيجَة سلبيّة	*n* nabat m'ammer نبات معمِّر
consequence	perennial
prose *n* nathr نثر	*n* nabatat khadrah نباتات خضرا
deliverance *n* najat نجاة	greenery
pass *n* najah نجاح	macrobiotic *adj* nabati نباتي
success *n* najah نجاح	vegan *n* nabati نَباتي
carpenter *n* najjar نجَّار	vegan *adj* nabati نَباتي
joiner *n* najjar نجَّار	vegetarian *n* nabati نَباتي
carpentry *n* nejarah نجارة	howl *n* nbah نباح
impurity *n* najaseh نَجَاسة	bay *n* nubah elkaleb نباح الكلب
relief *n* najdeh نجْدة	Neptune *n* nibtun نِبتون
defile *n* nejis نجس	pulse *n* nabd نبض
impure *adj* nejs نجس	palpitation *n* nabd نَبض
star *n* najm نجم	pulsation *n* nabdah نَبضَة
luminary *n* najm نَجم	fountain *n* nab'ah نبعَة
najm eldebb نجم الدبّ الأكبر	nobility *n* 'elnubala النبلاء
wain *n* elakbar	prophecy *n* nebuwweh نبُوّة

carious *adj* nakher نَخِر

palm *n* nakhleh نَخلة

date *n* nakhleh نَخلة

gallantry *n* nakhweh نَخوة

magnanimity *n* nakhweh نَخوة

counterpart *n* nidd نِدّ

moisture *n* nadaweh نَداوة

wetness *n* nadaweh نَداوة

elegy *n* nadbeh نَدبة

scar *n* nadbeh نَدبة

rareness *n* nedrah نَدرَة

rarity *n* nedrah نَدرَة

scoundrel *n* nadel نَذل

cad *n* nadel نَذل

regret *n* nadam نَدم

repentant *adj* nadman نَدمان

symposium *n* nadweh نَدوة

forum *n* nadweh نَدوة

wet *adj* nadyan نَديان

damp *adj* nadyan نَديان

moist *adj* nadyan نَديان

herald *n* nazir نَذير

omen *n* nazir نَذير

narcissus *n* narjes نَرجس

daffodil *n* narjis barri نَرجس بَرّي

narcissism *n* narjeseyyeh نَرجِسِيّة

impartiality *n* nazaha نَزَاهة

loadstar *n* najm elqutub نَجم القطب

asterisk *n* najmeh نَجمة

asteroid *adj* najmi نَجمي

stellar *adj* najmi نَجمي

starry *adj* najmi نَجمي

sculptor *n* nahhat نَحَّات

copper *n* nhas نُحاس

brass *n* nehas asfar نُحاس أَصفَر

coppery *adj* nehasi نُحاسي

sculptural *adj* nahti نَحتي

sculpture *n* nahti نَحتي

fatality *n* nahs نَحس

bee *n* nahleh نَحلة

grammar *n* nahu نَحو

grammarian *n* nahawi نَحوي

gaunt *adj* nahif نَحيف

meagre *adj* nahif نَحيف

thin *adj* nhif نَحيف

slender *n* nahif نَحيف

emaciated *adj* nahif نَحيف

scraggy *adj* nahil نَحيل

n nukha' elezam نُخاع العظام

marrow

spinal *adj* nukha'i نُخاعي

toast *n* nakhb نَخب

elite *n* elnughbeh النخبة

elitist *n* nakhbawi نَخبوي

elitism *n* elnakhbaweyyeh النخبوية

breed *n* nasel نِسل

breeze *n* nasmat نَسمات

aura *n* nismeh نِسمة

squire *n* neswanji نَسونجي

oblivion *n* nsyan نِسيان

forgetful *adj* nsyan نِسْيان

fabric *n* nasij نَسِيج

textile *n* nasij نَسِيج

sizzle *n* nashsh نَشّ

starch *n* nasha نَشًا

ammonia *n* nashadir نشادر

sawyer *n* nashshar نشّار

n nesharet khashab نشارة الخشب
sawdust

absonant *adj* nashaz نشاز

activity *n* nshat نشاط

alacrity *n* nashat نشاط

energy *n* nashat نشاط

vivacity *n* nashat نَشاط

publication *n* nashr نشر

brochure *n* nashra نشرة

bulletin *n* nashra نشرة

leaflet *n* nashrah نَشرة

n nashret iktitab نشرة اكتتاب
prospectus

active *adj* nshet نشط

ectasy *n* nashweh نشوة

euphoria *n* nashweh نشوة

n naze' slah نزع السلاح
disarmament

rash *adj* nezq نزق

levity *n* nezeq نَزَق

sally *n* nazweh نزوة

vagary *n* nazweh نزوة

freak *n* nazweh نزوة

caprice *n* nazweh نَزوة

feminist *n* elnisa'e النسائي

feminine *adj* nisa'e نسائي

feminist *adj* nisa'e نسائي

genealogy *n* nasab نَسَب

lineage *n* nasab نَسَب

ratio *n* nesbeh نسبة

n nesbeh me'aweyyeh نسبة مئويّة
percentage

relative *adj* 'nisbi نسبي

copy *n* naskh نسخ

transcription *n* naskh نسخ

reproduction *n* nasekh نسخ

version *n* neskhah نسخة

neskhah tebq نسخة طبق الأصل
replica *n* elasel

nesekha tbeq نُسْخَة طِبق الأصل
duplicate *n* elasel

eagle *n* nser نسر

condor *n* neser amriki نسر أمريكي

progeny *n* nasl نسل

n nasb tizkari نصب تذكاري	anthem n nashideh نشيدة
monument	chant n nashideh نشيدة
victory n nasr نصر	alacrious adj nashit نشيط
triumph n nasr نَصر	energetic adj nashit نشيط
n elnasraneyyeh النَصرانيّة	ginger adj nashit نشيط
Christendom	living adj nashit نشيط
n nesef da'era نصف دائرة	vivacious adj nashit نشيط
demicircle	lively adj nashit نَشِيط
n nesf da'erah نصف دائرة	half n ness نص
semicircle	half adj ness نص
advice n nsiha نصيحة	text n ness نص
naddarah la'eyn نضّارة لعين وحدة	midst n ness نص
monocle n wehdeh	n ness elsif نص الصيف
smug adj nedif نضيف	midsummer
spotless adj nedif نضيف	nuss elkurah نص الكرة الأرضيّة
stainless adj nedif نضيف	hemisphere n elardeyyeh
cavorting n natt نَط	midnight n ness ellil نص الليل
domain n netaq نطاق	script n nass barmaji نص برمجي
range n netaq نطاق	swindler n nassab نصّاب
scope n netaq نطاق	fraudulent adj nassab نَصّاب
sphere n nitaq نطاق	impostor n nassab نَصّاب
sideband n nitaq janbi نطاق جانبي	n nisab qanuni نصاب قانوني
jump n nattah نطّة	quorum
hop n nattah نطّة	recommendation n nasa'eh نصائح
skip n nattah نطّة	swindle n nasb نصب
butt n hateha نطحة	gimmick n nasb نَصْب
gore n nateha نطحة	n nasb tizkari نصب تذكاري
enunciation n nutuq نطق	memorial

boon *n* ne'meh نعمة

mint *n* 'na'na نَعْناع

obituary *n* na'weh نعوة

caw *n* naeyq نعيق

croak *n* naeyq نعيق

bliss *n* maeyem نعيم

hybrid *n* naghl نَغل

n naghmeh khafifeh نغمة خفيفة

undertone

nugget *n* nagit نغيت

n nafadet elghabra نفاضة الغبرا

duster

guile *n* nifaq نفاق

insincerity *n* nifaq نفاق

duplicity *n* nefaq نِفَاق

strut *n* nafekh elhal نفخ الحال

same *adj* nafs نفس

self *n* nafs نفس

breath *n* nafas نَفَس

psyche *n* nafs نَفْس

ditto *n* nafs eshshi نفس الشي

psychic *adj* nafsi نَفْسي

oil *n* neft نفط

petroleum *n* naft نَفْط

tunnel *n* nafaq نفق

alimony *n* nafaqa نفقة

expense *n* nafaqah نفقَة

ascendancy *n* nufuz نُفُوذ

enunciatory *adj* netqi نطقي

glasses *n* nazarat نظارات

n nazarat sbaha نظارات سباحة

goggles

optician *n* nazarrati نَظّارَاتي

cleanliness *n* elnazafeh النظافة

system *n* nizam نظام

n nizam eqta'e نظام إقطاعي

feudalism

regime *n* nizam elhukm نظام الحكم

ecosystem *n* nizam bi'e نظام بيئي

polity *n* nizam hukm نظام حكم

regular *adj* nizami نظامي

systematic *adj* nizami نظامي

methodical *adj* nizami نِظَامي

vision *n* nazar نظر

n nazrah khatfeh نظرة خاطفة

glimpse

theorem *n* nazari نظري

theory *n* nazareyyeh نظريّة

nadir *n* nazir نظير

clean *adj* nazif نظيف

ostrich *n* na'ameh نعامة

ewe *n* na'jeh نعجة

somnolence *n* na'as نعس

sleepy *adj* na'san نعسان

somnolent *n* na'san نَعسان

bier *n* na'esh نعش

decrement n neqsan نقصان	apathy n nufur نُفور
revocation n naqd نقض	reluctance n nufur نُفور
dot n nuqtah نقطة	banishment n nafi نَفي
drop n nuqtah نقطة	negation n nafi نَفي
point n nuqtah نقطّة	invaluable adj nafis نَفيس
n neqtet ettisal نقطة اتصال	nag n naqq نقّ
juncture	nagging n naqq نقّ
focus n nuqtet tarkiz نقطة تركيز	guild n naqabet eltejjar نقابة التجّار
n niqtet tawaqquf نقطة توقّف	unionist n naqabi نقابي
breakpoint	n naqqar elkhashab نقّار الخشَب
forte n neqtet qwweh نقطة قوّة	flicker
drip n nuqtah nuqtah نقطة نقطة	tackle n neqash نقاش
infusion n 'nafe نقّع	bicker v nikash نقاش
soak n naqe' belmay نقع بالمي	nagging adj naqqaq نقّاق
flip n naqf نقف	stretcher n naqqaleh نقّالة
transportation n naql نقل	litter n naqallet jarha نقّالة جرحى
conveyance n naql elhaki نقل الحكي	convalescence n naqaha نقاهة
n naql melkeyyeh نقل ملكيّة	purity n naqaweh نقاوة
transfer	criticism n naqed نقد
indignation n naqmeh نقمة	pecuniary adj naqdi نقدي
pure a naqi نقي	monetary adj naqdi نقّدي
catapult n neqqefeh نقّيفة	click n naqrah نقرة
matrimony n nikah نكاح	gout n nuqrus نقرُس
n nakkashet uzun نكّاشة أذن	inscription n naqsh نقش
aurilave	epitaph n naqesh a qabr نقش ع قبر
spite n nikayeh نكاية	lack n naqs نقص
anecdote n nekteh نكتة	deficiency n naqes نقص
gag n nekteh نكتة	imperfection n naqs نقّص

last *n* nihayeh نهاية	joke *n* nekteh نكتة
end *n* nihayeh نهاية	banter *n* nikteh نِكتة
conclusive *adj* nihaei نهائي	petulance *n* nakad نَكَد
final *adj* niha'e نهائي	petulant *adj* nekadi نكدي
terminal *adj* niha'i نِهائي	*n* neqran ejjamil نكران الفضل
plunder *n* nahb نهب	ingratitude
rifle *n* nahb نهب	poke *n* nakzeh نكزة
river *n* nahr نهر	relapse *n* nakseh نكسة
glacier *n* nahr jalidi نهر جليدى	setback *n* nakseh نكسة
renaissance *n* nahdah نهضَة	flavour *n* nakha نكهة
resurgence *n* nahdah نَهضَة	favour *n* nakha نكهَة
bray *n* nahiq elhimar نهيق الحمار	talebearer *n* nammam نَمَّام
kernel *n* nawat نَوَاة	telltale *n* nammam نَمَّام
nucleus *n* nawat نَوَاة	panther *n* nemer نمر
lament *n* nwah نواح	tiger *n* nemr نمر
mourner *n* nwah نوَّاح	tigress *n* nemrah نمرة
fit *n* nubeh نوبة	mongoose *n* nems نمس
brilliance *n* nuraneyeh نورانيّة	modality *n* namat نمط
seagull *n* nawras نورس	typical *adj* namati نَمَطِي
gull *n* nawras نورَس	termite *n* naml abyad نمل أبيض
vagabond *adj* nawari نُورِي	ant *n* namleh نملة
genre *n* 'nu نوع	emmet *n* namleh نملة
kind *n* 'nu نوع	growth *n* munwu نمُوّ
model *n* 'nu نوع	accrementition *n* nmweh نموة
sort *n* 'nu نوع	pattern *n* namuzaj نموذج
n nue' men essigar نوع من السيجار	*n* namuzaj asli نموذج أصلي
cheroot	prototype
	talebearing *n* namimeh نَميمة

نوع من القرود n nu' mn elqrud
gibbon

qualitative *adj* naw'e نَوْعِي

loom *n* nul نَوْل

sleep *n* num نوم

pot *n* nuneyyeh نُونِيّة

urinal *n* nuneyyeh نُونِيّة

nuclear *adj* nawawi نووي

aim *n* nyeh نِيّة

intent *n* neyyeh نِيّة

resplendent *adj* nayyer نَيِّر

April *n* nisan نيسان

nickel *n* nikl نِيكل

nicotine *n* nikutin نيكوتين

neutron *n* nyutrun نيوترون

neon *n* nyun نِيون

ه

abandoner *n* hajir هاجِر

spectre *n* hajes هاجِس

premonition *n* hajes هاجِس

both .*conj* had w had هاد وهاد

calm *n* hadi هادي

pacific *adj* hadi هادي

quiet *adj* hadi هادي

inactive *adj* hamed هامِد

---

margin *n* hamesh هامش

marginal *adj* hameshi هامشي

mortar *v* hawn هاوُن

amateur *n* hawi هاوي

abyss *n* hawyeh هاوِية

largesse *n* hebah هبة

gust *n* habbeh هبّة

landing *n* hubut هبوط

lampoon *n* 'hija هِجاء

satire *n* 'heja هِجَاء

satirical *adj* heja'i هِجائي

desert *n* hajer هجر

immigration *n* hijrah هجرة

emigration *n* hejrah هجرَة

migration *n* hejrah هجرَة

attack *n* hojum هجوم

offensive *n* hujum هجوم

offensive *adj* hujumi هجومي

hybrid *adj* hajin هجِين

mongrel *adj* hajin هجِين

scorer *n* haddaf هدّاف

marksman *n* haddaf هدّاف

wastage *n* hadr هدر

goal *n* hadaf هدف

objective *n* hadaf هدف

score *n* hadaf هدف

target *n* hadaf هدف

deconstruction *n* hadm هدم

hysteria *n* hesteryah هستيريا	demolition *n* hadem هدم
hiss *n* hasehaseh هسهسة	truce *n* hedneh هدنة
delicate *adj* hash هَشّ	armistice *n* hudneh هُدنة
brittle *adj* hashsh هَشّ	abatement *n* 'hudu هدوء
delicacy *n* hashasheh هشاشة	quiet *n* 'hudu هدوء
hill *n* hadabeh هضبة	gift *n* hadeyyeh هديّة
plateau *n* hadabeh هَضْبة	coo *n* hadil elhamam هديل الحمام
digestion *n* hadem هضم	deliriant *n* hazayan هذيان
indigestion *n* hadem هضم	pyramid *n* haram هَرَم
hacker *n* hakar هكر	*n* harmun zakari هرمون ذكري
lunar *adj* helali هلالي	testosterone
asparagus *n* hilyun هليون	hierarchy *n* harmeyyeh هرميّة
agony *n* hamm هم	escape *n* hurub هروب
mettle *n* hemmeh همّة	runaway *n* hurub هروب
rabble *n* hamaj همَج	dodge *n* hribeh هربية
savage *n* hamaj همَج	sway *n* hazz هزّ
bestial *adj* hamaji همجي	sneer *n* hazz elenf هزّ الإنف
barbarian *n* elhamaji الهَمَجي	nod *n* hazz elras هزّ الراس
barbarian *adj* hamaji همَجي	lull *n* 'hazz elrade هزّ الرضيع
inhuman *adj* hamaji همَجي	shrug *n* hazz elktaf هزّ الكتاف
barbarism *n* hamajeyeh همَجيّة	rocking *adj* hazzaz هزّاز
savagery *n* hamajeyyeh همَجيّة	quake *n* hazzeh هزّة
whisper *n* hams همس	wag *n* hazzeh هزّة
inaction *n* humud هُمُود	*n* hazzeh ardeyyeh هزّة أرضيّة
dandelion *n* hendbeh هندبة	earthquake
engineering *n* handaseh هندسة	defeat *n* hazimeh هزيمة
n hanadeh hayaweyeh هندسة حيويّة	rout *n* hazemeh هزَيمة
bioengineering	hysterical *adj* hestiri هستيري

solemnity n hybeh هَيبة

she pron heyyeh هيّة

outburst n hayajan هيجان

turmoil n hyajan هَيَجان

hydrogen n hydrojin هيدروجين

altar n haykal هيكل

temple n haykal هيكل

structure n haykal هيكل

n haykal azmi هيكل عظمي

skeleton

structural adj haykali هيكلي

cardamom n heal هيل

dormant adj hemid هيمِد

domination n haymaneh هيمنة

predominance n haymaneh هَيْمَنة

effortless adj hayyen هيّن

facile adj hayyem هيّن

n haye't elqudat هيئة القضاة

magistracy

و

and .conj wa و

confident adj wathiq واثق

adj watheq benafsuh واثق بنفسه

self-confident

duty n wajib واجِب

---

handaseh riyadeyyeh هندسة رياضيّة

geometry n

n handaseh ziraeih هندسة زراعية

agronomy

handaseh هندسة معماريّة

architecture n memareyeh

geometrical adj handasi هندسي

Indian adj hendi هندي

air n hawa هوا

wind n hwa هوا

hobby n hewayeh هوابة

aerobic adj hwaei هوائي

waft n hujeh هوجة

palanquin n hudaj هودج

sedan n hudaj هوْدج

xenomania n hawas هوس

obsession n hawas هوَس

mania n hawas هوَس

tumult n husheh هوشة

hockey n elhuki الهوكي

fright n hul هُوْل

here adv hun هون

there adv hunik هونيك

he pron hewweh هوّه

identity n haweyyeh هويّة

infatuation n hyam هيام

awe n haebeh هيبة

dignity n hebeh هيبة

adv waktar mn hik وأكتر من هيك	incumbent adj wajb واجِب
moreover	oasis n wahah واحَة
lest .conj w ella وإلا	somebody pron wahed واحد
otherwise .conj w ella وإلّا	eventually adv wa'akhiran وأخيرا
adv wel'aks sahih والعكس صحيح	vale n wadi وادي
vice-versa	valley n wadi وادي
jackal n wawi واوِي	canyon n wadi dayyeq وادي ضيِّق
epidemic n 'waba وَباء	ample adj wase'e واسع
pestilence n 'waba وَبَاء	large adj 'wase واسع
lastly adv wu belnihayeh وبالنهاية	roomy adj 'wase واسع
fuzz n wabar وبَر	vast adj 'wase واسع
only adv w bas وبس	n wase' elma'refeh واسع المعرفة
afterwards adv wba'da وبعدا	polymath
then adv wba'da وبعدا	apparent adj wadeh واضح
thence adv wba'da وبعدا	articulate adj wadeh واضح
thereafter adv wba'da وبعدا	evident adj wadeh واضح
adv w behal waqt وبهالوقت	obvious adj wadeh واضح
meanwhile	manifest adj wadeh واضح
pale n watad وتد	salient adj wadeh واضح
peg n watad وَتَد	watt n wat واط
wedge n watad وَتَد	aware adj waeii واعي
documentary adj wathaeiqi وَثائقي	mindful adj wa'i واعي
pagan n elwathani الوثني	dystopia n elwaqe' elmurr الواقع المرّ
idolater n wathani وثني	proof adj waqi واقي
pagan adj wathani وثني	protective adj waqi واقي
paganism n wathaneyyeh وَثنيّة	n waqi sadmat واقي صدمات
stove n wujaq وجاق	bumper
notability n wajaha وَجاهة	more adv waktar وأكثر

n wehdeh harariyeh وحدة حراريّة	meal n wajbeh وجبة
calorie	eureka int wajadtuha وجدتُها
monster n wahsh وحش	ache n 'waja وجع
cruel adj wahshi وحشي	torment n 'waja وجع
draconic adj wahshi وَحْشِي	pain n 'waja وجع
inhospitable adj wahshi وَحْشِي	headache n waja' ras وجع راس
savage adj wahshi وَحْشِي	toothache n waja' snen وجع سنين
cruelty n wahsheyyeh وحشيّة	n waja' adalat وجع عضلات
puddle n wahl وحل	myalgia
muse n wahi وحي	face n wajeh وجه
oracle n wahi وحي	n wajeh ta'beri وجه تعبيري
lonely adj wahid وحيد	emoticon
lone adj wahid وَحيد	babyface n wajeh tufuli وجه طفولي
single adj wahid وَحيد	tete- n wajhan lawajeh وجها لوجه
sole n wahid وَحيد	a-tete
sole adj wahid وَحيد	destination n elwejha الوجهة
n wahid elqarn وحيد القرن	standpoint n wejha وُجْهَة
rhinoceros	angle n wejhet nazar وجهة نظر
adj wahid ellun وحيد اللون	facial adj wajhi وجهي
monochromatic	existential adj wujudi وجودي
especially adv wekhsusan وخصوصا	ontological adj wujudi وُجُودي
goodwill n wedd وِدّ	n wujudeyyeh وجوديّة
farewell n 'wada وَداع	existentialism
farewell .interj wada'an وداعا	oneness n wehdaneyyeh وَحْدانيّة
neighbourly adj weddi وِدّي	loneliness n wehdeh وحدة
meek adj 'wade وديع	module n wehdeh وحدة
aft n wra ورا	unit n wehdeh وحدة
behind prep wara ورا	unity n wehdeh وحدة

oncogenic *adj* warami ورمي	beyond *prep* wara ورا
varnish *n* warnish ورنيش	by *prep* wara ورا
heir *n* warith وريث	heredity *n* wiratheh وراثة
successor *n* warith وريث	foliage *n* elnabat wraq وَرَاقُ النَّبات
vein *n* warid وَرِيد	*n* wraq nakdeyeh وراق نقديّة
gander *n* wazz وزّ	banknote
ministry *n* wazarah وزارة	inheritance *n* werteh ورِثة
goose *n* wazzeh وزّة	patrimony *n* werteh ورِثة
weight *n* wazn وزن	flower *n* wardeh وردة
weighty *adj* wezen وزِن	pink *adj* wardi وردي
minister *n* wazir وزير	roseate *adj* wardi وَرْدِي
mediation *n* wasatah وَسَاطَة	rosy *adj* wardi وَرْدِي
amplitude *n* wesa'yah وساعيّة	sprightly *adj* weresh ورِش
badge *n* wisam وِسام	*n* warshet amal ورشة عمل
slattern *n* elwesekh الوسخ	workshop
squalid *adj* wesekh وسخ	quandary *n* wartah ورطة
dirt *n* wasakh وسخ	fix *n* wartah وَرْطَة
dirty *adj* wesekh وسخ	quicksand *n* wartah وَرْطَة
middle *n* elwasat الوسط	stencil *n* waraq harir ورق حرير
middle *adj* wasat وسط	sandpaper *n* waraq qzaz ورق قزاز
mediocre *adj* wasat وَسَط	paper *n* waraqah ورقة
mid *adj* wasat وَسَط	sheet *n* waraqah وَرَقَة
average *adj* wasati وسطي	leaf *n* warqet shajar ورقة شجر
scruple *n* wuswas وَسْواس	hip *n* wrek ورك
insinuation *n* waswaseh وَسْوَسَة	sciatic *adj* werki وِرْكِي
median *adj* wasit وسيط	tumour *n* waram ورم
intermediary *n* elwasit الوَسِيط	*adj* waram lifi ورم لِيفِي
mediator *n* wasit وَسِيط	fibromuscular

legacy *n* waseyyeh وَصِيّة	intermediate *adj* wasit وَسِيط
will *n* waseyyeh وَصِيّة	*n* wasit ruhani وسيط روحاني
page *n* wasif وَصِيف	medium
maid *n* wasifeh وَصِيفة	means *n* wasileh وسيلة
conjuncture *n* 'wade وضع	shapely *adj* wasim وَسِيم
mode *n* 'wade وضع	tattoo *n* washm وَشْم
status *n* 'wade وَضع	bobbin *n* washi'a وشيعة
n wade' harbi وضع حربي	reel *n* washe'ah وَشِيعة
belligerency	imminent *adj* washik وَشيك
n wade' tabe'i وضع طبيعي	teachings *n* wasaya وَصَايا
normalcy	wardship *n* wesayeh وِصَاية
pose *n* wade'yyeh وضعِيّة	custody *n* wisayeh وِصَاية
ablution *n* 'wudu وضوء	description *n* wasef وصف
clarity *n* wuduh وضوح	recipe *n* wasfeh وصفة
clearance *n* wuduh وضوح	*n* wasfeh tebeyyeh وصفة طبيّة
ablutionary *adj* wudu'i وضوئي	prescription
carl *n* 'wadei وضيع	*n* wasleh asabeyeh وصلة عصبيّة
lowly *adj* 'wade وضيع	commissure
home *n* watan وطن	stigma *n* wasmeh وصمة
nationalist *n* elwatani الوطني	brand *n* wasmeh وصمة
national *adj* watani وطني	arrival *n* wusul وصول
patriot *n* watani وطني	opportunism *n* wusuleyyeh وُصُولِيّة
patriotic *adj* watani وطني	guardian *n* wasi وصي
n elwataneyyeh الوطنيّة	custodian *n* wasi وصي
nationalism	trustee *n* wasi وَصي
partiotism *n* wataneyyeh وطنِيّة	warden *n* wasi وصي
promise *n* wa'd وعد	testament *n* waseyyeh وصِيّة
bout *n* waekeh وعكة	commandment *n* waseyyeh وصِيّة

stumble *n* waq'ah وقعَة	malaise *n* wa'ekeh وَعكَة
waqef itlaq ennar النار إطلاق وقف	awareness *n* waei وعي
ceasefire *n*	otherwise *adv* w ghir hik وغير هيك
vigil *n* waqfet el'eyd العيد وقفة	mortality *n* wafat وفاة
n waqfeh bilddor بالدور وقفة	accord *n* wfq وفق
alignment	accordance *n* wfq وفق
n waqfeh zeghereh زغيرة وقفة	loyal *adj* wafi وَفِي
pause	cheek *n* waqahah وقاحَة
cuckoo *n* waqwaq وقوَاق	immodesty *n* waqahah وقاحَة
biofuel *n* wuqud hayawi حيوي وقود	audacity *n* waqaha وقَاحة
magisterial *adj* waqur وقور	flippancy *n* waqahah وَقَاحَة
fall *n* wuqu'e وقوع	prudence *n* weqayh وقاية
slide *n* 'wuqu وقوع	preventive *adj* weqa'i وقائي
standing *n* wuquf وُقُوف	prudential *adj* weqa'i وقائي
queue *n* wuquf aldur عالدور وقوف	preemptive *adj* weqa'i وِقَائي
ounce *n* weqeyyeh وُقِيّة	time *n* waqt وقت
agency *n* wkaleh وكالة	upon *prep* waqt وقت
den *n* waqer وَكْر	*adv* waqt elistehqaq الاستحقاق وقت
agent *n* wakil وكيل	due
neither *conj.* wla ولا	bed-time *n* waqet ennum النوم وقت
nor *conj.* wla ولا	opportune *adj* waqtuh وقته
nobody *pron* wla hada حدا ولا	momentary *adj* waqti وقتي
none *pron* wla hada حدا ولا	abusive *adj* weqeh وخ
aught *n* wla shi شي ولا	impolite *adj* weqh وخ
nothing *n* wla shi شي ولا	rude *adj* weqh وخ
nowhere *adv* wla makan مكان ولا	shameless *adj* weqh وخ
allegiance *n* 'wala ولاء	blatant *adj* weqeh وخ
birth *n* weladeh ولادة	immodest *adj* weqeh وَخ

already *adv* ya dub يا دوب

barely *adv* ya dub يا دوب

influence *v* ye'athther يَأْثِر

v ye'ajjer mn ajar يَأْجِر من آجار

sublet

adjourn *v* yeajil يَأْجِل

defer *v* ye'ajjil يَأْجِّل

postpone *v* ye'ajjel يَأْجِّل

prorogue *v* ye'ajjel يَأْجِّل

take *v* yakhud ياخد

obtain *v* yakhud ياخد

retaliate *v* yakhud beltar ياخد بالتّأر

v yakhud belmehayaleh ياخد بالمحايلة

coax

v yakhud hadanet ياخد حضانة

nurture

biopsy *v* yakhud khuza'a ياخد خزعة

sample *v* yakhud ayyeneh ياخد عيّنة

delay *v* ye'akhkhir يَأْخِر

post- *v* ye'akhkher tarikh يَأْخِر تاريخ

date

chastise *v* yeaddeb يَأَدّب

hardly *adv* yadub يادوب

perform *v* ye'addi يَأَدّي

permit *v* ye'zan يَأذن

reproduction *n* weladeh ولادة

obstetric *adj* welladi ولادِي

canton *n* welayeh ولاية

next *adv* wlaba'da ولبعدا

waldan ولدان بتّه ملعقة دهب

adj betumuh malaqet dahab

born rich

fecund *adj* walud وَلُود

prolific *adj* walud وَلُود

wail *n* walwaleh ولولة

banquet *n* walimeh وليمة

feast *n* walemeh وليمة

conj w ma' hik ومع هيك.

nevertheless

adv w ma' hik ومع هيك

nonetheless

adv w ma' hik ومع هيك

notwithstanding

aluminium *n* alumenyum الومنيوم

chimera *n* wahm وهم

illusion *n* wahm وهم

delusion *n* wahm وَهْم

phantom *n* wahm وَهْم

aeriform *adj* whmy وهمي

phantasmal *adj* wahmi وهمي

delusional *adj* wahmi وَهْمي

etcetera *adv* wuhik وهيك

whisky *n* wiski ويسكي

order v ye'mur يَأْمُر	harm v ye'zi يأذي
nationalize v ya'ammem يأمّم	yard n yard يارد
insure v ye'ammen يأمن	despair n ya's يأس
secure v ye'ammen يأمن	captivate v ya'sir يأسِر
lottery n yanasib ياناصيب	corroborate v yeassis يأسّس
divert v ye'anis يآنس	establish v ye'assis يأسّس
populate v ye'ahhel يأهّل	found v ye'assis يأسّس
qualify v ye'ahhel يأهّل	incorporate v ye'asses يأسّس
lodge v ye'wi يآوي	jasmine, jessamine n yasmin ياسمين
further v ya'ayyed يآيِّد	indicate v ye'ashsher يأشِّر
desperate adj ya'es يائِس	refer v ye'ashsher يأشِّر
hopeless adj ya'es يائِس	remark v ye'ashsher يأشِّر
stale v yebat يبات	advert v ya'asher birash يأشر براسه
initiate v yebader يبادِر	ruby n yaqut ياقوت
duel v yebariz يبارِز	topaz n yaqut asfar ياقوت أصفر
bless v yebarek يبارك	affirm v ya'kkd يأكّد
exaggerate v yebalegh يبالِغ	stress v ye'akked ala يأكِّد على
v yebalegh betaqdir يبالغ بتقدير	oxygenate v ye'aksij يأكسِج
overrate	oxidate v ye'aksed يأكسد
seem v bayan يبان	eat v yakul ياكُل
sound v yeban يبان	lunch v yakul elghada ياكل الغدا
adjudge v beit يبتَ	munch v yakul bsut ياكل بصوت
amputate v yabter يبتر	yakul luhum ياكل لحوم البشَر
mutilate v yebtur يبتُر	cannibalise v elbashar
sever v yebtur يبتُر	compose v yeallef يألِف
stump v yebtur يبتُر	v ye'allef hamyeh يألِف حامية
graft v yebtazz يبتزّ	garrisson
smile v yebtesm يبتسم	command v ye'mur يأمُر

seed *v* yebzur يبذُور	innovate *v* yebteker يبتكر
gibber *v* yebarbr يبرير	originate *v* yebtekr يبتكر
cackle *v* yebarber يبرير	invoke *v* yebtehel يبتهل
gabble *v* yebarber يبرير	transmit *v* yebethth يبث
babble *v* yebarber يبرير	*v* yebethth esharah يبث إشارة
cool *v* yebarred يبرّد	signal
rasp *v* yebrud يبرد	ennoble *v* yebajjel يجّل
v yebarred hemmet يبرّد همّة	research *v* yebhath يبحث
discourage	search *v* yebhath يبحث
justify *v* yebarrer يبرّر	navigate *v* yebhir يبحر
project *v* yebruz يبرز	stare *v* yebahleq يبحلق
sprout *v* yebare'm يبرعم	incense *v* yebakhkher يبخّر
glitter *v* yebruq يبرق	sublimate *v* yebakhkher يبخّر
twist *v* yebrum يبرم	vaporize *v* yebakhkher يبخّر
whirl *v* yebrum يبرم	*v* yebakhkher belbakhur يبخّر بالبخور
programme *v* yebarmej يبرمج	cense
adduce *v* yebrhin يبرهن	low *v* yebkhas يبخَس
prove *v* yebarhn يبرهن	creative *adj* 'yebde يُبدع
frame *v* yebarwez يبروز	alternate *v* yubaddil يبدّل
absolve *v* yebri يبري	*v* yebaddel elrish يبدّل الريش
taper *v* yebri يبري	moult
vindicate *v* yebarri يبرّي	begin *v* yebda يبدى
spit *v* yebzuq يبزق	commence *v* yebda يبدى
arid *adj* yabsan يَبسَان	star *v* yebda يبدى
elucidate *v* yebsit يبسّط	start *v* yebda يبدى
simplify *v* yebasset يبسّط	lavish *v* yebazzer يبذّر
elate *v* yebsit يبسط	squander *v* yebazzer يبذّر
gladden *v* yebsut يبسوط	waste *v* yebazzer يبذّر

stay v yebqah يبقى	portend v yebashsher يبشر
buckle v bebakkel shaer يبكّل الشعر	grate v yebshur يبشُر
cry v yebki يبكي	peep v yebasbes يبصبص
strip v yeblus يبلص	affix v ybsum يبصم
floor v yeballet يبلّط	v yebsum belibham يبصم بالإبهام
gorge v 'yebla يبلع	impress
swallow v 'yebla يبلع	disable v yebtil يبطل
avale v yabla' elehaneh يبلع الإهانة	invalidate v yebtel يبطل
devour v yebla' bala'e يبلع بلع	abolish v yebtil يبطل
notify v yeballegh يبلّغ	retard v 'yebatte يبطّئ
report v yeballegh يبلّغ	prattle v 'yeba'be يبعبع
apprise v yuballegh يبلّغ	send v yeb'at يبعت
polymerize v yebalmer يبلمر	mail v yeb'at belbarid يبعت بالبريد
construct v yebni يبني	post v yeb'at belbarid يبعت بالبريد
build v yebni يبني	fax v yeb'at belfaks يبعت بالفاكس
v yebni belismant يبني بالاسمنت	remit v yeb'at hwaleh يبعت حوالة
cement	telegraph v yeb'at faks يبعت فاكس
bridge v yebni jiser يبني جسر	expedite v labarra yebat يبعت لبرّا
nest v yebni ushsh يبني عشّ	man v yeb'atluh rejal يبعتله رجال
yebni kaedeh يبني قاعدة عسكرية	revive v yeb'ath يبعث
base v askaryeh	estrange v yeb'ed يبعد
astonish v yabhat يبهت	yeba'eed am elmarkaz يبعد عن المركز
pale v yebhat يبهت	decentre v
pepper v yebahher يبهّر	simmer v yebaqbeq يبقبق
spice v yebahher يبهّر	maculate v 'yebaqqe يبقّع
caress v yebawwes يبوّس	spot v 'yebaqqe يبقّع
kiss v yebus يبوّس	stain v 'yebaqqe يبقّع
osculate v yebawwes يبوّس	remain v yebqa يبقى

intrigue v yet'amar يتآمر	wallop v yebukes يوكس
scheme v yet'amr يتآمر	punch v yebukes يوكِس
conspire v yetamar يتآمَر	urinate v yebawwel يبوِّل
hope v yetammal يتأمَّل	ovulate v yebeid يبيض
meditate v yet'ammal يتأمَّل	blanch v yebayyed يبيِّض
ponder v yet'ammal يتأمَّل	whiten v yebayyed يبيِّض
contemplate v yetammal يتأمَّل	bleach v yebayyed يُبيِّض
premeditate v yet'anna يتأنَّى	v yebeid elsamak يبيض السمك
gape v yettawab يتثاوب	spawn
yawn v yettawab يتثاوب	v yebayyed eltanajer يبيِّض الطناجر
interchange v yetbadl يتبادل	tin
reciprocate v yetbadal يتبادل	sell v 'yebe يبيع
contest v yetbarah يتبارى	yabei belmazaad يبيع بالمزاد العلني
rival v yetbarah يتبارى	auction v elalani
lag v 'yetbata يتباطئ	v yebe' belmefarraq يبيع بالمفرَّق
slow v 'yetbata يتباطئ	retail
brag v yetbaha يتباهى	manifest v yebayyen يبيِّن
swagger v yetbaha يتباهى	spurn v yet'abbah an يتأبَّى عن
evaporate v yetbakhkhar يتبخَّر	stammer v 'yeta'te يتأتئ
steam v yetbakhkhar يتبخَّر	trade v yetajer يتاجر
vanish v yetbakhkhar يتبخَّر	traffic v yetajer يتاجر
repudiate v yetbarrah يتبرَّأ	loiter v yetakhkhar يتأخَّر
donate v 'yetbarra يتبرَّع	grumble v yetaffaf يتأفَّف
perfume v yetbarfan يتبرفَن	adapt v yet'aqlam يتأقلم
boast v yetbarwaz يتبروظ	ablate v yet'akal يتآكل
subordinate v 'yetba يتبع	fret v yet'akal يتآكل
season v yetabbel يتبِّل	erode v yettakal يتآكَل
jumble v yetbalbal يتبلبَل	glare v yetallaq يتألَّق

shun v yetehasha يتغاشى	crystalize v yetbalwar يتبلور
portion v yethasas يتحاصص	adopt v ytbnaa يتبنَى
ally v yatahalaf يتحالف	pursue v 'yettaba يتَّبع
mantle v yetehajjab يتحجّب	trace v 'yettabba يتَّبع
challenge v yetehadda يتحدّي	v yethabbet bewazefeh يتثبّت بوظيفة
harass v yeteharrash يتحرّش	tenure
move v yeteharrak يتحرّك	surpass v yetjawaz يتجاوز
yeteharrak mtel يتحرّك متل المكّوك	exceed v yetjawaz يتجاوَز
shuttle v elmakkuk	v yetjawaz elhadd يتجاوز الحدّ
investigate v yeteharrah يتحرّى	overdo
ferret v yetharrah يتحرّى	dare v 'yetjarra يتجرّأ
inspect v yeteharrah يتحرّى	spy v yetjassas يتجسّس
entrench v yetehassan يتحصّن	belch v 'yetejashae يتجشّأ
civilize v yetehaddar يتحضّر	burp v 'yejasha يتجشّأ
crash v yethattam يتحطّم	cockle v yetja'ad يتجعّد
materialize v yetehaqqaq يتحقّق	congeal v yetjammad يتجمّد
verify v yetehaqqaq يتحقّق	cluster v 'yetjamma يتجمّع
control v yetehakkam يتحكّم	flock v 'yetjamma يتجمّع
reign v yetehakkam يتحكّم	gather v 'yetjamma يتجمّع
bear v yetehammal يتحمّل	swarm v 'yetjamma يتجمّع
endure v yethammal يتحمّل	assemble v 'yatajammaa يتجمّع
withstand v yetehammal يتحمّل	mob v yetjamma' ennas يتجمّع الناس
bathe v yetehammam يتحمّم	avoid v yatajannab يتجنّب
shower v yetehammam يتحمّم	eschew v yetjannab يتجنّب
yetehammam يتحمّم بالشامبو	outrun v yetjannab يتجنّب
shampoo v belshambu	refrain v yetjannab يتجنّب
transform v yetehawwal يتحوّل	converse v yetehadath يتحادث
	avert v yatahasha يتحاشى

vacillate *v* yetzabzab يتذبذب	*v* yetehawwal la'azm يتحوّل لعظم
remember *v* yetzakkar يتذكّر	ossify
savour *v* yetzawwaq يتذوق	bias *v* yetehayyaz يتحيّز
correlate *v* yetrabat يترابط	blundering *v* yetkhabbat يتخبّط
revert *v* 'yetraja يتراجع	clot *v* yetkhaththar يتخثّر
undo *v* 'yetraja يتراجع	curd *v* yetekhaththar يتخثّر
yetraja' an يتراجع عن موقفه	graduate *v* yetkharraj يتخرّج
backtrack *v* elmawkif	specialize *v* yetkhassas يتخصّص
languish *v* yetrakha يتراخى	shake *v* yetkhadkhad يتخضخض
head *v* yetra'as يترأس	overtake *v* yetkhattah يتخطّى
preside *v* yetra'as يترأس	transgress *v* yetkhattah يتخطّى
plead *v* 'yetrafa يترافع	rarefy *v* yetkhalkhal يتخلخل
accompany *v* ytrafaq ma يترافق مع	forgo *v* yetkhallah يتخلّى
accumulate *v* yetrakam يتراكم	glut *v* yetkhum يتخُم
swing *v* yetrawah يتراوح	envisage *v* yetkhayyal يتخيّل
translate *v* yetarjem يترجم	fancy *v* yetkhayyal يتخيّل
adjure *v* yetrajja يترجّى	imagine *v* yetkhayyal يتخيّل
appeal *v* yetrajja يترجّى	overlap *v* yetdakhal يتداخل
entreat *v* yetrajja يترجّى	resent *v* yetdayaq يتدايق
please *v* yetrajjah يترجّى	roll *v* yetdahraj يتدحرج
date *v* yetarrekh يترّخ	infer *v* yetdakhkhal يتدخّل
shilly-shally *v* yetraddad يتردد	yetdakhkhal يتدخّل بشي مايخصُّه
thrive *v* 'yetra'ra يترعرع	pry *v* bshi ma beykhussuh
lurk *v* yetraqqab يترقّب	spurt *v* yetdaffaq يتدفّق
absist *v* ytruk يترك	droop *v* yetdallah يتدلّى
leave *v* yetruk يترك	lop *v* yetdallah يتدلّى
let *v* yetruk يترك	dangle *v* yetdandal يتدندل
cede *v* yetruk يترُك	backslide *v* yetdahwar يتّدهور

creep *v* yetsallal يَتَسَلَّل	relinquish *v* yetruk يَترُك
abut *v* yetsanad ala يَتَسنَد على	widow *v* yetrammal يَترَمَّل
shop *v* yetsawwaq يَتَسَوَّق	falter *v* yetrannah يَترَنَّح
cadge *v* yetsawwal يَتَسَوَّل	stagger *v* yetrannah يَترَنَّح
picnic *v* yetseran يَتَسيرَن	waver *v* yetrannah يَترَنَّح
quarrel *v* yetshakal يَتَشاكل	loll *v* yetrahhal يَترَهَّل
confer *v* yetshawar يَتَشاوَر	quit *v* yetruk يَترُوك
absorb *v* yetsharab يَتَشرب	coincide *v* yetzaman يَتزَامَن
shiver *v* yetshazzah يَتَشظَّى	budge *v* yezahzah يَتزَحزَح
somersault *v* yetshaqlab يَتَشقلَب	skid *v* yetzahlaq يَتزَحلَق
bask *v* yetshammas يَتَشمَّس	skate *v* yetzallaj يَتزَلَّج
constrict *v* yetshannaj يَتَشنَّج	espouse *v* yetzawwaj يَتزَوَّج
clutter *v* yetshawwash يَتَشوَّش	marry *v* yetzawwaj يَتزَوَّج
muddle *v* yetshawwash يَتَشوَّش	wed *v* yetzawwaj يَتزَوَّج
intersect *v* yetsalab يَتصالب	yetzayyan يَتزَيَّن بالمجوهرات
crack *v* 'yetsadda يَتصدَّع	bejewel *v* belmujawharat
fracture *v* 'yetsadda يَتصدَّع	inquire *v* yetsa'al يَتَساءل
dole *v* yetsaddaq يَتصدَّق	query *v* yetsa'al يَتَساءَل
act *v* yetsarraf يَتصرف	race *v* yetsabaq يَتَسابق
behave *v* yetsarraf يَتصرَّف	obscure *v* yetsattar ala يَتَستَّر على
dispose *v* yetsarraf يَتصرَّف	leak *v* yetsarrab يَتَسرَّب
v yetsarraf ghalat يَتصرَّف غلط	lie *v* yetsattah يَتَسطَّح
misbehave	prostrate *v* yetsattah يَتَسطَّح
browse *v* yesaffah يَتصفَّح	loaf *v* 'yetsakka يَتَسكَّع
explore *v* yestaffah يَتصفَّح	straggle *v* 'yetsakka يَتَسكَّع
surf *v* yetsaffah elnet يَتصفَّح النت	climb *v* yetsallaq يَتَسلَّق
contact *v* yettsel يَتَّصِل	*v* yesallaq besu'ubeh يَتَسلَّق بصعوبة
call *v* yettesel يَتَّصل	clamber

deal v yet'amal يتعامَل

cooperate v yetawan يتعاوَن

v yeta'awan ma يتعاون مع

collaborate

coexist v yetayash يتعايَش

strain v yet'ab يتعب

tire v yet'eb يتعّب

fatigue v yet'ab يتعب

enfeeble v yet'eb يتعّب

overwork v yet'eb يتعّب

toil v yet'ab يتعب

marvel v yet'ajjab يتعجّب

wonder v yet'ajjab يتعجّب

breach v yet'adda يتعدّى

sweat v yet'arraq يتعرّق

dine v yetashshah يتعشّى

learn v yet'allam يتعلّم

undertake v yet'ahhad يتعهّد

acclimatise v ytawaad يتعود

connive v yetghada يتغاضى

overlook v yetghadah يتغاضى

compliment v yetghazzal يتغزّل

flirt v yetghazzal يتغزّل

outdo v yetghallab يتغلّب

surmount v yetghallab يتغلّب

parry v yetfadah يتفادى

react v yetfa'al يتفاعل

parley v yetfawad يتفاوَض

dial n yettesel bi يتّصل ب

miscall v yettesel ghalat يتّصل غلط

overact v 'yetsanna يتصنّع

conceive v yetsawwar يتصوّر

damage v yetdarrar يتضرّر

imply v yetjamman يتضمّن

trespass v yettawal يتطاول

emanate v yettayar يتطايَر

intervene v yettaffal يتطفّل

meddle v yettaffal يتطفّل

merit v yetallab يتطلّب

require v yetallab يتطلّب

yettala' tatle'ah يتطلّع تطليعة غراميّة

ogle v gharameyyeh

volunteer v 'yettawwa يتطوّع

yettawwa' belshurtah يتطوّع بالشرطة

police v

pretend v yetzahar يتظاهر

v yetzahar bemasher يتظاهَر بمشاعِر

emote

conflict v 'yetarad ma يتعارَض مع

v yet'ataf ma يتعاطف مع

sympathize

convalesce v yetaafa يتعافى

recover v yet'afah يتعافى

contract v yetaaqad يتعاقَد

handle v yet'amal يتعامل

conduct v yeaamal يتعامَل

foretell v yetkahhan يتكهّن

prophesy v yetkahhan يتكهّن

conglomerate adj yetkawwar يتكوّر

consist v yekawwan mn يتكون من

dispute v yetlasan يتلاسَن

juggle v yetla'ab يتلاعب

v yetla'ab bel as'ar يتلاعب بالأسعار

manipulate

redress v yetlafa يتلافى

beam v 'yetla'l يتلالا

vitiate v yetlef يتلف

telecast v yetalfez يتلفز

televise v yetalfez يتلفز

telephone v yetalfn يتلفن

dawdle v 'yetlakka يتلكّع

orphanage n yetem يتم

bewind v yetmayal يتمايل

shamble v yetmayal يتمايل

relish v yetmatta' bi يتمتّع ب

rebel v yetmarrad يتمرّد

repel v yetmarrad يتمرّد

wallow v yetmarragh يتمرّغ

localize v yetmarkaz يتمركز

exercise v yetmarran يتمرّن

practise v yetmarran يتمرّن

jeer v yetmaskhar يتمسخَر

lounge v yetmashsha يتمشّى

pace v yetmashshah يتمشّى

crumble v yetfatfat يتفتفَت

view v yetfarraj يتفرّج

watch v yetfarraj يتفرّج

bifurcate v 'yetfarra يتفرّع

stampede v yetfarraq يتفرّق

v yetfaddal ala يتفضّل على

condescend

accord v 'ytfeq ma يتفق مع

mull v yetfakkar يتفكّر

excel v yetfawwaq يتفوّق

transcend v yetfawwaq يتفوّق

brawl v yetqatal يتقاتل

fight v yetqatal يتقاتَل

v yetqatal beljaww يتقاتل بالجوّ

dogfight

clash v 'yetqatal ma يتقاتل مع

lapse v yetqadm يتقادَم

partake v yetqasm يتقاسم

retire v yetqa'ad يتقاعد

outweigh v yetaqqel يتقِّل

perfect v yetqn يتقن

tick v yetekk يتك

presume v yetkabbar يتكبّر

agglomerate v ytkttal يتكتّل

accrue v yetkaddas يتكدّس

shatter v yetkassar يتكسّر

v yatakallam bewuduh يتكلّم بوضوح

articulate

heave v yetnahhad يِتَنَهَّد	saunter v yetmashshah يِتَمَشَّى
sigh v yetnahhad يِتَنَهَّد	smack v yetmattaq يِتَمَطَّق
ruck v yetni يِتْني	stretch v yetmatmat يِتَمَطْمَط
waddle v yetehadah يِتهادى	peruse v yetma'an يِتَمَعَّن
elude v yeteharrab mn يِتهرَّب من	evade v yetmallas يِتَمَلَّص
rock v yetehazhaz يِتهزهز	shirk v yetmallas يِتَمَلَّص
accuse v yetehm يِتهم	fidget v yetmalmal يِتَمَلْمَل
charge v yettehim يِتِّهِم	evaluate v yetammen يِتَمِّن
impeach v yettehm يِتِّهم	rate v yetammen يِتَمِّن
communicate v yetwasal يِتواصل	wish v yetmannah يِتَمَنَّى
proliferate v yetwalad يِتوالد	billow v yetmawwaj يِتَمَوَّج
repent v yetub يِتوب	ripple v yetmawwaj يِتَمَوَّج
enthrone v yetawwej يِتَوَّج	undulate v yetmawwaj يِتَمَوَّج
crown v yetawwej يِتَوَّج	abnegate v yetnazal يِتنازل
should v yetwajjab يِتَوَجَّب	waive v yetnazal يِتنازل
v yetwajjah lelshareq يِتوجَّه للشرق	yatanazal an يَتَنازَل عن ملكيّة
orientate	assign v mulkeyet
v yetwarrat bema'ziq يِتورَّط بمأزق	proportion v yetnasab يِتناسب
deadlock	deliberate v yetnaqash يِتناقش
mediate v yetwassat يِتوسَّط	forecast v 'yetnabba يِتنبَّأ
beseech v yetwassal يِتوسَّل	predict v 'yetnabba يِتنبَّأ
solicit v yetwassal يِتوسَّل	eavesdrop v yetnassat يِتنصَّت
anticipate v 'yatawaqa يِتوقَّع	traverse v yetnassal يِتنصَّل
expect v 'yetwaqqa يِتوقَّع	embitter v yetnaghghas يِتنغَّص
foresee v 'yetwaqqa يِتوقَّع	breathe v yetnaffas يِتنفَّس
administer v yetwalla يِتولَّى	respire v yetnaffas يِتنفَّس
shoulder v yetwallah يِتولَّى	disguise v yetnakkar يِتنكَّر
misdirect v yetuh يِتوه	bully v yetnammar يِتنمَّر

answer v yujawib يُجاوِب	misguide v yetawweh يِتوِّه
coerce v yejbur يُجبُر	orphan n yatim يَتِيم
enforce v yejbur يُجبُر	adhibit v yethbit يُثبِت
force v yejbur يُجبُر	steady v yethabbet يُثبِّت
compel v yejbir يُجبِر	clasp v yethabbit يُثبِّت
daub v yejabsen يُجبِصِن	fasten v yethabbit يُثبِّت
levy v yejbi يُجبي	demonstrate v yethbit يُثبِت
team v yejteme' befariq يُجتمِع بفريق	evince v yethabbit يُثبِّت
modernize v yejadded يُجدِّد	yethabbet bel mesmar يُثبِّت بالمسمار
regenerate v yejadded يُجدِّد	nail v
renew v yejadded يُجدِّد	v yethabbit bemesmar يُثبِّت بمسمار
paddle v yejaddef يُجدِّف	spike
ply v yejaddel يُجدِّل	peg v yethabbit se'er يُثبِّت سعر
v yejaddel elsaer يُجدِّل الشعر	puncture v yethqub يُثقُب
dreadlock	bore n yethqub يُثقُب
schedule v yejadwel يُجدوِل	pierce v yethqub يُثقُب
drag v yejurr يُجُر	revolt v yethur ala يثور على
draw v yejurr يُجُر	elicitate v yuthir يُثير
experience v yejarreb يُجرِّب	excite v yethir يُثير
essay v yejarreb يُجرِّب	yethir elgharezeh يثير الغريزة الجنسيّة
trail v yejarjer يُجرجِر	eroticize v eljinseyyeh
hurt v yejrah يُجرح	argue v yujadel يُجادِل
libel .vt yejarreh يُجرِّح	brangle v yejadel يُجادِل
wound v yejrah يُجرح	debate v yejadel يُجادِل
refute v yejarreh يُجرِّح	cope v yejari يُجاري
gash v yejrah يُجرح	peril v yejazef يُجازِف
injure v yejrah يُجرح	flatter v yejamel يُجامِل
offend v yejrah belhaki يُجرح بالحكي	respond v yejaweb يُجاوِب

sum v 'yejma يجمع	shovel v yejruf يجرُف
aggregate v 'yjmme يجمّع	clip v yejezz يجزّ
compile v 'yejammei يجمّع	mow v yejezz يجزّ
troop v 'yejamme يجمّع	fleece v yejzz elsuf يجزّ الصوف
pair v yejma' 2 sawa يجمع 2 سوا	segment v 'yejazze يجزّء
nut v yejma' juz يجمع الجوز	probe v yejess يجسّ
people v yejma' nas يجمع الناس	materialize v yejassed يجسّد
yejamme' bemajmu'at يجمّع بمجموعات	personify v yejassid يجسّد
group v	embody v yejassim يجسّم
combine v yejma' sawa يجمع سوا	incarnate v yejassem يجسّم
dement v yejenn يجنّ	substantiate v yejassem يجسّم
chain v yejanzir يجنزر	crimple v yeja'ed يجعّد
naturalize v yejannes يجنّس	create v yeja'lik يجعلك
madden v yejannin يجنّن	startle v yejfal يجفل
equip v yejahhez يجهّز	skin v yejalled يجلّد
prepare v yejahhiz يجهّز	birch v yajlud يجلُد
set v yejahhez يجهّز	flog v yejlud يجلُد
yejahhiz wajehet كّاب يجهّز واجهة كّاب	lace .vt yejlud يجلُد
dummy v ktab	scourge v yejalled يجلّد
aggrieve v yjur ala يجور على	thrash v yejlud يجلُد
persecute v yejur ala يجور على	straighten v yejalles يجلّس
may v yejuz يجوز	v yajles ma' elatfal يجلس مع الأطفال
come v yeji يجي	babysit
side v yeji a janb يجي ع جنب	galvanize v yejalfen يجلفن
ensue v yeji mn يجي من	freeze v yejammed يجمّد
v yeji mn nasab يجي من نَسَب	ice v yejammed يجمّد
descend	refrigerate v yejammed يجمّد
bring v yijib يجيب	lump v 'yejma يجمع

weave *v* yehbuk يحبُك	get *v* yejib يجيب
need *v* yehtaq يحتاج	fetch *v* yejib يجيب
hesitate *v* yehtar يحتار	incur *v* yejib a halu يجيب ع حاله
beware *v* yehtaat يحتاط	staff *v* yejib kader يجيب كادر
fend *v* yehtat يحتاط	father *v* yejib walad يجيب ولد
spare *v* yehtat يحتاط	endorse *v* yejayyer shik يجيّر شيك
fool *v* yehtal يحتال	skirt *v* yehazi يحاذي
hoax *v* yehetal يحتال	war *v* yehareb يحارِب
hoodwink *v* yehtal ala يحتال على	account *v* yuhaseb يحاسب
protest *v* yehtajj يحتجّ	besiege *v* yehaser يحاصِر
blaze *v* yehterq يحترِق	siege *v* yehaser يحاصِر
combust *v* yehteriq يحترِق	lecture *v* yehader يحاضِر
respect *v* yehterm يحترم	surround *v* yehawet يحاوط
revere *v* yehterm يحترم	attempt *v* yuhawil يحاوِل
retain *v* yehtefez يحتفظ	try *v* yehawel يحاوِل
celebrate *v* yehtifil يحتفل	endeavour *v* yehawel يحاوِل
scorn *v* yehteqer يحتقِر	like *v* yehb يحب
debase *v* yehteqir يحتقِر	love *v* yehebb يحبّ
engorge *v* yehtuqen يحتقِن	endear *v* yehabbeb يحبِّب
engross *v* yehteker يحتكِر	confine *v* yehbus يحبِس
monopolize *v* yehteker يحتكِر	occlude *v* yehbus يحبِس
court *v* yehtikim la يحتكِم ل	*v* yehbus beqafas يحبِس بقفص
occupy *v* yehtall يحتلّ	encage
contain *v* yehtwi يحتوي	cage *v* yehbus belqafas يحبِس بقفص
include *v* yehtwi يحتوي	depress *v* yehbit يحبِط
veil *v* yehajjeb يحجِّب	dishearten *v* yehbet يحبِط
v yehjub nur يحجب نور	frustrate *v* yehit يحبِط
overshadow	plot *v* yehbuk يحبُك

escort v yehrus يحرُس	hold v yehjuz يحجز
induce v yeharred يحرِّض	seize v yehjuz يحجز
instigate v yeharred يحرِّض	sequester v yehjuz يحجز
misrepresent v yeharref يحرُف	book v yehjuz يحجُز
yeharref an يحرُف عن الموضوع	undermine v yehajjem يحجِّم
digress v elmawdu'e	limit v yehedd يحدّ
burn v yahruq يحرق	delimit v yehaddid يحدِّد
fire v yehruq يحرُق	specify v yehadded يحدِّد
sear v yehruq يحرُق	v yehaddid elhudud يحدِّد الحدود
v yehruquh laramad يحرقه لرماد	demarcate
cremate	v yehadded elhudud يحدِّد الحدود
motion v yeharrik يحرِّك	border
mobilize v yeharrik يحرِّك	yehadded alkharitah يحدِّد عالخريطة
remove v yeharrek يحرِّك	map v
stir v yeharrek يحرِّك	doom v yehadded masir يحدِّد مصير
sway v yeharrek يحرِّك	gaze v yehaddeq يحدِّق
animate v yuharrek يُحرِّك	warn v yehazzer يحذِّر
v yeharrek elawatef يحرِّك العواطف	caution v yehzar يحذِر
commove	tip (off) v yehzar يحذِّر
v yeharrik shafayef يحرِّك شفايفه	delete v yehzuf يحذُف
mouth	omit v yehzuf يحذُف
v yeharrek yadaweyyen يحرِّك يدوياً	plough v yehruth يحرُث
manhandle	embarrass v yehrej يحرج
prohibit v yeharrem يحرِّم	edit v yeharrir يحرِّر
deprive v yehrum يحرُم	free v yeharrer يحرِّر
preclude v yehrum يحرُم	liberate v yeharrer يحرِّر
v yehrum kanaseyyan يحرِم كنسياً	release v yeharrer يحرِّر
excommunicate	guard v yehrus يحرس

stuff v yehshi يحشي	puzzle v yehzur يحزُر
fringe v yehshi ellebs يحشي اللبس	conjecture v yehzur يحزُر
cultivate v yehsud يحصد	bale v yahzum يحزُم
harvest v yehsud يحصد	pack v yehzum يحزُم
reap v yehsud يحصد	shear v yehzum يحزُم
acquire v yahsal يحصل	stow v yehzum يحزُم
collect v yehassil يحصّل	sorrow v yehzan يحزن
attain v yahsal ala يحصل على	perceive v yehess يحسّ
attend v yahdder يحضَر	sense v yehess يحسّ
present v yehdar يحضَر	calculate v yehsub يحسُب
nestle v yehdun يحضن	compute v yehsub يحسُب
cuddle v yehdun يحضُن	v yehsub ghalat يحسب غلط
embrace v yehdun يحضُن	miscalculate
incubate v yehdun يحضُن	v yahsub mu'addal يحسب معدّل
put v yehutt يحطّ	average
saddle v yehutt elsarj يحطّ السرج	begrudge v yehsud يحسُد
parcel v yehutt beltard يحطّ بالطرد	envy v yehsud يحسُد
v yehut bekatalug يحطّ بالكَالوج	deduct v yehsum يحسُم
catalogue	better v yehassin يحسّن
envelop v yehett bezarf يحطّ بظرف	enhance v yehassin يحسّن
enlist v yehut beqawaem يحطّ بقوائم	improve v yehassin يحسّن
v yehutt bekabsuleh يحطّ بكبسولة	meliorate v yehassen يحسّن
encapsulate	congregate v yehshud يحشُد
place v yehutt bemakan يحطّ بمكان	nose v yehshur enfu يحشر أنفه
v yehutt bemakan يحطّ بمكان	butt v yehshur infu يحشُر انفه
position	interfere v yehshur infuh يحشُر إنفه
v yehutt khatt tahtuh يحطّ خطّ تحته	cram v yehshi يحشي
underline	pad v yehshi يحشي

yeheff bewaraq qzaz قزاز بورق يحفّ	muffle v yehutt khimar خمار يحطّ
sandpaper v	staple v yehutt dabbus دبّوس يحطّ
gap v yehfur يحفر	yehett shi belmakan elghalat يحط شي بالمكان الغلط
dig v yehfur يحفر	misplace v belmakan elghalat
drill v yehfur يحفُر	yehutt shi jmb shi يحطّ شي جمب شي
excavate v yehfur يحفُر	juxtapose v
pit v yehfur يحفُر	yehet tuem طُعم للصيدة يحط
spade v yehfur يحفُر	bait v lelmasyadeh
carve v yehfur يحفُر	ground v yehett alard عاالأرض يحطّ
groove v yehfur akhdud أخدود يحفر	shelve v yehutt alraff عالرفّ يحطّ
well v yehfur bir بير يحفُر	v yehut fi elsanduq في الصندوق يحطّ
burrow n yehfur jeher جحر يحفُر	case
hole v yehfur hefrah حفرة يحفر	bag v yehut fi kis في كيس يحطّ
moat v yehfur khandaq خندق يحفر	v yehett kammadat كمّادات يحطّ
v yehfur khandaq خندق يحفر	foment
retrench	v yehutt kammameh كمّامة يحطّ
v yehfur khandaq خندق يحفر	muzzle
trench	v yehit lazqet jerh لزقة جرح يحط
etch v yehfur klisheh كليشيه يحفر	bandage
incite v yehaffez يحفّز	v yehutt lazqet jerh لزقة جرح يحطّ
motivate v yehaffez يحفّز	plaster
promote v yehaffez يحفّز	v yehutt nazareyyeh نظريّة يحطّ
spur v yehaffez يحفّز	theorize
adrenalise v yhffz يحفّز	shoe v yehutt na'el نعل يحطّ
keep v yehfaz يحفظ	ban v yahzur يحظُر
preserve v yehfaz يحفظ	block v yahzur يحظُر
reserve v yehfaz يحفظ	scrub v yeheff يحفّ
save v yehfaz يحفظ	

yehki metel السكارى متل يحكي
bleat v elsakara

address v 'yehki ma مع يحكي'

dissolve v yehhel يحل

solve v yehell يحل

supersede v yehell mahall محل يحل

milk v yehlub يحلب

swear v yehlif يحلف

forswear v yehlef kzeb كذب يحلف

perjure v yehlef kezb كذب يحلف

shave v yehliq يحلق

analyse v yuhallel يحلل

dream v yehlam يحلم

yehlam w hueh sahi صاحي وهو يحلم

daydream v

beautify v yehalli يحلّي

sweeten v yehalli يحلّي

candy v yehalli يحلّي

sugar v yehalli belsekkar بالسكّر يحلّي

redden v yehammer يحمّر

blush v yehmarr يحمّر

flush v yehammer يحمّر

v yehmarr mn elkhajal الخجل من يحمرّ
glow

v yehmarr wejhuh وجهه يحمرّ
crimson

lime v yehammed يحمّض

sour v yehammed يحمّض

v yehfaz bel edbarah بالإضبارة يحفظ
file

v yehfaz belsekkar بالسكّر يحفظ
conserve

grudge v yehqud يحقُد

fulfil v yehaqqeq يحقق

itch v yehekk يحكّ

rub v yehekk يحكّ

nuzzle v yehekk enfu إنفه يحكّ

sentence v yehkum يحكم

govern v yehakkim يحكّم

judge v yehkum يحكم

rule v yehkum يحكم

umpire ,.vt yehkum يحكم

arbitrate v yuhakkem يحكّم

misjudge v yehkum ghalat غلط يحكم

speak v yehki يحكي

talk v yehki يحكي

brazen v yehki bebaza'a بذاءة يحكي

blether v 'yehki beghabaa بغباء يحكي'

v yehki haki fadi فاضي حكي يحكي
blab

v yehki haki fadi فاضي حكي يحكي
bollocks

v yehki alhames عالهمس يحكي
commune

chatter v yehki ktir كتير يحكي

acidify v yehmidh يحمض

load v yehammel يحمّل

carry v yehmil يحمل

burden v yehmel hemel يحمل حمل

v yehammel zyadeh يحمّل زيادة
overload

v yahmil alzaher يحمل على الظهر
backpack

yehammluh fuq يحمّله فوق طاقته
overburden v taqtuh

protect v yehmi يحمي

safeguard v yehmi يحمي

shield v yehmi يحمي

commiserate v yehenn ala يحنّ على

relent v yehenn ala يحنّ على

embalm v yehannit يحنّط

bend n yehni يحني

bow v yehni يحني

crankle v yehni يحني

vault v yehni يحني

convert v yehawwel يحوّل

switch v yehawwel يحوّل

squint v yehwil يحول

gel v yehawwel lajell يحوّل لجلّ

v yehawwel lajilatin يحوّل لجيلاتين
gelatinize

gasify v yehawwel laghaz يحوّل لغاز

v yehawwel lafahim يحوّل لفحم
coke

comprise v yehwi يحوي

hold v yehwi يحوي

neutralize v yehid يحيّد

bewilder v yehayyer يحيّر

mystify v yehayyer يحيّر

nonplus v yehayyer يحيّر

perplex v yehayyer يحيّر

render v yehil يحيل

v yehil leltaqa'ud يحيل عالتقاعد
pension

v yehyi zikra يحيي ذكرى
commemorate

risk v yekhater يخاطر

hazard v yekhater يخاطر

fear v yekhaf يخاف

infringe v yekhalef يخالف

freak v yekhalef يخالف

inform v yekhayyer يخبّر

tell v yekhabber يخبّر

bake v yakhbuz يخبز

breaden v yekhbiz يخبز

thud v yekhbut يخبط

bash v yakhbut يخبط

slam v yekhbut elbab يخبط الباب

hide v yekhabbi يخبّي

yacht n yakht يخت

rave *v* yekharref يَخرَف	opt *v* yekhtar يختار
scratch *n* yekharmesh يخرمش	select *v* yekhtar يختار
claw *v* yekharmish يخرمِش	choose *v* yekhtar يختَار
yekharmesh يخرمش بالمخالب	test *v* yekhteber يختبر
paw *v* belmakhaleb	invent *v* 'yekhter يخترع
perforate *v* yekhazzeq يخزّق	penetrate *v* yekhteriq يخترق
store *v* yekhazzen يخزّن	abbreviate *v* yekhteser يختصر
stock *v* yekhazzen يخزّن	abscond *v* yekhtfi يختفي
v yekhsuf elqamar يخسُف القمر	disappear *v* yekhtifi يختفي
eclipse	fumble *v* yekhtall يختلّ
jingle *v* yekhashkhesh يخشخش	convulse *v* yekhtilij يختلج
clatter *v* yekhashekhis يخشخِش	misappropriate *v* yekhteles يختلس
toughen *v* yekhashshen يخشّن	differ *v* yekhtelef يختلف
pertain *v* yekhuss يخصّ	closet *v* yekhteli behalu يختلي بحاله
belong *v* yekhuss يخصّ	seal *v* yekhtum يختم
fertilize *v* yekhassib يخصّب	stamp *v* yekhtum يختم
allocate *v* yukhasses يخصّص	shy *v* yekhajjel يخجل
devote *v* yekhassis يخصّص	shame *v* yekhjal يخجّل
يخصص مصاري لتسديد دين	dope *v* yekhadder يخدّر
v yukhasses masari litasdid din	beguile *v* yakhdaa يخدع
amortise	deceive *v* 'yekhda يخدع
debit *v* yekhsum men يخصُم من	dupe *v* 'yekhda يخدع
geld *v* yekhsi يخصي	gull *v* 'yekhda يخدع
jolt *v* yekhudd يخضّ	page *v* yekhdum يخدم
acquiesce *v* 'yakhdha يخضع	serve *v* yekhdum يخدُم
betroth *v* yakhtub يخطُب	ruin *v* yekharreb يخرّب
plan *v* yekhattet يخطط	murmur *v* yekharkher يخرخر
abduct *v* yekhtuf يخطف	purr *v* yekharkher يخرخِر

v yekhfi belghabeh يخفي بالغابة embush	kidnap *v* yekhtuf يخطُف
palm *v* yekhfi bekaffuh يخفي بكفُه	abduct *v* yekhtuf يخطُف
eternalize *v* yekhalled يخلّد	step *v* yekhtu khetweh يخطو خطوة
immortalize *v* yekhalled يخلّد	yekhte' khata' kebir يخطئ خطأ كبير blunder *v*
perpetuate *v* yekhalled يخلّد	lessen *v* yekheff يخفّ
extricate *v* yekhalles يخلّص	decrease *v* yekhaffid يخفّض
rid *v* yekhalles يخلّص	lower *v* yekhaffed يخفّض
blend *v* yekhlut يخلُط	down *v* yekhaffef يخفّف
confuse *v* yekhlut يخلُط	lighten *v* yekhaffef يخفّف
intermingle *v* yekhlut يخلُط	moderate *v* yekhaffef يخفّف
mingle *v* yekhlut يخلُط	allay *v* yukhaffef يُخفّف
mix *v* yekhlut يخلُط	*v* yekhaffef elhukum يخفف الحُكم commute
shuffle *v* yekhlut يخلُط	
yakhlit mae maedan يخلط مع معدن amalgamate *v*	*v* yekhaffif essur'a يخفّف السرعة decelerate
dismiss *v* 'yekhla يخلَع	*v* 'yukhaffef alwaja يخفف الوجع alleviate
oust *v* 'yekhla يخلَع	
v yekhla' an elarsh يخلع عن العرش dethrone	*v* yekhaffef tawattur يخفف توتّر destress
rat *v* yekhlef bewa'duh يخلف بوعده	throb *v* yekhfuq يخفق
acetify *v* yekhalil يخلل	whisk *v* yekhfuq يخفق
pickle *v* yekhallel يخلّل	pulsate *v* yekhfuq يخفُق
discharge *v* yekhli يخلي	churn *v* yekhfuq ellaban يخفق اللبن
evacuate *v* yekhli يخلي	conceal *v* yekhfi يخفي
vacate *v* yekhli يخلي	harbour *v* yekhfi يخفي
yekhli sabil يخلي سبيل بشروط parole *v* beshrut	occult *v* yekhfi يخفي

tailor v yekhayyet يخيّط	v yekhallih faqir يخلّيه فقير
button v yekhayyet zerar يخيّط زرار	impoverish
camp v yekhayyem يخيّم	yekhalleyh kabsh الفدا يخلّيه كبش
arm n yad يدّ	scapegoat v elfeda
advocate v yudafie يدافع	v yekhalleh methali يخلّيه مثالي
defend v 'yedafe يدافع	idealize
champion v yedafe' am يدَافع عن	yekhalleyh meqarmesh يخلّيه مقرمش
remedy v yedawi يداوي	crispen v
bother v yedayeq يدايق	yekhalleh mu radyan يخلّيه مو رضيان
distress v yedayeq يدايق	dissatisfy v
disturb v yedayeq يدايق	brew v yekhammer يخمّر
dog v yedayeq يدايق	guess v yekhammen يخمّن
tease v yedayq يدايق	stifle v yekhnuq يخنق
upset v yedayeq يدايق	strangle v yekhnuq يخنق
massacre v yedbah يدبح	choke v yekhnuq يخنق
slaughter v yedbah يدبح	smother v yekhnuq يخنق
slay v yedbah يدبح	suffocate v yekhnuq يخنق
devise v yedabber يدبّر	asphyxiate v yakhnuq يخنَق
procure v yedabber يدبّر	bellow v yekhwwer يخوّر
v yedaberluh makideh يدبّرله مكيدة	cow v yekhawwif يخوّف
machinate	frighten v yekhawwef يخوّف
taw v yedbugh يدبغ	horrify v yekhawwef يخوّف
goo v yedabbeq يدبّق	intimidate v yekhawwef يخوّف
dub v yedablej يدبلج	overawe v yekhawwef يخوّف
access n yedkhul يدخل	terrify v yekhawwef يخوّف
enter v yedkhul يدخل	betray v yekhun يخون
insert v yedakhkhel يدخّل	disappoint v yekhayyeb يخيّب
	sew v yekhayyet يخيّط

invite v yed'e يدعي	يدخِّل الخيط بالإبرة yedakhkhel
allege v yaddaei يدّعي	thread v el'ebreh belkhit
purport v yedde'i يدّعي	v yedkhul munaqasah يدخل مناقصة
claim v 'yeddei يدّعي	tender
prosecute v yedde'i ala يدّعي على	yedakhkhluh يدخّله عالقائمة السودا
v 'yedei lelijtima يدعي لاجتماع	blacklist v alqaemeh elsuda
convene	smoke v yedakhkhen يدخِّن
v yedei leijtima'a يدعي لاجتماع	coach v yedarreb يُدرِّب
convoke	bolt v yedarbes elbab يدربِس الباب
scramble v yedfush يدفش	grade v yedarrej يدرِّج
thrust v yedfush يدفش	chat v yedardesh يدردِش
hurl v yedfush يدفُش	tack v yedruz يدرز
pound v yedfush يدفُش	seam v yedruz يدرُز
push v yedfush يدفُش	study v yedrus يدرس
pay v 'yedfa يدفع	instruct v yedarres يدرِّس
ransom v yedfa' fedyh يدفع فديِة	school v yedarres يدرِّس
cash v yeda' naqdi يدفع نقدي	teach v yedarres يدرِّس
entomb v yedfun يدفِن	realize v yudrek يدرك
bury v yedfun يدفِن	recognize v yedrek يدرك
warm v yedaffi يدفِّي	shove v yedess يدسّ
tap v yeduqq يدقّ	tread v yed'as يدعس
v yeduq belshakus يدقّ بالشاكوش	subsidize v yeda'am يدعم
hammer	support v yed'am يدعم
v yedeqq belmadaqq يدقّ بالمدقّ	prop v yed'am يدعِّم
maul	shore v yed'am يدعِّم
v yeduqq alderbakkeh يدِّق عالدربكّة	boost v yedaam يدعِّم
drum	back v yudae'm يُدعِّم
flap v yduqq kaff يدقّ كَفّ	auspicate v yaduu يدعو

thaw v yedawweb يدوِّب	wedge v yeduqq watad يدقّ وتد
daze v yedukh يدوخ	scrutinize v yedaqeq يدقّق
drizzle v yedukh يدوخ	v yudaqeq hesabat يدقّق حسابات
stun v yadawwekh يدوِّخ	audit
revolve v yedur يدور	tamper v yedekk يدكّ
stroll v yedur يدور	guide v yedell يدلّ
turn v yedur يدور	denote v yeddel يدِّل
circle v yedawwer يدوِّر	cocker v 'yedalle يدلّع
rotate v yedawwer يدوِّر	indulge v 'yedalle يدلّع
v yedawwer belgugel يدوِر بالغوغل	pamper v 'yedalle يدلّع
google	cherish v yedallel يدلّل
v yedur bedawreyyeh يدور بدوريّة	fondle v yedallel يدلّل
patrol	merge v yedmuj يدمج
pivot v yedur hula يدور حولى	growl v yedamdm يدمدم
v yedawwer atareqah يدوِّر عطريقه	destroy v yedammer يدمّر
grope	devastate v yedammer يدمّر
trample v yedus يدوس	ravage v yedammer يدمّر
pedal v yedawwes يدوِّس	annihilate v yudammer يُدمّر
undergo v yeduq يدوق	v yedamme' eleynin يُدمِع العينين
decorate v yedukir يدوكِر	blear
v yedawwen sutyyan يدوِّن صوتيًا	imprint v 'yedma يدمَغ
podcast	addict v yedmn يدمن
blare v yedwi يدوي	profane v yedannes يدنِّس
resound v yadawi يدوي	amaze v yudhish يُدهش
manual adj yadawi يدَوِي	paint v yedhan يدهن
administrate v yudir يدير	melt v yedub يدوب
manage v yedir يدير	dissolve v yedawweb يدوِّب
run v yedir يدير	smelt v yedawweb يدوِّب

stake *v* yerahn يراهن	narrow *v* yedayyeq يديّق
wager *v* yerahin يراهن	straiten *v* yedayyeq يديّق
bet *v* yerahin يراهن	tighten *v* yedayyeq يديّق
shuffle *v* yerawegh يراوغ	convict *v* yedin يدين
circumvent *v* yerawegh يراوغ	incriminate *v* yedin يدين
sham *v* yer'i يرائي	condemn *v* yedin يدين
profit *v* yerbah يربَح	butcher *v* yezbah يذبَح
win *v* yerbah يربَح	oscillate *v* yezabzeb يذبذب
gain *v* yerbah يربَح	remind *v* yezakker يذكّر
link *v* yerbut يربط	mention *v* yezkur يذكُر
strap *v* yerbut يربط	noteworthy *adj* yuzkar يُذكَر
shackle *v* yerbut يربِط	abject *v* yezell يذلّ
associate *v* yarbut يربُط	humiliate *v* yezll يذلّ
peg *v* yerbut يربُط	sin *v* yeznib يذنِب
yerbut elsafineh يربط السفينة بالحبل	astound *v* yuzhil يُذهِل
moor *v* belhabl	*v* yeze' al telfezyun يذيع عالتلفزيون
robe *v* yerbut belhabl يربط بالحبل	broadcast
rope *v* yerbut belhabl يربط بالحبل	review *v* 'yeraje يراجع
tie *v* yerbut krafeh يربط كرافة	correspond *v* yerasil يراسِل
square *v* 'yerabbe يربّع	content *v* yeradi يراضي
breed *v* yerabbi يربّي	convoy *v* yerafeq يرافِق
foster *v* yerabbi يربّي	mate *v* yerafeq يرافِق
raise *v* yerabbi يربّي	invigilate *v* yeraqib يراقب
yerabbi haywan alif يربّي حيوان أليف	superintend *v* yeraqib يراقب
pet *v*	censor *v* yeraqib يراقب
relax *v* yertah يرتاح	monitor *v* yeraqeb يراقِب
rest *v* yertah يرتاح	oversee *v* yeraqb يراقب
haunt *v* yertad يرتاد	proctor *v* yeraqb يراقب

yerja' mn mahal ما أجى محل من يرجع	declutter v yerattib يرتّب
return v ma eja	tidy v yeratteb يرتّب
v yerajje'u am ra'yu رأيه عن يرجّعه	arrange v yuratteb يُرتّب
dehort	mate v yertebet يرتبط
fibrillate v yerjuf يرجُف	couple v yertubet bi ب يرتبط
quiver v yerjuf يرجُف	tangle v yertebk يرتبك
tremble v yerjuf يرجُف	sag v yertekhi يرتخي
welcome v yerahheb يرحّب	slacken v yertekhi يرتخي
hail v yerahhib يرحّب	renounce v yertadd يرتدّ
deport v yerahhel يرحّل	abjure v yertadd an عن يرتدّ
depart v yerhal يرحَل	osmose v yertesheh يرتشح
decamp v yerhal faj'a فجأة يرحَل	flutter v yerte'esh يرتعش
v yerahhil mn elbalad البلد من يرحّل	thrill v yerte'sh يرتعش
expel	rise v 'yertefe يرتفع'
cheapen v yerakhkhes يرخّص	commit v yertikib يرتكب
license v yerakhkhes يرخّص	out-balance v yerajjeh يرجّح
reply v yerdd يردّ	preponderate v yerajjeh يرجّح
v yerudd e'tibar إعتبار يردّ	v yerajje' ezzekrayat الذكريات يرجّع
rehabilitate	evocate
inhibit v 'yerda يردع	v yerjje' elmasari المصاري يرجّع
restrain v 'yerda يردع	refund
subside v yersab يرسُب	v yerja' shabab شباب يرجع
consign v yersel يرسل	rejuvenate
figure v yersum يرسم	yerajje' lamanseb سابق لمنصب يرجّع
draw v yrsum يرسُم	reinstate v sabeq
sketch v yersum يرسُم	backlash v yurajje' lawara لورا يُرجّع
v yersum belkalam بالكلام يرسم	yerja' mn mahal ما أجى محل من يرجع
portray	retrace v ma eja

kick n yerfus يرفُس	dock v yersah يرسى
disapprove v yerfud يرفض	bestrew v yerush يرش
refuse v yerfud يرفض	sprinkle v yerushsh يرشّ
reject v yerfud يرفض	strew v yerushsh يرشّ
lever v 'yerfa يرفع	v yerushsh belmay يرشّ بالمي
lift v 'yerfa يرفع	splash
exalt v 'yeraffe يرفّع	spray v yerushsh sepray يرشّ سبراي
elevate v yerfa'e يرفَع	nominate v yerashsheh يرشّح
jack v 'yerfa يرفَع	ooze v yerashsheh يرشّح
suit v yerfa' qadeyyeh يرفع قضيّة	bribe v yershi يرشي
v yerfa' la'qsa hadd يرفع لأقصى حدّ	observe v yersud يرصُد
maximize	yarsud masari يرصُد مصاري لشي
v yerfa' ma'naweyyat يرفع معنويّات	appropriate v leshi
moralize	suckle v 'yeradde يرضّع
soothe v yeraffeh an يرفّه عن	consent v yerda يرضى
maggot n yaraqah يرقَة	satisfy v yerdi يرضي
nap v yerqud يرقُد	scare v yer'eb يرعب
dance v yerqus يرقُص	daunt v year'eeb يرعّب
tango v yerqus tangu يرقص تانغو	patronize v yer'ah يرعى
v yerqus elsamba يرقص سامبا	care v year'a يرعَى
samba	v yer'ah belmar'ah يرعَى بالمرعى
botch v 'yeraqqe يرقّع	pasture
cobble v 'yeraqqe يرقّع	graze v yer'a mwashi يرعى مواشي
patch v 'yeraqqe يرقّع	desire v yerghab يرغَب
number v yeraqqem يرقّم	covet v yerghab bi يرغَب ب
punctuate v yeraqqem يرقّم	foam v yerghi يرغي
v yeraqqim safhat يرقّم صفحات	scum v yerghi يرغي
page	flapping v yerafref يرفرف

sprint *v* yerkud beser'ah يركض بسرعة	ride *v* yerkab يركب
symbolize *v* yermuz يرمز	compose *v* yurakkeb يركّب
code *v* yerammiz يرمّز	compound *v* yerakkeb يركّب
blink *v* yermush يرمش	install *v* yerakkeb يركّب
mend *v* yerammem يرمّم	piece *v* yerakkeb يركّب
overhaul *v* yerammem يرمّم	mount *v* yerkab يركب
restore *v* yerammem يرمّم	boat *v* yerkab belzawareq يركب بالزورق
toss *v* yermi يرمي	airlift *v* yrkab blttayara يركب بالطيارة
lance *v* yermi harbeh يرمي الحربة	wheel *v* yerakkeb dulab يركّب دولاب
dart *v* yermi essahem يرمي السهم	embark *v* yerkab safeneh يركب سفينة
dread *n* yerheb يرهب	board *v* yerkab a'safineh يركب عسفينة
terrorize *v* yerheb يرهب	cycle *v* yerkab misklit يركب مسكليت
mortgage *v* yerhun يرهن	slump *v* yerkud يركد
pledge *v* yerhun يرهن	concentrate *v* yerakkiz يركّز
promote *v* yerawwej يروّج	focalize *v* yerakkiz يركّز
rumour *v* yerawwej isha'ah يروّج إشاعة	focus *v* yerakkiz يركّز
go *v* yruh يروح	station *v* yerakkez يركّز
decalcifiy *v* yerawweh elkles يروّح الكلس	gallop *v* yerkud يركض
demagnatize *v* yerawweh elmaghnatah يروّح المغنطة	run *v* yerkud يركض
emaculate *v* yerawweh elnamsh يروّح النمش	course *v* yerkud يركض
dematerialize *v* yerawweh madeyyet يروّح مادّية	rush *v* yerkud beser'ah يركض بسرعة

524

blazon v yezarkesh يزركش	v yerawweh mluhet يروّح ملوحة desalt
displease v yez'uj يزعُج	domesticate v yerawwedh يروّض
annoy v yuzeij يزعِج	subjugate v yerawwed يروّض
v yezaze' istiqrar يزعزع استقرار destabilize	tame v yerawwed يروّض
shriek v yez'aq يزعق	tranquillize v yerawweq يروّق
sadden v yeza'el يزعَل	quench v yerwi يروي
grieve v yez'al يزعَل	slake v yerwi يروي
pitch v yezaffet يزفّت	narrate v yerwi qessah يروي قصّة
tar v yezaffit يزفّت	comfort v yerayyeh يريّح
pave v yezaffet eltariq يزفّت الطريق	fallow v yerayyeh elard يريّح الأرض
cheep v yezaqzeq يزقزق	want v yrid يريد
slip v yezell يزلّ	v yezayed belmazad يزايِد بالمزاد outbid
glide v yezalleq يزلُق	
snarl v yezamjer يزمجِر	throw v yezett يزتّ
rancidify v yezannekh يزنِخ	discard v yezett يزتّ
begird v yezanner يزنِّر	cast v yezett يزتّ
prostitute v yezni يزني	shell v yezett qanabel يزتّ قنابل
visit v yezur يزور	crawl v yezhaf يزحَف
fake v yezawwer يزوّر	flourish v yezakhref يزخرف
forge v yezawwer يزوّر	ornament v yezakhref يزخرف
quibble v yezughel يزوغل	boom v yezdiher يزدهر
oil v yezayyet يزيّت	zip v yezerr elsahhab يزرّ السحّاب up
add v yzeed يزيد	
increase v yezid يزيد	plant v 'yezra يزرع
v yezid 4 marrat يزيد 4 مرّات quadruple	sow v 'yezra يزرع
	afforest v yzra shajar يزرع شجر
	transplant v yerra' udu يزرع عضو

tolerate *v* yesameh يسامح

share *v* yesahem يساهم

contribute *v* yesahem يساهِم

haggle *v* yesawm يساوِم

v yesawem belser يساوِم بالسعر

bargain

amount *v* yusawi يساوي

equal *v* yesawi يساوي

pacify *v* yesayer يساير

insult *v* yesbb يسُبّ

rail *v* yesebb يسُبّ

conduce *v* yesabbeb يسبِّب

effect *v* yesabbeb يسبِّب

reason *v* yesabbeb يسبِّب

cause *v* yesabbeb يسَبِّب

attaint *v* yusabib el'aar يسبب العَار

swim *v* yesbah يسبح

yesbah a luh يسبح ع لوح سباحة

bodyboard *v* sibaha

abuse *v* ysbseb يسبسب

precede *v* yesbuq يسبق

antecede *v* yasbuq يسبُق

prefix *v* yesbuq bi يسبق ب

lease *v* yesta'jer يستأجِر

hire *v* yesta'jer يستأجِر

rent *v* yesta'jer يستأجِر

agist *v* yestajr mazra'a يستأجِر مزرعة

eradicate *v* yesta'sel يستأصِل

v yezid 8 marrat يزيد 8 مرَّات

octuple

v yezid beladad يزيد بالعدد

outnumber

falsify *v* yezayyef يزيِّف

v yezil elrutubeh يزيل الرطوبة

dehumidify

v yezil eshshuhum يزيل الشحوم

delipidate

accessorise *v* yzyyen يزيِّن

adorn *v* yzyn يزيِّن

bedight *v* yuzayyen يزيِّن

deck *v* yezayyin يزيِّن

garnish *v* yezayyen يزيِّن

yezayyen يزيِّن بالمجوهرات

jewel *v* belmjawharat

left *n* elyasar اليسار

left *adj* yasar يسار

leftist *n* yasari يساري

aid *v* yusaed يساعد

assist *v* yusaed يساعد

help *v* yesa'ed يساعد

travel *v* yesafer يسافر

sail *v* yesafer belbahr يسافر بالبحر

v yesafer belbahr يسافر بالبحر

voyage

ask *v* yes'aal يسأل

forgive *v* yesameh يسامح

extract v yestakhles يستخلص	deserve v yetsahal يستاهل
decoy v yestadrij يستدرج	replace v yestabdel يستبدل
draw v yestadrej يستدرج	substitute v yestabdel يستبدل
arraign v yastade'i يستدعي	disqualify v yestabed يستبعد
prompt v yested'i يستدعي	exclude v yestab'ed يستبعد
summon v yestad'i يستدعي	forestall v yestebeq يسبق
call v yestadei يستَدعي	invest v yestathmer يستثمر
redeem v 'yestarje يسترجع	except v yestathni يستثني
restore v 'yestarje يسترجع	interrogate v yestajweb يستجوب
retrieve v 'yestarje يسترجع	question v yestajweb يستجوب
recover v yestredd يسترد	evoke v yestahder يستحضر
v yestredd melkeyyet يسترد ملكيّة	v yestahder arwah يستحضر أوراح
evict	conjure
placate v yestardi يسترضى	adj yastaheq eltaqdir يستحق التقدير
bed v yestrih يستريح	appreciable
break v yestrih يستريح	disdain v yestahqer يستحقر
succumb v yestaslim يستسلم	emulsify v yestahlib يستحلب
surrender v yestaslem يستسلم	implore v yestahlef يستحلف
v yestaslim beshrut يستَسلِم بشروط	harness v yestakhdem يستخدم
capitulate	use v yestakhdem يستخدم
consult v yestashir يستشير	v yestakhdem elvitu يستخدم الفيتو
counsel v yestishir يستشير	veto
reclaim v yestasleh يستصلح	yestakhdim يستخدم المكابح
belittle v yestasgher يستصغر	brake v elmakabeh
accommodate v ystadif يستضيف	n yestakhdem ghalat يستخدم غلط
house v yestadif يستضيف	misuse
taste v yestate'em يستطعم	derive v yestakhrej يستخرج
enslave v yesteid يستعبِد	deduce v yestakhlis يستخلص

abominate v yestanker يستنكر	slave v yesta'bed يستعبد
wait v yestannah يستنّى	hasten v yesta'jel يستعجل
hoot v 'yestahze يستهزء	hurry v yesta'jil يستعجل
ridicule v 'yestahze يستهزء	bustle v yesta'jil يستعجل
scoff v 'yestahze يستهزء	forearm v yesta'edd يستعدّ
consume v yestahlek يستهلك	beshame v yesta'err men يستعرّ من
despise v yestehin bi يستهين ب	borrow v yesta'ir يستعير
import v yestawred يستورد	profiteer v yesteghghel يستغلّ
settle v yestawten يستوطن	exploit v yestaghghel يستغلّ
apprehend v yastaweb يستوعب	vomit v yestafregh يستفرغ
comprehend v yestaweb يستوعب	provoke v yestfezz يستفزّ
capture v yestawli ala يستولي على	miss v yestafqed يستفقد
overwhelm v yestawli ala يستولي على	stabilize v yesteqrr يستقرّ
mature v yestwi يستوي	polarize v yestaqteb يستقطب
kneel v yesjud يسجد	abdicate ,vt yestaqil يستقيل
jot v yesajjel يسجّل	resign v yestqil يستقيل
record v yesajjel يسجّل	scout v yestakshef يستكشف
register v yesajjel يسجّل	replenish v yestakmil يستكمل
enrol v yesajjel bi يسجّل ب	receive v yestelm يستلم
log v yesajjel belsejl يسجّل بالسجل	last v yestmerr يستمرّ
yesajjel bara'et يسجّل براءة إختراع	progress v yestemerr يستمرّ
patent v 'ikhtera	continue v yestemerr يستمرّ
tape v yesajjel a shrit يسجّل ع شريط	conclude v yestantej يستنتج
imprison v yesjun يسجن	sniff v yestansheq يستنشق
jail v yesjun يسجن	inhale v yestansheq يستنشق
tow v yesehab يسحب	deplete v yestanfiz يستنفد
draft v yesehab يسحب	exhaust v yestanfiz يستنفذ
draw v yeshab يسحب	denounce v yestankir يستنكر

dumbfound v yesattel يسطّل	pull v yesehab يسحَب
intoxicate v yestul يسطّل	يسحب عالمكشوف yesehab
accommodate v ysae يِسع	overdraw v almakshuf
price v yesa'er يِسعِّر	yesehab men يسحب من التداول
salvage v yes'ef يِسعِف	demonetize v ettadawul
succour v yes'ef يِسعِف	bewitch v yasehar يِسحَر
ambulate v yuse'f يُسعِف	charm v yesehar يسحَر
cough v yesul يِسعُل	enchant v yeshar يسحَر
seek v yes'a يِسعى	beat v 'yaseha يِسحَق
spill v yesfah يِسفح	burlesque v yeskhar men يِسخَر من
culminate v yesaqqef يِسقِّف	soot v yesakhkhem يِسخِّم
roof v yesaqqef يِسقِّف	heat v yesakhkhen يِسخِّن
v yesquf belqashsh يِسقف بالقشّ	dead-end v yesedd يِسدّ
thatch	embank v yesedd يِسدّ
irrigate v yesqi يِسقي	reimburse v yesedd يِسدّ
water v yesqi يِسقي	repay v yesedd يِسدّ
shed v yeskub يِسكُب	tampon v yesedd يِسدّ
quiet .vt yesakket يِسكّت	score v yesadded hadaf يِسدّد هدف
hush v yesakket يِسكّت	demobilize v yesarreh يِسرِّح
silence v yesakket يِسكّت	discharge v yesarreh يِسرِّح
shut v yesakker يِسكّر	speed v 'yesarre يِسرِّع
inhabit v yeskun يِسكن	accelerate v 'ysarre يِسرِّع
live v yeskun يِسكن	steal v yesruq يِسرق
reside v yeskun يِسكن	yesruq mn يِسرق من الدكّان
ease v yeskun يِسكِّن	shoplift v eldekkan
mitigate v yesakken يِسكِّن	plane v yesatteh يِسطّح
relieve v yesakken يِسكِّن	surface v yesatteh يِسطّح
dwell v yeskun يِسكُن	stripe v yesatter يِسطِّر

name v yesammi يُسَمِّي

term v yesammi يُسَمِّي

sharpen v yesenn يُسِنّ

teethe v yesannen يُسَنِّن

wake v yesehar يُسِهر

facilitate v yesahhel يُسَهِّل

v yesahhel elam'a يُسَهِّل الأمعاء
purge

worsen v 'yesawwe يُسوء

journey v yesuh يُسوح

roam v yesuh يُسوح

blacken v yesawwed يُسوِّد

fence v yesawwer يُسوِّر

groom v yesus elhsan يُسوس الحصان

messiah n 'yasu يسُوع

drive v yesuq يُسوق

market v yesawweq يُسوِّق

motor v yesuq elmutur يُسوق الموتور

v yesawweq belhatef يُسوِّق بالهاتف
telemarket

even v yesawwi يُسوِّي

compromise v yesawwi يُسوِّي

level v yesawwi يُسوِّي

ripen v yesawwi يُسوِّي

settle v yesawwi يُسوِّي

enclose v yesayyej يُسيِّج

v yesayyej belshajr يُسيِّج بالشجر
hedge

populate v yesakken يُسكِّن

depredate v yeslub يَسلُب

infatuate v yeslub aqel يَسلُب عقل

sidearm v yesalleh يُسلِّح

arm v yusalleh يُسلِّح

deflesh v yeslakh يَسلخ

poach v yesluq elbidah يَسلق البيضة

deliver v yesallem يُسلِّم

hand v yesallem be'eyd يُسلِّم باليد

greet v yesallem ala يُسلِّم على

salute v yesallem ala يُسلِّم على

amuse v yusalli يُسلِّي

entertain v yesalli يُسلِّي

allow v yasmah يَسمح

permit v yesmah يَسمح

enable v yesmah يَسمح

manure v yesammed يُسمِّد

tan v yesammer يُسمِّر

hear v 'yesma يَسمع

listen v 'yesma يَسمع

v yesma' belsudefeh يَسمع بالصدفة
overhear

adhere v yesma' klmeh يَسمع كلمة

intensify v yesammek يُسمِّك

thicken v yesammek يُسمِّك

poison v yesammem يُسمِّم

bane v yesammem يُسمِّم

denominate v yesammi يُسمِّي

knit *v* yeshteghel suf يشتغل صوف	propel *v* yesayyer يسيّر
v yeshteghel alnul يشتغل ع النُّول	henpeck *v* yesyter يسيطر
loom	flow *v* yesil يسيل
v yeshtughil krusheh يشتغل كروشيه	drool *v* yesil rewelu يسيل رويله
crochet	participate *v* yesharek يشارك
yeshteghel يشتغل من قفا الكيف	share *v* yesharek يشارك
bungle *v* men qafa elkif	subscribe *v* yesharek يشارك
conjugate *v* yeshtaqq يشتقّ	satiate *v* 'yeshbe يشبع
complain *v* yeshtiki يشتكي	mesh *v* yeshabbek يشبّك
repute *v* yeshteher يشتهر	resemble *v* yeshbah يشبه
winter *v* yeshatti يشتّي	liken *v* yeshabbeh يشبّه
encourage *v* 'yeshajje يشجّع	assimilate *v* yushabbeh يشبّه
beg *v* yeshehad يشحد	hanker *v* yeshtaq يشتاق
grease *v* yeshahhim يشحّم	long *v* yeshtaq يشتاق
lubricate *v* yeshahhem يشحّم	crave *v* yeshtaq li يشتاق ل
lade *v* shahn يشحن	interlock *v* yeshtebek يشتبك
ship *v* yeshhan يشحن	combat *v* 'yeshtebek ma يشتبك مع
scrawl *v* yeshakhbet يشخبط	suspect *v* yeshtebeh bi يشتبه ب
snore *v* yeshkhur يشخر	indict *v* yeshtebeh be يشتبه ب
diagnose *v* yeshakhkhes يشخّص	deflect *v* yeshattit يشتّت
enthral *v* yeshedd يشدّ	disperse *v* yeshattet يشتّت
tense *v* yeshedd يشدّ	scatter *v* yeshattet يشتّت
v yeshedd elberghi يشدّ البرغي	stipulate *v* yeshteret يشترط
screw	buy *v* yeshteri يشتري
stress *v* yeshadded ala يشدّد على	purchase *v* yeshtri يشتري
prune *v* yeshazzeb يشذّب	function *v* yeshteghel يشتغل
drink *v* yeshrab يشرب	work *v* yeshteghel يشتغل
saturate *v* yesharreb يشرّب	labour *v* yeshteghl يشتغل

kindle v yesh'ul يشعل

yush'el adwaa' يُشعِل أضواء خلفيّة
backlight v khalfeyeh

accend v ysheul enaar يشعل النار

stoke v yesh'ul nar يشعل النار

yeshul ennar يشعل النار قبل وقتا
backfire v abel waqta

flash v yesh'ul flash يشعُل فلاش

yesh'ul qunblet يشعُل قنبلة إشارة
flare v isharah

flame v yesh'ul nar يشعل نار

v yesh'ul nar alakel يشعل نار عالأكل
flambé

reel v yeshaghghel يشغّل

cipher v yeshaffer يشفّر

encrypt v yeshaffer يشفّر

pity v yeshfuq ala يشفق على

lacerate v yesheqq يشقّ

tatter v yeshuqq يشقّ

tear v yeshuqq يشقّ

doubt v yeshekk يشكّ

prick v yeshekk يشكّ

jab v yeshekk ebreh يشكّ إبرة

v yeshekk bedabbus يشكّ بادبّوس
pin

thank v yeshkur يشكر

mistrust v yeshakkek يشكّك

misgive v yeshakkek يشكّك

bib v yashrab يشرَب

v yeshrab layeskar يشرَب ليسكَر
booze

toast v yeshrab nakhb يشرب نخب

explain v yeshrah يشرح

dissect v yesharreh يشرّح

slice v yesharreh يشرّح

illustrate v yeshrah يشرح

v yeshrah belsuwar يشرح بالصور
depict

yeshrah betreqah يشرح بطريقة تانية
paraphrase v tanyeh

displace v yesharred يشرّد

enact v 'yesharre يشرّع

legislate v 'yesharre يشرّع

honour v yesharref يشرّف

v yesharref bewjuduh يشرّف بوجوده
grace

supervise v yeshref ala يشرف على

sip v yeshruq يشرق

rip v yeshrum يشرُم

drift v yesh يشطّ عن

slash v yeshatteb يشطّب

flush v yeshtuf يشطّف

splinter v yeshazzi يشظّي

radiate v 'yeshe يشعّ

feel v yash'ur يشعر

shine v 'yesha'she يشعشع

scorch v yeshawwet يشوّط	brew v yeshakkel يشكّل
singe v yeshawwet يشوّط	form v yeshakkel يشكّل
see v yeshuf يشوف	shape v yeshakkel يشكّل
sight v yeshuf يشوف	v yeshakkel elma'dan يشكّل المعدن
deform v yeshawweh يشوّه	exude
disfigure v yeshawweh يشوّه	paralyse v yeshell يشلّ
distort v yeshawweh يشوّه	bare v yeshalleh يشلّح
mar v yeshawweh يشوّه	denude v yeshalleh يشلّح
v yeshwweh sem'ah يشوّه سمعة	rob v yeshalleh يشلّح
slander	smell v yeshemm يشمّ
v yeshawweh sem'et يشوّه سمعة	gloat v yeshmat يشمت
vilify	sun v yeshammes يشمّس
v yeshawweh sima'a يشوّه سمعة	involve v yeshmal يشمل
calumniate	encompass v yeshmal يشمَل
v yeshil istektab يشيل استقطاب	englobe v yeshmal يشمَل
depolarize	detest v yeshmaezz يشمئزّ
v yeshil elhashish يشيل الحشيش	loathe v yeshma'ezz يشمئزّ
weed	v yeshenn hamleh يشنّ حملة
wax v 'yeshil belshame يشيل بالشمع	campaign
pulp v yeshil lebb يشيل لبّ	certify v yeshehad يشهَد
yeshil men يشيل من قائمة المجرمين	witness v yeshhad يشهَد
v qaemet elmejrmin	testify v yeshhad يشهّد
decriminalize	defame v yeshahhir يشهّر
intimate v yesahib يصاحِب	popularize v yeshehur يشهُر
forfeit v yesader يصادِر	sob v yeshhaq يشهَق
confiscate v yusader يُصادِر	confuse v yeshawwesh يشوّش
ratify v yesadeq يصادق	disrupt v yeshawwesh يشوّش
cross v yusalib يصالِب	perturb v yeshawwesh يشوّش

proclaim v yesarreh يصرّح	pour v yesubb يصبّ
avow v yusarreh an يصرّح عن	tincture v yesbugh يصبغ
scream v yesrakh يصرخ	tint v yesbugh يصبغ
shout v yesarrekh يصرّخ	dye v yesbugh يصبغ
yield v yesarrekh يصرّخ	correct v yesahehhih يصحّح
creak v yesarsir يصرصر	emendate v yesahhih يصحّح
expend v yesruf يصرف	rectify v yesahheh يصحّح
spend v yesruf يصرف	deforest v yasahher يصحّر
v yesarref emleh عملة يصرّف	desert v yesahher يصحّر
exchange	yusahhi men ennum يصحّي من النوم
hunt v yestad يصطاد	awake v
v yestad belshabakeh بالشبكة يصطاد	v yesahhi mn elnum يصحّي من النوم
net	rouse
v yestad belsinnarah بالصنّارة يصطاد	obstruct v yesudd يصدّ
dib	repulse v yesudd يصدّ
dap v yestad berawaq يصطاد برواق	export v yesadder يصدّر
fish v yestad samk سمك يصطاد	issue v yesder يصدر
jostle v yestedem يصطدم	v yeder marsum يصدر مرسوم
line v yestaff يصطفّ	decree
ascend v yasa'ad يصعد	v yesaddeq altawqi'e يصدّق ع التوقيع
v yesaghgher elsurah الصورة يصغّر	countersign
zoom out	legalize v yesaddeq ala يصدّق على
array v yasuff يصفّ	shock v yesdum يصدم
park v yesuff sayyarah سيّارة يصفّ	dissuade v yesudduh an يصدّه عن
forge v yesaffeh يصفّح	rust v yesaddi يصدّي
laminate v yesaffeh يصفّح	determine v yeserr يصرّ
plate v yesaffeh يصفّح	insist v yeserr يصرّ
pardon v yesfah يصفح	declare v yesarreh يصرّح

يصوّر بالشاشة yesawwer belshasheh	whistle v yesaffer يصفِر
screen v	clap v yesaffiq يصفّق
film v yesawwer felm فِلم	applaud v yusaffeq يُصفّق
video v yesawwer vidyu يصوّر فيديو	clear v yesaffi يصفّي
fast v yesum يصوم	liquidate v yesaffi يصفّي
service v yesun يصون	arrive v yasil يصِل
inflict v yesib يصيب	approach v yasel ela يصِل إلى
befall v yusiib يُصيب	crucify v yeslub يصلُب
v yesib belgangarina يصيب بالغنغرينا	ameliorate v yusllih يصلِح
mortify	fix v yesalleh يصلِح
crow v yesih eddik يصيح الديك	reform v yesalleh يصلِح
become v yesir يصير	repair v yesalleh يصلِح
happen v yesir يصير	pray v yesalli يصلّي
occur v yesir يصير	clam v yesmut يصمت
cower v yesir jaban يصير جبان	design v yesammem يصمّم
vt yesir madyun la يصير مديون لـ	manufacture v 'yesanne يصنع
owe	sort v yesannef يصنّف
yesir martin يصير مرتين بالسنة	tabulate v yesannef يصنّف
biannually adv belseneh	assort v yusannif يُصنّف
formulate v yesegh يصيغ	classify v yesannif يصنّف
frame v yesigh يصيغ	fuse v yeshehar يصهر
model v yesigh يصيغ	v yesehal elhsan يصهل الحصان
speculate v yedareb يضارب	neigh
redouble v yeda'ef يضاعف	point .vt yesawweb يصوّب
double v yedaef يضاعف	soap v yesuben يصوبن
dup v yedaef يضاعف	vote v yesawwet يصوّت
duplicate v yedaef يضاعف	ballot v yesawwet يصوّت
geminate v yeda'ef يضاعف	picture v yesawwer يصوّر

biff v yedrub kaff كَفّ يضرُب	adjust v yadbt يضبط
thin v yed'af يضعف	v 'yedbut eliqaa الإيقاع يضبط
weaken i & .vt yedae'f يضعّف	cadence
press v yedghat يضغط	giggle v yedhak يضحك
depress v yedeghat ala على يضغَط	laugh v yedhak يضحك
braid v yedaffer يضفِّر	v yedhak belmekhfi بالمخفي يضحك
strand v yedaffer يضفِر	chuckle
benight v yudallel يضلِل	sacrifice v yedahhi يضحّي
tail v yedumm يضم	victimize v yedahhi bi ب يضحّي
annex v yaddum يضُم	pump v yedukhkh يضخّ
atrophy v yadmur يضمر	hit v yedrub يضرب
pine v yedmur يضمُر	strike v yedrub يضرب
assure v yadman يضمن	inject v yedrub ibreh إبرة يضرب
guarantee v yedman يضمن	syringe v yedrub ebreh إبرة يضرب
warrant v yedman يضمن	triple 3 3 bi yedrub vt., ب يضرب
ensure v yedman يضمَن	stone v yedrub belhajar بالحجر يضرب
enlighten v yedawwi يضوِّي	yedrub belkhizaran بالخيزرانة يضرب
gleam v yedawwi يضوِي	cane v
light v yedawwi يضوِي	yedrub بالرياضيّات يضرُب
lose v 'yedayye يضيع	multiply v belryadeyyat
fiddle v yedayye' elwaqt الوقت يضيع	v yedrub belkerbaj بالكرباج يضرُب
laze v yedayye' waqt وقت يضيع	whip
v yudef lekitab لكتاب يضيف	yedrub belmusaddas بالمسدّس يضرب
append	shoot v
match v yetabeq يطابق	v yadrub belmidrab بالمضرَب يضرُب
chase v yetared يطارِد	bat
stoop v yetati يطاطي	fist v yedrub boks بوكس يضرب
duck v tetati rasuh راسه يطاطي	slap v yedrub kaff كَفّ يضرب

stab v yet'an يطعن	v yetale' ahsha'a يطالع أحشاء
spear v yet'an beremeh يطعن برمح	eviscerate
skip v yetuff يطف	cook v yetbukh يطبخ
smoulder v yetaffi يطفي	yetbukh a nar يطبخ ع نار واطية
extinguish v yetaffi ennar يطفي النار	stew v wateyh
yetfi hariq يطفي حريق بالخرطوم	print v 'yetba يطبع
firehose v belkhartum	type v 'yetba يطبع
crepitate v yetuqq يطق	normalize v 'yetabbe يطبّع
brustle v yetaqteq يطقطق	vt yetba' el'emleh يطبع العملة.
clack v yetaqteq يطقطق	mint
quest vt. yetelub يطلب	apply v yutabbeq يُطبّق
request v yetlub يطلب	grind v yetehan يطحن
demand v yetlub يطلُب	mill v yetehan يطحن
v yetlub besut aali يطلب بصوت عالي	thresh v yetehan يطحن
clamour	v yetehan bisnanuh يطحن بسنانه
look v 'yetalle يطلّع	crunch
eject v 'yetalle يطلّع	v yetehan budrah يطحن بودرة
emerge v 'yetalle يطلَع	powder
yetalle' elruh يطلَع الروح من الجسم	pose v 'yetrah mawdu يطرح موضوع
disembody v mn eljesm	dismiss v yetrud يطرُد
dawn v yetla' elfajr يطلع الفجر	ostracize v yetrud يطرُد
exit v yetalle' labarrah يطلَع برّا	brocade v yutarriz يطرُز
glimmer v yetla' basis يطلع بصيص	deafen v yetrush يطرُش
yetla' beqareb يطلع بقارب العبّارة	forge v yetruq elhadid يطرق الحديد
ferry v elabbarah	tenderize v yetarri يطرّي
gawk v yettala' bihabal يطلّع بهبل	soften v yetarri يطرّي
lactate v yetalle' halib يطلّع حليب	vaccinate v yeta'em يطعّم
trip v yetla' rehleh يطلع رحلة	lunge v yet'an يطعن

cordon v yetawweq يطوّق	v yetalle' shararah يطلّع شرارة
encircle v yetawweq يطوّق	spark
ring n yetawweq يطوّق	echo v yetalle' sadah يطلّع صدى
heighten v yetawwil يطوّل	yetalle' sut يطلّع صوات ورا بعض
lengthen v yetawwel يطوّل	blip v wara baad
strengthen v yetawwel يطوّل	yetalle' sut tahen يطلّع صوت طحن
fold v yetwi يطوي	crump v
heal v yetayyeb يطيب	v yetalle' an essekkeh يطلع عن السكّة
fly v yetir يطير	derail
pilot v yetayyer يطيّر	divorce v yetalleq يطلّق
comply v 'yetei يطيع	emit v yetleq يطلق
obey v yet'e يطيع	evolve v yetleq يطلق
bear v 'yetiie يطيق	coat v yetli يطلي
stomach v yetiq يطيق	engulf v yetumm يطمّ
shade v yezallel يظلّل	aspire v yatmah ila يطمح إلى
shadow v yezallel يظلّل	efface v yetmus يطمس
brutify v yazlum يظلم	obliterate v yetmus يطمس
daresay v yezunn يظنّ	appease v yetammen يطمّن
distrust v yezunn يظنّ	buzz v yetanten يطنطن
surmise v yezunn يظنّ	cleanse v yetahher يطهّر
appear v yazhar يظهر	sanctify v yetahher يطهّر
admonish v yua'tb يعاتب	develop v yetawwir يطوّر
tantamount v ye'adel يعادل	draft v 'yetawwe يطوّع
equate v ye'adil يعادل	subject v 'yetawwe يطوّع
feud v ye'adi يعادي	v yetawwe' asaker يطوّع عساكر
oppose v ye'adi يعادي	induct
antagonize v yua'di يُعادي	float v yetuf يطوف
object v ye'ared يعارض	flood v yetuf يطوف

scowl *v* ye'bus يعبس

frown *v* ye'bus يعبس

fill *v* ya'abbi يعبّي

v ye'abbi besanduq يعبّي بصندوق

encase

bottle *v* yeabbi beqanani يعبّي بقناني

sack *v* ye'abbi belkis يعبّي بكياس

puddle *v* ye'abbi wahl يعبّي وحل

accustom *v* y'atad ala يعتاد على

deem *v* ye'teber يعتبر

regard *v* ye'tebr يعتبر

conceive *v* ye'teber يعتبر

consider *v* ye'teber يعتبر

assault *v* yatadi ala يعتدي على

encroach *v* ye'tedi ala يعتدي على

apologize *v* yaetazer يعتذر

demur *v* ye'terid يعترض

disagree *v* yetered يعترض

intercept *v* ye'terd يعترض

v yetured bisakhafeh يعترض بسخافة

cavil

acknowledge *v* yeateref يعترف

admit *v* yetirf يعترف

confess *v* yeteref يعترف

pride *v* ye'tazz bi يعتزّ ب

picket *v* ye'tesm يعتصم

manumit *v* ye'teq يعتق

emancipate *v* ye'tuq يعتق

contradict *v* yuaared يعارض

befriend *v* ye'aashir يعاشر

cohabit *v* ye'asher يعاشر

drab *v* yeasher qahbeh يعاشر قحبة

sanction *v* ye'aqeb يعاقب

castigate *v* yeaaqeb يعاقب

penalize *v* ye'aqeb يعاقب

punish *v* ye'aqib يعاقب

molest *v* ye'akes يعاكس

contrast *v* yuakes يعاكس

cure *v* yealij يعالج

physic *v* ye'alej يعالج

doctor *v* yealij يعالج

v ye'alej belashe'ah يعالج بالأشعّة

irradiate

ye'amel betariqah يعامل بطريقة سيئة

mistreat *v* saye'ah

opinionate *v* ye'aned يعاند

suffer *v* ye'ani يعاني

forward *v* ye'awen يعاون

calibrate *v* yeayir يعاير

standardize *v* ye'ayer يعاير

worship *v* ye'bud يعبد

deify *v* ye'bud يعبد

express *v* ye'abber يعبّر

phrase *v* ye'abber يعبّر

v ye'abber an ra'eyu يعبّر عن رأيه

opine

infect v ye'di يعدي	believe v ya'teked يعتقد
torture v ye'azzeb يعذّب	arrest v ya'taqil يعتقل
excuse v ye'zur يعذُر	nab v ye'teqel يعتقل
assoil v ya'zur يَعذُر	darken v ye'attem يعتّم
gimp v yu'ruj يعرُج	dim v yeattem يعتّم
lame v ye'ruj يعرُج	accredit v ye'tmd يعتمد
widen v ye'arred يعرّض	depend v ye'temed ala يعتمد على
display v ye'rud يعرُض	rely v ye'temed ala يعتمد على
exhibit v ye'rud يعرُض	profess v ye'teneq يعتنق
offer v ye'rud يعرُض	enamour v ye'jib يعجِب
pose v yer'ud su'al يعرُض سؤال	admire v yuejab be ب يعجب
v ye'arred lelkhatar يعرّض للخطر	thwart v ye'ajjez يعجِّز
endanger	teem v ye'juq يعجق
v ye'arred lelkhatar يعرّض للخطر	enumerate v ye'edd يعدّ
jeopardize	reckon v ye'edd يعدّ
know v ye'ref يعرف	count v yeudd يعدّ
define v ye'arrif يعرِّف	commute v yeaddel يعدّل
identify v ye'arref يعرِّف	modify v ye'addel يعدّل
perspire v ye'raq يعرَق	amend v yueaddil يُعدّل
foster v ye'azziz يعزز	v ye'addel eldaghet يعدّل الضغط
boost v yeazziz يعزِّز	pressurize
reinforce v ye'azzez يعزِّز	execute v ye'dim يعدُم
v ye'zuf almezmar يعزف عالمزمار	v ye'dim belkahraba يعدم بالكهربا
flute	electrocute
isolate v ye'zul يعزل	ye'dem bdun يعدم بدون محاكمة
seclude v ye'zul يعزل	lynch v muhakameh
insulate v ye'zul يعزُل	v ye'dim khanqan يعدم خنقا
segregate v ye'zul يعزُل	garrotte

mete v ye'ti hessah حصّة	depose v ye'zul يعزِل
'ye'ti haq eliqtera حق الاقتراع	comfort v ye'azzi يعزّي
enfranchise v	condole v yeazzi يعزّي
v ye'ti ared se'r عرض سعر	console v yeazzi يعزّي
quote	solace v ye'azzi يعزّي
endow v ye'ti mahr مهر	dragonfly n ya'sub يعسوب
magnify v ye'azzem يعظِّم	adore v 'yesha يعشق
chasten v ye'eff يعفّ	enrage v ye'assib يعصِّب
rot v ye'affen يعفِّن	v yaesub uyun عيون
acquit v ye'fo an يعفو عن	blindfold
exempt v ye'fi يعفي	compress v yu'sur يعصُر
remit v ye'fi يعفي	squeeze v ye'sur يعصِر
complicate v yeaqqid يعقِّد	storm v ye'suf يعصِّف
sophisticate v ye'aqqed يعقّد	v yaasuf zehneyan ذهنيًّا
gnarl v ye'qud يعقُد	brainstorm
knot v ye'qud يعقُد	disobey v ye'si يعصي
noose v ye'qud elhabl الحبل	mutiny v ye'si يعصي
sterilize v ye'aqqem يعقِّم	nibble v ye'add يعضّ
reflect v ye'kus يعكِس	bite v ye'add يعضّ
reverse v ye'kus يعكِس	scent v ye'atter يعطِّر
mirror v ye'kus suret صورة	sneeze v ye'tus يعطُس
curve v yekuf يعكُف	thirst v ye'tash يعطش
can v yealleb يعلّب	deactivate v yeattil يعطِّل
feed v ye'luf يعلِف	give v ye'ti يعطي
forage v ye'luf يعلِف	grant v ye'ti يعطي
hang v yealleq يعلِّق	bespeak v yeti esharah إشارة
comment v yualliq يُعلِّق	v ye'ti jer'ah zaydeh جرعة زايدة
	overdose

stage *v* ye'mel tadrib يعمل تدريب	يعلّق أسفل كتاب yualleq asfal elkitab
tour *v* ye'mel jawleh يعمل جولة	annotate *v*
contuse *v* yamul ridd يعمل رضّ	drape *v* yealleq bardayeh يعلّق برداية
sport *v* ye'mel ryadah يعمل رياضة	wall *v* ye'alleq al hit يعلّق عالحيط
diet *v* yemul rijim يعمل ريجيم	foul *v* ye'laq ma يعلّق مع
sauna *v* ye'mul sawnah يعمل ساونا	chew *v* yeallek يعلك
riot *v* ye'mel shaghab يعمل شغب	educate *v* yeallim يعلّم
transact *v* ye'mel safqah يعمل صفقة	mark *v* ye'allem يعلّم
conciliate *v* ye'mul silha يعمل صلحَة	advertise *v* yu'eln يعلن
v ye'mel syaneh يعمل صيانة	announce *v* yuelin يعلن
maintain	blare *v* yuelin يعلن
ye'mel ard يعمل عرض عسكري	soar *v* ye'alli يعلّي
parade *v* askari	immerse *v* ye'ammed يعمّد
ye'mul amal jirahi يعمل عمل جراحي	
operate *v*	erect *v* ye'ammer يعمّر
ye'mel fahes يعمل فحص شفهي	outlive *v* ye'ammer يعمّر
viva voce *adj* shafahi	deepen *v* yeammeq يعمّق
list *v* ye'mel qa'emeh يعمل قائمة	make *v* ye'mel يعمل
ye'mel يعمل مذاكرة صغيرة	do *v* yemil يعمل
quiz *v* muzakarah seghereh	ye'mel ashe'ah يعمل أشعّة سينيّة
massage *v* ye'mil massaj يعمل مسّاج	x-ray *v* sineyyeh
survey *v* ye'mel maseh يعمل مسح	handicap *v* ye'mel ey'aqa يعمل إعاقة
v ye'mul meshkleh يعمل مشكلة	ye'mel el'adeh يعمل العادة السريّة
trouble	masturbate *v* elserreyyeh
favour *v* ye'mel ma'ruf يعمل معروف	rehearse *v* ye'mel brufah يعمل بروفَة
v ye'mel muqabaleh يعمل مقابلة	agitate *v* ye'ml balbaleh يعمل بلبلة
interview	ye'mil tajmil يعمل تجميل للوجه
frolic *v* ye'mel maqlab يعمل مَقلَب	facelift *v* lelwajeh

yeish ma' يعيش مع شخص تاني chum v shakhes tani	v ye'mul munasabeh يعمل مُناسبِة occasion
impede v ye'yq يعيق	scar v ye'mul nadbeh يعمل ندبةٍ
roadblock v ye'iq يعيق	tattoo v ye'mul washm يعمل وشم
sustain v ye'yl يعيل	banquet v ye'mil walimeh يعمل وليمة
delimitate v yeayyin يعيّن	afflict v y'emllh msibeh يعمّله مصيبة
appoint v yuaeyyen يعيّن	circulate v ye'amem يعمّم
designate v yeayyen يعيّن	publicize v ye'ammem يعمّم
philander v yeghazel يغازل	label v y'anwen يعنون
venture v yeghamer يغامر	entitle v ye'anwen يعنون
dust v yeghabber يغبّر	mean v ye'ni يعني
blur v yeghabbesh يغبّش	habituate v yeawwed يعوّد
gossip v yeghtab يغتاب	ascribe v yaood lesabab يعود لسبب
asperse v yeghtab يَغتَاب	v yaood lesabab يعود لسبب
assassinate v yaghtal يغتال	attribute
flaunt v yeghtarr يغترّ	compensate v yeawwed يعوّض
rape v yeghteseb يغتصب	remunerate v ye'awwed يعوّض
violate v yeghteseb يغتصب	bark v yeawwi يعوّي
grab v yeghteseb يغتصب	taint v ye'ib يعيب
nourish v yeghazzi يغذّي	blemish v yeayyeb يعيب
riddle v yegharbel يغربل	repeat v ye'id يعيد
sieve v yegharbel يغربل	lend v ye'ir يعير
chirp v yegharred يغرّد	gibe v ye'ayyer يعيّر
warble v yegharred يغرّد	taunt v ye'ayyer يعيّر
entice v yegharrer يغرّر	live v ye'ish يعيش
instil v yeghrus يغرس	subsist v ye'ysh يعيش
tickle v yeghargher يغرغر	survive v ye'ysh يعيش
ladle v yeghruf يغرُف	

douse *v* yeghtus يغطُس	sink *v* yeghraq يغرق
cover *v* yeghatti يغطّي	drown *v* yeghraq يغرَق
cap *v* yeghatti يغطّي	*v* yegharreq safineh يغرق سفينة
v yeghatti belmasari يغطّي بالمصاري	shipwreck
hedge	allure *v* yughri يغري
v 'yeghatti beqenaa يغطّي بقِناع	lure *v* yeghri يغري
bemask	seduce *v* yeghri يغري
outshine *v* yeghatti ala يغطّي على	tempt *v* yeghri يغري
doze *v* yeghfah يغفى	glue *v* yegharri يغرّي
slumber *v* yeghfa يغفى	beckon *v* yughri يغري
master *v* yeghleb يغلب	spin *v* yeghzul يغزُل
goof *n* yeghlat يغلط	conquer *v* yaghzu يغزو
mislead *v* yeghallet يغلّط	invade *v* yeghzu يغزو
mistake *v* yeghlat يغلَط	overrun *vt* yeghzi يغزي
v yeghlat belteba'ah يغلط بالطباعة	wash *v* yeghsul يغسل
misprint	*v* yeghsel ellebes يغسل اللبس
sheathe *v* yeghallef يغلّف	launder
close *v* yughleq يغلق	rinse *v* yeghassel belmay يغسّل بالمي
surge *v* yeghli يغلي	adulterate *v* yghsh يغش
v yeghalli else'r يغلّي سعر	bluff *v* yeghush يغش
overcharge	cheat *v* yeghushsh يغش
v 'yeghli a'lbati يغلي عالبطيء	outwit *v* yegheshsh يغش
simmer	fuzz *v* yeghashshi يغشّي
decrepitate *v* yeghli ghali يغلي غلي	gulp *v* yeghuss يغص
boil *v* yeghli ghali يغلي غَلي	steep *v* yeghutt يغطّ
swamp *v* yeghmur يغمر	mire *v* yeghutt beltyn يغطّ بالطين
v yeghmur belmarqah يغمر بالمرقَة	submerge *v* yeghtus يغطس
dunk	dip *v* yeghtus يغطُس

open *v* yeftah يفتح

unfold *v* yeftah يفتح

brighten *v* yefatteh يفتّح

key *v* yeftah bel mftah يفتح بالمفتاح

preen *v* yeftekher bi يفتخر ب

prey *v* yefteres يفترس

assume *v* yaftared يفترض

suppose *v* yeftered يفترض

v yefterd jadalan يفترض جدلا

presuppose

malign *v* yefteri يفتري

ransack *v* yefattesh يفتّش

v yefattish alhajiz يفتّش عالحاجز

checkpoint

concoct *v* yefe'l يفتعل

beguile *v* yaftun يفتن

bomb *v* yefajjer يفجّر

detonate *v* yefajjer يفجّر

explode *v* yefajjer يفجّر

burst *v* yefajjer يفجّر

blast *v* yefajjer يُفجّر

scan *v* yefhas يفحص

check *v* yefhas يفحص

checkup *v* yefhas يفحص

revise *v* yefhas يفحص

yefhas يفحص صلاحيّة البيض

candle *v* salaheyet elbeid

show *v* yefarji يفرجي

plunge *v* yeghmus يغمُس

mumble *v* yeghamghem يغمغم

mutter *v* yeghamghem يغمغم

faint *v* yughma alyh يغمى عليه

swoon *v* yughma' alyh يغمى عليه

loot *v* yeghnam يغنَم

enrich *v* yeghanni يغنِي

sing *v* yeghanni يغنِّي

duet *v* yeghanni duwitto يغنّي دويتو

v yeghanni nashideh يغنِّي نشيدة

chant

dive *v* yeghus يغوص

v yeghus belwahel يغوص بالوَحل

bog

bedevil *v* yaghwi يغوي

absent *v* yeghib يغيب

foray *v* yeghayyer يغير

raid *v* yeghir يغير

alter *v* yughayir يغيّر

change *v* yeghayyer يغيّر

revise *v* yeghayyer يغيّر

vary *v* yeghayyer يغيّر

accost *v* yefateh يفاتح

surprise *v* 'yefaje يفاجئ

negotiate *v* yefawed يفاوض

flake *v* yefattet يفتّت

launch *v* yefteteh يفتتح

preface *v* yefteteh يفتتح

queer v yefsed يفسِد	cheer v yefarreh يفرِّح
spoil v yefsed يفسِد	delight v yefarreh يفرِّح
deprave v yefsed يفسِد	enrapture v yefarreh يفرِّح
v yefsid akhlaq أخلاق يفسِد	germinate v yefarrekh يفرِّخ
demoralize	single v yefred يفرِد
interpret v yefasser يفسِّر	secrete v yefruz يفرُز
v yefasser ghalat غلط يفسِّر	cushion v yefrush يفرُش
misconstrue	furnish v yefrush يفرُش
debauch v yefsuq يفسُق	brush v yefarshi يفرشي
fail v yefshal يفشَل	impose v yefrud يفرُض
spread v yefshi يفشي	yefrud rasm رسم زيادة
divulge v yefshi srr سرّ يفشي	surcharge v zyadeh
separate v yefsel يفصِل	tax v yefrud darebeh ضريبة يفرُض
detail v yefassil يفصِّل	v yefrud gharameh غرامة يفرُض
elaborate v yefassel يفصِّل	fine
disconnect v yefsil يفصِل	branch v 'yefarre يفرِّع
muster v yefsul يفصِل	disband v yefarreq يفرِّق
v yefudd elbakarah البكارَة يفُضّ	distinguish v yefarriq يفرِّق
deflower	crackle v yefarqi'e يفرقِع
scandalize v yefdah يفضَح	pop v 'yefarqe يفرقُع
expose v yefdah يفضَح	chop v yefrum يفرُم
prefer v yefaddel يفضِّل	mince v yefrum يفرُم
deign v yefaddel ala على يفضِّل	panic v 'yefazze يفزِّع
drain v yefaddi يفضِّي	repeal v yefsakh يفسَخ
empty v yefaddi يفضِّي	annul v yafsakh يفسَخ
void v yefaddi يفضِّي	overrule v yefsakh يفسَخ
v yefaddi men elhawa الهوا من يفضِّي	canary v yefassid يفسِّد
deflate	corrupt v yefsid يفسِد

ebulliate v yefur يفور

fizz v yefur يفور

seethe v yefur يفور

irritate v yefawwer damm يفوّر دمّ

delegate v yefawwid يفوّض

empower v yefawwed يفوّض

entrust v yefawwed يفوّض

vest v yefawwed يفوّض

benefit v yefid يفيد

arouse v yafiq يفيق

meet v yeqabel يقابل

v yeaatil bilmaarakeh يقاتل بالمعركة

battle

compare v yeqaren يقارن

litigate v yeqadi يقاضي

sue v yeqadi يقاضي

interrupt v 'yeqate يقاطع

boycott v 'yuqate يُقاطع

resist v yeqawm يقاوم

v yeqawm elhariq يقاوم الحريق

fireproof

buck v yeqawem beqweh يقاوم بقوّة

barter v yukayed يُقايض

v yeqbal beljam'ah يقبل في الجامعة

matriculate

intrude v yeqtehim يقتحم

scant v yeqatter ala يقتّر على

propose v yeqterh يقترح

ablactate v yeftum يفطم

wean v yeftum يفطم

outrage v 'yefazze يفظّع

v yafkud shakhes يفقد شخص

bereave

brood v yefaqqes elbid يفقّس البيض

detach v yefekk يفكّ

loosen v yefekk يفكّ

v yefkk daghet يفكّ الضغط

decompress

decrypt v yfekk tashfir يفكّ تشفير

think v yefakker يفكّر

brood v yefakker ktir يفكّر كتير

mope v yefakker ktir يفكّر كتير

decompose v yefakkik يفكّك

filter v yefalter يفلتر

prosper v yeflah يفلَح

bankrupt n yefallis يفلّس

perish v yefna يفنى

understand v yefham يفهم

perceive v yefham يفهَم

v yefham ghalat يفهم غلط

misapprehend

v yefham ghalat يفهم غلط

misconceive

v yefham ghalat يفهم غلط

misunderstand

bill v yefuter يفوتر

يقدِّم عمْناقَصَة yuqaddem ala	suggest v yeqterh يقترح
bid v munaqasa	poll v 'yeqtere يقترع
v yeqaddem ma'rud يقدِّم معروض	kill v yeqtul يقتل
petition	murder v yeqtul يقتِل
v yeqzuf elmani يقذف المني	yektel hashek w يقتِل حشك ولبك
ejaculate	belabour v labek
read .vt yeqrah يقرا	esteem v yeqadder يقدِّر
v yeqra' eshshifra يقرأ الشِفرَة	prize v yeqadder يقدِّر
decipher	fate v yeqadder يقدِّر
v yeqra' eshshifra يقرأ الشِفرَه	can v yeqder يقدِر
decode	could v yeqdir يقدِر
near v yeqarreb يقرِّب	appreciate v yuqadder يُقدِّر
offing n yeqarreb يقرِّب	yeqadder يقدِر بالاستدلال
decide v yeqarrer يقرِّر	extrapolate v bel'estedlal
resolve v yeqarrer يقرِّر	afford v yqdder ydfae يقدر يدفع
sting v yeqrus يقرص	canonize v yeqaddes يقدِّس
nettle v yeqrus يقرُص	enshrine v yeqaddes يقدِّس
nip v yeqrus يقرُص	hallow v yeqaddes يقدِّس
pinch v yeqrus يقرُص	confer v yeqaddem يقدِّم
pirate v yeqarsen يقرصِن	introduce v yeqaddem يقدِّم
gnaw v yeqrud يقرُض	provide v yeqaddem يقدِّم
loan v yuqred يُقرِض	submit v yeqaddem يقدِّم
squat v yeqarfes يقرفص	cater v yeqaddem akel يقدِّم أكل
cringe v yeqarfes يقرفص	v yukaddem eltalab يقدم طلب
crouch v yeqarfes يقرفص	apply
dwarf v yeqazzim يقزِّم	file v yeqaddem talab يقدِّم طلب
stunt v yeqazzem يقزِّم	yuqaddem ared se'r يقدِّم عرض سعر
sunder v yeqsum يقسم	bid v

feast *v* yuqsuf يقصُف

v yeksuf belkanabel يقصُف بالقنابل
bombard

v 'yeqsuf belmadafe يقصُف بالمدافع
cannonade

defecate *v* yeqdi hajtuh يقضي حاجته

distil *v* yeqatter يقطّر

leach *v* yeqatter يقطّر

seep *v* yeqatter يقطّر

slit *v* yeqatte' beltul يقطّع بالطول

v yeqta' belared يقطع بالعرض
crosscut

behead *v* yektaa ras يقطع راس

chip *v* yeqatte' sharayeh يقطّع شرايح

fillet *v* yeqatte' sharayeh يقطّع شرايح

gourd *n* yaqtin يقطين

pumpkin *n* yaqtin يقطين

locate *v* 'yeqa يقع

stumble *v* 'yeqa يقع

slide *v* 'yeqa يقع

v yeqa' belmasyadeh يقع بالمصيدة
trap

sit *v* yeq'ud يقعد

seat *v* yeqa'ed يقعّد

throne *v* yeq'ud al'arsh يقعد عالعرش

v yeq'ud al nuneyyeh يقعد عالنونيّة
pot

partition *v* yeqassem يقسم

divide *v* yeqassim يقسّم

split *v* yeqsum يقسُم

apportion *v* yukassem يقسّم

part *v* 'yeqassem ajza يقسّم أجزاء

v yuqassem beltasawi يقسّم بالتساوي
average

bisect *v* yeksem kesmin يقسم قسمين

quarter *v* 'yeqassem larba يقسّم لرباع

halve *v* yeqsm nessin يقسم نصّين

concrete *v* yeqassi يقسّي

harden *v* yeqassi يقسّي

scrape *v* yeqashsher يقشّر

peel *v* yeqshur يقشُر

cast *v* yeqshur eljeld يقشُر الجلد

yekasher lihaa' يقشر لحاء الشجر
bark *v* eshajar

graze *v* yeqshut يقشُط

shudder *v* yeqash'er يقشعر

cut *v* yequss يقُص

trim *v* yequss يقُص

v yequss belmenjal يقص بالمنجل
scythe

purpose *v* yeqsud يقصُد

signify *v* yeqsud يقصُد

shorten *v* yeqasser يقصّر

bob *v* yeqassir sharu يقصّر شعره

batter *v* yaqsuf يقصُف

concern *v* yuqliq يُقلِق

minimize *v* yeqallel يُقلِّل

reduce *v* yeqallel يُقلِّل

yeqallel lelhadd يُقلِّل لأدنى حدّ

minimum *adj* eladna

fry *v* yeqli يُقلِي

repress *v* 'yeqma يُقمَع

oppress *v* 'yeqma يُقمَع

quell *v* 'yeqma يُقمَع

shoot *v* yeqnus يُقنص

convince *v* 'yuqne يُقنِع

persuade *v* 'yeqne يُقنِع

conduct *v* yequd يُقود

lead *v* yequd يُقود

v yequd majmu'ah يُقود مجموعة

pioneer

trigger *v* yeqawwes يُقوِّس

arch *v* yuqawwes يُقوِّس

say *v* yequl يُقول

state *v* yequl يُقول

groan *v* byqul ah يُقول آه

stereotype *v* yequlib يُقولب

template *v* yequleb يُقولب

cast *v* yequlib يُقولب

mould *v* yequlib يُقورلِب

embolden *v* yeqawwi يُقوِّي

fortify *v* yeqawwi يُقوِّي

fester *v* yeqayyeh يُقيِّح

yeq'ud fatrah يُقعُد فترة مؤقّتة

sojourn *v* mu'aqqateh

hollow *v* yeqa'wir يُقعور

v yeqa'wer elkusah يُقعور الكوسا

ream

stand *v* yeqaf يُقف

queue *v* yeqaf beldur يُقف بالدور

leap *v* yeqfez يُقفز

bar *v* yukfil يُقفِل

lock *v* yeqfel يُقفِل

yeqful bequfel يُقفِل بقفل مركَّب

deadbolt *v* mrakkab

dwindle *v* yequll يُقلّ

turn *v* yeqlib يُقلب

invert *v* yeqaleb يُقلب

v yeqlub bi'ibhamuh يُقلب بإبهامه

thumb

evert *v* yeqleb labarrah يُقلب لبرًا

emulate *v* yeqalled يُقلِّد

imitate *v* yeqallid يُقلِّد

mime *v* yeqalled يُقلِّد

mimic *v* yeqallid يُقلِّد

mock *v* yeqalled يُقلِّد

ape *v* yukalled يُقلَّد

uproot *v* 'yeqla يُقلع

quarry *v* yeqla' hajar يُقلع حجارة

worry *v* yeqlaq يُقلق

ail *v* yuqlq يُقلق

cable *v* yekabbel يكّل	bound *v* yeqayyid يقيّد
v yekabbel beldyun يكّل بالديون	restrict *v* yeqayyed يقيّد
encumber	measure *v* yeqis يقيس
fade *v* yekbi يكبي	size *v* yeqis يقيس
write *v* yektub يكتب	span *v* yeqis belsheber يقيس بالشبر
v yektub Allah alyh يكتُب الله عليه	*v* yeqis umq elmay يقيس عمق المي
predetermine	fathom
v yektub beltabashir يكتب بالطباشير	estimate *v* yeqayyem يقيّم
chalk	value *v* yeqayym يقيّم
pen *v* yektub belqalam يكتب بالقلم	assess *v* yuqayyem يُقيّم
yektub beqalam يكتب بقلم رصاص	certainty *n* yaqin يقين
pencil *v* rsas	strive *v* yekafeh يكافح
v yektub bin qusin يكتب بين قوسين	struggle *v* yekafeh يكافح
bracket	contend *v* yekafeh يكافح
abound *v* yektar يكثَر	recompense *v* yekafi يكافي
detect *v* yekteshef يكتشف	reward *v* yekafi يكافي
discover *v* yekteshif يكتشف	award *v* 'yukafe يُكافى
mass *v* yekattel يكتّل	*v* yekebb elwasakh يكبّ الوسخ
v yektum a nafas يكتم ع نفَس	dump
burke	subdue *v* yekbut يكبت
condense *v* yekaththif يكثّف	bridle *n* yakbut يكبُت
moil *v* yekdah يكدَح	suppress *v* yekbah يكبح
confute *v* yekazzib يكذّب	enlarge *v* yekabber يكبّر
disprove *v* yekazzib يكذّب	grow *v* yekabber يكبَر
gainsay *v* yekazzib يكذّب	amplify *v* yukabber يُكبّر
lie *v* yekazzeb يكذّب	outgrow *v* yekbar aktar يكبَر أكثَر
fool *v* yekazzeb ala يكذُب على	*v* yekabber elsurah يكبّر الصورة
carbonize *v* yekarben يكربن	zoom in

shroud v yekaffen يكفّن

suffice v yekaffi يكفّي

cuff v yekalbesh يكلبش

handcuff v yekalbesh يكلبش

cost v yekallef يكلّف

v yekallel belghar يكلّل بالغار

garland

laurel n yekallel belghar يكلّل بالغار

complement n yekammil يكمّل

proceed v yekammel يكمّل

resume v yekammel يكمّل

supplement v yekammel يكمّل

gag v yekammem يكمّم

amass v yaknnuz يكنّز

scavenge v yekannes يكنّس

sweep v yeknus يكنّس

yeknus belmeknseh يكنّس بالمكنسة

vacuum v

electrify v yekahreb يكهرب

bank v yekawwem يكوّم

heap v yekawwem يكوّم

pile v yekawwem يكوّم

be v yekun يكون

exist v yekun يكون

iron v yekwi يكوي

deject v yek'ub يكتُب

note v yelahez يلاحظ

outlaw v yelaheq يلاحق

recur v yekarrer يكرّر

reiterate v yekarrer يكرّر

dedicate v yekarris يكرّس

v yekarres hayatuh يكرّس حياته

consecrate

accent v ykarek ala يكرك على

agonize v ykrkib يكركب

dignify v yekarrem يكرّم

hate v yekrah يكره

dislike v yekrah يكرَه

acquest n yeksab يكسب

earn v yeksab يكسَب

dull v yeksad يكسَد

stagnate v yeksud يكسَد

smash v yekasser يكسّر

break v yeksur يكسُر

clothe v yeksi يكسي

v yeksi belalwah يكسي بالألواح

panel

v yeksi belkhashab يكسي بالخشب

board

disclose v yekshuf يكشُف

expose v yekshuf يكشُف

forbear v yekeff an يكفّ عن

atone v yukaffir an يكفّر عن

vouch v yekfal يكفل

bail v yakfal يكفَل

sponsor v yekfal يكفَل

find v yelaqi يلاقي

wear v yelbes يلبس

attire v yulabbis يلبّس

dress v yelabbes يلبّس

encrust v yelabbes يلبّس

outfit v yelabbes يلبّس

girdle v yelabbes hizam يلبّس حزام

ferment v yelbes khimar يلبس خمار

gild v yelabbes dahab يلبّس دهب

gird v yelabbes zennar يلبّس زنّار

silver v yelabbes feddah يلبّس فضّة

mask v 'yelbes qina يلبس قناع

v yelbes lebes khas يلبس لبس خاص

apparel

garb v yelbs mantu يلبس مانطو

braze v yelabbes nehas يلبّس نحاس

mess v yelabbek يلبّك

bemuse v yelabbek يلبّك

meet v yelabbi يلبّي

accede v yelbie يلبي

abide v yeltezem يلتزم

cling v yeltezem bi يلتزم ب

resort v 'yelja يلجأ

curb v yeljum elhusan يلجم الحصان

persist v yelehh يلحّ

urge v yelehh يلحّ

disbelieve v yehid يلحد

lick v yelhas يلحس

follow v yelhaq يلحق

solder v yelhum يلحم

weld v yelhum يلحم

outline v yelakhkhes يلخّص

summarize v yelakhkhes يلخّص

abstract v yulakhkhes يُلخّص

stick v yelzuq يلزق

conglutinate v yelzuq يلزُق

paste v yelzuq يلزُق

v yelzuq ettihmeh bi يلزق التهمة ب

impute

adjoin v ylzq be يلزق ب

must v yelzam يلزم

oblige v yelzm يلزم

bind v yulzim يُلزم

commit v yulzim يُلزم

smear v yelattekh يلطخ

blot v yelattekh يلطّخ

blurt v yelattekh يلطّخ

play v yel'ab يلعب

game v yel'ab يلعب

dandle v yela'eeb elwalad يلعّب الولد

cajole v yelab beaqluh يلعَب بعقله

bowl v yelaab buling يلعب بولينغ

dice v yela'b tawleh يلعَب طاولة

gamble v yel'ab qmar يلعب قمار

curse v yelan يلعَن

damn v yel'an يلعَن

abrogate v yelghi يلغي

eliminate v yelghi يلغي

nullify v yelghi يلغي

cancel v yehlghi يلغي

v yeghi erraqabeh يلغي الرقابة

decontrol

v yeghi tajzy'et يلغي تجزأة

defragment

convolve v yeleff يلف

furl v yelff يلف

meander v yeleff يلف

reel v yeleff يلف

wrap v yeleff elhadeyyeh يلف الهدية

yelf bwaraq ma'dan يلف ورق معدن

foil v

v yeleff sindwesheh يلف صندويش

sandwich

attract v yalfit intibah يلفت انتباه

pronounce v yelfuz يلفظ

voice v yelfuz يلفظ

stitch v yelfuq يلفق

fabricate v yelaffeq يلفق

feign v yelaffeq يلفق

nickname v yelaqqeb يلقب

title v yelaqqeb يلقب

inoculate v yelaqqeh يلقح

immunize v yelaqqeh يلقح

snap v yelqutt يلقط

n yelqut surah يلقط صورة

photograph

tip v yelaqqim يلقم

fetter v yekalbesh يلكبش

glance v yelmah يلمح

hint v yelammeh يلمح

behold v yulammeh يلمح

allude v yulammih يلمح

finger v yelmes يلمس

touch v yelmus يلمس

twinkle v 'yelma يلمع

glaze v 'yelamme يلمع

polish v 'yelamme يلمع

sparkle v 'yelma يلمع

pant v yelhat يلهت

gasp v yelhat يلهت

inspire v yehem يلهم

bemire v yelawweth يلوث

contaminate v yelawweth يلوث

pollute v yelawweth يلوث

v yelawweh be'yduh يلوح بإيده

wave

reprimand v yelum يلوم

upbraid v yelum يلوم

censure v yelum يلوم

blame v yeluwm يلوم

colour v yelawwen يلون

arc n yalwi يلوي

wipe *v* yemsah يمسح	temper *v* yelayyn يليّن
mop *v* yemsah elaradi يمسح الأراضي	sex *v* yemares eljins يمارس الجنس
v yemsah belsfenjeh يمسح بالسفنجة	procrastinate *v* yematel يماطل
sponge	stall *v* yematel يماطل
adulate *v* ymssh jwkh يمسح جوخ	mind **.*vt*** 'yemane يمانع
butter *v* yemasseh jukh يمسّح جوخ	examine *v* yemtehen يمتحن
stroke *v* yemassed يمسّد	wander *v* yetmashshah يتمشّى
grapple *v* yemsik يمسك	consolidate *v* yemattin يمتّن
grasp *v* yemsik يمسك	abstain *v* 'yemtene يمتنع
hold *v* yemsik يمسك	*v* yemaththil bel jeththeh يمثّل بالجثّة
clutch *v* yemsuk يمسُك	mangle
catch *v* yemsik يمسك.	glorify *v* yemajjed يمجّد
grip *v* yemsek يمسك	clear *v* yemhi يمحي
comb *v* yemashshet يمشّط	erase *v* yemhi يمحي
foot *v* yemshi يمشي	acclaim *v* ymdah يمدح
march *v* yemshi يمشي	laud *v* yemdah يمدح
walk *v* yemshi يمشي	praise *v* yemdah يمدح
file *v* yemshi beldur يمشي بالدور	appraise *v* yamdah يمدح
stride *v* yemshi bser'ah يمشي بسرعة	commend *v* yemdah يمدح
dash *v* yemshi beajaleh يمشي بعجلة	extol *v* yemdah يمدح
linger *v* yemshi a mahl يمشي ع مهل	extend *v* yemadded يمدّد
advance *v* ymshi lqddam يمشي لقدام	humanize *v* yemadden يمدّن
suck *v* yemuss يمصّ	elapse *v* yemurr elwaqt يمرّ الوقت
sup *v* yemuss يمصّ	nurse *v* yemarred يمرّض
masticate *v* yemdagh يمضغ	sicken *v* yemarred يمرّض
spend *v* yemaddi يمضي	dilute *v* yemarreq يمرّق
salt *v* yemalleh يملّح	jest *v* yemzah يمزح
have *v* yemluk يملك	rag *v* yemsah يمسح

adj yamil liljinsin يميل للجنسين ambissexual

darkle v yemil lelsawad يميل للسواد

oath n yamin يمين

right adj yamin يمين

commune v yenaji يناجي

fit v yenasib يناسِب

militate v yenadel يناضِل

compete v yunafes ينافِس

discuss v yenaqesh يناقش

tackle v yenaqesh يناقش

counteract v yenaqid يناقِض

sleep v yenam ينام

v yenam almekhaddeh ينام عالمخدّة pillow

copulate v 'yenam ma ينام مع

manoeuvre v yenawer يناور

skirmish v yenawesh يناوش

howl v uyenbah ينبح

enjoy v yenbeset ينبسط

unearth v yenbush ينبُش

pulse v yenbud ينبض

v yenbud beser'ah ينبض بسرعة palpitate

spring v 'yenba ينبع

alarm v ynbbh ينبّه

forewarn v yenabbeh ينبّه

stimulate v yenabbeh ينبّه

possess v yemluk يملك

own v yemlik يملك

weary v yemallel يملّل

prime v yemalli يملّي

bestow v yemnah يمنح

concede v yemnah يمنح

prevent v 'yemna يمنع

taboo v 'yemna يمنع

debar v 'yemna يمنع

forbid v 'yemna يمنع

hinder v 'yemna يمنع

prelude v yemahhed يمهد

decease v yemut يموت

die v yemut يموت

v 'yemut bebute يموت ببطء euthanize

starve v 'yemut ju يموت جوع

parch v yemut atash يموت عطش

finance v yemawwel يموّل

camouflage v yemawweh يموّه

discriminate v yemayyez يميز

feature v yemayyez يميز

liquefy v 'yemayye يميع

lean v yemil يميل

lurch v yemil يميل

tend v yemil يميل

incline v yemil la يميل ل

shift v yenteql ينتقل	flabbergast v yenbehet ينبهت
revenge v yentqem ينتقم	dazzle v yenbher ينبهر
avenge v yantaqim men ينتقم من	wane v yetnaqas يتناقص
recede v yentekes ينتكس	heed v yentebeh ينتبه
relapse v yentekes ينتكس	notice v yentebeh ينتبه
belong v yentimi ينتمي	produce v yentej ينتج
v yentehi salahetuh ينتهي صلاحيته	result v yentij ينتج
expire	v yentehil shakhseyyet ينتحل شخصية
accomplish v ynthi mn ينتهي من	impersonate
ayield v yantahi men ينتهي من	elect v yentuhkib ينتخب
pass v yenjah ينجح	join v yentseb ينتسب
succeed v yenjah ينجح	affiliate v yntsib 'ila ينتسب إلى
gravitate v yenjzeb ينجذب	snatch v yentush ينتش
achieve v yenjez ينجز	pervade v yentesher ينتشر
besmirch v yenajjes ينجّس	prevail v yentesher ينتشر
sculpt v yenhat ينحت	propagate v yenteshr ينتشر
carve v yenhat ينحت	spread v yentesher ينتشر
chisel v yenhat ينحت	triumph v yentesr ينتصر
hew v yenhat ينحت	conquer v yentuser ala ينتصر على
decline v yenheder ينحدر	await v yantazir ينتظر
degrade v yenheder ينحدر	bide v yentuzer ينتظر
slant v yenheder ينحدر	pluck v yentuf ينتف
slope v yenheder ينحدر	shred v yentuf ينتف
infuriate v yenhar ينهر	swell v yentefekh ينتفخ
pervert v yenherif ينحرف	bag v yentafikh ينتفخ
stray v yenherf ينحرف	tap v 'yentefe ينتفع
deviate v yenhrif ينحرف	utilize v 'yentefe ينتفع
ebb v yenhsir elmadd ينحسر المدّ	lambaste v yentqed ينتقد

stream *v* yensab ينساب

tally *v* yensijm ينسجم

chime *v* yensijim ينسجِم

retreat *v* yenseheb ينسحب

withdraw *v* yensehb ينسحب

reproduce *v* yensakh ينسخ

transcribe *v* yensakh ينسخ

copy *v* yensakh ينسخ

torpedo *v* yensuf ينسف

concert *v* yenasseq ينسّق

coordinate *v* yenassiq ينسّق

marshal *vt* yenasseq ينسّق

sneak *v* yensall ينسلّ

slough *v* yenselekh ينسلخ

aniseed *n* yaansun ينسون

forget *v* yensa ينسى

sizzle *v* yeneshsh ينشّ

publish *v* yenshur ينشُر

diffuse *v* yenshur ينشُر

bruit *v* yeshur isha'a ينشُر إشاعة

v yeshur elasaker ينشُر العساكِر

deploy

v yenshur belmenshar ينشر بالمنشار

saw

energize *v* yenashshet ينشّط

reactivate *v* yenashshet ينشّط

vitalize *v* yenashshet ينشّط

activate *v* ynashet ينشّط

degenerate *v* yenhatt يحطّ

yenhatt bitarikh يحط بتاريخ أقدم

antedate *n* aqdam

slim *v* yenhaf يحف

emaciate *v* yenhaf ktir يحَف كثير

decay *v* yenhall يحلّ

engage *v* yenkhutib يخطب

sift *v* yenkhul يخل

cry *v* yendub يندب

regret *v* yendam يندم

dabble *v* yenaddi يندّي

damp *v* yenaddi يندّي

moisten *v* yenaddi يندّي

wet *v* yenaddi يندّي

v yenaddi shway يندّي شوي

dampen

herald *v* yenzir يندِر

disarm *v* yenza' slah ينزع سلاح

v yenza' mn eldalal ينزع من الدلال

spoil

yenza' waraq ينزع ورق الشجر

defoliate *v* eshshajar

bleed *v* yenzuf ينزُف

v yenazzil qimet ينزّل قيمة

depreciate

v yenazzil qimet ينزّل قيمة

devaluate

alight *v* yenzil min ينزل من

organize *v* yenazzem ينظّم	knuckle *v* yensheghel ينشغل
regulate *v* yenazzem ينظّم	preoccupy *v* yensheghel ينشغل
enliven *v* yen'esh ينعش	dehydrate *v* yenashshef ينشّف
refresh *v* yen'esh ينعش	dry *v* yenashshif ينشّف
caw *v* yea'q ينعق	towel *v* yenashshef ينشّف
smooth *v* yena'em ينعّم	pilfer *v* yenshul ينشل
inflame *v* yenghaz ينغاظ	yensab be abu ينصاب بأبو صفار
vex *v* yenaghghes ينغّص	jaundice *v* safar
hum *v* yenaghghem ينغّم	gimmick *v* yensub ينصُب
rupture *v* yenfetq ينفتق	swindle *v* yensub ينصُب
fascinate *v* yenften ينفتن	*v* yunsub kamin ينصب كمين
v yenfejr elburkan ينفجر البركان	ambuscade
erupt	advise *v* ynsah ينصح
v yenfukh belbuq ينفخ بالبوق	preach *v* yensah ينصح
trumpet	recommend *v* yensah ينصح
strut *v* yenfukh haluh ينفخ حاله	hop *v* yenutt ينطّ
implement *v* yenaffiz ينفّذ	jump *v* yenutt ينطّ
alienate *v* yunffer يُنفّر	skip *v* yenutt ينطّ
secede *v* yenfesl ينفصل	*v* yenutt mn alhajz ينطّ من عالحاجز
advantage *v* ynfae ينفع	hurdle
fuss *v* yenfe'el ينفعل	*v* yentebe' belras ينطبع بالراس
sprain *v* yenfekesh ينفكش	inculcate
exile *v* yenfi ينفي	gore *v* yentah ينطح
negate *v* yenfi ينفي	collide *v* yetureq bi ينطرق ب
banish *v* yanfi ينفي	bang *v* yentereq beshi ينطرق بشي
nag *v* yenuqq ينق	enunciate *v* yentuq ينطُق
debug *v* yenaqqeh ينقّح	cavort *v* yenatwet ينطوِط
emend *v* yenaqqeh ينقّح	clean *v* yenazzef يُنظّف

impart *v* yenqul ينقُل

v yenqul belmasurah ينقل بالماسورة
duct

convey *v* yenqul haki ينقل حكي

cite *v* yenqul an ينقُل عن

v yenqul melkeyyeh ينقل ملكيّة
transfer

overthrow *v* yenqeleb ala ينقلب على

topple *v* yenqelib ala ينقلب على

capsize *v* yeqelib qaleb ينقلب قلب

pick *v* yenaqqi ينقّي

purify *v* yenaqqi ينقّي

refine *v* yenaqqi ينقّي

banter *v* yenakket ينكّت

gag *v* yenakket ينكّت

joke *v* yenakket ينكّت

deny *v* yenkr ينكُر

poke *v* yenkuz ينكُز

nudge *v* yenkuz ينكُز

shrink *v* yenkemesh ينكمش

arise *v* yanmu ينمو

stem *v* yenmu ينمو

accrete *v* yenmou blzq ينمو بلزق

collapse *v* yenhar ينهار

plunder *v* yenhab ينهب

rifle *v* yenhab ينهب

maraud *v* yenhab ينهَب

chide *v* yenhar ينهر

retouch *v* yenaqqeh ينقّح

criticize *v* yenqud ينقُد

rescue *v* yenqez ينقذ

save *v* yenqez ينقذ

click *v* yequr ينقُر

v yenqur bemenqaruh ينقر بمنقاره
peck

engrave *v* yenqush ينقُش

inscribe *v* yenqush ينقُش

diminish *v* yenaqqis ينقّص

subtract *v* yenaqqes ينقّص

lack *v* yenaqqes ينقَص

revoke *v* yenqud ينقُض

pounce *v* yenqadd ala ينقضّ على

swoop *v* yenqadd ala ينقضّ على

dot *v* yenaqqet ينقّط

drip *v* yenaqqet ينقّط

drop *v* yenaqqet ينقّط

yenaqqet qatra ينقّط قطرة قطرة

dribble *v* qatra

puff *v* yenqete' nafasuh ينقطع نفَسُه

drench *v* yenqa'a ينقَع

infuse *v* 'yenfa ينقَع

soak *v* yenqa' belmay ينقع بالمي

catapult *v* yequf ينقُف

flip *v* yenquf ينقُف

transport *v* yenqul ينقل

dictate *v* yenaqqel ينقّل

migrate *v* yehajer يهاجِر

assail *v* yuhajim يُهاجِم

attack *v* yuhajim يُهاجِم

v yehajem eljanah يهاجم الجناح

flank

land *v* yehbut يهبِط

quake *v* yehtazz يهتزّ

wag *v* yehtazz يهتزّ

exclaim *v* yehtuf يهتِف

forsake *v* yehjur يهجُر

blow *v* yehjum يهجُم

lampoon *v* yehji يهجي

spell *v* yehajji يهجّي

menace *v* yehadded يهدّد

threaten *v* yehadded يهدّد

volley *v* yehadded يهدّد

waste *v* yehdur يهدُر

coo *v* yehdul elhamam يهدُل الحمام

deconstruct *v* yehdum يهدُم

demolish *v* yehdum يهدُم

subvert *v* yehdum يهدُم

cradle *n* yehadhid يهدهِد

gift *v* yehdi يهدي

assuage *v* yuhaddi يهدّي

becalm *v* yuhaddi يهدّي

abate *v* yehaddi يهدّي

calm *v* yehaddi يهدّي

still *v* yehaddi يهدّي

bray *v* yanhaq ينهَق

enervate *v* yenhik ينهِك

geek *v* yenhuwes ينهوس

obsess *v* yenhwes ينهوس

complete *v* yenhi ينهي

end *v* yenhi ينهي

finish *v* yenhi ينهي

terminate *v* yenhi ينهي

v yenhi eliste'mar ينهي الاستعمار

decolonize

v yenhi khedmet ينهي خدمة

decommission

lament *v* yenuh ينوح

mourn *v* yenuh ينوح

weep *v* yenuh ينوح

bewail *v* yenuuh ala ينوح على

illuminate *v* yenawwer ينوّر

opiate *v* yenawwem ينوّم

yenawwem ينوّم مغنطيسيا

mesmerize *v* maghnatiseyyan

yenawwim ينوّم مغنطيسياً

hypnotize *v* maghnatisyyan

aim *v* yenwi ينوي

intend *v* yenwi ينوي

mew *v* yenawwi ينوّي

depute *v* yenib ينيب

emigrate *v* yehajer يهاجِر

immigrate *v* yehajer يهاجِر

whisper *v* yehmus يهمس

disregard *v* yehmil يهمل

ignore *v* yehmil يهمل

neglect *v* yehmil يهمل

congratulate *v* yehanni يهنّي

felicitate *v* yehanni يهنّي

billow *v* yehuuj يهوج

waft *v* yehuj يهوج

Jew *n* yahudi يهودي

imperil *v* yehawwer يهوّر

aerify *v* yhwwy يهوّي

ventilate *v* yehawwi يهوّي

dominate *v* yehaymin يهيمن

predominate *v* yehaymn يهيمن

affront *v* yhin يهين

dishonour *v* yehin يهين

configure *v* 'yehayye يهيّئ

face *v* yewajeh يواجه

breast *v* yewajih يواجه

counter *v* yewajih يواجه

encounter *v* yewajeh يواجه

front *v* yewajeh يواجه

offset *v* yewazen يوازن

balance *v* yowazin يوازن

equalize *v* yewazin يوازن

poise *v* yewazin يوازن

parallel *v* yewazi يوازي

persevere *v* yewazeb يواظب

edify *v* yehazzib يهذّب

maunder *v* yehzi يهذي

dodge *v* yehrub يهرب

escape *v* yeharreb يهرّب

flee *v* yehrub يهرب

smuggle *v* yeharreb يهرّب

yehrub ma يهرب مع العشيقة

elope *v* elashiqah

crush *v* yehrus يهرس

jam *v* yehrus يهرس

mash *v* yehrus يهرس

squash *v* yehrus يهرس

sway *v* yehezz يهزّ

vibrate *v* yehezz يهزّ

lull *v* 'yehezz elrade يهزّ الرضيع

shrug *v* yehezz elktaf يهزّ الكتاف

sneer *v* yehezz enfuh يهزّ إنفه

nod *v* yehezz brasuh يهزّ براسه

rout *v* yehzum يهزم

vanquish *v* yehzum يهزم

defeat *v* yehzum يهزم

overcome *v* yehzem يهزم

beat *v* yahzim يهزم

hiss *v* yehasehes يهسهس

digest *v* yehdum يهضم

v yuhlik akbar qesem يهلك أكبر قسم

decimate

matter *v* yehemm يهمّ

bequeath v yowarreth يورّث	accept v ywafeq يوافق
supply v yewarred يورّد	approve v yuwafiq يوافق
implicate v yewarret يورّط	ywafiq rasmeyen ala يوافق رسمياً على
foliate v ywarreq يورّق	approbate v
varnish v yewarnesh يورنش	agree v ywafq ala يوافق على
distribute v 'yewazze يوزّع	assent v yuwafiq ala يوافق على
weigh v yuzen يوزن	jubilee n yubil يوبيل
soil v yewassekh يوسّخ	tension v yewatter يوتّر
constitute v yuassis يؤسّس	trust v yewaththeq يوثق
expand v 'yewasse يوسّع	attest v yuwaththiq يوثّق
space v 'yewasse يوسّع	confide v yuthaq bi ب يوثق
insinuate v yewaswes يوسوس	ordain v yujib يوجب
scruple v yewaswes يوسوس	abridge v yujez يوجز
beckon v yu'ashsher ala يؤشّر على	curtail v yujiz يوجز
describe v yusef يوصف	ache v 'yuje يوجع
prescribe v yusef ilaj يوصف علاج	pain v 'yewajje يوجّع
reach v yusel يوصل	torment v 'yewajje يوجّع
attach v yuwassil يوصّل	direct v yewajjeh يوجّه
connect v yewassel يوصّل	orient v yewajjeh يوجّه
plug v yewassel يوصّل	shoot v yewajjeh يوجّه
clarify v yewaddeh يوضّح	steer v yewajjeh يوجّه
employ v yewazzif يوظّف	unite v yewahhed يوحّد
recruit v yewazzef يوظّف	muse v yuhi يوحي
v yuwazzif fi safara يوظف في سفارة	bank v yude' belbank يودع بالبنك
attach	deposit v yude' belbank يودع بالبنك
promise v yu'id يوعد	yude' behsab يودع بحساب الضمان
sermonize v yu'ez يوعظ	escrow v eldaman
yoga n yuga يوغا	inherit v yewarret يورّت

confirm *v* yu'akkid يُؤَكِّد

emphasize *v* yeakkid يُؤَكِّد

assert *v* yuakkid ala يُؤَكِّد على

generate *v* yewalled يولِّد

born *v* yulad يولَد

reproduce *v* yulad يولَد

authorize *v* yuallef يؤلِّف

wail *v* yewalwel يولول

today *n* elyum اليوم

day *n* yum يوم

n yum elqyameh يوم القيامة

doomsday

flicker *v* yumed يومِض

believe *v* yu'emin يؤْمِن

daily *adj* yumi يومي

daily *adv* yumeyyan يومياً

diary *n* yawmeyyeh يوميّة

Greek *n* elyunan اليونان

Greek *adj* yunani يوناني

delude *v* yuhim يوهِم

shelter *v* ye'wi يؤْوي

despair *v* yey'as يأس

stiffen *v* yeyabbes بيبِّس

orphan *v* yeyattim يِتِّم

tang *n* ye'ezz يِثَزّ

moan *v* ye'en يِئِنّ

envoy *n* yufid يوفِد

avail *v* yuwaffer يوفِّر

fell *v* 'yewaqqe يوقِّع

sign *v* 'yewaqqe يوقِّع

fall *v* 'yuqa يوقَع

tumble *v* 'yuqa يوقَع

v yewaqqe' belfakhkh يوقِّع بالفخّ

snare

v yewaqqe' belfakh يوقِّع بالفَخّ

entangle

v yeqwaqqe' belfakh يوقِّع بالفَخّ

entrap

yewaqqe' beawwal يوقِّع بأوَّل حرف

initial *v* harf

yuwaqqee' bikhat يوقِّع بخط إيده

autograph *n* yadeh

baffle *v* yuke' fi hireh يوقِّع في حيرة

suspend *v* yuqef يوقِف

discontinue *v* yewaqqef يوقِّف

halt *v* yewaqqef يوقِّف

stop *v* yewaqqef يوقِّف

cease *v* yuqef يوقِف

align *v* ywqf bilddor يوقف بالدور

detain *v* yuqef belsejn يوقف بالسجن

v yewaqqef shway يوقِّف شوّي

pause

ascertain *v* yu'akkid يُؤَكِّد